Veterans in the United States

Statistics and Resources
2015

Veterans in the United States

Statistics and Resources 2015

Edited by
Shana Hertz Hattis

Lanham, MD

Published in the United States of America
by Bernan Press, a wholly owned subsidiary of
The Rowman & Littlefield Publishing Group, Inc.
4501 Forbes Boulevard, Suite 200
Lanham, Maryland 20706

Bernan Press
800-462-6420
www.rowman.com

ISBN-13: 978-1-59888-777-8
eISBN-13: 978-1-59888-778-5

♾™ The paper used in this publication meets the minimum requirements of American National Standard for Information Sciences—Permanence of Paper for Printed Library Materials, ANSI/NISO Z39.48-1992.

Manufactured in the United States of America.

Contents

INTRODUCTION

Bernan Press is pleased to present its first comprehensive collection of data related to veterans. This volume provides valuable information compiled by various government agencies including the Department of Veterans Affairs, the Department of Labor, and the U.S. Census Bureau.

Data related to veterans, while collected in great detail for the American Community Survey, is scattered between federal departments. This volume's mission is to present the most pertinent and compelling statistics in one easy-to-follow, useful, and informative volume. Each part is preceded by highlights of salient data, including figures, and its tables contain a wide range of information. Notes and definitions and a reference guide for veterans and those who work to support them are provided at the end of the book.

Part A comprises information from the American Community Survey. Information includes veteran status by age, race/ethnicity, period of service, and more. It looks at veterans living in poverty, educational attainment of veterans, and breakdowns of major topics by urban and rural areas and by state. When available and when not prohibitive in length, the 1-year, 3-year, and 5-year estimates are provided for all tables.

Part B uses data from the Bureau of Labor Statistics to investigate veterans in the labor force. The employment-population ratio, the unemployment rate, and employment by period of service and demographic characteristics are examined in these tables.

Part C represents the information collected by the Department of Veterans Affairs itself. This information covers a wide-ranging set of issues, including interments, veteran-related expenditures, projected population in the armed forces through September 2043, number of living veterans in each state, veterans employed in the federal government, and disability ratings and compensation.

ABOUT THE EDITOR

Shana Hertz Hattis is an editor with over a decade of experience in statistical and government research publications. Past titles include *State Profiles: The Population and Economy of Each U.S. State, Housing Statistics of the United States,* and *Crime in the United States.* She earned her bachelor of science in journalism and master of science in education degrees from Northwestern University.

PART A

Veterans in the American Community Survey

HIGHLIGHTS

Figure 1. States/Territories with the Highest and Lowest Percentages of Veterans in Their Populations, American Community Survey 5-Year Estimates, 2013

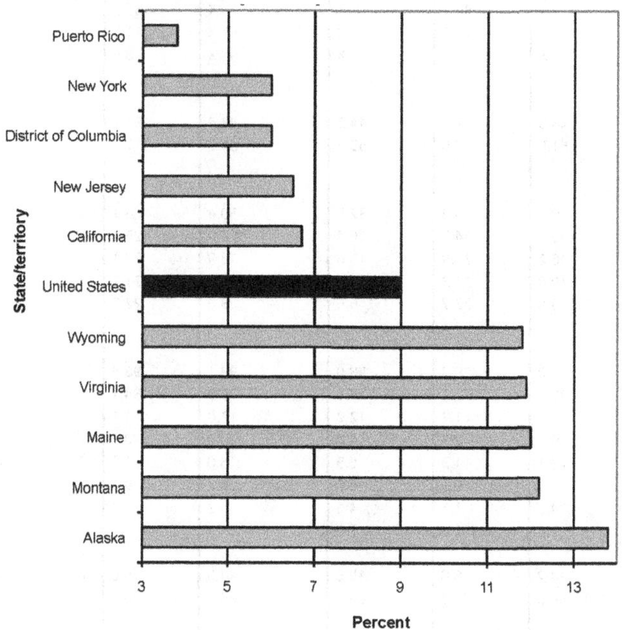

Figure 2. Period of Service for Veterans, United States, American Community Survey 5-Year Estimates, 2013

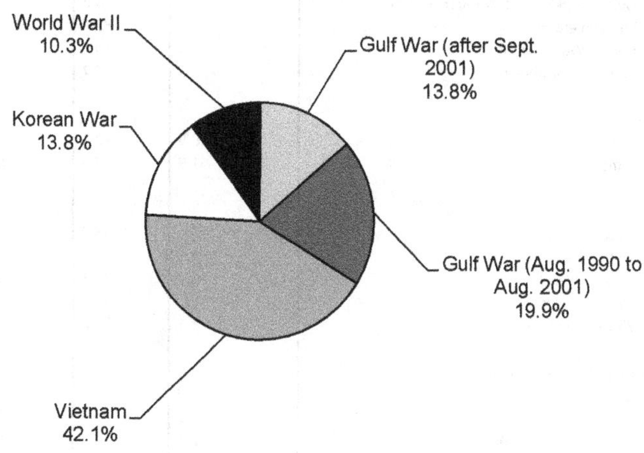

- In 2013, based on American Community Survey 5-year estimates, 9.0 percent of the U.S. population consisted of veterans. States and territories with the highest percentages of veterans included Alaska (13.8 percent), Montana (12.2 percent), Maine (12.0 percent), Virginia (11.9 percent), and Wyoming (11.8 percent). The states and territories with the lowest percentage of veterans included Puerto Rico (3.8 percent), New York (6.0 percent), the District of Columbia (6.0 percent), New Jersey (6.5 percent), and California (6.7 percent).

- Approximately 11.5 percent of all veterans in the United States in 2013 served in the post–September 2001 Gulf War era, while 16.6 percent served in the August 1990–August 2001 Gulf War era, 35.1 percent served in the Vietnam era, 11.5 percent served in the Korean War era, and 8.6 percent served in the World War II era. These numbers reflect the American Community Survey's 5-year estimates.

- In 2013, according to the American Community Survey's 5-year estimates, 7.7 percent of veterans had less than a high school diploma, 29.5 percent had graduated from high school, 36.4 percent had some college or an associate's degree, and 26.3 percent had a bachelor's degree or more. In contrast, 14.7 percent of nonveterans had less than a high school diploma, 28.0 percent had graduated from high school, 28.1 percent had some college or an associate's degree, and 29.1 percent had a bachelor's degree or more.

- Disabled veterans represented 28.5 percent of veterans in 2013 (according to the 1-year estimates from the American Community Survey). In the total population, 15.3 percent were disabled, and 14.1 percent of nonveterans were disabled.

- Whites accounted for 84.1 percent of veterans in 2013 (according to the 5-year estimates from the American Community Survey). Black or African-American veterans represented 11.1 percent of the veteran population, with American Indians and Alaska Natives comprising 0.7 percent, Asians accounting for 1.3 percent, Native Hawaiian and Other Pacific Islanders making up 0.1 percent, those of some other race comprising 1.2 percent, and those of two or more races accounting for 1.6 percent. Approximately 5.6 percent of veterans were of Hispanic or Latino ethnicity.

- Approximately 6.9 percent of veterans lived in poverty in 2013. In contrast, according to the 5-year estimates from the American Community Survey, 14.1 percent of nonveterans and 13.4 percent of the total population lived in poverty.

Table 1. Veteran Status, United States, American Community Survey Estimates, 2013

(Number; percent; dollars.)

Characteristic	1-year estimates			3-year estimates			5-year estimates		
	Total population	Veterans	Nonveterans	Total population	Veterans	Nonveterans	Total population	Veterans	Nonveterans
Civilian Population 18 Years and Over	241,556,724	19,588,586	221,968,138	239,133,187	20,757,863	218,375,324	236,576,902	21,263,779	215,313,123
Period of service									
Gulf War (9/2001 or later) veterans	X	14.0	X	X	12.8	X	X	11.5	X
Gulf War (8/1990 to 8/2001) veterans	X	18.2	X	X	17.2	X	X	16.6	X
Vietnam era veterans	X	35.6	X	X	35.2	X	X	35.1	X
Korean War veterans	X	10.7	X	X	11.0	X	X	11.5	X
World War II veterans	X	6.7	X	X	7.6	X	X	8.6	X
Sex									
Male	48.5	92.1	44.6	48.5	92.4	44.3	48.4	92.7	44.0
Female	51.5	7.9	55.4	51.5	7.6	55.7	51.6	7.3	56.0
Age									
18 to 34 years	30.4	8.3	32.4	30.4	8.4	32.5	30.4	8.1	32.6
35 to 54 years	34.8	24.1	35.7	35.4	24.7	36.4	36.0	25.1	37.0
55 to 64 years	16.3	20.3	15.9	16.2	21.9	15.6	15.9	23.1	15.2
65 to 74 years	10.4	24.1	9.2	10.0	22.3	8.8	9.7	21.2	8.6
75 years and over	8.1	23.2	6.7	8.0	22.7	6.6	8.0	22.5	6.6
Race and Hispanic/Latino origin									
One race	97.9	98.3	97.9	98.0	98.4	98.0	98.1	98.4	98.0
White	75.5	83.6	74.7	75.7	83.9	74.9	75.9	84.1	75.1
Black or African American	12.1	11.3	12.2	12.1	11.2	12.2	12.0	11.1	12.1
American Indian and Alaska Native	0.8	0.7	0.8	0.8	0.7	0.8	0.8	0.7	0.8
Asian	5.2	1.4	5.6	5.1	1.3	5.5	5.0	1.3	5.4
Native Hawaiian and Other Pacific Islander	0.2	0.2	0.2	0.2	0.1	0.2	0.2	0.1	0.2
Some other race	4.2	1.2	4.5	4.2	1.1	4.5	4.2	1.2	4.5
Two or more races	2.1	1.7	2.1	2.0	1.6	2.0	1.9	1.6	2.0
Hispanic or Latino (of any race)	15.0	6.0	15.7	14.7	5.8	15.6	14.5	5.6	15.4
White alone, not Hispanic or Latino	65.6	79.3	64.3	66.0	79.8	64.7	66.4	80.1	65.1
Median income in the past 12 months (in 2013 inflation-adjusted dollars)									
Civilian population 18 years and over with income	26,638	36,381	25,820	26,609	36,643	25,676	26,937	37,346	25,968
Male	X	36,740	31,898	X	37,043	31,853	X	37,815	32,347
Female	X	31,365	21,383	X	31,335	21,337	X	31,647	21,562
Educational attainment									
Civilian population 25 years and over	210,305,275	19,305,468	190,999,807	208,175,525	20,443,729	187,731,796	205,913,640	20,951,162	184,962,478
Less than high school graduate	13.4	7.3	14.1	13.8	7.4	14.4	14.0	7.7	14.7
High school graduate (includes equivalency)	27.9	29.1	27.7	28.1	29.3	28.0	28.2	29.5	28.0
Some college or associate's degree	29.1	36.8	28.3	29.1	36.7	28.2	29.0	36.4	28.1
Bachelor's degree or higher	29.6	26.8	29.9	29.1	26.6	29.4	28.8	26.3	29.1
Employment status									
Civilian population 18 to 64 years	196,892,734	10,320,312	186,572,422	196,076,801	11,406,215	184,670,586	194,725,860	11,977,656	182,748,204
Labor force participation rate	75.6	74.5	75.7	75.7	74.7	75.8	76.1	75.3	76.1
Civilian labor force 18 to 64 years	148,906,297	7,693,571	141,212,726	148,441,956	8,519,706	139,922,250	148,165,736	9,017,244	139,148,492
Unemployment rate	8.3	7.4	8.4	9.2	8.2	9.3	9.5	8.7	9.6
Poverty status in the past 12 months									
Civilian population 18 years and over for whom poverty status is determined	235,134,873	19,257,038	215,877,835	232,713,799	20,392,103	212,321,696	230,177,717	20,891,328	209,286,389
Below poverty in the past 12 months	13.9	7.3	14.5	13.9	7.2	14.5	13.4	6.9	14.1
Disability status									
Civilian population 18 years and over for whom poverty status is determined	235,134,873	19,257,038	215,877,835	232,713,799	20,392,103	212,321,696	230,177,717	20,891,328	209,286,389
Below poverty in the past 12 months	15.3	28.5	14.1	15.0	27.1	13.8	14.8	26.4	13.7
Group quarters population									
Total group quarters population	7,508,081	X	X	7,503,862	X	X	7,847,140	X	X
Percent veteran/nonveteran	X	5.5	94.5	X	6.1	93.9	X	6.2	93.8
Institutionalized group quarters population	3,820,222	X	X	3,838,073	X	X	3,845,120	X	X
Percent veteran/nonveteran	X	8.2	91.8	X	9.1	90.9	X	9.3	90.7
Noninstitutionalized group quarters population	3,687,859	X	X	3,665,789	X	X	3,642,020	X	X
Percent veteran/nonveteran	X	2.8	97.2	X	2.9	97.1	X	3.0	97.0

X = Not applicable/not available.
Note: The categories under period of service are not necessarily mutually exclusive. Veterans may have served in more than one period.

Table 2. Veteran Status, United States, American Community Survey Estimates, 2012

(Number; percent; dollars.)

Characteristic	1-year estimates			3-year estimates			5-year estimates		
	Total population	Veterans	Nonveterans	Total population	Veterans	Nonveterans	Total population	Veterans	Nonveterans
Civilian Population 18 Years and Over	239,178,768	21,230,865	217,947,903	236,680,744	21,500,559	215,180,185	234,029,580	21,853,912	212,175,668
Period of service									
Gulf War (9/2001 or later) veterans	X	12.9	X	X	11.7	X	X	10.3	X
Gulf War (8/1990 to 8/2001) veterans	X	17.1	X	X	16.4	X	X	16.0	X
Vietnam era veterans	X	34.9	X	X	34.9	X	X	35.0	X
Korean War veterans	X	10.9	X	X	11.3	X	X	11.9	X
World War II veterans	X	7.5	X	X	8.5	X	X	9.6	X
Sex									
Male	48.4	92.4	44.2	48.4	92.6	44.0	48.4	92.9	43.8
Female	51.6	7.6	55.8	51.6	7.4	56.0	51.6	7.1	56.2
Age									
18 to 34 years	30.4	8.6	32.6	30.4	8.3	32.6	30.4	7.9	32.7
35 to 54 years	35.4	24.8	36.4	36.0	25.1	37.1	36.6	25.5	37.7
55 to 64 years	16.1	21.5	15.6	16.0	23.3	15.3	15.6	24.2	14.8
65 to 74 years	10.0	22.6	8.8	9.6	20.9	8.5	9.4	20.2	8.3
75 years and over	8.0	22.5	6.6	8.0	22.4	6.5	8.0	22.2	6.5
Race and Hispanic/Latino origin									
One race	98.0	98.3	98.0	98.1	98.4	98.0	98.2	98.5	98.1
White	75.7	83.7	74.9	75.9	84.1	75.1	76.1	84.3	75.2
Black or African American	12.1	11.3	12.2	12.0	11.1	12.1	12.0	10.9	12.1
American Indian and Alaska Native	0.8	0.8	0.8	0.8	0.7	0.8	0.8	0.7	0.8
Asian	5.1	1.3	5.5	5.0	1.2	5.4	5.0	1.2	5.3
Native Hawaiian and Other Pacific Islander	0.2	0.2	0.2	0.2	0.1	0.2	0.2	0.1	0.2
Some other race	4.2	1.1	4.5	4.2	1.1	4.5	4.3	1.2	4.6
Two or more races	2.0	1.7	2.0	1.9	1.6	2.0	1.8	1.5	1.9
Hispanic or Latino (of any race)	14.7	5.7	15.6	14.5	5.5	15.4	14.2	5.4	15.2
White alone, not Hispanic or Latino	66.0	79.6	64.6	66.4	80.2	65.0	66.9	80.5	65.5
Median income in the past 12 months (in 2013 inflation-adjusted dollars)									
Civilian population 18 years and over with income	26,278	36,264	25,337	26,440	36,552	25,475	27,028	37,434	26,022
Male	X	36,672	31,586	X	36,961	31,588	X	37,943	32,444
Female	X	30,929	21,071	X	31,221	21,212	X	31,329	21,469
Educational attainment									
Civilian population 25 years and over	208,103,341	20,906,634	187,196,707	205,965,104	21,167,721	184,797,383	203,630,965	21,535,643	182,095,322
Less than high school graduate	13.7	7.1	14.4	14.1	7.6	14.8	14.3	8.1	15.1
High school graduate (includes equivalency)	28.1	29.2	27.9	28.3	29.6	28.2	28.3	29.6	28.1
Some college or associate's degree	29.2	36.9	28.3	29.0	36.5	28.1	28.9	36.2	28.1
Bachelor's degree or higher	29.1	26.7	29.3	28.6	26.3	28.9	28.5	26.1	28.7
Employment status									
Civilian population 18 to 64 years	196,038,291	11,659,939	184,378,352	195,028,385	12,190,149	182,838,236	193,358,139	12,594,826	180,763,313
Labor force participation rate	75.7	74.8	75.8	75.9	75.0	75.9	76.4	75.9	76.5
Civilian labor force 18 to 64 years	148,453,907	8,727,120	139,726,787	148,004,418	9,147,308	138,857,110	147,753,175	9,554,666	138,198,509
Unemployment rate	9.2	8.0	9.3	10.0	9.0	10.0	9.1	8.1	9.2
Poverty status in the past 12 months									
Civilian population 18 years and over for whom poverty status is determined	232,774,182	20,850,367	211,923,815	230,292,141	21,113,211	209,178,930	227,651,186	X	X
Below poverty in the past 12 months	13.9	7.2	14.6	13.7	6.9	14.4	0.6	X	X
Disability status									
Civilian population 18 years and over for whom poverty status is determined	232,774,182	20,850,367	211,923,815	230,292,141	X	X	227,651,186	X	X
Below poverty in the past 12 months	14.8	26.6	13.7	14.7	X	X	2.4	X	X
Group quarters population									
Total group quarters population	7,495,779	X	X	7,476,597	X	X	7,469,650	X	X
Percent veteran/nonveteran	X	6.4	93.6	X	6.4	93.6	X	6.5	93.5
Institutionalized group quarters population	3,845,829	X	X	3,849,087	X	X	3,859,296	X	X
Percent veteran/nonveteran	X	9.5	90.5	X	9.7	90.3	X	9.6	90.4
Noninstitutionalized group quarters population	3,649,950	X	X	3,627,510	X	X	3,610,354	X	X
Percent veteran/nonveteran	X	3.1	96.9	X	3.0	97.0	X	3.2	96.8

X = Not applicable/not available.

Note: The categories under period of service are not necessarily mutually exclusive. Veterans may have served in more than one period.

Table 3. Veteran Status, United States, American Community Survey Estimates, 2011

(Number; percent; dollars.)

Characteristic	1-year estimates			3-year estimates			5-year estimates		
	Total population	Veterans	Nonveterans	Total population	Veterans	Nonveterans	Total population	Veterans	Nonveterans
Civilian Population 18 Years and Over	236,665,774	21,458,427	215,207,347	234,063,189	21,797,348	212,265,841	231,421,987	22,215,303	209,206,684
Period of service									
Gulf War (9/2001 or later) veterans	X	11.6	X	X	10.2	X	X	9.2	X
Gulf War (8/1990 to 8/2001) veterans	X	16.5	X	X	15.9	X	X	15.5	X
Vietnam era veterans	X	35.0	X	X	35.0	X	X	34.8	X
Korean War veterans	X	11.3	X	X	11.9	X	X	12.4	X
World War II veterans	X	8.5	X	X	9.6	X	X	10.6	X
Sex									
Male	48.4	92.7	44.0	48.4	92.9	43.8	48.3	93.1	43.6
Female	51.6	7.3	56.0	51.6	7.1	56.2	51.7	6.9	56.4
Age									
18 to 34 years	30.4	8.2	32.6	30.4	7.9	32.7	30.4	7.8	32.8
35 to 54 years	36.0	25.1	37.1	36.6	25.5	37.7	37.1	25.9	38.3
55 to 64 years	16.1	23.7	15.3	15.7	24.5	14.8	15.3	25.1	14.3
65 to 74 years	9.5	20.6	8.4	9.3	19.9	8.3	9.1	19.4	8.1
75 years and over	8.0	22.4	6.6	8.0	22.2	6.5	8.0	21.8	6.5
Race and Hispanic/Latino origin									
One race	98.1	98.5	98.0	98.2	98.5	98.1	98.3	98.6	98.2
White	75.9	84.3	75.1	76.1	84.4	75.2	76.1	84.5	75.2
Black or African American	12.0	10.9	12.1	11.9	10.9	12.1	11.9	10.7	12.0
American Indian and Alaska Native	0.8	0.7	0.8	0.8	0.7	0.8	0.8	0.7	0.8
Asian	5.0	1.2	5.3	4.9	1.2	5.3	4.9	1.2	5.3
Native Hawaiian and Other Pacific Islander	0.1	0.1	0.2	0.2	0.1	0.2	0.2	0.1	0.2
Some other race	4.2	1.1	4.6	4.3	1.2	4.6	4.6	1.2	4.9
Two or more races	1.9	1.5	2.0	1.8	1.5	1.9	1.7	1.4	1.8
Hispanic or Latino (of any race)	14.5	5.6	15.4	14.3	5.4	15.2	14.0	5.2	14.9
White alone, not Hispanic or Latino	66.4	80.4	65.0	66.9	80.6	65.5	67.4	80.9	65.9
Median income in the past 12 months (in 2013 inflation-adjusted dollars)									
Civilian population 18 years and over with income	25,811	35,821	24,751	26,356	36,462	25,369	27,024	37,463	25,984
Male	X	36,202	31,083	X	36,865	31,619	X	37,973	32,795
Female	X	30,611	20,771	X	30,980	21,062	X	31,093	21,307
Educational attainment									
Civilian population 25 years and over	205,848,189	21,128,562	184,719,627	203,647,449	21,479,526	182,167,923	201,345,561	21,886,370	179,459,191
Less than high school graduate	14.1	7.6	14.9	14.4	8.1	15.2	14.7	8.6	15.4
High school graduate (includes equivalency)	28.4	29.7	28.3	28.5	29.8	28.3	28.7	30.1	28.5
Some college or associate's degree	28.9	36.3	28.1	28.9	36.2	28.0	28.5	35.5	27.6
Bachelor's degree or higher	28.5	26.3	28.8	28.2	26.0	28.5	28.2	25.8	28.5
Employment status									
Civilian population 18 to 64 years	195,280,748	12,242,199	183,038,549	193,573,774	12,621,774	180,952,000	191,813,167	13,052,588	178,760,579
Labor force participation rate	75.7	74.6	75.8	76.3	75.6	76.3	76.5	76.4	76.5
Civilian labor force 18 to 64 years	147,812,372	9,128,174	138,684,198	147,600,202	9,537,833	138,062,369	146,679,074	9,966,026	136,713,048
Unemployment rate	10.1	9.1	10.1	10.1	9.3	10.2	8.5	7.4	8.6
Poverty status in the past 12 months									
Civilian population 18 years and over for whom poverty status is determined	230,286,423	21,072,486	209,213,937	227,693,344	21,414,742	206,278,602	X	X	X
Below poverty in the past 12 months	13.9	7.0	14.6	13.3	6.7	13.9	X	X	X
Disability status									
Civilian population 18 years and over for whom poverty status is determined	230,286,423	21,072,486	209,213,937	227,693,344	21,414,742	206,278,602	X	X	X
Below poverty in the past 12 months	14.8	26.2	13.7	14.7	25.8	13.5	X	X	X
Group quarters population									
Total group quarters population	7,455,535	X	X	7,457,135	X	X	7,446,939	X	X
Percent veteran/nonveteran	X	6.4	93.6	X	6.4	93.6	X	6.6	93.4
Institutionalized group quarters population	3,862,830	X	X	3,860,898	X	X	3,870,484	X	X
Percent veteran/nonveteran	X	9.6	90.4	X	9.5	90.5	X	9.6	90.4
Noninstitutionalized group quarters population	3,592,705	X	X	3,596,237	X	X	3,576,455	X	X
Percent veteran/nonveteran	X	2.9	97.1	X	3.1	96.9	X	3.2	96.8

X = Not applicable/not available.

Note: The categories under period of service are not necessarily mutually exclusive. Veterans may have served in more than one period.

Table 4. Veteran Status, United States, American Community Survey Estimates, 2010

(Number; percent; dollars.)

Characteristic	1-year estimates			3-year estimates			5-year estimates		
	Total population	Veterans	Nonveterans	Total population	Veterans	Nonveterans	Total population	Veterans	Nonveterans
Civilian Population 18 Years and Over	234,137,287	21,798,077	212,339,210	231,412,378	22,168,038	209,244,340	228,808,831	22,652,496	206,156,335
Period of service									
Gulf War (9/2001 or later) veterans	X	10.5	X	X	9.0	X	X	8.4	X
Gulf War (8/1990 to 8/2001) veterans	X	15.8	X	X	15.4	X	X	15.0	X
Vietnam era veterans	X	34.9	X	X	34.9	X	X	34.4	X
Korean War veterans	X	11.8	X	X	12.4	X	X	12.8	X
World War II veterans	X	9.5	X	X	10.6	X	X	11.7	X
Sex									
Male	48.4	92.8	43.8	48.3	93.1	43.6	48.3	93.1	43.4
Female	51.6	7.2	56.2	51.7	6.9	56.4	51.7	6.9	56.6
Age									
18 to 34 years	30.4	8.0	32.7	30.4	7.6	32.8	30.4	7.8	32.9
35 to 54 years	36.7	25.5	37.8	37.2	26.0	38.4	37.7	26.3	38.9
55 to 64 years	15.7	24.5	14.8	15.3	25.2	14.3	15.0	25.4	13.8
65 to 74 years	9.3	19.7	8.3	9.2	19.3	8.1	9.0	19.0	7.9
75 years and over	7.9	22.2	6.5	8.0	22.0	6.5	8.0	21.4	6.5
Race and Hispanic/Latino origin									
One race	98.1	98.5	98.1	98.3	98.6	98.3	98.4	98.6	98.3
White	76.1	84.3	75.2	76.2	84.6	75.4	76.0	84.5	75.1
Black or African American	11.9	11.0	12.0	11.9	10.7	12.0	11.8	10.7	11.9
American Indian and Alaska Native	0.8	0.7	0.8	0.8	0.7	0.8	0.8	0.7	0.8
Asian	4.9	1.2	5.3	4.9	1.2	5.3	4.8	1.2	5.2
Native Hawaiian and Other Pacific Islander	0.2	0.1	0.2	0.2	0.1	0.2	0.2	0.1	0.2
Some other race	4.3	1.1	4.6	4.4	1.2	4.7	4.9	1.3	5.2
Two or more races	1.9	1.5	1.9	1.7	1.4	1.7	1.6	1.4	1.7
Hispanic or Latino (of any race)	14.3	5.3	15.2	14.0	5.2	14.9	13.7	5.1	14.6
White alone, not Hispanic or Latino	66.9	80.5	65.5	67.4	81.0	65.9	67.8	81.2	66.4
Median income in the past 12 months (in 2013 inflation-adjusted dollars)									
Civilian population 18 years and over with income	25,605	35,367	24,521	26,284	36,211	25,264	26,652	36,803	25,575
Male	X	35,725	30,822	X	36,635	31,759	X	37,321	32,415
Female	X	30,540	20,634	X	30,347	20,847	X	30,137	20,856
Educational attainment									
Civilian population 25 years and over	203,645,945	21,457,414	182,188,531	201,299,671	21,854,392	179,445,279	199,029,326	22,301,986	176,727,340
Less than high school graduate	14.5	8.0	15.2	14.7	8.5	15.5	15.0	9.1	15.8
High school graduate (includes equivalency)	28.5	29.9	28.4	28.5	29.8	28.3	29.0	30.4	28.9
Some college or associate's degree	28.8	36.1	28.0	28.8	35.9	27.9	28.1	34.9	27.2
Bachelor's degree or higher	28.2	25.9	28.4	28.0	25.7	28.3	27.9	25.6	28.2
Employment status									
Civilian population 18 to 64 years	193,703,762	12,662,865	181,040,897	191,810,677	13,022,303	178,788,374	190,059,418	13,497,353	176,562,065
Labor force participation rate	76.1	75.5	76.1	76.8	76.4	76.8	76.5	76.8	76.5
Civilian labor force 18 to 64 years	147,417,072	9,556,121	137,860,951	147,233,776	9,952,807	137,280,969	145,458,632	10,369,766	135,088,866
Unemployment rate	10.6	9.9	10.7	8.8	7.9	8.9	7.7	6.6	7.8
Poverty status in the past 12 months									
Civilian population 18 years and over for whom poverty status is determined	227,785,748	21,399,184	206,386,564	225,050,270	21,765,108	203,285,162	X	X	X
Below poverty in the past 12 months	13.4	6.7	14.1	12.6	6.4	13.2	X	X	X
Disability status									
Civilian population 18 years and over for whom poverty status is determined	227,785,748	21,399,184	206,386,564	225,050,270	21,765,108	203,285,162	X	X	X
Below poverty in the past 12 months	14.6	25.5	13.5	14.7	25.5	13.6	X	X	X
Group quarters population									
Total group quarters population	7,442,403	X	X	7,460,963	X	X	7,446,474	X	X
Percent veteran/nonveteran	X	6.6	93.4	X	6.8	93.2	X	7.0	93.0
Institutionalized group quarters population	3,851,131	X	X	3,867,067	X	X	3,869,994	X	X
Percent veteran/nonveteran	X	9.9	90.1	X	9.8	90.2	X	10.0	90.0
Noninstitutionalized group quarters population	3,591,272	X	X	3,593,896	X	X	3,576,480	X	X
Percent veteran/nonveteran	X	3.2	96.8	X	3.5	96.5	X	3.8	96.2

X = Not applicable/not available.

Note: The categories under period of service are not necessarily mutually exclusive. Veterans may have served in more than one period.

Table 5. Veteran Status, United States, American Community Survey Estimates, 2009

(Number; percent; dollars.)

Characteristic	1-year estimates			3-year estimates			5-year estimates		
	Total population	Veterans	Nonveterans	Total population	Veterans	Nonveterans	Total population	Veterans	Nonveterans
Civilian Population 18 Years and Over	231,222,799	21,854,374	209,368,425	228,727,364	22,382,962	206,344,402	226,148,027	22,894,578	203,253,449
Period of service									
Gulf War (9/2001 or later) veterans	X	8.7	X	X	8.2	X	X	7.7	X
Gulf War (8/1990 to 8/2001) veterans	X	15.6	X	X	15.2	X	X	14.7	X
Vietnam era veterans	X	34.7	X	X	34.3	X	X	33.8	X
Korean War veterans	X	12.4	X	X	12.8	X	X	13.1	X
World War II veterans	X	10.7	X	X	11.8	X	X	12.9	X
Sex									
Male	48.5	93.2	43.8	48.5	93.2	43.6	48.5	93.1	43.4
Female	51.5	6.8	56.2	51.5	6.8	56.4	51.5	6.9	56.6
Age									
18 to 34 years	30.7	7.6	33.1	30.6	7.9	33.1	30.7	8.1	33.3
35 to 54 years	37.2	26.2	38.3	37.7	26.4	38.9	38.1	26.8	39.3
55 to 64 years	15.0	24.9	14.0	14.7	25.4	13.6	14.4	25.4	13.2
65 to 74 years	9.0	19.0	8.0	8.8	18.6	7.7	8.7	18.6	7.5
75 years and over	8.1	22.2	6.6	8.1	21.7	6.7	8.1	21.2	6.7
Race and Hispanic/Latino origin									
One race	98.3	98.5	98.3	98.4	98.6	98.4	98.5	98.7	98.5
White	76.7	84.8	75.9	76.5	84.9	75.6	76.5	84.8	75.5
Black or African American	11.8	10.5	11.9	11.7	10.4	11.9	11.7	10.4	11.8
American Indian and Alaska Native	0.8	0.7	0.8	0.8	0.7	0.8	0.8	0.7	0.8
Asian	4.6	1.2	5.0	4.5	1.2	4.9	4.5	1.2	4.9
Native Hawaiian and Other Pacific Islander	0.1	0.1	0.1	0.1	0.1	0.1	0.1	0.1	0.1
Some other race	4.3	1.2	4.7	4.7	1.3	5.1	5.0	1.4	5.4
Two or more races	1.7	1.5	1.7	1.6	1.4	1.6	1.5	1.3	1.5
Hispanic or Latino (of any race)	13.6	5.2	14.5	13.3	5.0	14.3	13.1	4.9	14.0
White alone, not Hispanic or Latino	68.1	81.2	66.7	68.5	81.5	67.1	68.9	81.7	67.5
Median income in the past 12 months (in 2009 inflation-adjusted dollars)									
Civilian population 18 years and over with income	25,559	35,402	24,430	26,359	36,334	25,244	26,437	36,430	25,263
Male	X	35,869	30,845	X	36,841	31,943	X	37,009	32,315
Female	X	29,383	20,166	X	29,460	20,556	X	29,021	20,440
Educational attainment									
Civilian population 25 years and over	201,129,277	21,559,916	179,569,361	199,074,146	22,047,681	177,026,465	196,750,242	22,514,916	174,235,326
Less than high school graduate	14.8	8.5	15.6	15.1	9.1	15.9	15.5	9.8	16.2
High school graduate (includes equivalency)	28.6	29.9	28.4	29.1	30.4	28.9	29.4	30.6	29.2
Some college or associate's degree	28.8	36.0	27.9	28.1	35.0	27.2	27.7	34.3	26.8
Bachelor's degree or higher	27.9	25.6	28.2	27.7	25.5	28.0	27.5	25.3	27.8
Employment status									
Civilian population 18 to 64 years	191,716,151	12,842,337	178,873,814	190,007,905	13,362,579	176,645,326	188,147,157	13,798,460	174,348,697
Labor force participation rate	77.0	76.4	77	76.9	77.0	76.9	76.5	77.1	76.4
Civilian labor force 18 to 64 years	147,574,997	9,809,036	137,765,961	146,069,603	10,292,545	135,777,058	143,908,517	10,641,705	133,266,812
Unemployment rate	9.7	8.9	9.8	7.3	6.3	7.4	7.0	5.9	7.1
Poverty status in the past 12 months									
Civilian population 18 years and over for whom poverty status is determined	224,691,351	21,445,418	203,245,933	X	X	X	X	X	X
Below poverty in the past 12 months	12.5	6.5	13.2	X	X	X	X	X	X
Disability status									
Civilian population 18 years and over for whom poverty status is determined	224,691,351	21,445,418	203,245,933	X	X	X	X	X	X
Below poverty in the past 12 months	14.8	25.6	13.6	X	X	X	X	X	X
Group quarters population									
Total group quarters population	7,751,926	X	X	7,713,319	X	X	7,661,348	X	X
Percent veteran/nonveteran	X	6.8	93.2	X	7.3	92.7	X	7.5	92.5
Institutionalized group quarters population	4,088,784	X	X	4,079,373	X	X	4,054,452	X	X
Percent veteran/nonveteran	X	9.6	90.4	X	10.2	89.8	X	10.3	89.7
Noninstitutionalized group quarters population	3,663,142	X	X	3,633,946	X	X	3,606,896	X	X
Percent veteran/nonveteran	X	3.6	96.4	X	4.1	95.9	X	4.3	95.7

Note: The categories under period of service are not necessarily mutually exclusive. Veterans may have served in more than one period.
X = Not applicable/not available.

Table 6. Percent of the Civilian Population 18 Years and Over Who Are Veterans, United States, States, and Puerto Rico, American Community Survey Estimates, 2009–2013

(Percent.)

Geographic area	1-year estimates					3-year estimates					5-year estimates				
	2009	2010	2011	2012	2013	2009	2010	2011	2012	2013	2009	2010	2011	2012	2013
United States	9.5	9.3	9.1	8.9	8.1	9.8	9.6	9.3	9.1	8.7	10.1	9.9	9.6	9.3	9.0
Alabama	11.2	11.0	10.8	10.4	9.6	11.4	11.2	11.0	10.8	10.3	11.6	11.4	11.2	11.0	10.6
Alaska	14.1	14.1	14.0	13.6	11.9	14.5	14.4	14.3	13.9	13.2	15.0	14.7	14.5	14.2	13.8
Arizona	11.0	11.1	11.0	10.7	10.0	11.4	11.3	11.1	10.9	10.5	11.9	11.8	11.4	11.1	10.8
Arkansas	11.2	11.2	10.7	10.4	9.7	11.4	11.3	11.1	10.8	10.3	11.8	11.6	11.3	11.0	10.7
California	7.2	7.0	6.8	6.5	6.0	7.5	7.2	7.0	6.8	6.4	7.8	7.6	7.3	7.0	6.7
Colorado	10.5	10.3	10.7	10.4	9.5	11.0	10.8	10.6	10.5	10.2	11.4	11.1	10.9	10.7	10.4
Connecticut	8.2	8.2	8.2	7.7	6.8	8.7	8.5	8.3	8.0	7.6	9.2	9.0	8.6	8.3	7.9
Delaware	11.5	10.6	11.1	10.8	9.5	11.6	11.2	11.1	10.8	10.3	12.0	11.6	11.4	11.1	10.7
District of Columbia	6.8	6.1	5.8	6.0	5.2	6.9	6.4	6.2	6.0	5.7	7.3	6.9	6.4	6.2	6.0
Florida	11.0	10.9	10.5	10.2	9.4	11.5	11.1	10.8	10.5	10.0	11.9	11.6	11.2	10.8	10.4
Georgia	9.7	9.7	9.4	9.5	8.7	10.0	9.9	9.7	9.6	9.2	10.4	10.2	9.9	9.8	9.5
Hawaii	11.1	11.4	10.6	11.1	10.3	11.8	11.1	10.9	11.0	10.7	12.3	11.7	11.3	11.0	10.9
Idaho	10.9	11.0	10.5	10.6	10.1	11.7	11.3	10.8	10.7	10.4	12.2	11.8	11.4	11.1	10.7
Illinois	7.9	7.7	7.4	7.5	6.7	8.1	8.0	7.7	7.5	7.2	8.5	8.3	8.0	7.8	7.5
Indiana	9.8	9.6	9.3	9.2	8.4	10.1	9.9	9.6	9.4	9.0	10.4	10.2	9.9	9.6	9.3
Iowa	10.2	10.0	9.7	9.7	8.8	10.6	10.4	10.0	9.8	9.4	10.8	10.7	10.4	10.1	9.7
Kansas	10.4	10.2	9.9	10.0	9.1	10.9	10.7	10.2	10.0	9.7	11.2	11.0	10.6	10.3	9.9
Kentucky	9.7	9.6	9.3	9.4	8.7	10.1	9.9	9.6	9.5	9.2	10.4	10.2	9.9	9.7	9.4
Louisiana	9.4	9.2	9.1	8.9	7.7	9.5	9.4	9.2	9.0	8.6	9.8	9.6	9.4	9.2	8.9
Maine	12.7	12.2	12.2	11.6	11.2	13.2	12.7	12.4	12.0	11.7	13.5	13.2	12.8	12.4	12.0
Maryland	10.2	9.8	9.6	9.7	8.8	10.5	10.2	9.9	9.6	9.3	10.9	10.6	10.2	9.9	9.6
Massachusetts	8.0	7.8	7.5	7.3	6.4	8.4	8.1	7.8	7.5	7.0	8.7	8.5	8.1	7.8	7.4
Michigan	9.3	9.2	8.9	8.7	8.1	9.6	9.4	9.2	8.9	8.6	9.9	9.7	9.4	9.2	8.9
Minnesota	9.5	9.4	9.0	9.0	8.2	9.9	9.6	9.3	9.1	8.7	10.2	10.0	9.7	9.4	9.0
Mississippi	9.4	9.3	9.1	9.1	8.2	9.7	9.6	9.3	9.2	8.8	9.9	9.8	9.6	9.4	9.1
Missouri	11.0	10.9	10.7	10.4	9.4	11.3	11.2	10.9	10.7	10.2	11.6	11.4	11.2	10.9	10.5
Montana	12.9	12.5	12.3	12.7	10.5	13.4	13.1	12.6	12.5	11.9	13.7	13.5	13.1	12.8	12.2
Nebraska	11.0	10.6	10.6	10.4	8.9	11.1	11.0	10.8	10.5	10.0	11.4	11.2	11.0	10.8	10.3
Nevada	11.2	11.3	11.1	11.0	10.2	11.7	11.5	11.3	11.2	10.8	12.3	11.9	11.5	11.3	11.0
New Hampshire	11.1	11.1	11.1	10.6	10.1	11.7	11.5	11.2	11.0	10.6	12.3	12.0	11.6	11.2	10.9
New Jersey	7.0	6.7	6.6	6.4	5.6	7.3	7.1	6.8	6.5	6.2	7.7	7.4	7.1	6.8	6.5
New Mexico	11.4	11.6	11.4	11.4	10.2	11.7	11.6	11.5	11.4	11.0	12.0	11.9	11.7	11.5	11.2
New York	6.6	6.3	6.1	5.8	5.2	6.8	6.6	6.3	6.0	5.7	7.1	6.9	6.6	6.4	6.0
North Carolina	10.4	10.1	10.2	9.8	9.1	10.7	10.5	10.3	10.0	9.7	11.0	10.8	10.5	10.3	9.9
North Dakota	10.5	10.0	10.5	10.5	8.8	11.0	10.8	10.5	10.3	9.9	11.3	11.0	10.7	10.5	10.0
Ohio	10.2	10.1	9.9	9.6	8.9	10.6	10.4	10.1	9.9	9.4	10.9	10.7	10.4	10.1	9.8
Oklahoma	11.4	11.5	11.3	11.2	9.7	11.7	11.7	11.5	11.3	10.7	12.1	12.0	11.7	11.5	11.0
Oregon	11.7	11.2	10.6	10.7	9.5	11.9	11.6	11.2	10.9	10.3	12.2	11.9	11.5	11.2	10.8
Pennsylvania	10.1	9.9	9.6	9.3	8.5	10.5	10.2	9.9	9.6	9.1	10.8	10.6	10.2	9.9	9.5
Rhode Island	9.2	8.8	8.7	8.5	7.7	9.7	9.4	8.9	8.7	8.3	9.9	9.6	9.3	9.1	8.5
South Carolina	11.2	11.6	11.2	10.9	10.0	11.6	11.5	11.4	11.2	10.7	12.0	11.8	11.5	11.3	11.0
South Dakota	11.2	11.4	11.3	11.0	9.8	11.9	11.6	11.4	11.2	10.6	12.0	12.1	11.8	11.4	11.0
Tennessee	10.5	10.1	9.9	9.6	9.3	10.7	10.5	10.2	9.9	9.6	10.9	10.7	10.5	10.2	9.9
Texas	8.9	8.8	8.6	8.5	7.7	9.2	9.0	8.8	8.6	8.2	9.5	9.3	9.0	8.8	8.5
Utah	7.8	8.0	7.6	7.4	6.6	8.0	8.0	7.8	7.7	7.2	8.3	8.2	8.0	7.7	7.5
Vermont	10.5	9.8	10.3	9.6	8.2	10.8	10.4	10.3	9.9	9.3	11.0	10.7	10.5	10.2	9.7
Virginia	12.3	12.3	12.0	11.7	10.9	12.6	12.4	12.2	12.0	11.5	13.0	12.8	12.5	12.1	11.9
Washington	11.6	11.6	11.5	11.2	10.2	12.2	11.8	11.6	11.4	10.9	12.7	12.3	12.0	11.6	11.2
West Virginia	10.9	11.2	10.6	11.1	10.2	11.7	11.5	10.9	11.0	10.7	12.0	11.8	11.4	11.3	10.9
Wisconsin	9.9	9.7	9.4	9.2	8.3	10.2	10.0	9.7	9.4	9.0	10.4	10.3	10.0	9.7	9.3
Wyoming	12.4	12.3	12.2	11.1	11.1	12.8	12.5	12.3	11.9	11.5	13.3	13.0	12.6	12.0	11.8
Puerto Rico	4.0	4.0	3.8	3.8	3.2	4.1	4.1	4.0	3.9	3.6	4.3	4.2	4.1	4.0	3.8

Table 7. Period of Military Service for Civilian Veterans 18 Years and Over, United States, American Community Survey 5-Year Estimates, 2009–2013

(Number.)

Characteristic	2009	2010	2011	2012	2013
Total	22,894,578	22,652,496	22,215,303	21,853,912	21,263,779
Gulf War (9/2001 or later), no Gulf War (8/1990 to 8/2001), no Vietnam Era	1,008,410	1,097,201	1,204,865	1,361,146	1,496,810
Gulf War (9/2001 or later) and Gulf War (8/1990 to 8/2001), no Vietnam Era	706,039	752,325	787,537	832,727	887,159
Gulf War (9/2001 or later), and Gulf War (8/1990 to 8/2001), and Vietnam Era	48,788	50,437	50,400	51,104	52,634
Gulf War (8/1990 to 8/2001), no Vietnam Era	2,311,059	2,293,258	2,291,427	2,297,491	2,278,169
Gulf War (8/1990 to 8/2001) and Vietnam Era	300,126	309,843	313,438	312,156	309,495
Vietnam Era, no Korean War, no World War II	7,050,979	7,124,082	7,063,156	6,989,411	6,838,075
Vietnam Era and Korean War, no World War II	251,349	243,940	231,011	222,227	207,961
Vietnam Era and Korean War and World War II	81,117	73,633	66,733	63,234	53,473
Korean War, no Vietnam Era, no World War II	2,470,718	2,396,173	2,288,991	2,169,804	2,047,339
Korean War and World War II, no Vietnam Era	197,453	178,748	162,074	145,443	128,003
World War II, no Korean War, no Vietnam Era	2,676,493	2,394,097	2,132,905	1,891,533	1,653,181
Between Gulf War and Vietnam Era only	3,067,759	3,059,344	3,031,733	3,009,402	2,950,623
Between Vietnam Era and Korean War only	2,499,801	2,476,012	2,406,457	2,340,897	2,206,368
Between Korean War and World War II only	176,444	163,629	150,986	139,086	129,912
Pre-World War II only	48,043	39,774	33,590	28,251	24,577

Table 8. Service-Connected Disability-Rating Status and Ratings for Civilian Veterans 18 Years and Over, United States, American Community Survey Estimates, 2010–2013

(Number; percent.)

Characteristic	2010				2011			
	1-year estimates	Percent distribution	3-year estimates	Percent distribution	1-year estimates	Percent distribution	3-year estimates	Percent distribution
Total	21,798,077	100.0	22,168,038	100.0	21,458,427	100.0	21,797,348	100.0
Has no service-connected disability rating	18,397,255	84.4	18,797,570	84.8	17,993,755	83.9	18,407,153	84.4
Has a service-connected disability rating	3,400,822	15.6	3,370,468	15.2	3,464,672	16.1	3,390,195	15.6
0 percent	234,428	1.1	248,789	1.1	218,482	1.0	230,154	1.1
10 or 20 percent	1,259,686	5.8	1,298,462	5.9	1,156,848	5.4	1,211,805	5.6
30 or 40 percent	549,468	2.5	547,130	2.5	621,256	2.9	572,731	2.6
50 or 60 percent	330,552	1.5	319,962	1.4	386,231	1.8	347,074	1.6
70 percent or higher	697,681	3.2	653,136	2.9	810,245	3.8	724,077	3.3
Rating not reported	329,007	1.5	302,989	1.4	271,610	1.3	304,354	1.4

Characteristic	2012				2013			
	1-year estimates	Percent distribution	3-year estimates	Percent distribution	1-year estimates	Percent distribution	3-year estimates	Percent distribution
Total	21,230,865	100.0	21,500,559	100.0	19,588,586	100.0	20,757,863	100.0
Has no service-connected disability rating	17,633,991	83.1	18,011,153	83.8	16,012,592	81.7	17,210,837	82.9
Has a service-connected disability rating	3,596,874	16.9	3,489,406	16.2	3,575,994	18.3	3,547,026	17.1
0 percent	216,110	1.0	222,270	1.0	209,821	1.1	214,084	1.0
10 or 20 percent	1,168,920	5.5	1,197,985	5.6	1,132,920	5.8	1,155,274	5.6
30 or 40 percent	645,469	3.0	604,525	2.8	627,230	3.2	628,949	3.0
50 or 60 percent	422,800	2.0	379,753	1.8	436,466	2.2	416,065	2.0
70 percent or higher	881,981	4.2	796,074	3.7	957,504	4.9	883,202	4.3
Rating not reported	261,594	1.2	288,799	1.3	212,053	1.1	249,452	1.2

Note: Percentages may not sum to 100 due to rounding.

Table 9. Sex by Age by Veteran Status for the Civilian Population, United States, American Community Survey Estimates, 2009–2013

(Number.)

Characteristic	2009			2010			2011
	1-year estimates	3-year estimates	5-year estimates	1-year estimates	3-year estimates	5-year estimates	1-year estimates
Total	231,222,799	228,727,364	226,148,027	234,137,287	231,412,378	228,808,831	236,665,774
Veteran	X	X	X	21,798,077	22,168,038	22,652,496	21,458,427
Nonveteran	X	X	X	212,339,210	209,244,340	206,156,335	215,207,347
Male	112,139,727	110,922,446	109,597,111	113,212,564	111,827,661	110,549,178	114,569,587
Total, veteran	X	X	X	20,230,784	20,647,750	21,097,591	19,892,449
Total, nonveteran	X	X	X	92,981,780	91,179,911	89,451,587	94,677,138
18 to 34 years	36,019,549	35,572,913	35,229,059	35,697,801	35,272,947	34,943,711	36,235,526
Veteran	1,362,939	1,443,292	1,528,480	1,408,612	1,368,846	1,446,720	1,433,868
Nonveteran	34,656,610	34,129,621	33,700,579	34,289,189	33,904,101	33,496,991	34,801,658
35 to 54 years	42,574,094	42,714,327	42,634,670	42,362,228	42,465,436	42,523,468	42,076,425
Veteran	5,007,290	5,183,299	5,391,735	4,831,833	5,024,738	5,220,388	4,669,590
Nonveteran	37,566,804	37,531,028	37,242,935	37,530,395	37,440,698	37,303,080	37,406,835
55 to 64 years	16,764,909	16,247,146	15,706,052	17,718,890	17,079,215	16,518,862	18,341,390
Veteran	5,245,300	5,488,526	5,606,471	5,105,379	5,363,753	5,552,030	4,823,396
Nonveteran	11,519,609	10,758,620	10,099,581	12,613,511	11,715,462	10,966,832	13,517,994
65 to 74 years	9,611,008	9,272,824	9,007,829	10,155,596	9,837,971	9,489,102	10,474,911
Veteran	4,059,643	4,061,707	4,146,894	4,200,236	4,184,117	4,202,152	4,318,269
Nonveteran	5,551,365	5,211,117	4,860,935	5,955,360	5,653,854	5,286,950	6,156,642
75 years and over	7,170,167	7,115,236	7,019,501	7,278,049	7,172,092	7,074,035	7,441,335
Veteran	4,699,385	4,692,335	4,651,040	4,684,724	4,706,296	4,676,301	4,647,326
Nonveteran	2,470,782	2,422,901	2,368,461	2,593,325	2,465,796	2,397,734	2,794,009
Female	119,083,072	117,804,918	116,550,916	120,924,723	119,584,717	118,259,653	122,096,187
Total, veteran	X	X	X	1,567,293	1,520,288	1,554,905	1,565,978
Total, nonveteran	X	X	X	119,357,430	118,064,429	116,704,748	120,530,209
18 to 34 years	34,961,931	34,527,432	34,228,065	35,393,396	34,999,782	34,630,458	35,757,455
Veteran	307,572	318,126	331,639	339,980	317,056	328,433	335,393
Nonveteran	34,654,359	34,209,306	33,896,426	35,053,416	34,682,726	34,302,025	35,422,062
35 to 54 years	43,367,813	43,490,031	43,462,362	43,494,034	43,639,069	43,691,690	43,152,255
Veteran	716,032	731,632	741,705	737,352	733,752	740,760	719,325
Nonveteran	42,651,781	42,758,399	42,720,657	42,756,682	42,905,317	42,950,930	42,432,930
55 to 64 years	18,027,855	17,456,056	16,886,949	19,037,413	18,354,228	17,751,229	19,717,697
Veteran	203,204	197,704	198,430	239,709	214,158	209,022	260,627
Nonveteran	17,824,651	17,258,352	16,688,519	18,797,704	18,140,070	17,542,207	19,457,070
65 to 74 years	11,214,629	10,857,877	10,588,203	11,698,439	11,361,486	11,004,365	12,014,318
Veteran	92,830	95,680	106,770	99,302	95,365	102,871	100,297
Nonveteran	11,121,799	10,762,197	10,481,433	11,599,137	11,266,121	10,901,494	11,914,021
75 years and over	11,510,844	11,473,522	11,385,337	11,301,441	11,230,152	11,181,911	11,454,462
Veteran	160,179	170,661	191,414	150,950	159,957	173,819	150,336
Nonveteran	11,350,665	11,302,861	11,193,923	11,150,491	11,070,195	11,008,092	11,304,126

X = Not applicable/not available.

Table 9. Sex by Age by Veteran Status for the Civilian Population, United States, American Community Survey Estimates, 2009–2013—*Continued*

(Number.)

Characteristic	2011		2012			2013		
	3-year estimates	5-year estimates	1-year estimates	3-year estimates	5-year estimates	1-year estimates	3-year estimates	5-year estimates
Total	234,063,189	231,421,987	239,178,768	236,680,744	234,029,580	241,556,724	239,133,187	236,576,902
Veteran	21,797,348	22,215,303	21,230,865	21,500,559	21,853,912	19,588,586	20,757,863	21,263,779
Nonveteran	212,265,841	209,206,684	217,947,903	215,180,185	212,175,668	221,968,138	218,375,324	215,313,123
Male	113,204,009	111,874,993	115,846,470	114,585,505	113,202,658	117,124,074	115,882,380	114,530,194
Total, veteran	20,259,192	20,679,894	19,617,634	19,917,988	20,306,044	18,036,876	19,181,357	19,709,452
Total, nonveteran	92,944,817	91,195,099	96,228,836	94,667,517	92,896,614	99,087,198	96,701,023	94,820,742
18 to 34 years	35,748,681	35,337,119	36,646,425	36,241,723	35,769,216	37,082,660	36,689,853	36,213,953
Veteran	1,391,194	1,408,561	1,471,765	1,441,306	1,403,109	1,326,760	1,415,464	1,397,538
Nonveteran	34,357,487	33,928,558	35,174,660	34,800,417	34,366,107	35,755,900	35,274,389	34,816,415
35 to 54 years	42,274,463	42,413,848	41,816,824	42,055,032	42,236,359	41,519,834	41,786,295	42,014,910
Veteran	4,845,024	5,023,645	4,545,460	4,681,057	4,855,186	4,052,575	4,419,719	4,634,244
Nonveteran	37,429,439	37,390,203	37,271,364	37,373,975	37,381,173	37,467,259	37,366,576	37,380,666
55 to 64 years	17,711,835	17,114,811	18,577,958	18,228,321	17,641,437	18,947,363	18,633,809	18,140,850
Veteran	5,099,254	5,344,370	4,287,701	4,738,802	5,044,350	3,664,398	4,255,989	4,649,009
Nonveteran	12,612,581	11,770,441	14,290,257	13,489,519	12,597,087	15,282,965	14,377,820	13,491,841
65 to 74 years	10,166,322	9,816,070	11,212,220	10,612,787	10,238,746	11,795,606	11,160,105	10,699,722
Veteran	4,233,652	4,212,724	4,675,833	4,396,939	4,313,203	4,591,789	4,524,826	4,399,549
Nonveteran	5,932,670	5,603,346	6,536,387	6,215,848	5,925,543	7,203,817	6,635,279	6,300,173
						7,778,611		
75 years and over	7,302,708	7,193,145	7,593,043	7,447,642	7,316,900		7,612,318	7,460,759
Veteran	4,690,068	4,690,594	4,636,875	4,659,884	4,690,196	4,401,354	4,565,359	4,629,112
Nonveteran	2,612,640	2,502,551	2,956,168	2,787,758	2,626,704	3,377,257	3,046,959	2,831,647
Female	120,859,180	119,546,994	123,332,298	122,095,239	120,826,922	124,432,650	123,250,807	122,046,708
Total, veteran	1,538,156	1,535,409	1,613,231	1,582,571	1,547,868	1,551,710	1,576,506	1,554,327
Total, nonveteran	119,321,024	118,011,585	121,719,067	120,512,668	119,279,054	122,880,940	121,674,301	120,492,381
18 to 34 years	35,397,483	35,003,957	36,146,759	35,790,148	35,400,529	36,439,230	36,116,917	35,762,242
Veteran	326,821	323,823	346,493	342,223	327,488	300,902	328,306	325,905
Nonveteran	35,070,662	34,680,134	35,800,266	35,447,925	35,073,041	36,138,328	35,788,611	35,436,337
35 to 54 years	43,406,036	43,557,745	42,845,945	43,122,933	43,352,982	42,517,877	42,812,939	43,095,332
Veteran	723,024	731,220	722,578	724,701	727,180	665,161	701,080	711,580
Nonveteran	42,683,012	42,826,525	42,123,367	42,398,232	42,625,802	41,852,716	42,111,859	42,383,752
55 to 64 years	19,035,276	18,385,687	20,004,380	19,590,228	18,957,616	20,385,770	20,036,988	19,498,573
Veteran	236,457	220,969	285,942	262,060	237,513	310,516	285,657	259,380
Nonveteran	18,798,819	18,164,718	19,718,438	19,328,168	18,720,103	20,075,254	19,751,331	19,239,193
65 to 74 years	11,692,764	11,336,661	12,792,540	12,159,860	11,773,315	13,418,140	12,737,277	12,257,308
Veteran	98,508	98,457	111,820	104,250	100,144	123,496	112,239	106,138
Nonveteran	11,594,256	11,238,204	12,680,720	12,055,610	11,673,171	13,294,644	12,625,038	12,151,170
75 years and over	11,327,621	11,262,944	11,542,674	11,432,070	11,342,480	11,671,633	11,546,686	11,433,253
Veteran	153,346	160,940	146,398	149,337	155,543	151,635	149,224	151,324
Nonveteran	11,174,275	11,102,004	11,396,276	11,282,733	11,186,937	11,519,998	11,397,462	11,281,929

Table 10. Sex by Age by Veteran Status for the Civilian Population, United States, by Race and Hispanic Origin, American Community Survey Estimates, 2009–2013

(Number.)

Characteristic	White alone									
	2009		2010		2011		2012		2013	
	1-year estimates	3-year estimates	1-year estimates	3-year estimates	1-year estimates	3-year estimates	1-year estimates	3-year estimates	1-year estimates	3-year estimates
Total	177,352,027	175,071,191	178,109,255	176,421,474	179,679,273	178,037,060	181,055,755	179,601,297	182,277,317	180,976,600
Male	86,323,834	85,160,907	86,588,368	85,706,532	87,420,353	86,549,324	88,154,999	87,386,584	88,889,776	88,158,019
18 to 34 years	25,644,573	25,145,013	25,134,566	24,853,729	25,465,156	25,158,987	25,713,929	25,450,407	25,939,820	25,722,672
Veteran	1,047,841	1,101,331	1,083,836	1,050,797	1,104,600	1,068,478	1,135,762	1,108,583	1,026,941	1,092,844
Nonveteran	24,596,732	24,043,682	24,050,730	23,802,932	24,360,556	24,090,509	24,578,167	24,341,824	24,912,879	24,629,828
35 to 54 years	32,461,980	32,563,476	32,032,351	32,244,281	31,698,158	31,957,282	31,359,228	31,674,726	31,020,590	31,341,424
Veteran	3,861,796	3,988,578	3,681,638	3,840,992	3,598,609	3,713,465	3,475,797	3,585,526	3,120,509	3,394,678
Nonveteran	28,600,184	28,574,898	28,350,713	28,403,289	28,099,549	28,243,817	27,883,431	28,089,200	27,900,081	27,946,746
55 to 64 years	13,802,971	13,380,403	14,447,638	13,983,414	14,918,383	14,448,692	15,014,125	14,800,142	15,248,795	15,065,651
Veteran	4,528,397	4,774,367	4,346,768	4,614,290	4,075,624	4,345,054	3,545,753	3,986,450	2,984,672	3,531,970
Nonveteran	9,274,574	8,606,036	10,100,870	9,369,124	10,842,759	10,103,638	11,468,372	10,813,692	12,264,123	11,533,681
65 to 74 years	8,123,753	7,825,688	8,579,797	8,313,895	8,829,915	8,578,645	9,454,702	8,951,538	9,932,219	9,400,841
Veteran	3,669,534	3,666,549	3,786,443	3,775,975	3,890,947	3,817,828	4,188,769	3,954,605	4,090,701	4,053,906
Nonveteran	4,454,219	4,159,139	4,793,354	4,537,920	4,938,968	4,760,817	5,265,933	4,996,933	5,841,518	5,346,935
75 years and over	6,290,557	6,246,327	6,394,016	6,311,213	6,508,741	6,405,718	6,613,015	6,509,771	6,748,352	6,627,431
Veteran	4,334,894	4,336,091	4,332,501	4,352,626	4,295,265	4,334,018	4,268,745	4,301,716	4,035,998	4,203,497
Nonveteran	1,955,663	1,910,236	2,061,515	1,958,587	2,213,476	2,071,700	2,344,270	2,208,055	2,712,354	2,423,934
Female	91,028,193	89,910,284	91,520,887	90,714,942	92,258,920	91,487,736	92,900,756	92,214,713	93,387,541	92,818,581
18 to 34 years	24,779,187	24,317,877	24,669,944	24,408,804	24,952,153	24,690,594	25,141,654	24,932,057	25,266,380	25,120,176
Veteran	204,253	209,151	224,135	207,952	214,064	213,374	222,864	221,985	196,895	212,494
Nonveteran	24,574,934	24,108,726	24,445,809	24,200,852	24,738,089	24,477,220	24,918,790	24,710,072	25,069,485	24,907,682
35 to 54 years	32,513,904	32,629,989	32,243,726	32,479,012	31,881,387	32,175,763	31,517,172	31,854,912	31,093,054	31,474,046
Veteran	500,756	516,213	510,445	508,335	488,549	496,376	495,418	495,792	440,984	473,724
Nonveteran	32,013,148	32,113,776	31,733,281	31,970,677	31,392,838	31,679,387	31,021,754	31,359,120	30,652,070	31,000,322
55 to 64 years	14,489,736	14,051,144	15,185,371	14,700,716	15,689,305	15,189,249	15,810,872	15,567,809	16,038,971	15,850,067
Veteran	159,584	158,626	187,727	169,913	197,478	182,695	214,641	200,313	233,188	215,096
Nonveteran	14,330,152	13,892,518	14,997,644	14,530,803	15,491,827	15,006,554	15,596,231	15,367,496	15,805,783	15,634,971
65 to 74 years	9,281,826	8,972,043	9,663,528	9,396,024	9,902,261	9,659,924	10,550,373	10,038,333	11,037,582	10,496,386
Veteran	80,509	83,723	86,622	83,204	86,566	85,724	94,051	89,626	104,212	95,209
Nonveteran	9,201,317	8,888,320	9,576,906	9,312,820	9,815,695	9,574,200	10,456,322	9,948,707	10,933,370	10,401,177
75 years and over	9,963,540	9,939,231	9,758,318	9,730,386	9,833,814	9,772,206	9,880,685	9,821,602	9,951,554	9,877,906
Veteran	149,070	160,751	141,121	149,882	140,662	143,184	133,914	138,783	137,493	137,181
Nonveteran	9,814,470	9,778,480	9,617,197	9,580,504	9,693,152	9,629,022	9,746,771	9,682,819	9,814,061	9,740,725

Table 10. Sex by Age by Veteran Status for the Civilian Population, United States, by Race and Hispanic Origin, American Community Survey Estimates, 2009–2013—*Continued*

(Number.)

Characteristic	Black or African American alone									
	2009		2010		2011		2012		2013	
	1-year estimates	3-year estimates	1-year estimates	3-year estimates	1-year estimates	3-year estimates	1-year estimates	3-year estimates	1-year estimates	3-year estimates
Total	27,308,474	26,849,289	27,972,593	27,484,247	28,478,447	27,954,368	28,945,185	28,444,042	29,320,106	28,881,310
Male	12,622,311	12,402,515	12,921,380	12,679,201	13,206,135	12,928,651	13,445,220	13,197,827	13,624,362	13,421,170
18 to 34 years	4,855,030	4,745,107	4,737,976	4,655,075	4,911,617	4,766,942	5,005,424	4,898,453	5,082,805	5,002,839
Veteran	179,847	195,610	187,687	178,753	185,312	182,727	192,861	190,746	158,211	179,239
Nonveteran	4,675,183	4,549,497	4,550,289	4,476,322	4,726,305	4,584,215	4,812,563	4,707,707	4,924,594	4,823,600
35 to 54 years	4,882,514	4,876,409	5,059,513	5,018,400	5,024,156	5,021,938	5,020,609	5,022,288	4,986,291	5,002,372
Veteran	826,799	856,611	841,402	858,833	773,627	820,732	764,634	791,717	660,700	731,305
Nonveteran	4,055,715	4,019,798	4,218,111	4,159,567	4,250,529	4,201,206	4,255,975	4,230,571	4,325,591	4,271,067
55 to 64 years	1,596,710	1,524,915	1,778,425	1,692,174	1,867,523	1,781,282	1,946,305	1,867,433	2,010,206	1,939,335
Veteran	494,027	483,119	544,124	529,286	536,881	537,115	541,679	542,408	492,801	524,084
Nonveteran	1,102,683	1,041,796	1,234,301	1,162,888	1,330,642	1,244,167	1,404,626	1,325,025	1,517,405	1,415,251
65 to 74 years	806,528	779,749	860,464	835,318	892,703	865,836	946,125	898,678	1,001,950	946,964
Veteran	266,540	266,268	282,136	280,268	290,592	284,453	328,304	299,456	342,360	319,510
Nonveteran	539,988	513,481	578,328	555,050	602,111	581,383	617,821	599,222	659,590	627,454
75 years and over	481,529	476,335	485,002	478,234	510,136	492,653	526,757	510,975	543,110	529,660
Veteran	248,728	240,834	239,681	242,812	237,067	243,359	248,940	243,523	239,348	242,722
Nonveteran	232,801	235,501	245,321	235,422	273,069	249,294	277,817	267,452	303,762	286,938
Female	14,686,163	14,446,774	15,051,213	14,805,046	15,272,312	15,025,717	15,499,965	15,246,215	15,695,744	15,460,140
18 to 34 years	5,027,557	4,942,038	5,091,234	5,007,266	5,178,514	5,089,616	5,264,752	5,172,291	5,309,555	5,240,055
Veteran	71,974	75,598	74,461	72,836	79,701	74,622	81,879	78,313	63,948	74,326
Nonveteran	4,955,583	4,866,440	5,016,773	4,934,430	5,098,813	5,014,994	5,182,873	5,093,978	5,245,607	5,165,729
35 to 54 years	5,625,280	5,604,943	5,717,130	5,711,889	5,678,764	5,694,281	5,648,139	5,669,271	5,643,208	5,648,012
Veteran	162,901	165,896	174,502	172,081	179,416	173,811	172,819	176,709	168,791	173,862
Nonveteran	5,462,379	5,439,047	5,542,628	5,539,808	5,499,348	5,520,470	5,475,320	5,492,562	5,474,417	5,474,150
55 to 64 years	1,980,900	1,889,899	2,147,293	2,038,571	2,250,260	2,141,039	2,338,111	2,238,575	2,412,790	2,327,806
Veteran	31,823	27,898	39,694	33,077	47,338	40,464	53,915	46,439	57,131	52,657
Nonveteran	1,949,077	1,862,001	2,107,599	2,005,494	2,202,922	2,100,575	2,284,196	2,192,136	2,355,659	2,275,149
65 to 74 years	1,124,084	1,089,272	1,163,012	1,133,701	1,201,774	1,162,262	1,262,518	1,202,627	1,330,516	1,260,784
Veteran	7,861	7,250	8,202	7,487	7,994	7,868	11,650	9,177	13,259	10,920
Nonveteran	1,116,223	1,082,022	1,154,810	1,126,214	1,193,780	1,154,394	1,250,868	1,193,450	1,317,257	1,249,864
75 years and over	928,342	920,622	932,544	913,619	963,000	938,519	986,445	963,451	999,675	983,483
Veteran	6,281	5,905	6,713	6,364	6,114	6,492	7,841	6,786	8,263	7,400
Nonveteran	922,061	914,717	925,831	907,255	956,886	932,027	978,604	956,665	991,412	976,083

Table 10. Sex by Age by Veteran Status for the Civilian Population, United States, by Race and Hispanic Origin, American Community Survey Estimates, 2009–2013—*Continued*

(Number.)

Characteristic	American Indian and Alaska Native alone									
	2009		2010		2011		2012		2013	
	1-year estimates	3-year estimates	1-year estimates	3-year estimates	1-year estimates	3-year estimates	1-year estimates	3-year estimates	1-year estimates	3-year estimates
Total	1,744,086	1,736,388	1,804,775	1,762,413	1,804,173	1,785,380	1,832,136	1,815,497	1,814,586	1,821,454
Male	848,370	852,557	885,048	864,574	874,259	872,494	899,358	887,981	891,711	890,990
18 to 34 years	329,219	328,079	335,246	329,005	326,151	330,406	334,156	333,517	337,562	333,769
Veteran	12,977	14,295	9,940	12,216	12,383	11,643	12,721	11,634	11,873	12,616
Nonveteran	316,242	313,784	325,306	316,789	313,768	318,763	321,435	321,883	325,689	321,153
35 to 54 years	327,755	334,922	342,143	341,104	338,785	340,214	343,322	341,503	325,216	337,444
Veteran	46,765	51,738	46,987	49,491	46,622	46,599	48,028	47,139	34,544	43,938
Nonveteran	280,990	283,184	295,156	291,613	292,163	293,615	295,294	294,364	290,672	293,506
55 to 64 years	111,604	109,862	125,230	115,481	123,086	119,720	127,614	125,376	130,597	127,391
Veteran	42,089	42,215	40,795	41,171	39,457	40,340	37,040	39,614	32,878	36,765
Nonveteran	69,515	67,647	84,435	74,310	83,629	79,380	90,574	85,762	97,719	90,626
65 to 74 years	53,329	52,900	54,658	52,977	59,779	55,462	65,511	59,952	65,338	63,646
Veteran	22,361	23,158	24,381	22,890	24,991	24,033	30,436	26,950	28,453	27,803
Nonveteran	30,968	29,742	30,277	30,087	34,788	31,429	35,075	33,002	36,885	35,843
75 years and over	26,463	26,794	27,771	26,007	26,458	26,692	28,755	27,633	32,998	28,740
Veteran	13,530	14,653	16,788	14,782	14,079	14,785	15,875	15,456	16,184	14,863
Nonveteran	12,933	12,141	10,983	11,225	12,379	11,907	12,880	12,177	16,814	13,877
Female	895,716	883,831	919,727	897,839	929,914	912,886	932,778	927,516	922,875	930,464
18 to 34 years	318,219	310,435	327,533	318,312	332,723	324,169	323,995	327,888	319,987	325,923
Veteran	3,516	3,859	4,824	3,905	4,558	4,061	4,933	4,680	3,765	4,713
Nonveteran	314,703	306,576	322,709	314,407	328,165	320,108	319,062	323,208	316,222	321,210
35 to 54 years	346,967	349,306	357,808	355,866	352,441	354,387	347,667	353,011	335,756	347,818
Veteran	8,228	7,812	9,480	8,843	6,463	8,401	8,121	8,004	7,458	7,244
Nonveteran	338,739	341,494	348,328	347,023	345,978	345,986	339,546	345,007	328,298	340,574
55 to 64 years	125,760	121,434	131,153	123,442	132,821	129,964	143,616	135,946	146,166	140,641
Veteran	2,506	2,189	1,989	1,939	3,453	2,456	2,779	2,690	3,522	3,286
Nonveteran	123,254	119,245	129,164	121,503	129,368	127,508	140,837	133,256	142,644	137,355
65 to 74 years	62,349	61,619	63,330	61,612	67,844	63,874	72,532	67,994	75,863	71,998
Veteran	755	978	808	876	789	866	888	893	909	908
Nonveteran	61,594	60,641	62,522	60,736	67,055	63,008	71,644	67,101	74,954	71,090
75 years and over	42,421	41,037	39,903	38,607	44,085	40,492	44,968	42,677	45,103	44,084
Veteran	476	544	523	559	428	405	865	567	1,130	761
Nonveteran	41,945	40,493	39,380	38,048	43,657	40,087	44,103	42,110	43,973	43,323

Table 10. Sex by Age by Veteran Status for the Civilian Population, United States, by Race and Hispanic Origin, American Community Survey Estimates, 2009–2013—*Continued*

(Number.)

Characteristic	Asian alone									
	2009		2010		2011		2012		2013	
	1-year estimates	3-year estimates	1-year estimates	3-year estimates	1-year estimates	3-year estimates	1-year estimates	3-year estimates	1-year estimates	3-year estimates
Total	10,634,837	10,392,116	11,455,714	11,290,521	11,737,502	11,535,549	12,204,103	11,852,203	12,608,326	12,230,890
Male	5,012,155	4,914,173	5,324,051	5,259,904	5,454,118	5,367,210	5,663,414	5,507,681	5,865,008	5,686,104
18 to 34 years	1,749,297	1,739,925	1,911,384	1,919,922	1,931,320	1,931,438	2,007,813	1,967,343	2,071,170	2,015,582
Veteran	31,199	33,502	34,172	34,462	37,881	35,958	36,125	36,714	33,170	35,957
Nonveteran	1,718,098	1,706,423	1,877,212	1,885,460	1,893,439	1,895,480	1,971,688	1,930,629	2,038,000	1,979,625
35 to 54 years	2,050,006	2,011,386	2,110,088	2,085,569	2,153,958	2,121,251	2,206,686	2,159,993	2,254,312	2,210,786
Veteran	61,889	68,439	65,777	68,017	65,591	65,592	65,701	66,211	65,906	66,749
Nonveteran	1,988,117	1,942,947	2,044,311	2,017,552	2,088,367	2,055,659	2,140,985	2,093,782	2,188,406	2,144,037
55 to 64 years	638,320	612,806	695,624	668,607	730,464	700,136	758,591	731,687	797,589	766,750
Veteran	55,561	55,938	50,726	55,675	47,096	52,008	46,531	48,836	43,692	45,719
Nonveteran	582,759	556,868	644,898	612,932	683,368	648,128	712,060	682,851	753,897	721,031
65 to 74 years	354,981	339,160	379,668	369,313	396,813	385,633	430,254	405,383	463,183	432,830
Veteran	37,730	40,100	41,716	40,603	41,006	41,320	46,270	43,881	52,712	47,029
Nonveteran	317,251	299,060	337,952	328,710	355,807	344,313	383,984	361,502	410,471	385,801
75 years and over	219,551	210,896	227,287	216,493	241,563	228,752	260,070	243,275	278,754	260,156
Veteran	48,149	47,022	48,053	47,519	46,489	46,723	48,551	46,816	53,055	48,812
Nonveteran	171,402	163,874	179,234	168,974	195,074	182,029	211,519	196,459	225,699	211,344
		5,477,943								
Female	5,622,682		6,131,663	6,030,617	6,283,384	6,168,339	6,540,689	6,344,522	6,743,318	6,544,786
18 to 34 years	1,827,028	1,813,784	2,055,786	2,059,445	2,066,957	2,070,139	2,151,008	2,109,049	2,185,530	2,148,078
Veteran	8,730	8,057	8,381	8,702	9,959	9,167	9,292	9,126	9,681	9,397
Nonveteran	1,818,298	1,805,727	2,047,405	2,050,743	2,056,998	2,060,972	2,141,716	2,099,923	2,175,849	2,138,681
35 to 54 years	2,267,175	2,207,495	2,415,756	2,384,259	2,461,346	2,427,436	2,540,106	2,476,780	2,601,894	2,539,707
Veteran	9,698	9,512	10,717	10,463	11,297	10,826	10,833	10,992	10,749	11,099
Nonveteran	2,257,477	2,197,983	2,405,039	2,373,796	2,450,049	2,416,610	2,529,273	2,465,788	2,591,145	2,528,608
55 to 64 years	763,145	727,466	854,012	816,018	898,737	859,439	939,724	902,635	981,231	943,940
Veteran	2,594	2,717	3,326	2,718	2,700	3,003	3,877	3,317	4,712	3,720
Nonveteran	760,551	724,749	850,686	813,300	896,037	856,436	935,847	899,318	976,519	940,220
65 to 74 years	422,690	402,047	463,351	441,999	490,208	466,264	522,648	491,509	562,283	525,010
Veteran	916	1,155	1,272	1,286	1,574	1,268	1,879	1,595	1,466	1,690
Nonveteran	421,774	400,892	462,079	440,713	488,634	464,996	520,769	489,914	560,817	523,320
75 years and over	342,644	327,151	342,758	328,896	366,136	345,061	387,203	364,549	412,380	388,051
Veteran	1,717	1,541	1,058	1,398	1,102	1,281	1,571	1,198	1,724	1,436
Nonveteran	340,927	325,610	341,700	327,498	365,034	343,780	385,632	363,351	410,656	386,615

Table 10. Sex by Age by Veteran Status for the Civilian Population, United States, by Race and Hispanic Origin, American Community Survey Estimates, 2009–2013—*Continued*

(Number.)

	Native Hawaiian and Other Pacific Islander alone									
	2009		2010		2011		2012		2013	
Characteristic	1-year estimates	3-year estimates	1-year estimates	3-year estimates	1-year estimates	3-year estimates	1-year estimates	3-year estimates	1-year estimates	3-year estimates
Total	329,113	330,789	352,422	352,892	353,845	357,440	385,207	369,980	373,632	378,192
Male	163,941	163,643	174,089	174,081	175,049	175,848	188,084	181,421	184,182	186,058
18 to 34 years	68,041	69,904	76,308	76,020	73,335	75,769	81,928	78,203	77,630	78,715
Veteran	3,383	3,722	3,203	4,139	4,977	4,161	5,006	4,353	4,246	4,584
Nonveteran	64,658	66,182	73,105	71,881	68,358	71,608	76,922	73,850	73,384	74,131
35 to 54 years	63,374	62,127	65,563	66,346	67,286	66,997	69,741	68,383	69,255	69,734
Veteran	11,345	10,548	9,057	11,198	8,077	10,088	10,182	9,394	8,549	9,035
Nonveteran	52,029	51,579	56,506	55,148	59,209	56,909	59,559	58,989	60,706	60,699
55 to 64 years	20,025	19,068	19,116	19,161	20,353	19,773	21,724	20,456	21,671	22,173
Veteran	6,282	6,767	6,002	6,111	6,323	6,443	6,256	6,221	6,750	6,541
Nonveteran	13,743	12,301	13,114	13,050	14,030	13,330	15,468	14,235	14,921	15,632
65 to 74 years	8,133	8,516	9,189	8,534	10,902	9,528	9,666	10,244	10,704	10,801
Veteran	3,331	3,194	3,218	3,346	3,507	3,533	4,251	3,750	3,263	3,687
Nonveteran	4,802	5,322	5,971	5,188	7,395	5,995	5,415	6,494	7,441	7,114
75 years and over	4,368	4,028	3,913	4,020	3,173	3,781	5,025	4,135	4,922	4,635
Veteran	2,081	2,285	2,160	2,106	1,609	2,038	2,823	2,244	2,659	2,478
Nonveteran	2,287	1,743	1,753	1,914	1,564	1,743	2,202	1,891	2,263	2,157
Female	165,172	167,146	178,333	178,811	178,796	181,592	197,123	188,559	189,450	192,134
18 to 34 years	64,531	66,930	76,275	74,084	74,726	75,691	76,900	77,928	74,087	77,351
Veteran	1,148	1,124	1,805	1,457	900	1,408	1,517	1,566	1,200	1,291
Nonveteran	63,383	65,806	74,470	72,627	73,826	74,283	75,383	76,362	72,887	76,060
35 to 54 years	66,413	65,509	65,643	69,138	67,012	69,093	76,286	70,637	70,979	72,245
Veteran	1,709	1,870	1,614	1,942	1,582	1,748	1,381	1,466	2,084	1,677
Nonveteran	64,704	63,639	64,029	67,196	65,430	67,345	74,905	69,171	68,895	70,568
55 to 64 years	19,408	19,026	22,133	20,377	20,713	21,123	25,406	22,722	22,514	23,055
Veteran	507	339	406	384	315	454	538	506	681	550
Nonveteran	18,901	18,687	21,727	19,993	20,398	20,669	24,868	22,216	21,833	22,505
65 to 74 years	8,662	9,235	8,705	9,010	10,297	9,518	12,855	11,221	14,316	12,787
Veteran	282	270	222	252	124	235	277	224	392	271
Nonveteran	8,380	8,965	8,483	8,758	10,173	9,283	12,578	10,997	13,924	12,516
75 years and over	6,158	6,446	5,577	6,202	6,048	6,167	5,676	6,051	7,554	6,696
Veteran	42	42	86	52	55	93	72	84	197	116
Nonveteran	6,116	6,404	5,491	6,150	5,993	6,074	5,604	5,967	7,357	6,580

Table 10. Sex by Age by Veteran Status for the Civilian Population, United States, by Race and Hispanic Origin, American Community Survey Estimates, 2009–2013—*Continued*

(Number.)

	Some other race alone									
	2009		2010		2011		2012		2013	
Characteristic	1-year estimates	3-year estimates	1-year estimates	3-year estimates	1-year estimates	3-year estimates	1-year estimates	3-year estimates	1-year estimates	3-year estimates
Total	10,008,345	10,782,246	10,055,343	10,129,047	10,040,849	10,107,040	9,949,970	10,010,980	10,194,224	10,060,574
Male	5,301,755	5,695,367	5,202,004	5,231,887	5,213,482	5,238,053	5,164,570	5,199,733	5,263,260	5,217,476
18 to 34 years	2,498,512	2,734,150	2,511,516	2,544,167	2,469,781	2,509,848	2,391,953	2,458,175	2,404,976	2,421,243
Veteran	45,566	54,083	45,535	47,228	45,654	45,912	41,512	44,176	44,973	44,139
Nonveteran	2,452,946	2,680,067	2,465,981	2,496,939	2,424,127	2,463,936	2,350,441	2,413,999	2,360,003	2,377,104
35 to 54 years	2,128,689	2,252,063	2,009,824	2,032,901	2,046,528	2,046,315	2,040,063	2,033,972	2,074,263	2,053,572
Veteran	92,443	103,985	85,446	91,182	79,977	86,818	75,660	80,911	68,854	75,506
Nonveteran	2,036,246	2,148,078	1,924,378	1,941,719	1,966,551	1,959,497	1,964,403	1,953,061	2,005,409	1,978,066
55 to 64 years	408,450	427,308	433,784	408,547	436,742	426,631	459,227	445,682	482,975	462,489
Veteran	55,822	61,253	48,529	52,630	48,356	50,980	45,219	47,521	42,689	45,337
Nonveteran	352,628	366,055	385,255	355,917	388,386	375,651	414,008	398,161	440,286	417,152
65 to 74 years	172,179	179,601	165,652	162,326	171,340	168,493	179,461	172,623	202,279	184,929
Veteran	22,423	24,776	22,846	22,584	25,111	23,509	26,845	25,090	27,429	26,419
Nonveteran	149,756	154,825	142,806	139,742	146,229	144,984	152,616	147,533	174,850	158,510
75 years and over	93,925	102,245	81,228	83,946	89,091	86,766	93,866	89,281	98,767	95,243
Veteran	20,853	23,639	15,562	17,937	21,253	18,727	19,117	18,778	20,354	20,426
Nonveteran	73,072	78,606	65,666	66,009	67,838	68,039	74,749	70,503	78,413	74,817
Female	4,706,590	5,086,879	4,853,339	4,897,160	4,827,367	4,868,987	4,785,400	4,811,247	4,930,964	4,843,098
18 to 34 years	2,067,103	2,263,258	2,164,824	2,207,179	2,097,196	2,155,146	2,064,409	2,107,768	2,085,707	2,078,621
Veteran	9,591	10,391	12,353	10,799	10,176	11,266	11,573	11,405	10,946	10,876
Nonveteran	2,057,512	2,252,867	2,152,471	2,196,380	2,087,020	2,143,880	2,052,836	2,096,363	2,074,761	2,067,745
35 to 54 years	1,871,524	2,000,765	1,904,190	1,924,935	1,911,085	1,922,450	1,889,590	1,892,910	1,948,243	1,914,496
Veteran	12,480	12,546	8,478	11,289	11,408	10,864	11,227	10,254	10,364	10,718
Nonveteran	1,859,044	1,988,219	1,895,712	1,913,646	1,899,677	1,911,586	1,878,363	1,882,656	1,937,879	1,903,778
55 to 64 years	422,211	442,524	448,558	428,871	462,683	446,922	469,053	459,052	499,724	476,580
Veteran	1,481	1,933	1,974	1,873	2,590	2,040	2,026	2,225	4,028	2,884
Nonveteran	420,730	440,591	446,584	426,998	460,093	444,882	467,027	456,827	495,696	473,696
65 to 74 years	200,971	219,284	203,038	203,146	209,694	205,958	218,663	210,201	244,585	224,491
Veteran	523	589	240	415	833	525	957	631	1,156	920
Nonveteran	200,448	218,695	202,798	202,731	208,861	205,433	217,706	209,570	243,429	223,571
75 years and over	144,781	161,048	132,729	133,029	146,709	138,511	143,685	141,316	152,705	148,910
Veteran	862	605	524	616	608	624	340	503	610	561
Nonveteran	143,919	160,443	132,205	132,413	146,101	137,887	143,345	140,813	152,095	148,349

Table 10. Sex by Age by Veteran Status for the Civilian Population, United States, by Race and Hispanic Origin, American Community Survey Estimates, 2009–2013—*Continued*

(Number.)

Characteristic	Two or more races									
	2009		2010		2011		2012		2013	
	1-year estimates	3-year estimates	1-year estimates	3-year estimates	1-year estimates	3-year estimates	1-year estimates	3-year estimates	1-year estimates	3-year estimates
Total	3,845,917	3,565,345	4,387,185	3,971,784	4,571,685	4,286,352	4,806,412	4,586,745	4,968,533	4,784,167
Male	1,867,361	1,733,284	2,117,624	1,911,482	2,226,191	2,072,429	2,330,825	2,224,278	2,405,775	2,322,563
18 to 34 years	874,877	810,735	990,805	895,029	1,058,166	975,291	1,111,222	1,055,625	1,168,697	1,115,033
Veteran	42,126	40,749	44,239	41,251	43,061	42,315	47,778	45,100	47,346	46,085
Nonveteran	832,751	769,986	946,566	853,778	1,015,105	932,976	1,063,444	1,010,525	1,121,351	1,068,948
35 to 54 years	659,776	613,944	742,746	676,835	747,554	720,466	777,175	754,167	789,907	770,963
Veteran	106,253	103,400	101,526	105,025	97,087	101,730	105,458	100,159	93,513	98,508
Nonveteran	553,523	510,544	641,220	571,810	650,467	618,736	671,717	654,008	696,394	672,455
55 to 64 years	186,829	172,784	219,073	191,831	244,839	215,601	250,372	237,545	255,530	250,020
Veteran	63,122	64,867	68,435	64,590	69,659	67,314	65,223	67,752	60,916	65,573
Nonveteran	123,707	107,917	150,638	127,241	175,180	148,287	185,149	169,793	194,614	184,447
65 to 74 years	92,105	87,210	106,168	95,608	113,459	102,725	126,501	114,369	119,933	120,094
Veteran	37,724	37,662	39,496	38,451	42,115	38,976	50,958	43,207	46,871	46,472
Nonveteran	54,381	49,548	66,672	57,157	71,344	63,749	75,543	71,162	73,062	73,622
75 years and over	53,774	48,611	58,832	52,179	62,173	58,346	65,555	62,572	71,708	66,453
Veteran	31,150	27,811	29,979	28,514	31,564	30,418	32,824	31,351	33,756	32,561
Nonveteran	22,624	20,800	28,853	23,665	30,609	27,928	32,731	31,221	37,952	33,892
Female	1,978,556	1,832,061	2,269,561	2,060,302	2,345,494	2,213,923	2,475,587	2,362,467	2,562,758	2,461,604
18 to 34 years	878,306	813,110	1,007,800	924,692	1,055,186	992,128	1,124,041	1,063,167	1,197,984	1,126,713
Veteran	8,360	9,946	14,021	11,405	16,035	12,923	14,435	15,148	14,467	15,209
Nonveteran	869,946	803,164	993,779	913,287	1,039,151	979,205	1,109,606	1,048,019	1,183,517	1,111,504
35 to 54 years	676,550	632,024	789,781	713,970	800,220	762,626	826,985	805,412	824,743	816,615
Veteran	20,260	17,783	22,116	20,799	20,610	20,998	22,779	21,484	24,731	22,756
Nonveteran	656,290	614,241	767,665	693,171	779,610	741,628	804,206	783,928	800,012	793,859
55 to 64 years	226,695	204,563	248,893	226,233	263,178	247,540	277,598	263,489	284,374	274,899
Veteran	4,709	4,002	4,593	4,254	6,753	5,345	8,166	6,570	7,254	7,464
Nonveteran	221,986	200,561	244,300	221,979	256,425	242,195	269,432	256,919	277,120	267,435
65 to 74 years	114,047	104,377	133,475	115,994	132,240	124,964	152,951	137,975	152,995	145,821
Veteran	1,984	1,715	1,936	1,845	2,417	2,022	2,118	2,104	2,102	2,321
Nonveteran	112,063	102,662	131,539	114,149	129,823	122,942	150,833	135,871	150,893	143,500
75 years and over	82,958	77,987	89,612	79,413	94,670	86,665	94,012	92,424	102,662	97,556
Veteran	1,731	1,273	925	1,086	1,367	1,267	1,795	1,416	2,218	1,769
Nonveteran	81,227	76,714	88,687	78,327	93,303	85,398	92,217	91,008	100,444	95,787

Table 10. Sex by Age by Veteran Status for the Civilian Population, United States, by Race and Hispanic Origin, American Community Survey Estimates, 2009–2013—*Continued*

(Number.)

Characteristic	White alone, not Hispanic or Latino									
	2009		2010		2011		2012		2013	
	1-year estimates	3-year estimates	1-year estimates	3-year estimates	1-year estimates	3-year estimates	1-year estimates	3-year estimates	1-year estimates	3-year estimates
Total	157,421,169	156,665,739	156,589,477	155,862,438	157,215,880	156,528,746	157,808,374	157,191,302	158,357,567	157,771,345
Male	76,095,988	75,705,984	75,865,395	75,420,076	76,219,554	75,807,329	76,584,305	76,212,966	76,938,188	76,576,246
18 to 34 years	21,173,732	20,999,190	20,482,266	20,335,754	20,636,520	20,479,386	20,775,907	20,643,059	20,896,340	20,788,008
Veteran	947,686	1,000,811	955,556	938,424	972,699	949,107	1,001,414	978,104	905,613	962,518
Nonveteran	20,226,046	19,998,379	19,526,710	19,397,330	19,663,821	19,530,279	19,774,493	19,664,955	19,990,727	19,825,490
35 to 54 years	28,504,819	28,909,431	27,877,391	28,281,064	27,368,416	27,818,437	26,892,194	27,357,166	26,420,061	26,873,672
Veteran	3,625,884	3,762,573	3,441,985	3,600,582	3,346,187	3,468,693	3,221,223	3,335,142	2,885,731	3,147,166
Nonveteran	24,878,935	25,146,858	24,435,406	24,680,482	24,022,229	24,349,744	23,670,971	24,022,024	23,534,330	23,726,506
55 to 64 years	12,843,485	12,507,977	13,417,183	13,008,820	13,799,613	13,403,920	13,842,239	13,686,948	13,995,590	13,879,772
Veteran	4,356,765	4,612,386	4,178,998	4,442,171	3,909,863	4,174,563	3,389,338	3,822,751	2,832,995	3,374,060
Nonveteran	8,486,720	7,895,591	9,238,185	8,566,649	9,889,750	9,229,357	10,452,901	9,864,197	11,162,595	10,505,712
65 to 74 years	7,622,834	7,362,978	8,041,548	7,807,822	8,261,424	8,042,596	8,842,331	8,379,101	9,281,251	8,790,607
Veteran	3,560,037	3,562,264	3,669,863	3,664,384	3,769,623	3,702,071	4,058,529	3,832,391	3,952,230	3,924,669
Nonveteran	4,062,797	3,800,714	4,371,685	4,143,438	4,491,801	4,340,525	4,783,802	4,546,710	5,329,021	4,865,938
75 years and over	5,951,118	5,926,408	6,047,007	5,986,616	6,153,581	6,062,990	6,231,634	6,146,692	6,344,946	6,244,187
Veteran	4,225,045	4,231,405	4,229,320	4,249,058	4,194,710	4,230,549	4,160,032	4,197,248	3,919,256	4,093,463
Nonveteran	1,726,073	1,695,003	1,817,687	1,737,558	1,958,871	1,832,441	2,071,602	1,949,444	2,425,690	2,150,724
Female	81,325,181	80,959,755	80,724,082	80,442,362	80,996,326	80,721,417	81,224,069	80,978,336	81,419,379	81,195,099
18 to 34 years	20,925,704	20,751,053	20,332,375	20,259,126	20,466,076	20,366,746	20,536,956	20,463,625	20,577,371	20,538,499
Veteran	182,671	188,829	194,128	181,963	184,617	185,128	188,604	190,331	166,847	181,233
Nonveteran	20,743,033	20,562,224	20,138,247	20,077,163	20,281,459	20,181,618	20,348,352	20,273,294	20,410,524	20,357,266
35 to 54 years	28,848,334	29,247,421	28,142,272	28,575,674	27,608,559	28,091,311	27,090,907	27,591,493	26,590,059	27,077,691
Veteran	471,054	491,030	478,296	478,747	457,664	465,130	461,594	463,412	407,854	441,173
Nonveteran	28,377,280	28,756,391	27,663,976	28,096,927	27,150,895	27,626,181	26,629,313	27,128,081	26,182,205	26,636,518
55 to 64 years	13,442,314	13,100,165	14,029,624	13,610,611	14,441,686	14,024,627	14,502,749	14,327,433	14,662,689	14,537,946
Veteran	152,827	152,551	179,132	162,338	189,196	174,714	205,692	191,509	222,230	205,738
Nonveteran	13,289,487	12,947,614	13,850,492	13,448,273	14,252,490	13,849,913	14,297,057	14,135,924	14,440,459	14,332,208
65 to 74 years	8,668,849	8,406,113	8,990,324	8,762,737	9,200,864	8,990,240	9,796,387	9,329,261	10,251,853	9,748,609
Veteran	78,054	81,284	83,904	80,596	83,180	82,825	90,499	86,359	99,606	91,164
Nonveteran	8,590,795	8,324,829	8,906,420	8,682,141	9,117,684	8,907,415	9,705,888	9,242,902	10,152,247	9,657,445
75 years and over	9,439,980	9,455,003	9,229,487	9,234,214	9,279,141	9,248,493	9,297,070	9,266,524	9,337,407	9,292,354
Veteran	146,015	158,425	138,047	147,092	138,006	140,361	130,028	135,712	134,758	134,149
Nonveteran	9,293,965	9,296,578	9,091,440	9,087,122	9,141,135	9,108,132	9,167,042	9,130,812	9,202,649	9,158,205

Table 10. Sex by Age by Veteran Status for the Civilian Population, United States, by Race and Hispanic Origin, American Community Survey Estimates, 2009–2013—*Continued*

(Number.)

Characteristic	Hispanic or Latino (of any race)									
	2009		2010		2011		2012		2013	
	1-year estimates	3-year estimates	1-year estimates	3-year estimates	1-year estimates	3-year estimates	1-year estimates	3-year estimates	1-year estimates	3-year estimates
Total	31,507,868	30,534,030	33,411,311	32,334,362	34,408,616	33,412,365	35,244,521	34,351,274	36,122,468	35,255,428
Male	16,304,807	15,828,241	16,828,281	16,321,218	17,362,964	16,862,467	17,758,472	17,333,077	18,229,792	17,797,301
18 to 34 years	7,337,295	7,204,889	7,609,634	7,454,463	7,758,369	7,619,536	7,832,590	7,734,012	7,954,788	7,844,774
Veteran	159,502	168,400	187,207	173,497	194,151	180,164	194,198	190,797	182,317	191,821
Nonveteran	7,177,793	7,036,489	7,422,427	7,280,966	7,564,218	7,439,372	7,638,392	7,543,215	7,772,471	7,652,953
35 to 54 years	6,366,587	6,152,102	6,487,023	6,281,256	6,703,170	6,494,916	6,857,668	6,685,316	7,025,603	6,865,173
Veteran	353,985	358,465	355,045	360,645	364,215	360,954	363,832	362,956	333,522	355,490
Nonveteran	6,012,602	5,793,637	6,131,978	5,920,611	6,338,955	6,133,962	6,493,836	6,322,360	6,692,081	6,509,683
55 to 64 years	1,442,245	1,360,701	1,543,822	1,456,705	1,653,830	1,556,417	1,730,950	1,652,328	1,833,727	1,747,645
Veteran	243,694	237,993	234,378	241,685	233,874	239,862	219,754	230,207	210,602	221,626
Nonveteran	1,198,551	1,122,708	1,309,444	1,215,020	1,419,956	1,316,555	1,511,196	1,422,121	1,623,125	1,526,019
65 to 74 years	706,407	671,378	738,625	701,484	779,263	740,753	836,379	784,603	890,301	835,936
Veteran	139,983	137,255	147,118	142,546	156,312	148,091	169,651	157,315	174,695	166,219
Nonveteran	566,424	534,123	591,507	558,938	622,951	592,662	666,728	627,288	715,606	669,717
75 years and over	452,273	439,171	449,177	427,310	468,332	450,845	500,885	476,818	525,373	503,773
Veteran	135,819	133,556	124,671	127,134	128,451	128,166	135,905	130,342	144,203	138,073
Nonveteran	316,454	305,615	324,506	300,176	339,881	322,679	364,980	346,476	381,170	365,700
Female	15,203,061	14,705,789	16,583,030	16,013,144	17,045,652	16,549,898	17,486,049	17,018,197	17,892,676	17,458,127
18 to 34 years	6,279,351	6,130,494	6,926,355	6,741,566	7,026,368	6,899,614	7,137,009	7,019,318	7,234,243	7,117,378
Veteran	33,679	34,438	48,306	41,497	46,763	44,735	50,623	48,909	47,933	48,615
Nonveteran	6,245,672	6,096,056	6,878,049	6,700,069	6,979,605	6,854,879	7,086,386	6,970,409	7,186,310	7,068,763
35 to 54 years	5,811,937	5,618,816	6,342,143	6,127,704	6,517,384	6,329,313	6,663,194	6,497,249	6,791,236	6,651,358
Veteran	46,758	42,692	47,865	47,604	49,372	48,675	53,408	50,114	51,530	50,959
Nonveteran	5,765,179	5,576,124	6,294,278	6,080,100	6,468,012	6,280,638	6,609,786	6,447,135	6,739,706	6,600,399
55 to 64 years	1,552,880	1,460,785	1,693,995	1,602,859	1,805,663	1,702,525	1,887,842	1,798,002	1,984,685	1,893,890
Veteran	9,288	8,775	11,455	10,221	12,773	11,264	12,820	12,490	16,998	14,099
Nonveteran	1,543,592	1,452,010	1,682,540	1,592,638	1,792,890	1,691,261	1,875,022	1,785,512	1,967,687	1,879,791
65 to 74 years	856,807	822,062	924,380	880,236	958,770	922,170	1,031,504	970,619	1,080,856	1,024,595
Veteran	3,236	3,221	3,317	3,286	4,755	3,810	5,053	4,395	6,425	5,570
Nonveteran	853,571	818,841	921,063	876,950	954,015	918,360	1,026,451	966,224	1,074,431	1,019,025
75 years and over	702,086	673,632	696,157	660,779	737,467	696,276	766,500	733,009	801,656	770,906
Veteran	3,960	3,118	3,729	3,542	3,532	3,627	4,473	3,836	3,849	3,923
Nonveteran	698,126	670,514	692,428	657,237	733,935	692,649	762,027	729,173	797,807	766,983

Table 11. Veteran Status by Educational Attainment for the Civilian Population Age 25 Years and Over, United States, American Community Survey Estimates, 2010–2013

(Percent.)

Characteristic	2010 1-year estimates	2010 3-year estimates	2010 5-year estimates	2011 1-year estimates	2011 3-year estimates	2011 5-year estimates	2012 1-year estimates	2012 3-year estimates	2012 5-year estimates	2013 1-year estimates	2013 3-year estimates	2013 5-year estimates
Total	100.0	100.0	100.0	100.0	100.0	100.0	100.0	100.0	100.0	100.0	100.0	100.0
Veteran	10.5	10.9	11.2	10.3	10.5	10.9	10.0	10.3	10.6	9.2	9.8	10.2
Less than high school graduate	0.8	0.9	1.0	0.8	0.8	0.9	0.7	0.8	0.9	0.7	0.7	0.8
High school graduate (includes equivalency)	3.2	3.2	3.4	3.0	3.1	3.3	2.9	3.0	3.1	2.7	2.9	3.0
Some college or associate's degree	3.8	3.9	3.9	3.7	3.8	3.9	3.7	3.7	3.8	3.4	3.6	3.7
Bachelor's degree or higher	2.7	2.8	2.9	2.7	2.7	2.8	2.7	2.7	2.8	2.5	2.6	2.7
Nonveteran	89.5	89.1	88.8	89.7	89.5	89.1	90.0	89.7	89.4	90.8	90.2	89.8
Less than high school graduate	13.6	13.8	14.0	13.3	13.6	13.7	13.0	13.3	13.5	12.8	13.0	13.2
High school graduate (includes equivalency)	25.4	25.3	25.6	25.4	25.3	25.4	25.1	25.3	25.2	25.2	25.2	25.2
Some college or associate's degree	25.0	24.9	24.2	25.2	25.0	24.6	25.5	25.2	25.1	25.7	25.5	25.3
Bachelor's degree or higher	25.4	25.2	25.0	25.8	25.5	25.4	26.4	25.9	25.7	27.1	26.5	26.1

Note: Percentage totals may not sum to 100 due to rounding.

Table 12. Age by Veteran Status by Employment Status for the Civilian Population Age 18 to 64 Years, United States, American Community Survey Estimates, 2010–2013

(Number.)

Characteristic	2010 1-year estimates	2010 3-year estimates	2010 5-year estimates	2011 1-year estimates	2011 3-year estimates	2011 5-year estimates	2012 1-year estimates	2012 3-year estimates	2012 5-year estimates	2013 1-year estimates	2013 3-year estimates	2013 5-year estimates
Total	193,703,762	191,810,677	190,059,418	195,280,748	193,573,774	191,813,167	196,038,291	195,028,385	193,358,139	196,892,734	196,076,801	194,725,860
18 to 34 years	71,091,197	70,272,729	69,574,169	71,992,981	71,146,164	70,341,076	72,793,184	72,031,871	71,169,745	73,521,890	72,806,770	71,976,195
Veteran	1,748,592	1,685,902	1,775,153	1,769,261	1,718,015	1,732,384	1,818,258	1,783,529	1,730,597	1,627,662	1,743,770	1,723,443
In labor force	1,473,667	1,430,349	1,520,056	1,482,899	1,448,899	1,475,359	1,517,246	1,496,224	1,461,011	1,346,406	1,454,087	1,444,730
Employed	1,278,295	1,268,718	1,373,632	1,286,363	1,258,713	1,315,051	1,339,032	1,306,042	1,289,408	1,203,633	1,280,472	1,266,358
Unemployed	195,372	161,631	146,424	196,536	190,186	160,308	178,214	190,182	171,603	142,773	173,615	178,372
Not in labor force	274,925	255,553	255,097	286,362	269,116	257,025	301,012	287,305	269,586	281,256	289,683	278,713
Nonveteran	69,342,605	68,586,827	67,799,016	70,223,720	69,428,149	68,608,692	70,974,926	70,248,342	69,439,148	71,894,228	71,063,000	70,252,752
In labor force	52,146,838	52,189,412	51,588,324	52,605,253	52,370,613	52,058,920	53,353,539	52,795,281	52,606,237	54,160,666	53,421,186	52,999,518
Employed	44,717,258	45,871,093	45,998,231	45,337,640	45,192,268	45,923,902	46,511,671	45,609,287	46,001,941	47,843,174	46,612,673	46,058,607
Unemployed	7,429,580	6,318,319	5,590,093	7,267,613	7,178,345	6,135,018	6,841,868	7,185,994	6,604,296	6,317,492	6,808,513	6,940,911
Not in labor force	17,195,767	16,397,415	16,210,692	17,618,467	17,057,536	16,549,772	17,621,387	17,453,061	16,832,911	17,733,562	17,641,814	17,253,234
35 to 54 years	85,856,262	86,104,505	86,215,158	85,228,680	85,680,499	85,971,593	84,662,769	85,177,965	85,589,341	84,037,711	84,599,234	85,110,242
Veteran	5,569,185	5,758,490	5,961,148	5,388,915	5,568,048	5,754,865	5,268,038	5,405,758	5,582,366	4,717,736	5,120,799	5,345,824
In labor force	4,755,391	4,946,434	5,105,931	4,597,484	4,767,915	4,941,566	4,480,918	4,611,605	4,788,537	3,984,769	4,352,548	4,561,645
Employed	4,315,263	4,580,899	4,784,495	4,217,856	4,356,755	4,597,762	4,162,956	4,233,076	4,432,163	3,725,526	4,035,042	4,200,948
Unemployed	440,128	365,535	321,436	379,628	411,160	343,804	317,962	378,529	356,374	259,243	317,506	360,697
Not in labor force	813,794	812,056	855,217	791,431	800,133	813,299	787,120	794,153	793,829	732,967	768,251	784,179
Nonveteran	80,287,077	80,346,015	80,254,010	79,839,765	80,112,451	80,216,728	79,394,731	79,772,207	80,006,975	79,319,975	79,478,435	79,764,418
In labor force	65,394,486	65,798,614	65,418,129	64,753,771	65,343,970	65,451,986	64,385,864	64,819,496	65,329,535	64,149,988	64,406,846	64,924,870
Employed	59,702,816	61,159,529	61,480,210	59,524,616	60,010,143	61,066,410	59,692,875	59,637,002	60,595,301	59,961,322	59,716,481	59,967,512
Unemployed	5,691,670	4,639,085	3,937,919	5,229,155	5,333,827	4,385,576	4,692,989	5,182,494	4,734,234	4,188,666	4,690,365	4,957,358
Not in labor force	14,892,591	14,547,401	14,835,881	15,085,994	14,768,481	14,764,742	15,008,867	14,952,711	14,677,440	15,169,987	15,071,589	14,839,548
55 to 64 years	36,756,303	35,433,443	34,270,091	38,059,087	36,747,111	35,500,498	38,582,338	37,818,549	36,599,053	39,333,133	38,670,797	37,639,423
Veteran	5,345,088	5,577,911	5,761,052	5,084,023	5,335,711	5,565,339	4,573,643	5,000,862	5,281,863	3,974,914	4,541,646	4,908,389
In labor force	3,327,063	3,576,024	3,743,779	3,047,791	3,321,019	3,549,101	2,728,956	3,039,479	3,305,118	2,362,396	2,713,071	3,010,869
Employed	3,014,818	3,320,588	3,524,952	2,789,950	3,037,363	3,311,549	2,522,987	2,780,701	3,059,127	2,198,383	2,504,283	2,766,737
Unemployed	312,245	255,436	218,827	257,841	283,656	237,552	205,969	258,778	245,991	164,013	208,788	244,132
Not in labor force	2,018,025	2,001,887	2,017,273	2,036,232	2,014,692	2,016,238	1,844,687	1,961,383	1,976,745	1,612,518	1,828,575	1,897,520
Nonveteran	31,411,215	29,855,532	28,509,039	32,975,064	31,411,400	29,935,159	34,008,695	32,817,687	31,317,190	35,358,219	34,129,151	32,731,034
In labor force	20,319,627	19,292,943	18,082,413	21,325,174	20,347,786	19,202,142	21,987,384	21,242,333	20,262,737	22,902,072	22,094,218	21,224,104
Employed	18,705,585	18,070,937	17,104,554	19,753,995	18,844,406	18,028,998	20,550,885	19,703,692	18,929,638	21,574,937	20,650,108	19,770,041
Unemployed	1,614,042	1,222,006	977,859	1,571,179	1,503,380	1,173,144	1,436,499	1,538,641	1,333,099	1,327,135	1,444,110	1,454,063
Not in labor force	11,091,588	10,562,589	10,426,626	11,649,890	11,063,614	10,733,017	12,021,311	11,575,354	11,054,453	12,456,147	12,034,933	11,506,930

Table 13. Age by Veteran Status by Poverty Status in the Past 12 Months by Disability Status for the Civilian Population 18 Years and Over, United States, American Community Survey Estimates, 2010–2013

(Number; percent.)

Characteristic	2010				2011			
	1-year estimates	Percent distribution	3-year estimates	Percent distribution	1-year estimates	Percent distribution	3-year estimates	Percent distribution
Total	227,785,748	X	225,050,270	X	230,286,423	X	227,693,344	X
18 to 34 years, total	67,387,890	X	66,580,092	X	68,300,177	X	67,447,016	X
Veteran	1,705,513	100.0	1,632,850	100.0	1,731,106	100.0	1,677,852	100.0
Income in the past 12 months below poverty level	190,714	11.2	166,335	10.2	206,893	12.0	185,637	11.1
With a disability	25,424	1.5	24,616	1.5	30,233	1.7	26,956	1.6
No disability	165,290	9.7	141,719	8.7	176,660	10.2	158,681	9.5
Income in the past 12 months at or above poverty level	1,514,799	88.8	1,466,515	89.8	1,524,213	88.0	1,492,215	88.9
With a disability	104,560	6.1	104,510	6.4	116,393	6.7	110,743	6.6
No disability	1,410,239	82.7	1,362,005	83.4	1,407,820	81.3	1,381,472	82.3
Nonveteran	65,682,377	100.0	64,947,242	100.0	66,569,071	100.0	65,769,164	100.0
Income in the past 12 months below poverty level	13,322,253	20.3	12,256,518	18.9	13,808,855	20.7	13,124,931	20.0
With a disability	1,177,416	1.8	1,125,037	1.7	1,243,861	1.9	1,170,788	1.8
No disability	12,144,837	18.5	11,131,481	17.1	12,564,994	18.9	11,954,143	18.2
Income in the past 12 months at or above poverty level	52,360,124	79.7	52,690,724	81.1	52,760,216	79.3	52,644,233	80.0
With a disability	2,356,137	3.6	2,417,978	3.7	2,503,095	3.8	2,435,692	3.7
No disability	50,003,987	76.1	50,272,746	77.4	50,257,121	75.5	50,208,541	76.3
35 to 54 years, total	84,784,060	X	85,010,882	X	84,131,042	X	84,589,740	X
Veteran	5,472,508	100.0	5,653,224	100.0	5,298,096	100.0	5,474,176	100.0
Income in the past 12 months below poverty level	443,297	8.1	431,135	7.6	451,447	8.5	444,127	8.1
With a disability	148,094	2.7	151,512	2.7	149,618	2.8	150,769	2.8
No disability	295,203	5.4	279,623	4.9	301,829	5.7	293,358	5.4
Income in the past 12 months at or above poverty level	5,029,211	91.9	5,222,089	92.4	4,846,649	91.5	5,030,049	91.9
With a disability	569,369	10.4	597,205	10.6	550,350	10.4	573,984	10.5
No disability	4,459,842	81.5	4,624,884	81.8	4,296,299	81.1	4,456,065	81.4
Nonveteran	79,311,552	100.0	79,357,658	100.0	78,832,946	100.0	79,115,564	100.0
Income in the past 12 months below poverty level	9,407,172	11.9	8,568,198	10.8	9,970,467	12.6	9,275,090	11.7
With a disability	2,404,215	3.0	2,335,414	2.9	2,518,992	3.2	2,406,886	3.0
No disability	7,002,957	8.8	6,232,784	7.9	7,451,475	9.5	6,868,204	8.7
Income in the past 12 months at or above poverty level	69,904,380	88.1	70,789,460	89.2	68,862,479	87.4	69,840,474	88.3
With a disability	5,432,406	6.8	5,566,552	7.0	5,347,274	6.8	5,413,777	6.8
No disability	64,471,974	81.3	65,222,908	82.2	63,515,205	80.6	64,426,697	81.4
55 to 64 years, total	36,482,157	X	35,179,683	X	37,768,951	X	36,472,320	X
Veteran	5,288,779	100.0	5,526,489	100.0	5,027,316	100.0	5,282,650	100.0
Income in the past 12 months below poverty level	385,421	7.3	370,567	6.7	403,373	8.0	382,326	7.2
With a disability	156,545	3.0	153,795	2.8	165,339	3.3	157,547	3.0
No disability	228,876	4.3	216,772	3.9	238,034	4.7	224,779	4.3
Income in the past 12 months at or above poverty level	4,903,358	92.7	5,155,922	93.3	4,623,943	92.0	4,900,324	92.8
With a disability	1,066,750	20.2	1,089,607	19.7	1,062,652	21.1	1,072,474	20.3
No disability	3,836,608	72.5	4,066,315	73.6	3,561,291	70.8	3,827,850	72.5
Nonveteran	31,193,378	100.0	29,653,194	100.0	32,741,635	100.0	31,189,670	100.0
Income in the past 12 months below poverty level	3,165,016	10.1	2,862,790	9.7	3,480,267	10.6	3,143,545	10.1
With a disability	1,270,326	4.1	1,203,225	4.1	1,380,119	4.2	1,276,778	4.1
No disability	1,894,690	6.1	1,659,565	5.6	2,100,148	6.4	1,866,767	6.0
Income in the past 12 months at or above poverty level	28,028,362	89.9	26,790,404	90.3	29,261,368	89.4	28,046,125	89.9
With a disability	4,253,029	13.6	4,120,087	13.9	4,426,666	13.5	4,257,120	13.6
No disability	23,775,333	76.2	22,670,317	76.5	24,834,702	75.9	23,789,005	76.3
65 years and over, total	39,131,641	X	38,279,613	X	40,086,253	X	39,184,268	X
Veteran	8,932,384	100.0	8,952,545	100.0	9,015,968	100.0	8,980,064	100.0
Income in the past 12 months below poverty level	409,565	4.6	427,294	4.8	409,463	4.5	416,572	4.6
With a disability	198,752	2.2	209,818	2.3	193,695	2.1	200,527	2.2
No disability	210,813	2.4	217,476	2.4	215,768	2.4	216,045	2.4
Income in the past 12 months at or above poverty level	8,522,819	95.4	8,525,251	95.2	8,606,505	95.5	8,563,492	95.4
With a disability	3,195,697	35.8	3,210,805	35.9	3,249,964	36.0	3,227,174	35.9
No disability	5,327,122	59.6	5,314,446	59.4	5,356,541	59.4	5,336,318	59.4
Nonveteran	30,199,257	100.0	29,327,068	100.0	31,070,285	100.0	30,204,204	100.0
Income in the past 12 months below poverty level	3,128,008	10.4	3,189,029	10.9	3,320,993	10.7	3,210,150	100.0
With a disability	1,597,222	5.3	1,668,755	5.7	1,694,808	5.5	1,652,557	10.6
No disability	1,530,786	5.1	1,520,274	5.2	1,626,185	5.2	1,557,593	5.5
Income in the past 12 months at or above poverty level	27,071,249	89.6	26,138,039	89.1	27,749,292	89.3	26,994,054	5.2
With a disability	9,359,980	31.0	9,157,964	31.2	9,520,407	30.6	9,335,089	89.4
No disability	17,711,269	58.6	16,980,075	57.9	18,228,885	58.7	17,658,965	30.9

X = Not applicable.
Note: Percentages may not sum to 100 due to rounding.

Table 13. Age by Veteran Status by Poverty Status in the Past 12 Months by Disability Status for the Civilian Population 18 Years and Over, United States, American Community Survey Estimates, 2010–2013—*Continued*

(Number; percent.)

Characteristic	2012				2013			
	1-year estimates	Percent distribution	3-year estimates	Percent distribution	1-year estimates	Percent distribution	3-year estimates	Percent distribution
Total	232,774,182	X	230,292,141	X	235,134,873	X	225,050,270	X
18 to 34 years, total	69,064,364	X	68,309,726	X	69,758,263	X	66,580,092	X
Veteran	1,780,280	100.0	1,744,912	100.0	1,590,271	100.0	1,632,850	100.0
Income in the past 12 months below poverty level	211,449	11.9	203,291	11.7	178,385	11.2	166,335	10.2
With a disability	30,035	1.7	28,662	1.6	29,973	1.9	24,616	1.5
No disability	181,414	10.2	174,629	10.0	148,412	9.3	141,719	8.7
Income in the past 12 months at or above poverty level	1,568,831	88.1	1,541,621	88.3	1,411,886	88.8	1,466,515	89.8
With a disability	134,459	7.6	119,565	6.9	133,091	8.4	104,510	6.4
No disability	1,434,372	80.6	1,422,056	81.5	1,278,795	80.4	1,362,005	83.4
Nonveteran	67,284,084	100.0	66,564,814	100.0	68,167,992	100.0	64,947,242	100.0
Income in the past 12 months below poverty level	13,768,626	20.5	13,642,917	20.5	13,766,926	20.2	12,256,518	18.9
With a disability	1,273,382	1.9	1,225,491	1.8	1,315,133	1.9	1,125,037	1.7
No disability	12,495,244	18.6	12,417,426	18.7	12,451,793	18.3	11,131,481	17.1
Income in the past 12 months at or above poverty level	53,515,458	79.5	52,921,897	79.5	54,401,066	79.8	52,690,724	81.1
With a disability	2,527,511	3.8	2,453,705	3.7	2,709,383		2,417,978	3.7
No disability	50,987,947	75.8	50,468,192	75.8	51,691,683	75.8	50,272,746	77.4
35 to 54 years, total	83,590,679	X	84,099,626	X	82,994,070	X	85,010,882	X
Veteran	5,190,950	100.0	5,316,724	100.0	4,651,825	100.0	5,653,224	100.0
Income in the past 12 months below poverty level	441,296	8.5	444,700	8.4	396,641	8.5	431,135	7.6
With a disability	149,149	2.9	148,235	2.8	132,271	2.8	151,512	2.7
No disability	292,147	5.6	296,465	5.6	264,370	5.7	279,623	4.9
Income in the past 12 months at or above poverty level	4,749,654	91.5	4,872,024	91.6	4,255,184	91.5	5,222,089	92.4
With a disability	539,937	10.4	550,985	10.4	540,725	11.6	597,205	10.6
No disability	4,209,717	81.1	4,321,039	81.3	3,714,459	79.8	4,624,884	81.8
Nonveteran	78,399,729	100.0	78,782,902	100.0	78,342,245	100.0	79,357,658	100.0
Income in the past 12 months below poverty level	9,874,154	12.6	9,705,182	12.3	9,964,443	12.7	8,568,198	10.8
With a disability	2,511,007	3.2	2,467,875	3.1	2,513,874	3.2	2,335,414	2.9
No disability	7,363,147	9.4	7,237,307	9.2	7,450,569	9.5	6,232,784	7.9
Income in the past 12 months at or above poverty level	68,525,575	87.4	69,077,720	87.7	68,377,802	87.3	70,789,460	89.2
With a disability	5,234,286	6.7	5,320,229	6.8	5,408,869	6.9	5,566,552	7.0
No disability	63,291,289	80.7	63,757,491	80.9	62,968,933	80.4	65,222,908	82.2
55 to 64 years, total	38,279,311	X	37,533,102	X	39,028,973	X	35,179,683	X
Veteran	4,521,068	100.0	4,946,655	100.0	3,926,063	100.0	5,526,489	100.0
Income in the past 12 months below poverty level	400,890	8.9	392,610	7.9	366,108	9.3	370,567	6.7
With a disability	173,052	3.8	162,655	3.3	161,561	4.1	153,795	2.8
No disability	227,838	5.0	229,955	4.6	204,547	5.2	216,772	3.9
Income in the past 12 months at or above poverty level	4,120,178	91.1	4,554,045	92.1	3,559,955	90.7	5,155,922	93.3
With a disability	949,092	21.0	1,026,262	20.7	868,717	22.1	1,089,607	19.7
No disability	3,171,086	70.1	3,527,783	71.3	2,691,238	68.5	4,066,315	73.6
Nonveteran	33,758,243	100.0	32,586,447	100.0	35,102,910	100.0	29,653,194	100.0
Income in the past 12 months below poverty level	3,682,166	10.9	3,432,488	10.5	3,890,304	11.1	2,862,790	9.7
With a disability	1,473,311	4.4	1,369,348	4.2	1,558,305	4.4	1,203,225	4.1
No disability	2,208,855	6.5	2,063,140	6.3	2,331,999	6.6	1,659,565	5.6
Income in the past 12 months at or above poverty level	30,076,077	89.1	29,153,959	89.5	31,212,606	88.9	26,790,404	90.3
With a disability	4,514,245	13.4	4,392,148	13.5	4,847,437	13.8	4,120,087	13.9
No disability	25,561,832	75.7	24,761,811	76.0	26,365,169	75.1	22,670,317	76.5
65 years and over, total	41,839,828	X	40,349,687	X	43,353,567	X	38,279,613	X
Veteran	9,358,069	100.0	9,104,920	100.0	9,088,879	100.0	8,952,545	100.0
Income in the past 12 months below poverty level	453,273	4.8	425,206	4.7	471,085	5.2	427,294	4.8
With a disability	217,426	2.3	203,860	2.2	221,543	2.4	209,818	2.3
No disability	235,847	2.5	221,346	2.4	249,542	2.7	217,476	2.4
Income in the past 12 months at or above poverty level	8,904,796	95.2	8,679,714	95.3	8,617,794	94.8	8,525,251	95.2
With a disability	3,360,523	35.9	3,269,627	35.9	3,397,407	37.4	3,210,805	35.9
No disability	5,544,273	59.2	5,410,087	59.4	5,220,387	57.4	5,314,446	59.4
Nonveteran	32,481,759	100.0	31,244,767	100.0	34,264,688	100.0	29,327,068	100.0
Income in the past 12 months below poverty level	3,515,606	10.8	3,325,759	10.6	3,674,632	10.7	3,189,029	10.9
With a disability	1,772,945	5.5	1,691,120	5.4	1,795,304	5.2	1,668,755	5.7
No disability	1,742,661	5.4	1,634,639	5.2	1,879,328	5.5	1,520,274	5.2
Income in the past 12 months at or above poverty level	28,966,153	89.2	27,919,008	89.4	30,590,056	89.3	26,138,039	89.1
With a disability	9,657,305	29.7	9,506,181	30.4	10,361,534	30.2	9,157,964	31.2
No disability	19,308,848	59.4	18,412,827	58.9	20,228,522	59.0	16,980,075	57.9

Table 14. Median Income in the Past 12 Months (in Inflation-Adjusted Dollars), by Veteran Status and Sex for the Civilian Population Age 18 Years and Over with Income, United States, American Community Survey Estimates, 2010–2013

(Dollars.)

Characteristic	2010			2011			2012			2013		
	1-year estimates	3-year estimates	5-year estimates	1-year estimates	3-year estimates	5-year estimates	1-year estimates	3-year estimates	5-year estimates	1-year estimates	3-year estimates	5-year estimates
Total	25,605	26,284	26,652	25,811	26,356	27,024	26,278	26,440	27,028	26,638	26,609	26,937
Veterans	35,367	36,211	36,803	35,821	36,462	37,463	36,264	36,552	37,434	36,381	36,643	37,346
Male	35,725	36,635	37,321	36,202	36,865	37,973	36,672	36,961	37,943	36,740	37,043	37,815
Female	30,540	30,347	30,137	30,611	30,980	31,093	30,929	31,221	31,329	31,365	31,335	31,647
Nonveterans	24,521	25,264	25,575	24,751	25,369	25,984	25,337	25,475	26,022	25,820	25,676	25,968
Male	30,822	31,759	32,415	31,083	31,619	32,795	31,586	31,588	32,444	31,898	31,853	32,347
Female	20,634	20,847	20,856	20,771	21,062	21,307	21,071	21,212	21,469	21,383	21,337	21,562

This page is intentionally left blank

Table 15. Age by Veteran Status by Poverty Status in the Past 12 Months by Disability Status for the Civilian Population 18 Years and Over, United States, American Community Survey Estimates, 2010–2013

(Number; percent.)

Characteristic	2010				2011			
	1-year estimates	Percent distribution	3-year estimates	Percent distribution	1-year estimates	Percent distribution	3-year estimates	Percent distribution
Total	227,785,748	X	225,050,270	X	230,286,423	X	227,693,344	X
18 to 34 years, total	67,387,890	X	66,580,092	X	68,300,177	X	67,447,016	X
Veteran	1,705,513	100.0	1,632,850	100.0	1,731,106	100.0	1,677,852	100.0
Income in the past 12 months below poverty level	190,714	11.2	166,335	10.2	206,893	12.0	185,637	11.1
With a disability	25,424	1.5	24,616	1.5	30,233	1.7	26,956	1.6
No disability	165,290	9.7	141,719	8.7	176,660	10.2	158,681	9.5
Income in the past 12 months at or above poverty level	1,514,799	88.8	1,466,515	89.8	1,524,213	88.0	1,492,215	88.9
With a disability	104,560	6.1	104,510	6.4	116,393	6.7	110,743	6.6
No disability	1,410,239	82.7	1,362,005	83.4	1,407,820	81.3	1,381,472	82.3
Nonveteran	65,682,377	100.0	64,947,242	100.0	66,569,071	100.0	65,769,164	100.0
Income in the past 12 months below poverty level	13,322,253	20.3	12,256,518	18.9	13,808,855	20.7	13,124,931	20.0
With a disability	1,177,416	1.8	1,125,037	1.7	1,243,861	1.9	1,170,788	1.8
No disability	12,144,837	18.5	11,131,481	17.1	12,564,994	18.9	11,954,143	18.2
Income in the past 12 months at or above poverty level	52,360,124	79.7	52,690,724	81.1	52,760,216	79.3	52,644,233	80.0
With a disability	2,356,137	3.6	2,417,978	3.7	2,503,095	3.8	2,435,692	3.7
No disability	50,003,987	76.1	50,272,746	77.4	50,257,121	75.5	50,208,541	76.3
35 to 54 years, total	84,784,060	X	85,010,882	X	84,131,042	X	84,589,740	X
Veteran	5,472,508	100.0	5,653,224	100.0	5,298,096	100.0	5,474,176	100.0
Income in the past 12 months below poverty level	443,297	8.1	431,135	7.6	451,447	8.5	444,127	8.1
With a disability	148,094	2.7	151,512	2.7	149,618	2.8	150,769	2.8
No disability	295,203	5.4	279,623	4.9	301,829	5.7	293,358	5.4
Income in the past 12 months at or above poverty level	5,029,211	91.9	5,222,089	92.4	4,846,649	91.5	5,030,049	91.9
With a disability	569,369	10.4	597,205	10.6	550,350	10.4	573,984	10.5
No disability	4,459,842	81.5	4,624,884	81.8	4,296,299	81.1	4,456,065	81.4
Nonveteran	79,311,552	100.0	79,357,658	100.0	78,832,946	100.0	79,115,564	100.0
Income in the past 12 months below poverty level	9,407,172	11.9	8,568,198	10.8	9,970,467	12.6	9,275,090	11.7
With a disability	2,404,215	3.0	2,335,414	2.9	2,518,992	3.2	2,406,886	3.0
No disability	7,002,957	8.8	6,232,784	7.9	7,451,475	9.5	6,868,204	8.7
Income in the past 12 months at or above poverty level	69,904,380	88.1	70,789,460	89.2	68,862,479	87.4	69,840,474	88.3
With a disability	5,432,406	6.8	5,566,552	7.0	5,347,274	6.8	5,413,777	6.8
No disability	64,471,974	81.3	65,222,908	82.2	63,515,205	80.6	64,426,697	81.4
55 to 64 years, total	36,482,157	X	35,179,683	X	37,768,951	X	36,472,320	X
Veteran	5,288,779	100.0	5,526,489	100.0	5,027,316	100.0	5,282,650	100.0
Income in the past 12 months below poverty level	385,421	7.3	370,567	6.7	403,373	8.0	382,326	7.2
With a disability	156,545	3.0	153,795	2.8	165,339	3.3	157,547	3.0
No disability	228,876	4.3	216,772	3.9	238,034	4.7	224,779	4.3
Income in the past 12 months at or above poverty level	4,903,358	92.7	5,155,922	93.3	4,623,943	92.0	4,900,324	92.8
With a disability	1,066,750	20.2	1,089,607	19.7	1,062,652	21.1	1,072,474	20.3
No disability	3,836,608	72.5	4,066,315	73.6	3,561,291	70.8	3,827,850	72.5
Nonveteran	31,193,378	100.0	29,653,194	100.0	32,741,635	100.0	31,189,670	100.0
Income in the past 12 months below poverty level	3,165,016	10.1	2,862,790	9.7	3,480,267	10.6	3,143,545	10.1
With a disability	1,270,326	4.1	1,203,225	4.1	1,380,119	4.2	1,276,778	4.1
No disability	1,894,690	6.1	1,659,565	5.6	2,100,148	6.4	1,866,767	6.0
Income in the past 12 months at or above poverty level	28,028,362	89.9	26,790,404	90.3	29,261,368	89.4	28,046,125	89.9
With a disability	4,253,029	13.6	4,120,087	13.9	4,426,666	13.5	4,257,120	13.6
No disability	23,775,333	76.2	22,670,317	76.5	24,834,702	75.9	23,789,005	76.3
65 years and over, total	39,131,641	X	38,279,613	X	40,086,253	X	39,184,268	X
Veteran	8,932,384	100.0	8,952,545	100.0	9,015,968	100.0	8,980,064	100.0
Income in the past 12 months below poverty level	409,565	4.6	427,294	4.8	409,463	4.5	416,572	4.6
With a disability	198,752	2.2	209,818	2.3	193,695	2.1	200,527	2.2
No disability	210,813	2.4	217,476	2.4	215,768	2.4	216,045	2.4
Income in the past 12 months at or above poverty level	8,522,819	95.4	8,525,251	95.2	8,606,505	95.5	8,563,492	95.4
With a disability	3,195,697	35.8	3,210,805	35.9	3,249,964	36.0	3,227,174	35.9
No disability	5,327,122	59.6	5,314,446	59.4	5,356,541	59.4	5,336,318	59.4
Nonveteran	30,199,257	100.0	29,327,068	100.0	31,070,285	100.0	30,204,204	100.0
Income in the past 12 months below poverty level	3,128,008	10.4	3,189,029	10.9	3,320,993	10.7	3,210,150	100.0
With a disability	1,597,222	5.3	1,668,755	5.7	1,694,808	5.5	1,652,557	10.6
No disability	1,530,786	5.1	1,520,274	5.2	1,626,185	5.2	1,557,593	5.5
Income in the past 12 months at or above poverty level	27,071,249	89.6	26,138,039	89.1	27,749,292	89.3	26,994,054	5.2
With a disability	9,359,980	31.0	9,157,964	31.2	9,520,407	30.6	9,335,089	89.4
No disability	17,711,269	58.6	16,980,075	57.9	18,228,885	58.7	17,658,965	30.9

X = Not applicable.
Note: Percentages may not sum to 100 due to rounding.

Table 15. Age by Veteran Status by Poverty Status in the Past 12 Months by Disability Status for the Civilian Population 18 Years and Over, United States, American Community Survey Estimates, 2010–2013—*Continued*

(Number; percent.)

Characteristic	2012				2013			
	1-year estimates	Percent distribution	3-year estimates	Percent distribution	1-year estimates	Percent distribution	3-year estimates	Percent distribution
Total	232,774,182	X	230,292,141	X	235,134,873	X	225,050,270	X
18 to 34 years, total	69,064,364	X	68,309,726	X	69,758,263	X	66,580,092	X
Veteran	1,780,280	100.0	1,744,912	100.0	1,590,271	100.0	1,632,850	100.0
Income in the past 12 months below poverty level	211,449	11.9	203,291	11.7	178,385	11.2	166,335	10.2
With a disability	30,035	1.7	28,662	1.6	29,973	1.9	24,616	1.5
No disability	181,414	10.2	174,629	10.0	148,412	9.3	141,719	8.7
Income in the past 12 months at or above poverty level	1,568,831	88.1	1,541,621	88.3	1,411,886	88.8	1,466,515	89.8
With a disability	134,459	7.6	119,565	6.9	133,091	8.4	104,510	6.4
No disability	1,434,372	80.6	1,422,056	81.5	1,278,795	80.4	1,362,005	83.4
Nonveteran	67,284,084	100.0	66,564,814	100.0	68,167,992	100.0	64,947,242	100.0
Income in the past 12 months below poverty level	13,768,626	20.5	13,642,917	20.5	13,766,926	20.2	12,256,518	18.9
With a disability	1,273,382	1.9	1,225,491	1.8	1,315,133	1.9	1,125,037	1.7
No disability	12,495,244	18.6	12,417,426	18.7	12,451,793	18.3	11,131,481	17.1
Income in the past 12 months at or above poverty level	53,515,458	79.5	52,921,897	79.5	54,401,066	79.8	52,690,724	81.1
With a disability	2,527,511	3.8	2,453,705	3.7	2,709,383		2,417,978	3.7
No disability	50,987,947	75.8	50,468,192	75.8	51,691,683	75.8	50,272,746	77.4
35 to 54 years, total	83,590,679	X	84,099,626	X	82,994,070	X	85,010,882	X
Veteran	5,190,950	100.0	5,316,724	100.0	4,651,825	100.0	5,653,224	100.0
Income in the past 12 months below poverty level	441,296	8.5	444,700	8.4	396,641	8.5	431,135	7.6
With a disability	149,149	2.9	148,235	2.8	132,271	2.8	151,512	2.7
No disability	292,147	5.6	296,465	5.6	264,370	5.7	279,623	4.9
Income in the past 12 months at or above poverty level	4,749,654	91.5	4,872,024	91.6	4,255,184	91.5	5,222,089	92.4
With a disability	539,937	10.4	550,985	10.4	540,725	11.6	597,205	10.6
No disability	4,209,717	81.1	4,321,039	81.3	3,714,459	79.8	4,624,884	81.8
Nonveteran	78,399,729	100.0	78,782,902	100.0	78,342,245	100.0	79,357,658	100.0
Income in the past 12 months below poverty level	9,874,154	12.6	9,705,182	12.3	9,964,443	12.7	8,568,198	10.8
With a disability	2,511,007	3.2	2,467,875	3.1	2,513,874	3.2	2,335,414	2.9
No disability	7,363,147	9.4	7,237,307	9.2	7,450,569	9.5	6,232,784	7.9
Income in the past 12 months at or above poverty level	68,525,575	87.4	69,077,720	87.7	68,377,802	87.3	70,789,460	89.2
With a disability	5,234,286	6.7	5,320,229	6.8	5,408,869	6.9	5,566,552	7.0
No disability	63,291,289	80.7	63,757,491	80.9	62,968,933	80.4	65,222,908	82.2
55 to 64 years, total	38,279,311	X	37,533,102	X	39,028,973	X	35,179,683	X
Veteran	4,521,068	100.0	4,946,655	100.0	3,926,063	100.0	5,526,489	100.0
Income in the past 12 months below poverty level	400,890	8.9	392,610	7.9	366,108	9.3	370,567	6.7
With a disability	173,052	3.8	162,655	3.3	161,561	4.1	153,795	2.8
No disability	227,838	5.0	229,955	4.6	204,547	5.2	216,772	3.9
Income in the past 12 months at or above poverty level	4,120,178	91.1	4,554,045	92.1	3,559,955	90.7	5,155,922	93.3
With a disability	949,092	21.0	1,026,262	20.7	868,717	22.1	1,089,607	19.7
No disability	3,171,086	70.1	3,527,783	71.3	2,691,238	68.5	4,066,315	73.6
Nonveteran	33,758,243	100.0	32,586,447	100.0	35,102,910	100.0	29,653,194	100.0
Income in the past 12 months below poverty level	3,682,166	10.9	3,432,488	10.5	3,890,304	11.1	2,862,790	9.7
With a disability	1,473,311	4.4	1,369,348	4.2	1,558,305	4.4	1,203,225	4.1
No disability	2,208,855	6.5	2,063,140	6.3	2,331,999	6.6	1,659,565	5.6
Income in the past 12 months at or above poverty level	30,076,077	89.1	29,153,959	89.5	31,212,606	88.9	26,790,404	90.3
With a disability	4,514,245	13.4	4,392,148	13.5	4,847,437	13.8	4,120,087	13.9
No disability	25,561,832	75.7	24,761,811	76.0	26,365,169	75.1	22,670,317	76.5
65 years and over, total	41,839,828	X	40,349,687	X	43,353,567	X	38,279,613	X
Veteran	9,358,069	100.0	9,104,920	100.0	9,088,879	100.0	8,952,545	100.0
Income in the past 12 months below poverty level	453,273	4.8	425,206	4.7	471,085	5.2	427,294	4.8
With a disability	217,426	2.3	203,860	2.2	221,543	2.4	209,818	2.3
No disability	235,847	2.5	221,346	2.4	249,542	2.7	217,476	2.4
Income in the past 12 months at or above poverty level	8,904,796	95.2	8,679,714	95.3	8,617,794	94.8	8,525,251	95.2
With a disability	3,360,523	35.9	3,269,627	35.9	3,397,407	37.4	3,210,805	35.9
No disability	5,544,273	59.2	5,410,087	59.4	5,220,387	57.4	5,314,446	59.4
Nonveteran	32,481,759	100.0	31,244,767	100.0	34,264,688	100.0	29,327,068	100.0
Income in the past 12 months below poverty level	3,515,606	10.8	3,325,759	10.6	3,674,632	10.7	3,189,029	10.9
With a disability	1,772,945	5.5	1,691,120	5.4	1,795,304	5.2	1,668,755	5.7
No disability	1,742,661	5.4	1,634,639	5.2	1,879,328	5.5	1,520,274	5.2
Income in the past 12 months at or above poverty level	28,966,153	89.2	27,919,008	89.4	30,590,056	89.3	26,138,039	89.1
With a disability	9,657,305	29.7	9,506,181	30.4	10,361,534	30.2	9,157,964	31.2
No disability	19,308,848	59.4	18,412,827	58.9	20,228,522	59.0	16,980,075	57.9

Table 16. Percent of the Civilian Population 18 Years and Over Who Are Veterans, Urban/Rural and Inside/ Outside Metropolitan and Micropolitan Areas, United States, American Community Survey Estimates, 2009–2013

(Percent.)

Characteristic	2009			2010			2011			2012			2013		
	1-year estimates	3-year estimates	5-year estimates	1-year estimates	3-year estimates	5-year estimates	1-year estimates	3-year estimates	5-year estimates	1-year estimates	3-year estimates	5-year estimates	1-year estimates	3-year estimates	5-year estimates
Total, United States	9.5	9.8	10.1	9.3	9.6	9.9	9.1	9.3	9.6	8.9	9.1	9.3	8.1	8.7	9.0
Urban and Rural Areas															
Urban	8.9	9.2	9.6	8.7	9.0	9.3	8.5	8.7	9.0	8.4	8.6	8.8	7.6	8.2	8.5
Rural	11.2	11.6	11.9	11.2	11.5	11.8	11.0	11.2	11.5	11.0	11.2	11.5	10.1	10.8	11.1
Inside/Outside Metropolitan/ Micropolitan Areas															
In metropolitan or micropolitan statistical area	9.3	9.7	10.0	9.2	9.4	9.8	8.9	9.2	9.5	8.8	9.0	9.2	8.0	8.6	8.9
In metropolitan statistical area	9.1	9.4	9.8	9.0	9.2	9.5	8.7	9.0	9.2	8.5	8.7	9.0	7.8	8.4	8.7
In principal city	7.9	8.2	8.5	7.7	7.9	8.3	7.5	7.7	8.0	7.4	7.5	7.7	6.7	7.2	7.5
Not in principal city	9.9	10.3	10.6	9.8	10.0	10.4	9.5	9.8	10.1	9.3	9.5	9.8	8.5	9.1	9.4
In micropolitan statistical area	11.1	11.5	11.8	11.1	11.4	11.7	10.9	11.1	11.4	10.6	10.9	11.1	9.6	10.2	10.5
In principal city	10.2	10.7	10.9	10.1	10.5	10.8	10.1	10.2	10.5	9.8	9.9	10.2	8.8	9.4	9.7
Not in principal city	11.6	11.9	12.3	11.6	11.8	12.1	11.3	11.6	11.8	11.1	11.3	11.6	10.0	10.7	11.0
Not in metropolitan or micropolitan statistical area	11.2	11.5	11.8	11.1	11.5	11.7	11.0	11.2	11.5	10.7	10.9	11.2	9.8	10.5	10.8

Table 17. Percent of the Civilian Population 18 Years and Over Who Are Veterans, Selected Counties by State/Territory, United States, American Community Survey 1-Year Estimates, 2013

(Percent.)

Location	Percent veterans
United States	8.1
Alabama	9.6
Baldwin County	11.6
Calhoun County	11.5
Cullman County	7.9
DeKalb County	7.4
Elmore County	13.8
Etowah County	8.6
Houston County	11.4
Jefferson County	8.0
Lauderdale County	8.9
Lee County	7.4
Limestone County	9.0
Madison County	11.6
Marshall County	10.1
Mobile County	9.3
Montgomery County	10.6
Morgan County	8.5
St. Clair County	9.2
Shelby County	8.8
Talladega County	8.3
Tuscaloosa County	7.2
Walker County	10.3
Alaska	11.9
Anchorage Municipality	11.9
Fairbanks North Star Borough	13.6
Matanuska-Susitna Borough	14.8
Arizona	10.0
Apache County	6.6
Cochise County	17.6
Coconino County	7.3
Maricopa County	8.7
Mohave County	15.8
Navajo County	10.9
Pima County	11.5
Pinal County	11.6
Yavapai County	14.1
Yuma County	10.0
Arkansas	9.7
Benton County	9.7
Craighead County	9.0
Faulkner County	7.6
Garland County	15.0
Jefferson County	8.4
Lonoke County	13.4
Pulaski County	10.6
Saline County	12.2
Sebastian County	10.2
Washington County	6.0
White County	8.1
California	6.0
Alameda County	4.7
Butte County	8.7
Contra Costa County	6.1
El Dorado County	10.0
Fresno County	5.8
Humboldt County	9.5
Imperial County	4.8
Kern County	7.1
Kings County	9.5
Lake County	10.8
Los Angeles County	3.8
Madera County	7.4
California cnt'd	
Marin County	6.8
Mendocino County	7.6
Merced County	5.8
Monterey County	6.9
Napa County	8.2
Nevada County	12.5
Orange County	5.2
Placer County	10.5
Riverside County	7.4
Sacramento County	7.9
San Bernardino County	6.4
San Diego County	9.3
San Francisco County	3.4
San Joaquin County	6.4
San Luis Obispo County	8.3
San Mateo County	5.0
Santa Barbara County	7.3
Santa Clara County	4.3
Santa Cruz County	5.3
Shasta County	11.0
Solano County	10.7
Sonoma County	8.3
Stanislaus County	5.7
Sutter County	9.4
Tulare County	5.1
Ventura County	7.2
Yolo County	5.8
Yuba County	11.9
Colorado	9.5
Adams County	7.9
Arapahoe County	8.8
Boulder County	6.3
Denver County	6.1
Douglas County	8.6
El Paso County	18.7
Jefferson County	8.9
Larimer County	8.2
Mesa County	9.0
Pueblo County	12.4
Weld County	8.6
Connecticut	6.8
Fairfield County	5.2
Hartford County	6.4
Litchfield County	8.6
Middlesex County	8.8
New Haven County	6.6
New London County	11.3
Tolland County	7.4
Windham County	6.7
Delaware	9.5
Kent County	14.1
New Castle County	7.5
Sussex County	11.4
District of Columbia	5.2
District of Columbia	5.2
Florida	9.4
Alachua County	8.0
Bay County	16.3
Brevard County	14.2
Broward County	5.6
Charlotte County	16.8
Citrus County	17.6
Clay County	17.2
Florida cnt'd	
Collier County	11.1
Columbia County	13.3
Duval County	11.8
Escambia County	13.3
Flagler County	14.6
Hernando County	13.3
Highlands County	14.0
Hillsborough County	9.3
Indian River County	12.1
Lake County	12.6
Lee County	11.0
Leon County	7.5
Manatee County	11.2
Marion County	12.6
Martin County	11.2
Miami-Dade County	2.5
Monroe County	10.3
Nassau County	14.9
Okaloosa County	21.8
Orange County	6.7
Osceola County	6.3
Palm Beach County	8.1
Pasco County	13.1
Pinellas County	11.2
Polk County	10.1
Putnam County	12.4
St. Johns County	11.7
St. Lucie County	11.1
Santa Rosa County	17.2
Sarasota County	12.9
Seminole County	8.4
Sumter County	19.8
Volusia County	12.6
Georgia	8.7
Barrow County	9.0
Bartow County	8.5
Bibb County	7.8
Bulloch County	5.9
Carroll County	9.0
Catoosa County	7.1
Chatham County	11.2
Cherokee County	8.1
Clarke County	4.8
Clayton County	9.2
Cobb County	7.8
Columbia County	13.8
Coweta County	9.3
DeKalb County	7.5
Dougherty County	10.0
Douglas County	8.3
Fayette County	14.2
Floyd County	9.2
Forsyth County	7.7
Fulton County	5.9
Glynn County	12.6
Gwinnett County	6.5
Hall County	6.7
Henry County	11.0
Houston County	15.6
Liberty County	26.4
Lowndes County	11.9
Muscogee County	13.9
Newton County	10.0
Paulding County	8.3

Table 17. Percent of the Civilian Population 18 Years and Over Who Are Veterans, Selected Counties by State/Territory, United States, American Community Survey 1-Year Estimates, 2013—*Continued*

(Percent.)

Location	Percent veterans
Georgia cnt'd	
Richmond County	12.5
Rockdale County	7.9
Troup County	9.2
Walker County	7.4
Walton County	6.8
Whitfield County	7.3
Hawaii	10.3
Hawaii County	10.6
Honolulu County	11.0
Kauai County	7.5
Maui County	6.9
Idaho	10.1
Ada County	9.4
Bannock County	6.8
Bonneville County	8.7
Canyon County	9.1
Kootenai County	11.6
Twin Falls County	9.6
Illinois	6.7
Adams County	8.6
Champaign County	6.5
Cook County	4.7
DeKalb County	6.3
DuPage County	4.9
Kane County	5.6
Kankakee County	9.9
Kendall County	7.5
Lake County	6.0
LaSalle County	9.7
McHenry County	6.8
McLean County	6.7
Macon County	10.5
Madison County	10.2
Peoria County	7.3
Rock Island County	9.9
St. Clair County	15.0
Sangamon County	10.0
Tazewell County	9.5
Vermilion County	9.8
Will County	6.1
Williamson County	10.7
Winnebago County	9.5
Indiana	8.4
Allen County	7.8
Bartholomew County	7.1
Clark County	10.8
Delaware County	7.8
Elkhart County	7.3
Floyd County	10.9
Grant County	7.7
Hamilton County	6.9
Hancock County	8.6
Hendricks County	10.2
Howard County	11.6
Johnson County	9.3
Kosciusko County	7.5
Lake County	8.8
LaPorte County	8.8
Madison County	9.1
Marion County	7.4
Monroe County	6.2
Morgan County	11.0
Porter County	8.3
St. Joseph County	7.9
Tippecanoe County	5.9
Vanderburgh County	9.0
Vigo County	8.6
Wayne County	10.0
Iowa	8.8
Black Hawk County	6.6
Dallas County	7.8
Dubuque County	8.6
Johnson County	4.8
Linn County	10.2
Polk County	7.4
Pottawattamie County	9.1
Scott County	9.1
Story County	6.4
Woodbury County	9.3
Kansas	9.1
Butler County	9.2
Douglas County	5.0
Johnson County	7.8
Leavenworth County	17.1
Riley County	10.5
Sedgwick County	9.5
Shawnee County	10.7
Wyandotte County	7.3
Kentucky	8.7
Boone County	9.3
Bullitt County	10.0
Campbell County	8.1
Christian County	10.5
Daviess County	9.3
Fayette County	7.2
Hardin County	19.4
Jefferson County	8.7
Kenton County	8.5
McCracken County	11.3
Madison County	9.2
Pike County	7.0
Warren County	7.8
Louisiana	7.7
Ascension Parish	5.9
Bossier Parish	12.3
Caddo Parish	9.1
Calcasieu Parish	8.9
East Baton Rouge Parish	6.5
Iberia Parish	8.7
Jefferson Parish	6.7
Lafayette Parish	7.1
Lafourche Parish	4.8
Livingston Parish	8.0
Orleans Parish	5.9
Ouachita Parish	7.7
Rapides Parish	8.7
St. Landry Parish	6.8
St. Tammany Parish	8.9
Tangipahoa Parish	7.1
Terrebonne Parish	7.4
Maine	11.2
Androscoggin County	11.7
Aroostook County	12.6
Cumberland County	9.2
Kennebec County	10.3
Penobscot County	11.4
York County	12.2
Maryland	8.8
Allegany County	9.7
Anne Arundel County	12.4
Baltimore County	8.5
Calvert County	11.6
Carroll County	8.3
Cecil County	10.3
Charles County	14.9
Maryland cnt'd	
Frederick County	8.7
Harford County	10.3
Howard County	7.7
Montgomery County	6.0
Prince George's County	8.9
St. Mary's County	14.5
Washington County	10.8
Wicomico County	7.4
Baltimore city	6.2
Massachusetts	6.4
Barnstable County	10.9
Berkshire County	8.9
Bristol County	7.2
Essex County	6.4
Franklin County	8.4
Hampden County	8.3
Hampshire County	7.4
Middlesex County	5.3
Norfolk County	6.3
Plymouth County	8.0
Suffolk County	3.1
Worcester County	7.5
Michigan	8.1
Allegan County	7.0
Bay County	9.5
Berrien County	9.3
Calhoun County	11.5
Clinton County	7.5
Eaton County	7.6
Genesee County	8.6
Grand Traverse County	11.0
Ingham County	7.2
Isabella County	6.1
Jackson County	9.8
Kalamazoo County	8.1
Kent County	6.9
Lapeer County	10.2
Lenawee County	9.4
Livingston County	7.3
Macomb County	7.7
Marquette County	10.9
Midland County	8.2
Monroe County	8.7
Muskegon County	8.4
Oakland County	6.5
Ottawa County	7.7
Saginaw County	8.7
St. Clair County	9.4
Shiawassee County	8.2
Van Buren County	10.6
Washtenaw County	5.4
Wayne County	6.9
Minnesota	8.2
Anoka County	8.8
Blue Earth County	8.3
Carver County	7.1
Dakota County	7.6
Hennepin County	6.6
Olmsted County	8.0
Ramsey County	6.6
Rice County	9.8
St. Louis County	9.6
Scott County	7.7
Sherburne County	7.2
Stearns County	8.4
Washington County	8.7
Wright County	8.6

Table 17. Percent of the Civilian Population 18 Years and Over Who Are Veterans, Selected Counties by State/Territory, United States, American Community Survey 1-Year Estimates, 2013—*Continued*

(Percent.)

Location	Percent veterans
Mississippi	8.2
DeSoto County	8.0
Forrest County	7.2
Harrison County	18.0
Hinds County	5.5
Jackson County	11.8
Jones County	8.0
Lauderdale County	8.5
Lee County	8.4
Madison County	6.9
Rankin County	8.6
Missouri	9.4
Boone County	6.5
Buchanan County	9.7
Cape Girardeau County	9.5
Cass County	10.0
Christian County	7.8
Clay County	10.1
Cole County	9.6
Franklin County	8.4
Greene County	9.7
Jackson County	8.1
Jasper County	10.5
Jefferson County	9.8
Platte County	8.7
St. Charles County	9.1
St. Francois County	9.1
St. Louis County	8.1
St. Louis city	7.2
Montana	10.5
Cascade County	14.9
Flathead County	11.3
Gallatin County	5.8
Lewis and Clark County	10.8
Missoula County	7.3
Yellowstone County	9.7
Nebraska	8.9
Douglas County	7.6
Lancaster County	7.4
Sarpy County	12.8
Nevada	10.2
Clark County	9.7
Washoe County	9.5
New Hampshire	10.1
Cheshire County	13.4
Grafton County	9.3
Hillsborough County	9.0
Merrimack County	8.9
Rockingham County	9.1
Strafford County	10.1
New Jersey	5.6
Atlantic County	7.1
Bergen County	4.7
Burlington County	9.0
Camden County	7.0
Cape May County	9.8
Cumberland County	7.1
Essex County	3.8
Gloucester County	6.8
Hudson County	2.8
Hunterdon County	6.6
Mercer County	4.8
Middlesex County	4.4
Monmouth County	6.7
Morris County	5.3
Ocean County	9.8
New Jersey cnt'd	
Passaic County	3.6
Salem County	11.8
Somerset County	4.2
Sussex County	7.8
Union County	4.2
Warren County	7.4
New Mexico	10.2
Bernalillo County	9.8
Chaves County	10.1
Doña Ana County	8.7
Lea County	8.9
McKinley County	6.3
Otero County	18.0
Sandoval County	12.4
San Juan County	9.0
Santa Fe County	8.3
Valencia County	12.5
New York	5.2
Albany County	6.3
Bronx County	2.9
Broome County	7.5
Cattaraugus County	10.9
Cayuga County	11.4
Chautauqua County	10.0
Chemung County	7.8
Clinton County	9.3
Dutchess County	7.2
Erie County	8.0
Jefferson County	12.9
Kings County	2.3
Livingston County	8.2
Madison County	10.6
Monroe County	6.8
Nassau County	5.0
New York County	2.3
Niagara County	8.6
Oneida County	10.0
Onondaga County	7.6
Ontario County	9.9
Orange County	7.6
Oswego County	8.9
Putnam County	6.8
Queens County	2.5
Rensselaer County	7.5
Richmond County	4.8
Rockland County	4.5
St. Lawrence County	9.1
Saratoga County	9.3
Schenectady County	8.0
Steuben County	10.4
Suffolk County	6.3
Sullivan County	8.9
Tompkins County	5.0
Ulster County	6.3
Warren County	9.4
Wayne County	8.4
Westchester County	4.6
North Carolina	9.1
Alamance County	8.0
Brunswick County	13.4
Buncombe County	9.6
Burke County	8.5
Cabarrus County	8.3
Caldwell County	8.2
Carteret County	15.5
Catawba County	8.3
Chatham County	10.2
Cleveland County	9.7
North Carolina cnt'd	
Craven County	16.2
Cumberland County	19.4
Davidson County	8.4
Durham County	6.9
Forsyth County	8.1
Gaston County	9.1
Guilford County	7.3
Harnett County	14.0
Henderson County	11.1
Iredell County	8.8
Johnston County	10.1
Lincoln County	9.2
Mecklenburg County	6.4
Moore County	13.3
Nash County	10.2
New Hanover County	10.1
Onslow County	21.2
Orange County	4.4
Pitt County	7.4
Randolph County	9.3
Robeson County	7.0
Rockingham County	8.4
Rowan County	8.3
Rutherford County	8.6
Surry County	9.1
Union County	8.7
Wake County	7.1
Wayne County	11.8
Wilkes County	7.5
Wilson County	11.5
North Dakota	8.8
Burleigh County	8.2
Cass County	7.0
Grand Forks County	9.4
Ward County	11.0
Ohio	8.9
Allen County	9.6
Ashtabula County	11.0
Belmont County	10.0
Butler County	7.7
Clark County	10.7
Clermont County	9.3
Columbiana County	11.6
Cuyahoga County	7.7
Delaware County	7.8
Erie County	11.3
Fairfield County	9.7
Franklin County	6.9
Geauga County	8.6
Greene County	13.2
Hamilton County	7.3
Hancock County	8.6
Jefferson County	11.2
Lake County	8.9
Licking County	10.6
Lorain County	9.9
Lucas County	8.0
Mahoning County	10.1
Marion County	11.2
Medina County	9.8
Miami County	10.5
Montgomery County	9.6
Muskingum County	8.4
Portage County	9.1
Richland County	9.2
Ross County	10.2
Scioto County	10.3
Stark County	9.8
Summit County	8.8

Table 17. Percent of the Civilian Population 18 Years and Over Who Are Veterans, Selected Counties by State/Territory, United States, American Community Survey 1-Year Estimates, 2013—*Continued*

(Percent.)

Location	Percent veterans
Ohio cnt'd	
Trumbull County	10.6
Tuscarawas County	10.1
Warren County	8.6
Wayne County	8.9
Wood County	8.2
Oklahoma	9.7
Canadian County	9.7
Cleveland County	10.3
Comanche County	15.8
Creek County	9.4
Muskogee County	10.7
Oklahoma County	9.5
Payne County	6.7
Pottawatomie County	10.3
Rogers County	10.9
Tulsa County	8.6
Wagoner County	10.5
Oregon	9.5
Benton County	7.5
Clackamas County	9.5
Deschutes County	10.0
Douglas County	15.6
Jackson County	13.3
Josephine County	12.9
Klamath County	14.9
Lane County	9.9
Linn County	10.5
Marion County	10.1
Multnomah County	6.6
Polk County	9.5
Umatilla County	9.9
Washington County	6.9
Yamhill County	8.3
Pennsylvania	8.5
Adams County	10.1
Allegheny County	8.6
Armstrong County	10.7
Beaver County	11.0
Berks County	8.7
Blair County	11.9
Bucks County	7.4
Butler County	9.6
Cambria County	10.5
Carbon County	11.4
Centre County	6.1
Chester County	7.0
Clearfield County	9.7
Columbia County	8.3
Crawford County	10.9
Cumberland County	10.9
Dauphin County	8.6
Delaware County	6.4
Erie County	9.2
Fayette County	8.6
Franklin County	12.0
Indiana County	8.3
Lackawanna County	9.1
Lancaster County	7.8
Lawrence County	11.3
Lebanon County	9.9
Lehigh County	7.8
Luzerne County	9.5
Lycoming County	10.1
Mercer County	10.9
Monroe County	7.9
Montgomery County	7.1
Northampton County	7.4
Northumberland County	12.0
Pennsylvania cnt'd	
Philadelphia County	5.5
Schuylkill County	11.3
Somerset County	8.9
Washington County	10.1
Westmoreland County	9.9
York County	9.5
Rhode Island	7.7
Kent County	9.8
Newport County	14.4
Providence County	6.3
Washington County	8.1
South Carolina	10.0
Aiken County	10.2
Anderson County	9.3
Beaufort County	15.3
Berkeley County	14.2
Charleston County	9.8
Darlington County	8.6
Dorchester County	13.8
Florence County	7.0
Greenville County	8.8
Greenwood County	7.8
Horry County	11.2
Lancaster County	9.7
Laurens County	8.8
Lexington County	10.4
Oconee County	10.1
Orangeburg County	9.1
Pickens County	7.9
Richland County	10.7
Spartanburg County	8.2
Sumter County	15.2
York County	9.5
South Dakota	9.8
Minnehaha County	7.7
Pennington County	14.5
Tennessee	9.3
Anderson County	10.3
Blount County	11.2
Bradley County	8.7
Davidson County	6.8
Greene County	10.6
Hamilton County	9.5
Knox County	9.2
Madison County	9.0
Maury County	9.2
Montgomery County	21.2
Putnam County	6.1
Robertson County	7.2
Rutherford County	9.1
Sevier County	9.4
Shelby County	8.0
Sullivan County	10.7
Sumner County	8.8
Washington County	12.8
Williamson County	6.3
Wilson County	9.8
Texas	7.7
Angelina County	8.9
Bastrop County	11.3
Bell County	21.4
Bexar County	10.9
Bowie County	11.4
Brazoria County	7.8
Brazos County	5.5
Cameron County	5.6
Texas cnt'd	
Collin County	6.2
Comal County	12.9
Coryell County	19.8
Dallas County	5.4
Denton County	7.5
Ector County	6.6
Ellis County	8.1
El Paso County	8.7
Fort Bend County	5.7
Galveston County	8.7
Grayson County	10.8
Gregg County	9.9
Guadalupe County	14.9
Harris County	5.2
Harrison County	7.0
Hays County	8.6
Henderson County	10.7
Hidalgo County	4.0
Hunt County	12.2
Jefferson County	8.3
Johnson County	8.1
Kaufman County	8.4
Liberty County	10.5
Lubbock County	6.5
McLennan County	8.7
Midland County	7.1
Montgomery County	8.5
Nacogdoches County	6.4
Nueces County	10.9
Orange County	8.7
Parker County	9.0
Potter County	9.2
Randall County	10.5
Rockwall County	9.0
San Patricio County	9.0
Smith County	8.2
Tarrant County	8.1
Taylor County	11.9
Tom Green County	10.7
Travis County	6.2
Victoria County	9.2
Walker County	9.1
Webb County	3.0
Wichita County	11.5
Williamson County	8.6
Utah	6.6
Cache County	4.7
Davis County	8.3
Salt Lake County	5.7
Utah County	4.2
Washington County	10.5
Weber County	9.4
Vermont	8.2
Chittenden County	6.2
Virginia	10.9
Albemarle County	7.7
Arlington County	6.5
Augusta County	8.7
Bedford County	11.8
Chesterfield County	10.3
Fairfax County	9.4
Fauquier County	12.0
Frederick County	12.1
Hanover County	8.3
Henrico County	7.8
James City County	16.3
Loudoun County	8.4
Montgomery County	5.3

Table 17. Percent of the Civilian Population 18 Years and Over Who Are Veterans, Selected Counties by State/Territory, United States, American Community Survey 1-Year Estimates, 2013—*Continued*

(Percent.)

Location	Percent veterans	Location	Percent veterans	Location	Percent veterans
Virginia cnt'd		**Washington** cnt'd		**Wisconsin** cnt'd	
Prince William County	13.5	Lewis County	12.8	Outagamie County	8.4
Roanoke County	10.9	Pierce County	13.7	Ozaukee County	7.8
Rockingham County	7.4	Skagit County	11.0	Portage County	8.2
Spotsylvania County	15.3	Snohomish County	9.2	Racine County	8.1
Stafford County	19.3	Spokane County	11.3	Rock County	8.7
York County	20.0	Thurston County	14.4	St. Croix County	7.1
Alexandria city	8.2	Whatcom County	8.2	Sheboygan County	8.3
Chesapeake city	15.0	Yakima County	7.8	Walworth County	8.2
Hampton city	17.8			Washington County	8.8
Lynchburg city	8.4	**West Virginia**	10.2	Waukesha County	8.0
Newport News city	14.2	Berkeley County	13.8	Winnebago County	9.2
Norfolk city	15.6	Cabell County	8.7	Wood County	10.1
Portsmouth city	15.4	Harrison County	10.3		
Richmond city	6.1	Kanawha County	10.9	**Wyoming**	11.1
Roanoke city	10.6	Monongalia County	5.5	Laramie County	16.9
Suffolk city	16.5	Raleigh County	11.4	Natrona County	10.9
Virginia Beach city	18.2	Wood County	13.1		
				Puerto Rico	3.2
Washington	10.2	**Wisconsin**	8.3	Arecibo Municipio	2.2
Benton County	9.5	Brown County	7.6	Bayamón Municipio	4.1
Chelan County	9.1	Dane County	5.8	Caguas Municipio	3.4
Clallam County	15.9	Dodge County	7.8	Carolina Municipio	3.9
Clark County	10.0	Eau Claire County	8.7	Guaynabo Municipio	4.6
Cowlitz County	12.5	Fond du Lac County	9.6	Mayagüez Municipio	4.7
Franklin County	4.8	Jefferson County	8.1	Ponce Municipio	4.2
Grant County	8.3	Kenosha County	7.4	San Juan Municipio	3.4
Grays Harbor County	11.2	La Crosse County	9.0	Toa Alta Municipio	2.7
Island County	18.8	Manitowoc County	9.8	Toa Baja Municipio	4.0
King County	6.8	Marathon County	8.7	Trujillo Alto Municipio	3.5
Kitsap County	19.2	Milwaukee County	6.6		

Table 18. Percent of the Civilian Population 18 Years and Over Who Are Veterans, Selected Counties by State/ Territory, United States, American Community Survey 3-Year Estimates, 2013

(Percent.)

Location	Percent veterans
United States	8.7
Alabama	10.3
Autauga County	13.8
Baldwin County	12.8
Barbour County	9.3
Bibb County	7.3
Blount County	10.4
Butler County	9.1
Calhoun County	12.9
Chambers County	9.3
Cherokee County	10.4
Chilton County	10.5
Clarke County	8.1
Coffee County	17.8
Colbert County	9.6
Covington County	11.9
Cullman County	10.0
Dale County	18.8
Dallas County	8.7
DeKalb County	8.0
Elmore County	13.3
Escambia County	9.3
Etowah County	10.1
Franklin County	6.9
Geneva County	11.4
Houston County	11.9
Jackson County	9.5
Jefferson County	8.9
Lauderdale County	9.0
Lawrence County	7.7
Lee County	8.9
Limestone County	10.4
Macon County	8.8
Madison County	12.9
Marengo County	7.5
Marion County	9.1
Marshall County	9.9
Mobile County	10.6
Monroe County	7.1
Montgomery County	11.6
Morgan County	9.7
Pike County	9.8
Randolph County	9.2
Russell County	14.8
St. Clair County	10.0
Shelby County	9.1
Talladega County	10.0
Tallapoosa County	11.3
Tuscaloosa County	7.4
Walker County	10.6
Winston County	7.9
Alaska	13.2
Anchorage Municipality	13.6
Fairbanks North Star Borough	15.7
Juneau City and Borough	10.9
Kenai Peninsula Borough	14.1
Matanuska-Susitna Borough	14.7
Arizona	10.5
Apache County	8.0
Cochise County	19.5
Coconino County	7.9
Gila County	14.4
Graham County	9.0
La Paz County	16.4
Maricopa County	9.2
Mohave County	15.9
Navajo County	9.3
Arizona cnt'd	
Pima County	11.9
Pinal County	12.6
Santa Cruz County	6.9
Yavapai County	15.6
Yuma County	10.3
Arkansas	10.3
Ashley County	8.9
Baxter County	16.1
Benton County	9.6
Boone County	12.0
Carroll County	13.7
Clark County	9.5
Cleburne County	15.4
Columbia County	7.6
Conway County	8.6
Craighead County	8.4
Crawford County	11.7
Crittenden County	10.0
Faulkner County	8.8
Garland County	13.0
Greene County	10.8
Hempstead County	8.6
Hot Spring County	12.0
Independence County	9.1
Jefferson County	9.6
Johnson County	8.9
Logan County	11.8
Lonoke County	15.9
Miller County	9.8
Mississippi County	9.0
Ouachita County	9.0
Phillips County	6.9
Poinsett County	9.2
Polk County	13.7
Pope County	8.8
Pulaski County	10.5
St. Francis County	9.4
Saline County	12.3
Sebastian County	10.5
Union County	9.0
Washington County	7.1
White County	9.3
Yell County	7.9
California	6.4
Alameda County	5.1
Amador County	14.0
Butte County	9.7
Calaveras County	13.9
Colusa County	7.3
Contra Costa County	6.8
Del Norte County	11.3
El Dorado County	11.4
Fresno County	6.2
Glenn County	6.9
Humboldt County	8.9
Imperial County	4.8
Kern County	7.3
Kings County	9.6
Lake County	12.8
Lassen County	10.2
Los Angeles County	4.1
Madera County	7.9
Marin County	7.5
Mendocino County	9.7
Merced County	6.0
Monterey County	6.8
Napa County	8.2
Nevada County	12.6
California cnt'd	
Orange County	5.5
Placer County	10.7
Riverside County	8.0
Sacramento County	8.5
San Benito County	6.2
San Bernardino County	7.0
San Diego County	9.9
San Francisco County	3.8
San Joaquin County	6.7
San Luis Obispo County	9.0
San Mateo County	5.4
Santa Barbara County	7.7
Santa Clara County	4.6
Santa Cruz County	5.9
Shasta County	12.5
Siskiyou County	13.6
Solano County	10.9
Sonoma County	8.6
Stanislaus County	6.5
Sutter County	9.8
Tehama County	11.5
Tulare County	5.7
Tuolumne County	11.6
Ventura County	7.4
Yolo County	6.0
Yuba County	13.0
Colorado	10.2
Adams County	8.3
Arapahoe County	9.7
Boulder County	6.3
Broomfield County	8.3
Delta County	13.2
Denver County	6.7
Douglas County	9.0
Eagle County	4.5
Elbert County	14.0
El Paso County	18.9
Fremont County	13.6
Garfield County	7.2
Jefferson County	9.7
La Plata County	9.4
Larimer County	9.3
Logan County	10.1
Mesa County	12.2
Montezuma County	10.6
Montrose County	11.4
Morgan County	7.9
Pueblo County	12.8
Routt County	6.8
Summit County	6.4
Teller County	17.4
Weld County	9.0
Connecticut	7.6
Fairfield County	5.6
Hartford County	7.4
Litchfield County	9.4
Middlesex County	9.2
New Haven County	7.3
New London County	11.9
Tolland County	8.3
Windham County	9.8
Delaware	10.3
Kent County	15.4
New Castle County	8.1
Sussex County	12.2

Table 18. Percent of the Civilian Population 18 Years and Over Who Are Veterans, Selected Counties by State/ Territory, United States, American Community Survey 3-Year Estimates, 2013—*Continued*

(Percent.)

Location	Percent veterans
District of Columbia	5.7
District of Columbia	5.7
Florida	10.0
Alachua County	8.2
Baker County	9.8
Bay County	17.3
Bradford County	11.2
Brevard County	15.0
Broward County	6.2
Charlotte County	17.5
Citrus County	17.7
Clay County	17.9
Collier County	11.0
Columbia County	14.0
DeSoto County	8.8
Duval County	12.8
Escambia County	14.2
Flagler County	13.8
Gadsden County	9.3
Hardee County	7.4
Hendry County	6.4
Hernando County	14.7
Highlands County	15.5
Hillsborough County	9.5
Indian River County	13.3
Jackson County	12.6
Lake County	13.7
Lee County	11.9
Leon County	7.7
Levy County	14.0
Manatee County	12.7
Marion County	14.2
Martin County	12.9
Miami-Dade County	2.8
Monroe County	12.7
Nassau County	15.5
Okaloosa County	21.8
Okeechobee County	8.7
Orange County	6.9
Osceola County	7.5
Palm Beach County	8.8
Pasco County	13.1
Pinellas County	12.0
Polk County	10.7
Putnam County	13.2
St. Johns County	12.3
St. Lucie County	11.4
Santa Rosa County	17.9
Sarasota County	14.2
Seminole County	9.2
Sumter County	20.1
Suwannee County	13.2
Taylor County	12.1
Volusia County	13.2
Wakulla County	13.4
Walton County	14.8
Washington County	11.2
Georgia	9.2
Baldwin County	8.4
Barrow County	8.5
Bartow County	8.8
Bibb County	9.0
Bryan County	15.1
Bulloch County	6.6
Burke County	8.0
Butts County	8.3
Camden County	21.2
Carroll County	8.6
Catoosa County	9.6
Georgia cnt'd	
Chatham County	11.9
Chattooga County	8.4
Cherokee County	9.0
Clarke County	5.4
Clayton County	9.1
Cobb County	8.3
Coffee County	6.6
Colquitt County	6.9
Columbia County	14.5
Coweta County	10.4
Crisp County	9.7
Dawson County	9.4
Decatur County	7.3
DeKalb County	7.6
Dodge County	7.0
Dougherty County	10.2
Douglas County	10.5
Effingham County	12.4
Elbert County	9.6
Emanuel County	8.5
Fannin County	11.5
Fayette County	13.1
Floyd County	9.7
Forsyth County	7.8
Franklin County	7.9
Fulton County	6.2
Gilmer County	10.2
Glynn County	12.1
Gordon County	7.6
Grady County	8.6
Gwinnett County	6.3
Habersham County	9.5
Hall County	7.9
Haralson County	9.3
Harris County	15.1
Hart County	12.2
Henry County	11.8
Houston County	17.7
Jackson County	9.7
Jones County	8.0
Laurens County	9.1
Lee County	11.5
Liberty County	25.6
Lowndes County	11.7
Lumpkin County	9.2
McDuffie County	7.0
Madison County	8.5
Meriwether County	8.5
Mitchell County	9.4
Monroe County	11.3
Murray County	7.2
Muscogee County	14.6
Newton County	10.4
Oconee County	9.4
Paulding County	10.2
Peach County	11.0
Pickens County	12.9
Polk County	9.1
Putnam County	11.8
Richmond County	14.0
Rockdale County	9.6
Spalding County	9.7
Stephens County	8.0
Sumter County	8.5
Tattnall County	10.6
Thomas County	10.3
Tift County	6.4
Toombs County	7.7
Troup County	9.3
Union County	15.1
Georgia cnt'd	
Upson County	9.3
Walker County	10.7
Walton County	8.6
Ware County	8.4
Washington County	8.2
Wayne County	12.3
White County	8.0
Whitfield County	6.4
Worth County	9.4
Hawaii	10.7
Hawaii County	10.3
Honolulu County	11.3
Kauai County	8.6
Maui County	8.0
Idaho	10.4
Ada County	9.5
Bannock County	8.2
Bingham County	9.2
Blaine County	8.2
Bonner County	14.7
Bonneville County	9.0
Canyon County	10.0
Cassia County	8.0
Elmore County	28.3
Jefferson County	8.3
Jerome County	9.3
Kootenai County	12.5
Latah County	6.5
Madison County	3.3
Minidoka County	8.8
Nez Perce County	12.8
Payette County	12.3
Twin Falls County	9.6
Illinois	7.2
Adams County	10.4
Boone County	8.6
Bureau County	10.5
Champaign County	6.3
Christian County	11.3
Clinton County	11.4
Coles County	8.3
Cook County	5.1
DeKalb County	7.2
DuPage County	5.7
Effingham County	9.4
Fayette County	9.9
Franklin County	11.7
Fulton County	11.1
Grundy County	9.6
Henry County	11.0
Iroquois County	10.7
Jackson County	8.2
Jefferson County	11.1
Jersey County	13.3
Jo Daviess County	11.4
Kane County	6.6
Kankakee County	9.9
Kendall County	7.0
Knox County	11.1
Lake County	6.5
LaSalle County	9.8
Lee County	10.6
Livingston County	8.6
Logan County	8.7
McDonough County	8.7
McHenry County	7.3
McLean County	7.4

Table 18. Percent of the Civilian Population 18 Years and Over Who Are Veterans, Selected Counties by State/Territory, United States, American Community Survey 3-Year Estimates, 2013—*Continued*

(Percent.)

Location	Percent veterans
Illinois cnt'd	
Macon County	10.9
Macoupin County	11.4
Madison County	10.6
Marion County	10.9
Monroe County	11.1
Montgomery County	11.8
Morgan County	10.6
Ogle County	10.9
Peoria County	8.5
Perry County	10.9
Randolph County	11.5
Rock Island County	10.2
St. Clair County	14.7
Saline County	10.3
Sangamon County	10.3
Shelby County	13.7
Stephenson County	9.9
Tazewell County	9.7
Vermilion County	11.8
Whiteside County	11.4
Will County	6.7
Williamson County	12.0
Winnebago County	9.2
Woodford County	9.2
Indiana	9.0
Adams County	6.8
Allen County	8.7
Bartholomew County	9.1
Boone County	7.4
Carroll County	10.6
Cass County	10.5
Clark County	10.7
Clay County	8.9
Clinton County	7.7
Daviess County	8.7
Dearborn County	9.9
Decatur County	10.2
DeKalb County	9.2
Delaware County	8.4
Dubois County	9.6
Elkhart County	8.0
Fayette County	12.2
Floyd County	11.0
Franklin County	8.7
Fulton County	9.8
Gibson County	9.3
Grant County	10.3
Greene County	11.3
Hamilton County	7.2
Hancock County	9.2
Harrison County	9.6
Hendricks County	10.0
Henry County	11.0
Howard County	12.1
Huntington County	10.2
Jackson County	8.5
Jasper County	8.8
Jay County	9.1
Jefferson County	11.5
Jennings County	10.8
Johnson County	9.6
Knox County	8.8
Kosciusko County	7.9
LaGrange County	6.5
Lake County	8.6
LaPorte County	9.6
Lawrence County	11.5
Madison County	10.1
Marion County	8.2
Marshall County	8.3
Indiana cnt'd	
Miami County	12.7
Monroe County	6.4
Montgomery County	8.8
Morgan County	10.7
Noble County	8.1
Owen County	12.2
Porter County	10.0
Posey County	9.4
Putnam County	8.1
Randolph County	9.6
Ripley County	11.0
St. Joseph County	8.1
Scott County	9.4
Shelby County	9.5
Spencer County	10.6
Starke County	10.8
Steuben County	9.5
Sullivan County	8.8
Tippecanoe County	6.6
Vanderburgh County	9.0
Vigo County	9.1
Wabash County	8.9
Warrick County	9.9
Washington County	10.1
Wayne County	10.9
Wells County	8.9
White County	9.7
Whitley County	9.5
Iowa	9.4
Benton County	11.1
Black Hawk County	8.0
Boone County	11.7
Bremer County	9.4
Buchanan County	9.6
Buena Vista County	7.4
Carroll County	9.5
Cerro Gordo County	12.4
Clinton County	10.5
Dallas County	7.6
Des Moines County	11.1
Dubuque County	9.6
Fayette County	10.2
Henry County	8.7
Jackson County	11.4
Jasper County	10.1
Johnson County	5.5
Jones County	11.3
Lee County	13.3
Linn County	10.2
Mahaska County	8.2
Marion County	9.0
Marshall County	11.0
Muscatine County	8.5
Plymouth County	10.4
Polk County	8.1
Pottawattamie County	10.6
Scott County	9.8
Sioux County	7.3
Story County	6.3
Wapello County	9.4
Warren County	10.4
Washington County	9.0
Webster County	10.5
Winneshiek County	9.1
Woodbury County	9.1
Kansas	9.7
Barton County	9.1
Butler County	10.7
Kansas cnt'd	
Cherokee County	9.7
Cowley County	10.9
Crawford County	8.2
Douglas County	6.3
Ellis County	7.2
Finney County	5.0
Ford County	6.7
Franklin County	9.0
Geary County	22.8
Harvey County	8.8
Johnson County	8.1
Labette County	9.1
Leavenworth County	17.3
Lyon County	7.5
McPherson County	9.5
Miami County	8.8
Montgomery County	9.4
Pottawatomie County	10.4
Reno County	9.6
Riley County	9.5
Saline County	10.2
Sedgwick County	9.8
Seward County	4.2
Shawnee County	12.2
Sumner County	10.5
Wyandotte County	8.5
Kentucky	9.2
Allen County	10.5
Anderson County	9.1
Barren County	7.9
Bell County	8.3
Boone County	9.9
Boyd County	10.6
Boyle County	9.0
Breckinridge County	11.6
Bullitt County	10.7
Calloway County	8.5
Campbell County	8.5
Carter County	7.1
Christian County	13.7
Clark County	9.7
Clay County	5.4
Daviess County	9.8
Fayette County	7.2
Floyd County	5.5
Franklin County	10.5
Grant County	9.5
Graves County	9.8
Grayson County	10.2
Greenup County	8.4
Hardin County	19.7
Harlan County	8.2
Henderson County	8.7
Hopkins County	9.3
Jefferson County	9.2
Jessamine County	9.1
Johnson County	7.8
Kenton County	9.3
Knox County	5.5
Laurel County	8.8
Letcher County	6.7
Lincoln County	9.0
Logan County	9.2
McCracken County	11.5
Madison County	8.7
Marion County	8.8
Marshall County	11.1
Meade County	17.9
Mercer County	9.5

Table 18. Percent of the Civilian Population 18 Years and Over Who Are Veterans, Selected Counties by State/Territory, United States, American Community Survey 3-Year Estimates, 2013—*Continued*

(Percent.)

Location	Percent veterans
Kentucky cnt'd	
Montgomery County	7.6
Muhlenberg County	7.9
Nelson County	10.7
Ohio County	9.2
Oldham County	10.1
Perry County	7.5
Pike County	6.1
Pulaski County	9.4
Rowan County	6.0
Scott County	9.5
Shelby County	8.9
Taylor County	6.5
Warren County	7.6
Wayne County	8.0
Whitley County	8.9
Woodford County	11.3
Louisiana	8.6
Acadia Parish	6.6
Allen Parish	8.3
Ascension Parish	7.8
Assumption Parish	8.5
Avoyelles Parish	8.5
Beauregard Parish	12.8
Bossier Parish	13.8
Caddo Parish	10.1
Calcasieu Parish	9.5
Concordia Parish	10.0
De Soto Parish	11.1
East Baton Rouge Parish	7.1
East Feliciana Parish	7.8
Evangeline Parish	7.8
Franklin Parish	8.8
Grant Parish	8.9
Iberia Parish	8.7
Iberville Parish	6.9
Jefferson Parish	7.5
Jefferson Davis Parish	10.2
Lafayette Parish	8.6
Lafourche Parish	5.9
Lincoln Parish	7.5
Livingston Parish	9.5
Morehouse Parish	9.4
Natchitoches Parish	8.3
Orleans Parish	6.6
Ouachita Parish	8.8
Plaquemines Parish	9.6
Pointe Coupee Parish	7.5
Rapides Parish	9.9
Richland Parish	6.8
Sabine Parish	12.0
St. Bernard Parish	5.4
St. Charles Parish	8.2
St. James Parish	8.7
St. John the Baptist Parish	7.4
St. Landry Parish	7.1
St. Martin Parish	7.1
St. Mary Parish	8.2
St. Tammany Parish	10.7
Tangipahoa Parish	7.9
Terrebonne Parish	8.2
Union Parish	9.3
Vermilion Parish	7.3
Vernon Parish	20.7
Washington Parish	11.6
Webster Parish	11.2
West Baton Rouge Parish	7.6
Maine	11.7
Androscoggin County	11.8
Maine cnt'd	
Aroostook County	12.3
Cumberland County	9.7
Franklin County	12.1
Hancock County	11.8
Kennebec County	11.8
Knox County	13.3
Lincoln County	12.0
Oxford County	12.3
Penobscot County	11.6
Sagadahoc County	13.8
Somerset County	13.1
Waldo County	13.2
Washington County	12.8
York County	12.0
Maryland	9.3
Allegany County	10.6
Anne Arundel County	13.2
Baltimore County	8.8
Calvert County	12.9
Caroline County	10.8
Carroll County	9.9
Cecil County	10.7
Charles County	14.4
Dorchester County	12.6
Frederick County	10.0
Garrett County	9.5
Harford County	10.7
Howard County	7.9
Kent County	10.4
Montgomery County	6.3
Prince George's County	9.0
Queen Anne's County	11.1
St. Mary's County	16.4
Somerset County	9.8
Talbot County	13.2
Washington County	11.0
Wicomico County	9.3
Worcester County	12.5
Baltimore city	7.0
Massachusetts	7.0
Barnstable County	11.2
Berkshire County	9.9
Bristol County	7.7
Essex County	7.1
Franklin County	9.6
Hampden County	8.7
Hampshire County	7.5
Middlesex County	5.8
Norfolk County	6.8
Plymouth County	8.7
Suffolk County	3.7
Worcester County	8.3
Michigan	8.6
Allegan County	8.4
Alpena County	12.5
Antrim County	12.3
Barry County	10.1
Bay County	10.2
Berrien County	9.7
Branch County	9.1
Calhoun County	11.1
Cass County	10.8
Charlevoix County	11.2
Cheboygan County	12.1
Chippewa County	12.2
Clare County	12.1
Clinton County	7.9
Michigan cnt'd	
Delta County	14.9
Dickinson County	13.1
Eaton County	9.5
Emmet County	11.1
Genesee County	9.0
Gladwin County	11.8
Grand Traverse County	10.1
Gratiot County	8.9
Hillsdale County	10.4
Houghton County	10.4
Huron County	10.5
Ingham County	7.2
Ionia County	8.9
Iosco County	16.7
Isabella County	6.2
Jackson County	10.1
Kalamazoo County	7.9
Kent County	7.3
Lapeer County	9.8
Leelanau County	11.6
Lenawee County	9.9
Livingston County	8.2
Macomb County	8.4
Manistee County	13.6
Marquette County	11.3
Mason County	11.3
Mecosta County	10.8
Menominee County	12.9
Midland County	8.9
Monroe County	9.2
Montcalm County	10.0
Muskegon County	9.8
Newaygo County	11.1
Oakland County	6.9
Oceana County	11.7
Ogemaw County	13.1
Osceola County	12.6
Otsego County	11.2
Ottawa County	7.0
Roscommon County	13.0
Saginaw County	9.2
St. Clair County	10.2
St. Joseph County	8.9
Sanilac County	9.0
Shiawassee County	9.1
Tuscola County	10.5
Van Buren County	10.8
Washtenaw County	5.7
Wayne County	7.4
Wexford County	10.8
Minnesota	8.7
Anoka County	8.9
Becker County	12.8
Beltrami County	10.7
Benton County	10.8
Blue Earth County	8.0
Brown County	10.2
Carlton County	11.4
Carver County	7.1
Cass County	14.2
Chisago County	9.3
Clay County	6.7
Crow Wing County	12.2
Dakota County	8.6
Dodge County	10.3
Douglas County	10.8
Fillmore County	10.1
Freeborn County	11.6
Goodhue County	10.6

Table 18. Percent of the Civilian Population 18 Years and Over Who Are Veterans, Selected Counties by State/Territory, United States, American Community Survey 3-Year Estimates, 2013—*Continued*

(Percent.)

Location	Percent veterans
Minnesota cnt'd	
Hennepin County	6.9
Hubbard County	12.9
Isanti County	10.1
Itasca County	12.7
Kandiyohi County	8.6
Le Sueur County	9.5
Lyon County	7.3
McLeod County	10.0
Martin County	10.2
Meeker County	10.3
Mille Lacs County	11.7
Morrison County	10.9
Mower County	10.4
Nicollet County	7.2
Nobles County	7.9
Olmsted County	8.6
Otter Tail County	11.7
Pine County	12.8
Polk County	10.4
Ramsey County	7.1
Rice County	8.3
St. Louis County	10.6
Scott County	7.7
Sherburne County	8.5
Stearns County	9.6
Steele County	9.9
Todd County	11.0
Wabasha County	11.2
Washington County	8.9
Winona County	6.3
Wright County	8.5
Mississippi	8.8
Adams County	7.7
Alcorn County	8.1
Bolivar County	5.2
Clay County	7.5
Coahoma County	5.9
Copiah County	7.9
Covington County	8.9
DeSoto County	9.1
Forrest County	9.0
George County	8.2
Grenada County	5.7
Hancock County	12.8
Harrison County	16.6
Hinds County	7.5
Itawamba County	7.8
Jackson County	13.2
Jones County	8.5
Lafayette County	5.4
Lamar County	8.2
Lauderdale County	10.4
Leake County	8.7
Lee County	8.5
Leflore County	4.6
Lincoln County	7.2
Lowndes County	11.8
Madison County	7.4
Marion County	8.0
Marshall County	7.6
Monroe County	8.4
Neshoba County	7.6
Newton County	11.5
Oktibbeha County	6.2
Panola County	7.9
Pearl River County	11.4
Pike County	7.4
Pontotoc County	6.2
Prentiss County	5.1
Mississippi cnt'd	
Rankin County	8.5
Scott County	5.4
Simpson County	8.5
Sunflower County	5.1
Tate County	6.3
Tippah County	6.9
Union County	8.3
Warren County	8.1
Washington County	8.1
Wayne County	6.5
Yazoo County	6.7
Missouri	10.2
Adair County	7.4
Audrain County	10.1
Barry County	12.8
Boone County	6.6
Buchanan County	10.3
Butler County	13.1
Callaway County	10.6
Camden County	14.5
Cape Girardeau County	9.3
Cass County	11.6
Christian County	11.0
Clay County	10.1
Clinton County	13.2
Cole County	10.9
Crawford County	12.9
Dunklin County	9.5
Franklin County	9.9
Greene County	10.1
Henry County	13.2
Howell County	10.7
Jackson County	9.1
Jasper County	9.7
Jefferson County	10.6
Johnson County	16.5
Laclede County	11.3
Lafayette County	10.8
Lawrence County	14.5
Lincoln County	10.4
McDonald County	12.3
Marion County	10.5
Miller County	11.9
Morgan County	13.0
Newton County	10.4
Nodaway County	6.5
Pettis County	10.5
Phelps County	12.3
Platte County	10.3
Polk County	10.5
Pulaski County	26.3
Randolph County	10.5
Ray County	10.5
St. Charles County	10.0
St. Francois County	11.0
St. Louis County	8.8
Saline County	11.2
Scott County	9.5
Stoddard County	12.4
Stone County	14.1
Taney County	13.5
Texas County	14.4
Vernon County	10.4
Warren County	11.5
Washington County	13.0
Webster County	10.9
St. Louis city	7.2
Montana	11.9
Cascade County	16.4
Flathead County	12.1
Gallatin County	7.8
Lake County	12.8
Lewis and Clark County	12.9
Missoula County	9.8
Ravalli County	13.5
Silver Bow County	11.0
Yellowstone County	11.5
Nebraska	10.0
Adams County	10.3
Buffalo County	7.7
Cass County	16.8
Dakota County	8.0
Dawson County	6.9
Dodge County	10.3
Douglas County	8.7
Gage County	10.8
Hall County	9.3
Lancaster County	8.4
Lincoln County	11.7
Madison County	8.3
Platte County	10.0
Sarpy County	15.5
Saunders County	12.3
Scotts Bluff County	10.8
Washington County	10.6
Nevada	10.8
Churchill County	20.0
Clark County	10.1
Douglas County	14.1
Elko County	10.6
Lyon County	14.7
Nye County	20.5
Washoe County	10.9
Carson City	13.7
New Hampshire	10.6
Belknap County	12.8
Carroll County	15.0
Cheshire County	12.0
Coos County	12.8
Grafton County	10.3
Hillsborough County	9.5
Merrimack County	11.1
Rockingham County	10.0
Strafford County	10.1
Sullivan County	12.6
New Jersey	6.2
Atlantic County	7.6
Bergen County	5.0
Burlington County	10.3
Camden County	7.3
Cape May County	10.6
Cumberland County	6.8
Essex County	4.3
Gloucester County	8.3
Hudson County	3.1
Hunterdon County	7.0
Mercer County	5.8
Middlesex County	4.8
Monmouth County	7.0
Morris County	6.0
Ocean County	10.5
Passaic County	4.1
Salem County	11.1
Somerset County	5.3

Table 18. Percent of the Civilian Population 18 Years and Over Who Are Veterans, Selected Counties by State/ Territory, United States, American Community Survey 3-Year Estimates, 2013—*Continued*

(Percent.)

Location	Percent veterans	Location	Percent veterans	Location	Percent veterans
New Jersey cnt'd		**New York** cnt'd		**North Carolina** cnt'd	
Sussex County	8.3	St. Lawrence County	9.3	Montgomery County	8.2
Union County	4.5	Saratoga County	9.5	Moore County	14.6
Warren County	8.1	Schenectady County	8.6	Nash County	9.8
		Schoharie County	11.1	New Hanover County	10.5
New Mexico	11.0	Seneca County	10.3	Northampton County	9.0
Bernalillo County	10.7	Steuben County	12.0	Onslow County	21.6
Chaves County	9.5	Suffolk County	6.8	Orange County	5.2
Cibola County	9.2	Sullivan County	9.9	Pasquotank County	12.5
Curry County	17.9	Tioga County	10.5	Pender County	11.5
Doña Ana County	10.1	Tompkins County	5.0	Person County	8.8
Eddy County	10.2	Ulster County	7.8	Pitt County	7.2
Grant County	11.8	Warren County	9.7	Polk County	11.7
Lea County	8.2	Washington County	10.7	Randolph County	9.4
Lincoln County	12.1	Wayne County	9.3	Richmond County	11.1
Luna County	11.4	Westchester County	5.0	Robeson County	7.3
McKinley County	5.8	Wyoming County	9.2	Rockingham County	9.2
Otero County	18.8	Yates County	10.3	Rowan County	9.8
Rio Arriba County	8.2			Rutherford County	10.5
Roosevelt County	6.0	**North Carolina**	9.7	Sampson County	7.8
Sandoval County	14.7	Alamance County	8.8	Scotland County	9.8
San Juan County	9.4	Alexander County	8.5	Stanly County	8.5
San Miguel County	10.4	Anson County	10.1	Stokes County	9.4
Santa Fe County	8.8	Ashe County	10.2	Surry County	8.0
Taos County	12.6	Beaufort County	9.8	Transylvania County	12.9
Valencia County	13.6	Bertie County	7.0	Union County	8.0
		Bladen County	7.0	Vance County	8.7
New York	5.7	Brunswick County	13.8	Wake County	7.6
Albany County	7.0	Buncombe County	9.8	Warren County	9.4
Allegany County	11.3	Burke County	8.4	Watauga County	6.9
Bronx County	3.1	Cabarrus County	9.0	Wayne County	13.2
Broome County	8.8	Caldwell County	8.5	Wilkes County	8.8
Cattaraugus County	11.7	Carteret County	16.4	Wilson County	9.8
Cayuga County	10.8	Caswell County	7.2	Yadkin County	8.6
Chautauqua County	10.4	Catawba County	9.2		
Chemung County	10.0	Chatham County	10.8	**North Dakota**	9.9
Chenango County	9.8	Cherokee County	12.2	Burleigh County	9.5
Clinton County	10.5	Cleveland County	8.9	Cass County	8.3
Columbia County	9.5	Columbus County	8.8	Grand Forks County	9.8
Cortland County	9.4	Craven County	17.6	Morton County	9.8
Delaware County	10.0	Cumberland County	20.3	Stark County	8.7
Dutchess County	7.7	Currituck County	15.2	Stutsman County	10.0
Erie County	8.6	Dare County	10.0	Ward County	13.5
Essex County	12.3	Davidson County	9.5	Williams County	9.0
Franklin County	10.1	Davie County	10.6		
Fulton County	9.7	Duplin County	9.9	**Ohio**	9.4
Genesee County	8.8	Durham County	7.2	Adams County	9.1
Greene County	10.2	Edgecombe County	9.0	Allen County	9.6
Herkimer County	10.9	Forsyth County	9.0	Ashland County	9.9
Jefferson County	13.7	Franklin County	9.3	Ashtabula County	11.7
Kings County	2.5	Gaston County	9.5	Athens County	6.7
Lewis County	12.0	Granville County	11.3	Auglaize County	9.8
Livingston County	9.3	Greene County	8.0	Belmont County	10.8
Madison County	9.9	Guilford County	7.9	Brown County	10.4
Monroe County	7.3	Halifax County	7.9	Butler County	8.9
Montgomery County	9.7	Harnett County	13.8	Carroll County	11.1
Nassau County	5.6	Haywood County	12.1	Champaign County	10.8
New York County	2.7	Henderson County	12.8	Clark County	12.6
Niagara County	9.5	Hertford County	8.2	Clermont County	9.7
Oneida County	10.4	Hoke County	15.6	Clinton County	12.3
Onondaga County	8.0	Iredell County	8.8	Columbiana County	11.7
Ontario County	10.2	Jackson County	10.0	Coshocton County	12.0
Orange County	8.2	Johnston County	9.9	Crawford County	10.4
Orleans County	9.6	Lee County	11.0	Cuyahoga County	8.3
Oswego County	9.6	Lenoir County	9.0	Darke County	9.8
Otsego County	10.4	Lincoln County	9.9	Defiance County	10.4
Putnam County	6.5	McDowell County	10.8	Delaware County	8.0
Queens County	2.9	Macon County	14.4	Erie County	11.7
Rensselaer County	8.4	Madison County	8.4	Fairfield County	10.5
Richmond County	5.2	Martin County	7.6	Fayette County	10.1
Rockland County	4.9	Mecklenburg County	7.0	Franklin County	7.5

Table 18. Percent of the Civilian Population 18 Years and Over Who Are Veterans, Selected Counties by State/ Territory, United States, American Community Survey 3-Year Estimates, 2013—*Continued*

(Percent.)

Location	Percent veterans
Ohio cnt'd	
Fulton County	8.2
Gallia County	9.6
Geauga County	9.1
Greene County	13.7
Guernsey County	9.7
Hamilton County	8.1
Hancock County	8.9
Hardin County	8.9
Henry County	10.7
Highland County	10.3
Hocking County	12.8
Holmes County	5.6
Huron County	9.5
Jackson County	11.2
Jefferson County	12.3
Knox County	10.0
Lake County	9.4
Lawrence County	11.9
Licking County	11.7
Logan County	10.0
Lorain County	10.0
Lucas County	8.5
Madison County	10.4
Mahoning County	10.4
Marion County	11.0
Medina County	9.7
Meigs County	10.0
Mercer County	9.2
Miami County	10.5
Montgomery County	10.5
Morrow County	9.2
Muskingum County	9.6
Ottawa County	10.4
Perry County	10.7
Pickaway County	10.8
Pike County	10.2
Portage County	9.3
Preble County	12.0
Putnam County	8.6
Richland County	10.7
Ross County	10.8
Sandusky County	9.9
Scioto County	9.8
Seneca County	10.5
Shelby County	9.2
Stark County	10.3
Summit County	9.4
Trumbull County	11.3
Tuscarawas County	10.8
Union County	9.7
Van Wert County	10.2
Warren County	9.4
Washington County	10.5
Wayne County	8.8
Williams County	10.2
Wood County	7.8
Wyandot County	8.9
Oklahoma	10.7
Adair County	9.3
Beckham County	6.6
Bryan County	9.3
Caddo County	11.3
Canadian County	10.6
Carter County	10.6
Cherokee County	10.9
Cleveland County	10.6
Comanche County	18.3
Creek County	10.4
Custer County	7.9
Oklahoma cnt'd	
Delaware County	13.0
Garfield County	11.8
Garvin County	10.3
Grady County	11.4
Jackson County	19.9
Kay County	10.8
Le Flore County	10.2
Lincoln County	12.8
Logan County	11.2
McClain County	11.4
McCurtain County	9.7
McIntosh County	13.6
Mayes County	11.0
Muskogee County	11.2
Oklahoma County	10.4
Okmulgee County	11.0
Osage County	11.4
Ottawa County	11.4
Payne County	7.0
Pittsburg County	12.2
Pontotoc County	9.7
Pottawatomie County	11.6
Rogers County	12.7
Seminole County	10.0
Sequoyah County	10.2
Stephens County	11.7
Texas County	4.1
Tulsa County	9.4
Wagoner County	12.0
Washington County	10.5
Woodward County	7.7
Oregon	10.3
Benton County	7.6
Clackamas County	10.2
Clatsop County	13.3
Columbia County	14.2
Coos County	13.5
Crook County	16.7
Curry County	18.2
Deschutes County	11.5
Douglas County	15.6
Hood River County	8.2
Jackson County	13.8
Jefferson County	11.4
Josephine County	15.2
Klamath County	15.6
Lane County	10.5
Lincoln County	15.6
Linn County	12.6
Malheur County	10.0
Marion County	10.6
Multnomah County	7.1
Polk County	11.8
Tillamook County	12.2
Umatilla County	10.5
Union County	11.2
Wasco County	11.5
Washington County	7.7
Yamhill County	9.0
Pennsylvania	9.1
Adams County	10.6
Allegheny County	9.0
Armstrong County	11.4
Beaver County	11.6
Bedford County	10.3
Berks County	9.3
Blair County	12.6
Bradford County	12.5
Pennsylvania cnt'd	
Bucks County	8.1
Butler County	9.8
Cambria County	11.2
Carbon County	12.2
Centre County	7.1
Chester County	7.8
Clarion County	9.0
Clearfield County	11.5
Clinton County	9.5
Columbia County	9.0
Crawford County	11.2
Cumberland County	10.8
Dauphin County	9.4
Delaware County	7.4
Elk County	11.7
Erie County	9.8
Fayette County	10.9
Franklin County	11.0
Greene County	10.5
Huntingdon County	10.3
Indiana County	9.2
Jefferson County	10.8
Juniata County	8.4
Lackawanna County	10.4
Lancaster County	8.4
Lawrence County	10.8
Lebanon County	10.7
Lehigh County	8.2
Luzerne County	10.8
Lycoming County	10.8
McKean County	11.7
Mercer County	11.7
Mifflin County	10.8
Monroe County	9.5
Montgomery County	7.6
Northampton County	9.0
Northumberland County	12.3
Perry County	11.0
Philadelphia County	5.8
Pike County	11.3
Schuylkill County	11.3
Snyder County	7.9
Somerset County	10.5
Susquehanna County	11.4
Tioga County	11.5
Union County	8.7
Venango County	12.0
Warren County	12.5
Washington County	10.9
Wayne County	10.6
Westmoreland County	11.0
Wyoming County	11.1
York County	10.2
Rhode Island	8.3
Bristol County	8.0
Kent County	10.3
Newport County	13.3
Providence County	7.1
Washington County	8.7
South Carolina	10.7
Abbeville County	8.6
Aiken County	11.0
Anderson County	10.0
Barnwell County	9.4
Beaufort County	14.4
Berkeley County	15.7
Charleston County	10.6
Cherokee County	7.4

Table 18. Percent of the Civilian Population 18 Years and Over Who Are Veterans, Selected Counties by State/ Territory, United States, American Community Survey 3-Year Estimates, 2013—*Continued*

(Percent.)

Location	Percent veterans	Location	Percent veterans	Location	Percent veterans
South Carolina cnt'd		**Tennessee** cnt'd		**Texas** cnt'd	
Chester County	10.0	Hardin County	11.7	DeWitt County	10.9
Chesterfield County	7.5	Hawkins County	11.2	Ector County	6.9
Clarendon County	10.1	Henderson County	8.9	Ellis County	8.7
Colleton County	14.3	Henry County	15.1	El Paso County	8.8
Darlington County	9.3	Hickman County	8.9	Erath County	7.1
Dillon County	9.8	Jefferson County	11.2	Fannin County	11.4
Dorchester County	14.0	Knox County	8.3	Fayette County	10.3
Edgefield County	9.4	Lauderdale County	7.6	Fort Bend County	5.9
Fairfield County	10.8	Lawrence County	10.2	Galveston County	9.2
Florence County	8.6	Lincoln County	8.6	Gillespie County	12.1
Georgetown County	13.2	Loudon County	13.7	Gonzales County	7.1
Greenville County	8.8	McMinn County	10.8	Gray County	8.3
Greenwood County	8.2	McNairy County	11.6	Grayson County	10.9
Hampton County	9.4	Macon County	7.1	Gregg County	9.3
Horry County	12.0	Madison County	8.9	Grimes County	10.8
Jasper County	8.4	Marion County	8.7	Guadalupe County	15.6
Kershaw County	11.3	Marshall County	8.2	Hale County	6.7
Lancaster County	10.4	Maury County	10.1	Hardin County	10.6
Laurens County	9.3	Monroe County	11.2	Harris County	5.7
Lexington County	11.4	Montgomery County	20.3	Harrison County	8.8
Marion County	7.7	Morgan County	12.2	Hays County	8.2
Marlboro County	8.0	Obion County	9.7	Henderson County	11.4
Newberry County	8.8	Overton County	6.8	Hidalgo County	4.3
Oconee County	11.8	Putnam County	7.1	Hill County	10.9
Orangeburg County	9.2	Rhea County	9.1	Hockley County	6.3
Pickens County	8.8	Roane County	13.5	Hood County	15.1
Richland County	11.1	Robertson County	9.2	Hopkins County	10.2
Saluda County	9.0	Rutherford County	9.6	Houston County	12.3
Spartanburg County	9.7	Scott County	7.3	Howard County	9.8
Sumter County	15.6	Sevier County	10.1	Hunt County	12.6
Union County	9.7	Shelby County	8.1	Hutchinson County	11.2
Williamsburg County	7.6	Sullivan County	10.9	Jasper County	10.8
York County	9.8	Sumner County	10.0	Jefferson County	8.7
		Tipton County	11.4	Jim Wells County	7.3
South Dakota	10.6	Warren County	9.3	Johnson County	9.2
Brookings County	7.3	Washington County	11.9	Jones County	10.5
Brown County	8.8	Weakley County	10.4	Kaufman County	8.9
Codington County	11.2	White County	11.2	Kendall County	13.6
Lawrence County	12.5	Williamson County	6.2	Kerr County	15.4
Lincoln County	8.8	Wilson County	10.1	Kleberg County	8.0
Meade County	17.6			Lamar County	10.2
Minnehaha County	8.9	**Texas**	8.2	Lampasas County	21.9
Pennington County	14.7	Anderson County	8.7	Liberty County	9.4
Yankton County	9.5	Angelina County	10.2	Limestone County	10.1
		Aransas County	12.9	Lubbock County	7.2
Tennessee	9.6	Atascosa County	10.5	McLennan County	9.2
Anderson County	11.5	Austin County	8.0	Matagorda County	9.1
Bedford County	8.8	Bandera County	18.4	Maverick County	3.0
Blount County	12.3	Bastrop County	11.0	Medina County	11.8
Bradley County	9.3	Bee County	10.5	Midland County	8.4
Campbell County	9.5	Bell County	21.2	Milam County	11.8
Carroll County	9.5	Bexar County	11.6	Montgomery County	8.8
Carter County	11.0	Bowie County	10.8	Moore County	3.9
Cheatham County	9.7	Brazoria County	8.5	Nacogdoches County	6.7
Claiborne County	6.6	Brazos County	5.6	Navarro County	9.0
Cocke County	11.8	Brown County	11.1	Nueces County	10.8
Coffee County	11.0	Burnet County	13.0	Orange County	9.7
Cumberland County	14.6	Caldwell County	8.9	Palo Pinto County	11.2
Davidson County	7.5	Calhoun County	10.0	Panola County	10.0
Dickson County	10.2	Cameron County	5.7	Parker County	11.9
Dyer County	10.1	Cass County	12.7	Polk County	12.6
Fayette County	10.7	Chambers County	8.3	Potter County	8.3
Franklin County	12.2	Cherokee County	9.4	Randall County	10.2
Gibson County	10.3	Collin County	7.1	Rockwall County	8.9
Giles County	9.9	Colorado County	10.9	Rusk County	10.0
Grainger County	9.5	Comal County	14.5	San Jacinto County	9.6
Greene County	10.7	Cooke County	9.9	San Patricio County	10.2
Hamblen County	10.8	Coryell County	18.7	Shelby County	9.3
Hamilton County	9.5	Dallas County	5.8	Smith County	9.4
Hardeman County	7.8	Denton County	7.8	Starr County	2.7

Table 18. Percent of the Civilian Population 18 Years and Over Who Are Veterans, Selected Counties by State/Territory, United States, American Community Survey 3-Year Estimates, 2013—*Continued*

(Percent.)

Location	Percent veterans
Texas cnt'd	
Tarrant County	8.5
Taylor County	13.0
Titus County	6.7
Tom Green County	11.8
Travis County	6.5
Tyler County	10.9
Upshur County	11.3
Uvalde County	7.9
Val Verde County	9.1
Van Zandt County	11.8
Victoria County	8.8
Walker County	8.3
Waller County	6.3
Washington County	9.3
Webb County	3.7
Wharton County	6.4
Wichita County	13.1
Willacy County	5.6
Williamson County	10.3
Wilson County	14.5
Wise County	9.2
Wood County	14.4
Utah	7.2
Box Elder County	8.1
Cache County	5.5
Carbon County	7.6
Davis County	9.5
Duchesne County	6.9
Iron County	8.1
Salt Lake County	6.4
Sanpete County	7.7
Sevier County	9.3
Summit County	7.2
Tooele County	9.6
Uintah County	8.1
Utah County	4.8
Wasatch County	4.8
Washington County	10.7
Weber County	9.7
Vermont	9.3
Addison County	8.1
Bennington County	10.1
Caledonia County	10.8
Chittenden County	7.5
Franklin County	10.8
Lamoille County	8.6
Orange County	9.5
Orleans County	10.2
Rutland County	9.7
Washington County	9.9
Windham County	10.1
Windsor County	10.6
Virginia	11.5
Accomack County	11.4
Albemarle County	8.8
Amherst County	10.2
Arlington County	6.9
Augusta County	10.5
Bedford County	12.8
Botetourt County	10.5
Buchanan County	5.4
Campbell County	11.5
Caroline County	12.9
Carroll County	10.5
Chesterfield County	11.1
Culpeper County	11.5
Dinwiddie County	10.0
Virginia cnt'd	
Fairfax County	9.8
Fauquier County	12.6
Fluvanna County	11.1
Franklin County	10.1
Frederick County	12.4
Gloucester County	15.9
Goochland County	9.6
Halifax County	9.2
Hanover County	9.3
Henrico County	9.1
Henry County	9.3
Isle of Wight County	15.4
James City County	17.0
King George County	18.5
Lee County	8.9
Loudoun County	9.1
Louisa County	11.1
Mecklenburg County	11.3
Montgomery County	5.4
Orange County	11.7
Page County	9.2
Pittsylvania County	10.2
Powhatan County	10.4
Prince Edward County	7.4
Prince George County	15.4
Prince William County	13.8
Pulaski County	10.0
Roanoke County	11.7
Rockbridge County	13.8
Rockingham County	7.7
Russell County	6.0
Scott County	8.4
Shenandoah County	10.6
Smyth County	8.8
Spotsylvania County	15.1
Stafford County	20.0
Tazewell County	8.1
Warren County	12.9
Washington County	9.8
Wise County	7.8
Wythe County	9.3
York County	20.7
Alexandria city	8.6
Charlottesville city	4.9
Chesapeake city	15.2
Danville city	11.5
Fairfax city	9.4
Fredericksburg city	10.7
Hampton city	18.8
Harrisonburg city	3.3
Hopewell city	10.4
Lynchburg city	8.0
Manassas city	8.2
Newport News city	15.9
Norfolk city	16.3
Petersburg city	11.5
Portsmouth city	15.6
Richmond city	7.0
Roanoke city	9.8
Salem city	11.4
Staunton city	8.5
Suffolk city	17.0
Virginia Beach city	19.4
Waynesboro city	11.3
Winchester city	7.9
Washington	10.9
Asotin County	13.3
Benton County	10.2
Chelan County	10.4
Washington cnt'd	
Clallam County	15.9
Clark County	11.4
Cowlitz County	13.1
Douglas County	11.0
Franklin County	6.9
Grant County	8.7
Grays Harbor County	12.4
Island County	20.6
Jefferson County	16.1
King County	7.4
Kitsap County	18.8
Kittitas County	10.9
Klickitat County	12.9
Lewis County	13.2
Mason County	17.3
Okanogan County	12.8
Pacific County	18.3
Pierce County	14.9
Skagit County	11.9
Snohomish County	9.9
Spokane County	12.5
Stevens County	16.3
Thurston County	14.8
Walla Walla County	10.7
Whatcom County	8.8
Whitman County	6.8
Yakima County	7.9
West Virginia	10.7
Berkeley County	13.4
Boone County	9.1
Brooke County	10.5
Cabell County	9.6
Fayette County	10.0
Greenbrier County	13.4
Hampshire County	7.8
Hancock County	11.3
Harrison County	10.7
Jackson County	12.7
Jefferson County	11.6
Kanawha County	10.6
Lincoln County	12.0
Logan County	9.9
McDowell County	8.2
Marion County	11.5
Marshall County	11.9
Mason County	14.9
Mercer County	11.0
Mineral County	9.5
Mingo County	6.7
Monongalia County	6.3
Nicholas County	9.0
Ohio County	11.0
Preston County	10.2
Putnam County	11.4
Raleigh County	12.2
Randolph County	10.7
Upshur County	10.8
Wayne County	10.3
Wood County	12.0
Wyoming County	8.9
Wisconsin	9.0
Adams County	14.2
Barron County	10.3
Brown County	8.4
Calumet County	8.1
Chippewa County	11.1
Clark County	8.3
Columbia County	10.4

Table 18. Percent of the Civilian Population 18 Years and Over Who Are Veterans, Selected Counties by State/ Territory, United States, American Community Survey 3-Year Estimates, 2013—*Continued*

(Percent.)

Location	Percent veterans
Wisconsin cnt'd	
Dane County	6.9
Dodge County	8.8
Door County	10.0
Douglas County	11.1
Dunn County	8.0
Eau Claire County	9.1
Fond du Lac County	9.8
Grant County	7.7
Green County	8.0
Iowa County	8.4
Jackson County	11.7
Jefferson County	9.3
Juneau County	13.0
Kenosha County	8.0
Kewaunee County	10.5
La Crosse County	9.3
Langlade County	11.3
Lincoln County	11.5
Manitowoc County	10.9
Marathon County	9.7
Marinette County	13.0
Milwaukee County	7.0
Monroe County	15.5
Oconto County	12.1
Oneida County	13.2
Outagamie County	8.7
Ozaukee County	8.3
Pierce County	8.6
Polk County	11.2
Portage County	9.2
Racine County	9.3
Rock County	9.8
St. Croix County	8.9
Sauk County	11.2
Shawano County	10.8
Sheboygan County	9.1
Taylor County	9.6
Trempealeau County	9.7
Vernon County	9.6
Vilas County	13.4
Walworth County	8.4
Washington County	8.6
Wisconsin cnt'd	
Waukesha County	8.6
Waupaca County	11.9
Waushara County	12.8
Winnebago County	9.3
Wood County	10.4
Wyoming	11.5
Albany County	7.1
Campbell County	8.4
Fremont County	10.4
Laramie County	17.7
Natrona County	11.2
Park County	10.5
Sheridan County	13.6
Sweetwater County	10.7
Teton County	6.4
Uinta County	8.2
Puerto Rico	3.6
Aguada Municipio	2.1
Aguadilla Municipio	4.2
Aguas Buenas Municipio	3.7
Aibonito Municipio	2.5
Añasco Municipio	2.5
Arecibo Municipio	2.9
Barceloneta Municipio	2.1
Barranquitas Municipio	1.9
Bayamón Municipio	4.6
Cabo Rojo Municipio	3.0
Caguas Municipio	4.1
Camuy Municipio	1.9
Canóvanas Municipio	2.6
Carolina Municipio	4.7
Cataño Municipio	4.0
Cayey Municipio	4.1
Cidra Municipio	3.3
Coamo Municipio	3.9
Comerío Municipio	1.8
Corozal Municipio	2.8
Dorado Municipio	4.0
Fajardo Municipio	6.3
Guayama Municipio	2.3
Puerto Rico cnt'd	
Guayanilla Municipio	3.9
Guaynabo Municipio	3.8
Gurabo Municipio	3.5
Hatillo Municipio	3.8
Humacao Municipio	3.6
Isabela Municipio	4.2
Juana Díaz Municipio	3.7
Juncos Municipio	3.6
Lajas Municipio	3.6
Lares Municipio	2.4
Las Piedras Municipio	3.4
Loíza Municipio	2.8
Luquillo Municipio	4.6
Manatí Municipio	2.8
Mayagüez Municipio	3.9
Moca Municipio	3.0
Morovis Municipio	1.8
Naguabo Municipio	4.8
Naranjito Municipio	2.1
Orocovis Municipio	3.1
Peñuelas Municipio	3.7
Ponce Municipio	4.6
Quebradillas Municipio	3.8
Río Grande Municipio	2.6
Sabana Grande Municipio	4.1
Salinas Municipio	3.4
San Germán Municipio	4.5
San Juan Municipio	3.9
San Lorenzo Municipio	3.1
San Sebastián Municipio	3.4
Santa Isabel Municipio	4.2
Toa Alta Municipio	3.3
Toa Baja Municipio	4.4
Trujillo Alto Municipio	4.1
Utuado Municipio	2.2
Vega Alta Municipio	2.3
Vega Baja Municipio	1.6
Villalba Municipio	2.0
Yabucoa Municipio	2.2
Yauco Municipio	3.2

Table 19. Percent of the Civilian Population 18 Years and Over Who Are Veterans, Selected Counties by State/Territory, United States, American Community Survey 5-Year Estimates, 2013

(Percent.)

Location	Percent veterans
United States	9.0
Alabama	10.6
Autauga County	14.9
Baldwin County	13.4
Barbour County	9.9
Bibb County	7.5
Blount County	10.4
Bullock County	7.5
Butler County	9.5
Calhoun County	12.5
Chambers County	10.1
Cherokee County	10.5
Chilton County	10.0
Choctaw County	8.8
Clarke County	8.2
Clay County	10.1
Cleburne County	8.7
Coffee County	16.5
Colbert County	10.3
Conecuh County	10.9
Coosa County	10.4
Covington County	11.7
Crenshaw County	10.3
Cullman County	9.9
Dale County	19.0
Dallas County	9.1
DeKalb County	8.2
Elmore County	13.8
Escambia County	10.2
Etowah County	10.7
Fayette County	9.1
Franklin County	7.8
Geneva County	11.3
Greene County	7.4
Hale County	8.4
Henry County	11.1
Houston County	12.0
Jackson County	9.7
Jefferson County	9.2
Lamar County	10.1
Lauderdale County	9.6
Lawrence County	7.2
Lee County	9.0
Limestone County	10.8
Lowndes County	7.4
Macon County	10.0
Madison County	13.2
Marengo County	9.3
Marion County	9.5
Marshall County	10.2
Mobile County	10.8
Monroe County	7.2
Montgomery County	11.7
Morgan County	10.4
Perry County	8.5
Pickens County	10.7
Pike County	9.6
Randolph County	9.1
Russell County	14.8
St. Clair County	10.7
Shelby County	9.4
Sumter County	6.6
Talladega County	10.6
Tallapoosa County	11.2
Tuscaloosa County	7.9
Walker County	10.4
Washington County	7.9
Wilcox County	5.5
Winston County	9.0
Alaska	13.8
Aleutians East Borough	3.5
Aleutians West Census Area	7.6
Anchorage Municipality	14.4
Bethel Census Area	8.2
Bristol Bay Borough	13.4
Denali Borough	13.0
Dillingham Census Area	6.5
Fairbanks North Star Borough	16.2
Haines Borough	13.7
Hoonah-Angoon Census Area	10.1
Juneau City and Borough	11.3
Kenai Peninsula Borough	14.3
Ketchikan Gateway Borough	14.0
Kodiak Island Borough	11.9
Lake and Peninsula Borough	8.2
Matanuska-Susitna Borough	14.7
Nome Census Area	9.5
North Slope Borough	8.5
Northwest Arctic Borough	7.4
Petersburg Census Area	11.6
Prince of Wales-Hyder Census Area	11.6
Sitka City and Borough	11.3
Skagway Municipality	5.4
Southeast Fairbanks Census Area	19.6
Valdez-Cordova Census Area	12.3
Wade Hampton Census Area	7.9
Wrangell City and Borough	19.0
Yakutat City and Borough	12.5
Yukon-Koyukuk Census Area	10.3
Arizona	10.8
Apache County	8.2
Cochise County	19.4
Coconino County	7.8
Gila County	14.6
Graham County	10.1
Greenlee County	13.4
La Paz County	18.1
Maricopa County	9.4
Mohave County	16.3
Navajo County	9.4
Pima County	12.2
Pinal County	12.8
Santa Cruz County	6.7
Yavapai County	16.2
Yuma County	10.9
Arkansas	10.7
Arkansas County	9.5
Ashley County	8.3
Baxter County	16.9
Benton County	10.0
Boone County	11.5
Bradley County	8.8
Calhoun County	9.1
Carroll County	13.9
Chicot County	10.1
Clark County	9.8
Clay County	10.0
Cleburne County	15.3
Cleveland County	9.6
Columbia County	7.9
Conway County	9.5
Craighead County	9.1
Crawford County	11.6
Crittenden County	9.8
Cross County	8.9
Dallas County	7.3
Desha County	8.0
Arkansas cnt'd	
Drew County	6.9
Faulkner County	9.2
Franklin County	12.0
Fulton County	13.9
Garland County	13.9
Grant County	11.7
Greene County	11.9
Hempstead County	9.4
Hot Spring County	12.5
Howard County	8.7
Independence County	10.1
Izard County	14.6
Jackson County	9.6
Jefferson County	10.1
Johnson County	9.7
Lafayette County	9.1
Lawrence County	10.8
Lee County	5.9
Lincoln County	7.8
Little River County	12.2
Logan County	12.2
Lonoke County	15.1
Madison County	10.8
Marion County	16.6
Miller County	10.3
Mississippi County	9.0
Monroe County	10.2
Montgomery County	15.3
Nevada County	11.3
Newton County	12.8
Ouachita County	10.4
Perry County	12.6
Phillips County	8.3
Pike County	10.1
Poinsett County	9.9
Polk County	13.8
Pope County	9.3
Prairie County	12.3
Pulaski County	11.0
Randolph County	10.2
St. Francis County	8.9
Saline County	12.6
Scott County	11.5
Searcy County	11.5
Sebastian County	10.8
Sevier County	8.7
Sharp County	15.4
Stone County	13.7
Union County	9.8
Van Buren County	13.9
Washington County	7.8
White County	10.2
Woodruff County	10.5
Yell County	8.7
California	6.7
Alameda County	5.3
Alpine County	19.4
Amador County	14.8
Butte County	10.6
Calaveras County	14.3
Colusa County	7.5
Contra Costa County	7.1
Del Norte County	12.4
El Dorado County	11.9
Fresno County	6.5
Glenn County	7.5
Humboldt County	9.7
Imperial County	5.2
Inyo County	11.8

Table 19. Percent of the Civilian Population 18 Years and Over Who Are Veterans, Selected Counties by State/ Territory, United States, American Community Survey 5-Year Estimates, 2013—*Continued*

(Percent.)

Location	Percent veterans
California cnt'd	
Kern County	7.6
Kings County	10.1
Lake County	13.3
Lassen County	10.9
Los Angeles County	4.4
Madera County	7.6
Marin County	7.6
Mariposa County	14.4
Mendocino County	10.0
Merced County	6.2
Modoc County	13.5
Mono County	7.6
Monterey County	7.1
Napa County	8.8
Nevada County	12.6
Orange County	5.7
Placer County	11.0
Plumas County	14.2
Riverside County	8.4
Sacramento County	8.8
San Benito County	6.7
San Bernardino County	7.2
San Diego County	10.0
San Francisco County	4.2
San Joaquin County	7.2
San Luis Obispo County	9.6
San Mateo County	5.7
Santa Barbara County	8.0
Santa Clara County	4.8
Santa Cruz County	6.0
Shasta County	12.8
Sierra County	16.8
Siskiyou County	13.4
Solano County	11.2
Sonoma County	8.7
Stanislaus County	6.8
Sutter County	9.8
Tehama County	11.8
Trinity County	14.8
Tulare County	6.0
Tuolumne County	11.9
Ventura County	7.8
Yolo County	6.6
Yuba County	12.9
Colorado	10.4
Adams County	8.5
Alamosa County	9.3
Arapahoe County	9.9
Archuleta County	11.9
Baca County	11.2
Bent County	12.0
Boulder County	6.5
Broomfield County	9.0
Chaffee County	15.0
Cheyenne County	8.2
Clear Creek County	12.1
Conejos County	8.4
Costilla County	15.9
Crowley County	9.3
Custer County	22.1
Delta County	14.5
Denver County	7.0
Dolores County	12.5
Douglas County	9.6
Eagle County	4.4
Elbert County	13.3
El Paso County	18.4
Fremont County	14.0
Garfield County	8.4
Colorado cnt'd	
Gilpin County	16.2
Grand County	12.6
Gunnison County	8.2
Hinsdale County	15.8
Huerfano County	15.1
Jackson County	13.4
Jefferson County	10.0
Kiowa County	8.2
Kit Carson County	12.5
Lake County	9.4
La Plata County	9.5
Larimer County	9.5
Las Animas County	10.1
Lincoln County	10.9
Logan County	11.0
Mesa County	12.3
Mineral County	15.5
Moffat County	12.1
Montezuma County	11.8
Montrose County	10.5
Morgan County	8.0
Otero County	11.3
Ouray County	14.3
Park County	15.2
Phillips County	10.4
Pitkin County	6.7
Prowers County	11.2
Pueblo County	12.7
Rio Blanco County	10.7
Rio Grande County	11.2
Routt County	6.3
Saguache County	10.9
San Juan County	10.3
San Miguel County	6.6
Sedgwick County	12.3
Summit County	6.1
Teller County	18.1
Washington County	11.7
Weld County	9.0
Yuma County	8.5
Connecticut	7.9
Fairfield County	5.9
Hartford County	7.6
Litchfield County	9.9
Middlesex County	9.1
New Haven County	7.6
New London County	12.1
Tolland County	8.9
Windham County	10.3
Delaware	10.7
Kent County	15.1
New Castle County	8.7
Sussex County	12.8
District of Columbia	6.0
District of Columbia	6.0
Florida	10.4
Alachua County	8.3
Baker County	9.8
Bay County	17.0
Bradford County	12.2
Brevard County	15.7
Broward County	6.7
Calhoun County	13.8
Charlotte County	17.9
Citrus County	17.8
Clay County	18.4
Florida cnt'd	
Collier County	11.5
Columbia County	14.7
DeSoto County	10.4
Dixie County	15.9
Duval County	13.0
Escambia County	15.2
Flagler County	14.5
Franklin County	12.8
Gadsden County	9.1
Gilchrist County	13.7
Glades County	11.2
Gulf County	10.4
Hamilton County	11.1
Hardee County	7.0
Hendry County	6.6
Hernando County	15.4
Highlands County	16.2
Hillsborough County	9.9
Holmes County	11.8
Indian River County	13.6
Jackson County	12.8
Jefferson County	14.8
Lafayette County	11.1
Lake County	14.4
Lee County	12.5
Leon County	7.9
Levy County	14.4
Liberty County	9.7
Madison County	10.4
Manatee County	12.9
Marion County	14.8
Martin County	13.9
Miami-Dade County	3.0
Monroe County	12.4
Nassau County	15.7
Okaloosa County	22.2
Okeechobee County	10.1
Orange County	7.4
Osceola County	7.9
Palm Beach County	9.3
Pasco County	13.6
Pinellas County	12.5
Polk County	11.1
Putnam County	14.5
St. Johns County	12.6
St. Lucie County	12.1
Santa Rosa County	18.1
Sarasota County	14.6
Seminole County	9.2
Sumter County	20.1
Suwannee County	12.9
Taylor County	12.6
Union County	15.7
Volusia County	13.5
Wakulla County	14.3
Walton County	14.7
Washington County	10.7
Georgia	9.5
Appling County	7.4
Atkinson County	9.1
Bacon County	6.0
Baker County	5.2
Baldwin County	8.4
Banks County	9.1
Barrow County	9.9
Bartow County	8.9
Ben Hill County	8.9
Berrien County	10.2
Bibb County	9.9

Table 19. Percent of the Civilian Population 18 Years and Over Who Are Veterans, Selected Counties by State/ Territory, United States, American Community Survey 5-Year Estimates, 2013—*Continued*

(Percent.)

Location	Percent veterans
Georgia cnt'd	
Bleckley County	9.4
Brantley County	9.7
Brooks County	12.5
Bryan County	15.4
Bulloch County	7.1
Burke County	8.9
Butts County	8.4
Calhoun County	7.9
Camden County	19.5
Candler County	9.4
Carroll County	8.8
Catoosa County	9.9
Charlton County	11.9
Chatham County	12.0
Chattahoochee County	12.4
Chattooga County	7.8
Cherokee County	9.2
Clarke County	5.7
Clay County	10.3
Clayton County	9.6
Clinch County	9.6
Cobb County	8.5
Coffee County	7.8
Colquitt County	7.1
Columbia County	14.5
Cook County	9.2
Coweta County	11.0
Crawford County	9.1
Crisp County	9.5
Dade County	10.2
Dawson County	11.1
Decatur County	7.6
DeKalb County	7.8
Dodge County	8.9
Dooly County	10.5
Dougherty County	10.5
Douglas County	11.1
Early County	9.1
Echols County	10.2
Effingham County	12.1
Elbert County	10.1
Emanuel County	8.0
Evans County	9.0
Fannin County	12.1
Fayette County	14.4
Floyd County	10.1
Forsyth County	7.9
Franklin County	8.0
Fulton County	6.5
Gilmer County	10.8
Glascock County	7.9
Glynn County	13.0
Gordon County	7.6
Grady County	9.3
Greene County	11.3
Gwinnett County	6.7
Habersham County	10.1
Hall County	8.0
Hancock County	7.4
Haralson County	8.9
Harris County	14.5
Hart County	10.9
Heard County	9.8
Henry County	11.9
Houston County	18.0
Irwin County	12.6
Jackson County	8.9
Jasper County	8.4
Jeff Davis County	7.1
Jefferson County	9.0
Jenkins County	9.2
Georgia cnt'd	
Johnson County	9.3
Jones County	8.4
Lamar County	11.0
Lanier County	10.9
Laurens County	9.5
Lee County	11.0
Liberty County	26.0
Lincoln County	11.6
Long County	16.5
Lowndes County	11.2
Lumpkin County	10.1
McDuffie County	6.9
McIntosh County	13.0
Macon County	8.0
Madison County	8.4
Marion County	14.7
Meriwether County	8.3
Miller County	7.6
Mitchell County	8.6
Monroe County	10.0
Montgomery County	8.0
Morgan County	10.1
Murray County	7.3
Muscogee County	15.3
Newton County	10.2
Oconee County	8.9
Oglethorpe County	9.9
Paulding County	10.3
Peach County	11.1
Pickens County	12.0
Pierce County	10.0
Pike County	10.7
Polk County	9.2
Pulaski County	9.8
Putnam County	12.0
Quitman County	12.3
Rabun County	11.5
Randolph County	9.8
Richmond County	14.1
Rockdale County	10.5
Schley County	7.3
Screven County	8.7
Seminole County	9.5
Spalding County	10.6
Stephens County	9.2
Stewart County	6.5
Sumter County	8.1
Talbot County	10.2
Taliaferro County	7.2
Tattnall County	9.9
Taylor County	10.2
Telfair County	7.7
Terrell County	9.6
Thomas County	10.5
Tift County	6.6
Toombs County	9.5
Towns County	14.5
Treutlen County	6.8
Troup County	9.3
Turner County	7.6
Twiggs County	7.9
Union County	14.5
Upson County	9.4
Walker County	11.3
Walton County	9.3
Ware County	9.2
Warren County	7.6
Washington County	7.5
Wayne County	11.5
Webster County	5.3
Wheeler County	6.6
Georgia cnt'd	
White County	10.4
Whitfield County	7.3
Wilcox County	8.3
Wilkes County	7.9
Wilkinson County	8.5
Worth County	11.0
Hawaii	10.9
Hawaii County	10.9
Honolulu County	11.5
Kalawao County	4.8
Kauai County	8.9
Maui County	8.3
Idaho	10.7
Ada County	9.8
Adams County	17.1
Bannock County	9.3
Bear Lake County	10.2
Benewah County	14.4
Bingham County	9.4
Blaine County	8.3
Boise County	13.7
Bonner County	14.5
Bonneville County	9.6
Boundary County	15.5
Butte County	12.8
Camas County	13.7
Canyon County	10.1
Caribou County	9.8
Cassia County	8.6
Clark County	7.3
Clearwater County	14.6
Custer County	15.9
Elmore County	25.0
Franklin County	9.4
Fremont County	10.4
Gem County	12.9
Gooding County	10.4
Idaho County	14.5
Jefferson County	9.3
Jerome County	8.7
Kootenai County	12.5
Latah County	7.0
Lemhi County	15.8
Lewis County	15.4
Lincoln County	8.2
Madison County	3.5
Minidoka County	9.7
Nez Perce County	13.5
Oneida County	13.7
Owyhee County	11.2
Payette County	12.3
Power County	8.9
Shoshone County	15.9
Teton County	5.8
Twin Falls County	9.9
Valley County	14.4
Washington County	13.5
Illinois	7.5
Adams County	11.3
Alexander County	11.1
Bond County	10.8
Boone County	8.8
Brown County	7.8
Bureau County	10.5
Calhoun County	11.2
Carroll County	11.5
Cass County	9.7
Champaign County	6.5

Table 19. Percent of the Civilian Population 18 Years and Over Who Are Veterans, Selected Counties by State/ Territory, United States, American Community Survey 5-Year Estimates, 2013—*Continued*

(Percent.)

Location	Percent veterans	Location	Percent veterans	Location	Percent veterans
Illinois cnt'd		**Illinois** cnt'd		**Indiana** cnt'd	
Christian County	11.6	St. Clair County	14.9	Marion County	8.3
Clark County	11.7	Saline County	11.1	Marshall County	9.4
Clay County	10.0	Sangamon County	10.6	Martin County	11.8
Clinton County	12.1	Schuyler County	14.1	Miami County	12.2
Coles County	8.6	Scott County	10.5	Monroe County	6.4
Cook County	5.4	Shelby County	12.9	Montgomery County	9.5
Crawford County	11.5	Stark County	10.5	Morgan County	10.7
Cumberland County	11.7	Stephenson County	10.7	Newton County	9.0
DeKalb County	7.0	Tazewell County	10.3	Noble County	9.6
De Witt County	10.7	Union County	11.4	Ohio County	11.4
Douglas County	9.5	Vermilion County	11.9	Orange County	9.5
DuPage County	6.1	Wabash County	9.9	Owen County	12.3
Edgar County	11.4	Warren County	9.4	Parke County	10.3
Edwards County	10.8	Washington County	12.6	Perry County	9.2
Effingham County	10.1	Wayne County	11.3	Pike County	10.7
Fayette County	10.1	White County	12.0	Porter County	9.5
Ford County	10.9	Whiteside County	11.2	Posey County	9.7
Franklin County	12.4	Will County	7.0	Pulaski County	8.8
Fulton County	10.9	Williamson County	12.2	Putnam County	9.2
Gallatin County	10.5	Winnebago County	9.6	Randolph County	10.0
Greene County	10.2	Woodford County	9.3	Ripley County	11.1
Grundy County	9.5			Rush County	10.7
Hamilton County	11.0	**Indiana**	9.3	St. Joseph County	8.9
Hancock County	11.8	Adams County	7.5	Scott County	8.9
Hardin County	11.4	Allen County	8.9	Shelby County	10.3
Henderson County	14.4	Bartholomew County	9.4	Spencer County	11.7
Henry County	11.3	Benton County	9.7	Starke County	10.3
Iroquois County	10.5	Blackford County	11.6	Steuben County	10.0
Jackson County	8.8	Boone County	8.0	Sullivan County	8.6
Jasper County	9.7	Brown County	14.2	Switzerland County	11.2
Jefferson County	11.3	Carroll County	11.1	Tippecanoe County	6.8
Jersey County	13.7	Cass County	10.8	Tipton County	12.4
Jo Daviess County	12.6	Clark County	10.5	Union County	10.4
Johnson County	13.1	Clay County	9.7	Vanderburgh County	9.5
Kane County	6.6	Clinton County	8.4	Vermillion County	12.5
Kankakee County	9.9	Crawford County	10.0	Vigo County	9.4
Kendall County	7.3	Daviess County	8.5	Wabash County	9.9
Knox County	11.4	Dearborn County	9.9	Warren County	10.3
Lake County	7.0	Decatur County	10.1	Warrick County	10.4
LaSalle County	10.4	DeKalb County	9.8	Washington County	9.7
Lawrence County	9.2	Delaware County	9.1	Wayne County	10.9
Lee County	10.4	Dubois County	10.1	Wells County	8.8
Livingston County	9.3	Elkhart County	7.9	White County	11.1
Logan County	9.3	Fayette County	11.6	Whitley County	10.4
McDonough County	8.8	Floyd County	10.7		
McHenry County	7.7	Fountain County	9.6	**Iowa**	9.7
McLean County	7.7	Franklin County	8.5	Adair County	13.3
Macon County	11.4	Fulton County	10.5	Adams County	11.3
Macoupin County	12.0	Gibson County	9.7	Allamakee County	11.7
Madison County	11.2	Grant County	10.8	Appanoose County	10.5
Marion County	11.6	Greene County	12.1	Audubon County	11.8
Marshall County	11.4	Hamilton County	7.9	Benton County	11.1
Mason County	10.6	Hancock County	10.3	Black Hawk County	8.8
Massac County	10.7	Harrison County	11.1	Boone County	11.3
Menard County	11.6	Hendricks County	9.7	Bremer County	10.1
Mercer County	11.6	Henry County	11.1	Buchanan County	9.9
Monroe County	10.8	Howard County	11.8	Buena Vista County	7.9
Montgomery County	12.2	Huntington County	9.5	Butler County	8.8
Morgan County	10.7	Jackson County	8.7	Calhoun County	11.7
Moultrie County	9.3	Jasper County	10.1	Carroll County	9.2
Ogle County	10.2	Jay County	8.9	Cass County	10.9
Peoria County	9.0	Jefferson County	10.6	Cedar County	11.6
Perry County	10.6	Jennings County	10.5	Cerro Gordo County	11.6
Piatt County	10.4	Johnson County	9.5	Cherokee County	12.3
Pike County	9.1	Knox County	9.0	Chickasaw County	11.8
Pope County	12.0	Kosciusko County	8.5	Clarke County	9.9
Pulaski County	11.9	LaGrange County	7.2	Clay County	10.6
Putnam County	13.2	Lake County	8.9	Clayton County	11.3
Randolph County	11.5	LaPorte County	10.4	Clinton County	11.4
Richland County	11.7	Lawrence County	11.9	Crawford County	9.2
Rock Island County	10.6	Madison County	10.2	Dallas County	7.9

Table 19. Percent of the Civilian Population 18 Years and Over Who Are Veterans, Selected Counties by State/Territory, United States, American Community Survey 5-Year Estimates, 2013—*Continued*

(Percent.)

Location	Percent veterans
Iowa cnt'd	
Davis County	11.6
Decatur County	9.5
Delaware County	9.0
Des Moines County	11.6
Dickinson County	12.8
Dubuque County	9.8
Emmet County	9.8
Fayette County	10.6
Floyd County	12.3
Franklin County	9.9
Fremont County	13.8
Greene County	11.6
Grundy County	9.5
Guthrie County	10.8
Hamilton County	11.2
Hancock County	9.2
Hardin County	11.1
Harrison County	9.8
Henry County	10.1
Howard County	9.7
Humboldt County	12.5
Ida County	11.6
Iowa County	8.4
Jackson County	11.7
Jasper County	9.9
Jefferson County	11.5
Johnson County	6.2
Jones County	12.1
Keokuk County	9.9
Kossuth County	11.9
Lee County	12.7
Linn County	10.4
Louisa County	9.6
Lucas County	9.8
Lyon County	8.2
Madison County	11.9
Mahaska County	8.7
Marion County	9.9
Marshall County	11.6
Mills County	12.0
Mitchell County	11.0
Monona County	13.4
Monroe County	10.4
Montgomery County	10.9
Muscatine County	9.0
O'Brien County	10.3
Osceola County	10.1
Page County	12.8
Palo Alto County	10.7
Plymouth County	10.9
Pocahontas County	11.8
Polk County	8.2
Pottawattamie County	10.5
Poweshiek County	8.7
Ringgold County	10.3
Sac County	11.9
Scott County	9.8
Shelby County	11.2
Sioux County	7.3
Story County	6.4
Tama County	11.3
Taylor County	10.6
Union County	10.6
Van Buren County	11.5
Wapello County	9.6
Warren County	11.0
Washington County	9.6
Wayne County	11.7
Webster County	10.6
Winnebago County	9.9
Iowa cnt'd	
Winneshiek County	8.9
Woodbury County	9.5
Worth County	12.1
Wright County	9.3
Kansas	9.9
Allen County	12.0
Anderson County	10.5
Atchison County	9.1
Barber County	11.6
Barton County	9.1
Bourbon County	10.5
Brown County	11.2
Butler County	11.4
Chase County	13.2
Chautauqua County	12.6
Cherokee County	10.9
Cheyenne County	11.8
Clark County	11.1
Clay County	15.3
Cloud County	11.1
Coffey County	10.9
Comanche County	9.9
Cowley County	10.7
Crawford County	8.2
Decatur County	12.4
Dickinson County	14.7
Doniphan County	9.1
Douglas County	6.6
Edwards County	9.9
Elk County	14.0
Ellis County	8.8
Ellsworth County	10.6
Finney County	5.8
Ford County	6.4
Franklin County	9.8
Geary County	23.3
Gove County	10.8
Graham County	10.1
Grant County	4.1
Gray County	5.7
Greeley County	9.2
Greenwood County	11.5
Hamilton County	9.3
Harper County	10.3
Harvey County	8.6
Haskell County	5.0
Hodgeman County	11.1
Jackson County	13.5
Jefferson County	11.8
Jewell County	14.3
Johnson County	8.3
Kearny County	7.7
Kingman County	12.8
Kiowa County	8.0
Labette County	10.0
Lane County	10.4
Leavenworth County	17.5
Lincoln County	16.2
Linn County	12.6
Logan County	10.1
Lyon County	8.0
McPherson County	8.7
Marion County	9.8
Marshall County	10.8
Meade County	10.7
Miami County	9.8
Mitchell County	8.4
Montgomery County	10.0
Morris County	16.6
Kansas cnt'd	
Morton County	6.1
Nemaha County	8.7
Neosho County	12.0
Ness County	11.6
Norton County	12.1
Osage County	13.0
Osborne County	10.5
Ottawa County	10.8
Pawnee County	11.8
Phillips County	9.2
Pottawatomie County	10.2
Pratt County	10.3
Rawlins County	12.5
Reno County	10.1
Republic County	13.8
Rice County	10.4
Riley County	9.5
Rooks County	11.7
Rush County	12.0
Russell County	11.2
Saline County	10.3
Scott County	8.3
Sedgwick County	10.0
Seward County	4.9
Shawnee County	12.1
Sheridan County	12.4
Sherman County	10.0
Smith County	15.0
Stafford County	10.6
Stanton County	5.0
Stevens County	9.1
Sumner County	10.7
Thomas County	8.8
Trego County	13.3
Wabaunsee County	11.2
Wallace County	8.7
Washington County	11.5
Wichita County	9.4
Wilson County	10.7
Woodson County	12.0
Wyandotte County	9.0
Kentucky	9.4
Adair County	9.4
Allen County	9.9
Anderson County	9.3
Ballard County	11.5
Barren County	7.7
Bath County	6.7
Bell County	7.5
Boone County	9.9
Bourbon County	10.4
Boyd County	11.2
Boyle County	9.2
Bracken County	9.0
Breathitt County	5.3
Breckinridge County	11.2
Bullitt County	10.5
Butler County	8.2
Caldwell County	10.0
Calloway County	8.9
Campbell County	8.8
Carlisle County	10.2
Carroll County	9.5
Carter County	7.8
Casey County	9.9
Christian County	15.1
Clark County	9.7
Clay County	5.0

Table 19. Percent of the Civilian Population 18 Years and Over Who Are Veterans, Selected Counties by State/ Territory, United States, American Community Survey 5-Year Estimates, 2013—*Continued*

(Percent.)

Location	Percent veterans
Kentucky cnt'd	
Clinton County	9.7
Crittenden County	11.9
Cumberland County	8.8
Daviess County	10.2
Edmonson County	9.9
Elliott County	7.4
Estill County	8.3
Fayette County	7.6
Fleming County	8.7
Floyd County	6.7
Franklin County	10.4
Fulton County	9.4
Gallatin County	11.7
Garrard County	9.5
Grant County	9.7
Graves County	9.3
Grayson County	9.6
Green County	8.5
Greenup County	9.7
Hancock County	13.4
Hardin County	19.6
Harlan County	9.7
Harrison County	11.0
Hart County	8.7
Henderson County	8.8
Henry County	8.3
Hickman County	9.7
Hopkins County	9.7
Jackson County	7.2
Jefferson County	9.5
Jessamine County	8.8
Johnson County	7.6
Kenton County	9.8
Knott County	5.9
Knox County	6.5
Larue County	10.8
Laurel County	9.2
Lawrence County	6.5
Lee County	6.5
Leslie County	5.3
Letcher County	6.8
Lewis County	8.3
Lincoln County	8.8
Livingston County	7.5
Logan County	9.3
Lyon County	12.9
McCracken County	11.1
McCreary County	7.6
McLean County	10.4
Madison County	8.7
Magoffin County	4.7
Marion County	8.7
Marshall County	11.4
Martin County	6.4
Mason County	8.8
Meade County	17.4
Menifee County	9.8
Mercer County	10.5
Metcalfe County	7.3
Monroe County	8.8
Montgomery County	8.0
Morgan County	5.0
Muhlenberg County	8.4
Nelson County	9.6
Nicholas County	8.1
Ohio County	9.5
Oldham County	10.1
Owen County	8.3
Owsley County	6.5
Pendleton County	8.0
Kentucky cnt'd	
Perry County	7.0
Pike County	6.1
Powell County	6.9
Pulaski County	9.6
Robertson County	9.1
Rockcastle County	8.9
Rowan County	6.6
Russell County	8.4
Scott County	8.8
Shelby County	10.7
Simpson County	8.6
Spencer County	10.2
Taylor County	7.7
Todd County	9.7
Trigg County	15.0
Trimble County	8.8
Union County	10.7
Warren County	8.4
Washington County	7.8
Wayne County	7.7
Webster County	10.3
Whitley County	9.1
Wolfe County	7.6
Woodford County	11.0
Louisiana	8.9
Acadia Parish	7.6
Allen Parish	8.5
Ascension Parish	8.5
Assumption Parish	8.8
Avoyelles Parish	9.0
Beauregard Parish	13.3
Bienville Parish	10.5
Bossier Parish	14.2
Caddo Parish	10.2
Calcasieu Parish	9.9
Caldwell Parish	9.0
Cameron Parish	9.6
Catahoula Parish	8.6
Claiborne Parish	8.4
Concordia Parish	8.9
De Soto Parish	11.1
East Baton Rouge Parish	7.5
East Carroll Parish	4.4
East Feliciana Parish	7.9
Evangeline Parish	7.2
Franklin Parish	8.0
Grant Parish	10.2
Iberia Parish	8.4
Iberville Parish	7.6
Jackson Parish	11.3
Jefferson Parish	8.1
Jefferson Davis Parish	9.4
Lafayette Parish	8.2
Lafourche Parish	6.2
LaSalle Parish	9.2
Lincoln Parish	7.0
Livingston Parish	9.3
Madison Parish	8.2
Morehouse Parish	9.9
Natchitoches Parish	8.4
Orleans Parish	7.0
Ouachita Parish	8.9
Plaquemines Parish	10.5
Pointe Coupee Parish	7.8
Rapides Parish	11.0
Red River Parish	8.5
Richland Parish	6.5
Sabine Parish	11.3
St. Bernard Parish	5.4
Louisiana cnt'd	
St. Charles Parish	7.8
St. Helena Parish	9.0
St. James Parish	8.3
St. John the Baptist Parish	7.6
St. Landry Parish	7.4
St. Martin Parish	7.7
St. Mary Parish	8.8
St. Tammany Parish	11.2
Tangipahoa Parish	8.4
Tensas Parish	9.2
Terrebonne Parish	8.1
Union Parish	9.9
Vermilion Parish	7.7
Vernon Parish	20.2
Washington Parish	10.9
Webster Parish	10.9
West Baton Rouge Parish	7.6
West Carroll Parish	8.0
West Feliciana Parish	10.6
Winn Parish	8.0
Maine	12.0
Androscoggin County	12.3
Aroostook County	12.5
Cumberland County	9.9
Franklin County	11.7
Hancock County	12.3
Kennebec County	12.4
Knox County	13.3
Lincoln County	13.1
Oxford County	12.8
Penobscot County	11.8
Piscataquis County	14.6
Sagadahoc County	14.5
Somerset County	13.1
Waldo County	13.7
Washington County	13.9
York County	12.3
Maryland	9.6
Allegany County	11.1
Anne Arundel County	13.3
Baltimore County	9.2
Calvert County	13.0
Caroline County	11.6
Carroll County	10.4
Cecil County	11.1
Charles County	14.5
Dorchester County	12.9
Frederick County	9.9
Garrett County	9.7
Harford County	11.3
Howard County	8.7
Kent County	11.2
Montgomery County	6.5
Prince George's County	9.3
Queen Anne's County	11.4
St. Mary's County	16.7
Somerset County	9.5
Talbot County	13.6
Washington County	10.7
Wicomico County	9.7
Worcester County	12.5
Baltimore city	7.3
Massachusetts	7.4
Barnstable County	12.0
Berkshire County	9.8
Bristol County	7.8
Dukes County	7.1

Table 19. Percent of the Civilian Population 18 Years and Over Who Are Veterans, Selected Counties by State/ Territory, United States, American Community Survey 5-Year Estimates, 2013—*Continued*

(Percent.)

Location	Percent veterans
Massachusetts cnt'd	
Essex County	7.4
Franklin County	9.6
Hampden County	9.1
Hampshire County	7.5
Middlesex County	6.2
Nantucket County	6.3
Norfolk County	7.2
Plymouth County	9.2
Suffolk County	3.9
Worcester County	8.7
Michigan	8.9
Alcona County	18.4
Alger County	13.9
Allegan County	9.3
Alpena County	12.0
Antrim County	12.7
Arenac County	12.0
Baraga County	11.3
Barry County	10.7
Bay County	10.7
Benzie County	14.0
Berrien County	9.7
Branch County	9.3
Calhoun County	11.0
Cass County	11.6
Charlevoix County	11.6
Cheboygan County	13.0
Chippewa County	12.1
Clare County	13.1
Clinton County	8.4
Crawford County	14.3
Delta County	14.9
Dickinson County	13.6
Eaton County	9.8
Emmet County	11.2
Genesee County	9.3
Gladwin County	12.8
Gogebic County	14.4
Grand Traverse County	10.4
Gratiot County	9.2
Hillsdale County	10.4
Houghton County	10.3
Huron County	10.2
Ingham County	7.3
Ionia County	9.9
Iosco County	16.4
Iron County	15.1
Isabella County	6.2
Jackson County	10.1
Kalamazoo County	7.9
Kalkaska County	12.1
Kent County	7.6
Keweenaw County	19.6
Lake County	13.5
Lapeer County	9.7
Leelanau County	12.6
Lenawee County	9.9
Livingston County	8.9
Luce County	11.1
Mackinac County	14.0
Macomb County	8.5
Manistee County	14.1
Marquette County	11.9
Mason County	11.5
Mecosta County	10.1
Menominee County	13.7
Midland County	9.3
Missaukee County	10.9
Monroe County	9.9
Michigan cnt'd	
Montcalm County	10.2
Montmorency County	16.5
Muskegon County	10.3
Newaygo County	11.3
Oakland County	7.3
Oceana County	12.0
Ogemaw County	13.6
Ontonagon County	18.1
Osceola County	12.9
Oscoda County	15.9
Otsego County	11.7
Ottawa County	7.2
Presque Isle County	13.7
Roscommon County	15.5
Saginaw County	9.9
St. Clair County	10.2
St. Joseph County	9.7
Sanilac County	9.8
Schoolcraft County	13.2
Shiawassee County	9.8
Tuscola County	10.5
Van Buren County	11.1
Washtenaw County	6.1
Wayne County	7.8
Wexford County	11.8
Minnesota	9.0
Aitkin County	15.8
Anoka County	9.2
Becker County	12.8
Beltrami County	10.8
Benton County	10.2
Big Stone County	11.7
Blue Earth County	8.1
Brown County	10.9
Carlton County	11.9
Carver County	7.4
Cass County	14.6
Chippewa County	8.5
Chisago County	9.9
Clay County	7.5
Clearwater County	14.0
Cook County	12.2
Cottonwood County	9.9
Crow Wing County	12.1
Dakota County	9.2
Dodge County	10.6
Douglas County	11.5
Faribault County	11.0
Fillmore County	10.3
Freeborn County	11.7
Goodhue County	10.7
Grant County	12.1
Hennepin County	7.2
Houston County	10.8
Hubbard County	13.9
Isanti County	10.6
Itasca County	12.9
Jackson County	12.7
Kanabec County	12.4
Kandiyohi County	9.1
Kittson County	10.4
Koochiching County	11.7
Lac qui Parle County	10.8
Lake County	14.4
Lake of the Woods County	15.1
Le Sueur County	9.8
Lincoln County	12.2
Lyon County	7.7
McLeod County	10.4
Minnesota cnt'd	
Mahnomen County	11.0
Marshall County	9.4
Martin County	11.0
Meeker County	11.4
Mille Lacs County	11.4
Morrison County	11.5
Mower County	10.5
Murray County	12.2
Nicollet County	7.7
Nobles County	8.7
Norman County	11.0
Olmsted County	8.7
Otter Tail County	12.6
Pennington County	10.0
Pine County	13.1
Pipestone County	10.5
Polk County	10.5
Pope County	11.4
Ramsey County	7.3
Red Lake County	10.6
Redwood County	10.8
Renville County	10.4
Rice County	8.2
Rock County	12.6
Roseau County	10.8
St. Louis County	11.0
Scott County	7.8
Sherburne County	9.0
Sibley County	8.5
Stearns County	9.7
Steele County	9.8
Stevens County	8.2
Swift County	11.2
Todd County	10.9
Traverse County	13.9
Wabasha County	11.8
Wadena County	11.7
Waseca County	9.9
Washington County	8.9
Watonwan County	10.3
Wilkin County	11.1
Winona County	7.2
Wright County	9.0
Yellow Medicine County	11.6
Mississippi	9.1
Adams County	8.0
Alcorn County	8.5
Amite County	7.1
Attala County	9.8
Benton County	6.3
Bolivar County	5.6
Calhoun County	7.2
Carroll County	5.6
Chickasaw County	5.1
Choctaw County	9.9
Claiborne County	4.6
Clarke County	10.8
Clay County	8.0
Coahoma County	6.5
Copiah County	8.1
Covington County	10.1
DeSoto County	9.3
Forrest County	9.3
Franklin County	9.9
George County	9.8
Greene County	10.2
Grenada County	6.7
Hancock County	12.9
Harrison County	16.4

Table 19. Percent of the Civilian Population 18 Years and Over Who Are Veterans, Selected Counties by State/ Territory, United States, American Community Survey 5-Year Estimates, 2013—*Continued*

(Percent.)

Location	Percent veterans
Mississippi cnt'd	
Hinds County	7.7
Holmes County	4.2
Humphreys County	7.5
Issaquena County	7.5
Itawamba County	8.4
Jackson County	13.5
Jasper County	7.9
Jefferson County	5.2
Jefferson Davis County	6.3
Jones County	9.1
Kemper County	7.3
Lafayette County	5.7
Lamar County	9.4
Lauderdale County	11.0
Lawrence County	11.2
Leake County	8.1
Lee County	8.5
Leflore County	4.5
Lincoln County	7.9
Lowndes County	12.0
Madison County	7.8
Marion County	8.3
Marshall County	7.8
Monroe County	8.6
Montgomery County	9.4
Neshoba County	8.1
Newton County	11.5
Noxubee County	4.5
Oktibbeha County	5.6
Panola County	7.5
Pearl River County	11.9
Perry County	10.0
Pike County	7.6
Pontotoc County	6.9
Prentiss County	5.9
Quitman County	8.1
Rankin County	9.1
Scott County	6.1
Sharkey County	8.0
Simpson County	8.4
Smith County	7.7
Stone County	11.3
Sunflower County	6.1
Tallahatchie County	5.4
Tate County	7.4
Tippah County	7.7
Tishomingo County	10.2
Tunica County	6.9
Union County	8.3
Walthall County	6.2
Warren County	7.8
Washington County	7.7
Wayne County	7.7
Webster County	7.0
Wilkinson County	5.2
Winston County	7.7
Yalobusha County	9.7
Yazoo County	7.9
Missouri	10.5
Adair County	7.7
Andrew County	11.3
Atchison County	13.1
Audrain County	10.1
Barry County	12.7
Barton County	10.8
Bates County	8.9
Benton County	15.3
Bollinger County	11.6
Boone County	7.4
Missouri cnt'd	
Buchanan County	10.4
Butler County	12.8
Caldwell County	13.7
Callaway County	10.8
Camden County	14.3
Cape Girardeau County	9.9
Carroll County	12.4
Carter County	12.1
Cass County	11.8
Cedar County	13.9
Chariton County	10.8
Christian County	11.5
Clark County	13.1
Clay County	10.6
Clinton County	13.6
Cole County	11.2
Cooper County	10.2
Crawford County	13.9
Dade County	13.8
Dallas County	12.7
Daviess County	13.0
DeKalb County	12.0
Dent County	12.9
Douglas County	13.4
Dunklin County	9.9
Franklin County	10.5
Gasconade County	11.3
Gentry County	11.8
Greene County	10.9
Grundy County	10.5
Harrison County	12.2
Henry County	12.9
Hickory County	16.8
Holt County	13.4
Howard County	10.6
Howell County	11.8
Iron County	13.3
Jackson County	9.6
Jasper County	9.7
Jefferson County	10.8
Johnson County	16.2
Knox County	11.8
Laclede County	12.6
Lafayette County	10.5
Lawrence County	13.4
Lewis County	10.4
Lincoln County	10.1
Linn County	9.4
Livingston County	11.0
McDonald County	12.7
Macon County	11.8
Madison County	11.0
Maries County	13.1
Marion County	10.0
Mercer County	12.9
Miller County	13.3
Mississippi County	9.2
Moniteau County	10.7
Monroe County	12.6
Montgomery County	12.1
Morgan County	13.9
New Madrid County	11.8
Newton County	10.3
Nodaway County	6.7
Oregon County	13.2
Osage County	10.8
Ozark County	17.6
Pemiscot County	9.6
Perry County	10.8
Pettis County	11.4
Missouri cnt'd	
Phelps County	11.9
Pike County	12.8
Platte County	10.9
Polk County	10.4
Pulaski County	26.8
Putnam County	13.3
Ralls County	13.1
Randolph County	10.3
Ray County	10.5
Reynolds County	12.9
Ripley County	12.2
St. Charles County	10.0
St. Clair County	13.0
Ste. Genevieve County	12.1
St. Francois County	11.7
St. Louis County	9.1
Saline County	10.2
Schuyler County	9.1
Scotland County	8.8
Scott County	10.2
Shannon County	11.2
Shelby County	10.5
Stoddard County	12.5
Stone County	14.5
Sullivan County	8.8
Taney County	13.1
Texas County	13.5
Vernon County	10.0
Warren County	11.7
Washington County	11.9
Wayne County	12.3
Webster County	11.6
Worth County	13.1
Wright County	11.5
St. Louis city	7.7
Montana	12.2
Beaverhead County	13.1
Big Horn County	7.3
Blaine County	11.4
Broadwater County	16.3
Carbon County	14.5
Carter County	7.4
Cascade County	17.1
Chouteau County	13.3
Custer County	12.8
Daniels County	12.0
Dawson County	11.3
Deer Lodge County	16.2
Fallon County	9.6
Fergus County	13.3
Flathead County	12.4
Gallatin County	7.9
Garfield County	11.1
Glacier County	10.1
Golden Valley County	11.9
Granite County	15.5
Hill County	11.4
Jefferson County	15.8
Judith Basin County	14.7
Lake County	13.3
Lewis and Clark County	12.7
Liberty County	7.4
Lincoln County	15.8
McCone County	12.8
Madison County	12.6
Meagher County	15.2
Mineral County	18.4
Missoula County	10.1
Musselshell County	17.7

Table 19. Percent of the Civilian Population 18 Years and Over Who Are Veterans, Selected Counties by State/ Territory, United States, American Community Survey 5-Year Estimates, 2013—*Continued*

(Percent.)

Location	Percent veterans
Montana cnt'd	
Park County	11.1
Petroleum County	16.9
Phillips County	11.8
Pondera County	10.2
Powder River County	10.1
Powell County	15.3
Prairie County	16.5
Ravalli County	14.1
Richland County	9.6
Roosevelt County	6.9
Rosebud County	12.0
Sanders County	16.8
Sheridan County	10.9
Silver Bow County	11.7
Stillwater County	16.0
Sweet Grass County	11.1
Teton County	13.2
Toole County	17.1
Treasure County	13.4
Valley County	12.4
Wheatland County	13.0
Wibaux County	11.2
Yellowstone County	11.8
Nebraska	10.3
Adams County	10.5
Antelope County	11.7
Arthur County	9.3
Banner County	10.3
Blaine County	10.4
Boone County	12.3
Box Butte County	11.8
Boyd County	13.4
Brown County	13.9
Buffalo County	8.4
Burt County	12.6
Butler County	12.5
Cass County	16.5
Cedar County	11.1
Chase County	9.1
Cherry County	11.8
Cheyenne County	11.4
Clay County	10.3
Colfax County	8.5
Cuming County	10.5
Custer County	11.1
Dakota County	8.0
Dawes County	10.3
Dawson County	7.9
Deuel County	15.2
Dixon County	10.8
Dodge County	10.6
Douglas County	8.8
Dundy County	12.0
Fillmore County	11.2
Franklin County	14.6
Frontier County	12.7
Furnas County	13.4
Gage County	11.3
Garden County	15.0
Garfield County	11.9
Gosper County	10.6
Grant County	10.8
Greeley County	14.8
Hall County	9.6
Hamilton County	11.9
Harlan County	12.1
Hayes County	14.9
Hitchcock County	13.5
Holt County	10.3
Nebraska cnt'd	
Hooker County	13.4
Howard County	12.7
Jefferson County	10.8
Johnson County	11.0
Kearney County	12.0
Keith County	11.3
Keya Paha County	9.9
Kimball County	13.2
Knox County	12.6
Lancaster County	8.8
Lincoln County	12.2
Logan County	9.3
Loup County	15.3
McPherson County	10.8
Madison County	9.1
Merrick County	13.8
Morrill County	10.0
Nance County	8.3
Nemaha County	11.8
Nuckolls County	13.2
Otoe County	10.1
Pawnee County	9.2
Perkins County	6.8
Phelps County	10.4
Pierce County	13.2
Platte County	9.5
Polk County	10.4
Red Willow County	10.5
Richardson County	12.6
Rock County	10.6
Saline County	8.4
Sarpy County	16.1
Saunders County	12.2
Scotts Bluff County	10.8
Seward County	8.7
Sheridan County	12.9
Sherman County	10.5
Sioux County	12.8
Stanton County	7.1
Thayer County	11.6
Thomas County	12.5
Thurston County	9.0
Valley County	11.5
Washington County	11.8
Wayne County	10.5
Webster County	11.3
Wheeler County	10.3
York County	11.1
Nevada	11.0
Churchill County	19.9
Clark County	10.2
Douglas County	15.1
Elko County	11.3
Esmeralda County	13.2
Eureka County	14.8
Humboldt County	11.0
Lander County	12.5
Lincoln County	15.5
Lyon County	15.6
Mineral County	21.0
Nye County	21.5
Pershing County	13.3
Storey County	18.6
Washoe County	11.1
White Pine County	14.8
Carson City	14.5
New Hampshire	10.9
Belknap County	13.4
New Hampshire cnt'd	
Carroll County	14.7
Cheshire County	11.7
Coos County	13.7
Grafton County	10.7
Hillsborough County	9.9
Merrimack County	11.2
Rockingham County	10.2
Strafford County	10.6
Sullivan County	12.9
New Jersey	6.5
Atlantic County	7.9
Bergen County	5.3
Burlington County	10.5
Camden County	7.6
Cape May County	11.3
Cumberland County	7.2
Essex County	4.6
Gloucester County	8.8
Hudson County	3.2
Hunterdon County	7.4
Mercer County	6.1
Middlesex County	5.2
Monmouth County	7.3
Morris County	6.3
Ocean County	11.0
Passaic County	4.3
Salem County	11.0
Somerset County	5.6
Sussex County	8.5
Union County	4.9
Warren County	8.5
New Mexico	11.2
Bernalillo County	10.9
Catron County	15.9
Chaves County	10.1
Cibola County	9.1
Colfax County	12.9
Curry County	16.5
De Baca County	10.2
Doña Ana County	10.5
Eddy County	11.1
Grant County	13.0
Guadalupe County	11.4
Harding County	17.7
Hidalgo County	9.4
Lea County	8.2
Lincoln County	13.2
Los Alamos County	13.2
Luna County	11.8
McKinley County	6.3
Mora County	10.1
Otero County	19.2
Quay County	12.5
Rio Arriba County	8.8
Roosevelt County	8.0
Sandoval County	14.5
San Juan County	8.4
San Miguel County	10.7
Santa Fe County	9.7
Sierra County	18.2
Socorro County	9.7
Taos County	11.8
Torrance County	13.4
Union County	9.8
Valencia County	13.3
New York	6.0
Albany County	7.5

Table 19. Percent of the Civilian Population 18 Years and Over Who Are Veterans, Selected Counties by State/ Territory, United States, American Community Survey 5-Year Estimates, 2013—*Continued*

(Percent.)

Location	Percent veterans
New York cnt'd	
Allegany County	11.4
Bronx County	3.4
Broome County	9.2
Cattaraugus County	11.7
Cayuga County	10.5
Chautauqua County	11.2
Chemung County	11.2
Chenango County	10.5
Clinton County	11.3
Columbia County	10.6
Cortland County	8.8
Delaware County	10.6
Dutchess County	8.1
Erie County	9.0
Essex County	11.6
Franklin County	9.7
Fulton County	10.5
Genesee County	9.4
Greene County	11.4
Hamilton County	15.7
Herkimer County	11.2
Jefferson County	13.8
Kings County	2.6
Lewis County	11.4
Livingston County	9.4
Madison County	10.2
Monroe County	7.5
Montgomery County	9.7
Nassau County	6.0
New York County	3.1
Niagara County	10.3
Oneida County	10.8
Onondaga County	8.5
Ontario County	10.6
Orange County	8.5
Orleans County	10.1
Oswego County	9.7
Otsego County	10.5
Putnam County	6.6
Queens County	3.2
Rensselaer County	9.1
Richmond County	5.5
Rockland County	5.2
St. Lawrence County	9.1
Saratoga County	9.8
Schenectady County	9.2
Schoharie County	10.7
Schuyler County	11.3
Seneca County	10.7
Steuben County	12.3
Suffolk County	7.3
Sullivan County	9.7
Tioga County	11.3
Tompkins County	5.6
Ulster County	8.2
Warren County	10.7
Washington County	11.6
Wayne County	9.3
Westchester County	5.3
Wyoming County	9.5
Yates County	10.5
North Carolina	9.9
Alamance County	9.2
Alexander County	8.7
Alleghany County	8.8
Anson County	9.6
Ashe County	10.6
Avery County	9.6
Beaufort County	10.7
North Carolina cnt'd	
Bertie County	7.2
Bladen County	8.0
Brunswick County	14.9
Buncombe County	10.6
Burke County	9.0
Cabarrus County	9.4
Caldwell County	8.7
Camden County	14.7
Carteret County	16.9
Caswell County	7.7
Catawba County	9.3
Chatham County	10.9
Cherokee County	12.4
Chowan County	10.7
Clay County	15.9
Cleveland County	9.1
Columbus County	9.1
Craven County	17.9
Cumberland County	20.3
Currituck County	14.8
Dare County	11.4
Davidson County	9.4
Davie County	10.8
Duplin County	9.4
Durham County	7.0
Edgecombe County	9.2
Forsyth County	9.4
Franklin County	9.2
Gaston County	9.8
Gates County	12.3
Graham County	9.4
Granville County	10.8
Greene County	9.0
Guilford County	8.3
Halifax County	8.4
Harnett County	13.7
Haywood County	12.9
Henderson County	13.3
Hertford County	8.8
Hoke County	14.8
Hyde County	5.7
Iredell County	9.2
Jackson County	9.4
Johnston County	10.2
Jones County	13.3
Lee County	10.9
Lenoir County	9.7
Lincoln County	9.9
McDowell County	10.3
Macon County	14.8
Madison County	9.0
Martin County	8.9
Mecklenburg County	7.4
Mitchell County	8.0
Montgomery County	8.5
Moore County	14.7
Nash County	9.5
New Hanover County	10.5
Northampton County	8.3
Onslow County	21.6
Orange County	5.5
Pamlico County	13.5
Pasquotank County	12.9
Pender County	11.9
Perquimans County	14.9
Person County	9.3
Pitt County	7.3
Polk County	12.1
Randolph County	9.6
Richmond County	11.5
North Carolina cnt'd	
Robeson County	7.6
Rockingham County	9.4
Rowan County	9.8
Rutherford County	10.6
Sampson County	9.2
Scotland County	9.7
Stanly County	9.2
Stokes County	8.6
Surry County	8.4
Swain County	10.1
Transylvania County	13.7
Tyrrell County	9.6
Union County	8.4
Vance County	9.5
Wake County	7.9
Warren County	11.5
Washington County	10.1
Watauga County	7.2
Wayne County	13.4
Wilkes County	8.9
Wilson County	9.9
Yadkin County	8.5
Yancey County	9.1
North Dakota	10.0
Adams County	11.5
Barnes County	10.9
Benson County	9.6
Billings County	10.1
Bottineau County	14.6
Bowman County	9.9
Burke County	10.0
Burleigh County	9.9
Cass County	8.4
Cavalier County	12.5
Dickey County	9.8
Divide County	10.2
Dunn County	9.9
Eddy County	11.0
Emmons County	12.5
Foster County	8.5
Golden Valley County	7.1
Grand Forks County	10.0
Grant County	12.7
Griggs County	14.5
Hettinger County	12.1
Kidder County	10.9
LaMoure County	8.6
Logan County	11.9
McHenry County	12.3
McIntosh County	10.4
McKenzie County	9.9
McLean County	12.0
Mercer County	11.3
Morton County	9.5
Mountrail County	12.1
Nelson County	15.1
Oliver County	10.5
Pembina County	11.9
Pierce County	9.7
Ramsey County	9.3
Ransom County	10.3
Renville County	13.9
Richland County	8.7
Rolette County	7.1
Sargent County	10.2
Sheridan County	9.7
Sioux County	7.8
Slope County	8.7
Stark County	9.2

Table 19. Percent of the Civilian Population 18 Years and Over Who Are Veterans, Selected Counties by State/Territory, United States, American Community Survey 5-Year Estimates, 2013—*Continued*

(Percent.)

Location	Percent veterans
North Dakota cnt'd	
Steele County	12.3
Stutsman County	9.8
Towner County	9.4
Traill County	11.8
Walsh County	10.5
Ward County	13.5
Wells County	9.2
Williams County	9.1
Ohio	9.8
Adams County	9.1
Allen County	10.3
Ashland County	10.1
Ashtabula County	12.0
Athens County	6.6
Auglaize County	10.3
Belmont County	11.0
Brown County	10.9
Butler County	9.2
Carroll County	10.8
Champaign County	11.3
Clark County	13.0
Clermont County	9.9
Clinton County	12.3
Columbiana County	12.0
Coshocton County	11.9
Crawford County	10.6
Cuyahoga County	8.8
Darke County	9.5
Defiance County	10.9
Delaware County	8.1
Erie County	11.5
Fairfield County	10.9
Fayette County	10.0
Franklin County	7.7
Fulton County	8.7
Gallia County	9.9
Geauga County	9.1
Greene County	14.3
Guernsey County	11.0
Hamilton County	8.5
Hancock County	9.4
Hardin County	9.4
Harrison County	12.8
Henry County	11.4
Highland County	11.0
Hocking County	12.9
Holmes County	5.5
Huron County	10.5
Jackson County	11.8
Jefferson County	12.2
Knox County	9.7
Lake County	10.3
Lawrence County	11.7
Licking County	11.6
Logan County	10.1
Lorain County	10.3
Lucas County	8.7
Madison County	10.2
Mahoning County	10.6
Marion County	10.6
Medina County	10.0
Meigs County	11.0
Mercer County	10.3
Miami County	10.9
Monroe County	12.5
Montgomery County	10.9
Morgan County	11.4
Morrow County	11.1
Muskingum County	10.0
Ohio cnt'd	
Noble County	13.8
Ottawa County	10.9
Paulding County	10.4
Perry County	10.3
Pickaway County	10.1
Pike County	10.4
Portage County	9.4
Preble County	11.8
Putnam County	7.9
Richland County	11.1
Ross County	11.9
Sandusky County	10.2
Scioto County	10.5
Seneca County	10.9
Shelby County	9.6
Stark County	10.8
Summit County	9.8
Trumbull County	11.6
Tuscarawas County	10.9
Union County	9.2
Van Wert County	9.9
Vinton County	8.6
Warren County	9.6
Washington County	11.0
Wayne County	9.4
Williams County	10.9
Wood County	8.6
Wyandot County	9.4
Oklahoma	11.0
Adair County	10.4
Alfalfa County	12.4
Atoka County	10.6
Beaver County	7.6
Beckham County	7.8
Blaine County	10.2
Bryan County	9.9
Caddo County	12.3
Canadian County	11.4
Carter County	11.3
Cherokee County	10.8
Choctaw County	9.1
Cimarron County	8.2
Cleveland County	10.9
Coal County	11.6
Comanche County	18.8
Cotton County	13.8
Craig County	12.2
Creek County	10.9
Custer County	7.8
Delaware County	13.4
Dewey County	9.7
Ellis County	10.3
Garfield County	12.2
Garvin County	10.3
Grady County	11.3
Grant County	10.5
Greer County	10.7
Harmon County	10.1
Harper County	8.7
Haskell County	11.3
Hughes County	9.4
Jackson County	18.7
Jefferson County	9.6
Johnston County	11.2
Kay County	11.1
Kingfisher County	7.9
Kiowa County	11.5
Latimer County	11.1
Le Flore County	10.1
Oklahoma cnt'd	
Lincoln County	13.2
Logan County	11.1
Love County	9.0
McClain County	11.4
McCurtain County	10.6
McIntosh County	13.5
Major County	10.7
Marshall County	12.2
Mayes County	11.9
Murray County	13.1
Muskogee County	11.8
Noble County	11.3
Nowata County	11.5
Okfuskee County	12.0
Oklahoma County	10.7
Okmulgee County	11.2
Osage County	11.2
Ottawa County	11.4
Pawnee County	12.2
Payne County	7.5
Pittsburg County	13.0
Pontotoc County	10.3
Pottawatomie County	11.8
Pushmataha County	12.8
Roger Mills County	9.3
Rogers County	13.0
Seminole County	10.2
Sequoyah County	10.1
Stephens County	12.8
Texas County	5.5
Tillman County	11.0
Tulsa County	9.6
Wagoner County	12.2
Washington County	11.5
Washita County	10.9
Woods County	10.2
Woodward County	8.7
Oregon	10.8
Baker County	16.3
Benton County	7.8
Clackamas County	10.5
Clatsop County	13.6
Columbia County	14.6
Coos County	15.8
Crook County	16.9
Curry County	18.9
Deschutes County	12.5
Douglas County	15.9
Gilliam County	14.2
Grant County	15.0
Harney County	12.6
Hood River County	8.9
Jackson County	14.1
Jefferson County	12.6
Josephine County	15.5
Klamath County	15.4
Lake County	14.9
Lane County	10.9
Lincoln County	15.2
Linn County	13.1
Malheur County	10.1
Marion County	11.0
Morrow County	13.2
Multnomah County	7.5
Polk County	11.8
Sherman County	15.8
Tillamook County	13.7
Umatilla County	11.3
Union County	11.4

Table 19. Percent of the Civilian Population 18 Years and Over Who Are Veterans, Selected Counties by State/Territory, United States, American Community Survey 5-Year Estimates, 2013—*Continued*

(Percent.)

Location	Percent veterans	Location	Percent veterans	Location	Percent veterans
Oregon cnt'd		**Pennsylvania** cnt'd		**South Dakota** cnt'd	
Wallowa County	15.1	Wayne County	12.2	Campbell County	11.3
Wasco County	12.5	Westmoreland County	11.4	Charles Mix County	10.6
Washington County	8.2	Wyoming County	11.1	Clark County	10.0
Wheeler County	14.9	York County	10.3	Clay County	8.2
Yamhill County	10.0			Codington County	11.4
		Rhode Island	8.5	Corson County	11.8
Pennsylvania	9.5	Bristol County	8.4	Custer County	17.5
Adams County	11.2	Kent County	10.4	Davison County	10.2
Allegheny County	9.5	Newport County	13.3	Day County	12.9
Armstrong County	11.3	Providence County	7.1	Deuel County	13.6
Beaver County	11.5	Washington County	9.7	Dewey County	8.7
Bedford County	11.2			Douglas County	11.9
Berks County	9.4	**South Carolina**	11.0	Edmunds County	9.8
Blair County	12.8	Abbeville County	9.9	Fall River County	18.4
Bradford County	12.0	Aiken County	11.3	Faulk County	10.0
Bucks County	8.4	Allendale County	7.8	Grant County	10.4
Butler County	10.5	Anderson County	10.3	Gregory County	13.0
Cambria County	12.0	Bamberg County	10.7	Haakon County	8.1
Cameron County	15.0	Barnwell County	9.2	Hamlin County	10.3
Carbon County	12.0	Beaufort County	15.2	Hand County	10.4
Centre County	7.3	Berkeley County	15.5	Hanson County	11.0
Chester County	8.2	Calhoun County	10.8	Harding County	6.9
Clarion County	9.4	Charleston County	11.1	Hughes County	10.1
Clearfield County	12.0	Cherokee County	8.6	Hutchinson County	9.0
Clinton County	10.6	Chester County	10.5	Hyde County	11.2
Columbia County	9.4	Chesterfield County	9.0	Jackson County	9.6
Crawford County	11.4	Clarendon County	10.7	Jerauld County	11.3
Cumberland County	11.2	Colleton County	13.8	Jones County	15.1
Dauphin County	10.1	Darlington County	9.2	Kingsbury County	12.0
Delaware County	7.9	Dillon County	8.8	Lake County	10.5
Elk County	11.4	Dorchester County	14.5	Lawrence County	12.5
Erie County	9.9	Edgefield County	10.2	Lincoln County	9.0
Fayette County	11.1	Fairfield County	11.3	Lyman County	13.0
Forest County	14.7	Florence County	9.0	McCook County	11.3
Franklin County	11.3	Georgetown County	12.8	McPherson County	11.4
Fulton County	11.1	Greenville County	9.3	Marshall County	10.9
Greene County	11.8	Greenwood County	9.4	Meade County	17.8
Huntingdon County	10.6	Hampton County	8.4	Mellette County	11.0
Indiana County	9.8	Horry County	12.6	Miner County	10.4
Jefferson County	10.8	Jasper County	8.4	Minnehaha County	9.2
Juniata County	8.8	Kershaw County	11.7	Moody County	11.4
Lackawanna County	10.6	Lancaster County	10.5	Pennington County	15.0
Lancaster County	8.7	Laurens County	9.7	Perkins County	10.8
Lawrence County	10.9	Lee County	7.7	Potter County	13.0
Lebanon County	10.6	Lexington County	11.5	Roberts County	10.8
Lehigh County	8.7	McCormick County	13.3	Sanborn County	14.7
Luzerne County	11.2	Marion County	8.6	Shannon County	7.9
Lycoming County	11.4	Marlboro County	8.4	Spink County	10.5
McKean County	12.4	Newberry County	9.2	Stanley County	10.6
Mercer County	11.8	Oconee County	12.4	Sully County	9.3
Mifflin County	11.2	Orangeburg County	9.2	Todd County	8.5
Monroe County	10.3	Pickens County	8.9	Tripp County	7.8
Montgomery County	8.1	Richland County	11.5	Turner County	10.9
Montour County	10.4	Saluda County	9.4	Union County	11.4
Northampton County	9.4	Spartanburg County	9.6	Walworth County	14.4
Northumberland County	12.8	Sumter County	15.4	Yankton County	9.7
Perry County	11.5	Union County	9.3	Ziebach County	7.5
Philadelphia County	6.2	Williamsburg County	7.9		
Pike County	12.5	York County	9.8	**Tennessee**	9.9
Potter County	12.7			Anderson County	12.0
Schuylkill County	11.7	**South Dakota**	11.0	Bedford County	9.3
Snyder County	8.8	Aurora County	11.0	Benton County	12.9
Somerset County	10.9	Beadle County	10.3	Bledsoe County	10.5
Sullivan County	14.2	Bennett County	9.1	Blount County	12.2
Susquehanna County	11.8	Bon Homme County	12.0	Bradley County	9.3
Tioga County	12.3	Brookings County	7.8	Campbell County	9.3
Union County	9.4	Brown County	9.0	Cannon County	9.4
Venango County	12.2	Brule County	12.0	Carroll County	10.9
Warren County	12.7	Buffalo County	6.6	Carter County	11.1
Washington County	11.1	Butte County	13.7	Cheatham County	9.3

Table 19. Percent of the Civilian Population 18 Years and Over Who Are Veterans, Selected Counties by State/ Territory, United States, American Community Survey 5-Year Estimates, 2013—*Continued*

(Percent.)

Location	Percent veterans
Tennessee cnt'd	
Chester County	8.5
Claiborne County	8.4
Clay County	8.1
Cocke County	12.1
Coffee County	11.0
Crockett County	7.7
Cumberland County	14.3
Davidson County	7.8
Decatur County	10.8
DeKalb County	9.2
Dickson County	10.3
Dyer County	10.7
Fayette County	9.9
Fentress County	10.2
Franklin County	13.6
Gibson County	10.3
Giles County	9.8
Grainger County	8.9
Greene County	10.8
Grundy County	9.5
Hamblen County	11.0
Hamilton County	9.6
Hancock County	9.2
Hardeman County	8.4
Hardin County	10.7
Hawkins County	11.6
Haywood County	7.9
Henderson County	9.9
Henry County	14.1
Hickman County	10.0
Houston County	11.9
Humphreys County	10.7
Jackson County	8.6
Jefferson County	12.3
Johnson County	10.1
Knox County	8.4
Lake County	8.7
Lauderdale County	8.6
Lawrence County	9.9
Lewis County	13.7
Lincoln County	9.3
Loudon County	13.4
McMinn County	10.8
McNairy County	11.0
Macon County	7.6
Madison County	9.3
Marion County	9.3
Marshall County	9.6
Maury County	9.5
Meigs County	11.0
Monroe County	10.7
Montgomery County	21.3
Moore County	11.9
Morgan County	11.4
Obion County	10.5
Overton County	8.0
Perry County	11.0
Pickett County	12.8
Polk County	8.9
Putnam County	7.5
Rhea County	8.4
Roane County	14.4
Robertson County	9.6
Rutherford County	9.6
Scott County	7.0
Sequatchie County	7.8
Sevier County	10.2
Shelby County	8.5
Smith County	8.0
Stewart County	16.4
Tennessee cnt'd	
Sullivan County	11.5
Sumner County	10.6
Tipton County	11.7
Trousdale County	9.6
Unicoi County	9.9
Union County	6.8
Van Buren County	10.8
Warren County	9.0
Washington County	12.0
Wayne County	9.4
Weakley County	9.5
White County	11.3
Williamson County	7.0
Wilson County	10.8
Texas	8.5
Anderson County	9.8
Andrews County	8.9
Angelina County	10.1
Aransas County	14.9
Archer County	12.8
Armstrong County	13.5
Atascosa County	10.1
Austin County	8.8
Bailey County	8.6
Bandera County	18.7
Bastrop County	12.1
Baylor County	8.9
Bee County	9.7
Bell County	21.3
Bexar County	12.0
Blanco County	15.3
Borden County	11.2
Bosque County	13.4
Bowie County	11.6
Brazoria County	9.0
Brazos County	5.7
Brewster County	9.5
Briscoe County	7.4
Brooks County	7.9
Brown County	11.9
Burleson County	10.0
Burnet County	12.9
Caldwell County	9.2
Calhoun County	10.7
Callahan County	13.1
Cameron County	5.8
Camp County	10.9
Carson County	10.3
Cass County	12.7
Castro County	7.4
Chambers County	8.9
Cherokee County	9.4
Childress County	9.2
Clay County	10.4
Cochran County	6.5
Coke County	11.5
Coleman County	11.7
Collin County	7.4
Collingsworth County	9.2
Colorado County	10.6
Comal County	14.7
Comanche County	11.2
Concho County	7.6
Cooke County	10.2
Coryell County	19.2
Cottle County	8.1
Crane County	7.1
Crockett County	7.2
Crosby County	6.9
Texas cnt'd	
Culberson County	8.4
Dallam County	6.3
Dallas County	6.1
Dawson County	4.7
Deaf Smith County	5.3
Delta County	13.5
Denton County	8.0
DeWitt County	11.0
Dickens County	11.3
Dimmit County	6.0
Donley County	10.2
Duval County	7.3
Eastland County	11.5
Ector County	7.1
Edwards County	9.2
Ellis County	9.2
El Paso County	8.9
Erath County	7.6
Falls County	9.8
Fannin County	12.5
Fayette County	10.7
Fisher County	9.7
Floyd County	6.9
Foard County	11.0
Fort Bend County	6.1
Franklin County	12.4
Freestone County	11.6
Frio County	7.1
Gaines County	4.0
Galveston County	9.8
Garza County	5.1
Gillespie County	13.3
Glasscock County	4.6
Goliad County	12.5
Gonzales County	7.5
Gray County	8.6
Grayson County	10.6
Gregg County	9.5
Grimes County	11.9
Guadalupe County	16.0
Hale County	7.3
Hall County	9.4
Hamilton County	10.7
Hansford County	6.9
Hardeman County	9.9
Hardin County	10.2
Harris County	6.0
Harrison County	9.7
Hartley County	9.9
Haskell County	7.6
Hays County	8.7
Hemphill County	7.7
Henderson County	12.3
Hidalgo County	4.5
Hill County	11.3
Hockley County	6.9
Hood County	14.7
Hopkins County	10.4
Houston County	11.3
Howard County	10.4
Hudspeth County	7.5
Hunt County	12.3
Hutchinson County	11.8
Irion County	15.4
Jack County	10.7
Jackson County	8.9
Jasper County	12.3
Jeff Davis County	13.8
Jefferson County	9.2
Jim Hogg County	7.5

Table 19. Percent of the Civilian Population 18 Years and Over Who Are Veterans, Selected Counties by State/ Territory, United States, American Community Survey 5-Year Estimates, 2013—*Continued*

(Percent.)

Location	Percent veterans	Location	Percent veterans	Location	Percent veterans
Texas cnt'd		**Texas** cnt'd		**Utah** cnt'd	
Jim Wells County	7.4	Reeves County	5.6	Garfield County	11.8
Johnson County	9.7	Refugio County	10.7	Grand County	8.6
Jones County	10.9	Roberts County	4.5	Iron County	8.2
Karnes County	10.0	Robertson County	7.7	Juab County	8.2
Kaufman County	9.3	Rockwall County	8.8	Kane County	12.7
Kendall County	14.1	Runnels County	11.2	Millard County	8.9
Kenedy County	8.1	Rusk County	10.6	Morgan County	11.7
Kent County	8.3	Sabine County	17.4	Piute County	14.6
Kerr County	15.8	San Augustine County	12.9	Rich County	11.3
Kimble County	10.8	San Jacinto County	11.3	Salt Lake County	6.7
King County	2.2	San Patricio County	11.4	San Juan County	6.1
Kinney County	17.8	San Saba County	9.5	Sanpete County	8.7
Kleberg County	9.5	Schleicher County	7.3	Sevier County	8.9
Knox County	10.0	Scurry County	8.4	Summit County	7.1
Lamar County	10.0	Shackelford County	7.8	Tooele County	10.0
Lamb County	6.1	Shelby County	9.7	Uintah County	8.6
Lampasas County	21.9	Sherman County	8.5	Utah County	5.0
La Salle County	5.3	Smith County	9.8	Wasatch County	5.3
Lavaca County	8.6	Somervell County	12.1	Washington County	10.8
Lee County	11.2	Starr County	2.5	Wayne County	10.6
Leon County	14.3	Stephens County	8.6	Weber County	10.3
Liberty County	9.5	Sterling County	2.3		
Limestone County	10.1	Stonewall County	11.9	**Vermont**	9.7
Lipscomb County	9.7	Sutton County	6.6	Addison County	8.8
Live Oak County	13.1	Swisher County	10.6	Bennington County	11.3
Llano County	17.0	Tarrant County	8.9	Caledonia County	10.9
Loving County	2.5	Taylor County	12.4	Chittenden County	7.4
Lubbock County	7.4	Terrell County	8.9	Essex County	13.0
Lynn County	6.1	Terry County	5.3	Franklin County	10.9
McCulloch County	9.3	Throckmorton County	10.6	Grand Isle County	9.9
McLennan County	9.1	Titus County	7.7	Lamoille County	8.5
McMullen County	8.9	Tom Green County	11.0	Orange County	9.7
Madison County	8.1	Travis County	6.6	Orleans County	11.0
Marion County	14.2	Trinity County	12.5	Rutland County	10.6
Martin County	6.8	Tyler County	11.0	Washington County	10.1
Mason County	12.7	Upshur County	11.8	Windham County	10.6
Matagorda County	9.7	Upton County	6.6	Windsor County	11.6
Maverick County	3.2	Uvalde County	7.5		
Medina County	12.7	Val Verde County	9.1	**Virginia**	11.9
Menard County	17.2	Van Zandt County	12.0	Accomack County	12.4
Midland County	8.6	Victoria County	9.4	Albemarle County	8.7
Milam County	10.6	Walker County	8.8	Alleghany County	11.1
Mills County	11.2	Waller County	6.8	Amelia County	10.9
Mitchell County	8.3	Ward County	10.9	Amherst County	10.0
Montague County	12.2	Washington County	9.1	Appomattox County	12.6
Montgomery County	9.4	Webb County	3.6	Arlington County	7.1
Moore County	3.9	Wharton County	6.6	Augusta County	10.8
Morris County	12.1	Wheeler County	7.7	Bath County	10.8
Motley County	8.4	Wichita County	12.6	Bedford County	13.1
Nacogdoches County	6.8	Wilbarger County	8.9	Bland County	12.9
Navarro County	8.9	Willacy County	6.6	Botetourt County	12.2
Newton County	13.7	Williamson County	10.6	Brunswick County	6.4
Nolan County	8.9	Wilson County	14.3	Buchanan County	6.0
Nueces County	11.4	Winkler County	5.7	Buckingham County	9.3
Ochiltree County	7.0	Wise County	10.3	Campbell County	11.2
Oldham County	5.9	Wood County	14.5	Caroline County	12.8
Orange County	10.5	Yoakum County	6.6	Carroll County	10.6
Palo Pinto County	11.5	Young County	9.6	Charles City County	11.9
Panola County	9.6	Zapata County	5.1	Charlotte County	10.5
Parker County	12.0	Zavala County	5.2	Chesterfield County	11.4
Parmer County	5.2			Clarke County	14.8
Pecos County	7.0	**Utah**	7.5	Craig County	16.3
Polk County	12.6	Beaver County	8.8	Culpeper County	11.0
Potter County	8.6	Box Elder County	8.2	Cumberland County	10.9
Presidio County	6.8	Cache County	5.4	Dickenson County	7.6
Rains County	15.8	Carbon County	8.5	Dinwiddie County	11.2
Randall County	10.1	Daggett County	16.4	Essex County	10.5
Reagan County	3.8	Davis County	9.8	Fairfax County	10.1
Real County	14.5	Duchesne County	7.4	Fauquier County	13.0
Red River County	10.6	Emery County	7.3	Floyd County	10.8

Table 19. Percent of the Civilian Population 18 Years and Over Who Are Veterans, Selected Counties by State/Territory, United States, American Community Survey 5-Year Estimates, 2013—*Continued*

(Percent.)

Location	Percent veterans
Virginia cnt'd	
Fluvanna County	11.4
Franklin County	10.5
Frederick County	12.5
Giles County	9.8
Gloucester County	15.6
Goochland County	11.7
Grayson County	8.7
Greene County	13.3
Greensville County	10.0
Halifax County	9.7
Hanover County	10.5
Henrico County	9.3
Henry County	10.1
Highland County	13.5
Isle of Wight County	15.4
James City County	16.9
King and Queen County	12.5
King George County	17.7
King William County	9.9
Lancaster County	15.3
Lee County	8.9
Loudoun County	9.0
Louisa County	11.3
Lunenburg County	11.5
Madison County	13.1
Mathews County	15.5
Mecklenburg County	11.1
Middlesex County	13.9
Montgomery County	6.1
Nelson County	11.0
New Kent County	13.2
Northampton County	11.5
Northumberland County	16.5
Nottoway County	9.9
Orange County	13.5
Page County	9.9
Patrick County	10.6
Pittsylvania County	10.3
Powhatan County	10.8
Prince Edward County	7.5
Prince George County	16.4
Prince William County	13.8
Pulaski County	11.4
Rappahannock County	11.6
Richmond County	6.8
Roanoke County	11.7
Rockbridge County	14.2
Rockingham County	8.2
Russell County	6.4
Scott County	8.1
Shenandoah County	11.0
Smyth County	9.4
Southampton County	14.8
Spotsylvania County	14.6
Stafford County	19.6
Surry County	12.8
Sussex County	11.1
Tazewell County	9.1
Warren County	12.4
Washington County	10.4
Westmoreland County	12.5
Wise County	8.9
Wythe County	9.5
York County	21.7
Alexandria city	9.3
Bedford city	12.9
Bristol city	10.4
Buena Vista city	8.8
Charlottesville city	4.7
Chesapeake city	16.0
Virginia cnt'd	
Colonial Heights city	14.6
Covington city	13.7
Danville city	12.0
Emporia city	7.4
Fairfax city	9.7
Falls Church city	7.3
Franklin city	13.0
Fredericksburg city	9.4
Galax city	10.3
Hampton city	19.8
Harrisonburg city	3.9
Hopewell city	11.3
Lexington city	5.2
Lynchburg city	9.0
Manassas city	9.3
Manassas Park city	8.2
Martinsville city	9.7
Newport News city	16.7
Norfolk city	16.5
Norton city	8.3
Petersburg city	10.7
Poquoson city	15.0
Portsmouth city	15.3
Radford city	6.4
Richmond city	7.2
Roanoke city	10.2
Salem city	11.1
Staunton city	9.4
Suffolk city	17.6
Virginia Beach city	19.4
Waynesboro city	11.4
Williamsburg city	7.3
Winchester city	8.0
Washington	11.2
Adams County	7.1
Asotin County	12.8
Benton County	11.1
Chelan County	10.4
Clallam County	15.5
Clark County	11.5
Columbia County	12.7
Cowlitz County	13.5
Douglas County	11.0
Ferry County	14.5
Franklin County	6.3
Garfield County	15.1
Grant County	9.1
Grays Harbor County	13.3
Island County	21.5
Jefferson County	17.4
King County	7.7
Kitsap County	19.1
Kittitas County	10.7
Klickitat County	13.8
Lewis County	13.6
Lincoln County	15.1
Mason County	17.5
Okanogan County	12.4
Pacific County	18.3
Pend Oreille County	14.5
Pierce County	14.9
San Juan County	11.5
Skagit County	12.9
Skamania County	14.7
Snohomish County	10.5
Spokane County	12.7
Stevens County	16.6
Thurston County	15.0
Wahkiakum County	13.0
Washington cnt'd	
Walla Walla County	11.6
Whatcom County	9.2
Whitman County	6.5
Yakima County	8.3
West Virginia	10.9
Barbour County	10.0
Berkeley County	13.4
Boone County	9.4
Braxton County	11.3
Brooke County	10.5
Cabell County	10.2
Calhoun County	10.4
Clay County	9.6
Doddridge County	12.2
Fayette County	10.8
Gilmer County	10.0
Grant County	9.8
Greenbrier County	13.6
Hampshire County	7.8
Hancock County	11.7
Hardy County	9.7
Harrison County	11.1
Jackson County	12.6
Jefferson County	11.5
Kanawha County	10.9
Lewis County	11.3
Lincoln County	10.6
Logan County	10.0
McDowell County	8.5
Marion County	11.1
Marshall County	12.6
Mason County	13.9
Mercer County	10.9
Mineral County	11.2
Mingo County	6.9
Monongalia County	6.6
Monroe County	9.8
Morgan County	9.7
Nicholas County	9.2
Ohio County	10.5
Pendleton County	12.2
Pleasants County	11.1
Pocahontas County	12.9
Preston County	11.5
Putnam County	11.2
Raleigh County	12.6
Randolph County	11.9
Ritchie County	12.9
Roane County	10.4
Summers County	11.5
Taylor County	12.3
Tucker County	12.4
Tyler County	11.3
Upshur County	10.1
Wayne County	10.7
Webster County	9.2
Wetzel County	11.4
Wirt County	11.5
Wood County	12.1
Wyoming County	8.8
Wisconsin	9.3
Adams County	14.6
Ashland County	11.8
Barron County	10.7
Bayfield County	13.9
Brown County	8.9
Buffalo County	10.4
Burnett County	15.6

Table 19. Percent of the Civilian Population 18 Years and Over Who Are Veterans, Selected Counties by State/ Territory, United States, American Community Survey 5-Year Estimates, 2013—*Continued*

(Percent.)

Location	Percent veterans	Location	Percent veterans	Location	Percent veterans
Wisconsin cnt'd		**Wisconsin** cnt'd		**Puerto Rico** cnt'd	
Calumet County	8.7	Walworth County	8.9	Coamo Municipio	4.4
Chippewa County	11.3	Washburn County	13.3	Comerío Municipio	1.7
Clark County	9.0	Washington County	8.8	Corozal Municipio	2.7
Columbia County	10.8	Waukesha County	8.9	Culebra Municipio	5.8
Crawford County	12.1	Waupaca County	12.2	Dorado Municipio	4.9
Dane County	7.3	Waushara County	13.3	Fajardo Municipio	6.6
Dodge County	9.6	Winnebago County	9.8	Florida Municipio	2.2
Door County	10.6	Wood County	10.7	Guánica Municipio	3.8
Douglas County	11.5			Guayama Municipio	3.0
Dunn County	8.3	**Wyoming**	11.8	Guayanilla Municipio	3.4
Eau Claire County	9.5	Albany County	7.5	Guaynabo Municipio	4.1
Florence County	15.1	Big Horn County	12.2	Gurabo Municipio	3.8
Fond du Lac County	10.0	Campbell County	8.2	Hatillo Municipio	3.9
Forest County	13.0	Carbon County	13.2	Hormigueros Municipio	4.5
Grant County	8.1	Converse County	12.8	Humacao Municipio	3.4
Green County	8.8	Crook County	9.8	Isabela Municipio	4.4
Green Lake County	10.4	Fremont County	11.5	Jayuya Municipio	3.1
Iowa County	8.8	Goshen County	11.8	Juana Díaz Municipio	4.3
Iron County	15.3	Hot Springs County	17.5	Juncos Municipio	3.3
Jackson County	12.1	Johnson County	13.8	Lajas Municipio	3.8
Jefferson County	9.6	Laramie County	17.7	Lares Municipio	2.1
Juneau County	13.3	Lincoln County	8.2	Las Marías Municipio	3.1
Kenosha County	9.0	Natrona County	10.8	Las Piedras Municipio	2.9
Kewaunee County	10.7	Niobrara County	9.4	Loíza Municipio	2.6
La Crosse County	9.6	Park County	11.4	Luquillo Municipio	4.3
Lafayette County	8.6	Platte County	13.6	Manatí Municipio	3.2
Langlade County	12.1	Sheridan County	13.6	Maricao Municipio	3.5
Lincoln County	11.8	Sublette County	9.5	Maunabo Municipio	1.8
Manitowoc County	11.1	Sweetwater County	11.4	Mayagüez Municipio	3.9
Marathon County	9.7	Teton County	7.8	Moca Municipio	3.0
Marinette County	13.4	Uinta County	9.2	Morovis Municipio	2.0
Marquette County	13.9	Washakie County	11.9	Naguabo Municipio	4.2
Menominee County	11.4	Weston County	13.8	Naranjito Municipio	2.0
Milwaukee County	7.4			Orocovis Municipio	3.0
Monroe County	15.9	**Puerto Rico**	3.8	Patillas Municipio	3.6
Oconto County	11.8	Adjuntas Municipio	2.0	Peñuelas Municipio	3.5
Oneida County	14.4	Aguada Municipio	2.3	Ponce Municipio	4.8
Outagamie County	9.1	Aguadilla Municipio	4.1	Quebradillas Municipio	3.5
Ozaukee County	9.1	Aguas Buenas Municipio	3.2	Rincón Municipio	3.8
Pepin County	9.7	Aibonito Municipio	3.7	Río Grande Municipio	2.9
Pierce County	8.5	Añasco Municipio	2.6	Sabana Grande Municipio	4.3
Polk County	10.8	Arecibo Municipio	3.4	Salinas Municipio	4.1
Portage County	8.5	Arroyo Municipio	2.5	San Germán Municipio	4.2
Price County	13.2	Barceloneta Municipio	3.6	San Juan Municipio	4.1
Racine County	9.6	Barranquitas Municipio	2.6	San Lorenzo Municipio	3.1
Richland County	9.9	Bayamón Municipio	4.7	San Sebastián Municipio	3.2
Rock County	9.9	Cabo Rojo Municipio	3.5	Santa Isabel Municipio	4.1
Rusk County	11.6	Caguas Municipio	4.2	Toa Alta Municipio	3.2
St. Croix County	9.4	Camuy Municipio	2.6	Toa Baja Municipio	4.7
Sauk County	10.4	Canóvanas Municipio	2.6	Trujillo Alto Municipio	4.2
Sawyer County	12.6	Carolina Municipio	4.8	Utuado Municipio	2.3
Shawano County	11.3	Cataño Municipio	3.7	Vega Alta Municipio	2.6
Sheboygan County	9.7	Cayey Municipio	4.2	Vega Baja Municipio	2.3
Taylor County	9.6	Ceiba Municipio	5.9	Vieques Municipio	5.4
Trempealeau County	9.6	Ciales Municipio	2.4	Villalba Municipio	2.4
Vernon County	10.6	Cidra Municipio	3.1	Yabucoa Municipio	2.7
Vilas County	14.5			Yauco Municipio	4.2

Table 20. Percent of the Civilian Population 18 Years and Over Who Are Veterans, Selected Places by State/Territory, United States, American Community Survey 1-Year Estimates, 2013

(Percent.)

Location	Percent veterans
United States	8.1
Alabama	9.6
Birmingham city	7.1
Dothan city	11.2
Hoover city	9.6
Huntsville city	11.5
Mobile city	8.8
Montgomery city	10.1
Tuscaloosa city	6.4
Alaska	11.9
Anchorage municipality	11.9
Arizona	10.0
Avondale city	8.3
Casas Adobes CDP	13.1
Chandler city	7.4
Flagstaff city	5.3
Gilbert town	6.3
Glendale city	9.3
Goodyear city	11.8
Mesa city	9.4
Peoria city	11.0
Phoenix city	6.6
San Tan Valley CDP	9.7
Scottsdale city	9.4
Surprise city	16.6
Tempe city	5.6
Tucson city	9.0
Yuma city	11.6
Arkansas	9.7
Fayetteville city	4.0
Fort Smith city	8.4
Jonesboro city	9.2
Little Rock city	7.6
North Little Rock city	11.8
Springdale city	7.0
California	6.0
Alameda city	7.4
Alhambra city	2.9
Anaheim city	4.6
Antioch city	5.8
Apple Valley town	11.4
Arden-Arcade CDP	7.3
Bakersfield city	5.7
Baldwin Park city	1.9
Bellflower city	5.6
Berkeley city	3.1
Buena Park city	5.3
Burbank city	6.5
Camarillo city	13.3
Carlsbad city	8.5
Carmichael CDP	11.5
Carson city	4.9
Chico city	5.3
Chino city	5.5
Chino Hills city	5.4
Chula Vista city	9.4
Citrus Heights city	13.3
Clovis city	7.7
Compton city	2.9
Concord city	7.2
Corona city	5.8
Costa Mesa city	5.4
Daly City city	4.8
Davis city	3.7
Downey city	4.7
California cnt'd	
East Los Angeles CDP	1.7
El Cajon city	8.0
Elk Grove city	7.1
El Monte city	2.4
Escondido city	7.0
Fairfield city	9.7
Folsom city	7.1
Fontana city	4.2
Fremont city	3.9
Fresno city	5.5
Fullerton city	4.2
Garden Grove city	4.0
Glendale city	2.8
Hawthorne city	3.3
Hayward city	5.0
Hemet city	8.5
Hesperia city	4.2
Huntington Beach city	6.6
Indio city	6.7
Inglewood city	4.7
Irvine city	3.6
Jurupa Valley city	4.8
Lake Forest city	7.5
Lakewood city	5.0
Lancaster city	8.6
Livermore city	6.1
Long Beach city	4.9
Los Angeles city	3.2
Lynwood city	1.5
Manteca city	5.4
Menifee city	11.1
Merced city	4.0
Milpitas city	4.2
Mission Viejo city	9.1
Modesto city	6.8
Moreno Valley city	6.3
Mountain View city	3.9
Murrieta city	10.0
Napa city	7.7
Newport Beach city	5.0
Norwalk city	4.0
Oakland city	4.1
Oceanside city	11.4
Ontario city	3.5
Orange city	5.0
Oxnard city	5.9
Palmdale city	5.1
Palo Alto city	5.5
Pasadena city	4.1
Perris city	5.3
Pittsburg city	5.1
Pleasanton city	6.7
Pomona city	2.7
Rancho Cordova city	8.7
Rancho Cucamonga city	5.8
Redding city	9.5
Redlands city	8.7
Redondo Beach city	5.3
Redwood City city	6.6
Rialto city	4.9
Richmond city	4.3
Riverside city	5.4
Roseville city	9.7
Sacramento city	6.9
Salinas city	4.2
San Bernardino city	5.8
San Buenaventura (Ventura) city	7.8
San Clemente city	7.2
San Diego city	8.7
San Francisco city	3.4
California cnt'd	
San Jose city	4.0
San Leandro city	4.4
San Marcos city	8.0
San Mateo city	4.8
San Ramon city	4.4
Santa Ana city	2.4
Santa Barbara city	6.3
Santa Clara city	3.8
Santa Clarita city	5.2
Santa Maria city	6.4
Santa Monica city	3.7
Santa Rosa city	7.5
Simi Valley city	6.9
South Gate city	1.7
South San Francisco city	5.1
South Whittier CDP	3.4
Stockton city	5.1
Sunnyvale city	5.2
Temecula city	9.2
Thousand Oaks city	6.5
Torrance city	6.3
Tracy city	8.0
Turlock city	4.5
Tustin city	3.4
Union City city	3.5
Upland city	6.9
Vacaville city	13.8
Vallejo city	9.3
Victorville city	5.8
Visalia city	5.5
Vista city	7.7
Walnut Creek city	8.0
West Covina city	4.8
Westminster city	4.9
Whittier city	5.1
Yorba Linda city	6.6
Yuba City city	10.1
Colorado	9.5
Arvada city	10.0
Aurora city	9.1
Boulder city	4.2
Centennial city	7.3
Colorado Springs city	16.7
Denver city	6.1
Fort Collins city	6.6
Greeley city	7.4
Highlands Ranch CDP	6.7
Lakewood city	9.4
Longmont city	7.7
Loveland city	9.7
Pueblo city	11.5
Thornton city	8.0
Westminster city	7.7
Connecticut	6.8
Bridgeport city	4.3
Danbury city	5.4
Hartford city	2.3
New Britain city	5.3
New Haven city	3.8
Norwalk city	4.9
Stamford city	3.3
Waterbury city	6.2
Delaware	9.5
Wilmington city	6.5
District of Columbia	5.2
Washington city	5.2

Table 20. Percent of the Civilian Population 18 Years and Over Who Are Veterans, Selected Places by State/ Territory, United States, American Community Survey 1-Year Estimates, 2013—*Continued*

(Percent.)

Location	Percent veterans
Florida	9.4
Alafaya CDP	8.3
Boca Raton city	7.5
Boynton Beach city	8.5
Brandon CDP	11.3
Cape Coral city	10.6
Clearwater city	9.2
Coral Springs city	6.0
Davie town	5.1
Deerfield Beach city	7.0
Deltona city	12.8
Fort Lauderdale city	7.3
Fort Myers city	8.3
Gainesville city	6.1
Hialeah city	1.1
Hollywood city	6.2
Jacksonville city	12.0
Kendall CDP	5.0
Kissimmee city	3.6
Lakeland city	9.6
Largo city	12.7
Lauderhill city	5.1
Lehigh Acres CDP	5.3
Melbourne city	14.7
Miami city	1.9
Miami Beach city	1.9
Miami Gardens city	3.0
Miramar city	3.9
Orlando city	6.5
Palm Bay city	10.5
Palm Coast city	13.4
Pembroke Pines city	4.8
Pine Hills CDP	4.3
Plantation city	3.8
Pompano Beach city	8.6
Port St. Lucie city	9.6
Riverview CDP	12.6
St. Petersburg city	9.6
Spring Hill CDP	12.6
Sunrise city	6.3
Tallahassee city	6.3
Tampa city	8.5
Town 'n' Country CDP	7.9
Weston city	5.9
West Palm Beach city	5.1
Georgia	8.7
Albany city	9.2
Athens-Clarke County unified government (balance)	4.7
Atlanta city	6.0
Augusta-Richmond County consolidated government (balance)	12.6
Columbus city	13.9
Johns Creek city	3.8
Macon city	6.3
Roswell city	7.4
Sandy Springs city	4.6
Savannah city	10.8
Warner Robins city	14.7
Hawaii	10.3
Urban Honolulu CDP	8.5
Idaho	10.1
Boise City city	10.0
Meridian city	7.7
Nampa city	9.3
Illinois	6.7
Arlington Heights village	5.7
Illinois cnt'd	
Aurora city	4.1
Bloomington city	7.4
Bolingbrook village	4.5
Champaign city	5.6
Chicago city	3.9
Cicero town	2.0
Decatur city	10.3
Elgin city	5.7
Evanston city	3.6
Joliet city	5.9
Naperville city	4.6
Palatine village	3.9
Peoria city	5.6
Rockford city	8.9
Schaumburg village	4.4
Skokie village	3.5
Springfield city	10.1
Waukegan city	5.9
Indiana	8.4
Bloomington city	4.4
Carmel city	6.0
Evansville city	8.9
Fishers town	6.6
Fort Wayne city	7.7
Gary city	10.5
Hammond city	7.8
Indianapolis city (balance)	7.2
Lafayette city	6.5
Muncie city	6.9
South Bend city	6.4
Iowa	8.8
Cedar Rapids city	9.7
Davenport city	9.1
Des Moines city	6.6
Iowa City city	2.7
Sioux City city	9.0
Waterloo city	6.2
Kansas	9.1
Kansas City city	6.7
Lawrence city	4.5
Olathe city	7.1
Overland Park city	7.4
Topeka city	10.4
Wichita city	9.0
Kentucky	8.7
Lexington-Fayette urban county	7.2
Louisville/Jefferson County metro government (balance)	8.8
Louisiana	7.7
Baton Rouge city	6.0
Bossier City city	12.4
Kenner city	6.5
Lafayette city	6.6
Lake Charles city	6.9
Metairie CDP	6.5
New Orleans city	5.9
Shreveport city	8.3
Maine	11.2
Portland city	5.5
Maryland	8.8
Baltimore city	6.2
Bethesda CDP	6.0
Columbia CDP	8.4
Ellicott City CDP	8.1
Maryland cnt'd	
Frederick city	9.5
Gaithersburg city	6.3
Germantown CDP	4.3
Glen Burnie CDP	10.5
Silver Spring CDP	5.9
Waldorf CDP	16.1
Massachusetts	6.4
Boston city	2.8
Brockton city	6.3
Cambridge city	1.5
Fall River city	5.7
Framingham CDP	5.5
Lawrence city	2.2
Lowell city	3.8
Lynn city	4.9
New Bedford city	6.4
Newton city	3.6
Quincy city	6.1
Somerville city	3.8
Springfield city	5.4
Worcester city	4.9
Michigan	8.1
Ann Arbor city	3.4
Dearborn city	5.2
Detroit city	6.0
Farmington Hills city	6.5
Flint city	7.1
Grand Rapids city	5.9
Kalamazoo city	6.3
Lansing city	7.6
Livonia city	8.1
Rochester Hills city	5.2
Southfield city	8.0
Sterling Heights city	6.3
Troy city	4.5
Warren city	7.6
Westland city	6.2
Wyoming city	4.3
Minnesota	8.2
Bloomington city	9.1
Brooklyn Park city	6.2
Duluth city	7.8
Eagan city	6.3
Maple Grove city	8.4
Minneapolis city	5.1
Plymouth city	5.6
Rochester city	7.0
St. Cloud city	8.1
St. Paul city	4.7
Woodbury city	9.5
Mississippi	8.2
Gulfport city	16.7
Jackson city	5.6
Missouri	9.4
Columbia city	5.3
Independence city	9.3
Kansas City city	8.5
Lee's Summit city	8.9
O'Fallon city	9.4
St. Charles city	7.9
St. Joseph city	9.4
St. Louis city	7.2
Springfield city	8.5
Montana	10.5
Billings city	9.5

Table 20. Percent of the Civilian Population 18 Years and Over Who Are Veterans, Selected Places by State/ Territory, United States, American Community Survey 1-Year Estimates, 2013—*Continued*

(Percent.)

Location	Percent veterans
Montana cnt'd	
Missoula city	6.2
Nebraska	8.9
Lincoln city	7.1
Omaha city	7.8
Nevada	10.2
Enterprise CDP	7.8
Henderson city	11.8
Las Vegas city	10.0
North Las Vegas city	11.0
Paradise CDP	7.4
Reno city	7.6
Sparks city	10.7
Spring Valley CDP	6.9
Sunrise Manor CDP	9.8
New Hampshire	10.1
Manchester city	7.1
Nashua city	9.2
New Jersey	5.6
Bayonne city	7.1
Camden city	4.7
Clifton city	4.2
East Orange city	5.0
Elizabeth city	2.3
Jersey City city	2.5
Newark city	2.9
Passaic city	2.0
Paterson city	1.7
Toms River CDP	8.1
Trenton city	5.2
Union City city	1.1
New Mexico	10.2
Albuquerque city	9.9
Las Cruces city	9.7
Rio Rancho city	13.6
Santa Fe city	8.4
New York	5.2
Albany city	4.1
Buffalo city	7.0
Cheektowaga CDP	9.9
Mount Vernon city	3.9
New Rochelle city	5.3
New York city	2.6
Rochester city	4.5
Schenectady city	5.8
Syracuse city	5.3
Yonkers city	3.7
North Carolina	9.1
Asheville city	8.2
Cary town	6.2
Charlotte city	6.1
Concord city	6.8
Durham city	6.3
Fayetteville city	21.5
Gastonia city	7.7
Greensboro city	7.0
Greenville city	4.6
High Point city	7.2
Jacksonville city	19.9
Raleigh city	5.8
Wilmington city	8.5
Winston-Salem city	7.4
North Dakota	8.8
Bismarck city	8.6
Fargo city	6.4
Ohio	8.9
Akron city	8.0
Canton city	10.0
Cincinnati city	5.3
Cleveland city	7.2
Columbus city	6.4
Dayton city	8.8
Lorain city	9.3
Parma city	8.8
Toledo city	8.3
Youngstown city	8.2
Oklahoma	9.7
Broken Arrow city	8.2
Edmond city	9.7
Lawton city	15.7
Norman city	9.0
Oklahoma City city	9.2
Tulsa city	8.1
Oregon	9.5
Beaverton city	5.4
Bend city	6.8
Eugene city	7.4
Gresham city	8.1
Hillsboro city	7.2
Medford city	11.6
Portland city	6.2
Salem city	9.7
Pennsylvania	8.5
Allentown city	5.7
Bethlehem city	4.5
Erie city	8.6
Philadelphia city	5.5
Pittsburgh city	7.4
Reading city	4.6
Scranton city	7.4
Rhode Island	7.7
Cranston city	8.6
Pawtucket city	4.3
Providence city	2.9
Warwick city	9.0
South Carolina	10.0
Charleston city	8.9
Columbia city	8.4
Mount Pleasant town	8.4
North Charleston city	11.6
Rock Hill city	9.5
South Dakota	9.8
Rapid City city	13.5
Sioux Falls city	7.5
Tennessee	9.3
Chattanooga city	8.2
Clarksville city	21.4
Franklin city	5.9
Jackson city	9.5
Johnson City city	13.4
Knoxville city	7.1
Memphis city	6.9
Murfreesboro city	9.0
Nashville-Davidson metropolitan government (balance)	6.7
Texas	7.7
Abilene city	11.5
Allen city	6.6
Amarillo city	10.4
Arlington city	7.2
Atascocita CDP	9.0
Austin city	5.3
Baytown city	7.0
Beaumont city	7.7
Brownsville city	3.7
Bryan city	6.9
Carrollton city	5.9
College Station city	4.3
Corpus Christi city	11.0
Dallas city	4.8
Denton city	6.1
Edinburg city	5.5
El Paso city	9.6
Flower Mound town	7.0
Fort Worth city	7.4
Frisco city	6.1
Garland city	6.5
Grand Prairie city	6.3
Harlingen city	7.8
Houston city	4.7
Irving city	3.6
Killeen city	31.7
Laredo city	3.0
League City city	9.2
Lewisville city	5.1
Longview city	8.8
Lubbock city	6.7
McAllen city	5.2
McKinney city	6.7
Mesquite city	6.3
Midland city	6.6
Mission city	4.6
Missouri City city	7.4
North Richland Hills city	9.4
Odessa city	6.7
Pasadena city	5.6
Pearland city	7.0
Pharr city	3.7
Plano city	5.9
Richardson city	6.1
Round Rock city	7.7
San Angelo city	10.8
San Antonio city	9.7
Sugar Land city	4.6
Temple city	13.1
The Woodlands CDP	6.5
Tyler city	7.7
Victoria city	9.2
Waco city	6.4
Wichita Falls city	10.9
Utah	6.6
Layton city	9.5
Ogden city	9.7
Orem city	3.9
Provo city	2.9
St. George city	10.8
Salt Lake City city	5.9
Sandy city	7.1
West Jordan city	5.2
West Valley City city	6.0
Vermont	8.2

Table 20. Percent of the Civilian Population 18 Years and Over Who Are Veterans, Selected Places by State/Territory, United States, American Community Survey 1-Year Estimates, 2013—*Continued*

(Percent.)

Location	Percent veterans
Virginia	10.9
Alexandria city	8.2
Arlington CDP	6.5
Centreville CDP	6.2
Chesapeake city	15.0
Dale City CDP	14.0
Hampton city	17.8
Lynchburg city	8.4
Newport News city	14.2
Norfolk city	15.6
Portsmouth city	15.4
Richmond city	6.1
Roanoke city	10.6
Suffolk city	16.5
Virginia Beach city	18.2
Washington	10.2
Auburn city	11.2
Bellevue city	5.4
Bellingham city	7.4
Washington cnt'd	
Everett city	8.3
Federal Way city	8.8
Kennewick city	7.0
Kent city	7.9
Kirkland city	5.3
Pasco city	3.9
Renton city	6.8
Seattle city	5.6
Spokane city	9.9
Spokane Valley city	12.1
Tacoma city	12.7
Vancouver city	9.6
Yakima city	8.3
West Virginia	10.2
Wisconsin	8.3
Appleton city	7.2
Eau Claire city	9.0
Wisconsin cnt'd	
Green Bay city	7.8
Kenosha city	7.0
Madison city	4.5
Milwaukee city	5.8
Oshkosh city	7.6
Racine city	7.6
Waukesha city	6.1
Wyoming	11.1
Puerto Rico	3.2
Bayamón zona urbana	4.2
Caguas zona urbana	4.3
Carolina zona urbana	4.3
Guaynabo zona urbana	5.1
Mayagüez zona urbana	5.1
Ponce zona urbana	4.9
San Juan zona urbana	3.4

Table 21. Percent of the Civilian Population 18 Years and Over Who Are Veterans, Selected Places by State/Territory, United States, American Community Survey 3-Year Estimates, 2013

(Percent.)

Location	Percent veterans
United States	8.7
Alabama	10.3
Alabaster city	9.5
Albertville city	8.2
Anniston city	13.4
Athens city	9.4
Auburn city	4.5
Bessemer city	9.8
Birmingham city	7.7
Daphne city	11.4
Decatur city	8.9
Dothan city	12.0
Enterprise city	21.7
Florence city	8.9
Gadsden city	10.5
Homewood city	4.3
Hoover city	10.0
Huntsville city	11.8
Madison city	15.5
Mobile city	10.2
Montgomery city	11.4
Mountain Brook city	7.8
Northport city	7.7
Opelika city	10.0
Oxford city	11.8
Pelham city	7.8
Phenix City city	12.6
Prattville city	14.3
Prichard city	8.7
Selma city	6.6
Tillmans Corner CDP	9.1
Trussville city	9.8
Tuscaloosa city	6.3
Vestavia Hills city	8.4
Alaska	13.2
Anchorage municipality	13.6
Badger CDP	22.7
Fairbanks city	14.1
Juneau city and borough	10.9
Arizona	10.5
Anthem CDP	12.6
Apache Junction city	17.6
Avondale city	9.7
Buckeye town	7.9
Bullhead City city	17.2
Casa Grande city	13.1
Casas Adobes CDP	13.0
Catalina Foothills CDP	12.8
Chandler city	8.1
Drexel Heights CDP	11.6
El Mirage city	8.3
Flagstaff city	5.6
Florence town	12.7
Fortuna Foothills CDP	21.4
Fountain Hills town	13.4
Gilbert town	8.2
Glendale city	9.5
Goodyear city	14.6
Green Valley CDP	22.2
Kingman city	15.1
Lake Havasu City city	18.2
Marana town	13.9
Maricopa city	14.3
Mesa city	10.2
Nogales city	3.5
Oro Valley town	14.8
Peoria city	10.7
Arizona cnt'd	
Phoenix city	7.0
Prescott city	18.6
Prescott Valley town	14.1
Queen Creek town	10.7
Sahuarita town	13.6
San Luis city	2.0
San Tan Valley CDP	10.4
Scottsdale city	9.4
Sierra Vista city	27.6
Sun City CDP	21.7
Sun City West CDP	26.5
Surprise city	15.0
Tempe city	6.4
Tucson city	10.1
Yuma city	10.5
Arkansas	10.3
Bella Vista town	16.0
Benton city	10.5
Bentonville city	6.7
Cabot city	19.8
Conway city	7.2
Fayetteville city	5.4
Fort Smith city	9.1
Hot Springs city	11.9
Jacksonville city	17.3
Jonesboro city	8.3
Little Rock city	8.3
North Little Rock city	11.5
Paragould city	10.7
Pine Bluff city	8.9
Rogers city	7.0
Russellville city	7.1
Searcy city	6.5
Sherwood city	11.4
Springdale city	7.2
Texarkana city	10.3
Van Buren city	8.8
West Memphis city	10.8
California	6.4
Adelanto city	5.3
Agoura Hills city	4.1
Alameda city	7.2
Alhambra city	2.6
Aliso Viejo city	4.4
Altadena CDP	4.9
American Canyon city	7.1
Anaheim city	4.6
Antelope CDP	8.3
Antioch city	6.7
Apple Valley town	12.5
Arcadia city	3.8
Arden-Arcade CDP	8.3
Arvin city	1.1
Ashland CDP	3.3
Atascadero city	10.8
Atwater city	8.3
Azusa city	2.5
Bakersfield city	6.0
Baldwin Park city	2.3
Banning city	13.3
Barstow city	14.3
Bay Point CDP	6.8
Beaumont city	6.6
Bell city	1.9
Bellflower city	4.8
Bell Gardens city	1.0
Belmont city	6.9
Benicia city	8.8
California cnt'd	
Berkeley city	3.9
Beverly Hills city	4.2
Bloomington CDP	3.6
Blythe city	6.7
Brawley city	5.1
Brea city	6.3
Brentwood city	8.5
Buena Park city	4.8
Burbank city	5.5
Burlingame city	4.1
Calabasas city	5.3
Calexico city	1.2
Camarillo city	11.1
Campbell city	5.6
Carlsbad city	8.5
Carmichael CDP	11.1
Carson city	5.9
Casa de Oro-Mount Helix CDP	12.4
Castro Valley CDP	7.2
Cathedral City city	6.2
Ceres city	5.1
Cerritos city	5.2
Chico city	6.0
Chino city	6.0
Chino Hills city	5.5
Chula Vista city	10.6
Citrus Heights city	12.0
Claremont city	7.3
Clovis city	8.8
Coachella city	0.9
Colton city	4.5
Compton city	3.2
Concord city	7.9
Corcoran city	7.3
Corona city	5.6
Coronado city	19.9
Costa Mesa city	4.9
Covina city	6.1
Cudahy city	1.0
Culver City city	4.4
Cupertino city	2.6
Cypress city	7.1
Daly City city	4.3
Dana Point city	10.1
Danville town	7.6
Davis city	3.7
Delano city	2.3
Desert Hot Springs city	6.8
Diamond Bar city	4.5
Dinuba city	3.4
Downey city	4.1
Duarte city	3.7
Dublin city	4.5
East Los Angeles CDP	1.8
East Palo Alto city	3.3
Eastvale city	4.6
El Cajon city	8.5
El Centro city	3.7
El Cerrito city	5.9
El Dorado Hills CDP	9.2
Elk Grove city	8.4
El Monte city	2.1
El Paso de Robles (Paso Robles) city	10.3
Encinitas city	7.8
Escondido city	7.2
Eureka city	11.9
Fairfield city	11.0
Fair Oaks CDP	9.6
Fallbrook CDP	10.8
Florence-Graham CDP	1.0

Table 21. Percent of the Civilian Population 18 Years and Over Who Are Veterans, Selected Places by State/Territory, United States, American Community Survey 3-Year Estimates, 2013—*Continued*

(Percent.)

Location	Percent veterans
California cnt'd	
Florin CDP	6.3
Folsom city	7.8
Fontana city	4.3
Foothill Farms CDP	7.8
Foster City city	4.3
Fountain Valley city	6.8
Fremont city	4.3
French Valley CDP	12.9
Fresno city	5.9
Fullerton city	4.6
Galt city	9.1
Gardena city	5.5
Garden Grove city	4.3
Gilroy city	5.0
Glendale city	3.2
Glendora city	7.4
Goleta city	6.9
Granite Bay CDP	7.9
Hacienda Heights CDP	5.1
Hanford city	9.0
Hawthorne city	4.0
Hayward city	5.3
Hemet city	11.5
Hercules city	5.4
Hesperia city	7.2
Highland city	7.1
Hollister city	5.2
Huntington Beach city	7.6
Huntington Park city	1.0
Imperial Beach city	12.6
Indio city	6.6
Inglewood city	5.1
Irvine city	3.8
Isla Vista CDP	N
Jurupa Valley city	5.7
La Cañada Flintridge city	5.2
La Crescenta-Montrose CDP	3.9
Ladera Ranch CDP	7.8
Lafayette city	7.6
Laguna Beach city	7.0
Laguna Hills city	6.7
Laguna Niguel city	5.8
La Habra city	5.3
Lake Elsinore city	7.3
Lake Forest city	6.3
Lakeside CDP	13.0
Lakewood city	6.7
La Mesa city	13.2
La Mirada city	5.3
Lancaster city	8.2
La Presa CDP	11.6
La Puente city	3.3
La Quinta city	11.1
La Verne city	7.6
Lawndale city	3.7
Lemon Grove city	12.9
Lemoore city	16.4
Lennox CDP	0.9
Lincoln city	14.9
Livermore city	7.4
Lodi city	8.0
Loma Linda city	6.2
Lomita city	7.4
Lompoc city	10.2
Long Beach city	5.6
Los Altos city	6.9
Los Angeles city	3.4
Los Banos city	6.4
Los Gatos town	7.4
Lynwood city	1.6
California cnt'd	
Madera city	4.5
Manhattan Beach city	6.6
Manteca city	8.3
Marina city	12.5
Martinez city	10.0
Maywood city	0.9
Mead Valley CDP	4.1
Menifee city	12.2
Menlo Park city	5.6
Merced city	5.5
Millbrae city	5.5
Milpitas city	3.5
Mission Viejo city	8.7
Modesto city	6.9
Monrovia city	5.5
Montclair city	3.7
Montebello city	4.0
Monterey city	13.2
Monterey Park city	3.6
Moorpark city	5.4
Moreno Valley city	6.7
Morgan Hill city	6.2
Mountain View city	4.4
Murrieta city	10.5
Napa city	7.8
National City city	5.4
Newark city	4.8
Newport Beach city	7.4
Norco city	8.1
North Highlands CDP	10.4
North Tustin CDP	7.3
Norwalk city	4.3
Novato city	7.9
Oakdale city	10.8
Oakland city	4.6
Oakley city	7.0
Oceanside city	12.7
Oildale CDP	8.1
Ontario city	3.8
Orange city	5.0
Orangevale CDP	9.9
Orcutt CDP	13.4
Oxnard city	6.0
Pacifica city	5.9
Palmdale city	5.8
Palm Desert city	12.2
Palm Springs city	11.7
Palo Alto city	4.8
Paradise town	13.2
Paramount city	2.8
Pasadena city	5.0
Patterson city	3.8
Perris city	3.9
Petaluma city	8.2
Pico Rivera city	4.7
Pittsburg city	5.8
Placentia city	5.7
Pleasant Hill city	5.6
Pleasanton city	6.7
Pomona city	2.8
Porterville city	7.3
Port Hueneme city	9.6
Poway city	11.5
Ramona CDP	8.9
Rancho Cordova city	10.8
Rancho Cucamonga city	6.3
Rancho Palos Verdes city	8.7
Rancho San Diego CDP	13.8
Rancho Santa Margarita city	4.4
Redding city	11.5
California cnt'd	
Redlands city	8.7
Redondo Beach city	6.0
Redwood City city	6.0
Reedley city	4.2
Rialto city	5.6
Richmond city	4.5
Ridgecrest city	17.7
Riverbank city	6.1
Riverside city	6.1
Rocklin city	10.3
Rohnert Park city	5.5
Rosamond CDP	13.7
Rosemead city	1.8
Rosemont CDP	9.9
Roseville city	9.6
Rowland Heights CDP	3.6
Sacramento city	7.2
Salinas city	4.1
San Bernardino city	5.9
San Bruno city	5.2
San Buenaventura (Ventura) city	8.7
San Carlos city	6.8
San Clemente city	8.9
San Diego city	9.2
San Dimas city	9.5
San Fernando city	2.5
San Francisco city	3.8
San Gabriel city	2.3
Sanger city	5.4
San Jacinto city	7.5
San Jose city	4.2
San Juan Capistrano city	6.7
San Leandro city	5.8
San Lorenzo CDP	5.4
San Luis Obispo city	6.1
San Marcos city	7.0
San Mateo city	5.4
San Pablo city	5.6
San Rafael city	5.7
San Ramon city	5.0
Santa Ana city	2.3
Santa Barbara city	5.9
Santa Clara city	4.2
Santa Clarita city	6.1
Santa Cruz city	3.7
Santa Maria city	6.2
Santa Monica city	4.6
Santa Paula city	4.7
Santa Rosa city	8.1
Santee city	12.5
Saratoga city	7.2
Seal Beach city	12.1
Seaside city	7.6
Selma city	4.6
Simi Valley city	7.0
Soledad city	5.6
South El Monte city	2.6
South Gate city	1.3
South Lake Tahoe city	7.0
South Pasadena city	4.7
South San Francisco city	5.7
South San Jose Hills CDP	3.6
South Whittier CDP	5.0
Spring Valley CDP (San Diego County)	15.5
Stanton city	4.3
Stockton city	5.8
Suisun City city	11.7
Sunnyvale city	5.0
Temecula city	9.7
Temescal Valley CDP	10.3

Table 21. Percent of the Civilian Population 18 Years and Over Who Are Veterans, Selected Places by State/ Territory, United States, American Community Survey 3-Year Estimates, 2013—*Continued*

(Percent.)

Location	Percent veterans
California cnt'd	
Temple City city	3.5
Thousand Oaks city	7.0
Torrance city	6.4
Tracy city	6.1
Tulare city	5.7
Turlock city	6.0
Tustin city	4.1
Twentynine Palms city	20.5
Union City city	3.7
Upland city	7.2
Vacaville city	13.6
Valinda CDP	3.5
Vallejo city	9.0
Victorville city	6.9
Vineyard CDP	5.9
Visalia city	6.7
Vista city	6.8
Walnut city	3.6
Walnut Creek city	7.9
Wasco city	4.2
Watsonville city	3.5
West Carson CDP	6.0
West Covina city	5.3
West Hollywood city	3.0
Westminster city	5.0
Westmont CDP	4.3
West Puente Valley CDP	5.0
West Rancho Dominguez CDP	4.7
West Sacramento city	7.7
West Whittier-Los Nietos CDP	4.2
Whittier city	6.0
Wildomar city	10.3
Willowbrook CDP	1.7
Windsor town	9.2
Winter Gardens CDP	13.6
Woodland city	7.8
Yorba Linda city	5.6
Yuba City city	9.9
Yucaipa city	10.2
Yucca Valley town	16.9
Colorado	10.2
Arvada city	10.6
Aurora city	9.9
Boulder city	3.8
Brighton city	5.9
Broomfield city	8.3
Castle Rock town	8.7
Centennial city	9.2
Clifton CDP	10.8
Colorado Springs city	17.2
Columbine CDP	9.8
Commerce City city	7.9
Dakota Ridge CDP	8.5
Denver city	6.7
Englewood city	9.3
Fort Collins city	6.5
Fountain city	27.2
Grand Junction city	11.8
Greeley city	8.1
Highlands Ranch CDP	7.4
Ken Caryl CDP	9.8
Lafayette city	8.0
Lakewood city	9.9
Littleton city	9.9
Longmont city	8.5
Loveland city	11.3
Northglenn city	11.0
Parker town	9.7
Pueblo city	11.5
Colorado cnt'd	
Pueblo West CDP	17.0
Security-Widefield CDP	25.4
Thornton city	8.3
Westminster city	8.9
Wheat Ridge city	9.8
Windsor town	10.2
Connecticut	7.6
Bridgeport city	4.2
Bristol city	8.7
Danbury city	5.0
Darien CDP	4.5
East Hartford CDP	6.4
East Haven CDP	8.7
Hartford city	3.1
Manchester CDP	6.9
Meriden city	7.8
Middletown city	7.6
Milford city (balance)	7.8
Naugatuck borough	10.3
New Britain city	5.8
New Haven city	4.3
Newington CDP	9.1
New London city	7.2
North Haven CDP	9.3
Norwalk city	5.5
Norwich city	10.2
Shelton city	7.9
Stamford city	3.9
Stratford CDP	8.6
Torrington city	9.8
Trumbull CDP	8.5
Waterbury city	5.8
West Hartford CDP	6.4
West Haven city	7.6
Westport CDP	5.2
Wethersfield CDP	9.8
Delaware	10.3
Bear CDP	8.0
Dover city	14.4
Newark city	4.2
Wilmington city	6.7
District of Columbia	5.7
Washington city	5.7
Florida	10.0
Alafaya CDP	7.4
Altamonte Springs city	8.3
Apopka city	8.1
Aventura city	5.1
Bayonet Point CDP	17.5
Bellview CDP	14.9
Bloomingdale CDP	15.2
Boca Raton city	7.7
Bonita Springs city	11.7
Boynton Beach city	10.2
Bradenton city	11.8
Brandon CDP	10.4
Brent CDP	12.1
Buenaventura Lakes CDP	5.6
Cape Coral city	11.6
Carrollwood CDP	9.0
Casselberry city	9.6
Citrus Park CDP	6.5
Clearwater city	10.0
Clermont city	12.9
Coconut Creek city	6.6
Cooper City city	5.2
Florida cnt'd	
Coral Gables city	4.2
Coral Springs city	6.0
Coral Terrace CDP	3.3
Country Club CDP	1.9
Crestview city	22.4
Cutler Bay town	5.1
Dania Beach city	7.0
Davie town	6.2
Daytona Beach city	10.2
Deerfield Beach city	8.1
DeLand city	12.2
Delray Beach city	8.7
Deltona city	11.9
Doral city	1.5
Dunedin city	13.8
East Lake CDP	10.8
East Lake-Orient Park CDP	5.5
Edgewater city	16.5
Egypt Lake-Leto CDP	4.5
Ensley CDP	9.1
Estero CDP	15.8
Ferry Pass CDP	15.1
Fleming Island CDP	16.1
Fort Lauderdale city	7.9
Fort Myers city	9.1
Fort Pierce city	8.3
Fort Walton Beach city	20.0
Fountainebleau CDP	1.2
Four Corners CDP	11.1
Fruit Cove CDP	14.7
Gainesville city	6.1
Golden Gate CDP	3.2
Golden Glades CDP	2.3
Greenacres city	5.1
Haines City city	7.1
Hallandale Beach city	5.0
Hialeah city	1.1
Hialeah Gardens city	0.6
Holiday CDP	14.7
Hollywood city	6.3
Homestead city	4.2
Hunters Creek CDP	4.9
Immokalee CDP	1.3
Ives Estates CDP	2.8
Jacksonville city	12.8
Jacksonville Beach city	13.5
Jupiter town	10.4
Kendale Lakes CDP	2.0
Kendall CDP	4.7
Kendall West CDP	1.3
Keystone CDP	8.5
Key West city	10.0
Kissimmee city	5.0
Lakeland city	11.4
Lake Magdalene CDP	10.2
Lakeside CDP	18.1
Lake Worth city	5.6
Land O' Lakes CDP	11.9
Largo city	13.0
Lauderdale Lakes city	3.3
Lauderhill city	5.8
Lealman CDP	9.7
Leesburg city	10.8
Lehigh Acres CDP	6.8
Leisure City CDP	3.5
Margate city	7.4
Meadow Woods CDP	7.1
Melbourne city	14.5
Merritt Island CDP	16.4
Miami city	2.1

Table 21. Percent of the Civilian Population 18 Years and Over Who Are Veterans, Selected Places by State/Territory, United States, American Community Survey 3-Year Estimates, 2013—*Continued*

(Percent.)

Location	Percent veterans
Florida cnt'd	
Miami Beach city	2.7
Miami Gardens city	4.1
Miami Lakes town	2.7
Miramar city	4.1
Naples city	15.9
Navarre CDP	24.4
New Smyrna Beach city	17.6
Northdale CDP	8.5
North Fort Myers CDP	16.7
North Lauderdale city	2.8
North Miami city	2.5
North Miami Beach city	3.0
North Port city	15.2
Oakland Park city	5.7
Oakleaf Plantation CDP	22.2
Oak Ridge CDP	3.2
Ocala city	11.0
Ocoee city	7.2
Orlando city	6.3
Ormond Beach city	13.9
Oviedo city	9.9
Pace CDP	13.9
Palm Bay city	12.3
Palm Beach Gardens city	10.2
Palm City CDP	12.2
Palm Coast city	13.2
Palmetto Bay village	6.2
Palm Harbor CDP	12.4
Palm River-Clair Mel CDP	9.7
Palm Springs village	4.5
Palm Valley CDP	13.2
Panama City city	14.8
Parkland city	4.0
Pembroke Pines city	5.7
Pensacola city	13.5
Pine Hills CDP	6.5
Pinellas Park city	12.5
Plantation city	5.1
Plant City city	10.2
Poinciana CDP	7.6
Pompano Beach city	7.8
Port Charlotte CDP	14.5
Port Orange city	13.6
Port St. Lucie city	9.9
Princeton CDP	6.5
Richmond West CDP	3.1
Riverview CDP	13.7
Riviera Beach city	7.7
Rockledge city	17.5
Royal Palm Beach village	6.5
Ruskin CDP	7.1
St. Cloud city	9.9
St. Petersburg city	10.7
Sanford city	8.8
Sarasota city	9.5
Sebastian city	14.9
South Bradenton CDP	11.8
South Miami Heights CDP	3.5
Spring Hill CDP	13.8
Sun City Center CDP	23.4
Sunny Isles Beach city	4.6
Sunrise city	6.5
Sweetwater city	0.5
Tallahassee city	6.1
Tamarac city	8.1
Tamiami CDP	1.8
Tampa city	8.4
Tarpon Springs city	14.9
Temple Terrace city	8.2
The Acreage CDP	6.8
Florida cnt'd	
The Crossings CDP	6.0
The Hammocks CDP	2.7
The Villages CDP	26.3
Titusville city	14.7
Town 'n' Country CDP	8.2
University CDP (Hillsborough County)	6.4
University CDP (Orange County)	4.3
University Park CDP	1.6
Valrico CDP	13.8
Venice city	18.8
Vero Beach South CDP	13.2
Wekiwa Springs CDP	10.0
Wellington village	5.9
Wesley Chapel CDP	9.9
Westchase CDP	7.5
Westchester CDP	0.8
West Little River CDP	3.6
Weston city	5.3
West Palm Beach city	6.6
West Pensacola CDP	11.7
Winter Garden city	7.3
Winter Haven city	10.9
Winter Park city	8.9
Winter Springs city	9.4
Wright CDP	21.3
Georgia	9.2
Acworth city	8.6
Albany city	9.1
Alpharetta city	5.2
Athens-Clarke County unified government (balance)	5.3
Atlanta city	5.6
Augusta-Richmond County consolidated government (balance)	13.9
Brookhaven city	5.1
Candler-McAfee CDP	8.3
Canton city	6.3
Carrollton city	4.9
Cartersville city	9.8
Columbus city	14.6
Dalton city	7.5
Decatur city	5.5
Douglasville city	8.0
Duluth city	4.5
Dunwoody city	8.0
East Point city	7.9
Evans CDP	12.0
Gainesville city	6.8
Griffin city	9.1
Hinesville city	27.7
Johns Creek city	5.0
Kennesaw city	9.0
LaGrange city	8.0
Lawrenceville city	9.5
Mableton CDP	9.1
McDonough city	13.0
Macon city	9.0
Marietta city	6.0
Martinez CDP	11.6
Milton city	6.7
Newnan city	8.2
Peachtree City city	12.9
Peachtree Corners city	5.9
Pooler city	12.1
Redan CDP	8.2
Rome city	7.6
Roswell city	7.3
Sandy Springs city	5.9
Savannah city	10.9
Georgia cnt'd	
Smyrna city	6.5
Statesboro city	2.9
Stockbridge city	11.5
Sugar Hill city	5.6
Tucker CDP	9.6
Union City city	5.5
Valdosta city	9.5
Warner Robins city	17.8
Woodstock city	8.2
Hawaii	10.7
East Honolulu CDP	10.0
Ewa Gentry CDP	13.0
Hilo CDP	9.9
Kahului CDP	6.3
Kailua CDP (Honolulu County)	11.2
Kaneohe CDP	11.3
Kihei CDP	6.5
Mililani Mauka CDP	10.9
Mililani Town CDP	15.8
Pearl City CDP	15.0
Schofield Barracks CDP	N
Urban Honolulu CDP	8.9
Waipahu CDP	8.5
Idaho	10.4
Boise City city	9.8
Caldwell city	8.3
Coeur d'Alene city	11.3
Eagle city	9.4
Idaho Falls city	10.1
Lewiston city	13.3
Meridian city	8.4
Moscow city	5.0
Nampa city	10.0
Pocatello city	8.4
Post Falls city	12.2
Rexburg city	2.1
Twin Falls city	9.9
Illinois	7.2
Addison village	3.5
Algonquin village	6.6
Alton city	10.5
Arlington Heights village	6.9
Aurora city	4.6
Bartlett village	4.9
Batavia city	6.8
Belleville city	14.4
Belvidere city	6.6
Berwyn city	4.9
Bloomingdale village	4.4
Bloomington city	7.7
Blue Island city	4.3
Bolingbrook village	5.4
Buffalo Grove village	4.5
Burbank city	4.2
Calumet City city	7.7
Carbondale city	4.1
Carol Stream village	5.4
Carpentersville village	2.9
Champaign city	4.9
Charleston city	4.2
Chicago city	4.1
Chicago Heights city	6.6
Cicero town	2.1
Collinsville city	10.1
Crest Hill city	6.9
Crystal Lake city	6.4
Danville city	10.1

Table 21. Percent of the Civilian Population 18 Years and Over Who Are Veterans, Selected Places by State/ Territory, United States, American Community Survey 3-Year Estimates, 2013—*Continued*

(Percent.)

Location	Percent veterans
Illinois cnt'd	
Darien city	9.4
Decatur city	11.0
DeKalb city	5.2
Des Plaines city	6.6
Dolton village	6.5
Downers Grove village	6.0
East Moline city	9.6
East Peoria city	7.7
East St. Louis city	10.0
Edwardsville city	8.8
Elgin city	5.8
Elk Grove Village village	8.0
Elmhurst city	6.7
Elmwood Park village	5.7
Evanston city	4.0
Freeport city	10.7
Galesburg city	10.7
Geneva city	9.0
Glendale Heights village	4.1
Glen Ellyn village	5.6
Glenview village	7.2
Granite City city	9.5
Grayslake village	4.9
Gurnee village	7.1
Hanover Park village	4.0
Harvey city	6.4
Highland Park city	7.6
Hoffman Estates village	4.9
Homer Glen village	7.3
Huntley village	12.0
Joliet city	6.2
Kankakee city	9.6
Lake Forest city	7.3
Lake in the Hills village	6.4
Lake Zurich village	5.4
Lansing village	9.1
Libertyville village	6.8
Lisle village	5.6
Lockport city	4.5
Lombard village	7.0
Loves Park city	9.1
McHenry city	7.9
Machesney Park village	9.1
Maywood village	6.2
Melrose Park village	3.8
Moline city	10.2
Morton Grove village	5.5
Mount Prospect village	5.6
Mundelein village	5.7
Naperville city	4.6
New Lenox village	7.8
Niles village	5.2
Normal town	5.4
Northbrook village	7.2
North Chicago city	9.7
Oak Forest city	6.3
Oak Lawn village	8.3
Oak Park village	5.5
O'Fallon city	21.3
Orland Park village	6.9
Oswego village	5.8
Palatine village	5.4
Park Forest village	7.4
Park Ridge city	5.8
Pekin city	10.3
Peoria city	7.6
Plainfield village	5.9
Quincy city	10.6
Rockford city	8.8
Rock Island city	9.4
Illinois cnt'd	
Rolling Meadows city	5.6
Romeoville village	5.0
Roselle village	6.3
Round Lake Beach village	5.3
St. Charles city	8.4
Schaumburg village	5.5
Skokie village	4.6
South Elgin village	5.0
South Holland village	7.9
Springfield city	10.4
Streamwood village	4.6
Tinley Park village	6.9
Urbana city	4.5
Vernon Hills village	3.2
Villa Park village	6.5
Waukegan city	5.6
West Chicago city	4.1
Westmont village	5.1
Wheaton city	6.1
Wheeling village	3.6
Wilmette village	5.9
Woodridge village	5.6
Woodstock city	6.6
Zion city	9.6
Indiana	9.0
Anderson city	9.7
Bloomington city	4.1
Brownsburg town	9.8
Carmel city	6.6
Clarksville town	10.6
Columbus city	8.2
Crown Point city	9.2
East Chicago city	5.7
Elkhart city	8.4
Evansville city	8.9
Fishers town	6.0
Fort Wayne city	8.9
Franklin city	10.7
Gary city	9.7
Goshen city	7.1
Granger CDP	8.3
Greenfield city	9.6
Greenwood city	10.0
Hammond city	7.4
Highland town	9.2
Hobart city	10.4
Indianapolis city (balance)	8.0
Jeffersonville city	10.1
Kokomo city	12.6
Lafayette city	8.0
La Porte city	9.8
Lawrence city	11.3
Marion city	8.9
Merrillville town	9.9
Michigan City city	8.5
Mishawaka city	8.9
Muncie city	7.2
Munster town	8.5
New Albany city	11.1
Noblesville city	8.3
Plainfield town	11.3
Portage city	9.7
Richmond city	10.5
Schererville town	8.5
South Bend city	7.3
Terre Haute city	8.0
Valparaiso city	8.1
Westfield city	6.9
West Lafayette city	3.7
Indiana cnt'd	
Zionsville town	5.0
Iowa	9.4
Ames city	4.4
Ankeny city	8.8
Bettendorf city	9.9
Burlington city	11.5
Cedar Falls city	5.7
Cedar Rapids city	10.2
Clinton city	10.3
Coralville city	6.2
Council Bluffs city	9.9
Davenport city	9.2
Des Moines city	7.8
Dubuque city	9.7
Fort Dodge city	9.9
Iowa City city	3.9
Marion city	9.8
Marshalltown city	11.1
Mason City city	11.8
Muscatine city	7.6
Ottumwa city	9.0
Sioux City city	8.5
Urbandale city	8.3
Waterloo city	8.9
West Des Moines city	6.5
Kansas	9.7
Derby city	15.2
Dodge City city	6.0
Emporia city	6.5
Garden City city	5.0
Gardner city	10.3
Hays city	5.9
Hutchinson city	9.1
Junction City city	21.6
Kansas City city	8.3
Lawrence city	5.8
Leavenworth city	22.3
Leawood city	8.9
Lenexa city	9.4
Liberal city	4.3
Manhattan city	7.6
Olathe city	7.7
Overland Park city	7.2
Pittsburg city	6.7
Prairie Village city	7.5
Salina city	10.0
Shawnee city	8.1
Topeka city	11.5
Wichita city	9.4
Kentucky	9.2
Ashland city	9.0
Bowling Green city	6.4
Covington city	10.3
Elizabethtown city	17.4
Florence city	11.5
Frankfort city	10.6
Georgetown city	8.6
Henderson city	8.6
Hopkinsville city	11.0
Independence city	7.8
Jeffersontown city	8.0
Lexington-Fayette urban county	7.2
Louisville/Jefferson County metro government (balance)	9.2
Nicholasville city	8.6
Owensboro city	9.9
Paducah city	12.6

Table 21. Percent of the Civilian Population 18 Years and Over Who Are Veterans, Selected Places by State/Territory, United States, American Community Survey 3-Year Estimates, 2013—*Continued*

(Percent.)

Location	Percent veterans
Kentucky cnt'd	
Radcliff city	28.1
Richmond city	7.1
Louisiana	8.6
Alexandria city	8.4
Baton Rouge city	6.4
Bayou Cane CDP	10.5
Bossier City city	14.2
Central city	8.4
Hammond city	5.6
Harvey CDP	6.2
Houma city	8.6
Kenner city	7.0
Lafayette city	8.4
Lake Charles city	9.1
Laplace CDP	7.9
Marrero CDP	6.2
Metairie CDP	7.5
Monroe city	8.3
New Iberia city	8.3
New Orleans city	6.6
Prairieville CDP	8.9
Ruston city	5.9
Shreveport city	9.1
Slidell city	10.5
Sulphur city	9.9
Terrytown CDP	5.9
Maine	11.7
Auburn city	11.1
Bangor city	10.6
Biddeford city	9.2
Lewiston city	10.2
Portland city	6.7
South Portland city	9.1
Maryland	9.3
Annapolis city	9.7
Arnold CDP	13.4
Aspen Hill CDP	6.0
Baltimore city	7.0
Bel Air North CDP	7.8
Bel Air South CDP	8.9
Bethesda CDP	6.8
Bowie city	10.6
Carney CDP	10.1
Catonsville CDP	9.1
Chillum CDP	3.3
Clinton CDP	14.9
College Park city	3.4
Columbia CDP	8.5
Crofton CDP	12.7
Cumberland city	10.8
Dundalk CDP	10.0
Edgewood CDP	12.2
Eldersburg CDP	11.6
Ellicott City CDP	8.3
Essex CDP	9.1
Fairland CDP	7.9
Fort Washington CDP	15.9
Frederick city	9.7
Gaithersburg city	5.7
Germantown CDP	4.5
Glen Burnie CDP	11.2
Greenbelt city	6.8
Hagerstown city	10.4
Ilchester CDP	6.9
Landover CDP	6.8
Langley Park CDP	1.1
Laurel city	8.6

Location	Percent veterans
Maryland cnt'd	
Lochearn CDP	10.3
Middle River CDP	10.0
Milford Mill CDP	10.5
Montgomery Village CDP	5.4
North Bethesda CDP	6.8
North Laurel CDP	8.1
North Potomac CDP	4.6
Odenton CDP	20.2
Olney CDP	5.9
Owings Mills CDP	6.8
Parkville CDP	10.3
Pasadena CDP	11.4
Perry Hall CDP	7.4
Pikesville CDP	8.5
Potomac CDP	7.3
Randallstown CDP	8.9
Reisterstown CDP	6.9
Rockville city	6.6
Salisbury city	7.7
Severn CDP	16.6
Severna Park CDP	11.2
Silver Spring CDP	5.1
South Laurel CDP	9.4
Suitland CDP	6.6
Towson CDP	6.3
Waldorf CDP	14.8
Wheaton CDP	5.4
Woodlawn CDP (Baltimore County)	9.2
Massachusetts	7.0
Agawam Town city	9.8
Arlington CDP	5.5
Attleboro city	8.7
Barnstable Town city	10.2
Belmont CDP	4.9
Beverly city	7.0
Boston city	3.5
Braintree Town city	6.8
Brockton city	6.7
Brookline CDP	2.8
Burlington CDP	7.7
Cambridge city	2.6
Chelsea city	4.0
Chicopee city	11.2
Danvers CDP	9.8
Dedham CDP	6.8
Everett city	4.8
Fall River city	7.0
Fitchburg city	7.5
Framingham CDP	5.6
Franklin Town city	6.0
Gardner city	12.4
Gloucester city	8.9
Haverhill city	8.2
Holyoke city	7.4
Lawrence city	2.9
Leominster city	9.5
Lexington CDP	4.9
Lowell city	5.5
Lynn city	5.4
Malden city	3.9
Marblehead CDP	7.6
Marlborough city	6.4
Medford city	4.7
Melrose city	7.3
Methuen Town city	7.0
Milford CDP	6.6
Milton CDP	7.0
Needham CDP	5.3
New Bedford city	6.8

Location	Percent veterans
Massachusetts cnt'd	
Newton city	4.3
Northampton city	7.2
Norwood CDP	6.6
Peabody city	8.2
Pittsfield city	8.9
Quincy city	7.2
Randolph CDP	6.0
Reading CDP	7.8
Revere city	4.3
Salem city	7.4
Saugus CDP	9.7
Somerville city	3.5
Springfield city	6.5
Stoneham CDP	9.4
Taunton city	6.9
Wakefield CDP	7.5
Waltham city	4.3
Watertown Town city	4.8
Wellesley CDP	5.1
Westfield city	9.7
West Springfield Town city	9.3
Weymouth Town city	9.4
Wilmington CDP	7.8
Winchester CDP	7.9
Woburn city	7.4
Worcester city	6.4
Michigan	8.6
Adrian city	8.8
Allen Park city	8.8
Ann Arbor city	3.8
Auburn Hills city	7.5
Battle Creek city	10.8
Bay City city	9.7
Birmingham city	4.4
Burton city	9.3
Dearborn city	5.7
Dearborn Heights city	7.3
Detroit city	6.6
East Lansing city	2.2
Eastpointe city	8.3
Farmington Hills city	7.2
Ferndale city	5.2
Flint city	7.8
Forest Hills CDP	7.5
Garden City city	8.4
Grand Rapids city	6.5
Hamtramck city	2.1
Haslett CDP	9.7
Holland city	5.8
Holt CDP	12.4
Inkster city	7.6
Jackson city	7.5
Kalamazoo city	5.9
Kentwood city	7.2
Lansing city	6.9
Lincoln Park city	8.1
Livonia city	9.0
Madison Heights city	7.3
Marquette city	7.7
Midland city	7.7
Monroe city	8.7
Mount Pleasant city	4.2
Muskegon city	7.9
Norton Shores city	10.3
Novi city	6.1
Oak Park city	6.8
Okemos CDP	7.2
Pontiac city	7.1
Portage city	8.7

Table 21. Percent of the Civilian Population 18 Years and Over Who Are Veterans, Selected Places by State/Territory, United States, American Community Survey 3-Year Estimates, 2013—*Continued*

(Percent.)

Location	Percent veterans
Michigan cnt'd	
Port Huron city	10.6
Rochester Hills city	5.8
Romulus city	8.5
Roseville city	7.9
Royal Oak city	6.3
Saginaw city	8.0
St. Clair Shores city	10.0
Southfield city	7.9
Southgate city	9.5
Sterling Heights city	7.1
Taylor city	8.5
Troy city	4.8
Walker city	6.6
Warren city	8.7
Waverly CDP	10.3
Westland city	7.7
Wyandotte city	7.2
Wyoming city	6.0
Ypsilanti city	5.4
Minnesota	8.7
Andover city	7.5
Apple Valley city	8.8
Austin city	10.3
Blaine city	8.8
Bloomington city	9.6
Brooklyn Center city	6.6
Brooklyn Park city	6.6
Burnsville city	8.5
Champlin city	6.9
Chanhassen city	8.1
Chaska city	4.4
Coon Rapids city	9.0
Cottage Grove city	11.2
Crystal city	9.5
Duluth city	8.7
Eagan city	7.6
Eden Prairie city	6.2
Edina city	7.8
Elk River city	6.8
Faribault city	8.3
Farmington city	8.8
Fridley city	7.8
Golden Valley city	6.9
Hastings city	8.4
Inver Grove Heights city	9.8
Lakeville city	8.1
Lino Lakes city	8.0
Mankato city	6.7
Maple Grove city	6.7
Maplewood city	9.5
Minneapolis city	5.5
Minnetonka city	8.1
Moorhead city	5.5
New Brighton city	6.8
New Hope city	7.3
Northfield city	7.0
Oakdale city	7.6
Owatonna city	9.6
Plymouth city	6.8
Prior Lake city	9.1
Ramsey city	9.3
Richfield city	8.1
Rochester city	8.4
Rosemount city	7.8
Roseville city	10.1
St. Cloud city	9.8
St. Louis Park city	7.4
St. Paul city	5.6
Savage city	5.9
Minnesota cnt'd	
Shakopee city	5.9
Shoreview city	9.5
South St. Paul city	8.3
White Bear Lake city	11.8
Winona city	5.3
Woodbury city	8.4
Mississippi	8.8
Biloxi city	18.0
Brandon city	9.5
Clinton city	8.0
Columbus city	12.2
Greenville city	8.7
Gulfport city	15.9
Hattiesburg city	8.3
Horn Lake city	10.2
Jackson city	7.3
Madison city	9.2
Meridian city	10.2
Olive Branch city	5.8
Oxford city	5.4
Pascagoula city	9.8
Pearl city	10.0
Ridgeland city	6.4
Southaven city	9.4
Starkville city	5.5
Tupelo city	10.0
Vicksburg city	6.8
Missouri	10.2
Affton CDP	8.8
Arnold city	10.0
Ballwin city	8.8
Belton city	13.2
Blue Springs city	9.8
Cape Girardeau city	7.8
Chesterfield city	10.2
Columbia city	5.7
Ferguson city	9.6
Florissant city	9.0
Gladstone city	11.6
Grandview city	9.8
Hazelwood city	8.7
Independence city	11.1
Jefferson City city	11.4
Joplin city	9.3
Kansas City city	8.7
Kirkwood city	7.8
Lee's Summit city	9.2
Liberty city	8.1
Maryland Heights city	6.6
Mehlville CDP	8.7
Nixa city	8.1
Oakville CDP	10.5
O'Fallon city	10.3
Old Jamestown CDP	11.6
Raytown city	9.2
St. Charles city	9.7
St. Joseph city	10.3
St. Louis city	7.2
St. Peters city	9.5
Sedalia city	8.4
Spanish Lake CDP	10.4
Springfield city	9.2
University City city	7.0
Webster Groves city	7.5
Wentzville city	8.5
Wildwood city	7.1
Montana	11.9
Billings city	11.4
Bozeman city	5.4
Butte-Silver Bow (balance)	11.0
Great Falls city	15.9
Helena city	10.7
Kalispell city	10.0
Missoula city	8.2
Nebraska	10.0
Bellevue city	18.5
Columbus city	9.9
Fremont city	9.3
Grand Island city	9.2
Hastings city	10.3
Kearney city	6.9
Lincoln city	8.2
Norfolk city	8.2
North Platte city	12.4
Omaha city	8.7
Papillion city	15.5
Nevada	10.8
Carson City	13.7
Elko city	8.8
Enterprise CDP	7.8
Henderson city	11.4
Las Vegas city	10.5
North Las Vegas city	11.0
Pahrump CDP	20.9
Paradise CDP	8.7
Reno city	9.7
Sparks city	11.3
Spring Valley CDP	7.5
Summerlin South CDP	10.6
Sunrise Manor CDP	9.5
Whitney CDP	8.6
Winchester CDP	9.0
New Hampshire	10.6
Concord city	11.8
Derry CDP	8.8
Dover city	9.6
Keene city	6.8
Manchester city	7.9
Nashua city	9.4
Portsmouth city	8.7
Rochester city	11.9
New Jersey	6.2
Atlantic City city	6.0
Bayonne city	6.8
Bergenfield borough	5.4
Bridgeton city	4.3
Camden city	3.9
Carteret borough	4.4
Cliffside Park borough	4.5
Clifton city	4.3
East Orange city	5.3
Elizabeth city	2.6
Elmwood Park borough	5.3
Englewood city	3.3
Fair Lawn borough	4.8
Fort Lee borough	4.5
Garfield city	3.6
Hackensack city	3.8
Hoboken city	1.8
Iselin CDP	4.6
Jersey City city	3.1
Kearny town	4.1
Lakewood CDP	2.5

Table 21. Percent of the Civilian Population 18 Years and Over Who Are Veterans, Selected Places by State/Territory, United States, American Community Survey 3-Year Estimates, 2013—*Continued*

(Percent.)

Location	Percent veterans	Location	Percent veterans	Location	Percent veterans
New Jersey cnt'd		**New York** cnt'd		**North Carolina** cnt'd	
Linden city	6.2	Harrison village	3.8	Chapel Hill town	3.7
Lodi borough	4.1	Hauppauge CDP	9.7	Charlotte city	6.8
Long Branch city	5.2	Hempstead village	3.6	Concord city	9.1
Millville city	7.1	Hicksville CDP	5.8	Cornelius town	9.0
Newark city	3.2	Holbrook CDP	5.7	Durham city	6.4
New Brunswick city	2.0	Holtsville CDP	7.5	Fayetteville city	21.8
North Plainfield borough	5.0	Huntington Station CDP	5.6	Fuquay-Varina town	12.6
Old Bridge CDP	4.1	Irondequoit CDP	8.1	Garner town	10.4
Palisades Park borough	1.2	Ithaca city	1.9	Gastonia city	8.4
Paramus borough	6.6	Jamestown city	9.7	Goldsboro city	14.4
Passaic city	1.8	Kingston city	6.4	Greensboro city	7.5
Paterson city	1.9	Kiryas Joel village	N	Greenville city	5.8
Perth Amboy city	2.6	Lake Ronkonkoma CDP	7.9	Havelock city	28.7
Plainfield city	4.2	Levittown CDP	6.9	Hickory city	7.1
Pleasantville city	5.1	Lindenhurst village	7.1	High Point city	7.5
Princeton	3.1	Lockport city	10.1	Holly Springs town	11.4
Rahway city	5.0	Long Beach city	5.5	Huntersville town	7.1
Ridgewood village	6.0	Massapequa CDP	7.5	Indian Trail town	8.4
Roselle borough	3.1	Medford CDP	7.4	Jacksonville city	22.7
Sayreville borough	5.8	Melville CDP	6.3	Kannapolis city	9.4
Somerset CDP	4.4	Merrick CDP	6.1	Kernersville town	10.4
South Plainfield borough	5.7	Middletown city	6.0	Kinston city	9.2
Summit city	6.0	Mount Vernon city	4.2	Lumberton city	7.6
Toms River CDP	9.5	Newburgh city	4.4	Matthews town	8.5
Trenton city	5.9	New City CDP	6.0	Mint Hill town	10.8
Union City city	1.7	New Rochelle city	5.1	Monroe city	7.8
Vineland city	7.1	New York city	2.9	Mooresville town	8.5
Westfield town	5.1	Niagara Falls city	9.2	Morrisville town	6.6
West New York town	1.7	North Amityville CDP	5.4	New Bern city	12.4
Woodbridge CDP	5.4	North Bay Shore CDP	3.2	Raleigh city	6.4
		North Bellmore CDP	6.2	Rocky Mount city	10.9
New Mexico	11.0	North Tonawanda city	9.8	Salisbury city	10.5
Alamogordo city	22.2	Oceanside CDP	6.2	Sanford city	9.5
Albuquerque city	10.8	Ossining village	4.4	Shelby city	9.7
Carlsbad city	11.0	Peekskill city	6.3	Statesville city	9.4
Clovis city	17.7	Plainview CDP	6.1	Thomasville city	8.7
Farmington city	9.6	Port Chester village	3.6	Wake Forest town	9.9
Gallup city	9.9	Poughkeepsie city	6.5	Wilmington city	9.1
Hobbs city	7.8	Rochester city	5.3	Wilson city	10.2
Las Cruces city	11.1	Rockville Centre village	5.5	Winston-Salem city	8.2
Rio Rancho city	15.9	Rome city	12.9		
Roswell city	9.9	Ronkonkoma CDP	7.7	**North Dakota**	9.9
Santa Fe city	8.4	Rotterdam CDP	9.4	Bismarck city	9.2
South Valley CDP	7.4	Saratoga Springs city	10.3	Dickinson city	7.9
		Schenectady city	7.0	Fargo city	7.8
New York	5.7	Selden CDP	4.7	Grand Forks city	8.5
Albany city	4.5	Shirley CDP	4.8	Minot city	12.5
Auburn city	9.9	Smithtown CDP	7.9	West Fargo city	10.2
Baldwin CDP	5.2	Spring Valley village	2.6	Williston city	9.0
Bay Shore CDP	5.4	Syosset CDP	5.3		
Binghamton city	7.6	Syracuse city	5.7	**Ohio**	9.4
Brentwood CDP	3.9	Tonawanda CDP	9.0	Akron city	9.2
Brighton CDP	6.5	Troy city	5.9	Alliance city	8.8
Buffalo city	7.2	Uniondale CDP	2.6	Ashland city	10.5
Centereach CDP	7.1	Utica city	6.8	Athens city	2.4
Central Islip CDP	4.5	Valley Stream village	5.4	Austintown CDP	12.1
Cheektowaga CDP	10.3	Watertown city	12.1	Avon city	8.7
Commack CDP	8.0	West Babylon CDP	6.5	Avon Lake city	9.2
Copiague CDP	5.0	West Islip CDP	6.1	Barberton city	8.4
Coram CDP	5.6	West Seneca CDP	9.2	Beavercreek city	19.0
Deer Park CDP	7.2	White Plains city	3.9	Boardman CDP	10.0
Dix Hills CDP	4.1	Yonkers city	4.4	Bowling Green city	4.0
East Meadow CDP	7.2			Brunswick city	9.1
East Patchogue CDP	8.1	**North Carolina**	9.7	Canton city	9.5
Elmira city	7.1	Apex town	6.9	Centerville city	13.3
Elmont CDP	2.6	Asheboro city	8.7	Chillicothe city	12.3
Franklin Square CDP	6.0	Asheville city	8.7	Cincinnati city	6.7
Freeport village	4.8	Burlington city	9.0	Cleveland city	7.5
Garden City village	7.0	Carrboro town	3.8	Cleveland Heights city	6.4
Glen Cove city	5.1	Cary town	6.5	Columbus city	7.0

Table 21. Percent of the Civilian Population 18 Years and Over Who Are Veterans, Selected Places by State/Territory, United States, American Community Survey 3-Year Estimates, 2013—*Continued*

(Percent.)

Location	Percent veterans
Ohio cnt'd	
Cuyahoga Falls city	9.8
Dayton city	8.9
Delaware city	9.7
Dublin city	6.4
Elyria city	10.4
Euclid city	8.9
Fairborn city	14.3
Fairfield city	8.6
Findlay city	8.7
Gahanna city	8.0
Garfield Heights city	10.7
Green city	9.8
Grove City city	7.7
Hamilton city	9.7
Hilliard city	7.6
Huber Heights city	15.3
Hudson city	6.9
Kent city	5.2
Kettering city	10.2
Lakewood city	7.7
Lancaster city	10.8
Lebanon city	8.9
Lima city	8.9
Lorain city	9.1
Mansfield city	11.1
Maple Heights city	7.9
Marion city	11.0
Marysville city	9.7
Mason city	8.1
Massillon city	10.4
Medina city	10.3
Mentor city	9.2
Miamisburg city	10.5
Middletown city	8.6
Newark city	10.5
North Olmsted city	9.0
North Ridgeville city	9.4
North Royalton city	8.6
Norwood city	8.9
Oregon city	9.5
Oxford city	2.6
Parma city	9.8
Parma Heights city	7.4
Perrysburg city	6.7
Piqua city	9.8
Portsmouth city	8.7
Reynoldsburg city	10.5
Riverside city	13.7
Rocky River city	10.2
Sandusky city	11.4
Shaker Heights city	6.5
Sidney city	9.8
Solon city	5.2
South Euclid city	5.7
Springfield city	10.3
Stow city	9.6
Strongsville city	8.9
Toledo city	8.3
Trotwood city	11.3
Troy city	11.2
Upper Arlington city	6.4
Wadsworth city	10.7
Warren city	10.1
Westerville city	8.9
Westlake city	7.5
Willoughby city	8.0
Wooster city	7.7
Xenia city	10.6
Youngstown city	9.5
Zanesville city	7.5
Oklahoma	10.7
Ardmore city	11.2
Bartlesville city	10.1
Bixby city	8.5
Broken Arrow city	10.3
Del City city	13.7
Duncan city	10.7
Edmond city	9.6
Enid city	11.8
Lawton city	18.5
Midwest City city	15.5
Moore city	11.3
Muskogee city	10.1
Norman city	9.5
Oklahoma City city	9.9
Owasso city	11.1
Ponca City city	9.9
Sapulpa city	10.2
Shawnee city	9.2
Stillwater city	5.3
Tulsa city	8.9
Yukon city	9.8
Oregon	10.3
Albany city	10.7
Aloha CDP	7.3
Ashland city	7.9
Beaverton city	6.7
Bend city	9.5
Bethany CDP	6.3
Corvallis city	6.3
Eugene city	7.7
Forest Grove city	8.1
Grants Pass city	13.4
Gresham city	8.6
Hillsboro city	7.1
Keizer city	11.8
Klamath Falls city	12.1
Lake Oswego city	8.3
McMinnville city	9.9
Medford city	13.8
Milwaukie city	10.0
Newberg city	5.1
Oregon City city	8.3
Portland city	6.7
Redmond city	13.1
Roseburg city	16.2
Salem city	10.8
Springfield city	10.3
Tigard city	8.5
Tualatin city	8.0
West Linn city	10.2
Wilsonville city	7.9
Woodburn city	8.7
Pennsylvania	9.1
Allentown city	6.2
Allison Park CDP	9.9
Altoona city	11.9
Bethel Park municipality	8.8
Bethlehem city	7.2
Chambersburg borough	9.5
Chester city	6.7
Drexel Hill CDP	6.6
Easton city	5.9
Erie city	9.1
Harrisburg city	6.0
Hazleton city	7.0
Johnstown city	12.1
Lancaster city	5.2
Pennsylvania cnt'd	
Lebanon city	10.7
Levittown CDP	8.8
McKeesport city	12.2
Monroeville municipality	11.4
Murrysville municipality	7.9
New Castle city	9.2
Norristown borough	5.8
Philadelphia city	5.8
Pittsburgh city	7.1
Plum borough	9.9
Pottstown borough	9.6
Reading city	5.4
Scranton city	9.3
State College borough	1.8
West Mifflin borough	12.1
Wilkes-Barre city	10.4
Williamsport city	8.4
York city	6.0
Rhode Island	8.3
Cranston city	7.9
East Providence city	7.6
Newport city	11.6
Pawtucket city	6.5
Providence city	3.4
Warwick city	9.9
Woonsocket city	8.0
South Carolina	10.7
Aiken city	11.2
Anderson city	8.2
Charleston city	9.4
Columbia city	8.8
Easley city	13.1
Florence city	9.7
Goose Creek city	18.2
Greenville city	7.3
Greenwood city	5.7
Greer city	6.7
Hilton Head Island town	12.4
Mauldin city	11.6
Mount Pleasant town	10.4
Myrtle Beach city	10.3
North Augusta city	12.5
North Charleston city	12.3
Rock Hill city	9.0
St. Andrews CDP	8.8
Socastee CDP	12.9
Spartanburg city	9.0
Summerville town	13.4
Sumter city	15.2
Taylors CDP	8.9
South Dakota	10.6
Aberdeen city	9.0
Brookings city	6.3
Rapid City city	14.4
Sioux Falls city	8.3
Watertown city	11.6
Tennessee	9.6
Bartlett city	12.6
Brentwood city	6.7
Bristol city	9.5
Chattanooga city	9.1
Clarksville city	20.6
Cleveland city	7.4
Collierville town	9.6
Columbia city	9.4
Cookeville city	5.7

Table 21. Percent of the Civilian Population 18 Years and Over Who Are Veterans, Selected Places by State/Territory, United States, American Community Survey 3-Year Estimates, 2013—*Continued*

(Percent.)

Location	Percent veterans
Tennessee cnt'd	
East Ridge city	9.2
Farragut town	11.0
Franklin city	5.8
Gallatin city	8.2
Germantown city	10.8
Hendersonville city	9.4
Jackson city	8.2
Johnson City city	11.4
Kingsport city	11.1
Knoxville city	6.3
La Vergne city	9.3
Lebanon city	7.4
Maryville city	11.2
Memphis city	7.0
Morristown city	8.3
Mount Juliet city	9.7
Murfreesboro city	8.8
Nashville-Davidson metropolitan government (balance)	7.4
Oak Ridge city	12.9
Shelbyville city	6.5
Smyrna town	9.7
Spring Hill city	5.1
Texas	8.2
Abilene city	12.4
Allen city	8.6
Alvin city	8.3
Amarillo city	9.2
Arlington city	7.5
Atascocita CDP	10.2
Austin city	5.8
Balch Springs city	4.3
Baytown city	6.2
Beaumont city	7.8
Bedford city	11.2
Benbrook city	12.9
Big Spring city	9.2
Brownsville city	3.8
Brushy Creek CDP	8.0
Bryan city	6.8
Burleson city	10.2
Canyon Lake CDP	18.9
Carrollton city	6.0
Cedar Hill city	8.0
Cedar Park city	10.0
Channelview CDP	6.3
Cibolo city	23.1
Cleburne city	8.5
Cloverleaf CDP	4.2
College Station city	4.3
Colleyville city	10.0
Conroe city	7.5
Converse city	20.8
Coppell city	6.1
Copperas Cove city	27.7
Corinth city	7.4
Corpus Christi city	11.0
Corsicana city	8.2
Dallas city	5.3
Deer Park city	7.9
Del Rio city	8.5
Denison city	12.0
Denton city	7.4
DeSoto city	8.8
Duncanville city	7.9
Eagle Pass city	3.7
Edinburg city	5.1
El Paso city	9.6
Euless city	7.3
Texas cnt'd	
Farmers Branch city	7.0
Flower Mound town	6.4
Fort Hood CDP	N
Fort Worth city	7.6
Fresno CDP	7.0
Friendswood city	8.2
Frisco city	6.1
Galveston city	9.2
Garland city	6.6
Georgetown city	15.2
Grand Prairie city	6.8
Grapevine city	8.1
Greenville city	10.1
Haltom City city	8.3
Harker Heights city	26.2
Harlingen city	7.9
Houston city	5.2
Huntsville city	7.2
Hurst city	8.3
Irving city	4.6
Keller city	10.8
Kerrville city	15.3
Killeen city	29.3
Kingsville city	7.4
Kyle city	8.4
Lake Jackson city	8.6
Lancaster city	7.9
La Porte city	9.4
Laredo city	3.8
League City city	8.7
Leander city	9.9
Lewisville city	6.5
Little Elm city	9.2
Longview city	8.8
Lubbock city	7.1
Lufkin city	9.8
McAllen city	5.4
McKinney city	7.7
Mansfield city	10.0
Marshall city	6.1
Mesquite city	6.3
Midland city	7.5
Mission city	5.6
Mission Bend CDP	4.8
Missouri City city	7.5
Nacogdoches city	4.5
New Braunfels city	11.3
North Richland Hills city	10.7
Odessa city	7.4
Paris city	10.1
Pasadena city	5.8
Pearland city	8.3
Pflugerville city	10.9
Pharr city	4.3
Plainview city	7.3
Plano city	6.7
Port Arthur city	7.2
Richardson city	6.8
Rockwall city	9.7
Rosenberg city	4.9
Round Rock city	7.4
Rowlett city	7.7
Sachse city	5.4
Saginaw city	13.9
San Angelo city	11.7
San Antonio city	10.4
San Benito city	7.2
San Juan city	3.4
San Marcos city	5.1
Schertz city	21.8
Texas cnt'd	
Seguin city	9.1
Sherman city	9.9
Socorro city	2.9
Southlake city	9.4
Spring CDP	8.4
Sugar Land city	4.6
Temple city	13.6
Texarkana city	7.9
Texas City city	8.7
The Colony city	9.7
The Woodlands CDP	7.1
Timberwood Park CDP	11.5
Tyler city	8.3
University Park city	2.7
Victoria city	8.9
Waco city	7.6
Watauga city	8.2
Waxahachie city	7.4
Weatherford city	11.4
Weslaco city	7.1
West Odessa CDP	5.7
Wichita Falls city	12.5
Wylie city	7.8
Utah	7.2
American Fork city	6.3
Bountiful city	7.9
Cedar City city	6.9
Clearfield city	14.3
Clinton city	12.9
Cottonwood Heights city	7.5
Draper city	7.2
Eagle Mountain city	6.2
Farmington city	6.4
Herriman city	7.5
Holladay city	7.5
Kaysville city	5.6
Kearns CDP	5.4
Layton city	12.0
Lehi city	4.2
Logan city	4.4
Magna CDP	5.6
Midvale city	5.4
Millcreek CDP	6.7
Murray city	7.1
Ogden city	9.5
Orem city	5.0
Pleasant Grove city	3.8
Provo city	3.2
Riverton city	5.0
Roy city	10.0
St. George city	10.5
Salt Lake City city	6.2
Sandy city	7.6
Saratoga Springs city	6.4
South Jordan city	6.3
South Salt Lake city	4.4
Spanish Fork city	4.8
Springville city	6.7
Syracuse city	11.3
Taylorsville city	6.8
Tooele city	11.2
Washington city	10.3
West Jordan city	5.5
West Valley City city	5.9
Vermont	9.3
Burlington city	5.6

Table 21. Percent of the Civilian Population 18 Years and Over Who Are Veterans, Selected Places by State/Territory, United States, American Community Survey 3-Year Estimates, 2013—*Continued*

(Percent.)

Location	Percent veterans
Virginia	11.5
Alexandria city	8.6
Annandale CDP	6.9
Arlington CDP	6.9
Ashburn CDP	8.3
Bailey's Crossroads CDP	6.7
Blacksburg town	3.3
Burke CDP	14.1
Cave Spring CDP	12.3
Centreville CDP	7.8
Chantilly CDP	10.1
Charlottesville city	4.9
Cherry Hill CDP	12.1
Chesapeake city	15.2
Chester CDP	11.8
Christiansburg town	5.4
Dale City CDP	13.2
Danville city	11.5
Fairfax city	9.4
Fair Oaks CDP	7.5
Franklin Farm CDP	7.4
Fredericksburg city	10.7
Hampton city	18.8
Harrisonburg city	3.3
Herndon town	8.4
Hopewell city	10.4
Lake Ridge CDP	17.3
Leesburg town	8.3
Lincolnia CDP	6.5
Linton Hall CDP	14.4
Lynchburg city	8.0
McLean CDP	9.7
McNair CDP	9.5
Manassas city	8.2
Marumsco CDP	9.9
Mechanicsville CDP	9.8
Montclair CDP	20.3
Newport News city	15.9
Norfolk city	16.3
Oakton CDP	10.0
Petersburg city	11.5
Portsmouth city	15.6
Reston CDP	8.7
Richmond city	7.0
Roanoke city	9.8
Salem city	11.4
Short Pump CDP	7.0
South Riding CDP	5.9
Springfield CDP	9.9
Staunton city	8.5
Sterling CDP	10.2
Suffolk city	17.0
Tuckahoe CDP	8.7
Tysons Corner CDP	4.8
Virginia Beach city	19.4
Waynesboro city	11.3
West Falls Church CDP	6.0
West Springfield CDP	15.5
Winchester city	7.9
Woodlawn CDP (Fairfax County)	7.5
Washington	10.9
Auburn city	11.8
Bainbridge Island city	10.3
Bellevue city	6.9
Bellingham city	7.5
Washington cnt'd	
Bothell city	8.0
Bremerton city	17.0
Burien city	8.5
Camas city	11.1
Cottage Lake CDP	8.4
Des Moines city	9.2
Eastmont CDP	8.1
Edmonds city	11.3
Everett city	9.1
Fairwood CDP (King County)	10.0
Federal Way city	9.7
Five Corners CDP	10.6
Graham CDP	15.9
Hazel Dell CDP	9.6
Issaquah city	5.8
Kenmore city	7.6
Kennewick city	8.8
Kent city	8.0
Kirkland city	6.5
Lacey city	18.1
Lake Stevens city	11.6
Lakewood city	20.9
Longview city	11.9
Lynnwood city	8.4
Maple Valley city	8.5
Marysville city	11.6
Mercer Island city	8.5
Moses Lake city	9.7
Mountlake Terrace city	9.2
Mount Vernon city	10.7
Mukilteo city	11.6
Oak Harbor city	27.1
Olympia city	9.8
Orchards CDP	11.0
Parkland CDP	13.0
Pasco city	6.3
Pullman city	3.9
Puyallup city	12.7
Redmond city	5.3
Renton city	8.1
Richland city	11.9
Salmon Creek CDP	10.4
Sammamish city	5.4
SeaTac city	7.5
Seattle city	6.0
Shoreline city	9.3
Silver Firs CDP	6.9
South Hill CDP	15.1
Spanaway CDP	19.0
Spokane city	11.4
Spokane Valley city	13.1
Tacoma city	13.0
Union Hill-Novelty Hill CDP	8.4
University Place city	15.0
Vancouver city	11.7
Walla Walla city	10.9
Wenatchee city	10.8
Yakima city	8.3
West Virginia	10.7
Charleston city	8.7
Huntington city	10.3
Morgantown city	4.1
Parkersburg city	11.3
Wheeling city	11.9
Wisconsin	9.0
Appleton city	7.5
Beloit city	8.4
Brookfield city	9.7
Caledonia village	9.4
De Pere city	9.0
Eau Claire city	8.3
Fitchburg city	4.5
Fond du Lac city	10.0
Franklin city	7.0
Green Bay city	8.2
Greenfield city	10.3
Janesville city	9.4
Kenosha city	7.6
La Crosse city	8.0
Madison city	5.4
Manitowoc city	11.6
Menomonee Falls village	8.3
Mequon city	8.1
Milwaukee city	6.2
Mount Pleasant village	10.6
Muskego city	9.7
Neenah city	8.4
New Berlin city	7.7
Oak Creek city	8.8
Oshkosh city	8.6
Pleasant Prairie village	9.9
Racine city	8.8
Sheboygan city	8.2
South Milwaukee city	10.0
Stevens Point city	7.2
Sun Prairie city	8.5
Superior city	8.9
Watertown city	9.9
Waukesha city	6.9
Wausau city	10.5
Wauwatosa city	7.6
West Allis city	7.9
West Bend city	9.3
Wyoming	11.5
Casper city	11.1
Cheyenne city	17.8
Gillette city	8.7
Laramie city	6.9
Rock Springs city	10.9
Puerto Rico	3.6
Arecibo zona urbana	2.3
Bayamón zona urbana	4.9
Caguas zona urbana	4.9
Carolina zona urbana	4.9
Cataño zona urbana	4.0
Fajardo zona urbana	5.4
Guayama zona urbana	3.2
Guaynabo zona urbana	4.2
Levittown comunidad	6.1
Mayagüez zona urbana	3.9
Ponce zona urbana	5.1
San Juan zona urbana	3.9
Trujillo Alto zona urbana	4.2
Vega Baja zona urbana	2.1

Table 22. Percent of the Civilian Population 18 Years and Over Who Are Veterans, Selected Places by American Indian Area/Alaska Native Area/Alaska Native Regional Corporation, United States, American Community Survey 1-Year Estimates, 2013

(Percent.)

Area	Percent veterans
American Indian Reservation and Off-Reservation Trust Land—Federal	
All areas	7.6
Navajo Nation Reservation and Off-Reservation Trust Land, AZ—NM—UT	4.1
Oklahoma Tribal Statistical Area	
All areas	10.1
Cherokee OTSA, OK	10.0
Cheyenne-Arapaho OTSA, OK	8.4
Chickasaw OTSA, OK	10.5
Choctaw OTSA, OK	8.6
Citizen Potawatomi Nation-Absentee Shawnee OTSA, OK	14.9
Creek OTSA, OK	8.8
Kiowa-Comanche-Apache-Fort Sill Apache OTSA, OK	15.5
Alaska Native Village Statistical Area	
All areas	11.3
Knik ANVSA, AK	14.8
State Designated Tribal Statistical Area	
All areas	11.9
Cher-O-Creek SDTSA, AL	11.1
Coharie SDTSA, NC	10.8
Lumbee SDTSA, NC	15.0
United Houma Nation SDTSA, LA	6.8
Alaska Native Regional Corporation	
Cook Inlet ANRC, AK	12.5
Doyon ANRC, AK	13.3
Sealaska ANRC, AK	10.6

Table 23. Percent of the Civilian Population 18 Years and Over Who Are Veterans, Selected Places by American Indian Area/Alaska Native Area/Alaska Native Regional Corporation, United States, American Community Survey 3-Year Estimates, 2013

(Percent.)

Area	Percent veterans
American Indian Reservation and Off-Reservation Trust Land—Federal	
All areas	8.5
Agua Caliente Indian Reservation and Off-Reservation Trust Land, CA	14.8
Flathead Reservation, MT	12.6
Isabella Reservation and Off-Reservation Trust Land, MI	8.0
Navajo Nation Reservation and Off-Reservation Trust Land, AZ—NM—UT	4.8
Oneida (WI) Reservation and Off-Reservation Trust Land, WI	9.8
Osage Reservation, OK	11.4
Puyallup Reservation and Off-Reservation Trust Land, WA	11.0
Uintah and Ouray Reservation and Off-Reservation Trust Land, UT	6.5
Wind River Reservation and Off-Reservation Trust Land, WY	9.8
Yakama Nation Reservation and Off-Reservation Trust Land, WA	5.7
Oklahoma Tribal Statistical Area	
All areas	11.2
Cherokee OTSA, OK	11.3
Cheyenne-Arapaho OTSA, OK	9.3
Chickasaw OTSA, OK	10.9
Choctaw OTSA, OK	10.4
Citizen Potawatomi Nation-Absentee Shawnee OTSA, OK	15.7
Creek OTSA, OK	9.9
Kickapoo OTSA, OK	10.6
Kiowa-Comanche-Apache-Fort Sill Apache OTSA, OK	17.0
Sac and Fox OTSA, OK	11.0
Seminole OTSA, OK	9.7
Kaw/Ponca joint-use OTSA, OK	10.3
Alaska Native Village Statistical Area	
All areas	12.0
Chickaloon ANVSA, AK	13.6
Kenaitze ANVSA, AK	13.5
Knik ANVSA, AK	15.0
Tribal Designated Statistical Area	
All areas	12.8
Samish TDSA, WA	13.3
State Designated Tribal Statistical Area	
All areas	12.6
Cher-O-Creek SDTSA, AL	11.3
Coharie SDTSA, NC	11.2
Echota Cherokee SDTSA, AL	12.0
Four Winds Cherokee SDTSA, LA	19.3
Lumbee SDTSA, NC	15.5
MaChis Lower Creek SDTSA, AL	13.7
United Houma Nation SDTSA, LA	7.7
Alaska Native Regional Corporation	
Calista ANRC, AK	7.3
Cook Inlet ANRC, AK	13.8
Doyon ANRC, AK	15.6
Sealaska ANRC, AK	11.6

Table 24. Percent of the Civilian Population 18 Years and Over Who Are Veterans, Selected Places by American Indian Area/Alaska Native Area/Alaska Native Regional Corporation, United States, American Community Survey 5-Year Estimates, 2013

(Percent.)

Area	Percent veterans
American Indian Reservation and Off-Reservation Trust Land — Federal	
All areas	
Acoma Pueblo and Off-Reservation Trust Land, NM	8.4
Agua Caliente Indian Reservation and Off-Reservation Trust Land, CA	15.5
Alabama-Coushatta Reservation and Off-Reservation Trust Land, TX	7.3
Allegany Reservation, NY	11.1
Alturas Indian Rancheria, CA	-
Annette Island Reserve, AK	9.1
Aroostook Band of Micmac Trust Land, ME	3.0
Auburn Rancheria and Off-Reservation Trust Land, CA	-
Augustine Reservation, CA	-
Bad River Reservation, WI	11.7
Barona Reservation, CA	7.3
Battle Mountain Reservation, NV	20.0
Bay Mills Reservation and Off-Reservation Trust Land, MI	12.8
Benton Paiute Reservation and Off-Reservation Trust Land, CA	10.7
Berry Creek Rancheria and Off-Reservation Trust Land, CA	9.4
Big Bend Rancheria, CA	-
Big Cypress Reservation, FL	0.0
Big Lagoon Rancheria, CA	0.0
Big Pine Reservation, CA	9.8
Big Sandy Rancheria, CA	1.7
Big Valley Rancheria, CA	15.3
Bishop Reservation, CA	7.3
Blackfeet Indian Reservation and Off-Reservation Trust Land, MT	8.7
Blue Lake Rancheria and Off-Reservation Trust Land, CA	11.8
Bois Forte Reservation, MN	9.3
Bridgeport Reservation, CA	2.2
Brighton Reservation, FL	6.2
Burns Paiute Indian Colony and Off-Reservation Trust Land, OR	0.0
Cabazon Reservation, CA	0.8
Cahuilla Reservation, CA	7.6
Campbell Ranch, NV	15.5
Campo Indian Reservation, CA	3.6
Capitan Grande Reservation, CA	-
Carson Colony, NV	7.7
Catawba Reservation, SC	6.1
Cattaraugus Reservation, NY	8.5
Cedarville Rancheria and Off-Reservation Trust Land, CA	0.0
Celilo Village, OR	0.0
Chehalis Reservation and Off-Reservation Trust Land, WA	6.7
Chemehuevi Reservation, CA	6.4
Cheyenne River Reservation and Off-Reservation Trust Land, SD	8.3
Chicken Ranch Rancheria and Off-Reservation Trust Land, CA	-
Chitimacha Reservation, LA	8.3
Pueblo de Cochiti, NM	11.8
Coconut Creek Trust Land, FL	-
Cocopah Reservation, AZ	17.4
Coeur d'Alene Reservation, ID	15.5
Cold Springs Rancheria, CA	9.1
Colorado River Indian Reservation, AZ--CA	13.0
Colusa Rancheria, CA	6.1
Colville Reservation and Off-Reservation Trust Land, WA	13.1
Coos, Lower Umpqua, and Siuslaw Reservation and Off-Reservation Trust Land, OR	7.9
Coquille Reservation, OR	21.1
Cortina Indian Rancheria, CA	0.0
Coushatta Reservation and Off-Reservation Trust Land, LA	5.9
Cow Creek Reservation and Off-Reservation Trust Land, OR	21.1
Coyote Valley Reservation, CA	0.0
Crow Reservation and Off-Reservation Trust Land, MT	5.3
Crow Creek Reservation, SD	5.3
Dresslerville Colony, NV	14.6
Dry Creek Rancheria and Off-Reservation Trust Land, CA	-
Duck Valley Reservation, NV--ID	12.5
Duckwater Reservation, NV	9.0
Eastern Cherokee Reservation, NC	6.5
Elko Colony, NV	7.6
Elk Valley Rancheria and Off-Reservation Trust Land, CA	20.7
Ely Reservation, NV	7.8
Enterprise Rancheria, CA	0.0
Ewiiaapaayp Reservation, CA	-
Fallon Paiute-Shoshone Colony and Off-Reservation Trust Land, NV	2.0
Fallon Paiute-Shoshone Reservation and Off-Reservation Trust Land, NV	11.0
Flandreau Reservation, SD	13.8
Flathead Reservation, MT	12.9
Fond du Lac Reservation and Off-Reservation Trust Land, MN--WI	10.8
Forest County Potawatomi Community and Off-Reservation Trust Land, WI	8.0
Fort Apache Reservation, AZ	3.2
Fort Belknap Reservation and Off-Reservation Trust Land, MT	10.6
Fort Berthold Reservation, ND	9.4
Fort Bidwell Reservation and Off-Reservation Trust Land, CA	3.0
Fort Hall Reservation and Off-Reservation Trust Land, ID	6.4
Fort Independence Reservation, CA	23.3
Fort McDermitt Indian Reservation, NV--OR	2.5
Fort McDowell Yavapai Nation Reservation, AZ	3.3
Fort Mojave Reservation and Off-Reservation Trust Land, AZ--CA--NV	15.9
Fort Peck Indian Reservation and Off-Reservation Trust Land, MT	6.5
Fort Pierce Reservation, FL	0.0
Fort Sill Apache Indian Reservation, NM	-
Fort Yuma Indian Reservation, CA--AZ	7.9
Gila River Indian Reservation, AZ	5.1
Goshute Reservation, NV--UT	0.8
Grand Portage Reservation and Off-Reservation Trust Land, MN	14.9
Grand Ronde Community and Off-Reservation Trust Land, OR	9.9
Grand Traverse Reservation and Off-Reservation Trust Land, MI	9.3
Greenville Rancheria, CA	0.0
Grindstone Indian Rancheria, CA	1.2
Guidiville Rancheria and Off-Reservation Trust Land, CA	0.0
Hannahville Indian Community and Off-Reservation Trust Land, MI	8.6
Havasupai Reservation, AZ	2.5
Ho-Chunk Nation Reservation and Off-Reservation Trust Land, WI--MN	10.5
Hoh Indian Reservation and Off-Reservation Trust Land, WA	2.3
Hollywood Reservation, FL	12.1
Hoopa Valley Reservation, CA	6.1
Hopi Reservation and Off-Reservation Trust Land, AZ	8.0
Hopland Rancheria, CA	5.2
Houlton Maliseet Reservation and Off-Reservation Trust Land, ME	15.4
Hualapai Indian Reservation and Off-Reservation Trust Land, AZ	1.7
Huron Potawatomi Reservation and Off-Reservation Trust Land, MI	13.5
Immokalee Reservation, FL	0.0
Inaja and Cosmit Reservation, CA	-
Indian Township Reservation, ME	6.3
Iowa (KS-NE) Reservation and Off-Reservation Trust Land, KS--NE	6.8
Isabella Reservation and Off-Reservation Trust Land, MI	7.9
Isleta Pueblo, NM	9.3
Jackson Rancheria, CA	-
Jamestown S'Klallam Reservation and Off-Reservation Trust Land, WA	2.6
Jamul Indian Village, CA	-
Jemez Pueblo, NM	10.6
Jena Band of Choctaw Reservation, LA	-
Jicarilla Apache Nation Reservation and Off-Reservation Trust Land, NM	5.5
Kaibab Indian Reservation, AZ	3.9
Kalispel Reservation and Off-Reservation Trust Land, WA	7.3
Karuk Reservation and Off-Reservation Trust Land, CA	7.3
Kickapoo (KS) Reservation, KS	13.4
Kickapoo (TX) Reservation, TX	0.0
Klamath Reservation, OR	0.0
Kootenai Reservation and Off-Reservation Trust Land, ID	12.5
Lac Courte Oreilles Reservation and Off-Reservation Trust Land, WI	8.5
Lac du Flambeau Reservation, WI	11.6
Lac Vieux Desert Reservation, MI	1.7
Laguna Pueblo and Off-Reservation Trust Land, NM	9.5
La Jolla Reservation, CA	3.1
Lake Traverse Reservation and Off-Reservation Trust Land, SD--ND	10.1
L'Anse Reservation and Off-Reservation Trust Land, MI	13.3
La Posta Indian Reservation, CA	0.0
Las Vegas Indian Colony, NV	2.8

Table 24. Percent of the Civilian Population 18 Years and Over Who Are Veterans, Selected Places by American Indian Area/Alaska Native Area/Alaska Native Regional Corporation, United States, American Community Survey 5-Year Estimates, 2013—*Continued*

(Percent.)

Area	Percent veterans	Area	Percent veterans
Laytonville Rancheria, CA	11.7	Port Madison Reservation, WA	14.2
Leech Lake Reservation and Off-Reservation Trust Land, MN	13.3	Prairie Band of Potawatomi Nation Reservation, KS	10.8
Likely Rancheria, CA	-	Prairie Island Indian Community and Off-Reservation Trust Land, MN	7.6
Little River Reservation and Off-Reservation Trust Land, MI	3.0	Pueblo of Pojoaque and Off-Reservation Trust Land, NM	11.9
Little Traverse Bay Reservation and Off-Reservation Trust Land, MI	12.5	Puyallup Reservation and Off-Reservation Trust Land, WA	11.3
Lone Pine Reservation, CA	8.5	Pyramid Lake Paiute Reservation, NV	12.1
Lookout Rancheria, CA	0.0	Quartz Valley Reservation and Off-Reservation Trust Land, CA	12.1
Los Coyotes Reservation, CA	10.3	Quileute Reservation, WA	4.2
Lovelock Indian Colony, NV	1.7	Quinault Reservation, WA	6.7
Lower Brule Reservation and Off-Reservation Trust Land, SD	11.2	Ramona Village, CA	-
Lower Elwha Reservation and Off-Reservation Trust Land, WA	6.4	Red Cliff Reservation and Off-Reservation Trust Land, WI	8.1
Lower Sioux Indian Community, MN	4.0	Redding Rancheria, CA	0.0
Lummi Reservation, WA	10.7	Red Lake Reservation, MN	4.8
Lytton Rancheria, CA	-	Redwood Valley Rancheria, CA	6.9
Makah Indian Reservation, WA	12.7	Reno-Sparks Indian Colony, NV	7.3
Manchester-Point Arena Rancheria, CA	0.6	Resighini Rancheria, CA	0.0
Manzanita Reservation and Off-Reservation Trust Land, CA	0.0	Rincon Reservation, CA	8.3
Maricopa (Ak Chin) Indian Reservation, AZ	2.9	Roaring Creek Rancheria, CA	0.0
Mashantucket Pequot Reservation and Off-Reservation Trust Land, CT	8.4	Robinson Rancheria and Off-Reservation Trust Land, CA	5.2
Match-e-be-nash-she-wish Band of Pottawatomi Reservation, MI	-	Rocky Boy's Reservation and Off-Reservation Trust Land, MT	7.8
Menominee Reservation and Off-Reservation Trust Land, WI	9.8	Rohnerville Rancheria, CA	10.0
Mesa Grande Reservation, CA	9.6	Rosebud Indian Reservation and Off-Reservation Trust Land, SD	9.2
Mescalero Reservation, NM	6.2	Round Valley Reservation and Off-Reservation Trust Land, CA	8.5
Miccosukee Reservation and Off-Reservation Trust Land, FL	-	Rumsey Indian Rancheria, CA	-
Middletown Rancheria, CA	0.0	Sac and Fox/Meskwaki Settlement and Off-Reservation Trust Land, IA	9.6
Mille Lacs Reservation and Off-Reservation Trust Land, MN	13.6	Sac and Fox Nation Reservation and Off-Reservation Trust Land, NE—KS	7.2
Minnesota Chippewa Trust Land, MN	17.7	St. Croix Reservation and Off-Reservation Trust Land, WI	6.1
Mississippi Choctaw Reservation and Off-Reservation Trust Land, MS	4.4	St. Regis Mohawk Reservation, NY	10.0
Moapa River Indian Reservation, NV	7.1	Salt River Reservation, AZ	6.4
Mohegan Reservation and Off-Reservation Trust Land, CT	0.0	San Carlos Reservation, AZ	6.6
Montgomery Creek Rancheria, CA	-	Sandia Pueblo, NM	8.6
Mooretown Rancheria and Off-Reservation Trust Land, CA	13.7	San Felipe Pueblo, NM	5.0
Morongo Reservation and Off-Reservation Trust Land, CA	4.6	San Ildefonso Pueblo and Off-Reservation Trust Land, NM	7.5
Muckleshoot Reservation and Off-Reservation Trust Land, WA	11.7	San Manuel Reservation and Off-Reservation Trust Land, CA	6.3
Nambe Pueblo and Off-Reservation Trust Land, NM	11.2	San Pasqual Reservation, CA	7.1
Narragansett Reservation, RI	14.3	Santa Ana Pueblo, NM	5.2
Navajo Nation Reservation and Off-Reservation Trust Land, AZ--NM--UT	4.8	Santa Clara Pueblo, NM	9.3
Nez Perce Reservation, ID	13.7	Santa Rosa Rancheria, CA	6.6
Nisqually Reservation, WA	15.9	Santa Rosa Reservation, CA	0.0
Nooksack Reservation and Off-Reservation Trust Land, WA	4.4	Santa Ynez Reservation, CA	7.0
Northern Cheyenne Indian Reservation and Off-Reservation Trust Land, MT--SD	7.4	Santa Ysabel Reservation, CA	8.9
North Fork Rancheria and Off-Reservation Trust Land, CA	16.1	Santee Reservation, NE	11.4
Northwestern Shoshone Reservation, UT	-	Santo Domingo Pueblo, NM	5.7
Ohkay Owingeh, NM	7.5	Sauk-Suiattle Reservation, WA	17.5
Oil Springs Reservation, NY	0.0	Sault Ste. Marie Reservation and Off-Reservation Trust Land, MI	8.6
Omaha Reservation, NE--IA	8.2	Seminole (FL) Trust Land, FL	-
Oneida Nation Reservation, NY	-	Shakopee Mdewakanton Sioux Community and Off-Reservation Trust Land, MN	16.9
Oneida (WI) Reservation and Off-Reservation Trust Land, WI	10.1	Sherwood Valley Rancheria and Off-Reservation Trust Land, CA	2.4
Onondaga Nation Reservation, NY	0.0	Shingle Springs Rancheria and Off-Reservation Trust Land, CA	4.3
Ontonagon Reservation, MI	-	Shoalwater Bay Indian Reservation and Off-Reservation Trust Land, WA	3.8
Osage Reservation, OK	11.2	Siletz Reservation and Off-Reservation Trust Land, OR	9.0
Paiute (UT) Reservation, UT	7.6	Skokomish Reservation, WA	7.0
Pala Reservation, CA	5.8	Skull Valley Reservation, UT	0.0
Pascua Pueblo Yaqui Reservation and Off-Reservation Trust Land, AZ	5.7	Smith River Rancheria and Off-Reservation Trust Land, CA	9.8
Paskenta Rancheria, CA	-	Snoqualmie Reservation, WA	-
Passamaquoddy Trust Land, ME	0.0	Soboba Reservation and Off-Reservation Trust Land, CA	3.7
Pauma and Yuima Reservation, CA	5.3	Sokaogon Chippewa Community and Off-Reservation Trust Land, WI	9.7
Pechanga Reservation, CA	8.3	Southern Ute Reservation, CO	11.4
Penobscot Reservation and Off-Reservation Trust Land, ME	10.3	South Fork Reservation and Off-Reservation Trust Land, NV	10.1
Picayune Rancheria and Off-Reservation Trust Land, CA	31.6	Spirit Lake Reservation, ND	7.4
Picuris Pueblo, NM	12.4	Spokane Reservation and Off-Reservation Trust Land, WA	18.0
Pine Ridge Reservation, SD--NE	8.0	Squaxin Island Reservation and Off-Reservation Trust Land, WA	7.4
Pinoleville Rancheria, CA	11.0	Standing Rock Reservation, SD--ND	9.8
Pit River Trust Land, CA	-	Stewart Community, NV	7.4
Pleasant Point Reservation, ME	6.7	Stewarts Point Rancheria, CA	6.7
Poarch Creek Reservation and Off-Reservation Trust Land, AL--FL	7.5	Stillaguamish Reservation and Off-Reservation Trust Land, WA	100.0
Pokagon Reservation and Off-Reservation Trust Land, MI	13.4	Stockbridge Munsee Community and Off-Reservation Trust Land, WI	11.8
Ponca (NE) Trust Land, NE--IA	0.0	Sulphur Bank Rancheria, CA	14.6
Port Gamble Reservation and Off-Reservation Trust Land, WA	10.7	Summit Lake Reservation and Off-Reservation Trust Land, NV	-

Table 24. Percent of the Civilian Population 18 Years and Over Who Are Veterans, Selected Places by American Indian Area/Alaska Native Area/Alaska Native Regional Corporation, United States, American Community Survey 5-Year Estimates, 2013—*Continued*

(Percent.)

Area	Percent veterans
Susanville Indian Rancheria and Off-Reservation Trust Land, CA	15.9
Swinomish Reservation and Off-Reservation Trust Land, WA	15.7
Sycuan Reservation and Off-Reservation Trust Land, CA	1.7
Table Bluff Reservation, CA	2.8
Table Mountain Rancheria, CA	48.5
Tampa Reservation, FL	-
Taos Pueblo and Off-Reservation Trust Land, NM	10.5
Tesuque Pueblo and Off-Reservation Trust Land, NM	6.3
Timbi-Sha Shoshone Reservation and Off-Reservation Trust Land, CA—NV	4.0
Tohono O'odham Nation Reservation and Off-Reservation Trust Land, AZ	7.6
Tonawanda Reservation, NY	12.7
Tonto Apache Reservation and Off-Reservation Trust Land, AZ	0.0
Torres-Martinez Reservation, CA	0.7
Trinidad Rancheria and Off-Reservation Trust Land, CA	7.2
Tulalip Reservation and Off-Reservation Trust Land, WA	12.1
Tule River Reservation and Off-Reservation Trust Land, CA	5.5
Tunica-Biloxi Reservation and Off-Reservation Trust Land, LA	1.6
Tuolumne Rancheria, CA	11.1
Turtle Mountain Reservation and Off-Reservation Trust Land, MT—ND—SD	6.5
Tuscarora Nation Reservation, NY	7.7
Twenty-Nine Palms Reservation, CA	0.0
Uintah and Ouray Reservation and Off-Reservation Trust Land, UT	6.9
Umatilla Reservation and Off-Reservation Trust Land, OR	10.1
Upper Lake Rancheria, CA	4.8
Upper Sioux Community and Off-Reservation Trust Land, MN	5.5
Upper Skagit Reservation, WA	12.3
Ute Mountain Reservation and Off-Reservation Trust Land, CO--NM--UT	2.2
Viejas Reservation, CA	3.3
Walker River Reservation, NV	10.5
Wampanoag-Aquinnah Trust Land, MA	3.9
Warm Springs Reservation and Off-Reservation Trust Land, OR	7.8
Washoe Ranches Trust Land, NV--CA	20.5
Wells Colony, NV	0.0
White Earth Reservation and Off-Reservation Trust Land, MN	11.5
Wind River Reservation and Off-Reservation Trust Land, WY	10.6
Winnebago Reservation and Off-Reservation Trust Land, NE--IA	9.6
Winnemucca Indian Colony, NV	5.9
Woodfords Community, CA	5.9
XL Ranch Rancheria, CA	0.0
Yakama Nation Reservation and Off-Reservation Trust Land, WA	5.5
Yankton Reservation, SD	10.4
Yavapai-Apache Nation Reservation, AZ	7.4
Yavapai-Prescott Reservation, AZ	17.2
Yerington Colony, NV	0.4
Yomba Reservation, NV	0.0
Ysleta del Sur Pueblo and Off-Reservation Trust Land, TX	4.2
Yurok Reservation, CA	8.2
Zia Pueblo and Off-Reservation Trust Land, NM	10.8
Zuni Reservation and Off-Reservation Trust Land, NM--AZ	6.4
Kickapoo (KS) Reservation/Sac and Fox Nation Trust Land joint-use area, KS	-
San Felipe Pueblo/Santa Ana Pueblo joint-use area, NM	-
San Felipe Pueblo/Santo Domingo Pueblo joint-use area, NM	-
American Indian Reservation — State	
All areas	
Golden Hill Paugussett (state) Reservation, CT	0.0
Hassanamisco (state) Reservation, MA	0.0
Mattaponi (state) Reservation, VA	4.2
MOWA Choctaw (state) Reservation, AL	3.5
Pamunkey (state) Reservation, VA	23.4
Paucatuck Eastern Pequot (state) Reservation, CT	6.5
Poospatuck (state) Reservation, NY	5.8
Schaghticoke (state) Reservation, CT	0.0
Shinnecock (state) Reservation, NY	11.8
Tama (state) Reservation, GA	0.0
Oklahoma Tribal Statistical Area	
All areas	
Caddo-Wichita-Delaware OTSA, OK	10.9
Cherokee OTSA, OK	11.6
Cheyenne-Arapaho OTSA, OK	10.0
Chickasaw OTSA, OK	11.3
Choctaw OTSA, OK	10.9
Citizen Potawatomi Nation-Absentee Shawnee OTSA, OK	15.6
Creek OTSA, OK	10.1
Eastern Shawnee OTSA, OK	10.7
Iowa OTSA, OK	13.1
Kaw OTSA, OK	12.8
Kickapoo OTSA, OK	11.7
Kiowa-Comanche-Apache-Fort Sill Apache OTSA, OK	17.1
Miami OTSA, OK	10.3
Modoc OTSA, OK	5.1
Otoe-Missouria OTSA, OK	7.1
Ottawa OTSA, OK	9.9
Pawnee OTSA, OK	12.2
Peoria OTSA, OK	10.5
Ponca OTSA, OK	9.9
Quapaw OTSA, OK	11.3
Sac and Fox OTSA, OK	11.4
Seminole OTSA, OK	10.0
Seneca-Cayuga OTSA, OK	18.1
Tonkawa OTSA, OK	8.8
Wyandotte OTSA, OK	13.7
Creek/Seminole joint-use OTSA, OK	12.3
Kaw/Ponca joint-use OTSA, OK	10.9
Kiowa-Comanche-Apache-Ft Sill Apache/Caddo-Wichita-Delaware joint-use OTSA, OK	11.8
Miami/Peoria joint-use OTSA, OK	10.8
Alaska Native Village Statistical Area	
All areas	
Akhiok ANVSA, AK	0.0
Akiachak ANVSA, AK	7.1
Akiak ANVSA, AK	6.8
Akutan ANVSA, AK	1.3
Alakanuk ANVSA, AK	15.7
Alatna ANVSA, AK	0.0
Aleknagik ANVSA, AK	8.3
Algaaciq ANVSA, AK	8.2
Allakaket ANVSA, AK	0.0
Ambler ANVSA, AK	5.5
Anaktuvuk Pass ANVSA, AK	2.8
Andreafsky ANVSA, AK	4.5
Angoon ANVSA, AK	9.4
Aniak ANVSA, AK	10.5
Anvik ANVSA, AK	10.7
Arctic Village ANVSA, AK	10.5
Atka ANVSA, AK	4.2
Atmautluak ANVSA, AK	6.7
Atqasuk ANVSA, AK	6.5
Barrow ANVSA, AK	3.5
Beaver ANVSA, AK	12.8
Belkofski ANVSA, AK	-
Bethel ANVSA, AK	11.7
Bill Moore's ANVSA, AK	-
Birch Creek ANVSA, AK	0.0
Brevig Mission ANVSA, AK	8.2
Buckland ANVSA, AK	4.7
Cantwell ANVSA, AK	9.6
Canyon Village ANVSA, AK	-
Chalkyitsik ANVSA, AK	0.0
Chefornak ANVSA, AK	7.5
Chenega ANVSA, AK	5.6
Chevak ANVSA, AK	4.9
Chickaloon ANVSA, AK	14.1
Chignik ANVSA, AK	11.5

Table 24. Percent of the Civilian Population 18 Years and Over Who Are Veterans, Selected Places by American Indian Area/Alaska Native Area/Alaska Native Regional Corporation, United States, American Community Survey 5-Year Estimates, 2013—*Continued*

(Percent.)

Area	Percent veterans	Area	Percent veterans
Chignik Lagoon ANVSA, AK	2.0	Kotlik ANVSA, AK	8.2
Chignik Lake ANVSA, AK	2.6	Kotzebue ANVSA, AK	7.7
Chilkat ANVSA, AK	10.1	Koyuk ANVSA, AK	8.6
Chilkoot ANVSA, AK	12.9	Koyukuk ANVSA, AK	14.9
Chistochina ANVSA, AK	16.9	Kwethluk ANVSA, AK	2.3
Chitina ANVSA, AK	25.0	Kwigillingok ANVSA, AK	4.8
Chuathbaluk ANVSA, AK	0.0	Kwinhagak ANVSA, AK	8.6
Chulloonawick ANVSA, AK	-	Lake Minchumina ANVSA, AK	37.5
Circle ANVSA, AK	5.2	Larsen Bay ANVSA, AK	21.1
Clarks Point ANVSA, AK	0.0	Lesnoi ANVSA, AK	-
Copper Center ANVSA, AK	14.5	Levelock ANVSA, AK	4.4
Council ANVSA, AK	-	Lime Village ANVSA, AK	0.0
Craig ANVSA, AK	13.4	Lower Kalskag ANVSA, AK	5.8
Crooked Creek ANVSA, AK	1.5	McGrath ANVSA, AK	9.9
Deering ANVSA, AK	1.5	Manley Hot Springs ANVSA, AK	10.0
Dillingham ANVSA, AK	9.7	Manokotak ANVSA, AK	4.1
Dot Lake ANVSA, AK	18.5	Marshall ANVSA, AK	9.9
Douglas ANVSA, AK	10.2	Mary's Igloo ANVSA, AK	-
Eagle ANVSA, AK	25.0	Mekoryuk ANVSA, AK	10.6
Eek ANVSA, AK	6.4	Mentasta Lake ANVSA, AK	6.6
Egegik ANVSA, AK	6.4	Minto ANVSA, AK	4.8
Eklutna ANVSA, AK	0.0	Mountain Village ANVSA, AK	5.7
Ekuk ANVSA, AK	-	Naknek ANVSA, AK	12.9
Ekwok ANVSA, AK	4.2	Nanwalek ANVSA, AK	0.0
Elim ANVSA, AK	5.3	Napaimute ANVSA, AK	-
Emmonak ANVSA, AK	8.6	Napakiak ANVSA, AK	5.7
Evansville ANVSA, AK	21.6	Napaskiak ANVSA, AK	7.3
Eyak ANVSA, AK	4.5	Nelson Lagoon ANVSA, AK	0.0
False Pass ANVSA, AK	23.1	Nenana ANVSA, AK	15.7
Fort Yukon ANVSA, AK	6.1	Newhalen ANVSA, AK	7.4
Gakona ANVSA, AK	19.0	New Koliganek ANVSA, AK	5.9
Galena ANVSA, AK	8.7	New Stuyahok ANVSA, AK	2.9
Gambell ANVSA, AK	6.0	Newtok ANVSA, AK	1.9
Georgetown ANVSA, AK	-	Nightmute ANVSA, AK	10.7
Golovin ANVSA, AK	13.5	Nikolai ANVSA, AK	0.0
Goodnews Bay ANVSA, AK	5.5	Nikolski ANVSA, AK	9.4
Grayling ANVSA, AK	5.0	Ninilchik ANVSA, AK	14.3
Gulkana ANVSA, AK	9.2	Noatak ANVSA, AK	5.1
Hamilton ANVSA, AK	-	Nome ANVSA, AK	12.7
Healy Lake ANVSA, AK	-	Nondalton ANVSA, AK	5.9
Holy Cross ANVSA, AK	9.5	Noorvik ANVSA, AK	6.7
Hoonah ANVSA, AK	12.1	Northway ANVSA, AK	3.3
Hooper Bay ANVSA, AK	8.3	Nuiqsut ANVSA, AK	2.2
Hughes ANVSA, AK	0.0	Nulato ANVSA, AK	6.7
Huslia ANVSA, AK	11.4	Nunam Iqua ANVSA, AK	7.1
Hydaburg ANVSA, AK	6.4	Nunapitchuk ANVSA, AK	3.0
Igiugig ANVSA, AK	0.0	Ohogamiut ANVSA, AK	-
Iliamna ANVSA, AK	23.0	Old Harbor ANVSA, AK	7.4
Inalik ANVSA, AK	25.0	Oscarville ANVSA, AK	0.0
Ivanof Bay ANVSA, AK	-	Ouzinkie ANVSA, AK	11.3
Kake ANVSA, AK	13.5	Paimiut ANVSA, AK	-
Kaktovik ANVSA, AK	7.4	Pedro Bay ANVSA, AK	25.0
Kalskag ANVSA, AK	1.5	Perryville ANVSA, AK	2.9
Kaltag ANVSA, AK	8.5	Petersburg ANVSA, AK	10.0
Karluk ANVSA, AK	0.0	Pilot Point ANVSA, AK	6.5
Kasaan ANVSA, AK	5.0	Pilot Station ANVSA, AK	6.0
Kasigluk ANVSA, AK	8.7	Pitkas Point ANVSA, AK	6.6
Kenaitze ANVSA, AK	13.8	Platinum ANVSA, AK	22.5
Ketchikan ANVSA, AK	14.2	Point Hope ANVSA, AK	8.3
Kiana ANVSA, AK	6.8	Point Lay ANVSA, AK	5.6
King Cove ANVSA, AK	6.2	Portage Creek ANVSA, AK	-
King Salmon ANVSA, AK	12.9	Port Alsworth ANVSA, AK	2.2
Kipnuk ANVSA, AK	3.5	Port Graham ANVSA, AK	13.7
Kivalina ANVSA, AK	3.6	Port Heiden ANVSA, AK	21.2
Klawock ANVSA, AK	9.8	Port Lions ANVSA, AK	5.9
Knik ANVSA, AK	14.9	Rampart ANVSA, AK	15.0
Kobuk ANVSA, AK	3.0	Red Devil ANVSA, AK	11.5
Kodiak ANVSA, AK	-	Ruby ANVSA, AK	15.2
Kokhanok ANVSA, AK	6.8	Russian Mission ANVSA, AK	4.9
Kongiganak ANVSA, AK	3.7	St. George ANVSA, AK	13.3

Table 24. Percent of the Civilian Population 18 Years and Over Who Are Veterans, Selected Places by American Indian Area/Alaska Native Area/Alaska Native Regional Corporation, United States, American Community Survey 5-Year Estimates, 2013—*Continued*

(Percent.)

Area	Percent veterans
St. Michael ANVSA, AK	6.8
St. Paul ANVSA, AK	7.4
Salamatof ANVSA, AK	11.7
Sand Point ANVSA, AK	2.7
Savoonga ANVSA, AK	4.2
Saxman ANVSA, AK	7.5
Scammon Bay ANVSA, AK	8.3
Selawik ANVSA, AK	7.6
Seldovia ANVSA, AK	14.7
Shageluk ANVSA, AK	9.4
Shaktoolik ANVSA, AK	7.3
Shishmaref ANVSA, AK	7.2
Shungnak ANVSA, AK	5.9
Sitka ANVSA, AK	10.2
Skagway ANVSA, AK	5.4
Sleetmute ANVSA, AK	6.0
Solomon ANVSA, AK	-
South Naknek ANVSA, AK	7.7
Stebbins ANVSA, AK	2.6
Stevens Village ANVSA, AK	6.7
Stony River ANVSA, AK	11.5
Takotna ANVSA, AK	7.1
Tanacross ANVSA, AK	20.0
Tanana ANVSA, AK	9.9
Tatitlek ANVSA, AK	15.4
Tazlina ANVSA, AK	17.5
Telida ANVSA, AK	0.0
Teller ANVSA, AK	6.3
Tetlin ANVSA, AK	9.2
Togiak ANVSA, AK	1.6
Toksook Bay ANVSA, AK	1.3
Tuluksak ANVSA, AK	8.4
Tuntutuliak ANVSA, AK	2.3
Tununak ANVSA, AK	13.2
Twin Hills ANVSA, AK	10.0
Tyonek ANVSA, AK	6.9
Ugashik ANVSA, AK	13.3
Unalakleet ANVSA, AK	11.4
Unalaska ANVSA, AK	6.0
Venetie ANVSA, AK	5.1
Wainwright ANVSA, AK	10.2
Wales ANVSA, AK	8.0
White Mountain ANVSA, AK	12.3
Wrangell ANVSA, AK	17.4
Yakutat ANVSA, AK	13.6
Tribal Designated Statistical Area	
All areas	
Cayuga Nation TDSA, NY	11.5
Ione Band of Miwok TDSA, CA	0.0
Mechoopda TDSA, CA	7.2
Samish TDSA, WA	14.1
State Designated Tribal Statistical Area	
All areas	
Adais Caddo SDTSA, LA	9.3
Apache Choctaw SDTSA, LA	8.3
Beaver Creek SDTSA, SC	12.1
Cher-O-Creek SDTSA, AL	11.6
Cherokee Tribe of Northeast Alabama SDTSA, AL	11.1
Chickahominy SDTSA, VA	12.5
Clifton Choctaw SDTSA, LA	9.5
Coharie SDTSA, NC	11.5
Eastern Chickahominy SDTSA, VA	17.6
Echota Cherokee SDTSA, AL	11.5
Four Winds Cherokee SDTSA, LA	19.4
Haliwa-Saponi SDTSA, NC	6.1
Lenape Indian Tribe of Delaware SDTSA, DE	12.9
Lumbee SDTSA, NC	15.6
MaChis Lower Creek SDTSA, AL	13.7
Meherrin SDTSA, NC	8.7
Nanticoke Indian Tribe SDTSA, DE	14.9
Nanticoke Lenni Lenape SDTSA, NJ	8.5
Occaneechi-Saponi SDTSA, NC	10.3
Pee Dee SDTSA, SC	7.2
Ramapough SDTSA, NJ	5.9
Sappony SDTSA, NC	10.4
Santee SDTSA, SC	5.6
Star Muskogee Creek SDTSA, AL	13.0
United Cherokee Ani-Yun-Wiya Nation SDTSA, AL	11.6
United Houma Nation SDTSA, LA	7.8
Upper South Carolina Pee Dee SDTSA, SC	6.3
Waccamaw SDTSA, SC	4.9
Waccamaw Siouan SDTSA, NC	8.1
Wassamasaw SDTSA, SC	21.4
Alaska Native Regional Corporation	
Ahtna ANRC, AK	17.0
Aleut ANRC, AK	6.1
Arctic Slope ANRC, AK	8.5
Bering Straits ANRC, AK	9.5
Bristol Bay ANRC, AK	7.9
Calista ANRC, AK	8.1
Chugach ANRC, AK	13.9
Cook Inlet ANRC, AK	14.4
Doyon ANRC, AK	16.2
Koniag ANRC, AK	11.9
NANA ANRC, AK	7.4
Sealaska ANRC, AK	12.1

- = Either no sample observations or too few sample observations were available to compute an estimate, or a ratio of medians cannot be calculated because one or both of the median estimates falls in the lowest interval or upper interval of an open-ended distribution.

Table 25. Period of Military Service for Civilian Veterans 18 Years and Over, States and Puerto Rico, American Community Survey Estimates, 2013

(Number.)

Geographic area	1-year estimates							
	Total	Gulf War (9/2001 or later), no Gulf War (8/1990 to 8/2001), no Vietnam Era	Gulf War (9/2001 or later) and Gulf War (8/1990 to 8/2001), no Vietnam Era	Gulf War (9/2001 or later), and Gulf War (8/1990 to 8/2001), and Vietnam Era	Gulf War (8/1990 to 8/2001), no Vietnam Era	Gulf War (8/1990 to 8/2001) and Vietnam Era	Vietnam Era, no Korean War, no World War II	Vietnam Era and Korean War, no World War II
Alabama	355,396	32,728	20,766	2,587	46,732	8,564	115,126	5,411
Alaska	63,023	10,227	5,647	520	9,554	981	18,877	374
Arizona	498,885	40,885	25,541	1,895	54,102	8,166	165,695	7,441
Arkansas	218,589	20,999	9,327	868	25,504	3,380	72,059	3,879
California	1,743,333	166,120	73,385	3,741	173,247	18,208	583,549	17,619
Colorado	380,210	40,264	28,408	1,237	50,249	8,067	121,045	4,568
Connecticut	190,782	11,388	6,672	629	15,402	1,791	62,516	769
Delaware	68,666	4,671	4,426	94	6,973	1,234	22,548	926
District of Columbia	27,846	3,430	2,539	0	3,293	125	6,928	191
Florida	1,455,002	98,460	71,395	4,581	153,693	26,103	459,577	20,991
Georgia	645,822	61,102	44,927	1,561	99,084	14,672	192,174	6,932
Hawaii	107,791	17,400	11,963	984	8,384	1,940	32,176	1,243
Idaho	119,403	11,150	6,631	592	12,418	2,676	41,528	837
Illinois	655,291	47,335	21,419	860	71,789	5,438	223,625	2,473
Indiana	420,596	28,124	12,492	782	53,493	3,459	143,763	1,144
Iowa	208,602	19,010	7,613	855	19,385	2,150	70,925	1,025
Kansas	197,302	22,060	12,656	512	20,233	3,728	60,984	1,504
Kentucky	293,162	24,927	14,959	901	37,168	4,194	97,886	2,615
Louisiana	268,553	27,838	14,233	565	32,794	2,441	87,613	2,105
Maine	119,540	7,297	5,484	349	11,476	2,077	43,248	1,450
Maryland	400,934	37,107	37,313	2,371	49,314	7,491	112,431	3,406
Massachusetts	340,282	23,434	8,287	992	26,411	1,645	113,002	1,550
Michigan	618,433	36,123	16,729	691	62,094	4,762	222,442	2,840
Minnesota	337,197	23,485	13,095	406	27,305	2,538	122,684	1,261
Mississippi	183,405	17,188	11,819	653	23,835	3,598	59,762	3,600
Missouri	436,545	30,539	19,404	1,066	47,213	5,522	149,783	2,644
Montana	82,659	6,421	3,540	242	7,961	734	31,026	699
Nebraska	124,987	11,045	6,533	544	14,057	2,920	38,351	1,016
Nevada	215,452	20,637	14,184	801	23,095	3,681	71,600	3,023
New Hampshire	106,113	5,176	4,632	361	10,187	1,583	36,022	950
New Jersey	384,726	25,968	10,427	900	28,916	2,263	128,565	1,878
New Mexico	160,570	15,356	10,584	257	18,479	3,265	51,415	2,654
New York	804,646	66,295	20,162	1,154	63,048	6,696	255,552	1,906
North Carolina	681,275	56,967	41,195	2,043	89,355	13,871	224,490	8,402
North Dakota	48,892	7,363	2,544	9	3,887	915	16,092	333
Ohio	790,615	52,259	28,816	1,523	80,389	6,648	273,933	2,211
Oklahoma	280,509	28,764	14,559	1,120	35,596	5,848	93,829	3,439
Oregon	293,024	17,115	10,667	1,000	30,067	4,285	106,888	1,762
Pennsylvania	849,690	53,472	26,295	2,220	81,338	6,331	284,457	2,972
Rhode Island	64,325	5,825	2,628	137	4,925	422	19,923	402
South Carolina	366,802	35,748	20,532	1,745	46,445	8,804	119,002	5,655
South Dakota	61,883	7,452	2,971	301	6,077	1,660	19,295	425
Tennessee	465,435	41,696	23,726	2,240	53,982	9,694	160,474	4,437
Texas	1,483,389	164,860	101,164	4,962	220,589	25,748	455,256	17,011
Utah	131,033	15,423	7,591	593	13,257	2,213	41,528	1,070
Vermont	41,028	1,635	940	30	3,205	342	16,025	379
Virginia	687,158	83,625	88,114	3,312	96,243	24,400	181,884	7,757
Washington	541,551	52,543	35,969	1,663	63,789	10,964	181,456	6,024
West Virginia	150,576	8,334	6,555	327	18,494	1,968	55,180	999
Wisconsin	368,679	26,777	11,034	658	35,014	3,154	129,770	1,253
Wyoming	48,979	5,386	4,009	11	6,621	892	16,328	221
Puerto Rico	88,933	7,798	2,319	382	5,451	366	27,032	486

Table 25. Period of Military Service for Civilian Veterans 18 Years and Over, States and Puerto Rico, American Community Survey Estimates, 2013—*Continued*

(Number.)

Geographic area	1-year estimates							
	Vietnam Era and Korean War and World War II	Korean War, no Vietnam Era, no World War II	Korean War and World War II, no Vietnam Era	World War II, no Korean War, no Vietnam Era	Between Gulf War and Vietnam Era only	Between Vietnam Era and Korean War only	Between Korean War and World War II only	Pre-World War II only
Alabama	1,260	25,281	1,499	14,959	50,154	28,669	1,536	124
Alaska	247	1,705	73	1,872	9,520	3,420	6	0
Arizona	1,432	47,890	2,649	27,169	62,322	50,973	1,975	750
Arkansas	611	19,941	457	9,475	30,873	19,802	996	418
California	7,208	168,079	10,840	117,691	228,835	162,770	10,325	1,716
Colorado	921	24,652	1,378	16,212	52,099	29,461	1,587	62
Connecticut	70	21,553	1,888	18,414	26,174	21,975	1,376	165
Delaware	104	5,588	185	4,075	9,970	7,263	490	119
District of Columbia	128	2,474	161	1,892	4,234	2,096	253	102
Florida	4,569	154,363	8,957	104,205	191,108	147,224	8,336	1,440
Georgia	1,602	41,729	2,375	22,165	105,697	49,054	2,293	455
Hawaii	343	7,262	574	4,882	11,185	8,606	707	142
Idaho	117	9,971	301	7,177	14,817	10,720	468	0
Illinois	488	69,993	2,148	47,211	90,485	67,014	4,348	665
Indiana	220	38,755	1,119	26,693	67,704	39,767	2,853	228
Iowa	304	24,400	789	16,449	22,867	21,647	1,061	122
Kansas	488	18,251	885	12,535	25,017	16,691	1,485	273
Kentucky	420	23,689	544	15,619	40,941	26,781	2,361	157
Louisiana	770	23,687	854	14,440	35,216	24,456	1,411	130
Maine	156	11,342	304	7,849	18,064	9,486	944	14
Maryland	682	29,861	1,513	22,206	62,100	33,069	1,941	129
Massachusetts	466	41,034	3,237	30,778	47,172	39,089	2,637	548
Michigan	414	63,300	2,767	44,921	94,072	63,154	3,875	249
Minnesota	106	37,816	1,193	22,231	48,063	35,373	1,573	68
Mississippi	260	11,895	1,007	9,090	25,171	14,763	616	148
Missouri	1,233	40,914	2,893	23,944	68,712	39,561	2,795	322
Montana	66	7,331	668	3,776	11,036	8,432	580	147
Nebraska	199	14,028	433	7,228	16,975	11,300	353	5
Nevada	268	15,217	1,109	8,844	31,882	20,305	643	163
New Hampshire	187	10,535	642	5,877	18,330	11,453	105	73
New Jersey	327	50,028	2,001	37,430	45,955	46,614	3,009	445
New Mexico	590	12,740	931	6,719	22,579	14,156	683	162
New York	392	97,641	3,648	72,099	119,907	89,124	6,114	908
North Carolina	1,257	52,735	2,024	29,349	100,703	55,649	2,869	366
North Dakota	0	4,992	82	2,433	5,021	5,197	24	0
Ohio	964	78,489	3,898	53,991	125,655	76,694	4,229	916
Oklahoma	259	24,055	1,163	11,772	35,118	22,994	1,829	164
Oregon	463	25,693	1,092	19,197	41,377	31,588	1,541	289
Pennsylvania	851	94,478	4,272	67,558	119,677	97,049	7,737	983
Rhode Island	344	8,649	327	5,806	9,167	5,163	607	0
South Carolina	813	26,214	2,207	14,530	52,609	30,472	1,714	312
South Dakota	0	7,340	550	2,410	7,912	5,041	363	86
Tennessee	581	35,854	1,631	21,443	67,335	40,850	1,343	149
Texas	3,117	101,536	7,528	62,653	200,421	108,590	9,066	888
Utah	161	12,356	626	8,039	14,697	12,509	923	47
Vermont	82	3,854	537	2,960	6,641	4,089	260	49
Virginia	2,673	37,069	2,114	24,721	90,658	41,872	1,966	750
Washington	1,299	38,832	1,816	24,356	75,524	44,354	2,655	307
West Virginia	27	13,031	1,122	7,282	21,297	14,988	972	0
Wisconsin	351	39,224	1,454	26,622	49,915	41,561	1,758	134
Wyoming	0	3,703	205	1,994	5,644	3,803	162	0
Puerto Rico	51	18,021	309	4,082	11,271	10,385	601	379

Table 25. Period of Military Service for Civilian Veterans 18 Years and Over, States and Puerto Rico, American Community Survey Estimates, 2013—*Continued*

(Number.)

Geographic area	3-year estimates							
	Total	Gulf War (9/2001 or later), no Gulf War (8/1990 to 8/2001), no Vietnam Era	Gulf War (9/2001 or later) and Gulf War (8/1990 to 8/2001), no Vietnam Era	Gulf War (9/2001 or later), and Gulf War (8/1990 to 8/2001), and Vietnam Era	Gulf War (8/1990 to 8/2001), no Vietnam Era	Gulf War (8/1990 to 8/2001) and Vietnam Era	Vietnam Era, no Korean War, no World War II	Vietnam Era and Korean War, no World War II
Alabama	380,869	33,231	21,404	2,020	49,313	8,550	120,946	6,321
Alaska	69,354	10,287	6,761	361	10,979	1,201	20,018	490
Arizona	517,913	42,000	24,018	1,243	54,190	8,493	166,559	7,473
Arkansas	229,403	21,182	7,918	1,001	26,250	3,545	74,225	3,790
California	1,839,029	158,361	72,623	3,518	179,885	20,582	598,975	19,477
Colorado	400,149	37,789	26,631	1,110	51,583	8,896	127,916	5,583
Connecticut	210,645	11,795	5,517	414	16,887	1,965	69,768	778
Delaware	73,407	5,311	3,812	177	7,496	1,117	23,890	858
District of Columbia	29,635	3,317	1,936	16	3,455	270	8,073	280
Florida	1,530,401	95,923	66,118	3,983	157,764	26,553	465,836	21,768
Georgia	679,209	60,416	43,384	1,931	101,519	14,559	205,945	7,700
Hawaii	111,312	17,599	11,382	576	8,927	1,954	32,089	1,249
Idaho	121,363	9,879	5,434	418	13,698	2,068	42,222	1,245
Illinois	700,445	51,643	21,469	765	71,411	5,585	238,130	3,115
Indiana	444,835	30,787	12,118	898	47,106	4,556	148,046	1,995
Iowa	220,580	17,180	6,730	555	20,474	2,070	74,714	1,042
Kansas	207,521	20,651	10,402	452	22,894	3,496	65,573	1,798
Kentucky	306,527	24,295	13,218	782	35,868	4,345	103,635	2,810
Louisiana	297,393	29,338	14,496	550	37,596	3,090	96,610	2,831
Maine	123,884	6,827	4,556	270	12,493	1,931	43,441	1,373
Maryland	420,257	38,795	32,943	1,700	52,481	7,714	119,201	3,386
Massachusetts	368,700	23,565	8,184	966	27,978	2,096	118,050	2,045
Michigan	650,663	34,931	15,575	858	61,848	4,620	231,300	2,763
Minnesota	357,324	23,102	10,643	495	30,035	2,880	127,632	1,571
Mississippi	195,828	18,976	9,022	694	23,926	3,735	62,020	2,986
Missouri	469,128	32,211	17,612	982	50,368	6,508	158,305	3,898
Montana	92,510	7,162	3,286	272	9,746	1,413	32,336	808
Nebraska	138,188	12,336	7,199	338	15,779	2,486	43,052	1,159
Nevada	224,263	19,003	10,965	666	25,325	4,088	73,333	3,078
New Hampshire	110,556	6,154	3,768	368	10,577	1,501	37,240	1,202
New Jersey	420,197	27,237	10,169	826	29,409	2,999	136,481	2,040
New Mexico	171,112	15,662	8,937	497	19,799	2,994	56,364	2,343
New York	870,137	63,393	20,496	1,564	67,752	6,029	272,513	2,566
North Carolina	713,723	59,899	40,573	1,806	91,994	15,304	226,209	8,013
North Dakota	53,278	7,211	2,420	160	4,593	795	17,760	323
Ohio	838,539	51,038	24,853	1,485	86,369	6,829	285,959	3,466
Oklahoma	306,485	27,442	15,362	1,059	36,369	5,807	101,547	3,487
Oregon	312,755	18,231	9,036	748	30,530	3,592	114,220	2,458
Pennsylvania	908,924	53,699	25,748	1,777	79,662	7,774	298,992	4,097
Rhode Island	69,036	5,055	2,429	249	5,219	727	21,567	503
South Carolina	386,543	34,631	20,114	1,616	48,140	8,640	124,147	6,390
South Dakota	66,432	6,252	3,030	268	6,618	1,373	20,842	557
Tennessee	475,435	38,471	21,683	1,857	54,783	8,739	159,786	5,337
Texas	1,561,756	167,905	90,994	4,329	219,943	28,130	483,267	20,076
Utah	140,739	15,441	7,239	553	14,702	2,359	43,906	1,250
Vermont	46,825	2,738	1,075	81	3,650	496	16,492	321
Virginia	717,295	80,002	85,462	4,467	101,734	25,380	188,619	9,680
Washington	574,914	51,490	32,591	1,567	68,131	12,136	189,175	6,312
West Virginia	156,983	10,028	5,181	393	17,427	1,605	55,567	1,395
Wisconsin	395,187	27,432	10,722	717	37,074	3,474	133,478	1,481
Wyoming	50,277	4,962	3,154	48	6,713	827	16,893	393
Puerto Rico	100,988	9,271	2,762	328	7,147	484	28,046	697

Table 25. Period of Military Service for Civilian Veterans 18 Years and Over, States and Puerto Rico, American Community Survey Estimates, 2013—*Continued*

(Number.)

Geographic area	3-year estimates							
	Vietnam Era and Korean War and World War II	Korean War, no Vietnam Era, no World War II	Korean War and World War II, no Vietnam Era	World War II, no Korean War, no Vietnam Era	Between Gulf War and Vietnam Era only	Between Vietnam Era and Korean War only	Between Korean War and World War II only	Pre-Word War II only
Alabama	1,233	29,127	1,573	18,771	53,062	33,312	1,760	246
Alaska	102	2,883	245	1,592	10,329	3,955	144	7
Arizona	1,569	50,876	3,619	32,553	66,707	55,402	2,712	499
Arkansas	678	20,388	1,061	12,436	32,374	22,995	1,232	328
California	6,328	177,402	14,286	138,796	245,797	187,261	12,766	2,972
Colorado	1,018	27,436	1,413	20,216	55,176	33,551	1,671	160
Connecticut	230	24,495	1,702	22,566	28,061	24,701	1,457	309
Delaware	136	6,299	272	4,831	10,421	8,195	458	134
District of Columbia	69	2,781	165	1,903	4,675	2,439	163	93
Florida	5,974	166,567	11,311	125,673	201,505	169,314	10,093	2,019
Georgia	1,794	44,705	2,320	27,229	112,057	52,567	2,665	418
Hawaii	390	7,494	572	6,313	12,036	9,509	1,002	220
Idaho	243	10,753	612	7,967	14,545	11,601	629	49
Illinois	740	74,076	3,241	56,129	91,204	77,062	5,001	874
Indiana	396	43,643	1,860	29,657	74,526	46,146	2,803	298
Iowa	242	25,974	992	18,478	27,158	23,481	1,352	138
Kansas	603	19,262	1,176	15,328	24,818	19,441	1,447	180
Kentucky	445	26,744	614	17,243	45,496	28,746	2,000	286
Louisiana	527	24,864	1,791	17,857	37,965	27,892	1,751	235
Maine	287	11,685	672	9,098	18,686	11,571	983	11
Maryland	1,071	32,278	1,893	26,772	64,147	35,743	1,840	293
Massachusetts	419	45,482	3,467	37,630	51,038	44,764	2,519	497
Michigan	571	68,211	2,901	52,961	96,555	72,500	4,510	559
Minnesota	304	39,761	1,703	27,211	47,887	41,696	2,137	267
Mississippi	377	15,603	1,231	10,281	28,465	17,427	895	190
Missouri	721	44,938	2,644	31,507	69,094	47,368	2,567	405
Montana	52	7,925	487	5,302	12,655	10,399	519	148
Nebraska	189	15,045	692	9,583	17,262	12,409	604	55
Nevada	625	18,660	1,078	10,465	32,771	22,985	1,118	103
New Hampshire	247	10,810	629	7,265	18,274	11,978	400	143
New Jersey	469	54,873	2,628	44,004	50,651	54,249	3,545	617
New Mexico	450	13,214	971	8,837	25,118	14,758	734	434
New York	750	105,768	4,452	86,883	124,445	105,764	6,697	1,065
North Carolina	1,215	55,106	2,705	35,199	107,657	64,584	2,861	598
North Dakota	99	5,234	100	3,361	5,513	5,502	151	56
Ohio	829	82,731	3,993	64,822	131,156	89,561	4,613	835
Oklahoma	438	25,929	1,839	16,708	39,744	28,776	1,757	221
Oregon	609	28,332	1,864	24,037	42,224	35,046	1,552	276
Pennsylvania	981	102,617	5,537	84,116	124,590	110,485	7,786	1,063
Rhode Island	238	8,514	494	6,636	9,493	7,276	520	116
South Carolina	1,055	28,191	1,794	17,689	57,027	35,079	1,803	227
South Dakota	107	7,183	363	4,251	8,720	6,496	292	80
Tennessee	651	38,208	1,696	24,267	69,987	47,938	1,712	320
Texas	4,150	109,575	7,921	78,438	210,386	126,883	8,448	1,311
Utah	244	13,845	750	9,881	14,592	15,022	741	214
Vermont	60	4,723	367	3,330	7,711	5,400	351	30
Virginia	2,663	40,742	2,863	29,852	93,306	49,461	2,517	547
Washington	1,771	40,504	3,444	31,934	83,305	49,391	2,767	396
West Virginia	236	15,320	720	9,356	20,241	18,319	1,096	99
Wisconsin	348	41,387	1,722	30,207	54,980	49,677	2,267	221
Wyoming	56	4,174	332	2,188	5,531	4,834	169	3
Puerto Rico	190	20,765	675	4,644	12,331	12,622	689	337

Table 25. Period of Military Service for Civilian Veterans 18 Years and Over, States and Puerto Rico, American Community Survey Estimates, 2013—*Continued*

(Number.)

Geographic area	5-year estimates							
	Total	Gulf War (9/2001 or later), no Gulf War (8/1990 to 8/2001), no Vietnam Era	Gulf War (9/2001 or later) and Gulf War (8/1990 to 8/2001), no Vietnam Era	Gulf War (9/2001 or later), and Gulf War (8/1990 to 8/2001), and Vietnam Era	Gulf War (8/1990 to 8/2001), no Vietnam Era	Gulf War (8/1990 to 8/2001) and Vietnam Era	Vietnam Era, no Korean War, no World War II	Vietnam Era and Korean War, no World War II
Alabama	388,865	29,633	20,535	1,793	48,597	8,364	123,581	6,045
Alaska	71,004	9,440	7,338	372	11,315	1,350	21,159	539
Arizona	522,382	36,351	22,590	1,127	54,835	8,183	166,084	7,612
Arkansas	237,311	19,161	7,901	971	26,568	3,715	77,179	3,977
California	1,893,539	144,322	68,777	3,347	181,850	20,685	613,467	20,820
Colorado	399,458	31,810	23,777	1,095	52,656	8,604	129,827	5,591
Connecticut	217,947	10,728	5,094	347	16,252	1,982	72,292	794
Delaware	75,081	4,915	3,848	216	7,367	1,131	24,140	902
District of Columbia	30,520	2,864	1,745	50	3,233	293	8,421	271
Florida	1,569,406	86,923	62,951	3,937	156,838	27,705	468,402	22,995
Georgia	690,208	55,124	39,958	1,769	101,578	14,094	214,131	8,138
Hawaii	112,625	15,286	10,514	560	9,481	2,006	32,975	1,516
Idaho	122,955	8,852	5,348	348	13,339	1,952	42,341	1,599
Illinois	727,919	46,292	21,230	786	72,822	5,788	243,041	3,152
Indiana	455,105	26,979	11,471	660	48,083	4,348	151,430	2,010
Iowa	226,175	14,741	6,592	502	20,855	2,236	75,756	1,084
Kansas	211,113	17,722	9,305	448	22,839	3,667	67,999	2,011
Kentucky	312,365	21,586	12,314	775	36,411	4,342	104,622	3,043
Louisiana	304,271	27,318	13,414	591	38,082	3,493	99,220	3,004
Maine	126,842	6,470	4,058	355	12,741	1,908	43,029	1,372
Maryland	427,068	35,123	31,845	1,708	51,056	7,509	123,631	3,493
Massachusetts	383,087	21,360	8,011	937	27,813	2,131	122,157	2,246
Michigan	672,213	32,031	14,480	962	63,518	4,751	235,645	2,982
Minnesota	366,990	20,826	9,316	492	30,877	2,818	129,654	1,469
Mississippi	200,748	18,495	8,436	745	23,671	3,735	61,818	3,164
Missouri	479,828	29,763	16,339	1,104	50,029	6,260	160,570	3,981
Montana	94,404	6,465	3,427	201	9,888	1,538	32,991	833
Nebraska	142,176	11,432	7,078	253	15,791	2,458	44,040	1,104
Nevada	226,555	16,836	10,167	564	26,006	4,198	73,882	3,251
New Hampshire	112,790	5,487	3,574	328	10,323	1,416	38,182	1,267
New Jersey	437,652	23,894	9,371	703	29,885	2,948	140,349	1,993
New Mexico	172,717	14,149	8,139	515	18,940	3,098	57,156	2,490
New York	912,499	56,351	20,281	1,540	70,551	5,892	285,290	2,682
North Carolina	724,295	53,615	38,742	2,058	92,481	14,186	228,790	8,695
North Dakota	53,157	6,072	2,318	138	4,921	922	17,459	307
Ohio	864,923	45,078	23,670	1,333	86,326	6,971	292,447	3,489
Oklahoma	312,492	25,072	14,508	959	35,254	5,626	104,563	3,863
Oregon	323,205	16,164	8,722	674	30,926	3,599	116,892	2,686
Pennsylvania	943,417	50,240	24,312	1,729	80,146	8,247	305,659	4,126
Rhode Island	70,621	4,710	2,310	189	5,182	775	22,130	553
South Carolina	391,660	30,209	18,373	1,605	49,187	8,903	125,640	6,368
South Dakota	67,886	5,817	2,789	309	6,595	1,344	21,445	479
Tennessee	484,901	34,317	19,778	1,612	54,250	8,859	162,121	5,899
Texas	1,583,272	146,383	85,998	4,236	218,412	28,447	495,443	21,375
Utah	143,771	14,140	6,725	480	15,006	2,408	44,466	1,260
Vermont	48,456	2,490	1,047	69	3,682	470	16,957	334
Virginia	726,470	71,629	81,280	4,647	102,158	25,779	195,277	10,665
Washington	582,265	44,311	29,852	1,413	68,830	12,364	194,211	6,784
West Virginia	159,448	9,128	4,614	332	16,259	1,521	56,205	1,515
Wisconsin	408,870	24,228	10,109	679	37,786	3,504	136,989	1,657
Wyoming	50,852	4,478	2,788	71	6,678	972	16,920	476
Puerto Rico	105,823	8,915	2,519	401	7,288	772	29,589	890

Table 25. Period of Military Service for Civilian Veterans 18 Years and Over, States and Puerto Rico, American Community Survey Estimates, 2013—*Continued*

(Number.)

Geographic area	5-year estimates							
	Vietnam Era and Korean War and World War II	Korean War, no Vietnam Era, no World War II	Korean War and World War II, no Vietnam Era	World War II, no Korean War, no Vietnam Era	Between Gulf War and Vietnam Era only	Between Vietnam Era and Korean War only	Between Korean War and World War II only	Pre-World War II only
Alabama	1,153	32,280	2,402	22,090	55,249	34,971	1,858	314
Alaska	145	2,841	148	1,783	10,280	4,117	174	3
Arizona	1,870	53,512	3,787	38,284	67,732	57,029	2,860	526
Arkansas	714	21,734	1,349	14,767	33,415	24,027	1,446	387
California	7,161	188,736	15,784	161,466	253,645	197,212	12,883	3,384
Colorado	1,349	29,080	1,854	23,105	54,264	34,645	1,626	175
Connecticut	282	26,628	1,732	25,359	28,508	26,127	1,456	366
Delaware	145	7,038	396	5,383	10,916	8,153	412	119
District of Columbia	67	3,023	144	2,529	5,068	2,583	165	64
Florida	6,699	174,723	13,425	146,565	206,349	178,443	11,381	2,070
Georgia	1,944	46,424	2,820	31,658	113,930	55,074	3,091	475
Hawaii	482	8,697	486	7,041	12,367	10,165	862	187
Idaho	214	11,433	639	9,050	14,413	12,636	697	94
Illinois	811	79,900	3,531	66,591	95,623	82,120	5,318	914
Indiana	397	46,180	2,441	35,037	74,539	48,337	2,851	342
Iowa	301	27,749	1,190	21,051	27,763	24,925	1,252	178
Kansas	628	20,156	1,437	17,919	25,030	20,316	1,445	191
Kentucky	546	28,109	919	19,694	46,418	31,118	2,122	346
Louisiana	767	26,182	1,672	20,402	37,965	29,919	1,956	286
Maine	322	12,348	819	10,314	19,488	12,731	795	92
Maryland	1,221	33,928	2,143	30,370	65,019	37,683	2,029	310
Massachusetts	660	47,881	3,609	43,247	51,176	48,287	2,982	590
Michigan	705	74,143	3,315	61,414	96,614	76,188	4,805	660
Minnesota	358	42,049	1,994	31,688	48,904	44,087	2,106	352
Mississippi	390	17,692	1,118	12,303	29,158	18,709	1,049	265
Missouri	852	48,717	2,853	36,357	69,961	49,731	2,906	405
Montana	93	9,054	512	6,018	11,940	10,601	733	110
Nebraska	296	15,946	844	11,472	17,251	13,350	727	134
Nevada	731	19,751	1,213	11,831	32,914	23,794	1,205	212
New Hampshire	255	11,041	639	8,642	18,970	12,027	452	187
New Jersey	711	58,361	2,823	51,494	53,076	57,641	3,631	772
New Mexico	594	14,617	1,150	10,654	24,975	15,143	783	314
New York	884	112,464	5,090	102,401	127,320	113,410	6,985	1,358
North Carolina	1,400	57,098	3,031	42,484	110,181	67,257	3,641	636
North Dakota	136	5,395	115	3,743	5,441	5,883	223	84
Ohio	1,099	89,496	4,364	74,595	133,638	95,845	5,380	1,192
Oklahoma	746	27,528	2,142	19,822	39,640	30,522	1,900	347
Oregon	719	29,711	2,254	28,130	43,618	37,115	1,666	329
Pennsylvania	1,254	109,200	6,105	99,191	127,054	116,853	7,997	1,304
Rhode Island	192	8,905	532	7,477	9,537	7,506	512	111
South Carolina	1,158	30,759	2,076	20,658	56,926	37,474	2,086	238
South Dakota	107	7,568	468	4,894	8,587	7,020	383	81
Tennessee	917	41,153	2,104	28,771	72,279	50,257	2,164	420
Texas	5,501	116,372	9,010	89,904	217,070	135,273	8,245	1,603
Utah	271	14,615	855	11,284	15,503	15,807	786	165
Vermont	76	4,843	330	3,903	7,791	6,002	404	58
Virginia	3,305	43,781	3,289	34,484	94,982	51,615	2,878	701
Washington	2,007	44,155	3,823	35,847	83,736	51,523	2,776	633
West Virginia	314	16,141	806	11,301	20,912	19,213	1,103	84
Wisconsin	463	43,751	2,117	35,826	57,505	51,354	2,519	383
Wyoming	61	4,451	304	2,888	5,983	4,550	206	26
Puerto Rico	290	21,908	914	5,039	12,517	13,865	654	262

PART B

Veterans in the Bureau of Labor Statistics (BLS)

HIGHLIGHTS

Figure 1. Unemployment Rate, by Selected Race/Ethnicity, United States, 2014

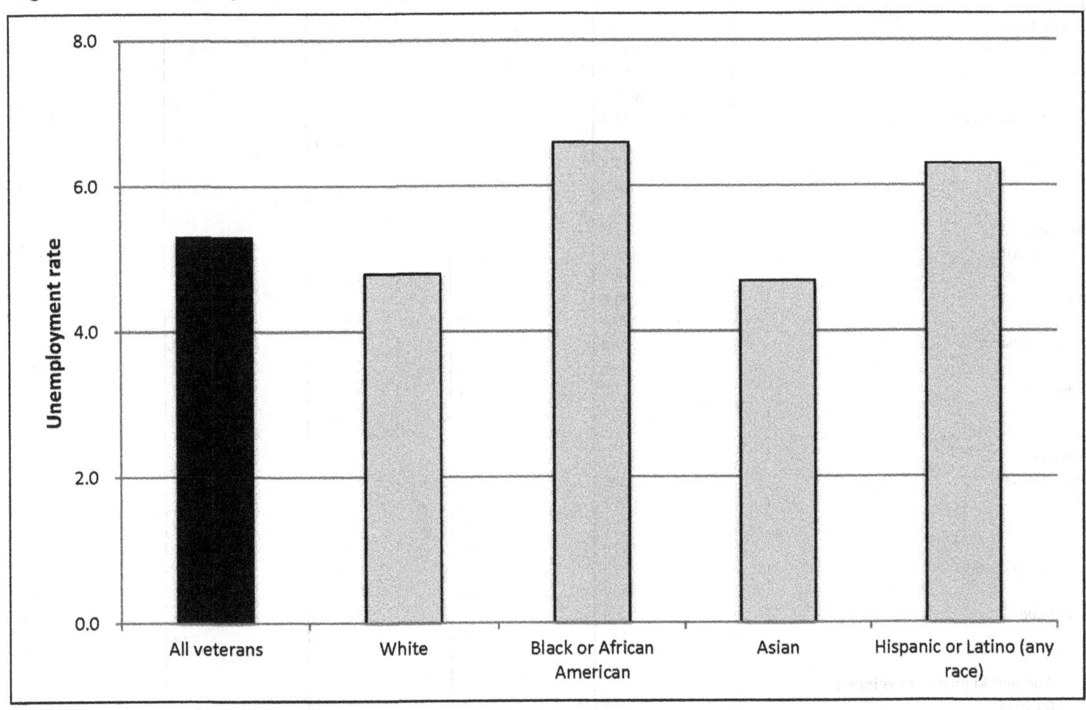

- In 2014, according to the Bureau of Labor Statistics, the total unemployment rate for veterans declined to 5.3 percent. The unemployment rate for veterans who served in the Gulf War II era (identified as after September 2001), declined 1.8 percentage points to 7.2 percent.

- Among the 573,000 unemployed veterans in 2014, 59 percent were age 45 and over, 37 percent were age 25 to 44, and 4 percent were age 18 to 24.

- Male veterans were unemployed at a rate of 5.2 percent and female veterans were unemployed at a rate of 6.0 percent in 2014.

- The unemployment rates in 2014 were 4.8 percent for White veterans, 6.6 percent for Black or African American veterans, 4.7 percent for Asian veterans, and 6.3 percent for veterans of Hispanic or Latino ethnicity.

Table 26. Employment Status of the Civilian Population 18 Years and Over, by Veteran Status, Period of Service, and Sex, Not Seasonally Adjusted, June 2014 and June 2015

(Numbers in thousands.)

Characteristic	Total		Men		Women	
	June 2014	June 2015	June 2014	June 2015	June 2014	June 2015
Veterans, 18 Years and Over						
Civilian nonsitutional population	21,181	21,224	18,930	19,227	2,251	1,997
Civilian labor force	10,621	10,541	9,245	9,407	1,377	1,133
Participation rate	50.1	49.7	48.8	48.9	61.2	56.8
Employed	10,043	10,082	8,771	9,025	1,273	1,057
Employment-population ratio	47.4	47.5	46.2	46.9	56.5	52.9
Unemployed	578	459	474	382	104	77
Unemployment rate	5.4	4.4	5.1	4.1	7.5	6.8
Not in labor force	10,560	10,683	9,685	9,820	874	864
Gulf War—era II veterans						
Civilian nonsitutional population	3,093	3,576	2,461	2,951	632	626
Civilian labor force	2,492	2,796	2,061	2,409	432	387
Participation rate	80.6	78.2	83.7	81.6	68.3	61.9
Employed	2,317	2,645	1,930	2,302	387	343
Employment-population ratio	74.9	74.0	78.4	78.0	61.2	54.8
Unemployed	175	151	131	107	44	44
Unemployment rate	7.0	5.4	6.3	4.5	10.3	11.4
Not in labor force	601	780	400	542	201	238
Gulf War—era I veterans						
Civilian nonsitutional population	3,380	3,449	2,712	2,911	668	537
Civilian labor force	2,797	2,746	2,280	2,373	518	373
Participation rate	82.8	79.6	84.1	81.5	77.6	69.4
Employed	2,670	2,630	2,192	2,278	478	352
Employment-population ratio	79.0	76.3	80.8	78.3	71.5	65.4
Unemployed	127	116	87	95	40	22
Unemployment rate	4.6	4.2	3.8	4.0	7.8	5.8
Not in labor force	582	702	432	538	150	164
World War II, Korean War, and Vietnam-era veterans						
Civilian nonsitutional population	9,399	8,920	9,046	8,603	353	317
Civilian labor force	2,623	2,348	2,519	2,261	104	87
Participation rate	27.9	26.3	27.8	26.3	29.4	27.5
Employed	2,489	2,250	2,397	2,164	92	86
Employment-population ratio	26.5	25.2	26.5	25.2	26.2	27.0
Unemployed	133	98	122	96	11	1
Unemployment rate	5.1	4.2	4.8	4.3	10.9	1.7
Not in labor force	6,776	6,572	6,527	6,342	249	230
Veterans of other service periods						
Civilian nonsitutional population	5,309	5,279	4,711	4,762	598	517
Civilian labor force	2,709	2,650	2,386	2,364	323	286
Participation rate	51.0	50.2	50.6	49.7	54.1	55.3
Employed	2,567	2,557	2,252	2,280	315	277
Employment-population ratio	48.4	48.4	47.8	47.9	52.7	53.5
Unemployed	142	93	134	84	8	9
Unemployment rate	5.2	3.5	5.6	3.6	2.4	3.3
Not in labor force	2,600	2,629	2,325	2,398	275	231
Nonveterans, 18 Year and Over						
Civilian nonsitutional population	217,844	220,583	96,293	97,257	121,550	123,326
Civilian labor force	144,013	145,295	73,460	73,791	70,553	71,505
Participation rate	66.1	65.9	76.3	75.9	58.0	58.0
Employed	135,399	137,702	69,006	69,934	66,393	67,768
Employment-population ratio	62.2	62.4	71.7	71.9	54.6	54.9
Unemployed	8,614	7,594	4,453	3,857	4,161	3,737
Unemployment rate	6.0	5.2	6.1	5.2	5.9	5.2
Not in labor force	73,831	75,288	22,834	23,466	50,997	51,882

Note: Veterans served on active duty in the U.S. Armed Forces and were not on active duty at the time of the survey. Nonveterans never served on active duty in the U.S. Armed Forces. Veterans could have served anywhere in the world during these periods of service: Gulf War era II (September 2001-present), Gulf War era I (August 1990-August 2001), Vietnam era (August 1964-April 1975), Korean War (July 1950-January 1955), World War II (December 1941-December 1946), and other service periods (all other time periods). Veterans who served in more than one wartime period are classified only in the most recent one. Veterans who served during one of the selected wartime periods and another period are classified only in the wartime period.

Table 27. Employment Status of Persons 18 Years and Over by Veteran Status, Period of Service, Sex, Race, and Hispanic or Latino Ethnicity, 2014 Annual Averages

(Numbers in thousands; percent.)

Characteristic	Civilian noninstitutionalized population	Civilian labor force						Not in labor force
		Total	Percent of population	Employed		Unemployed		
				Total	Percent of population	Total	Percent of labor force	
TOTAL								
Total, 18 years and over	239,049	153,951	64.4	144,760	60.6	9,191	6.0	85,098
Veterans	21,229	10,744	50.6	10,171	47.9	573	5.3	10,485
Gulf War era, total	6,540	5,302	81.1	5,003	76.5	298	5.6	1,238
Gulf War era II	3,185	2,535	79.6	2,353	73.9	182	7.2	649
Gulf War era I	3,356	2,766	82.4	2,650	79.0	117	4.2	589
WWII, Korean War, and Vietnam era	9,372	2,654	28.3	2,522	26.9	132	5.0	6,718
Other service periods	5,317	2,788	52.4	2,645	49.7	143	5.1	2,529
Nonveterans	217,820	143,207	65.7	134,589	61.8	8,618	6.0	74,613
MEN								
Total, 18 years and over	115,235	81,924	71.1	76,963	66.8	4,960	6.1	33,311
Veterans	19,023	9,358	49.2	8,868	46.6	490	5.2	9,664
Gulf War era, total	5,268	4,393	83.4	4,157	78.9	236	5.4	875
Gulf War era II	2,549	2,096	82.2	1,952	76.6	144	6.9	453
Gulf War era I	2,719	2,297	84.5	2,205	81.1	92	4.0	421
WWII, Korean War, and Vietnam era	9,023	2,559	28.4	2,432	27.0	127	5.0	6,464
Other service periods	4,732	2,406	50.8	2,270	48.2	127	5.3	2,326
Nonveterans	96,213	72,565	75.4	68,095	70.8	4,470	6.2	23,647
WOMEN								
Total, 18 years and over	123,814	72,027	58.2	67,796	54.8	4,231	5.9	51,787
Veterans	2,206	1,386	62.8	1,303	59.0	83	6.0	821
Gulf War era, total	1,272	909	71.4	847	66.5	62	6.8	463
Gulf War era II	635	439	69.2	402	63.3	37	8.5	196
Gulf War era I	637	469	73.7	445	69.8	25	5.2	168
WWII, Korean War, and Vietnam era	349	95	27.2	90	25.7	5	5.4	254
Other service periods	585	382	65.3	366	62.6	16	4.2	203
Nonveterans	121,607	70,641	58.1	66,494	54.7	4,184	5.9	50,966
WHITE								
Total, 18 years and over	188,848	121,736	64.5	115,499	61.2	6,237	5.1	67,112
Veterans	17,786	8,735	49.1	8,317	46.8	418	4.8	9,050
Gulf War era, total	5,039	4,128	81.9	3,915	77.7	213	5.2	910
Gulf War era II	2,449	1,977	80.7	1,849	75.5	127	6.4	472
Gulf War era I	2,590	2,152	83.1	2,066	79.8	85	4.0	438
WWII, Korean War, and Vietnam era	8,317	2,360	28.4	2,251	27.1	109	4.6	5,957
Other service periods	4,430	2,247	50.7	2,151	48.6	96	4.3	2,183
Nonveterans	171,062	113,001	66.1	107,182	62.7	5,819	5.1	58,062
BLACK OR AFRICAN AMERICAN								
Total, 18 years and over	2,516	1,445	57.4	1,334	53.0	111	7.7	1,071
Veterans	1,049	815	77.6	761	72.5	54	6.6	235
Gulf War era, total	490	366	74.6	331	67.5	35	9.5	124
Gulf War era II	559	449	80.3	430	76.9	19	4.2	110
Gulf War era I	768	204	26.6	188	24.4	17	8.2	564
WWII, Korean War, and Vietnam era	699	426	61.0	386	55.2	41	9.6	272
Other service periods	27,047	17,253	63.8	15,309	56.6	1,944	11.3	9,794
Nonveterans								
ASIAN								
Total, 18 years and over	13,288	8,651	65.1	8,226	61.9	425	4.9	4,637
Veterans	335	217	64.9	207	61.8	10	4.7	118
Gulf War era, total	166	141	85.1	134	80.7	7	5.2	25
Gulf War era II	90	74	82.7	69	76.6	5	7.4	16
Gulf War era I	77	67	87.9	65	85.4	2	2.8	9
WWII, Korean War, and Vietnam era	112	39	35.1	37	33.2	2	5.3	73
Other service periods	57	37	64.4	36	62.9	1	2.3	20
Nonveterans	12,952	8,434	65.1	8,019	61.9	414	4.9	4,519
HISPANIC OR LATINO ETHNICITY								
Total, 18 years and over	3,633	24,952	68.7	23,168	63.8	1,784	7.1	11,381
Veterans	1,395	897	64.3	841	60.3	56	6.3	498
Gulf War era, total	716	581	81.1	543	75.9	38	6.5	135
Gulf War era II	423	331	78.2	306	72.3	25	7.6	92
Gulf War era I	293	250	85.4	238	81.1	12	5.0	43
WWII, Korean War, and Vietnam era	381	130	34.1	122	32.0	8	6.1	251
Other service periods	298	186	62.4	175	58.8	11	5.9	112
Nonveterans	34,938	24,055	68.9	22,327	63.9	1,727	7.2	10,883

Note: Veterans are men and women who served on active duty in the U.S. Armed Forces and were not on active duty at the time of the survey. Nonveterans never served on active duty in the U.S. Armed Forces. Veterans could have served anywhere in the world during these periods of service: Gulf War era II (September 2001-present), Gulf War era I (August 1990-August 2001), Vietnam era (August 1964-April 1975), Korean War (July 1950-January 1955), World War II (December 1941–December 1946), and other service periods (all other time periods). Veterans are counted in only one period of service, their most recent wartime period. Veterans who served in more than one wartime period are classified in the most recent one. Veterans who served in both a wartime period and any other service period are classified in the wartime period. Estimates for the above race groups (white, black or African American, and Asian) do not sum to totals because data are not presented for all races. Persons whose ethnicity is identified as Hispanic or Latino may be of any race.

Table 28. Employment Status of Persons 25 Years and Over by Veteran Status, Period of Service, and Educational Attainment, 2014 Annual Averages

(Numbers in thousands; percent.)

Characteristic	Civilian noninstitutionalized population	Civilian labor force						Not in labor force
		Total	Percent of population	Employed		Unemployed		
				Total	Percent of population	Total	Percent of labor force	
VETERANS								
Total, 25 years and over	21,018	10,602	50.4	10,052	47.8	550	5.2	10,416
Less than a high school diploma	1,154	260	22.5	244	21.2	16	6.3	894
High school graduates, no college	6,497	2,948	45.4	2,772	42.7	176	6.0	3,548
Some college or associate's degree	7,376	4,032	54.7	3,802	51.5	230	5.7	3,344
Bachelor's degree or higher	5,991	3,361	56.1	3,234	54.0	128	3.8	2,630
Gulf War era, total								
Total, 25 years and over	6,329	5,160	81.5	4,884	77.2	375	5.3	1,169
Less than a high school diploma	87	56	64.5	50	58.1	5	9.8	31
High school graduates, no college	1,540	1,226	79.7	1,149	74.6	78	6.3	313
Some college or associate's degree	2,728	2,167	79.5	2,039	74.8	128	5.9	560
Bachelor's degree or higher	1,975	1,710	86.6	1,646	83.3	64	3.7	265
Gulf War era II								
Total, 25 years and over	2,973	2,393	80.5	2,234	75.2	159	6.6	580
Less than a high school diploma	35	22	65.1	20	57.8	3	-	12
High school graduates, no college	695	556	80.0	511	73.4	46	8.2	139
Some college or associate's degree	1,338	1,029	76.9	956	71.5	73	7.0	309
Bachelor's degree or higher	905	785	86.8	747	82.6	38	4.8	119
Gulf War era I								
Total, 25 years and over	3,356	2,766	82.4	2,650	79.0	117	4.2	589
Less than a high school diploma	52	33	64.0	30	58.4	3	-	19
High school graduates, no college	844	670	79.4	638	75.6	32	4.8	174
Some college or associate's degree	1,389	1,138	82.0	1,083	77.9	56	4.9	251
Bachelor's degree or higher	1,070	925	86.4	899	84.0	26	2.8	146
WWII, Korean War, and Vietnam era								
Total, 25 years and over	9,372	2,654	28.3	2,522	46.9	132	5.0	6,718
Less than a high school diploma	738	111	15.1	106	14.4	5	4.7	626
High school graduates, no college	3,028	759	24.7	709	23.4	40	5.3	2,279
Some college or associate's degree	2,913	894	30.7	838	28.8	55	6.2	2,019
Bachelor's degree or higher	2,693	900	33.4	869	32.3	32	3.5	1,793
Other service periods								
Total, 25 years and over	5,317	2,788	52.4	2,645	49.7	143	5.1	2,529
Less than a high school diploma	330	93	28.2	87	26.5	6	6.0	237
High school graduates, no college	1,929	973	50.4	915	47.4	58	6.0	956
Some college or associate's degree	1,735	971	55.9	924	53.3	47	4.8	764
Bachelor's degree or higher	1,323	751	56.8	719	54.3	32	4.3	572
NONVETERANS								
Total, 25 years and over	188,217	124,025	65.9	117,812	62.6	6,213	5.0	64,191
Less than a high school diploma	22,835	10,455	45.8	9,506	41.6	949	9.1	12,380
High school graduates, no college	55,469	33,030	59.5	31,043	56.0	1,987	6.0	22,439
Some college or associate's degree	48,593	33,499	68.9	31,693	65.2	1,806	5.4	15,093
Bachelor's degree or higher	61,320	47,041	76.7	45,570	74.3	1,471	3.1	14,279

- = No data or data that do not meet publication criteria (values not shown where base is less than 35,000).

Note: Veterans are men and women who served on active duty in the U.S. Armed Forces and were not on active duty at the time of the survey. Nonveterans never served on active duty in the U.S. Armed Forces. Veterans could have served anywhere in the world during these periods of service: Gulf War era II (September 2001-present), Gulf War era I (August 1990-August 2001), Vietnam era (August 1964-April 1975), Korean War (July 1950-January 1955), World War II (December 1941–December 1946), and other service periods (all other time periods). Veterans are counted in only one period of service, their most recent wartime period. Veterans who served in more than one wartime period are classified in the most recent one. Veterans who served in both a wartime period and any other service period are classified in the wartime period.

PART C

Veterans in the Department of Veterans Affairs (VA), National Center for Veterans Analysis and Statistics

HIGHLIGHTS

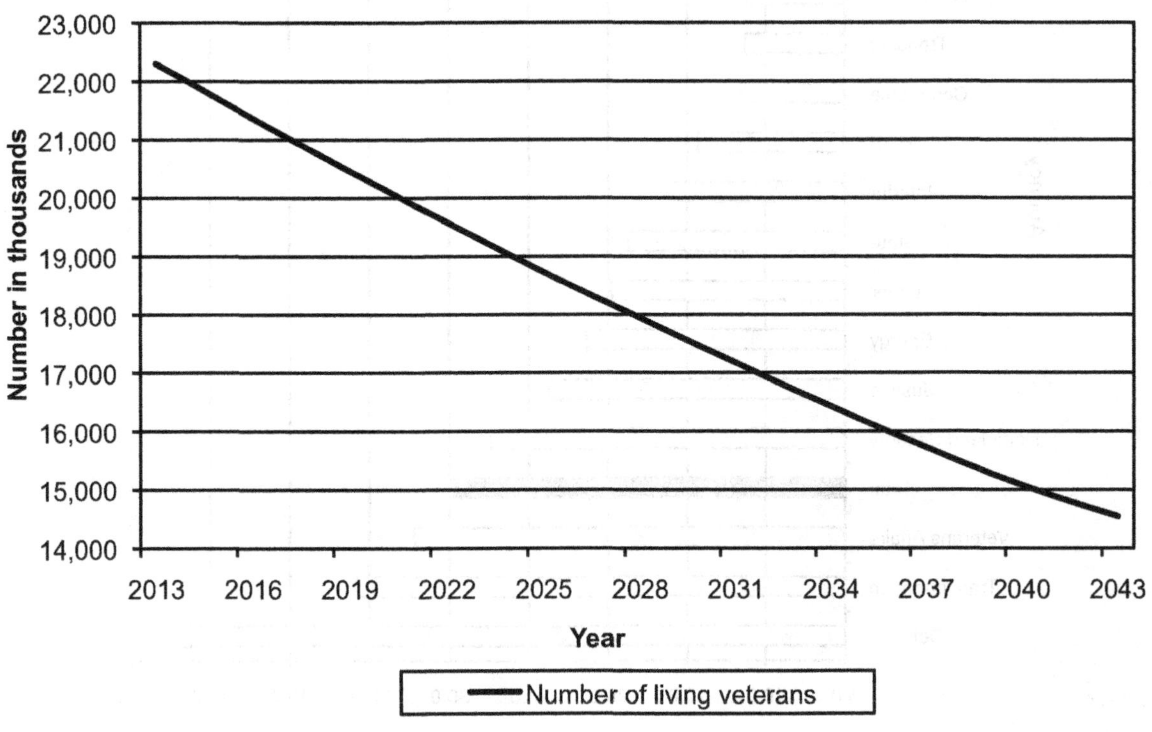

- As of 2013, there were 22,299,350 living veterans in the United States. Projections by the Department of Veterans Affairs show a decline to 20,170,355 by 2020, 17,421,211 by 2030, and 14,539,505 by 2043.

- There were 1,376,048 living officers and 20,923,301 living enlisted servicemembers in 2013. These numbers are projected to decrease to 1,303,204 officers and 13,236,301 enlisted servicemembers by 2043. These number represent declines of 5.3 percent and 36.7 percent, respectively. However, for females (comprising 164,686 living officers and 1,836,566 living enlisted servicemembers in 2013), these number are expected to rise: 33.7 percent for officers and 18.9 percent for enlisted servicemembers.

- In fiscal year 2014, Texas had the highest spending on veteran-related expenditures, of all states and territories with $15.4 billion spent. California ($14.3 billion), Florida ($11.7 billion), Ohio ($7.5 billion), and New York ($6.1 billion) rounded out the five highest-spending states and territories. States and territories spending the least included Guam ($88.6 million), Vermont ($295 million), North Dakota ($367 million), Wyoming ($383 million), and Delaware ($398 million).

- In 2013, there were 3,743,259 veterans with a service-connected disability. Of these, 34.2 percent had disability ratings of 0 to 20 percent, 20.0 percent had disability ratings of 30 to 40 percent, 15.3 percent had disability ratings of 50 to 60 percent, and 30.4 percent had disability ratings of 70 to 100 percent. The rest involved cremated remains.

Figure 2. Percent of On-Board Federal Employees Who Are Veterans, United States, 2013

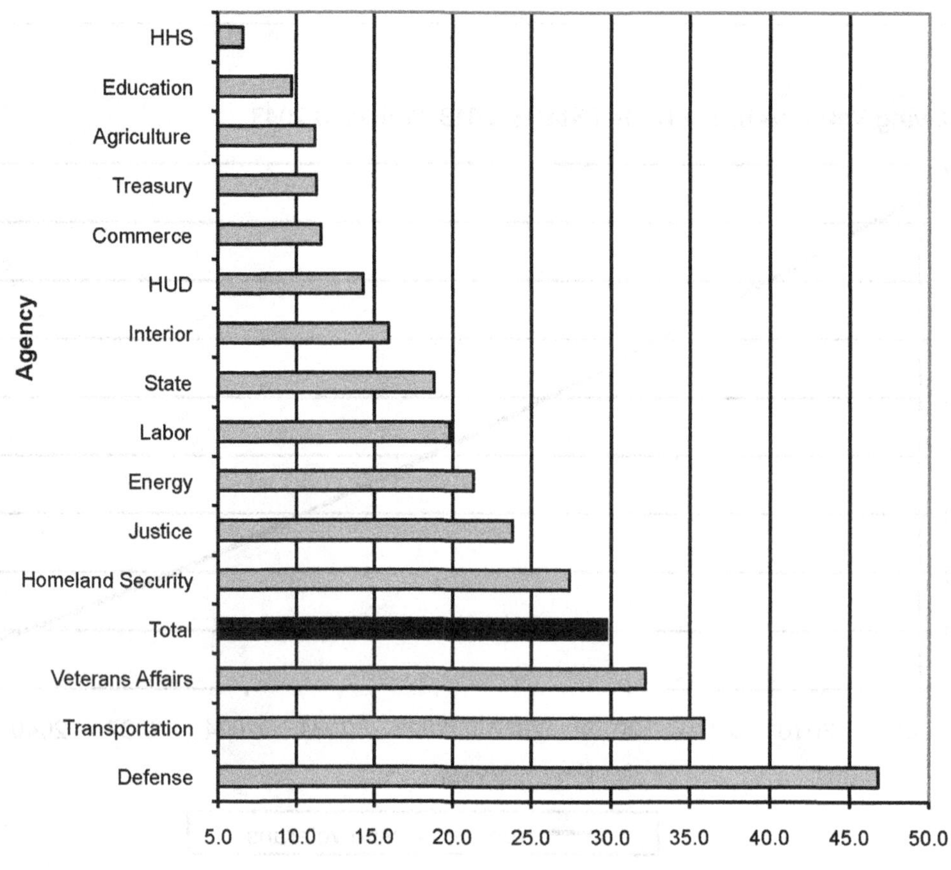

- The Department of Defense employed the highest proportion of veterans in 2013; veterans comprised 46.8 percent of its employees. The Department of Health and Human Services, at 6.6 percent, had the smallest percentage of veterans. The Department of Veterans Affairs was comprised of 32.2 percent veterans, while the percentage for all federal agencies was 29.7 percent.
- Of the 124,787 veteran and nonveteran interments in 2013 that were analyzed by the National Cemetery Administration, just under half (49.4 percent) were casket interments.

Table 29. Veterans in the Population: Living Veterans, by Gender, 2013–Projected 2043

(Number.)

Age groups	2013	2014	2015	2016	2017	2018	2019	2020	2021	2022	2023
TOTAL	22,299,350	21,999,108	21,680,534	21,368,156	21,065,561	20,761,269	20,461,616	20,170,355	19,874,602	19,583,789	19,295,709
Under 20 years	10,384	5,898	5,820	5,793	5,743	5,708	5,955	5,938	6,070	6,063	6,021
20 to 24 years	310,194	283,586	253,907	231,391	214,429	201,136	196,171	196,988	196,527	196,344	195,911
25 to 29 years	742,643	753,686	760,952	761,053	750,579	724,816	688,404	653,523	624,594	600,964	582,152
30 to 34 years	1,069,813	1,057,946	1,033,276	1,005,899	989,530	988,783	994,130	998,531	992,115	973,527	942,103
35 to 39 years	1,077,475	1,094,850	1,122,265	1,145,089	1,163,499	1,164,358	1,148,884	1,124,177	1,094,889	1,075,326	1,072,087
40 to 44 years	1,377,770	1,313,037	1,233,924	1,187,405	1,166,689	1,167,802	1,180,624	1,208,168	1,231,102	1,249,921	1,252,338
45 to 49 years	1,625,754	1,587,894	1,580,049	1,555,295	1,511,631	1,451,281	1,384,339	1,307,782	1,262,814	1,242,628	1,244,455
50 to 54 years	1,908,350	1,877,874	1,821,286	1,758,347	1,693,931	1,639,211	1,600,375	1,593,638	1,569,752	1,527,220	1,468,580
55 to 59 years	2,007,152	1,989,491	1,954,589	1,915,263	1,882,950	1,861,470	1,831,792	1,777,923	1,717,835	1,656,006	1,603,933
60 to 64 years	2,303,000	2,085,187	1,980,933	1,956,181	1,928,430	1,924,252	1,908,006	1,875,856	1,839,386	1,809,686	1,790,128
65 to 69 years	3,151,898	3,195,675	3,120,427	2,767,254	2,441,272	2,157,624	1,957,192	1,862,380	1,841,368	1,817,282	1,814,605
70 to 74 years	2,036,905	2,127,179	2,239,849	2,531,807	2,736,936	2,861,351	2,902,386	2,833,712	2,515,481	2,222,901	1,968,036
75 to 79 years	1,685,148	1,647,745	1,623,302	1,636,010	1,696,984	1,749,745	1,832,088	1,932,684	2,192,217	2,375,477	2,484,940
80 to 84 years	1,514,202	1,486,228	1,436,873	1,377,425	1,325,702	1,304,387	1,280,590	1,265,936	1,280,379	1,334,880	1,382,247
85 years and over	1,478,662	1,492,832	1,513,081	1,533,944	1,557,256	1,559,344	1,550,682	1,533,118	1,510,074	1,495,564	1,488,175
MALE	20,298,098	19,979,030	19,645,321	19,316,672	18,996,873	18,674,575	18,356,104	18,045,489	17,731,010	17,421,294	17,114,937
Under 20 years	7,725	4,187	4,134	4,116	4,081	4,084	4,278	4,265	4,389	4,369	4,321
20 to 24 years	249,354	227,476	203,113	184,561	170,709	159,456	154,999	155,287	154,674	154,318	153,850
25 to 29 years	607,502	618,894	627,132	628,529	620,667	598,246	566,787	536,449	510,919	489,956	473,344
30 to 34 years	864,941	857,948	841,026	822,789	813,798	817,440	823,646	828,728	823,460	807,350	779,300
35 to 39 years	883,192	893,984	913,745	930,806	945,450	946,719	936,592	919,245	898,773	886,455	887,489
40 to 44 years	1,170,890	1,109,740	1,037,799	992,082	968,027	962,916	969,582	989,516	1,006,417	1,021,108	1,023,426
45 to 49 years	1,401,226	1,367,400	1,356,703	1,332,307	1,291,259	1,236,424	1,173,434	1,103,760	1,059,394	1,035,591	1,031,039
50 to 54 years	1,642,435	1,614,682	1,566,884	1,513,516	1,460,176	1,412,815	1,378,268	1,368,690	1,345,150	1,305,038	1,251,664
55 to 59 years	1,778,611	1,751,930	1,709,802	1,664,063	1,625,335	1,598,724	1,571,759	1,526,530	1,475,744	1,424,712	1,379,711
60 to 64 years	2,147,730	1,914,922	1,794,327	1,754,522	1,713,927	1,701,271	1,676,181	1,636,956	1,594,167	1,558,133	1,533,488
65 to 69 years	3,056,197	3,089,405	3,002,305	2,640,557	2,304,197	2,008,423	1,793,664	1,683,191	1,647,709	1,611,311	1,600,422
70 to 74 years	1,975,799	2,062,140	2,171,940	2,456,300	2,654,967	2,770,708	2,801,901	2,722,096	2,396,063	2,093,845	1,827,700
75 to 79 years	1,638,816	1,601,885	1,576,202	1,586,669	1,643,940	1,694,202	1,772,881	1,870,669	2,123,125	2,300,498	2,402,223
80 to 84 years	1,474,011	1,445,162	1,396,178	1,337,636	1,286,619	1,265,415	1,241,936	1,226,062	1,238,576	1,289,828	1,334,969
85 years and over	1,399,669	1,419,274	1,444,031	1,468,219	1,493,721	1,497,732	1,490,195	1,474,047	1,452,449	1,438,781	1,431,993
FEMALE	2,001,252	2,020,077	2,035,213	2,051,484	2,068,688	2,086,694	2,105,512	2,124,866	2,143,592	2,162,495	2,180,772
Under 20 years	2,660	1,711	1,686	1,677	1,662	1,624	1,677	1,673	1,681	1,694	1,700
20 to 24 years	60,839	56,110	50,795	46,830	43,720	41,680	41,172	41,701	41,852	42,026	42,061
25 to 29 years	135,141	134,792	133,821	132,523	129,913	126,570	121,617	117,075	113,675	111,008	108,807
30 to 34 years	204,872	199,998	192,249	183,110	175,732	171,343	170,484	169,803	168,655	166,177	162,803
35 to 39 years	194,283	200,866	208,520	214,283	218,049	217,639	212,292	204,932	196,116	188,871	184,598
40 to 44 years	206,880	203,298	196,124	195,323	198,662	204,886	211,041	218,653	224,685	228,813	228,912
45 to 49 years	224,528	220,494	223,346	222,988	220,371	214,857	210,905	204,022	203,419	207,037	213,417
50 to 54 years	265,914	263,192	254,402	244,831	233,754	226,397	222,107	224,948	224,602	222,182	216,916
55 to 59 years	228,542	237,561	244,788	251,200	257,615	262,747	260,033	251,393	242,090	231,294	224,222
60 to 64 years	155,270	170,265	186,606	201,659	214,503	222,981	231,825	238,900	245,220	251,552	256,640
65 to 69 years	95,702	106,270	118,122	126,697	137,075	149,201	163,527	179,189	193,660	205,972	214,184
70 to 74 years	61,106	65,038	67,909	75,507	81,969	90,644	100,485	111,616	119,417	129,056	140,336
75 to 79 years	46,332	45,860	47,100	49,341	53,044	55,543	59,206	62,015	69,092	74,979	82,717
80 to 84 years	40,191	41,065	40,694	39,789	39,083	38,972	38,654	39,874	41,803	45,052	47,278
85 years and over	78,992	73,558	69,050	65,725	63,535	61,612	60,487	59,071	57,625	56,783	56,182

Table 29. Veterans in the Population: Living Veterans, by Gender, 2013–Projected 2043—*Continued*

(Number.)

Age groups	2024	2025	2026	2027	2028	2029	2030	2031	2032	2033
TOTAL	19,011,203	18,731,298	18,457,094	18,194,043	17,933,835	17,676,075	17,421,211	17,169,150	16,919,502	16,671,719
Under 20 years	5,973	5,926	5,888	5,852	5,818	5,784	5,752	5,722	5,692	5,664
20 to 24 years	195,121	194,039	192,848	191,753	190,716	189,766	188,935	188,225	187,661	187,224
25 to 29 years	572,426	568,186	564,978	563,255	561,349	559,166	556,905	554,679	552,623	550,913
30 to 34 years	900,885	860,732	829,969	807,608	790,033	781,548	778,342	776,002	773,645	771,216
35 to 39 years	1,075,573	1,077,805	1,071,697	1,055,180	1,026,548	988,902	952,284	924,507	902,117	884,542
40 to 44 years	1,238,332	1,214,221	1,186,586	1,169,096	1,167,895	1,173,321	1,177,358	1,172,666	1,155,954	1,127,303
45 to 49 years	1,257,693	1,284,874	1,308,002	1,327,013	1,329,837	1,316,429	1,293,127	1,266,158	1,248,626	1,247,231
50 to 54 years	1,403,443	1,328,513	1,284,918	1,265,354	1,267,477	1,280,732	1,307,642	1,330,540	1,349,154	1,351,893
55 to 59 years	1,566,941	1,560,908	1,538,111	1,497,216	1,440,686	1,378,043	1,305,902	1,264,139	1,245,609	1,248,103
60 to 64 years	1,762,667	1,711,669	1,654,712	1,596,067	1,546,807	1,512,100	1,507,078	1,485,787	1,446,996	1,393,126
65 to 69 years	1,800,658	1,771,781	1,738,898	1,712,327	1,695,073	1,670,138	1,622,552	1,569,357	1,514,647	1,468,951
70 to 74 years	1,789,068	1,705,792	1,688,947	1,669,107	1,667,876	1,656,420	1,631,355	1,602,766	1,579,915	1,565,304
75 to 79 years	2,519,565	2,456,609	2,182,706	1,932,956	1,715,259	1,564,201	1,495,700	1,483,898	1,469,264	1,469,433
80 to 84 years	1,451,209	1,533,421	1,748,019	1,900,351	1,988,666	2,013,941	1,958,330	1,741,853	1,547,571	1,378,174
85 years and over	1,471,648	1,456,822	1,460,816	1,500,906	1,539,797	1,585,583	1,639,948	1,802,851	1,940,026	2,022,643
MALE	16,812,427	16,514,957	16,223,420	15,942,709	15,665,523	15,391,592	15,121,356	14,854,842	14,591,672	14,331,405
Under 20 years	4,271	4,221	4,180	4,140	4,102	4,066	4,031	3,998	3,966	3,934
20 to 24 years	153,050	152,017	150,840	149,815	148,850	148,000	147,261	146,655	146,183	145,842
25 to 29 years	464,332	460,036	456,799	455,075	453,253	451,255	449,218	447,224	445,450	444,022
30 to 34 years	743,125	707,668	680,394	660,535	644,981	637,084	633,702	631,264	628,984	626,714
35 to 39 years	891,808	894,765	889,675	875,263	849,539	816,415	784,061	759,404	739,504	723,935
40 to 44 years	1,014,333	997,271	978,135	967,462	970,086	975,965	980,336	976,371	961,674	935,827
45 to 49 years	1,037,952	1,057,338	1,074,357	1,089,121	1,091,697	1,083,017	1,066,503	1,047,786	1,036,952	1,039,286
50 to 54 years	1,190,304	1,122,066	1,079,009	1,055,870	1,051,619	1,058,574	1,077,744	1,094,526	1,108,927	1,111,404
55 to 59 years	1,346,839	1,337,932	1,315,446	1,276,908	1,225,516	1,166,548	1,100,929	1,059,655	1,037,578	1,033,778
60 to 64 years	1,508,539	1,465,841	1,417,880	1,369,678	1,327,254	1,296,485	1,288,592	1,267,572	1,231,068	1,182,182
65 to 69 years	1,577,820	1,541,961	1,502,867	1,470,101	1,447,886	1,425,278	1,385,640	1,341,046	1,296,290	1,257,075
70 to 74 years	1,635,345	1,537,308	1,506,860	1,475,447	1,466,445	1,446,720	1,414,941	1,380,371	1,351,589	1,332,277
75 to 79 years	2,428,030	2,355,221	2,074,240	1,815,801	1,587,987	1,424,807	1,342,881	1,318,726	1,293,608	1,286,701
80 to 84 years	1,400,824	1,480,690	1,689,088	1,836,186	1,917,810	1,935,511	1,871,598	1,649,121	1,447,530	1,269,629
85 years and over	1,415,854	1,400,621	1,403,650	1,441,307	1,478,499	1,521,867	1,573,920	1,731,121	1,862,369	1,938,799
FEMALE	2,198,776	2,216,341	2,233,674	2,251,334	2,268,312	2,284,483	2,299,854	2,314,307	2,327,830	2,340,314
Under 20 years	1,703	1,705	1,708	1,712	1,715	1,718	1,721	1,724	1,727	1,730
20 to 24 years	42,071	42,022	42,007	41,938	41,866	41,766	41,675	41,570	41,478	41,382
25 to 29 years	108,094	108,150	108,179	108,180	108,096	107,911	107,687	107,454	107,173	106,891
30 to 34 years	157,760	153,064	149,575	147,073	145,051	144,464	144,640	144,738	144,661	144,502
35 to 39 years	183,765	183,040	182,022	179,918	177,009	172,487	168,222	165,103	162,613	160,607
40 to 44 years	223,998	216,950	208,451	201,634	197,809	197,356	197,022	196,295	194,281	191,476
45 to 49 years	219,741	227,536	233,645	237,893	238,141	233,412	226,623	218,372	211,674	207,945
50 to 54 years	213,140	206,447	205,909	209,484	215,858	222,158	229,899	236,014	240,227	240,489
55 to 59 years	220,102	222,975	222,665	220,308	215,170	211,495	204,973	204,484	208,031	214,325
60 to 64 years	254,128	245,828	236,831	226,389	219,552	215,615	218,486	218,215	215,928	210,944
65 to 69 years	222,838	229,820	236,032	242,226	247,187	244,860	236,912	228,311	218,357	211,876
70 to 74 years	153,723	168,484	182,087	193,659	201,431	209,699	216,415	222,395	228,326	233,028
75 to 79 years	91,535	101,388	108,466	117,155	127,272	139,395	152,819	165,172	175,655	182,731
80 to 84 years	50,385	52,732	58,931	64,166	70,856	78,430	86,732	92,732	100,041	108,545
85 years and over	55,794	56,200	57,167	59,600	61,298	63,717	66,027	71,729	77,657	83,844

Table 29. Veterans in the Population: Living Veterans, by Gender, 2013–Projected 2043—*Continued*

(Number.)

Age groups	2034	2035	2036	2037	2038	2039	2040	2041	2042	2043
TOTAL	16,427,119	16,186,677	15,951,470	15,719,014	15,493,002	15,276,966	15,072,875	14,882,168	14,704,879	14,539,505
Under 20 years	5,636	5,608	5,581	5,566	5,553	5,540	5,527	5,515	5,503	5,491
20 to 24 years	186,921	186,740	186,681	186,675	186,769	186,984	187,329	187,785	188,341	188,986
25 to 29 years	549,601	548,658	548,093	547,698	547,465	547,398	547,529	547,894	548,521	549,434
30 to 34 years	768,627	766,058	763,622	761,288	759,206	757,383	755,770	754,373	753,188	752,204
35 to 39 years	876,062	872,879	870,604	868,288	865,850	863,190	860,474	857,787	855,215	852,902
40 to 44 years	1,089,764	1,053,269	1,025,568	1,003,193	985,578	976,959	973,569	971,033	968,476	965,817
45 to 49 years	1,252,401	1,256,206	1,251,397	1,234,742	1,206,325	1,169,123	1,132,922	1,105,360	1,083,076	1,065,508
50 to 54 years	1,338,763	1,315,985	1,289,672	1,272,645	1,271,450	1,276,673	1,280,501	1,275,829	1,259,577	1,231,809
55 to 59 years	1,261,419	1,287,935	1,310,550	1,328,955	1,331,900	1,319,415	1,297,558	1,272,311	1,256,158	1,255,438
60 to 64 years	1,333,438	1,264,628	1,225,070	1,207,857	1,210,886	1,224,358	1,250,514	1,272,884	1,291,161	1,294,505
65 to 69 years	1,437,165	1,433,348	1,413,790	1,377,407	1,326,650	1,270,573	1,205,935	1,169,175	1,153,588	1,157,227
70 to 74 years	1,543,389	1,500,132	1,451,778	1,402,148	1,361,017	1,332,894	1,330,446	1,313,001	1,279,717	1,233,072
75 to 79 years	1,460,839	1,440,510	1,417,379	1,399,270	1,387,941	1,369,870	1,332,241	1,290,250	1,247,379	1,212,359
80 to 84 years	1,263,186	1,213,474	1,207,730	1,199,452	1,201,108	1,195,968	1,181,598	1,165,370	1,153,219	1,145,960
85 years and over	2,059,908	2,041,246	1,983,953	1,923,830	1,845,304	1,780,639	1,730,961	1,693,600	1,661,760	1,628,793
MALE	14,075,317	13,824,448	13,579,869	13,339,273	13,106,314	12,884,504	12,675,802	12,481,605	12,301,922	12,135,240
Under 20 years	3,903	3,873	3,843	3,825	3,809	3,794	3,778	3,764	3,749	3,735
20 to 24 years	145,626	145,528	145,541	145,611	145,775	146,058	146,464	146,983	147,602	148,311
25 to 29 years	442,977	442,296	441,991	441,852	441,871	442,051	442,415	442,995	443,824	444,930
30 to 34 years	624,367	622,063	619,878	617,837	616,041	614,508	613,193	612,099	611,211	610,521
35 to 39 years	716,021	712,636	710,228	707,943	705,615	703,141	700,628	698,126	695,784	693,704
40 to 44 years	902,690	870,364	845,712	825,758	810,078	801,959	798,297	795,560	792,960	790,333
45 to 49 years	1,044,859	1,048,948	1,044,816	1,030,101	1,004,401	971,494	939,362	914,768	894,834	879,136
50 to 54 years	1,102,904	1,086,768	1,068,521	1,058,032	1,060,448	1,066,007	1,070,047	1,065,993	1,051,598	1,026,480
55 to 59 years	1,040,854	1,059,731	1,076,293	1,090,513	1,093,147	1,085,149	1,069,746	1,052,331	1,042,512	1,045,267
60 to 64 years	1,126,041	1,063,505	1,024,348	1,003,605	1,000,427	1,007,731	1,026,375	1,042,792	1,056,931	1,059,878
65 to 69 years	1,228,977	1,222,312	1,202,955	1,168,741	1,122,747	1,070,029	1,011,335	974,850	955,771	953,353
70 to 74 years	1,312,482	1,276,671	1,236,351	1,195,984	1,160,831	1,136,057	1,130,799	1,113,486	1,082,226	1,040,041
75 to 79 years	1,270,446	1,243,819	1,215,074	1,191,429	1,175,795	1,159,567	1,128,677	1,093,915	1,059,317	1,029,542
80 to 84 years	1,144,284	1,083,038	1,066,695	1,049,435	1,045,008	1,033,097	1,013,066	991,788	974,697	963,713
85 years and over	1,968,886	1,942,896	1,877,625	1,808,608	1,720,320	1,643,863	1,581,621	1,532,154	1,488,906	1,446,297
FEMALE	2,351,802	2,362,228	2,371,601	2,379,741	2,386,689	2,392,462	2,397,073	2,400,564	2,402,958	2,404,266
Under 20 years	1,732	1,735	1,738	1,741	1,744	1,746	1,749	1,751	1,754	1,756
20 to 24 years	41,295	41,212	41,140	41,064	40,994	40,926	40,866	40,802	40,738	40,675
25 to 29 years	106,624	106,362	106,102	105,846	105,594	105,347	105,114	104,899	104,698	104,504
30 to 34 years	144,261	143,995	143,744	143,452	143,164	142,875	142,577	142,274	141,977	141,684
35 to 39 years	160,041	160,243	160,376	160,345	160,235	160,048	159,846	159,661	159,431	159,197
40 to 44 years	187,074	182,905	179,856	177,435	175,499	175,000	175,271	175,473	175,516	175,484
45 to 49 years	207,541	207,258	206,582	204,640	201,925	197,630	193,559	190,592	188,242	186,372
50 to 54 years	235,859	229,217	221,152	214,613	211,002	210,666	210,455	209,837	207,979	205,328
55 to 59 years	220,565	228,205	234,257	238,442	238,753	234,266	227,812	219,979	213,646	210,171
60 to 64 years	207,397	201,123	200,722	204,252	210,459	216,627	224,140	230,092	234,231	234,627
65 to 69 years	208,188	211,035	210,835	208,666	203,903	200,544	194,600	194,325	197,818	203,874
70 to 74 years	230,907	223,461	215,427	206,164	200,187	196,837	199,648	199,515	197,491	193,032
75 to 79 years	190,393	196,691	202,306	207,842	212,146	210,302	203,564	196,335	188,062	182,817
80 to 84 years	118,902	130,436	141,035	150,017	156,101	162,871	168,533	173,582	178,522	182,247
85 years and over	91,022	98,350	106,328	115,222	124,985	136,776	149,340	161,446	172,854	182,496

Note: Numbers from this table should be reported to the nearest 1,000. Numbers and projections are for September 30th of the applicable year.

Table 30. Veterans in the Population: Living Veterans, by Period of Service and Gender, 2013–Projected 2043

(Number.)

Year	Between KC & VNE	Between VNE & GW era	Between WWII & KC	GW era: post-9/11 only	GW era: pre-9/11 & GW era: post-9/11 only	GW era: pre-9/11 only	KC & VNE only	KC only	Post-GW era	Pre-WWII	WNE & GW era: pre-9/11 only	VNE only	WNE, GW era: pre-9/11, GW era: post-9/11	WWII & KC only	WWII only	WW'II, KC, VNE
TOTAL																
2013	2,083,858	3,406,845	102,614	2,401,605	1,213,773	2,799,822	185,260	1,722,990	0	14,078	317,347	6,789,871	56,441	87,309	1,079,397	38,140
2014	2,008,458	3,383,568	93,055	2,604,055	1,271,146	2,789,415	173,018	1,606,022	0	11,213	312,869	6,673,279	55,697	74,808	909,878	32,628
2015	1,929,987	3,359,303	83,630	2,794,947	1,315,019	2,778,508	160,685	1,487,553	0	8,884	308,191	6,551,490	54,919	63,326	756,529	27,565
2016	1,848,490	3,333,888	74,388	2,985,460	1,358,341	2,766,869	148,297	1,368,070	0	6,987	303,302	6,424,320	54,106	52,842	619,816	22,979
2017	1,763,880	3,307,343	65,301	3,178,426	1,401,801	2,754,476	135,888	1,248,038	0	5,506	298,186	6,291,291	53,254	43,331	499,979	18,862
2018	1,676,146	3,279,678	56,226	3,364,349	1,443,138	2,741,298	123,409	1,127,104	0	4,347	292,818	6,151,818	52,359	34,906	398,442	15,233
2019	1,585,419	3,250,864	47,433	3,546,449	1,484,570	2,727,298	110,869	1,005,314	0	3,438	287,182	6,005,444	51,418	27,795	315,985	12,140
2020	1,491,816	3,220,847	39,171	3,707,375	1,526,978	2,712,451	98,340	883,669	21,548	2,723	281,257	5,851,676	50,427	22,034	250,441	9,599
2021	1,395,498	3,189,643	31,850	3,843,322	1,567,750	2,696,824	86,018	764,621	59,013	2,161	275,006	5,689,789	49,380	17,461	198,664	7,603
2022	1,296,878	3,157,072	25,606	3,970,107	1,590,405	2,680,288	74,197	651,019	122,413	1,717	268,428	5,519,650	48,274	13,859	157,845	6,030
2023	1,196,208	3,123,007	20,495	4,060,700	1,603,723	2,662,805	63,086	545,415	227,982	1,367	261,503	5,340,895	47,107	11,016	125,609	4,790
2024	1,093,628	3,087,304	16,323	4,140,082	1,611,187	2,644,352	52,914	450,813	347,439	1,090	254,212	5,153,294	45,874	8,770	100,111	3,811
2025	989,704	3,049,817	13,019	4,209,012	1,614,883	2,624,903	43,761	368,655	478,927	870	246,537	4,956,705	44,572	6,992	79,905	3,036
2026	885,902	3,010,399	10,398	4,272,436	1,614,736	2,604,443	35,717	298,895	618,822	696	238,468	4,751,106	43,198	5,583	63,872	2,423
2027	783,752	2,968,871	8,318	4,331,633	1,612,254	2,582,960	28,849	240,772	770,123	557	229,999	4,536,675	41,749	4,464	51,131	1,936
2028	684,441	2,925,051	6,663	4,385,439	1,606,665	2,560,425	23,166	193,323	927,195	447	221,121	4,313,563	40,221	3,574	40,993	1,549
2029	589,718	2,878,733	5,345	4,433,777	1,598,873	2,536,810	18,557	155,005	1,089,235	359	211,839	4,082,193	38,614	2,866	32,910	1,241
2030	501,630	2,829,715	4,293	4,478,190	1,589,120	2,512,060	14,887	124,456	1,254,590	289	202,178	3,843,114	36,933	2,301	26,460	996
2031	421,729	2,777,787	3,454	4,518,893	1,577,887	2,486,107	11,958	100,065	1,422,575	233	192,121	3,597,219	35,168	1,850	21,305	800
2032	350,598	2,722,741	2,782	4,557,968	1,563,856	2,458,842	9,619	80,564	1,592,480	188	181,704	3,345,519	33,330	1,490	17,177	643
2033	288,414	2,664,381	2,244	4,594,703	1,548,463	2,430,153	7,748	64,953	1,763,572	152	170,925	3,088,994	31,428	1,201	13,869	518
2034	235,497	2,602,538	1,813	4,628,982	1,531,991	2,399,898	6,249	52,436	1,935,718	123	159,850	2,829,949	29,474	970	11,213	418
2035	191,542	2,537,016	1,466	4,660,546	1,514,486	2,367,931	5,046	42,387	2,109,128	99	148,538	2,570,838	27,453	784	9,078	338
2036	155,538	2,467,639	1,187	4,690,393	1,495,901	2,334,139	4,081	34,307	2,282,851	80	137,076	2,314,617	25,393	635	7,360	273
2037	126,242	2,394,249	963	4,718,369	1,476,042	2,298,375	3,304	27,805	2,456,628	65	125,447	2,061,523	23,291	514	5,975	221
2038	102,453	2,316,722	782	4,744,371	1,455,080	2,260,521	2,679	22,563	2,630,373	53	113,783	1,816,986	21,182	417	4,856	179
2039	83,252	2,234,902	636	4,751,668	1,432,942	2,220,478	2,174	18,333	2,820,842	43	102,250	1,585,948	19,061	339	3,952	145
2040	67,728	2,148,667	517	4,749,615	1,409,541	2,178,111	1,767	14,913	3,018,731	35	90,997	1,371,677	16,961	276	3,221	118
2041	55,169	2,057,922	422	4,740,857	1,384,770	2,133,306	1,438	12,147	3,221,407	29	80,106	1,176,719	14,930	225	2,628	96
2042	44,992	1,962,616	344	4,727,080	1,358,545	2,085,923	1,171	9,905	3,427,188	24	69,723	1,001,948	13,012	183	2,146	78
2043	36,736	1,862,722	281	4,708,289	1,330,753	2,035,865	955	8,087	3,636,031	19	59,955	846,622	11,221	150	1,755	64
MALE																
2013	13,255	1,017,061	84,451	37,484	98,804	1,671,300	182,069	2,017,041	6,555,220	296,802	52,703	2,946,790	2,349,599	1,013,092	1,962,429	0
2014	10,540	857,543	72,376	32,075	89,569	1,556,836	170,003	1,943,023	6,440,697	292,484	51,988	2,925,821	2,340,625	1,063,289	2,132,160	0
2015	8,334	713,085	61,266	27,106	80,477	1,441,174	157,861	1,866,222	6,321,323	287,988	51,242	2,903,795	2,331,042	1,101,797	2,292,609	0
2016	6,539	583,940	51,097	22,600	71,550	1,324,621	145,666	1,786,478	6,196,691	283,291	50,463	2,880,740	2,320,823	1,139,764	2,452,410	0
2017	5,141	470,465	41,908	18,548	62,760	1,207,580	133,456	1,703,720	6,066,322	278,377	49,648	2,856,674	2,309,944	1,178,098	2,614,232	0
2018	4,049	374,209	33,718	14,974	53,975	1,089,758	121,176	1,617,949	5,929,717	273,229	48,792	2,831,610	2,298,379	1,214,537	2,768,502	0
2019	3,194	296,128	26,821	11,924	45,446	971,152	108,848	1,529,281	5,786,366	267,826	47,893	2,805,537	2,286,101	1,250,881	2,918,706	0
2020	2,524	234,162	21,235	9,423	37,450	852,786	96,524	1,437,848	5,635,819	262,149	46,947	2,778,420	2,273,081	1,288,101	3,052,245	16,774
2021	1,997	185,318	16,806	7,458	30,362	737,079	84,415	1,343,950	5,477,625	256,177	45,949	2,750,206	2,259,288	1,323,626	3,164,370	46,383
2022	1,583	146,888	13,321	5,911	24,363	626,769	72,792	1,247,889	5,311,415	249,897	44,896	2,720,802	2,244,692	1,343,291	3,269,772	97,013
2023	1,257	116,600	10,575	4,693	19,461	524,372	61,866	1,149,907	5,136,854	243,291	43,785	2,690,101	2,229,262	1,354,817	3,345,756	182,340
2024	999	92,693	8,407	3,731	15,471	432,791	51,865	1,050,153	4,953,728	236,341	42,613	2,657,979	2,212,977	1,361,186	3,412,542	278,952
2025	795	73,794	6,693	2,970	12,317	353,396	42,870	949,176	4,761,931	229,031	41,377	2,624,319	2,195,819	1,364,247	3,470,813	385,407
2026	634	58,831	5,336	2,368	9,819	286,121	34,967	848,406	4,561,447	221,354	40,073	2,588,997	2,177,782	1,363,929	3,524,666	498,689
2027	506	46,967	4,260	1,891	7,839	230,170	28,220	749,383	4,352,447	213,304	38,700	2,551,863	2,158,857	1,361,548	3,575,179	621,575
2028	405	37,548	3,405	1,511	6,267	184,531	22,641	653,292	4,135,116	204,879	37,255	2,512,763	2,139,035	1,356,444	3,621,240	749,191
2029	324	30,060	2,726	1,210	5,017	147,727	18,123	561,790	3,909,896	196,084	35,735	2,471,521	2,118,290	1,349,415	3,662,731	880,941
2030	260	24,097	2,185	970	4,022	118,421	14,527	476,910	3,677,348	186,925	34,144	2,427,961	2,096,585	1,340,675	3,700,881	1,015,446
2031	208	19,342	1,754	778	3,228	95,056	11,660	400,128	3,438,353	177,417	32,480	2,381,909	2,073,859	1,330,640	3,735,844	1,152,185
2032	168	15,547	1,410	626	2,595	76,401	9,371	331,938	3,193,929	167,579	30,747	2,333,207	2,050,033	1,318,172	3,769,405	1,290,546
2033	135	12,512	1,135	503	2,088	61,486	7,541	272,471	2,945,092	157,419	28,955	2,281,669	2,025,012	1,304,525	3,800,922	1,429,939
2034	109	10,082	914	406	1,683	49,547	6,077	222,006	2,694,113	146,992	27,105	2,227,141	1,998,671	1,289,950	3,830,278	1,570,244
2035	88	8,135	738	327	1,358	39,977	4,903	180,209	2,443,390	136,364	25,202	2,169,466	1,970,899	1,274,480	3,857,246	1,711,667
2036	71	6,572	596	264	1,097	32,296	3,961	146,049	2,195,828	125,620	23,263	2,108,507	1,941,592	1,258,083	3,882,670	1,853,400
2037	57	5,316	482	214	887	26,123	3,204	118,295	1,951,724	114,747	21,288	2,044,116	1,910,632	1,240,599	3,906,403	1,995,184

Table 30. Veterans in the Population: Living Veterans, by Period of Service and Gender, 2013–Projected 2043—*Continued*

(Number.)

Year	Between KC & VNE	Between VNE & GW era	Between WWII & KC	GW era: post-9/11 only	GW era: pre-9/11 & GW era: post-9/11 only	GW era: pre-9/11 only	KC & VNE only	KC only	Post-GW era	Pre-WWII	WNE & GW era: pre-9/11 only	VNE only	WNE, GW era: pre-9/11, GW era: post-9/11	WWII & KC only	WWII only	WW'II, KC, VNE
MALE cnt'd																
2038	46	4,305	390	173	718	21,156	2,595	95,801	1,716,329	103,879	19,308	1,976,203	1,877,925	1,222,180	3,928,363	2,136,943
2039	38	3,491	317	140	583	17,154	2,104	77,679	1,494,467	93,158	17,323	1,904,655	1,843,366	1,202,763	3,934,211	2,293,056
2040	31	2,834	257	114	473	13,926	1,708	63,061	1,289,330	82,725	15,362	1,829,353	1,806,850	1,182,272	3,931,957	2,455,550
2041	25	2,303	209	93	384	11,319	1,388	51,256	1,103,295	72,649	13,474	1,750,216	1,768,289	1,160,621	3,923,903	2,622,182
2042	20	1,874	170	75	313	9,211	1,130	41,710	937,071	63,073	11,694	1,667,262	1,727,577	1,137,734	3,911,498	2,791,511
2043	16	1,527	138	61	255	7,504	920	33,981	789,833	54,092	10,045	1,580,467	1,684,613	1,113,514	3,894,756	2,963,516
FEMALE																
2013	823	62,336	2,858	656	3,811	51,690	3,191	66,817	234,651	20,545	3,738	460,055	450,223	200,682	439,177	0
2014	673	52,335	2,432	553	3,486	49,186	3,015	65,436	232,581	20,384	3,709	457,746	448,789	207,857	471,894	0
2015	550	43,444	2,059	459	3,153	46,379	2,825	63,765	230,167	20,203	3,677	455,508	447,466	213,222	502,338	0
2016	448	35,876	1,745	379	2,839	43,449	2,631	62,013	227,629	20,011	3,643	453,148	446,046	218,577	533,050	0
2017	366	29,513	1,423	313	2,541	40,458	2,432	60,160	224,969	19,809	3,606	450,669	444,532	223,703	564,194	0
2018	298	24,233	1,187	258	2,251	37,345	2,232	58,197	222,102	19,588	3,567	448,068	442,919	228,601	595,846	0
2019	244	19,856	973	215	1,988	34,162	2,021	56,138	219,077	19,355	3,525	445,327	441,197	233,689	627,743	0
2020	200	16,279	799	176	1,721	30,883	1,816	53,968	215,856	19,108	3,480	442,427	439,370	238,877	655,130	4,774
2021	163	13,346	655	145	1,488	27,542	1,603	51,548	212,164	18,829	3,431	439,437	437,536	244,123	678,952	12,630
2022	134	10,958	538	119	1,243	24,250	1,405	48,990	208,235	18,531	3,378	436,271	435,595	247,114	700,335	25,400
2023	110	9,009	442	98	1,034	21,043	1,220	46,301	204,041	18,212	3,321	432,905	433,543	248,905	714,945	45,642
2024	91	7,417	364	80	852	18,022	1,049	43,475	199,566	17,871	3,260	429,325	431,375	250,001	727,540	68,487
2025	75	6,111	300	66	702	15,259	891	40,528	194,774	17,506	3,195	425,497	429,083	250,636	738,199	93,520
2026	62	5,041	247	55	579	12,773	750	37,496	189,660	17,114	3,125	421,402	426,662	250,807	747,770	120,133
2027	51	4,164	204	45	478	10,602	629	34,369	184,228	16,695	3,049	417,007	424,103	250,706	756,454	148,548
2028	42	3,445	169	37	396	8,792	525	31,149	178,447	16,241	2,966	412,288	421,390	250,220	764,199	178,004
2029	35	2,851	140	31	328	7,279	434	27,927	172,296	15,755	2,878	407,212	418,520	249,457	771,046	208,294
2030	29	2,363	116	26	271	6,035	360	24,720	165,766	15,254	2,789	401,754	415,475	248,445	777,309	239,143
2031	24	1,962	96	21	225	5,009	298	21,601	158,866	14,704	2,688	395,878	412,248	247,247	783,048	270,391
2032	20	1,631	80	18	187	4,163	248	18,660	151,590	14,125	2,583	389,534	408,809	245,685	788,562	301,934
2033	17	1,358	67	15	156	3,466	207	15,943	143,902	13,506	2,473	382,712	405,141	243,939	793,781	333,633
2034	14	1,131	55	12	130	2,889	172	13,491	135,836	12,858	2,369	375,398	401,228	242,041	798,703	365,474
2035	12	943	46	10	108	2,410	144	11,333	127,448	12,173	2,251	367,550	397,032	240,006	803,301	397,460
2036	10	788	39	9	91	2,012	120	9,488	118,789	11,455	2,130	359,132	392,547	237,818	807,724	429,451
2037	8	659	32	7	76	1,682	100	7,947	109,798	10,700	2,004	350,133	387,743	235,443	811,965	461,444
2038	7	551	27	6	63	1,408	84	6,652	100,657	9,905	1,874	340,520	382,596	232,901	816,008	493,430
2039	6	462	23	5	53	1,179	70	5,572	91,481	9,093	1,738	330,247	377,112	230,179	817,457	527,786
2040	5	387	19	4	44	988	59	4,667	82,347	8,271	1,599	319,314	371,262	227,268	817,658	563,181
2041	4	324	16	4	37	828	49	3,913	73,424	7,457	1,456	307,706	365,017	224,149	816,954	599,225
2042	3	272	13	3	31	695	41	3,283	64,878	6,650	1,318	295,354	358,346	220,811	815,582	635,677
2043	3	228	11	2	26	583	35	2,755	56,789	5,863	1,176	282,255	351,251	217,239	813,534	672,515

Note: Numbers from this table should be reported to the nearest 1,000. Numbers and projections are for September 30th of the applicable year.
WWII = World War II; KC = Korean Conflict; VNE = Vietnam War; GW = Gulf War.

Table 31. Veterans in the Population: Living Veterans, by Race, Ethnicity, and Gender, 2013–Projected 2043

(Number.)

Year	White alone	Black or African American alone	American Indian and Alaska Native alone	Asian alone	Native Hawaiian and Other Pacific Islander alone	Some other race alone	Two or more races	Hispanic or Latino (of any race)	White alone, not Hispanic or Latino	All veterans
TOTAL										
2013	18,405,156	2,687,057	178,224	300,251	42,168	277,487	409,007	1,475,828	17,349,880	22,299,350
2014	18,095,704	2,688,702	178,183	299,857	42,643	281,655	412,364	1,488,615	17,032,870	21,999,108
2015	17,773,882	2,686,072	177,887	299,129	43,032	285,490	415,042	1,499,441	16,704,939	21,680,534
2016	17,458,264	2,683,046	177,567	298,541	43,409	289,593	417,736	1,511,085	16,382,745	21,368,156
2017	17,151,289	2,680,267	177,265	298,271	43,775	294,130	420,563	1,524,257	16,068,293	21,065,561
2018	16,843,990	2,676,178	176,889	298,075	44,084	298,805	423,247	1,537,392	15,753,802	20,761,269
2019	16,541,267	2,671,604	176,467	298,081	44,353	303,876	425,968	1,551,164	15,443,842	20,461,616
2020	16,245,819	2,667,060	176,042	298,421	44,595	309,523	428,895	1,566,234	15,140,728	20,170,355
2021	15,947,855	2,660,760	175,435	298,790	44,766	315,351	431,646	1,580,739	14,835,973	19,874,602
2022	15,654,480	2,654,047	174,761	299,383	44,898	321,660	434,559	1,596,084	14,535,719	19,583,789
2023	15,364,054	2,646,519	174,004	300,153	44,990	328,395	437,595	1,611,958	14,238,561	19,295,709
2024	15,077,387	2,638,185	173,157	301,094	45,049	335,540	440,790	1,628,316	13,945,349	19,011,203
2025	14,795,386	2,629,101	172,211	302,215	45,067	343,122	444,196	1,645,307	13,656,862	18,731,298
2026	14,518,915	2,619,397	171,178	303,502	45,065	351,165	447,873	1,663,111	13,373,814	18,457,094
2027	14,251,946	2,609,858	170,117	305,125	45,072	359,908	452,017	1,682,700	13,099,526	18,194,043
2028	13,988,338	2,599,235	168,949	306,870	45,049	369,038	456,356	1,702,752	12,828,722	17,933,835
2029	13,727,826	2,587,479	167,679	308,700	44,997	378,510	460,885	1,723,238	12,561,108	17,676,075
2030	13,470,861	2,574,594	166,311	310,606	44,927	388,299	465,613	1,744,151	12,297,108	17,421,211
2031	13,217,396	2,560,568	164,849	312,588	44,843	398,375	470,529	1,765,488	12,036,645	17,169,150
2032	12,967,190	2,545,309	163,293	314,625	44,747	408,726	475,612	1,787,234	11,779,461	16,919,502
2033	12,719,789	2,528,734	161,663	316,728	44,634	419,323	480,847	1,809,359	11,525,090	16,671,719
2034	12,476,438	2,510,935	159,954	318,900	44,507	430,154	486,232	1,831,901	11,274,722	16,427,119
2035	12,237,966	2,492,056	158,185	321,142	44,356	441,212	491,761	1,854,889	11,029,159	16,186,677
2036	12,005,303	2,472,181	156,370	323,486	44,179	452,501	497,450	1,878,387	10,789,287	15,951,470
2037	11,776,276	2,451,159	154,499	325,884	43,986	463,975	503,236	1,902,171	10,553,068	15,719,014
2038	11,554,314	2,429,165	152,581	328,379	43,779	475,649	509,135	1,926,362	10,323,828	15,493,002
2039	11,342,484	2,406,532	150,670	331,006	43,560	487,528	515,186	1,951,033	10,104,582	15,276,966
2040	11,142,525	2,383,470	148,784	333,756	43,333	499,597	521,410	1,976,190	9,897,051	15,072,875
2041	10,955,628	2,360,178	146,930	336,634	43,095	511,881	527,822	2,001,921	9,702,361	14,882,168
2042	10,781,626	2,336,811	145,115	339,655	42,849	524,388	534,435	2,028,242	9,520,333	14,704,879
2043	10,619,071	2,313,370	143,331	342,796	42,601	537,103	541,234	2,055,100	9,349,551	14,539,505
MALE										
2013	16,978,124	2,272,848	155,955	265,230	36,578	243,582	345,780	1,307,863	16,035,237	20,298,098
2014	16,660,837	2,267,244	155,453	264,260	36,879	246,720	347,638	1,315,535	15,714,031	19,979,030
2015	16,333,410	2,258,441	154,718	263,066	37,111	249,660	348,914	1,321,696	15,383,852	19,645,321
2016	16,011,042	2,249,327	153,927	262,039	37,332	252,880	350,125	1,328,577	15,058,351	19,316,672
2017	15,696,312	2,240,606	153,112	261,355	37,541	256,557	351,389	1,336,914	14,739,663	18,996,873
2018	15,380,440	2,230,717	152,163	260,768	37,689	260,396	352,402	1,345,099	14,420,209	18,674,575
2019	15,068,417	2,220,408	151,110	260,396	37,790	264,629	353,354	1,353,869	14,104,552	18,356,104
2020	14,763,217	2,210,217	149,987	260,371	37,859	269,427	354,411	1,363,863	13,795,266	18,045,489
2021	14,455,935	2,198,516	148,669	260,400	37,853	274,397	355,238	1,373,354	13,484,646	17,731,010
2022	14,153,086	2,186,559	147,238	260,664	37,803	279,814	356,130	1,383,626	13,178,304	17,421,294
2023	13,853,638	2,174,062	145,690	261,126	37,706	285,632	357,083	1,394,471	12,875,345	17,114,937
2024	13,558,183	2,160,943	144,022	261,772	37,565	291,819	358,124	1,405,787	12,576,429	16,812,427
2025	13,267,746	2,147,291	142,230	262,606	37,378	298,398	359,308	1,417,724	12,282,457	16,514,957
2026	12,983,063	2,133,176	140,331	263,616	37,164	305,386	360,683	1,430,431	11,994,030	16,223,420
2027	12,707,769	2,119,238	138,380	264,965	36,939	312,998	362,418	1,444,754	11,714,217	15,942,709
2028	12,436,387	2,104,438	136,313	266,464	36,687	320,947	364,287	1,459,539	11,438,297	15,665,523
2029	12,168,756	2,088,732	134,141	268,076	36,404	329,193	366,290	1,474,764	11,166,075	15,391,592
2030	11,905,337	2,072,117	131,873	269,777	36,098	337,714	368,442	1,490,410	10,897,999	15,121,356
2031	11,646,168	2,054,581	129,522	271,574	35,773	346,486	370,739	1,506,479	10,634,083	14,854,842
2032	11,390,974	2,036,072	127,088	273,448	35,432	355,498	373,159	1,522,955	10,374,050	14,591,672
2033	11,139,341	2,016,566	124,589	275,412	35,075	364,730	375,692	1,539,820	10,117,483	14,331,405
2034	10,892,476	1,996,134	122,020	277,465	34,701	374,176	378,347	1,557,109	9,865,549	14,075,317
2035	10,651,283	1,974,896	119,397	279,616	34,303	383,829	381,124	1,574,864	9,619,110	13,824,448
2036	10,416,660	1,952,965	116,736	281,890	33,879	393,703	384,036	1,593,156	9,379,025	13,579,869
2037	10,186,577	1,930,192	114,025	284,254	33,438	403,749	387,038	1,611,780	9,143,393	13,339,273

Table 31. Veterans in the Population: Living Veterans, by Race, Ethnicity, and Gender, 2013–Projected 2043 —*Continued*

(Number.)

Year	White alone	Black or African American alone	American Indian and Alaska Native alone	Asian alone	Native Hawaiian and Other Pacific Islander alone	Some other race alone	Two or more races	Hispanic or Latino (of any race)	White alone, not Hispanic or Latino	All veterans
MALE cnt'd										
2038	9,964,402	1,906,774	111,283	286,743	32,984	413,977	390,149	1,630,851	8,915,483	13,106,314
2039	9,753,164	1,883,070	108,557	289,385	32,519	424,397	393,411	1,650,447	8,698,272	12,884,504
2040	9,554,586	1,859,284	105,863	292,170	32,046	435,000	396,853	1,670,587	8,493,458	12,675,802
2041	9,369,792	1,835,635	103,209	295,109	31,567	445,807	400,486	1,691,372	8,302,090	12,481,605
2042	9,198,620	1,812,268	100,605	298,204	31,081	456,827	404,316	1,712,818	8,123,989	12,301,922
2043	9,039,652	1,789,153	98,040	301,437	30,591	468,047	408,321	1,734,865	7,957,779	12,135,240
FEMALE										
2013	1,427,032	414,209	22,269	35,021	5,590	33,905	63,227	167,965	1,314,642	2,001,252
2014	1,434,867	421,457	22,730	35,597	5,765	34,935	64,726	173,081	1,318,839	2,020,077
2015	1,440,472	427,631	23,168	36,063	5,921	35,829	66,128	177,746	1,321,087	2,035,213
2016	1,447,222	433,719	23,640	36,502	6,077	36,713	67,611	182,508	1,324,394	2,051,484
2017	1,454,977	439,661	24,153	36,916	6,234	37,573	69,174	187,343	1,328,629	2,068,688
2018	1,463,550	445,460	24,726	37,308	6,396	38,410	70,844	192,293	1,333,593	2,086,694
2019	1,472,850	451,196	25,357	37,685	6,563	39,246	72,614	197,295	1,339,290	2,105,512
2020	1,482,602	456,843	26,054	38,050	6,737	40,096	74,484	202,370	1,345,462	2,124,866
2021	1,491,920	462,243	26,766	38,389	6,912	40,953	76,408	207,385	1,351,327	2,143,592
2022	1,501,394	467,489	27,523	38,719	7,095	41,846	78,429	212,459	1,357,415	2,162,495
2023	1,510,416	472,458	28,314	39,027	7,285	42,763	80,511	217,487	1,363,216	2,180,772
2024	1,519,205	477,242	29,135	39,322	7,484	43,721	82,666	222,529	1,368,919	2,198,776
2025	1,527,640	481,811	29,981	39,609	7,688	44,724	84,888	227,583	1,374,405	2,216,341
2026	1,535,852	486,220	30,846	39,886	7,901	45,779	87,190	232,680	1,379,784	2,233,674
2027	1,544,177	490,620	31,737	40,160	8,133	46,909	89,599	237,947	1,385,309	2,251,334
2028	1,551,951	494,796	32,636	40,405	8,362	48,091	92,070	243,213	1,390,425	2,268,312
2029	1,559,070	498,746	33,538	40,624	8,593	49,317	94,595	248,474	1,395,033	2,284,483
2030	1,565,524	502,477	34,438	40,829	8,829	50,585	97,171	253,741	1,399,109	2,299,854
2031	1,571,228	505,988	35,327	41,015	9,071	51,889	99,790	259,009	1,402,562	2,314,307
2032	1,576,215	509,237	36,206	41,177	9,314	53,228	102,453	264,279	1,405,411	2,327,830
2033	1,580,447	512,168	37,073	41,316	9,560	54,593	105,156	269,539	1,407,607	2,340,314
2034	1,583,962	514,802	37,934	41,435	9,806	55,978	107,885	274,792	1,409,172	2,351,802
2035	1,586,683	517,160	38,788	41,526	10,053	57,383	110,637	280,025	1,410,048	2,362,228
2036	1,588,643	519,216	39,634	41,596	10,300	58,798	113,414	285,230	1,410,263	2,371,601
2037	1,589,699	520,966	40,475	41,630	10,548	60,226	116,198	290,390	1,409,675	2,379,741
2038	1,589,912	522,391	41,297	41,635	10,795	61,671	118,986	295,511	1,408,345	2,386,689
2039	1,589,320	523,462	42,113	41,621	11,041	63,130	121,775	300,586	1,406,311	2,392,462
2040	1,587,940	524,186	42,921	41,586	11,287	64,596	124,557	305,603	1,403,593	2,397,073
2041	1,585,837	524,543	43,721	41,525	11,527	66,074	127,336	310,550	1,400,271	2,400,564
2042	1,583,006	524,543	44,510	41,451	11,768	67,561	130,119	315,423	1,396,344	2,402,958
2043	1,579,419	524,217	45,290	41,359	12,011	69,056	132,913	320,236	1,391,772	2,404,266

Note: Numbers from this table should be reported to the nearest 1,000. Numbers and projections are for September 30th of the applicable year.

Table 32. Veterans in the Population: Living Veterans, by Branch of Service and Gender, 2010–Projected 2040

(Number.)

Year	Army	Navy	Air Force	Marine	Nondefense[1]	Reserve[2]	Total
TOTAL							
2010	10,239,140	5,201,127	4,213,998	2,439,345	265,574	672,708	23,031,892
2011	9,998,660	5,108,372	4,155,292	2,418,707	263,926	731,192	22,676,149
2012	9,759,735	5,015,179	4,090,492	2,397,001	262,027	803,845	22,328,279
2013	9,525,802	4,923,984	4,022,747	2,375,157	260,195	865,080	21,972,964
2014	9,297,060	4,834,178	3,951,850	2,353,283	258,307	925,052	21,619,731
2015	9,076,380	4,747,710	3,880,662	2,332,063	256,561	998,583	21,291,961
2016	8,863,262	4,664,308	3,809,275	2,311,402	254,897	1,063,105	20,966,249
2017	8,654,419	4,582,000	3,736,294	2,290,716	253,175	1,098,666	20,615,270
2018	8,450,358	4,501,240	3,662,818	2,270,211	251,470	1,134,752	20,270,850
2019	8,252,774	4,423,020	3,590,268	2,250,283	249,853	1,166,275	19,932,474
2020	8,062,784	4,347,788	3,519,607	2,231,201	248,366	1,194,529	19,604,276
2021	7,883,292	4,277,597	3,453,414	2,213,681	247,234	1,219,238	19,294,455
2022	7,711,488	4,210,641	3,389,905	2,197,040	246,270	1,238,411	18,993,756
2023	7,544,192	4,145,142	3,327,646	2,180,633	245,321	1,252,622	18,695,556
2024	7,382,527	4,081,897	3,267,529	2,164,776	244,473	1,264,726	18,405,928
2025	7,225,803	4,020,299	3,209,006	2,149,308	243,635	1,273,909	18,121,959
2026	7,073,518	3,960,039	3,151,825	2,134,119	242,782	1,280,555	17,842,838
2027	6,927,952	3,903,423	3,098,789	2,119,786	242,237	1,284,669	17,576,857
2028	6,783,366	3,846,370	3,045,554	2,104,991	241,624	1,286,293	17,308,199
2029	6,642,606	3,790,872	2,993,966	2,090,479	240,997	1,285,856	17,044,776
2030	6,502,402	3,734,279	2,941,153	2,075,433	240,082	1,283,547	16,776,896
2031	6,366,507	3,679,088	2,890,023	2,060,705	239,207	1,280,686	16,516,215
2032	6,229,150	3,621,944	2,837,379	2,045,061	238,127	1,277,178	16,248,838
2033	6,094,867	3,565,621	2,785,979	2,029,495	237,058	1,272,985	15,986,005
2034	5,966,010	3,511,173	2,736,529	2,014,568	236,018	1,268,195	15,732,492
2035	5,841,359	3,457,520	2,687,970	1,999,936	234,903	1,262,718	15,484,406
2036	5,723,208	3,406,014	2,641,695	1,986,139	233,826	1,256,649	15,247,531
2037	5,612,948	3,357,557	2,598,540	1,973,554	232,853	1,250,052	15,025,505
2038	5,510,351	3,312,025	2,558,400	1,962,120	232,010	1,242,866	14,817,771
2039	5,418,356	3,271,536	2,523,574	1,952,572	231,524	1,235,146	14,632,708
2040	5,334,208	3,234,320	2,492,054	1,944,263	231,203	1,226,757	14,462,805
MALE							
2010	9,323,380	4,720,430	3,694,913	2,309,364	233,202	545,812	20,827,101
2011	9,080,362	4,625,890	3,631,185	2,288,319	231,152	594,694	20,451,602
2012	8,838,055	4,530,419	3,561,384	2,266,032	228,811	654,998	20,079,700
2013	8,600,530	4,436,766	3,489,000	2,243,551	226,518	705,377	19,701,743
2014	8,367,894	4,344,238	3,413,681	2,220,934	224,149	754,526	19,325,423
2015	8,142,717	4,254,678	3,337,919	2,198,842	221,897	815,105	18,971,157
2016	7,924,330	4,167,653	3,261,699	2,177,138	219,691	868,057	18,618,568
2017	7,710,303	4,081,692	3,184,061	2,155,407	217,429	897,001	18,245,891
2018	7,501,244	3,997,371	3,106,203	2,133,893	215,195	926,315	17,880,221
2019	7,298,947	3,915,683	3,029,593	2,112,968	213,059	951,768	17,522,017
2020	7,104,362	3,837,046	2,954,997	2,092,906	211,066	974,598	17,174,975
2021	6,920,464	3,763,511	2,885,029	2,074,441	209,432	994,505	16,847,382
2022	6,744,041	3,693,048	2,817,726	2,056,776	207,956	1,009,779	16,529,327
2023	6,572,715	3,624,384	2,752,084	2,039,453	206,526	1,020,949	16,216,111
2024	6,407,673	3,558,307	2,689,055	2,022,773	205,228	1,030,341	15,913,378
2025	6,247,598	3,493,868	2,627,727	2,006,458	203,945	1,037,391	15,616,987
2026	6,092,442	3,431,010	2,568,062	1,990,497	202,670	1,042,345	15,327,026
2027	5,944,517	3,372,054	2,512,861	1,975,474	201,720	1,045,195	15,051,820
2028	5,797,835	3,312,819	2,457,693	1,960,006	200,715	1,045,983	14,775,051
2029	5,655,416	3,255,336	2,404,512	1,944,849	199,719	1,045,050	14,504,883
2030	5,513,435	3,196,705	2,350,132	1,929,095	198,439	1,042,615	14,230,421
2031	5,376,273	3,139,743	2,297,768	1,913,733	197,217	1,039,739	13,964,474
2032	5,238,067	3,081,024	2,244,211	1,897,482	195,806	1,036,323	13,692,913
2033	5,102,988	3,023,150	2,192,028	1,881,265	194,417	1,032,381	13,426,229
2034	4,973,124	2,967,009	2,141,773	1,865,572	193,055	1,027,964	13,168,497

Table 32. Veterans in the Population: Living Veterans, by Branch of Service and Gender, 2010–Projected 2040—*Continued*

(Number.)

Year	Army	Navy	Air Force	Marine	Nondefense[1]	Reserve[2]	Total
MALE cnt'd							
2035	4,848,003	2,911,982	2,092,761	1,850,256	191,647	1,023,065	12,917,715
2036	4,730,071	2,859,513	2,046,455	1,835,896	190,311	1,017,728	12,679,973
2037	4,620,725	2,810,494	2,003,678	1,822,866	189,111	1,012,004	12,458,878
2038	4,519,559	2,764,736	1,964,247	1,811,074	188,071	1,005,860	12,253,548
2039	4,429,509	2,724,337	1,930,438	1,801,251	187,416	999,340	12,072,292
2040	4,347,373	2,687,290	1,900,014	1,792,660	186,940	992,363	11,906,640
FEMALE							
2010	915,760	480,697	519,085	129,981	32,372	126,896	2,204,790
2011	918,297	482,482	524,107	130,388	32,775	136,498	2,224,547
2012	921,680	484,760	529,107	130,969	33,216	148,847	2,248,579
2013	925,272	487,218	533,747	131,606	33,677	159,703	2,271,222
2014	929,167	489,939	538,169	132,349	34,158	170,526	2,294,308
2015	933,664	493,033	542,743	133,222	34,664	183,478	2,320,804
2016	938,932	496,655	547,576	134,265	35,206	195,049	2,347,681
2017	944,116	500,308	552,234	135,309	35,746	201,666	2,369,379
2018	949,114	503,869	556,615	136,318	36,276	208,437	2,390,629
2019	953,827	507,338	560,675	137,316	36,794	214,507	2,410,457
2020	958,423	510,742	564,610	138,296	37,300	219,931	2,429,301
2021	962,828	514,085	568,385	139,240	37,802	224,734	2,447,073
2022	967,447	517,593	572,179	140,264	38,314	228,632	2,464,429
2023	971,477	520,758	575,562	141,180	38,795	231,673	2,479,445
2024	974,854	523,591	578,473	142,003	39,245	234,384	2,492,550
2025	978,206	526,431	581,278	142,850	39,689	236,517	2,504,972
2026	981,076	529,030	583,763	143,621	40,112	238,210	2,515,812
2027	983,435	531,369	585,928	144,312	40,518	239,475	2,525,037
2028	985,531	533,552	587,861	144,985	40,909	240,310	2,533,148
2029	987,190	535,535	589,454	145,630	41,278	240,806	2,539,893
2030	988,967	537,574	591,021	146,338	41,644	240,932	2,546,476
2031	990,233	539,344	592,255	146,972	41,990	240,947	2,551,741
2032	991,082	540,921	593,167	147,579	42,321	240,854	2,555,925
2033	991,879	542,471	593,952	148,230	42,641	240,604	2,559,777
2034	992,886	544,165	594,756	148,995	42,962	240,231	2,563,995
2035	993,357	545,537	595,210	149,680	43,255	239,653	2,566,692
2036	993,137	546,501	595,240	150,244	43,516	238,921	2,567,558
2037	992,224	547,062	594,862	150,688	43,742	238,048	2,566,627
2038	990,791	547,290	594,152	151,046	43,939	237,005	2,564,223
2039	988,847	547,199	593,135	151,321	44,108	235,806	2,560,416
2040	986,834	547,030	592,040	151,603	44,264	234,394	2,556,166

Note: Numbers from this table should be reported to the nearest 1,000. Numbers and projections are for September 30th of the applicable year.
[1]Nondefense includes Coast Guard, Public Health Service (PHS) and National Oceanic and Atmospheric Administration (NOAA).
[2]Reserve Forces include only those who have had active federal military service (other than for training) as a result of their membership in the reserves or National Guard. Reserve forces with prior active military service in the regular military, are classified according to the branch (Army, Navy, Air Force, Marines) in which they served while in the regular military, notwithstanding their subsequent service in the Reserve Forces.

Table 33. Veterans in the Population: Living Veterans, by Officer/Enlisted and Gender, 2013–Projected 2043

(Number.)

Year	Officer	Enlisted	Total
TOTAL			
2013	1,376,048	20,923,301	22,299,350
2014	1,374,000	20,625,108	21,999,108
2015	1,368,136	20,312,398	21,680,534
2016	1,363,564	20,004,592	21,368,156
2017	1,360,406	19,705,156	21,065,561
2018	1,356,346	19,404,923	20,761,269
2019	1,351,753	19,109,864	20,461,616
2020	1,348,113	18,822,242	20,170,355
2021	1,343,821	18,530,781	19,874,602
2022	1,339,925	18,243,864	19,583,789
2023	1,336,327	17,959,382	19,295,709
2024	1,332,867	17,678,336	19,011,203
2025	1,329,958	17,401,340	18,731,298
2026	1,327,287	17,129,807	18,457,094
2027	1,326,271	16,867,772	18,194,043
2028	1,325,315	16,608,520	17,933,835
2029	1,324,290	16,351,785	17,676,075
2030	1,323,215	16,097,996	17,421,211
2031	1,322,373	15,846,777	17,169,150
2032	1,321,491	15,598,011	16,919,502
2033	1,320,406	15,351,313	16,671,719
2034	1,319,626	15,107,493	16,427,119
2035	1,317,494	14,869,183	16,186,677
2036	1,315,318	14,636,152	15,951,470
2037	1,313,264	14,405,750	15,719,014
2038	1,311,213	14,181,789	15,493,002
2039	1,308,988	13,967,978	15,276,966
2040	1,306,825	13,766,049	15,072,875
2041	1,305,114	13,577,054	14,882,168
2042	1,303,903	13,400,977	14,704,879
2043	1,303,204	13,236,301	14,539,505
MALE			
2013	1,211,362	19,086,736	20,298,098
2014	1,206,785	18,772,245	19,979,030
2015	1,199,061	18,446,260	19,645,321
2016	1,192,457	18,124,215	19,316,672
2017	1,187,170	17,809,704	18,996,873
2018	1,181,037	17,493,537	18,674,575
2019	1,174,364	17,181,740	18,356,104
2020	1,168,571	16,876,918	18,045,489
2021	1,162,108	16,568,902	17,731,010
2022	1,155,986	16,265,307	17,421,294
2023	1,150,179	15,964,758	17,114,937
2024	1,144,489	15,667,938	16,812,427
2025	1,139,324	15,375,633	16,514,957
2026	1,134,410	15,089,010	16,223,420
2027	1,130,996	14,811,713	15,942,709
MALE cnt'd			
2028	1,127,688	14,537,835	15,665,523
2029	1,124,390	14,267,202	15,391,592
2030	1,121,116	14,000,240	15,121,356
2031	1,118,127	13,736,715	14,854,842
2032	1,115,182	13,476,490	14,591,672
2033	1,112,145	13,219,260	14,331,405
2034	1,109,468	12,965,849	14,075,317
2035	1,105,723	12,718,726	13,824,448
2036	1,102,056	12,477,813	13,579,869
2037	1,098,606	12,240,667	13,339,273
2038	1,095,280	12,011,034	13,106,314
2039	1,091,947	11,792,558	12,884,504
2040	1,088,837	11,586,965	12,675,802
2041	1,086,299	11,395,305	12,481,605
2042	1,084,368	11,217,553	12,301,922
2043	1,083,042	11,052,198	12,135,240
FEMALE			
2013	164,686	1,836,566	2,001,252
2014	167,215	1,852,863	2,020,077
2015	169,074	1,866,139	2,035,213
2016	171,107	1,880,377	2,051,484
2017	173,236	1,895,452	2,068,688
2018	175,309	1,911,386	2,086,694
2019	177,389	1,928,123	2,105,512
2020	179,542	1,945,325	2,124,866
2021	181,713	1,961,879	2,143,592
2022	183,938	1,978,557	2,162,495
2023	186,148	1,994,624	2,180,772
2024	188,378	2,010,398	2,198,776
2025	190,634	2,025,706	2,216,341
2026	192,877	2,040,798	2,233,674
2027	195,275	2,056,059	2,251,334
2028	197,627	2,070,685	2,268,312
2029	199,900	2,084,583	2,284,483
2030	202,098	2,097,756	2,299,854
2031	204,246	2,110,061	2,314,307
2032	206,309	2,121,521	2,327,830
2033	208,260	2,132,053	2,340,314
2034	210,157	2,141,644	2,351,802
2035	211,771	2,150,457	2,362,228
2036	213,262	2,158,339	2,371,601
2037	214,658	2,165,083	2,379,741
2038	215,933	2,170,755	2,386,689
2039	217,042	2,175,420	2,392,462
2040	217,989	2,179,084	2,397,073
2041	218,815	2,181,749	2,400,564
2042	219,534	2,183,423	2,402,958
2043	220,162	2,184,104	2,404,266

Note: Numbers from this table should be reported to the nearest 1,000. Numbers and projections are for September 30th of the applicable year.

Table 34. Veterans in the Population: Living Veterans, by State/Territory and Age Group, 2013 and Projected 2023, 2033, and 2043

(Number.)

State	Under 20 years	20 to 24 years	25 to 29 years	30 to 34 years	35 to 39 years	40 to 44 years	45 to 49 years	50 to 54 years	55 to 59 years	60 to 64 years	65 to 69 years	70 to 74 years	75 to 79 years	80 to 84 years	85 years and over	Total
2013 Total	5,898	283,586	753,686	1,057,946	1,094,850	1,313,037	1,587,894	1,877,874	1,989,491	2,085,187	3,195,675	2,127,179	1,647,745	1,486,228	1,492,832	21,999,108
Alabama	85	5,922	14,654	20,559	21,839	27,795	32,464	38,791	41,572	42,347	56,024	37,832	28,289	25,010	20,435	413,618
Alaska	31	1,551	4,747	5,845	5,315	5,751	6,731	7,778	7,869	8,197	7,847	5,114	3,162	1,922	1,536	73,397
Arizona	124	5,512	16,462	23,653	24,621	29,090	34,455	40,851	45,495	49,603	81,752	57,114	46,186	40,731	36,557	532,206
Arkansas	61	4,490	9,675	12,530	12,929	15,979	18,467	21,156	23,059	25,012	33,201	23,009	18,957	17,413	13,337	249,274
California	622	25,549	70,613	95,893	92,641	97,125	114,250	139,115	161,698	172,807	270,345	185,704	147,794	135,235	142,079	1,851,470
Colorado	73	4,634	14,780	21,846	22,808	28,465	33,341	37,236	39,799	41,293	58,915	37,307	27,347	23,527	21,900	413,271
Connecticut	59	2,392	6,069	8,072	8,774	10,145	12,455	16,856	18,088	16,679	33,221	24,195	17,532	17,242	21,643	213,420
Delaware	16	834	2,188	3,228	3,351	4,021	5,531	7,586	7,576	7,000	10,610	8,215	6,267	6,154	5,522	78,099
District of Columbia	9	314	871	1,639	1,892	1,715	1,970	2,690	3,349	3,091	3,136	2,742	1,919	2,249	2,241	29,825
Florida	304	13,616	41,050	62,891	68,377	84,231	103,368	135,519	145,224	135,209	216,820	169,631	143,071	130,135	134,250	1,583,697
Georgia	184	10,858	28,415	38,579	42,902	55,617	67,418	78,103	78,536	70,000	100,206	67,141	45,440	37,085	32,399	752,882
Hawaii	54	2,398	6,748	8,724	7,660	7,453	8,566	10,015	10,284	11,734	16,513	9,509	7,179	6,481	7,689	121,007
Idaho	53	2,311	5,181	6,526	6,537	7,823	9,690	10,796	11,070	14,126	20,492	12,851	9,428	8,185	7,326	132,395
Illinois	261	9,821	23,807	34,531	34,384	41,656	50,731	56,259	57,206	65,347	111,894	73,045	53,506	52,956	56,171	721,575
Indiana	135	7,328	16,830	21,272	20,897	28,791	36,838	45,271	45,407	46,557	68,783	42,749	33,326	30,518	31,581	476,283
Iowa	37	4,013	8,361	10,809	10,756	12,418	16,600	18,544	18,009	23,025	36,153	19,860	17,096	17,997	17,977	231,655
Kansas	48	3,432	9,380	12,196	11,910	13,931	15,759	17,555	18,662	22,445	31,752	19,510	14,431	14,015	16,181	221,206
Kentucky	75	4,669	11,721	15,419	16,561	21,305	25,761	30,220	30,482	32,441	51,128	29,825	21,557	20,727	18,708	330,599
Louisiana	108	5,623	12,749	20,618	20,839	24,036	26,063	23,469	26,997	33,518	47,700	28,356	21,922	19,693	18,455	330,145
Maine	33	1,395	3,437	4,592	5,368	6,904	8,653	11,785	12,536	12,536	19,854	12,571	9,361	9,121	9,086	127,234
Maryland	113	4,768	13,569	22,311	25,234	29,624	36,076	45,588	44,934	40,470	57,092	37,617	27,643	25,467	27,257	437,762
Massachusetts	95	3,887	10,396	14,102	14,583	17,858	22,260	30,845	32,274	32,287	58,995	40,200	32,797	32,212	36,981	379,772
Michigan	123	6,268	16,517	22,280	23,287	34,658	46,735	56,729	57,735	67,068	110,769	67,451	49,422	47,801	51,626	658,469
Minnesota	79	5,430	11,892	15,215	14,496	18,049	24,808	29,823	31,590	37,213	58,957	37,166	29,046	26,913	28,474	369,149
Mississippi	69	4,411	9,321	12,448	12,575	15,246	17,331	20,066	20,994	21,057	27,530	18,881	15,748	12,929	11,784	220,389
Missouri	110	6,024	16,146	22,075	23,031	28,702	34,887	42,438	45,665	48,818	76,362	49,009	35,705	33,434	31,940	494,346
Montana	25	1,596	3,662	4,967	5,067	5,573	6,608	7,667	8,061	10,192	15,005	10,445	7,913	6,722	6,144	99,646
Nebraska	13	2,382	5,670	7,492	7,164	8,846	11,207	12,325	11,624	14,162	20,357	12,302	9,255	10,487	10,087	143,375
Nevada	56	2,579	6,927	10,708	11,300	12,621	16,103	19,530	20,905	22,597	35,117	24,582	18,981	13,970	12,050	228,027
New Hampshire	22	1,191	3,216	4,052	4,534	6,160	7,725	11,013	11,974	10,120	15,950	12,090	9,252	8,079	8,283	113,660
New Jersey	87	4,475	11,585	16,485	16,975	18,369	23,748	31,956	34,058	34,284	68,950	46,416	39,542	39,969	41,496	428,396
New Mexico	49	2,101	5,178	7,991	8,190	9,741	11,674	15,022	16,273	18,362	26,935	16,073	13,465	10,527	9,947	171,528
New York	263	9,798	26,710	37,914	38,416	41,732	56,390	73,787	76,176	74,444	135,030	91,378	76,644	72,016	81,523	892,221
North Carolina	214	10,820	32,855	41,005	43,238	54,164	61,450	69,849	73,032	72,298	110,107	68,465	54,025	43,516	39,982	775,020
North Dakota	9	1,387	3,016	3,635	3,119	3,513	4,232	4,438	4,373	6,070	7,650	4,716	4,349	3,309	3,579	57,395
Ohio	257	9,868	25,817	35,376	36,460	49,224	64,807	75,993	79,222	84,838	135,935	84,128	63,312	60,131	61,114	866,481
Oklahoma	99	5,536	13,492	20,059	19,454	21,683	23,718	25,558	29,800	33,425	48,699	33,014	24,572	19,999	18,463	337,571
Oregon	58	3,151	9,071	13,181	13,958	17,355	21,660	25,534	28,868	34,266	54,133	36,951	26,589	21,557	25,300	331,632
Pennsylvania	242	10,891	25,154	36,194	38,889	47,213	63,075	76,413	77,829	84,914	145,132	100,575	76,056	73,846	82,646	939,069
Rhode Island	9	977	2,248	2,697	3,044	3,425	4,500	6,369	6,452	5,817	10,836	7,706	5,902	5,896	6,086	71,966
South Carolina	160	6,428	15,212	19,660	22,014	27,127	31,704	38,500	39,139	41,875	59,715	40,082	31,089	25,248	19,599	417,554
South Dakota	16	1,419	3,055	4,177	3,850	4,291	5,481	6,340	6,147	7,238	8,768	5,967	4,957	4,960	5,364	72,030
Tennessee	81	6,136	17,641	23,675	24,520	32,294	39,508	46,147	49,321	53,116	72,257	46,659	37,070	31,181	26,734	506,340
Texas	505	23,188	70,234	106,122	108,274	124,009	132,991	136,401	152,660	162,763	227,447	146,341	106,046	94,887	88,549	1,680,418
Utah	43	2,662	6,457	9,121	9,200	9,561	10,177	11,224	11,909	13,771	19,403	14,637	12,339	10,591	10,624	151,719
Vermont	4	540	1,377	1,733	1,941	2,519	3,383	4,785	4,956	4,183	7,332	5,283	3,651	3,182	3,732	48,602
Virginia	352	12,116	33,227	48,023	52,574	62,213	70,865	82,040	80,332	71,319	94,872	59,405	43,731	36,385	33,934	781,388
Washington	183	6,909	21,304	31,069	32,010	37,337	45,903	52,552	58,075	61,533	87,167	58,829	42,318	34,350	34,084	603,623
West Virginia	42	2,042	5,093	7,173	8,293	10,309	11,509	12,184	12,892	19,007	26,047	17,379	13,662	11,233	10,491	167,355
Wisconsin	85	5,168	13,309	17,272	16,769	21,281	29,863	34,308	35,821	40,929	64,031	39,809	34,799	29,465	30,814	413,723
Wyoming	18	1,020	2,259	3,024	2,982	3,303	3,924	4,015	4,329	4,726	7,370	4,648	3,241	2,585	2,264	49,708
Puerto Rico	21	1,189	2,370	2,839	3,143	3,152	3,253	4,748	6,265	8,111	13,564	11,677	12,397	11,232	9,280	93,240
Island Areas & Foreign	22	569	1,968	4,453	5,906	7,633	11,226	14,092	12,883	10,947	11,816	11,018	8,457	5,754	7,531	114,275

Table 34. Veterans in the Population: Living Veterans, by State/Territory and Age Group, 2013 and Projected 2023, 2033, and 2043—*Continued*

(Number.)

State	Under 20 years	20 to 24 years	25 to 29 years	30 to 34 years	35 to 39 years	40 to 44 years	45 to 49 years	50 to 54 years	55 to 59 years	60 to 64 years	65 to 69 years	70 to 74 years	75 to 79 years	80 to 84 years	85 years and over	Total
2023 Projected total	6,021	195,911	582,152	942,103	1,072,087	1,252,338	1,244,455	1,468,580	1,603,933	1,790,128	1,814,605	1,968,036	2,484,940	1,382,247	1,488,175	19,295,709
Alabama	87	3,097	9,638	18,441	21,895	26,800	27,427	33,681	35,282	39,144	39,986	40,302	45,396	25,556	25,897	392,629
Alaska	32	1,234	3,876	6,235	7,002	7,022	6,171	6,274	6,197	6,450	5,959	6,139	4,683	2,770	1,984	72,028
Arizona	127	4,475	13,800	21,700	25,582	30,001	29,997	34,353	37,153	42,848	45,884	52,424	70,409	42,340	44,568	495,662
Arkansas	62	2,067	6,390	12,920	13,982	15,450	15,233	18,933	19,514	21,503	22,586	24,431	27,147	16,018	17,848	234,084
California	633	23,061	63,193	84,488	88,576	98,242	91,145	95,285	102,383	121,139	135,567	147,117	189,280	109,665	121,532	1,471,306
Colorado	75	3,283	11,117	18,454	22,471	26,440	26,484	31,546	32,670	35,359	36,698	37,813	46,956	23,484	24,149	376,997
Connecticut	60	1,529	4,301	6,986	7,929	8,786	8,854	10,038	11,884	14,909	14,941	15,218	24,343	14,448	15,892	160,118
Delaware	16	603	1,790	2,861	3,363	4,066	4,140	4,691	6,015	7,739	7,170	7,186	9,179	5,737	6,519	71,075
District of Columbia	9	369	1,274	1,838	1,558	1,883	1,812	1,655	1,813	2,582	3,137	2,711	2,365	1,790	1,967	26,761
Florida	311	10,754	33,225	52,452	62,498	78,209	82,523	97,483	109,557	135,095	134,558	129,990	182,423	121,680	139,197	1,369,953
Georgia	190	7,056	22,626	38,400	42,079	48,587	52,276	65,157	70,312	78,378	74,346	68,205	82,658	46,033	40,785	737,086
Hawaii	55	2,158	6,592	9,357	9,458	9,946	9,004	8,629	8,378	9,278	8,810	10,661	12,220	5,887	6,347	116,780
Idaho	55	1,641	4,583	7,581	7,752	8,315	8,049	9,375	10,385	11,169	11,115	14,571	17,243	8,663	9,000	129,499
Illinois	265	7,038	19,066	28,725	31,448	37,468	35,630	43,681	48,012	50,935	49,584	62,317	83,379	44,550	49,231	591,329
Indiana	137	4,132	12,083	20,924	22,721	23,910	23,112	31,552	37,593	42,600	41,189	43,853	53,045	27,939	30,351	415,141
Iowa	38	1,719	5,249	10,591	11,650	12,679	11,984	14,149	17,038	17,646	16,655	23,071	27,383	12,673	17,117	199,642
Kansas	49	2,146	6,723	11,310	13,151	14,322	13,990	15,570	15,770	16,556	17,190	20,868	24,488	12,449	13,583	198,165
Kentucky	78	3,011	8,919	14,965	17,094	19,077	19,721	24,952	27,495	29,918	29,148	32,316	40,497	19,967	20,728	307,885
Louisiana	110	3,372	9,334	15,314	16,996	23,151	22,341	26,272	24,505	22,688	25,909	32,015	37,056	18,269	20,028	297,359
Maine	34	933	2,638	4,306	4,950	5,663	6,291	7,606	8,986	11,378	11,451	11,861	15,663	7,884	8,886	108,530
Maryland	115	3,639	12,425	19,892	21,523	27,501	29,031	32,533	35,330	40,365	36,500	33,671	41,217	21,906	23,191	378,839
Massachusetts	97	2,703	7,545	11,591	13,068	14,493	14,590	17,747	21,516	27,607	26,801	29,476	42,975	24,358	29,474	284,039
Michigan	126	3,793	10,460	16,824	19,921	22,544	23,708	35,651	44,092	50,842	51,193	63,827	83,685	41,250	45,312	513,229
Minnesota	82	2,518	7,466	14,353	15,971	17,018	15,378	19,647	24,689	27,610	28,502	35,255	44,570	23,381	26,149	302,588
Mississippi	71	2,101	6,073	11,503	12,435	14,792	15,062	18,241	18,422	20,088	19,581	20,495	21,068	12,441	14,033	206,405
Missouri	112	3,518	10,814	19,191	23,023	26,958	26,652	33,275	36,477	42,187	42,601	47,365	60,892	31,825	33,487	438,377
Montana	25	905	2,580	4,623	5,503	6,476	6,108	6,727	7,224	7,718	8,045	10,341	12,258	7,260	7,254	93,048
Nebraska	14	1,227	3,845	6,946	7,876	8,851	8,330	9,768	10,960	11,324	10,442	13,583	15,265	7,651	9,325	125,407
Nevada	57	1,581	5,198	9,198	10,462	13,173	13,133	14,844	16,966	18,418	18,944	20,925	26,962	16,011	15,041	200,913
New Hampshire	22	650	2,011	3,892	4,650	4,799	5,163	6,695	8,091	10,352	10,431	9,292	12,294	7,573	8,259	94,174
New Jersey	90	2,907	8,381	13,166	14,613	17,119	16,408	18,126	22,294	27,612	27,277	30,635	49,126	27,750	34,656	310,160
New Mexico	51	1,594	4,869	7,580	7,906	10,283	10,171	11,991	12,523	15,031	15,369	17,961	21,122	10,442	11,685	158,577
New York	268	6,876	19,313	29,381	33,043	37,928	36,539	41,722	53,416	64,245	62,109	65,868	96,273	53,201	65,122	665,305
North Carolina	216	8,051	23,837	38,136	45,300	50,190	52,717	63,059	65,288	71,348	71,626	72,586	92,496	48,407	49,056	752,313
North Dakota	9	802	2,405	4,063	4,274	4,616	3,878	4,177	4,342	4,189	3,986	5,664	5,691	3,292	3,533	54,921
Ohio	260	6,487	18,080	28,980	33,327	38,314	38,528	52,073	62,923	70,092	70,635	80,019	102,673	52,219	57,617	712,229
Oklahoma	102	3,529	10,689	17,953	20,238	24,538	23,149	25,339	24,789	25,524	29,046	32,554	39,066	22,366	21,347	320,227
Oregon	58	2,067	6,341	10,767	13,071	15,362	15,275	18,988	22,161	25,190	28,318	33,365	44,865	24,809	24,324	284,962
Pennsylvania	249	6,444	17,955	30,243	33,855	41,606	41,519	51,552	64,280	70,680	69,095	82,256	110,386	64,370	71,369	755,858
Rhode Island	10	493	1,537	2,695	2,708	2,904	3,125	3,491	4,452	5,710	5,238	5,096	7,981	4,682	5,283	55,404
South Carolina	162	4,118	11,838	19,883	21,711	25,220	27,366	32,460	34,605	40,301	39,228	43,322	51,672	29,082	28,674	409,643
South Dakota	17	773	2,250	4,159	4,776	5,389	4,764	5,354	5,938	6,430	5,977	7,504	6,765	4,118	5,191	69,405
Tennessee	83	3,257	10,636	20,707	25,669	29,202	29,749	38,614	42,430	47,574	48,435	51,613	60,683	32,855	33,760	475,265
Texas	511	16,460	52,468	88,482	109,862	132,743	126,154	142,301	134,504	135,944	148,128	154,970	185,069	97,447	99,052	1,624,095
Utah	44	1,615	5,100	8,946	10,070	11,809	10,862	11,233	10,883	11,183	11,307	13,359	15,786	10,234	11,520	143,950
Vermont	4	209	685	1,613	2,040	2,155	2,267	2,802	3,572	4,608	4,460	3,905	5,725	3,400	3,220	40,666
Virginia	359	11,495	33,832	49,616	53,252	65,055	68,874	75,491	73,615	76,265	70,235	62,900	72,455	38,127	37,236	788,805
Washington	187	6,323	19,242	28,629	33,210	38,542	37,087	42,086	45,938	49,954	54,418	57,776	67,538	38,174	36,885	555,989
West Virginia	43	1,278	3,955	6,984	8,015	9,599	9,975	11,999	12,340	11,990	12,434	19,171	19,991	11,967	11,826	151,565
Wisconsin	88	2,727	7,898	14,558	17,884	19,466	18,303	23,703	30,121	32,194	32,783	39,717	48,504	26,950	30,268	345,164
Wyoming	19	794	2,245	3,572	3,739	4,292	3,873	4,149	4,180	3,924	3,982	4,257	5,813	2,808	2,697	50,344
Puerto Rico	22	782	2,104	3,200	2,965	3,221	3,637	3,515	3,294	4,700	5,716	7,870	10,397	7,531	10,829	69,781
Island Areas & Foreign	24	517	1,659	2,931	3,971	6,165	6,896	8,347	11,337	11,620	9,881	8,374	7,859	6,556	5,895	92,032

Table 34. Veterans in the Population: Living Veterans, by State/Territory and Age Group, 2013 and Projected 2023, 2033, and 2043—*Continued*

(Number.)

State	Under 20 years	20 to 24 years	25 to 29 years	30 to 34 years	35 to 39 years	40 to 44 years	45 to 49 years	50 to 54 years	55 to 59 years	60 to 64 years	65 to 69 years	70 to 74 years	75 to 79 years	80 to 84 years	85 years and over	Total
2033 Projected total	5,664	187,224	550,913	771,216	884,542	1,127,303	1,247,231	1,351,893	1,248,103	1,393,126	1,468,951	1,565,304	1,469,433	1,378,174	2,022,643	16,671,719
Alabama	82	2,969	9,125	13,523	16,537	24,306	28,091	31,700	29,902	33,920	33,974	35,929	33,966	29,636	38,835	362,494
Alaska	30	1,183	3,673	5,354	6,156	7,518	7,990	7,260	5,607	5,014	4,648	4,641	3,978	3,567	3,116	69,735
Arizona	119	4,286	13,121	18,919	22,343	28,128	32,675	35,421	33,065	36,043	37,887	41,761	41,461	41,027	65,545	451,800
Arkansas	58	1,968	5,983	8,840	10,481	15,822	16,758	17,535	16,232	19,024	18,883	19,894	19,338	18,106	23,998	212,918
California	597	22,013	59,945	76,698	80,767	86,884	90,234	93,847	80,729	80,079	83,484	94,151	97,228	90,769	137,313	1,174,737
Colorado	70	3,131	10,483	15,495	18,131	22,922	26,599	28,527	26,157	29,304	29,364	30,285	29,087	25,972	36,071	331,600
Connecticut	56	1,454	4,050	5,480	6,061	7,565	8,150	8,444	7,968	8,593	9,813	11,766	10,934	9,529	18,068	117,933
Delaware	15	570	1,678	2,432	2,909	3,702	4,199	4,605	4,346	4,743	5,945	7,352	6,362	5,529	8,703	63,089
District of Columbia	8	351	1,224	1,894	2,003	1,930	1,636	1,770	1,579	1,423	1,520	2,039	2,289	1,721	1,922	23,309
Florida	292	10,286	31,553	45,085	52,859	66,929	77,930	88,586	85,629	95,621	104,615	123,874	114,665	97,026	173,050	1,168,002
Georgia	177	6,797	21,538	31,042	36,505	48,544	52,089	55,016	54,369	64,578	67,748	72,195	63,566	50,602	70,144	694,909
Hawaii	52	2,078	6,295	8,579	9,256	10,376	10,980	10,733	8,615	7,744	7,349	7,803	6,898	7,275	9,229	113,261
Idaho	51	1,566	4,315	5,990	6,943	9,341	9,386	9,357	8,502	9,596	10,392	10,682	9,830	11,081	14,740	121,771
Illinois	250	6,716	18,029	23,772	26,290	31,686	33,446	37,451	33,746	39,452	42,082	42,540	38,145	41,269	63,631	478,505
Indiana	129	3,923	11,334	15,652	17,809	23,832	24,776	24,901	22,994	29,885	34,482	37,253	33,287	30,690	42,470	353,418
Iowa	36	1,643	4,926	7,032	8,285	12,493	13,138	13,599	12,198	13,538	15,644	15,523	13,541	16,110	21,539	169,245
Kansas	46	2,061	6,378	9,019	10,393	13,537	15,250	15,515	13,960	14,592	14,241	14,274	13,734	14,483	19,158	176,641
Kentucky	73	2,877	8,411	11,930	13,988	18,437	20,414	21,400	20,590	24,690	26,255	27,282	24,551	23,424	32,815	277,137
Louisiana	104	3,223	8,837	11,901	13,372	17,496	19,036	24,142	22,096	25,091	22,881	20,181	21,242	22,712	29,636	261,948
Maine	32	884	2,470	3,469	4,102	5,302	5,773	6,113	6,314	7,252	8,282	9,995	9,320	8,351	12,443	90,102
Maryland	109	3,490	11,845	17,569	20,226	24,564	26,242	29,536	27,617	28,022	28,843	31,497	26,507	21,270	29,619	326,956
Massachusetts	91	2,587	7,156	9,542	10,255	12,040	13,150	13,959	13,266	15,383	18,047	22,111	19,864	18,697	32,270	208,419
Michigan	118	3,618	9,861	12,904	13,947	17,440	20,059	21,887	21,937	31,972	38,821	42,812	39,926	42,870	63,062	381,234
Minnesota	76	2,413	7,012	9,741	11,221	16,418	17,203	17,388	15,020	18,254	22,139	23,540	22,437	23,854	34,429	241,145
Mississippi	67	2,016	5,749	8,157	9,451	13,795	15,281	17,204	16,121	18,035	17,410	18,115	16,360	14,813	18,116	190,690
Missouri	106	3,358	10,181	14,624	17,196	23,534	27,125	29,738	27,600	32,455	34,233	37,700	35,158	33,653	49,239	375,898
Montana	24	861	2,424	3,462	4,233	6,049	6,821	7,437	6,569	6,785	6,997	7,139	6,888	7,667	10,645	84,001
Nebraska	13	1,176	3,639	5,109	5,957	8,384	9,109	9,338	8,112	9,025	9,833	9,707	8,281	9,280	11,909	108,869
Nevada	54	1,506	4,906	7,258	8,499	11,440	12,761	14,788	13,589	14,413	15,847	16,490	15,726	15,081	22,817	175,174
New Hampshire	21	616	1,872	2,774	3,268	4,602	5,168	5,068	5,107	6,195	7,170	8,776	8,217	6,317	10,049	75,218
New Jersey	84	2,783	7,942	10,627	11,490	13,742	14,624	16,058	14,454	15,195	18,045	21,400	19,645	19,000	36,165	221,253
New Mexico	48	1,530	4,617	6,554	7,618	9,590	10,228	12,099	10,821	11,780	11,803	13,550	12,839	12,937	17,308	143,324
New York	252	6,568	18,242	24,091	25,669	30,067	32,579	35,592	32,701	35,680	44,048	50,479	45,181	41,057	69,958	492,163
North Carolina	205	7,675	22,494	31,060	35,690	46,507	54,470	56,533	55,166	63,592	64,420	67,479	62,779	55,134	79,596	702,800
North Dakota	8	773	2,287	3,103	3,687	5,131	5,181	5,128	3,964	3,952	3,929	3,620	3,192	3,917	4,638	52,512
Ohio	246	6,177	17,025	22,869	25,414	31,953	35,290	38,468	36,843	47,808	56,102	59,508	55,389	54,152	78,793	566,035
Oklahoma	96	3,383	10,103	14,421	16,782	21,999	24,374	27,553	24,213	24,970	23,469	23,056	24,212	23,618	32,638	294,886
Oregon	55	1,960	5,945	8,454	9,780	12,653	14,441	16,077	15,389	18,507	21,080	22,912	23,776	24,276	37,549	232,853
Pennsylvania	233	6,171	16,942	23,019	26,265	34,743	37,258	43,226	41,079	48,258	57,769	60,557	54,743	56,032	89,334	595,630
Rhode Island	9	471	1,445	1,990	2,161	2,787	2,829	2,910	2,892	3,057	3,746	4,578	3,903	3,257	6,063	42,099
South Carolina	153	3,931	11,232	15,922	18,791	25,225	27,250	29,333	29,552	33,662	34,974	38,990	35,227	33,853	46,927	385,022
South Dakota	16	747	2,148	3,134	3,829	5,491	5,966	6,245	5,183	5,491	5,877	6,084	5,239	5,634	6,207	67,291
Tennessee	78	3,110	10,056	15,049	17,953	26,121	31,161	33,325	31,833	39,175	41,604	44,560	42,006	38,929	52,487	427,447
Texas	483	15,694	49,672	73,960	88,342	113,608	132,756	147,364	131,063	140,395	128,535	124,008	124,712	112,958	153,143	1,536,693
Utah	41	1,533	4,791	7,044	8,478	11,460	12,414	13,559	11,659	11,171	10,266	10,020	9,377	9,639	14,177	135,629
Vermont	4	201	646	1,008	1,232	1,990	2,350	2,343	2,315	2,682	3,248	3,982	3,570	2,689	4,599	32,860
Virginia	338	11,001	32,108	45,407	53,140	65,312	70,896	75,907	69,401	68,946	64,729	64,718	55,707	43,739	57,459	778,808
Washington	176	6,038	18,234	25,888	30,095	35,586	39,252	41,579	36,852	39,546	41,811	43,517	43,873	40,495	54,961	497,902
West Virginia	40	1,223	3,746	5,676	6,918	9,051	9,765	10,929	10,663	11,919	11,674	10,853	10,369	13,693	16,903	133,424
Wisconsin	82	2,627	7,476	10,356	11,907	16,841	19,493	20,208	18,171	22,343	27,418	28,047	26,394	27,532	39,369	278,264
Wyoming	17	761	2,120	2,967	3,611	4,785	4,751	5,060	4,203	4,011	3,760	3,379	3,171	2,931	4,406	49,934
Puerto Rico	21	746	1,984	2,625	2,828	3,460	3,540	3,641	3,589	3,231	2,919	3,960	4,460	5,288	9,232	51,524
Island Areas & Foreign	22	506	1,646	2,749	3,422	4,181	4,896	6,492	6,555	7,034	8,896	8,744	6,884	5,035	6,146	73,209

Table 34. Veterans in the Population: Living Veterans, by State/Territory and Age Group, 2013 and Projected 2023, 2033, and 2043—*Continued*

(Number.)

State	Under 20 years	20 to 24 years	25 to 29 years	30 to 34 years	35 to 39 years	40 to 44 years	45 to 49 years	50 to 54 years	55 to 59 years	60 to 64 years	65 to 69 years	70 to 74 years	75 to 79 years	80 to 84 years	85 years and over	Total
2043 Projected total	5,491	188,986	549,434	752,204	852,902	965,817	1,065,508	1,231,809	1,255,438	1,294,505	1,157,227	1,233,072	1,212,359	1,145,960	1,628,793	14,539,505
Alabama	80	2,983	9,071	13,189	15,965	19,265	22,478	29,046	30,597	32,233	29,121	31,391	29,314	27,495	37,321	329,550
Alaska	30	1,193	3,659	5,224	5,953	6,748	7,246	7,669	7,126	5,775	4,126	3,519	3,074	2,740	3,254	67,336
Arizona	117	4,327	13,073	18,464	21,638	25,462	29,082	33,508	36,672	38,237	34,638	35,634	34,832	34,054	53,612	413,349
Arkansas	56	1,995	5,986	8,616	10,028	11,572	13,104	17,977	17,875	17,810	15,872	17,731	16,418	15,341	22,070	192,452
California	577	22,281	59,915	74,818	77,935	81,250	83,862	83,740	79,834	79,550	66,485	62,489	60,616	60,462	94,178	987,992
Colorado	68	3,168	10,460	15,109	17,466	20,176	22,394	25,152	26,501	26,816	23,698	25,285	23,642	21,572	30,474	291,981
Connecticut	54	1,469	4,047	5,331	5,823	6,235	6,482	7,341	7,341	7,253	6,587	6,736	7,138	7,604	10,838	90,279
Delaware	15	582	1,688	2,372	2,797	3,307	3,757	4,239	4,397	4,706	4,383	4,525	5,281	5,844	7,585	55,477
District of Columbia	8	354	1,222	1,846	1,956	2,008	1,998	1,777	1,419	1,505	1,314	1,110	1,099	1,305	1,928	20,849
Florida	284	10,371	31,439	43,992	51,098	60,071	68,518	77,563	81,702	87,691	82,386	88,099	90,539	95,715	135,140	1,004,606
Georgia	175	6,815	21,363	30,335	35,341	41,260	46,669	55,254	54,326	54,955	52,941	60,000	58,721	55,534	68,379	642,068
Hawaii	51	2,084	6,248	8,375	9,015	9,896	10,816	10,941	10,185	9,554	7,520	6,432	5,725	5,427	7,590	109,857
Idaho	51	1,592	4,316	5,834	6,673	7,657	8,490	10,374	9,839	9,564	8,501	9,175	9,304	8,474	12,626	112,467
Illinois	241	6,769	17,989	23,170	25,266	27,256	28,876	32,262	31,875	34,304	30,061	33,411	33,224	29,677	43,111	397,491
Indiana	124	3,984	11,360	15,235	17,014	18,640	19,987	24,837	24,606	23,818	21,331	26,406	28,415	27,194	36,038	298,989
Iowa	35	1,662	4,911	6,853	7,947	8,933	9,791	13,439	13,354	13,124	11,310	11,975	12,925	11,413	16,452	144,123
Kansas	45	2,076	6,341	8,797	10,048	11,461	12,674	14,745	15,131	14,592	12,664	12,661	11,543	10,265	15,541	158,585
Kentucky	71	2,912	8,402	11,626	13,455	15,449	17,291	20,752	21,315	21,338	19,824	22,704	22,500	20,720	27,986	246,345
Louisiana	100	3,250	8,820	11,609	12,878	14,314	15,605	18,680	18,928	23,229	20,798	22,536	19,246	14,967	24,715	229,675
Maine	31	899	2,481	3,377	3,923	4,493	4,952	5,758	5,809	5,888	5,883	6,428	6,839	7,318	10,169	74,249
Maryland	105	3,500	11,766	17,178	19,683	22,676	25,121	26,786	25,041	25,395	22,393	21,586	20,791	20,286	24,187	286,493
Massachusetts	89	2,609	7,132	9,303	9,897	10,332	10,712	11,777	11,973	12,134	11,125	12,224	13,351	14,544	20,288	157,491
Michigan	114	3,659	9,850	12,566	13,398	14,114	14,802	17,338	18,809	20,067	19,645	27,099	30,660	30,043	45,065	277,229
Minnesota	75	2,430	6,977	9,495	10,741	11,844	12,681	16,908	16,843	16,394	13,679	15,759	17,787	16,722	25,309	193,643
Mississippi	66	2,034	5,729	7,972	9,145	10,645	12,304	16,165	16,348	17,162	15,351	16,316	14,732	13,612	17,668	175,250
Missouri	102	3,391	10,158	14,255	16,518	19,009	21,256	26,309	28,159	29,362	26,254	29,332	28,843	28,080	39,785	320,814
Montana	23	876	2,429	3,379	4,058	4,805	5,485	6,990	7,279	7,521	6,397	6,294	6,063	5,498	8,613	75,710
Nebraska	13	1,187	3,628	4,988	5,750	6,636	7,294	8,891	8,852	8,710	7,359	7,798	7,931	6,941	9,479	95,457
Nevada	51	1,515	4,889	7,073	8,176	9,504	10,799	13,049	13,262	14,444	12,819	13,024	13,363	12,366	18,195	152,530
New Hampshire	20	630	1,882	2,701	3,113	3,502	3,817	4,857	5,111	4,747	4,574	5,285	5,700	6,203	8,152	60,295
New Jersey	82	2,809	7,918	10,369	11,086	11,657	12,027	13,137	12,895	13,479	11,706	11,669	12,911	13,687	20,509	165,942
New Mexico	47	1,540	4,589	6,399	7,364	8,620	9,967	11,378	10,874	11,953	10,269	10,672	10,008	10,212	14,891	128,782
New York	244	6,617	18,183	23,478	24,680	25,569	26,295	28,969	29,289	30,399	26,955	27,985	32,241	32,784	44,682	378,370
North Carolina	196	7,777	22,476	30,288	34,362	39,596	44,684	52,591	56,543	57,085	54,638	60,191	57,036	53,159	72,633	643,256
North Dakota	8	774	2,270	3,032	3,567	4,150	4,612	5,651	5,224	4,865	3,612	3,444	3,200	2,607	3,810	50,826
Ohio	237	6,237	17,003	22,258	24,347	26,361	28,015	32,640	33,953	35,713	33,206	40,968	44,825	42,026	59,983	447,773
Oklahoma	94	3,413	10,064	14,072	16,171	18,575	20,864	24,870	25,429	27,274	23,078	22,733	19,941	17,350	27,693	271,621
Oregon	53	1,993	5,962	8,223	9,331	10,343	11,195	13,478	14,636	15,832	14,777	16,899	17,980	17,351	28,677	186,731
Pennsylvania	228	6,217	16,872	22,440	25,195	27,718	29,904	36,653	37,126	40,850	37,351	41,756	46,535	43,245	62,325	474,415
Rhode Island	9	480	1,447	1,940	2,078	2,223	2,367	2,787	2,634	2,576	2,452	2,443	2,780	3,021	3,877	33,115
South Carolina	147	3,955	11,199	15,519	18,143	21,334	24,304	29,279	29,360	30,597	30,090	32,629	31,635	31,376	43,309	352,878
South Dakota	15	746	2,128	3,064	3,713	4,390	4,997	6,389	6,454	6,439	5,182	5,219	5,216	4,796	6,285	65,033
Tennessee	76	3,143	10,033	14,682	17,322	20,293	23,087	30,112	33,291	34,108	31,506	36,884	36,569	34,762	48,775	374,645
Texas	464	15,837	49,560	72,106	85,174	99,172	110,782	128,008	138,647	147,086	126,667	129,661	111,052	94,813	139,809	1,448,836
Utah	40	1,558	4,797	6,860	8,150	9,501	10,705	13,163	13,319	13,647	11,161	10,137	8,676	7,492	11,126	130,331
Vermont	4	203	643	983	1,189	1,394	1,569	2,184	2,393	2,277	2,140	2,340	2,637	2,872	3,619	26,446
Virginia	327	11,091	32,005	44,373	51,513	61,705	70,837	75,827	70,876	69,070	60,485	57,911	51,374	46,127	55,545	759,066
Washington	170	6,105	18,197	25,239	29,068	33,110	36,159	38,420	38,808	39,352	33,779	34,592	34,182	31,611	47,351	446,143
West Virginia	40	1,236	3,736	5,539	6,677	7,764	8,719	10,410	10,521	10,962	10,177	10,851	9,905	8,188	13,369	118,093
Wisconsin	81	2,636	7,417	10,103	11,456	12,656	13,660	17,744	19,347	19,236	16,730	19,599	22,461	20,431	30,286	223,844
Wyoming	17	772	2,116	2,897	3,468	4,075	4,610	5,564	5,067	4,899	3,818	3,478	3,043	2,433	3,439	49,698
Puerto Rico	20	754	1,982	2,558	2,733	3,054	3,445	3,846	3,503	3,368	3,212	2,759	2,320	2,770	5,460	41,784
Island Areas & Foreign	22	495	1,610	2,699	3,415	4,039	4,358	4,585	4,736	5,562	5,201	5,288	6,213	5,429	5,591	59,245

Note: Numbers from this table should be reported to the nearest 1,000. Numbers and projections are for September 30th of the applicable year.

This page is intentionally left blank

Table 35. Veterans in the Population: Living Veterans, by State/Territory, Period of Service and Gender, 2013 and Projected 2023, 2033, and 2043

(Number.)

State and year	(a) All veterans (b+c)	(b) Wartime veterans (i+j+k+m+n+p+q+r+t+u+v)	(c) Peacetime veterans (h+l+o+s+w)	(d) WWII (i+j+k)	(e) Korean Conflict (KC) (j+k+m+n)	(f) Vietnam Era (VNE) (k+n+p+q+r)	(g) Gulf War Era (GW) (q+r+t+u+v)	(h) Pre-WWII	(i) WWII only	(j) WWII & KC only	(k) WWII, KC, & VNE only
2013 Total	22,299,350	16,691,955	5,607,395	1,204,846	2,033,699	7,387,059	6,788,988	14,078	1,079,397	87,309	38,140
Alabama	414,913	317,559	97,354	15,130	35,215	135,621	150,108	107	13,203	1,158	769
Alaska	73,309	57,492	15,817	1,297	2,614	21,320	34,619	13	1,104	73	120
Arizona	535,470	403,781	131,689	29,880	57,295	187,683	153,340	274	25,213	3,210	1,456
Arkansas	250,397	187,539	62,858	10,343	21,667	84,026	81,545	259	9,047	631	665
California	1,899,632	1,420,262	479,369	116,785	190,240	643,939	534,404	1,809	100,204	12,292	4,288
Colorado	416,636	323,269	93,366	18,187	32,069	143,608	146,814	65	15,989	1,507	690
Connecticut	220,332	159,279	61,053	18,377	22,905	72,335	49,861	120	17,282	933	163
District of Columbia	30,156	21,756	8,399	1,500	2,809	8,080	9,995	86	1,499	1	0
Delaware	78,744	57,865	20,879	4,158	7,565	25,322	23,338	41	3,768	234	156
Florida	1,607,945	1,192,656	415,289	111,623	181,258	523,743	444,435	1,119	97,091	8,213	6,319
Georgia	752,192	569,897	182,295	25,102	51,235	237,533	283,951	226	22,479	1,314	1,310
Hawaii	121,164	96,199	24,965	6,169	8,067	38,721	48,395	73	5,419	375	375
Idaho	132,242	103,738	28,504	6,367	11,515	48,831	41,363	12	5,533	571	262
Illinois	737,385	550,859	186,526	44,564	70,769	247,246	200,520	749	41,474	2,387	703
Indiana	483,113	343,888	139,226	24,279	42,354	151,933	135,382	233	22,120	1,583	575
Iowa	235,168	176,471	58,697	14,002	24,046	79,165	63,856	111	13,144	654	204
Kansas	223,743	174,276	49,467	12,867	19,762	74,980	74,469	97	11,272	1,156	439
Kentucky	332,404	250,496	81,908	13,823	27,378	112,650	105,614	212	12,912	519	392
Louisiana	333,535	262,927	70,608	15,374	27,285	107,947	121,704	226	13,250	1,783	341
Maine	129,308	96,065	33,243	7,475	12,711	45,660	34,344	0	6,545	680	251
Maryland	444,479	334,162	110,317	22,961	33,606	131,241	161,192	317	20,635	1,406	920
Massachusetts	392,079	283,174	108,906	31,017	46,499	129,074	84,260	320	28,427	2,281	308
Michigan	676,170	490,147	186,023	41,278	64,513	242,562	153,324	466	38,449	2,298	532
Minnesota	377,165	279,431	97,734	22,118	37,050	132,246	94,944	147	20,379	1,338	401
Mississippi	221,519	168,406	53,112	8,821	17,615	68,829	80,671	94	8,009	541	271
Missouri	500,120	369,207	130,913	26,204	45,591	169,806	142,382	286	24,073	1,739	391
Montana	100,150	75,472	24,677	4,666	8,373	35,513	29,850	47	4,326	309	30
Nebraska	145,411	113,861	31,550	7,791	14,853	47,566	48,230	90	6,994	620	178
Nevada	230,760	170,517	60,243	9,088	21,991	82,218	68,276	94	7,735	728	624
New Hampshire	115,877	83,329	32,548	7,183	11,303	38,361	30,238	122	6,286	634	263
New Jersey	443,741	323,534	120,207	32,856	53,943	146,977	99,180	389	30,443	2,039	374
New Mexico	172,727	128,960	43,767	7,788	13,446	63,368	50,164	438	7,287	237	264
New York	921,854	654,919	266,935	68,730	96,748	286,312	217,861	875	64,736	3,235	759
North Carolina	774,958	590,831	184,126	29,969	58,382	251,247	279,265	273	26,935	2,081	954
North Dakota	57,603	45,375	12,228	2,694	4,966	18,125	20,993	0	2,481	117	96
Ohio	884,580	642,548	242,032	49,513	78,294	299,668	232,035	694	46,344	2,634	535
Oklahoma	338,763	258,356	80,407	15,094	27,450	115,532	112,023	101	13,261	1,442	392
Oregon	336,869	251,251	85,618	21,689	31,459	125,255	83,308	385	19,154	1,836	699
Pennsylvania	961,373	692,701	268,671	68,435	100,183	315,323	229,871	891	63,158	4,409	868
Rhode Island	74,052	53,699	20,352	5,301	8,346	23,097	19,115	23	4,730	472	99
South Carolina	416,917	313,899	103,018	15,296	32,871	142,632	142,114	203	13,404	1,170	721
South Dakota	72,221	55,024	17,197	3,897	7,539	22,129	23,815	6	3,465	244	188
Tennessee	508,445	375,011	133,434	20,060	42,021	169,959	160,699	479	18,304	1,297	459
Texas	1,683,409	1,307,552	375,857	70,233	125,553	549,930	629,630	708	60,880	5,430	3,923
Utah	152,376	118,752	33,624	8,301	15,327	46,981	54,246	116	7,236	716	349
Vermont	49,512	34,941	14,571	2,976	4,165	16,284	12,819	28	2,699	204	74
Virginia	777,314	623,170	154,144	27,091	47,998	228,291	364,460	113	23,180	2,316	1,595
Washington	608,026	461,706	146,320	29,382	47,499	212,419	199,508	189	25,035	2,897	1,450
West Virginia	168,832	126,647	42,185	8,073	15,957	60,844	46,393	62	7,329	435	310
Wisconsin	421,584	305,921	115,663	25,702	38,233	142,463	108,090	69	23,830	1,609	263
Wyoming	49,491	38,678	10,813	1,907	3,748	17,280	17,494	0	1,459	383	65
Puerto Rico	96,071	72,720	23,351	3,859	20,456	30,608	20,174	108	3,345	425	89
Island Areas & Foreign	117,113	81,775	35,338	7,571	8,961	34,574	34,307	114	6,838	512	221

Table 35. Veterans in the Population: Living Veterans, by State/Territory, Period of Service and Gender, 2013 and Projected 2023, 2033, and 2043—*Continued*

(Number.)

State and year	(l) Between WWII & KC	(m) KC only	(n) KC & VNE only	(o) Between KC & VNE	(p) VNE only	(q) VNE & GW (Pre 9/11) only	(r) VNE, GW (Pre 9/11), & GW (Post 9/11) only	(s) Between VNE & GW (Pre 9/11)	(t) GW (Pre 9/11) only	(u) GW (Pre 9/11) & GW (Post 9/11) only	(v) GW (Post 9/11) only	(w) Post-GW Era
2013 Total	102,614	1,722,990	185,260	2,083,858	6,789,871	317,347	56,441	3,406,845	2,799,822	1,213,773	2,401,605	0
Alabama	1,395	27,815	5,474	32,071	119,033	8,880	1,466	63,780	62,903	29,361	47,498	0
Alaska	139	2,132	290	4,104	19,154	1,312	444	11,560	11,200	8,107	13,555	0
Arizona	2,119	45,712	6,917	54,756	167,933	9,922	1,456	74,541	63,945	28,737	49,280	0
Arkansas	1,486	17,131	3,241	21,899	75,280	3,579	1,262	39,214	33,774	11,621	31,310	0
California	10,559	155,592	18,068	181,820	595,414	22,337	3,832	285,181	208,258	91,907	208,070	0
Colorado	1,175	24,599	5,273	30,870	128,397	7,913	1,335	61,256	58,476	34,075	45,016	0
Connecticut	1,432	21,131	679	24,889	69,231	2,071	191	34,613	22,320	5,911	19,368	0
District of Columbia	89	2,622	186	2,576	7,452	442	0	5,648	4,088	2,270	3,196	0
Delaware	607	6,284	891	8,198	23,194	1,007	74	12,033	8,959	4,735	8,563	0
Florida	9,578	147,838	18,887	171,299	469,873	25,388	3,276	233,293	191,122	86,432	138,217	0
Georgia	2,163	41,066	7,545	50,632	212,232	14,329	2,117	129,274	119,680	57,735	90,090	0
Hawaii	920	6,114	1,203	8,758	34,318	2,352	472	15,214	11,244	14,678	19,649	0
Idaho	496	9,511	1,170	11,214	45,326	1,932	140	16,783	17,948	6,343	15,000	0
Illinois	4,461	64,402	3,276	74,130	238,095	4,425	747	107,186	88,391	30,558	76,399	0
Indiana	2,312	38,460	1,736	46,961	144,032	4,336	1,255	89,721	60,576	17,271	51,945	0
Iowa	876	22,007	1,181	22,653	75,425	1,858	498	35,056	26,496	8,645	26,359	0
Kansas	1,133	16,463	1,704	19,217	68,773	3,566	497	29,020	28,467	13,829	28,110	0
Kentucky	1,226	24,059	2,408	27,762	104,592	4,376	882	52,708	46,428	16,392	37,535	0
Louisiana	1,691	22,333	2,828	26,195	100,688	3,419	671	42,497	54,076	19,125	44,413	0
Maine	718	10,640	1,141	11,306	42,465	1,620	184	21,219	16,030	4,980	11,531	0
Maryland	1,288	28,677	2,603	35,546	118,729	7,348	1,641	73,166	62,090	39,526	50,586	0
Massachusetts	2,036	42,264	1,646	42,293	123,987	2,060	1,073	64,257	36,411	10,243	34,475	0
Michigan	3,976	58,935	2,749	70,340	233,861	4,587	833	111,241	75,203	20,529	52,172	0
Minnesota	1,662	34,085	1,226	40,056	127,058	2,954	607	55,869	41,008	11,809	38,565	0
Mississippi	1,048	14,514	2,290	17,092	62,111	3,750	408	34,879	30,064	12,469	33,980	0
Missouri	1,946	39,261	4,199	48,243	157,161	7,191	864	80,438	63,183	21,178	49,966	0
Montana	428	7,196	837	10,449	32,923	1,311	412	13,754	12,956	3,996	11,176	0
Nebraska	474	12,932	1,124	11,397	43,785	2,246	234	19,589	18,731	9,829	17,190	0
Nevada	756	17,439	3,200	22,673	72,515	5,046	832	36,719	28,524	11,095	22,779	0
New Hampshire	383	9,634	771	11,549	35,502	1,338	486	20,494	13,704	4,794	9,916	0
New Jersey	2,961	49,509	2,021	52,899	139,968	3,902	711	63,958	38,169	15,237	41,161	0
New Mexico	362	11,091	1,853	14,799	58,064	2,981	207	28,168	21,137	8,386	17,453	0
New York	4,696	90,379	2,374	108,176	275,575	5,862	1,742	153,188	90,174	31,626	88,457	0
North Carolina	2,406	48,563	6,785	61,974	226,249	15,645	1,615	119,473	115,208	52,404	94,394	0
North Dakota	231	4,578	175	5,423	16,936	642	277	6,574	6,778	3,466	9,830	0
Ohio	4,038	71,828	3,298	89,873	285,874	8,278	1,684	147,427	109,679	32,973	79,421	0
Oklahoma	1,227	22,280	3,336	31,281	105,623	5,283	898	47,798	41,929	19,751	44,161	0
Oregon	1,257	25,811	3,113	34,171	117,330	3,642	471	49,804	41,056	11,371	26,769	0
Pennsylvania	6,955	90,545	4,361	107,983	299,489	8,681	1,924	152,842	101,389	35,153	82,723	0
Rhode Island	438	7,175	601	8,056	21,508	503	386	11,835	6,711	4,115	7,400	0
South Carolina	1,485	24,879	6,101	35,535	125,509	8,358	1,944	65,795	58,390	25,392	48,031	0
South Dakota	204	6,467	641	6,645	20,204	952	144	10,342	8,076	4,981	9,662	0
Tennessee	1,715	34,797	5,468	46,623	153,987	8,247	1,797	84,617	69,613	26,555	54,487	0
Texas	7,004	97,443	18,757	125,264	491,489	30,651	5,110	242,880	250,603	111,832	231,433	0
Utah	338	13,126	1,135	14,987	41,943	3,031	523	18,182	17,951	10,995	21,747	0
Vermont	362	3,604	284	5,600	15,258	543	126	8,581	5,332	1,706	5,112	0
Virginia	2,358	35,508	8,579	47,893	187,531	25,720	4,866	103,781	122,193	108,956	102,726	0
Washington	2,004	36,513	6,639	50,453	189,664	13,222	1,443	93,674	78,992	37,948	67,903	0
West Virginia	1,007	13,601	1,611	18,513	56,969	1,629	325	22,603	21,233	6,067	17,138	0
Wisconsin	1,945	34,867	1,494	48,625	135,768	3,722	1,215	65,025	47,595	13,573	41,985	0
Wyoming	82	2,935	365	4,498	15,978	835	37	6,234	7,402	3,452	5,767	0
Puerto Rico	542	19,237	705	12,226	28,745	536	532	10,475	7,000	2,791	9,315	0
Island Areas & Foreign	428	7,408	820	11,415	31,669	1,586	279	23,381	16,958	6,862	8,622	0

Table 35. Veterans in the Population: Living Veterans, by State/Territory, Period of Service and Gender, 2013 and Projected 2023, 2033, and 2043—*Continued*

(Number.)

State and year	(a) All veterans (b+c)	(b) Wartime veterans (i+j+k+m+n+p+q+r+t+u+v)	(c) Peacetime veterans (h+l+o+s+w)	(d) WWII (i+j+k)	(e) Korean Conflict (KC) (j+k+m+n)	(f) Vietnam Era (VNE) (k+n+p+q+r)	(g) Gulf War Era (GW) (q+r+t+u+v)	(h) Pre-WWII	(i) WWII only	(j) WWII & KC only	(k) WWII, KC, & VNE only
2023 Projected total	X	X	X	X	X	X	X	1,367	125,609	11,016	4,790
Alabama	X	X	X	X	X	X	X	11	1,626	153	86
Alaska	X	X	X	X	X	X	X	1	111	8	17
Arizona	X	X	X	X	X	X	X	29	3,388	440	198
Arkansas	X	X	X	X	X	X	X	27	1,126	97	81
California	X	X	X	X	X	X	X	154	10,416	1,339	472
Colorado	X	X	X	X	X	X	X	7	1,883	197	76
Connecticut	X	X	X	X	X	X	X	11	1,820	110	22
District of Columbia	X	X	X	X	X	X	X	8	176	0	0
Delaware	X	X	X	X	X	X	X	5	483	41	23
Florida	X	X	X	X	X	X	X	114	12,193	1,101	841
Georgia	X	X	X	X	X	X	X	23	2,948	188	192
Hawaii	X	X	X	X	X	X	X	7	603	46	40
Idaho	X	X	X	X	X	X	X	1	717	90	28
Illinois	X	X	X	X	X	X	X	67	4,590	281	84
Indiana	X	X	X	X	X	X	X	25	2,558	208	65
Iowa	X	X	X	X	X	X	X	10	1,600	89	28
Kansas	X	X	X	X	X	X	X	9	1,279	146	48
Kentucky	X	X	X	X	X	X	X	21	1,542	68	54
Louisiana	X	X	X	X	X	X	X	22	1,608	238	35
Maine	X	X	X	X	X	X	X	0	777	91	34
Maryland	X	X	X	X	X	X	X	29	2,225	164	99
Massachusetts	X	X	X	X	X	X	X	33	3,106	273	29
Michigan	X	X	X	X	X	X	X	44	4,299	291	67
Minnesota	X	X	X	X	X	X	X	15	2,253	166	47
Mississippi	X	X	X	X	X	X	X	9	955	70	37
Missouri	X	X	X	X	X	X	X	30	2,853	230	56
Montana	X	X	X	X	X	X	X	5	552	43	3
Nebraska	X	X	X	X	X	X	X	8	797	75	23
Nevada	X	X	X	X	X	X	X	9	915	101	73
New Hampshire	X	X	X	X	X	X	X	11	764	84	31
New Jersey	X	X	X	X	X	X	X	35	3,184	247	40
New Mexico	X	X	X	X	X	X	X	44	877	31	39
New York	X	X	X	X	X	X	X	76	6,769	368	83
North Carolina	X	X	X	X	X	X	X	30	3,477	283	139
North Dakota	X	X	X	X	X	X	X	0	275	12	14
Ohio	X	X	X	X	X	X	X	68	5,253	325	65
Oklahoma	X	X	X	X	X	X	X	10	1,612	188	58
Oregon	X	X	X	X	X	X	X	44	2,372	242	97
Pennsylvania	X	X	X	X	X	X	X	91	7,235	546	111
Rhode Island	X	X	X	X	X	X	X	2	503	63	12
South Carolina	X	X	X	X	X	X	X	24	1,805	169	119
South Dakota	X	X	X	X	X	X	X	1	442	30	27
Tennessee	X	X	X	X	X	X	X	49	2,310	181	63
Texas	X	X	X	X	X	X	X	73	7,526	723	512
Utah	X	X	X	X	X	X	X	12	912	92	35
Vermont	X	X	X	X	X	X	X	3	313	24	11
Virginia	X	X	X	X	X	X	X	12	2,698	282	196
Washington	X	X	X	X	X	X	X	18	3,004	354	169
West Virginia	X	X	X	X	X	X	X	7	883	60	41
Wisconsin	X	X	X	X	X	X	X	6	2,798	205	29
Wyoming	X	X	X	X	X	X	X	0	164	54	8
Puerto Rico	X	X	X	X	X	X	X	10	325	51	9
Island Areas & Foreign	X	X	X	X	X	X	X	10	707	58	25

Table 35. Veterans in the Population: Living Veterans, by State/Territory, Period of Service and Gender, 2013 and Projected 2023, 2033, and 2043—*Continued*

(Number.)

State and year	(l) Between WWII & KC	(m) KC only	(n) KC & VNE only	(o) Between KC & VNE	(p) VNE only	(q) VNE & GW (Pre 9/11) only	(r) VNE, GW (Pre 9/11), & GW (Post 9/11) only	(s) Between VNE & GW (Pre 9/11)	(t) GW (Pre 9/11) only	(u) GW (Pre 9/11) & GW (Post 9/11) only	(v) GW (Post 9/11) only	(w) Post-GW Era
2023 Projected total	20,495	545,415	63,086	1,196,208	5,340,895	261,503	47,107	3,123,007	2,662,805	1,603,723	4,060,700	227,982
Alabama	273	9,411	1,974	19,642	98,321	7,617	1,267	61,716	63,345	42,169	81,335	3,684
Alaska	29	594	90	2,069	12,481	902	269	9,030	9,535	10,395	24,971	1,528
Arizona	471	16,890	2,629	35,661	146,050	9,034	1,340	75,279	66,207	39,400	93,490	5,158
Arkansas	372	5,998	1,105	13,535	63,117	2,959	1,125	38,402	34,294	16,882	52,536	2,426
California	1,933	43,843	5,319	92,815	413,781	16,103	2,885	232,205	173,654	108,111	342,458	25,819
Colorado	241	8,232	1,634	17,680	101,832	6,414	1,141	56,219	55,090	42,119	80,122	4,112
Connecticut	250	6,016	227	12,741	49,590	1,504	132	29,191	19,483	7,533	29,748	1,739
District of Columbia	19	711	75	1,411	5,752	361	0	4,918	3,347	2,783	6,735	465
Delaware	138	2,118	356	5,187	19,843	874	63	11,794	8,792	6,499	14,145	714
Florida	2,104	51,632	6,857	106,364	385,889	21,301	2,800	221,469	186,872	116,316	241,344	12,757
Georgia	447	14,522	2,786	31,685	178,171	12,674	1,926	125,761	118,081	78,280	160,875	8,528
Hawaii	161	1,838	380	4,592	25,736	1,832	347	13,164	9,650	18,971	36,648	2,763
Idaho	139	3,574	463	7,121	39,557	1,754	128	16,922	18,447	9,491	29,192	1,875
Illinois	813	18,913	1,084	40,294	180,287	3,389	603	94,339	80,303	36,832	121,841	7,607
Indiana	474	11,827	614	27,296	115,022	3,541	996	82,642	57,776	22,701	84,830	4,567
Iowa	161	6,761	408	12,623	60,796	1,559	414	32,883	25,909	11,930	42,501	1,968
Kansas	200	4,893	567	10,926	54,174	2,900	397	26,535	26,836	19,046	47,602	2,607
Kentucky	260	7,747	898	16,580	86,786	3,769	764	51,461	46,498	23,127	64,815	3,496
Louisiana	314	7,607	944	15,466	81,156	2,836	560	39,473	51,508	23,952	67,890	3,751
Maine	150	3,490	420	6,364	33,659	1,301	148	19,632	15,243	6,937	19,240	1,044
Maryland	237	8,306	644	18,305	84,000	5,420	1,228	61,346	54,662	49,564	87,783	4,827
Massachusetts	342	12,467	495	22,130	89,828	1,539	798	54,451	31,745	12,836	50,941	3,024
Michigan	742	17,584	876	39,195	180,316	3,707	685	97,420	66,182	23,625	73,975	4,221
Minnesota	290	10,069	383	22,312	98,257	2,366	489	50,339	38,202	15,279	59,331	2,789
Mississippi	261	4,768	750	10,092	50,052	3,125	353	33,213	29,596	19,070	51,605	2,450
Missouri	397	12,774	1,398	28,961	127,964	6,123	745	76,643	62,715	29,711	83,709	4,069
Montana	90	2,383	316	6,259	27,588	1,157	376	13,595	13,425	6,474	19,755	1,027
Nebraska	78	3,974	344	6,417	34,135	1,821	191	17,705	17,332	12,604	28,436	1,468
Nevada	145	5,793	1,084	13,485	56,068	4,061	667	33,871	27,979	15,190	39,582	1,888
New Hampshire	99	3,168	234	6,552	27,110	1,074	400	18,466	12,860	6,102	16,459	759
New Jersey	601	13,577	566	26,400	97,135	3,009	517	52,402	32,303	17,732	59,073	3,340
New Mexico	72	3,619	620	8,712	46,625	2,462	179	26,861	21,104	13,098	32,340	1,893
New York	815	25,417	734	54,342	194,046	4,363	1,334	127,169	77,140	36,326	128,622	7,699
North Carolina	570	16,417	2,685	38,691	193,330	14,030	1,472	118,648	116,081	72,216	164,715	9,529
North Dakota	50	1,415	58	3,050	13,398	529	227	6,128	6,615	5,202	17,002	947
Ohio	763	21,753	1,095	50,069	221,989	6,636	1,366	131,912	100,702	39,575	123,559	7,099
Oklahoma	251	7,539	1,151	19,126	86,929	4,486	770	46,253	42,302	28,073	77,349	4,130
Oregon	264	8,912	1,165	21,124	97,033	3,112	395	47,597	40,301	14,353	45,644	2,306
Pennsylvania	1,386	27,792	1,398	61,062	232,407	6,745	1,581	138,484	96,179	43,529	130,291	7,021
Rhode Island	87	2,135	204	4,383	15,479	342	289	9,884	5,718	4,824	10,881	599
South Carolina	350	9,217	2,341	23,382	110,484	7,566	1,796	66,712	59,917	36,803	84,249	4,708
South Dakota	44	2,117	229	4,019	17,315	845	132	10,369	8,362	7,117	17,453	902
Tennessee	328	11,837	2,033	29,487	131,999	7,240	1,638	83,879	70,837	37,917	91,488	3,978
Texas	1,519	32,466	6,457	75,588	404,314	26,231	4,441	234,999	251,354	151,896	406,063	19,934
Utah	73	4,342	365	9,159	34,342	2,613	449	17,390	17,921	15,392	38,934	1,918
Vermont	63	1,082	106	3,173	11,965	429	95	7,791	5,028	2,628	7,698	258
Virginia	448	11,223	2,586	26,877	143,744	20,541	4,016	93,600	113,178	147,557	207,794	14,053
Washington	435	12,182	2,207	29,622	150,846	10,758	1,223	86,126	74,833	50,888	125,700	7,623
West Virginia	205	4,545	615	11,373	46,678	1,361	280	22,105	22,111	8,955	30,864	1,483
Wisconsin	342	10,870	517	27,642	108,090	3,004	1,029	60,046	45,515	17,605	64,446	3,021
Wyoming	16	948	120	2,541	12,629	697	31	5,927	7,851	5,249	13,226	883
Puerto Rico	106	5,823	219	6,708	21,195	366	407	8,981	6,083	4,652	13,957	889
Island Areas & Foreign	79	2,282	261	5,918	21,605	1,120	201	19,659	15,802	8,202	15,462	639

Table 35. Veterans in the Population: Living Veterans, by State/Territory, Period of Service and Gender, 2013 and Projected 2023, 2033, and 2043—*Continued*

(Number.)

State and year	(a) All veterans (b+c)	(b) Wartime veterans (i+j+k+m+n+p+q+r+t+u+v)	(c) Peacetime veterans (h+l+o+s+w)	(d) WWII (i+j+k)	(e) Korean Conflict (KC) (j+k+m+n)	(f) Vietnam Era (VNE) (k+n+p+q+r)	(g) Gulf War Era (GW) (q+r+t+u+v)	(h) Pre-WWII	(i) WWII only	(j) WWII & KC only	(k) WWII, KC, & VNE only
2033 Projected total	X	X	X	X	X	X	X	152	13,869	1,201	518
Alabama	X	X	X	X	X	X	X	1	190	17	9
Alaska	X	X	X	X	X	X	X	0	11	1	1
Arizona	X	X	X	X	X	X	X	3	432	54	24
Arkansas	X	X	X	X	X	X	X	3	131	11	9
California	X	X	X	X	X	X	X	15	1,019	129	44
Colorado	X	X	X	X	X	X	X	1	205	22	8
Connecticut	X	X	X	X	X	X	X	1	182	11	2
District of Columbia	X	X	X	X	X	X	X	1	17	0	0
Delaware	X	X	X	X	X	X	X	1	62	5	3
Florida	X	X	X	X	X	X	X	14	1,486	133	98
Georgia	X	X	X	X	X	X	X	3	345	22	21
Hawaii	X	X	X	X	X	X	X	1	66	5	4
Idaho	X	X	X	X	X	X	X	0	86	11	3
Illinois	X	X	X	X	X	X	X	7	477	29	8
Indiana	X	X	X	X	X	X	X	3	283	23	7
Iowa	X	X	X	X	X	X	X	1	179	10	3
Kansas	X	X	X	X	X	X	X	1	139	16	5
Kentucky	X	X	X	X	X	X	X	2	176	8	6
Louisiana	X	X	X	X	X	X	X	2	177	27	4
Maine	X	X	X	X	X	X	X	0	88	10	4
Maryland	X	X	X	X	X	X	X	3	222	16	9
Massachusetts	X	X	X	X	X	X	X	4	316	27	3
Michigan	X	X	X	X	X	X	X	5	457	31	7
Minnesota	X	X	X	X	X	X	X	2	243	18	5
Mississippi	X	X	X	X	X	X	X	1	108	8	4
Missouri	X	X	X	X	X	X	X	4	318	25	6
Montana	X	X	X	X	X	X	X	1	65	5	0
Nebraska	X	X	X	X	X	X	X	1	86	8	2
Nevada	X	X	X	X	X	X	X	1	103	11	8
New Hampshire	X	X	X	X	X	X	X	1	87	9	3
New Jersey	X	X	X	X	X	X	X	3	320	24	4
New Mexico	X	X	X	X	X	X	X	5	100	3	4
New York	X	X	X	X	X	X	X	7	662	37	8
North Carolina	X	X	X	X	X	X	X	4	421	33	16
North Dakota	X	X	X	X	X	X	X	0	29	1	1
Ohio	X	X	X	X	X	X	X	7	557	34	7
Oklahoma	X	X	X	X	X	X	X	1	185	22	6
Oregon	X	X	X	X	X	X	X	6	281	28	11
Pennsylvania	X	X	X	X	X	X	X	11	776	58	11
Rhode Island	X	X	X	X	X	X	X	0	52	6	1
South Carolina	X	X	X	X	X	X	X	3	223	21	14
South Dakota	X	X	X	X	X	X	X	0	56	3	3
Tennessee	X	X	X	X	X	X	X	6	273	21	7
Texas	X	X	X	X	X	X	X	8	872	81	57
Utah	X	X	X	X	X	X	X	1	108	10	4
Vermont	X	X	X	X	X	X	X	0	34	3	1
Virginia	X	X	X	X	X	X	X	2	297	30	21
Washington	X	X	X	X	X	X	X	2	338	38	18
West Virginia	X	X	X	X	X	X	X	1	99	7	4
Wisconsin	X	X	X	X	X	X	X	1	310	23	3
Wyoming	X	X	X	X	X	X	X	0	18	6	1
Puerto Rico	X	X	X	X	X	X	X	1	34	5	1
Island Areas & Foreign	X	X	X	X	X	X	X	1	66	5	2

Table 35. Veterans in the Population: Living Veterans, by State/Territory, Period of Service and Gender, 2013 and Projected 2023, 2033, and 2043—*Continued*

(Number.)

State and year	(l) Between WWII & KC	(m) KC only	(n) KC & VNE only	(o) Between KC & VNE	(p) VNE only	(q) VNE & GW (Pre 9/11) only	(r) VNE, GW (Pre 9/11), & GW (Post 9/11) only	(s) Between VNE & GW (Pre 9/11)	(t) GW (Pre 9/11) only	(u) GW (Pre 9/11) & GW (Post 9/11) only	(v) GW (Post 9/11) only	(w) Post-GW Era
2033 Projected total	2,244	64,953	7,748	288,414	3,088,994	170,925	31,428	2,664,381	2,430,153	1,548,463	4,594,703	1,763,572
Alabama	31	1,181	251	5,106	59,324	5,186	851	55,039	60,491	43,038	100,894	30,884
Alaska	3	61	9	479	6,209	511	99	6,362	7,333	8,713	27,661	12,282
Arizona	57	2,298	363	9,752	92,711	6,561	980	71,390	67,295	41,675	116,126	42,079
Arkansas	45	752	137	3,443	38,863	1,837	800	34,711	33,214	17,346	61,862	19,752
California	186	4,597	561	19,612	209,029	9,048	1,738	175,338	140,556	92,992	339,978	179,896
Colorado	26	973	181	4,070	57,847	3,992	785	47,021	49,209	39,613	92,915	34,732
Connecticut	24	648	26	2,625	25,186	867	61	22,591	16,130	6,679	30,242	12,659
District of Columbia	2	73	9	320	2,865	204	0	3,705	2,621	2,358	7,042	4,092
Delaware	16	271	47	1,378	12,431	572	37	10,930	8,416	6,631	16,647	5,642
Florida	255	6,832	907	28,264	234,182	14,433	1,925	197,701	175,628	116,159	287,295	102,689
Georgia	52	1,856	361	8,322	107,566	8,968	1,451	113,376	111,731	78,430	191,795	70,608
Hawaii	19	212	42	981	14,444	1,147	190	10,723	8,070	17,197	39,596	20,565
Idaho	16	464	60	1,897	25,794	1,284	92	15,918	18,182	9,798	34,390	13,775
Illinois	83	2,110	127	9,023	99,722	1,976	395	77,483	70,403	34,014	128,162	54,486
Indiana	51	1,383	78	6,734	68,292	2,263	583	71,012	52,878	22,041	92,852	34,937
Iowa	18	789	54	2,718	36,188	1,041	265	28,524	24,020	11,778	47,832	15,826
Kansas	21	557	65	2,584	31,632	1,909	241	22,468	24,169	18,197	53,847	20,790
Kentucky	30	946	117	4,071	52,334	2,541	526	46,312	44,074	23,218	75,372	27,405
Louisiana	36	926	114	3,914	48,445	1,861	360	33,963	47,531	23,255	73,817	27,515
Maine	18	422	51	1,490	19,675	818	90	16,979	13,842	6,742	21,917	7,957
Maryland	23	899	66	4,066	42,953	3,140	717	46,531	44,539	43,491	99,793	40,488
Massachusetts	33	1,374	54	4,799	46,925	899	447	42,660	26,604	11,514	50,816	21,944
Michigan	78	1,979	101	8,957	102,518	2,439	462	80,877	57,611	21,578	74,186	29,949
Minnesota	31	1,140	42	5,053	55,981	1,494	312	42,173	34,112	14,567	64,155	21,818
Mississippi	29	588	90	2,423	30,068	2,011	248	29,093	27,755	19,427	59,838	19,000
Missouri	43	1,522	169	7,253	76,015	4,202	510	67,098	58,858	29,813	97,174	32,888
Montana	10	298	43	1,563	16,776	819	285	12,305	13,026	6,789	24,106	7,910
Nebraska	8	453	38	1,498	19,546	1,167	119	14,976	15,375	11,762	32,070	11,760
Nevada	16	730	136	3,658	33,453	2,713	427	29,660	26,272	15,082	46,899	16,003
New Hampshire	10	378	27	1,597	15,084	707	275	15,374	11,333	5,781	18,403	6,148
New Jersey	62	1,431	60	5,423	48,348	1,816	295	39,597	26,040	15,183	58,182	24,464
New Mexico	8	446	78	2,155	27,767	1,601	127	23,621	19,835	13,362	39,174	15,038
New York	79	2,659	87	11,232	99,665	2,571	846	97,754	63,200	31,693	126,333	55,330
North Carolina	68	2,088	359	10,056	119,605	10,010	1,071	109,248	112,688	73,459	191,525	72,149
North Dakota	5	166	7	694	7,877	356	147	5,238	6,010	5,032	19,640	7,308
Ohio	80	2,479	124	11,599	126,900	4,252	880	110,062	89,509	36,996	130,649	51,902
Oklahoma	28	924	143	4,948	52,520	2,972	512	40,943	40,255	28,301	90,323	32,805
Oregon	34	1,132	148	5,500	58,855	2,119	252	42,436	38,165	14,177	51,276	18,435
Pennsylvania	148	3,232	165	14,345	132,056	4,026	1,039	116,368	87,177	41,539	142,487	52,192
Rhode Island	9	236	24	1,023	8,115	147	165	7,659	4,725	4,277	11,081	4,579
South Carolina	42	1,244	307	6,607	70,776	5,314	1,299	63,130	59,214	38,573	101,887	36,366
South Dakota	5	274	28	1,017	11,200	599	94	9,717	8,248	7,433	21,409	7,205
Tennessee	39	1,498	271	7,829	83,343	5,003	1,229	76,759	68,761	39,191	109,349	33,867
Texas	172	4,035	787	18,966	242,572	17,620	3,048	209,176	239,886	152,619	481,517	165,277
Utah	9	548	47	2,273	20,387	1,803	307	15,186	16,686	15,583	46,827	15,850
Vermont	7	127	13	778	6,888	256	45	6,578	4,524	2,581	8,764	2,261
Virginia	48	1,329	303	6,251	80,185	12,874	2,689	77,623	97,810	136,901	254,559	107,886
Washington	50	1,474	260	7,159	87,851	6,897	836	72,981	67,589	48,764	144,182	59,463
West Virginia	23	554	80	3,099	28,439	878	192	19,688	21,361	9,186	37,407	12,407
Wisconsin	37	1,289	63	6,351	63,766	1,880	715	51,579	41,582	17,008	70,377	23,281
Wyoming	2	112	13	594	7,461	490	22	4,991	7,375	5,343	16,748	6,756
Puerto Rico	12	711	27	1,525	11,111	179	225	6,991	5,138	4,386	14,868	6,311
Island Areas & Foreign	8	253	30	1,342	11,251	653	121	14,761	13,097	7,198	18,459	5,963

Table 35. Veterans in the Population: Living Veterans, by State/Territory, Period of Service and Gender, 2013 and Projected 2023, 2033, and 2043—*Continued*

(Number.)

State and year	(a) All veterans (b+c)	(b) Wartime veterans (i+j+k+m+n+p+q+r+t+u+v)	(c) Peacetime veterans (h+l+o+s+w)	(d) WWII (i+j+k)	(e) Korean Conflict (KC) (j+k+m+n)	(f) Vietnam Era (VNE) (k+n+p+q+r)	(g) Gulf War Era (GW) (q+r+t+u+v)	(h) Pre-WWII	(i) WWII only	(j) WWII & KC only	(k) WWII, KC, & VNE only
2043 Projected total	X	X	X	X	X	X	X	19	1,755	150	64
Alabama	X	X	X	X	X	X	X	0	25	2	1
Alaska	X	X	X	X	X	X	X	0	1	0	0
Arizona	X	X	X	X	X	X	X	0	63	8	3
Arkansas	X	X	X	X	X	X	X	0	17	1	1
California	X	X	X	X	X	X	X	2	112	14	5
Colorado	X	X	X	X	X	X	X	0	25	3	1
Connecticut	X	X	X	X	X	X	X	0	20	1	0
District of Columbia	X	X	X	X	X	X	X	0	2	0	0
Delaware	X	X	X	X	X	X	X	0	9	1	0
Florida	X	X	X	X	X	X	X	2	208	19	13
Georgia	X	X	X	X	X	X	X	0	46	3	3
Hawaii	X	X	X	X	X	X	X	0	8	1	0
Idaho	X	X	X	X	X	X	X	0	12	2	0
Illinois	X	X	X	X	X	X	X	1	56	3	1
Indiana	X	X	X	X	X	X	X	0	36	3	1
Iowa	X	X	X	X	X	X	X	0	23	1	0
Kansas	X	X	X	X	X	X	X	0	17	2	1
Kentucky	X	X	X	X	X	X	X	0	23	1	1
Louisiana	X	X	X	X	X	X	X	0	22	4	0
Maine	X	X	X	X	X	X	X	0	12	1	0
Maryland	X	X	X	X	X	X	X	0	25	2	1
Massachusetts	X	X	X	X	X	X	X	1	36	3	0
Michigan	X	X	X	X	X	X	X	1	55	4	1
Minnesota	X	X	X	X	X	X	X	0	30	2	1
Mississippi	X	X	X	X	X	X	X	0	14	1	0
Missouri	X	X	X	X	X	X	X	0	40	3	1
Montana	X	X	X	X	X	X	X	0	9	1	0
Nebraska	X	X	X	X	X	X	X	0	11	1	0
Nevada	X	X	X	X	X	X	X	0	13	1	1
New Hampshire	X	X	X	X	X	X	X	0	11	1	0
New Jersey	X	X	X	X	X	X	X	0	37	3	0
New Mexico	X	X	X	X	X	X	X	1	13	0	1
New York	X	X	X	X	X	X	X	1	74	4	1
North Carolina	X	X	X	X	X	X	X	1	58	4	2
North Dakota	X	X	X	X	X	X	X	0	4	0	0
Ohio	X	X	X	X	X	X	X	1	67	4	1
Oklahoma	X	X	X	X	X	X	X	0	24	3	1
Oregon	X	X	X	X	X	X	X	1	38	4	1
Pennsylvania	X	X	X	X	X	X	X	1	95	7	1
Rhode Island	X	X	X	X	X	X	X	0	6	1	0
South Carolina	X	X	X	X	X	X	X	1	31	3	2
South Dakota	X	X	X	X	X	X	X	0	8	0	0
Tennessee	X	X	X	X	X	X	X	1	37	3	1
Texas	X	X	X	X	X	X	X	1	116	10	7
Utah	X	X	X	X	X	X	X	0	15	1	0
Vermont	X	X	X	X	X	X	X	0	4	0	0
Virginia	X	X	X	X	X	X	X	0	38	4	2
Washington	X	X	X	X	X	X	X	0	43	5	2
West Virginia	X	X	X	X	X	X	X	0	13	1	1
Wisconsin	X	X	X	X	X	X	X	0	39	3	0
Wyoming	X	X	X	X	X	X	X	0	2	1	0
Puerto Rico	X	X	X	X	X	X	X	0	4	1	0
Island Areas & Foreign	X	X	X	X	X	X	X	0	7	1	0

Table 35. Veterans in the Population: Living Veterans, by State/Territory, Period of Service and Gender, 2013 and Projected 2023, 2033, and 2043—*Continued*

(Number.)

State and year	(l) Between WWII & KC	(m) KC only	(n) KC & VNE only	(o) Between KC & VNE	(p) VNE only	(q) VNE & GW (Pre 9/11) only	(r) VNE, GW (Pre 9/11), & GW (Post 9/11) only	(s) Between VNE & GW (Pre 9/11)	(t) GW (Pre 9/11) only	(u) GW (Pre 9/11) & GW (Post 9/11) only	(v) GW (Post 9/11) only	(w) Post-GW Era
2043 Projected total	281	8,087	955	36,736	846,622	59,955	11,221	1,862,722	2,035,865	1,330,753	4,708,289	3,636,031
Alabama	4	153	32	689	16,968	1,966	276	39,623	52,342	38,249	111,088	68,131
Alaska	0	6	1	50	1,534	144	18	3,564	4,917	6,084	25,770	25,246
Arizona	8	323	50	1,400	27,524	2,549	346	54,959	63,136	39,914	132,104	90,963
Arkansas	6	98	17	463	11,569	603	290	25,769	29,441	15,676	66,354	42,146
California	20	498	59	2,174	50,096	2,696	561	106,574	104,594	71,097	309,271	340,219
Colorado	3	118	21	510	15,741	1,315	312	32,009	39,866	33,180	95,259	73,618
Connecticut	3	72	3	288	5,771	280	9	14,063	12,090	5,150	27,718	24,811
District of Columbia	0	8	1	37	695	52	0	2,114	1,868	1,745	6,275	8,052
Delaware	2	38	6	201	3,665	195	8	8,148	7,372	6,045	17,759	12,027
Florida	35	939	120	3,970	67,597	5,400	746	145,179	150,625	103,814	307,259	218,681
Georgia	7	243	46	1,116	30,578	3,546	687	83,330	96,398	70,680	205,203	150,184
Hawaii	3	26	5	120	3,751	385	52	6,991	6,020	13,937	38,691	39,867
Idaho	2	61	8	254	8,244	505	32	12,308	16,574	9,081	36,888	28,495
Illinois	10	247	14	1,068	25,568	604	145	52,574	57,284	28,252	123,998	107,665
Indiana	6	170	10	856	19,079	743	172	50,300	44,612	18,956	92,829	71,218
Iowa	2	97	6	336	9,916	366	85	20,538	20,443	10,253	48,945	33,110
Kansas	3	67	8	320	8,794	673	73	15,641	19,948	15,285	54,791	42,962
Kentucky	4	120	14	526	14,628	871	186	34,264	37,911	20,607	79,942	57,246
Louisiana	5	116	14	507	13,660	677	100	23,668	40,516	20,568	74,500	55,318
Maine	2	53	6	192	5,410	272	25	12,085	11,438	5,752	22,344	16,659
Maryland	2	102	7	476	10,145	974	207	28,147	32,078	32,421	97,498	84,408
Massachusetts	4	154	6	539	11,152	268	121	26,965	20,414	8,948	46,535	42,347
Michigan	9	236	12	1,072	26,945	875	186	55,290	46,854	17,799	70,102	57,787
Minnesota	4	135	5	611	14,978	522	115	28,915	28,024	12,306	63,210	44,784
Mississippi	4	75	11	312	9,009	629	95	20,884	23,518	17,076	63,801	39,820
Missouri	5	190	20	928	20,955	1,624	189	48,003	50,504	26,561	102,193	69,597
Montana	1	39	5	212	4,814	323	128	9,086	11,528	6,240	26,157	17,168
Nebraska	1	54	4	184	5,259	373	31	10,424	12,538	9,818	32,221	24,537
Nevada	2	94	17	482	9,665	930	125	21,504	22,444	13,227	49,696	34,329
New Hampshire	1	46	3	198	3,978	279	122	10,505	9,045	4,803	18,348	12,953
New Jersey	7	159	7	593	10,774	587	84	23,952	19,125	11,258	51,933	47,423
New Mexico	1	57	10	287	7,840	562	52	16,921	16,884	11,895	42,502	31,757
New York	9	289	10	1,241	23,248	771	310	60,940	47,220	24,069	114,337	105,847
North Carolina	9	280	46	1,401	34,787	3,813	376	81,414	100,335	67,220	204,722	148,787
North Dakota	1	20	1	87	2,135	133	45	3,727	4,956	4,231	20,233	15,255
Ohio	9	296	14	1,417	34,081	1,451	285	75,151	73,541	30,875	127,254	103,326
Oklahoma	3	118	18	643	15,253	1,024	159	29,627	35,036	25,279	95,746	68,687
Oregon	5	147	19	724	16,878	784	78	30,938	33,525	12,664	52,457	38,469
Pennsylvania	18	394	20	1,766	34,439	1,215	340	80,150	72,772	34,873	142,206	106,118
Rhode Island	1	27	3	116	1,964	23	35	4,744	3,573	3,314	10,323	8,986
South Carolina	6	172	41	942	21,524	1,987	455	48,938	53,323	36,159	111,820	77,475
South Dakota	1	36	4	135	3,478	226	30	7,513	7,421	6,958	23,590	15,632
Tennessee	5	197	35	1,070	25,242	1,853	537	57,195	60,901	35,987	118,440	73,142
Texas	22	523	98	2,523	70,140	6,291	1,098	152,016	210,721	137,861	511,840	355,569
Utah	1	72	6	301	5,736	652	125	10,935	14,009	13,845	50,454	34,178
Vermont	1	16	2	100	1,913	73	11	4,513	3,768	2,148	8,916	4,982
Virginia	6	166	36	791	20,978	4,106	998	52,383	75,330	110,679	266,420	227,129
Washington	7	185	31	908	24,743	2,394	324	50,194	55,793	41,693	146,531	123,290
West Virginia	3	69	10	408	8,204	283	63	14,564	18,699	8,164	40,307	27,304
Wisconsin	5	160	8	790	17,731	607	278	36,605	35,034	14,504	70,254	47,827
Wyoming	0	13	2	74	2,168	215	8	3,515	6,159	4,619	18,363	14,559
Puerto Rico	1	86	3	185	2,641	44	45	4,180	3,879	3,562	14,824	12,327
Island Areas & Foreign	1	26	3	144	3,038	222	42	9,182	9,515	5,378	18,069	13,616

Note: Numbers from this table should be reported to the nearest 1,000. Numbers and projections are for September 30th of the applicable year.
X = Not applicable/not available.
WWII = World War II; KC = Korean Conflict; VNE = Vietnam War; GW = Gulf War.

Table 36. Veterans in the Population: Living Veterans, by State/Territory, Race, Ethnicity, and Gender, 2013 and Projected 2023, 2033, and 2043

(Number.)

State and year	White alone	Black or African American alone	American Indian and Alaska Native alone	Asian alone	Native Hawaiian and Other Pacific Islander alone	Some other race alone	Two or more races	Hispanic or Latino (of any race)	White alone, not Hispanic or Latino	All veterans
2013 Total	18,405,156	2,687,057	178,224	300,251	42,168	277,487	409,007	1,475,828	17,349,880	22,299,350
Alabama	308,687	94,909	1,887	1,795	127	993	6,515	6,717	303,406	414,913
Alaska	60,308	3,377	5,377	638	544	603	2,462	3,042	58,768	73,309
Arizona	470,649	26,803	10,635	5,271	1,321	11,173	9,620	62,027	422,891	535,470
Arkansas	211,625	31,708	1,942	1,117	0	616	3,389	3,547	209,258	250,397
California	1,456,984	175,966	21,157	106,621	8,238	70,480	60,187	295,987	1,262,066	1,899,632
Colorado	368,618	21,955	4,335	5,043	255	7,557	8,874	42,695	337,371	416,636
Connecticut	194,345	17,742	870	1,107	0	2,806	3,463	11,964	186,786	220,332
District of Columbia	60,738	15,211	516	438	13	1,036	793	2,879	58,499	78,744
Delaware	10,539	18,322	72	230	1	238	752	1,285	9,748	30,156
Florida	1,375,220	175,410	6,390	11,312	1,780	12,980	24,853	126,675	1,271,879	1,607,945
Georgia	485,811	240,874	2,592	5,557	499	6,144	10,714	22,745	472,833	752,192
Hawaii	45,732	7,046	620	37,792	9,487	2,168	18,319	10,135	43,026	121,164
Idaho	125,084	2,455	1,214	295	126	726	2,343	3,465	122,482	132,242
Illinois	609,330	99,927	1,975	5,987	180	11,315	8,672	34,879	587,695	737,385
Indiana	433,171	38,876	1,708	1,722	170	3,051	4,416	10,528	426,194	483,113
Iowa	224,744	5,923	683	603	176	843	2,197	3,392	222,602	235,168
Kansas	197,457	15,942	2,481	1,036	197	1,212	5,417	7,027	192,381	223,743
Kentucky	297,286	28,793	871	792	229	662	3,771	5,919	292,769	332,404
Louisiana	239,364	84,443	2,008	670	312	2,022	4,717	9,890	231,804	333,535
Maine	124,995	939	1,253	393	0	47	1,682	1,488	123,780	129,308
Maryland	287,928	134,505	1,649	6,615	235	2,894	10,653	13,243	279,971	444,479
Massachusetts	362,033	16,850	718	2,785	320	3,763	5,610	11,111	355,299	392,079
Michigan	583,769	75,703	3,730	1,613	126	2,599	8,631	11,452	575,381	676,170
Minnesota	352,494	12,098	3,372	3,649	92	1,112	4,349	6,415	347,584	377,165
Mississippi	155,197	61,725	1,078	810	142	999	1,568	2,790	152,979	221,519
Missouri	440,539	44,651	3,721	1,987	323	1,766	7,133	10,151	433,244	500,120
Montana	92,619	884	4,023	398	0	575	1,650	2,383	90,999	100,150
Nebraska	134,415	6,457	1,448	486	124	828	1,654	3,917	131,676	145,411
Nevada	190,406	19,971	2,665	7,934	1,102	2,649	6,034	18,513	176,481	230,760
New Hampshire	112,755	735	541	201	0	199	1,446	1,396	111,996	115,877
New Jersey	362,465	61,099	1,477	5,717	40	7,847	5,096	35,080	338,878	443,741
New Mexico	141,308	5,767	8,869	1,396	34	11,267	4,087	48,771	105,934	172,727
New York	764,046	105,856	3,062	10,753	551	22,702	14,885	69,219	725,669	921,854
North Carolina	582,161	165,824	7,555	3,883	620	3,206	11,709	20,371	568,749	774,958
North Dakota	52,700	1,026	2,466	326	206	135	744	874	51,992	57,603
Ohio	772,821	91,728	2,808	2,316	294	3,400	11,213	14,017	763,464	884,580
Oklahoma	276,809	22,724	17,860	1,668	347	1,885	17,470	9,401	270,443	338,763
Oregon	314,618	5,835	3,820	3,084	319	1,065	8,128	9,254	307,576	336,869
Pennsylvania	859,904	82,052	1,588	3,687	54	4,253	9,835	24,151	843,239	961,373
Rhode Island	68,902	2,380	246	465	2	1,262	795	2,139	67,517	74,052
South Carolina	302,712	102,824	1,643	1,514	0	3,331	4,891	11,798	295,430	416,917
South Dakota	64,982	842	4,520	60	2	358	1,457	1,156	64,225	72,221
Tennessee	423,569	71,666	1,777	1,420	476	2,461	7,076	9,703	417,645	508,445
Texas	1,350,636	242,730	11,011	13,026	2,310	36,020	27,676	296,161	1,105,961	1,683,409
Utah	140,489	2,859	1,829	2,408	656	1,807	2,328	9,791	134,654	152,376
Vermont	48,250	160	267	179	1	25	630	456	47,831	49,512
Virginia	577,597	163,156	2,908	12,726	942	7,178	12,807	30,167	558,413	777,314
Washington	533,693	29,335	6,642	12,789	3,306	5,270	16,990	24,277	517,601	608,026
West Virginia	159,006	5,882	221	184	160	253	3,126	1,186	157,932	168,832
Wisconsin	392,026	18,093	4,392	1,420	71	1,756	3,826	7,151	387,456	421,584
Wyoming	46,597	556	341	507	2	517	972	1,647	45,671	49,491
Puerto Rico	72,217	8,362	420	207	0	6,044	8,821	93,820	1,842	96,071
Island Areas & Foreign	84,807	16,102	972	5,621	5,655	1,392	2,563	7,580	79,911	117,113

Table 36. Veterans in the Population: Living Veterans, by State/Territory, Race, Ethnicity, and Gender, 2013 and Projected 2023, 2033, and 2043—*Continued*

(Number.)

State and year	White alone	Black or African American alone	American Indian and Alaska Native alone	Asian alone	Native Hawaiian and Other Pacific Islander alone	Some other race alone	Two or more races	Hispanic or Latino (of any race)	White alone, not Hispanic or Latino	All veterans
2023 Projected total	15,364,054	2,646,519	174,004	300,153	44,990	328,395	437,595	1,611,958	14,238,561	19,295,709
Alabama	279,878	100,131	1,739	2,842	136	1,254	6,649	7,994	273,283	392,629
Alaska	57,781	5,252	4,604	491	710	596	2,594	3,409	55,972	72,028
Arizona	419,893	28,582	10,919	12,201	1,496	12,320	10,251	68,027	367,203	495,662
Arkansas	192,543	34,060	1,816	1,260	1	775	3,630	4,430	189,542	234,084
California	1,056,717	149,594	17,007	96,436	8,228	86,343	56,981	295,170	881,269	1,471,306
Colorado	329,604	20,126	4,049	4,686	606	7,322	10,603	46,341	296,020	376,997
Connecticut	136,957	15,688	653	987	2	2,603	3,228	13,985	128,164	160,118
District of Columbia	52,263	15,865	427	585	5	1,150	779	3,178	49,868	71,075
Delaware	10,860	14,488	79	269	7	345	714	1,669	9,796	26,761
Florida	1,122,517	185,089	8,925	12,613	1,915	13,626	25,267	142,660	1,005,010	1,369,953
Georgia	448,630	258,766	2,720	6,370	441	8,126	12,033	32,637	427,834	737,086
Hawaii	46,709	10,540	699	29,038	8,905	2,565	18,324	12,184	43,957	116,780
Idaho	120,440	3,117	1,611	369	173	1,143	2,645	4,207	117,560	129,499
Illinois	474,143	84,515	1,762	5,829	164	14,219	10,697	41,555	448,630	591,329
Indiana	369,894	33,403	2,086	1,601	169	3,407	4,582	10,361	363,264	415,141
Iowa	189,109	5,520	638	529	137	954	2,755	3,832	186,720	199,642
Kansas	171,588	15,110	2,462	1,055	199	1,160	6,589	8,430	165,300	198,165
Kentucky	271,965	28,934	877	1,016	360	773	3,960	8,473	265,457	307,885
Louisiana	209,827	77,750	1,789	667	335	2,154	4,838	10,119	201,916	297,359
Maine	102,804	1,241	2,567	364	1	51	1,502	1,548	101,520	108,530
Maryland	232,155	119,789	1,297	7,157	214	3,384	14,843	15,384	222,348	378,839
Massachusetts	257,623	13,967	589	2,467	257	3,783	5,353	12,758	249,660	284,039
Michigan	438,006	60,791	3,580	1,237	115	2,307	7,194	10,703	429,830	513,229
Minnesota	277,571	11,324	3,214	4,803	85	1,109	4,481	6,516	272,570	302,588
Mississippi	137,776	63,313	1,205	896	124	1,482	1,609	3,515	134,939	206,405
Missouri	382,595	40,755	3,501	2,084	356	2,375	6,710	13,197	372,895	438,377
Montana	85,227	1,097	3,993	375	1	657	1,697	3,022	83,072	93,048
Nebraska	114,720	6,057	1,417	563	103	736	1,810	3,668	112,136	125,407
Nevada	162,416	18,142	2,241	7,560	1,112	2,877	6,565	21,576	145,735	200,913
New Hampshire	89,414	2,037	491	274	1	166	1,790	1,337	88,724	94,174
New Jersey	241,641	45,705	1,267	5,568	27	8,061	7,892	39,451	214,431	310,160
New Mexico	120,978	6,350	9,660	1,443	604	15,555	3,986	49,497	88,815	158,577
New York	525,467	84,416	2,491	9,974	499	28,734	13,723	73,513	487,610	665,305
North Carolina	534,296	187,684	7,807	5,179	687	4,597	12,064	26,985	519,050	752,313
North Dakota	48,529	1,540	2,479	319	273	151	1,631	1,372	47,379	54,921
Ohio	614,636	77,324	2,338	2,108	352	3,344	12,127	13,315	605,735	712,229
Oklahoma	252,037	28,178	17,131	1,921	336	2,667	17,957	10,580	245,067	320,227
Oregon	260,873	5,410	3,865	3,144	407	1,106	10,157	12,598	253,014	284,962
Pennsylvania	663,394	67,972	1,406	7,069	52	4,340	11,625	25,971	644,477	755,858
Rhode Island	49,132	3,563	208	384	2	1,325	790	2,698	47,537	55,404
South Carolina	284,424	111,176	1,620	1,689	0	4,725	6,009	20,137	270,307	409,643
South Dakota	60,966	1,136	4,409	86	5	528	2,274	1,417	60,126	69,405
Tennessee	387,270	73,511	1,808	1,615	523	2,768	7,771	10,535	380,964	475,265
Texas	1,270,555	253,791	11,735	15,161	2,557	40,300	29,996	340,514	989,044	1,624,095
Utah	130,170	2,976	1,982	2,283	1,298	2,670	2,569	11,020	124,110	143,950
Vermont	39,206	277	259	208	2	49	665	458	38,838	40,666
Virginia	548,865	192,965	2,841	14,113	1,268	10,786	17,966	38,923	525,349	788,805
Washington	474,908	32,071	5,921	13,298	3,315	7,316	19,159	34,587	451,596	555,989
West Virginia	142,097	5,454	253	238	184	300	3,039	1,399	140,879	151,565
Wisconsin	314,434	19,120	4,138	1,639	72	1,891	3,871	7,173	310,416	345,164
Wyoming	46,353	653	313	501	3	1,384	1,137	3,059	45,054	50,344
Puerto Rico	50,833	6,055	266	153	1	4,648	7,825	67,580	1,481	69,781
Island Areas & Foreign	61,363	14,146	851	5,434	6,165	1,384	2,687	7,293	57,087	92,032

Table 36. Veterans in the Population: Living Veterans, by State/Territory, Race, Ethnicity, and Gender, 2013 and Projected 2023, 2033, and 2043—*Continued*

(Number.)

State and year	White alone	Black or African American alone	American Indian and Alaska Native alone	Asian alone	Native Hawaiian and Other Pacific Islander alone	Some other race alone	Two or more races	Hispanic or Latino (of any race)	White alone, not Hispanic or Latino	All veterans
2033 Projected total	12,719,789	2,528,734	161,663	316,728	44,634	419,323	480,847	1,809,359	11,525,090	16,671,719
Alabama	249,609	96,447	1,497	6,484	144	1,686	6,628	9,188	242,960	362,494
Alaska	55,726	5,531	3,472	337	745	477	3,448	3,084	54,250	69,735
Arizona	367,431	27,419	10,252	22,827	1,474	12,456	9,942	67,880	316,188	451,800
Arkansas	170,632	33,195	1,643	1,547	5	1,788	4,110	6,570	166,918	212,918
California	760,866	121,855	12,175	97,431	6,944	124,709	50,758	291,995	626,852	1,174,737
Colorado	284,488	16,345	3,277	4,012	774	6,574	16,129	52,157	250,140	331,600
Connecticut	99,041	12,427	542	818	6	2,235	2,865	14,377	89,728	117,933
District of Columbia	42,162	18,036	284	689	5	1,144	769	3,299	39,768	63,089
Delaware	11,219	10,213	77	354	9	661	776	2,345	9,853	23,309
Florida	908,703	192,683	14,444	13,885	1,885	13,088	23,314	169,951	764,629	1,168,002
Georgia	404,484	258,739	2,506	6,389	432	10,128	12,231	42,460	375,620	694,909
Hawaii	49,626	13,371	758	21,611	7,264	3,410	17,221	13,749	46,851	113,261
Idaho	110,350	3,830	1,862	563	200	1,966	3,000	5,537	107,280	121,771
Illinois	373,159	66,960	1,639	5,197	143	15,184	16,223	42,290	349,261	478,505
Indiana	314,642	26,654	2,049	1,388	165	3,598	4,920	10,084	308,679	353,418
Iowa	158,147	5,279	562	569	69	1,540	3,079	5,451	154,949	169,245
Kansas	151,795	13,348	2,215	1,029	200	1,135	6,920	9,129	145,093	176,641
Kentucky	240,331	27,600	903	1,461	410	1,977	4,455	13,700	230,575	277,137
Louisiana	188,124	65,110	1,401	586	338	2,111	4,279	9,458	180,617	261,948
Maine	80,089	2,524	5,840	298	3	87	1,261	1,632	78,640	90,102
Maryland	194,854	101,370	1,177	6,975	184	3,778	18,618	16,800	184,397	326,956
Massachusetts	183,925	11,759	546	2,358	185	4,495	5,150	14,087	175,998	208,419
Michigan	324,621	45,140	2,927	940	93	1,960	5,552	9,204	317,462	381,234
Minnesota	218,503	9,574	2,691	5,134	68	1,005	4,171	5,927	214,119	241,145
Mississippi	124,061	60,521	1,325	936	92	1,940	1,815	4,332	120,769	190,690
Missouri	323,837	35,326	3,008	2,475	356	4,241	6,656	18,346	311,610	375,898
Montana	75,133	1,815	3,551	500	4	1,214	1,783	4,432	72,319	84,001
Nebraska	99,542	5,176	1,177	558	62	595	1,759	3,251	97,209	108,869
Nevada	138,096	16,311	1,853	7,085	1,027	3,791	7,011	24,080	120,179	175,174
New Hampshire	66,213	6,216	472	305	2	131	1,878	1,216	65,653	75,218
New Jersey	156,708	31,250	919	4,734	11	7,038	20,593	41,963	129,447	221,253
New Mexico	95,470	6,068	9,232	1,476	2,291	25,177	3,610	52,993	68,765	143,324
New York	357,887	62,337	1,712	8,613	424	49,598	11,591	96,066	316,987	492,163
North Carolina	461,419	211,582	7,077	5,665	713	5,064	11,279	31,770	445,906	702,800
North Dakota	43,413	2,024	2,189	343	302	383	3,858	2,090	42,093	52,512
Ohio	486,715	59,099	1,693	1,745	346	3,021	13,417	11,578	479,895	566,035
Oklahoma	218,710	39,602	14,599	1,957	307	3,181	16,530	10,556	212,137	294,886
Oregon	201,170	4,882	3,426	2,852	377	1,111	19,035	22,405	193,405	232,853
Pennsylvania	504,888	51,888	1,122	17,358	45	3,914	16,415	26,032	488,169	595,630
Rhode Island	33,107	6,529	178	294	2	1,258	730	2,891	31,643	42,099
South Carolina	262,570	107,364	1,429	1,668	0	5,739	6,251	40,022	229,525	385,022
South Dakota	57,682	1,619	3,949	188	10	935	2,908	2,153	56,687	67,291
Tennessee	340,824	70,030	1,739	2,067	547	4,169	8,071	12,786	334,002	427,447
Texas	1,192,195	245,078	11,805	16,167	2,602	39,888	28,958	409,356	844,496	1,536,693
Utah	119,858	3,454	1,941	2,218	1,586	3,739	2,834	12,270	113,830	135,629
Vermont	30,956	527	241	257	3	188	688	679	30,584	32,860
Virginia	477,529	240,534	2,469	13,702	1,373	12,365	30,835	41,561	453,302	778,808
Washington	416,267	31,343	4,859	12,362	2,961	10,635	19,477	45,128	386,886	497,902
West Virginia	124,640	4,726	318	292	195	410	2,843	1,843	123,285	133,424
Wisconsin	247,028	20,765	3,464	1,626	65	1,827	3,490	6,603	243,674	278,264
Wyoming	41,775	766	304	427	4	5,457	1,201	7,282	40,493	49,934
Puerto Rico	36,860	4,119	146	176	1	3,769	6,453	48,308	2,138	51,524
Island Areas & Foreign	42,712	12,372	727	5,801	7,181	1,354	3,062	7,012	39,176	73,209

Table 36. Veterans in the Population: Living Veterans, by State/Territory, Race, Ethnicity, and Gender, 2013 and Projected 2023, 2033, and 2043—*Continued*

(Number.)

State and year	White alone	Black or African American alone	American Indian and Alaska Native alone	Asian alone	Native Hawaiian and Other Pacific Islander alone	Some other race alone	Two or more races	Hispanic or Latino (of any race)	White alone, not Hispanic or Latino	All veterans
2043 Projected total	10,619,071	2,313,370	143,331	342,796	42,601	537,103	541,234	2,055,100	9,349,551	14,539,505
Alabama	222,496	83,111	1,338	13,368	150	2,325	6,762	10,337	218,472	329,550
Alaska	53,633	5,304	2,364	177	684	336	4,838	2,455	53,130	67,336
Arizona	327,901	23,931	8,959	31,015	1,337	11,497	8,709	62,810	282,748	413,349
Arkansas	149,575	30,130	1,346	2,045	10	4,255	5,091	10,502	145,280	192,452
California	559,247	94,457	7,647	105,696	5,388	174,305	41,252	289,662	475,265	987,992
Colorado	243,751	11,720	2,246	3,085	854	5,373	24,951	57,736	212,228	291,981
Connecticut	75,883	9,020	457	616	9	1,778	2,516	13,199	67,288	90,279
District of Columbia	31,997	20,593	219	740	7	1,104	818	3,164	29,880	55,477
Delaware	11,647	6,582	74	487	9	1,177	872	3,042	10,191	20,849
Florida	751,488	186,800	19,885	14,247	1,613	10,907	19,665	213,223	560,756	1,004,606
Georgia	372,652	238,119	2,041	5,993	431	11,291	11,541	47,619	339,102	642,068
Hawaii	53,083	14,737	720	15,653	5,238	5,310	15,116	15,717	50,234	109,857
Idaho	97,460	4,626	2,002	963	215	3,638	3,562	7,737	94,506	112,467
Illinois	304,725	48,693	1,581	4,468	104	15,197	22,723	40,692	285,662	397,491
Indiana	267,662	19,024	1,946	1,216	153	3,720	5,269	9,850	262,726	298,989
Iowa	131,016	5,112	438	927	31	3,115	3,484	8,473	126,803	144,123
Kansas	136,697	10,656	1,858	892	184	1,216	7,083	9,491	130,168	158,585
Kentucky	207,363	24,675	856	2,359	430	5,164	5,497	20,521	195,243	246,345
Louisiana	174,261	48,211	943	477	301	1,986	3,496	8,258	167,690	229,675
Maine	57,987	5,200	9,597	214	5	159	1,088	1,757	56,291	74,249
Maryland	172,387	81,340	1,206	6,106	138	4,146	21,170	17,794	162,203	286,493
Massachusetts	132,229	9,913	513	2,698	129	6,527	5,483	16,618	124,763	157,491
Michigan	239,303	29,634	2,173	677	60	1,500	3,882	7,323	233,472	277,229
Minnesota	175,018	7,125	2,040	5,009	35	866	3,551	5,026	171,524	193,643
Mississippi	115,338	52,804	1,377	930	60	2,459	2,281	5,140	111,870	175,250
Missouri	269,876	28,898	2,538	3,265	319	8,415	7,502	25,605	256,161	320,814
Montana	65,101	2,573	2,845	779	7	2,380	2,026	6,387	61,864	75,710
Nebraska	88,119	3,980	878	515	12	391	1,561	2,720	86,064	95,457
Nevada	116,364	14,244	1,500	6,274	864	5,726	7,557	26,738	98,351	152,530
New Hampshire	45,613	11,984	430	314	3	128	1,823	1,083	45,178	60,295
New Jersey	97,702	18,493	592	3,804	1	5,449	39,900	41,035	74,087	165,942
New Mexico	68,500	5,273	8,255	1,383	4,686	37,750	2,935	58,115	48,340	128,782
New York	242,099	41,610	1,079	7,070	318	77,277	8,918	125,062	198,458	378,370
North Carolina	385,054	231,452	5,591	5,802	655	5,202	9,500	33,619	369,752	643,256
North Dakota	38,567	2,526	1,756	446	299	1,054	6,177	3,386	37,274	50,826
Ohio	387,163	40,198	1,037	1,364	319	2,449	15,243	9,292	383,573	447,773
Oklahoma	187,397	53,252	11,327	1,816	292	3,425	14,112	9,591	181,354	271,621
Oregon	142,511	4,234	2,779	2,468	313	1,166	33,260	36,957	135,595	186,731
Pennsylvania	380,620	34,922	751	32,783	30	3,294	22,015	23,664	372,958	474,415
Rhode Island	21,050	9,889	152	218	3	1,116	688	2,853	19,750	33,115
South Carolina	245,944	92,058	1,068	1,510	0	6,273	6,025	69,043	184,333	352,878
South Dakota	53,697	2,245	3,252	423	14	1,808	3,594	3,586	52,531	65,033
Tennessee	293,702	59,747	1,495	3,050	523	7,667	8,461	17,125	286,638	374,645
Texas	1,141,866	216,453	10,831	15,797	2,358	35,600	25,932	501,669	698,066	1,448,836
Utah	110,776	4,326	1,756	2,397	1,806	5,813	3,459	14,462	105,099	130,331
Vermont	23,844	808	204	340	4	501	744	1,140	23,452	26,446
Virginia	383,374	294,584	1,840	11,410	1,280	12,431	54,146	38,739	361,570	759,066
Washington	369,490	27,945	3,634	10,498	2,346	13,405	18,824	50,485	338,704	446,143
West Virginia	110,009	3,800	407	330	192	622	2,733	2,448	108,661	118,093
Wisconsin	193,340	21,874	2,566	1,465	42	1,656	2,901	5,582	190,862	223,844
Wyoming	34,956	807	291	331	6	12,151	1,157	13,838	33,903	49,698
Puerto Rico	29,491	3,032	48	312	1	3,283	5,618	35,985	4,071	41,784
Island Areas & Foreign	28,047	10,647	602	6,575	8,333	1,317	3,723	6,746	25,409	59,245

Note: Numbers from this table should be reported to the nearest 1,000. Numbers and projections are for September 30th of the applicable year.

Table 37. Veterans in the Population: Living Veterans, by Veteran Integrated Service Network, by Age Group, 2013–Projected 2043

(Number.)

Age group and VISN	VISN description	2013	2014	2015	2016	2017	2018	2019	2020	2021	2022	2023	2024	2025	2026	2027
TOTAL	**Total**	22,299,350	21,999,108	21,680,534	21,368,156	21,065,561	20,761,269	20,461,616	20,170,355	19,874,602	19,583,789	19,295,709	19,011,203	18,731,298	18,457,094	18,194,043
1	VA New England Healthcare System	981,160	954,654	928,073	902,395	877,628	853,411	829,957	807,347	785,222	763,782	742,931	722,711	703,114	684,145	665,969
2	VA Healthcare Network Upstate New York	467,256	456,614	445,821	435,268	425,023	414,914	405,054	395,500	386,242	377,230	368,420	359,784	351,337	343,099	335,148
3	VA NY/NJ Veterans Healthcare Network	759,466	728,386	697,858	668,753	640,956	614,205	588,663	564,338	541,482	519,634	498,709	478,716	459,656	441,523	424,408
4	VA Healthcare - VISN 4	1,246,623	1,219,472	1,191,987	1,165,029	1,138,776	1,112,845	1,087,513	1,062,882	1,038,957	1,015,594	992,704	970,345	948,516	927,242	906,677
5	VA Capitol Health Care Network	728,307	721,049	712,522	704,533	697,003	689,311	681,798	674,693	667,413	660,342	653,349	646,475	639,746	633,219	627,245
6	VA Mid-Atlantic Health Care Network	1,358,211	1,362,529	1,363,876	1,364,634	1,365,334	1,364,795	1,363,734	1,362,603	1,359,165	1,355,431	1,351,186	1,346,524	1,341,565	1,336,417	1,331,627
7	VA Southeast Network	1,457,909	1,458,074	1,456,079	1,453,455	1,450,686	1,446,894	1,442,490	1,437,831	1,431,793	1,425,349	1,418,350	1,410,877	1,403,013	1,394,890	1,386,960
8	VA Sunshine Healthcare Network	1,621,606	1,593,926	1,565,530	1,537,286	1,509,653	1,482,099	1,455,054	1,428,617	1,403,776	1,379,225	1,354,874	1,330,825	1,307,161	1,283,955	1,261,498
9	VA Mid South Healthcare Network	976,619	971,396	965,101	958,523	951,888	944,730	937,314	929,818	921,500	913,009	904,265	895,347	886,301	877,176	868,220
10	VA Healthcare System of Ohio	832,744	816,285	799,588	783,179	767,192	751,348	735,794	720,610	705,292	690,263	675,466	660,888	646,551	632,489	618,814
11	Veterans In Partnership	1,179,313	1,154,108	1,128,722	1,103,787	1,079,523	1,055,498	1,031,976	1,009,085	986,201	963,825	941,836	920,257	899,101	878,391	858,288
12	VA Great Lakes Health Care System	912,716	891,874	870,934	850,524	830,752	811,324	792,436	774,132	755,696	737,758	720,248	703,176	686,536	670,354	654,735
15	VA Heartland Network	853,682	843,433	832,444	821,626	811,113	800,475	789,933	779,653	768,643	757,787	747,008	736,334	725,814	715,478	705,524
16	South Central VA Health Care Network	1,760,091	1,749,686	1,736,870	1,724,219	1,711,764	1,698,575	1,685,130	1,671,801	1,656,758	1,641,608	1,626,202	1,610,598	1,594,934	1,579,343	1,564,328
17	VA Heart of Texas Health Care Network	1,079,927	1,082,345	1,083,236	1,084,077	1,085,095	1,085,522	1,085,762	1,086,070	1,084,672	1,083,143	1,081,357	1,079,359	1,077,232	1,075,065	1,073,236
18	VA Southwest Health Care Network	873,321	867,833	861,448	854,828	848,335	841,500	834,588	827,782	821,101	814,336	807,432	800,408	793,358	786,329	779,533
19	Rocky Mountain Network	737,576	733,139	727,905	722,680	717,660	712,383	707,058	701,851	695,155	688,464	681,705	674,899	668,111	661,386	654,955
20	Northwest Network	1,132,458	1,123,190	1,112,692	1,102,204	1,092,007	1,081,411	1,070,726	1,060,197	1,048,936	1,037,599	1,026,030	1,014,271	1,002,420	990,566	979,037
21	Sierra Pacific Network	1,098,733	1,073,498	1,047,739	1,023,093	999,421	976,156	953,591	931,844	909,771	888,309	867,355	846,962	827,159	807,980	789,705
22	Desert Pacific Healthcare Network	1,257,215	1,228,659	1,199,124	1,170,725	1,143,600	1,116,875	1,090,924	1,066,055	1,043,982	1,022,730	1,002,142	982,238	963,076	944,715	927,517
23	VA Midwest Health Care Network	984,415	968,957	952,985	937,339	922,154	906,999	892,119	877,645	862,844	848,372	834,140	820,209	806,596	793,331	780,617
UNDER 20 YEARS	**Total**	10,384	5,898	5,820	5,793	5,743	5,708	5,955	5,938	6,070	6,063	6,021	5,973	5,926	5,888	5,852
1	VA New England Healthcare System	396	222	219	218	216	215	224	223	228	228	227	225	223	222	220
2	VA Healthcare Network Upstate New York	182	103	101	100	99	99	104	104	106	106	106	107	105	104	105
3	VA NY/NJ Veterans Healthcare Network	372	226	224	223	222	220	229	228	232	232	230	227	226	225	222
4	VA Healthcare - VISN 4	519	278	274	271	268	268	280	280	287	286	285	285	281	279	279
5	VA Capitol Health Care Network	318	198	195	194	192	192	200	199	204	204	202	201	199	198	197
6	VA Mid-Atlantic Health Care Network	847	529	524	525	520	515	536	533	544	544	537	530	528	525	519
7	VA Southeast Network	737	396	389	385	382	381	399	398	408	407	406	405	400	398	397
8	VA Sunshine Healthcare Network	476	277	273	271	269	268	280	279	285	285	283	282	279	277	276
9	VA Mid South Healthcare Network	386	191	188	186	184	184	193	192	197	197	197	197	194	193	193
10	VA Healthcare System of Ohio	409	240	238	239	237	234	243	242	246	247	243	240	239	238	235
11	Veterans In Partnership	477	256	252	252	250	248	258	257	263	263	261	258	257	255	253
12	VA Great Lakes Health Care System	514	298	293	292	289	288	300	300	306	306	304	301	299	297	295
15	VA Heartland Network	359	186	183	182	180	179	187	187	191	191	190	189	187	186	185
16	South Central VA Health Care Network	1,054	574	566	565	560	556	579	577	590	590	585	579	575	572	567
17	VA Heart of Texas Health Care Network	521	297	294	295	293	289	300	299	305	305	301	297	296	294	290
18	VA Southwest Health Care Network	355	215	211	207	205	206	217	217	222	221	222	222	219	218	218
19	Rocky Mountain Network	319	164	162	161	160	159	165	165	169	168	167	166	165	164	163
20	Northwest Network	520	321	316	315	312	310	324	323	330	330	328	325	322	320	319
21	Sierra Pacific Network	476	310	308	304	302	301	314	314	321	320	319	318	314	312	311
22	Desert Pacific Healthcare Network	696	441	437	437	434	430	447	444	454	454	448	441	440	438	432
23	VA Midwest Health Care Network	449	175	172	169	168	168	176	176	180	180	180	180	177	176	176
20 TO 24 YEARS	**Total**	310,194	283,586	253,907	231,391	214,429	201,136	196,171	196,988	196,527	196,344	195,911	195,121	194,039	192,848	191,753
1	VA New England Healthcare System	11,672	10,382	8,983	7,972	7,239	6,711	6,524	6,548	6,534	6,532	6,517	6,488	6,447	6,402	6,361
2	VA Healthcare Network Upstate New York	5,980	5,302	4,677	4,275	3,981	3,713	3,627	3,641	3,630	3,627	3,618	3,602	3,582	3,559	3,538
3	VA NY/NJ Veterans Healthcare Network	8,270	7,509	6,629	5,992	5,557	5,286	5,130	5,151	5,138	5,132	5,122	5,105	5,077	5,048	5,019
4	VA Healthcare - VISN 4	15,440	13,907	12,195	10,700	9,540	8,736	8,467	8,499	8,480	8,477	8,462	8,429	8,384	8,331	8,283
5	VA Capitol Health Care Network	7,922	7,746	7,311	6,900	6,668	6,428	6,284	6,310	6,301	6,299	6,290	6,270	6,239	6,204	6,170
6	VA Mid-Atlantic Health Care Network	22,383	21,161	20,033	19,395	18,888	18,246	17,949	18,033	17,950	17,905	17,848	17,768	17,666	17,561	17,468
7	VA Southeast Network	23,824	21,222	18,337	16,162	14,546	13,332	12,931	12,986	12,973	12,971	12,957	12,924	12,869	12,805	12,743
8	VA Sunshine Healthcare Network	15,017	13,747	12,350	11,459	10,904	10,453	10,230	10,273	10,259	10,255	10,236	10,197	10,143	10,082	10,027
9	VA Mid South Healthcare Network	14,789	12,727	10,631	9,181	8,065	7,258	7,036	7,064	7,052	7,050	7,036	7,007	6,970	6,926	6,887
10	VA Healthcare System of Ohio	10,553	9,417	8,187	7,361	6,782	6,383	6,194	6,216	6,202	6,197	6,182	6,154	6,115	6,073	6,033
11	Veterans In Partnership	15,847	13,943	11,932	10,313	9,237	8,501	8,258	8,286	8,265	8,260	8,239	8,197	8,144	8,084	8,031
12	VA Great Lakes Health Care System	12,232	11,212	10,014	9,082	8,264	7,691	7,455	7,486	7,468	7,462	7,449	7,427	7,390	7,350	7,310
15	VA Heartland Network	12,779	11,262	9,760	8,607	7,697	7,103	6,904	6,932	6,920	6,916	6,902	6,876	6,839	6,798	6,761
16	South Central VA Health Care Network	30,571	27,694	24,215	21,402	19,211	17,667	17,136	17,202	17,163	17,150	17,112	17,040	16,940	16,830	16,728
17	VA Heart of Texas Health Care Network	16,076	14,864	13,470	12,444	11,698	11,052	10,798	10,848	10,832	10,819	10,794	10,753	10,694	10,633	10,575
18	VA Southwest Health Care Network	11,333	10,510	9,669	9,074	8,724	8,367	8,199	8,233	8,216	8,213	8,199	8,169	8,129	8,081	8,037
19	Rocky Mountain Network	11,183	10,233	9,128	8,221	7,497	6,891	6,707	6,732	6,709	6,700	6,680	6,647	6,605	6,559	6,518
20	Northwest Network	14,226	13,634	12,878	12,276	11,875	11,427	11,207	11,253	11,223	11,211	11,181	11,128	11,060	10,984	10,917
21	Sierra Pacific Network	12,231	11,417	10,579	10,019	9,658	9,319	9,145	9,190	9,174	9,169	9,155	9,131	9,089	9,044	9,000
22	Desert Pacific Healthcare Network	19,610	19,546	19,223	18,992	18,845	18,410	18,142	18,221	18,170	18,144	18,089	17,996	17,881	17,758	17,651
23	VA Midwest Health Care Network	18,256	16,147	13,708	11,561	9,552	8,162	7,851	7,885	7,867	7,858	7,842	7,814	7,777	7,735	7,696

Table 37. Veterans in the Population: Living Veterans, by Veteran Integrated Service Network, by Age Group, 2013–Projected 2043—*Continued*

(Number.)

Age group and VISN	VISN description	2028	2029	2030	2031	2032	2033	2034	2035	2036	2037	2038	2039	2040	2041	2042	2043
TOTAL	**Total**	17,933,835	17,676,075	17,421,211	17,169,150	16,919,502	16,671,719	16,427,119	16,186,677	15,951,470	15,719,014	15,493,002	15,276,966	15,072,875	14,882,168	14,704,879	14,539,505
1	VA New England Healthcare System	648,288	631,054	614,308	598,005	582,120	566,631	551,588	537,033	522,995	509,370	496,286	483,904	472,266	461,409	451,308	441,876
2	VA Healthcare Network Upstate New York	327,380	319,768	312,321	305,023	297,873	290,844	283,962	277,248	270,723	264,333	258,164	252,284	246,724	241,511	236,634	232,052
3	VA NY/NJ Veterans Healthcare Network	408,073	392,482	377,619	363,458	349,945	337,049	324,772	313,118	302,082	291,588	281,715	272,535	264,062	256,296	249,191	242,668
4	VA Healthcare - VISN 4	886,500	866,694	847,280	828,215	809,487	791,051	773,003	755,407	738,327	721,595	705,426	689,987	675,406	661,764	649,067	637,216
5	VA Capitol Health Care Network	621,322	615,462	609,614	603,822	598,055	592,321	586,651	581,047	575,557	570,118	564,800	559,720	554,899	550,369	546,117	542,106
6	VA Mid-Atlantic Health Care Network	1,326,420	1,320,782	1,314,771	1,308,410	1,301,728	1,294,663	1,287,302	1,279,724	1,271,992	1,263,901	1,255,720	1,247,743	1,240,111	1,232,920	1,226,197	1,219,877
7	VA Southeast Network	1,378,568	1,369,721	1,360,437	1,350,762	1,340,656	1,330,117	1,319,244	1,308,138	1,296,905	1,285,387	1,273,819	1,262,484	1,251,526	1,241,087	1,231,194	1,221,746
8	VA Sunshine Healthcare Network	1,239,341	1,217,459	1,195,870	1,174,608	1,153,630	1,132,867	1,112,493	1,092,573	1,073,170	1,054,083	1,035,627	1,018,026	1,001,422	985,965	971,552	958,046
9	VA Mid South Healthcare Network	859,087	849,734	840,238	830,589	820,795	810,804	800,684	790,492	780,264	769,895	759,559	749,463	739,739	730,450	721,648	713,285
10	VA Healthcare System of Ohio	605,332	592,031	578,916	565,953	553,129	540,434	527,896	515,564	503,496	491,599	479,996	468,844	458,236	448,238	438,851	430,022
11	Veterans In Partnership	838,480	818,904	799,606	780,560	761,742	743,126	724,775	706,712	689,017	671,609	654,679	638,419	622,988	608,446	594,813	582,021
12	VA Great Lakes Health Care System	639,460	624,498	609,851	595,539	581,528	567,787	554,362	541,299	528,625	516,243	504,301	492,927	482,200	472,195	462,916	454,287
15	VA Heartland Network	695,651	685,837	676,094	666,405	656,751	647,108	637,527	628,052	618,730	609,482	600,444	591,791	583,597	575,916	568,751	562,050
16	South Central VA Health Care Network	1,549,222	1,533,990	1,518,718	1,503,380	1,487,946	1,472,372	1,456,732	1,441,158	1,425,741	1,410,292	1,395,140	1,380,535	1,366,641	1,353,584	1,341,420	1,330,043
17	VA Heart of Texas Health Care Network	1,071,211	1,069,005	1,066,607	1,063,997	1,061,186	1,058,132	1,054,891	1,051,529	1,048,098	1,044,477	1,040,848	1,037,405	1,034,263	1,031,454	1,028,995	1,026,793
18	VA Southwest Health Care Network	772,644	765,709	758,711	751,694	744,645	737,551	730,442	723,381	716,407	709,453	702,689	696,291	690,346	684,947	680,077	675,678
19	Rocky Mountain Network	648,524	642,105	635,720	629,360	623,000	616,643	610,331	604,082	597,959	591,868	585,934	580,303	575,041	570,177	565,706	561,582
20	Northwest Network	967,375	955,559	943,671	931,706	919,676	907,579	895,528	883,563	871,789	860,062	848,588	837,534	827,043	817,222	808,087	799,582
21	Sierra Pacific Network	771,893	754,528	737,606	721,163	705,179	689,635	674,581	660,055	646,074	632,504	619,514	607,244	595,755	585,099	575,292	566,250
22	Desert Pacific Healthcare Network	910,933	894,928	879,533	864,726	850,455	836,708	823,579	811,064	799,178	787,783	777,056	767,058	757,831	749,400	741,744	734,786
23	VA Midwest Health Care Network	768,130	755,825	743,718	731,774	719,975	708,299	696,773	685,437	674,341	663,369	652,695	642,467	632,777	623,719	615,320	607,538
UNDER 20 YEARS	**Total**	5,818	5,784	5,752	5,722	5,692	5,664	5,636	5,608	5,581	5,566	5,553	5,540	5,527	5,515	5,503	5,491
1	VA New England Healthcare System	219	218	216	215	214	213	212	211	210	209	209	208	208	208	207	207
2	VA Healthcare Network Upstate New York	105	103	102	101	101	99	98	97	98	98	98	99	98	98	98	97
3	VA NY/NJ Veterans Healthcare Network	220	220	220	218	217	217	217	216	214	213	212	211	211	210	210	209
4	VA Healthcare - VISN 4	279	275	273	272	270	268	265	263	263	264	264	264	263	262	262	261
5	VA Capitol Health Care Network	195	194	193	192	191	190	189	188	187	187	187	186	186	185	185	185
6	VA Mid-Atlantic Health Care Network	514	515	513	510	508	507	508	506	500	497	495	492	492	491	490	489
7	VA Southeast Network	397	391	388	387	384	381	377	374	375	375	375	375	374	373	372	371
8	VA Sunshine Healthcare Network	274	272	271	269	268	266	264	263	262	262	261	261	260	260	259	259
9	VA Mid South Healthcare Network	193	189	188	187	186	184	182	181	181	182	181	182	181	181	180	180
10	VA Healthcare System of Ohio	232	233	232	231	230	230	231	230	227	225	224	223	223	222	222	221
11	Veterans In Partnership	252	250	249	248	246	245	245	244	242	241	240	240	239	239	238	238
12	VA Great Lakes Health Care System	293	292	290	289	287	286	284	283	282	281	280	280	279	278	278	277
15	VA Heartland Network	184	183	181	181	179	178	177	176	176	175	175	175	174	174	174	173
16	South Central VA Health Care Network	563	561	559	555	553	550	549	546	543	540	539	537	536	535	534	533
17	VA Heart of Texas Health Care Network	287	288	288	286	285	284	286	285	281	278	277	276	275	275	274	274
18	VA Southwest Health Care Network	219	214	212	212	210	208	204	202	204	205	205	206	205	204	204	204
19	Rocky Mountain Network	162	161	160	159	158	157	157	156	155	155	154	154	154	153	153	153
20	Northwest Network	317	315	313	311	310	308	306	305	304	303	302	301	301	300	299	299
21	Sierra Pacific Network	310	307	305	304	302	300	297	295	295	295	295	294	294	293	292	292
22	Desert Pacific Healthcare Network	426	429	428	425	424	423	424	422	418	414	413	410	410	409	408	407
23	VA Midwest Health Care Network	177	173	172	171	170	168	166	165	166	166	166	166	166	165	165	165
20 TO 24 YEARS	**Total**	190,716	189,766	188,935	188,225	187,661	187,224	186,921	186,740	186,681	186,675	186,769	186,984	187,329	187,785	188,341	188,986
1	VA New England Healthcare System	6,325	6,289	6,263	6,241	6,223	6,212	6,208	6,206	6,207	6,208	6,210	6,217	6,230	6,247	6,267	6,290
2	VA Healthcare Network Upstate New York	3,521	3,504	3,489	3,476	3,466	3,458	3,453	3,450	3,448	3,448	3,450	3,455	3,465	3,476	3,489	3,502
3	VA NY/NJ Veterans Healthcare Network	4,989	4,962	4,940	4,920	4,904	4,892	4,883	4,878	4,875	4,874	4,875	4,879	4,883	4,890	4,900	4,914
4	VA Healthcare - VISN 4	8,240	8,198	8,162	8,132	8,107	8,088	8,075	8,066	8,062	8,060	8,063	8,072	8,090	8,113	8,139	8,167
5	VA Capitol Health Care Network	6,137	6,108	6,080	6,056	6,037	6,020	6,007	5,998	5,993	5,991	5,993	5,999	6,008	6,022	6,038	6,057
6	VA Mid-Atlantic Health Care Network	17,375	17,294	17,218	17,155	17,106	17,065	17,034	17,019	17,015	17,017	17,027	17,049	17,077	17,117	17,168	17,228
7	VA Southeast Network	12,679	12,628	12,567	12,516	12,476	12,435	12,395	12,370	12,354	12,348	12,352	12,366	12,386	12,415	12,448	12,486
8	VA Sunshine Healthcare Network	9,973	9,925	9,881	9,844	9,814	9,790	9,772	9,761	9,757	9,756	9,761	9,773	9,792	9,817	9,846	9,880
9	VA Mid South Healthcare Network	6,851	6,819	6,789	6,763	6,743	6,727	6,715	6,707	6,705	6,704	6,708	6,717	6,732	6,751	6,773	6,798
10	VA Healthcare System of Ohio	5,996	5,960	5,935	5,913	5,895	5,885	5,882	5,881	5,884	5,885	5,886	5,890	5,898	5,908	5,924	5,943
11	Veterans In Partnership	7,986	7,939	7,908	7,880	7,858	7,846	7,844	7,843	7,846	7,848	7,852	7,860	7,878	7,901	7,928	7,958
12	VA Great Lakes Health Care System	7,270	7,235	7,202	7,173	7,150	7,130	7,113	7,102	7,096	7,093	7,094	7,101	7,111	7,125	7,142	7,163
15	VA Heartland Network	6,725	6,693	6,664	6,638	6,618	6,601	6,589	6,581	6,577	6,577	6,580	6,588	6,600	6,617	6,637	6,659
16	South Central VA Health Care Network	16,633	16,543	16,472	16,411	16,362	16,327	16,310	16,299	16,298	16,299	16,305	16,321	16,350	16,389	16,437	16,493
17	VA Heart of Texas Health Care Network	10,514	10,464	10,416	10,375	10,342	10,315	10,296	10,286	10,283	10,284	10,291	10,302	10,312	10,329	10,353	10,385
18	VA Southwest Health Care Network	7,997	7,961	7,926	7,896	7,872	7,852	7,834	7,822	7,816	7,813	7,817	7,828	7,847	7,871	7,897	7,926
19	Rocky Mountain Network	6,482	6,446	6,420	6,397	6,379	6,368	6,364	6,362	6,363	6,365	6,368	6,376	6,391	6,409	6,431	6,455
20	Northwest Network	10,857	10,798	10,754	10,715	10,684	10,664	10,656	10,651	10,653	10,656	10,664	10,677	10,699	10,727	10,761	10,801
21	Sierra Pacific Network	8,953	8,917	8,874	8,838	8,810	8,782	8,755	8,739	8,729	8,725	8,729	8,739	8,752	8,771	8,793	8,820
22	Desert Pacific Healthcare Network	17,553	17,456	17,387	17,327	17,279	17,250	17,240	17,236	17,242	17,250	17,263	17,285	17,319	17,364	17,419	17,484
23	VA Midwest Health Care Network	7,658	7,626	7,591	7,561	7,538	7,517	7,497	7,484	7,478	7,476	7,480	7,491	7,506	7,526	7,549	7,575

Table 37. Veterans in the Population: Living Veterans, by Veteran Integrated Service Network, by Age Group, 2013–Projected 2043—*Continued*

(Number.)

Age group and VISN	VISN description	2013	2014	2015	2016	2017	2018	2019	2020	2021	2022	2023	2024	2025	2026	2027
25 TO 29 YEARS	**Total**	742,643	753,686	760,952	761,053	750,579	724,816	688,404	653,523	624,594	600,964	582,152	572,426	568,186	564,978	563,255
1	VA New England Healthcare System	26,349	26,744	26,949	26,630	25,890	24,675	23,102	21,563	20,358	19,417	18,717	18,380	18,243	18,136	18,075
2	VA Healthcare Network Upstate New York	13,591	13,978	14,148	14,004	13,702	13,066	12,243	11,548	11,044	10,643	10,285	10,113	10,032	9,970	9,935
3	VA NY/NJ Veterans Healthcare Network	21,177	20,414	19,697	19,173	18,542	17,817	16,890	15,958	15,247	14,711	14,340	14,077	13,974	13,897	13,856
4	VA Healthcare - VISN 4	32,710	33,154	33,464	33,585	33,214	31,992	30,094	28,195	26,481	25,073	24,057	23,597	23,424	23,292	23,219
5	VA Capitol Health Care Network	23,194	23,734	24,419	25,128	25,439	25,136	24,623	24,023	23,373	22,912	22,475	22,141	21,980	21,864	21,813
6	VA Mid-Atlantic Health Care Network	56,139	58,768	60,023	60,309	59,735	58,305	56,008	54,330	52,941	51,730	50,540	49,792	49,376	49,061	48,899
7	VA Southeast Network	51,402	53,408	55,058	55,806	55,379	53,261	49,933	46,628	44,023	41,955	40,348	39,626	39,357	39,165	39,075
8	VA Sunshine Healthcare Network	39,545	39,836	40,249	40,138	39,348	37,772	35,969	34,286	33,048	32,147	31,404	30,929	30,714	30,551	30,466
9	VA Mid South Healthcare Network	32,870	33,694	34,206	33,953	32,898	31,094	28,625	26,258	24,509	23,083	22,025	21,618	21,461	21,342	21,278
10	VA Healthcare System of Ohio	24,356	24,483	24,548	24,217	23,423	22,335	20,972	19,613	18,630	17,875	17,323	17,000	16,876	16,780	16,722
11	Veterans In Partnership	34,297	34,413	34,551	34,396	33,457	31,759	29,565	27,401	25,589	24,295	23,369	22,945	22,770	22,633	22,550
12	VA Great Lakes Health Care System	28,300	27,915	27,688	27,185	26,722	25,695	24,363	23,015	21,905	20,872	20,116	19,720	19,580	19,476	19,419
15	VA Heartland Network	29,516	30,118	30,237	30,145	29,530	28,184	26,362	24,695	23,275	22,087	21,277	20,900	20,749	20,635	20,575
16	South Central VA Health Care Network	67,399	67,796	68,627	68,903	68,232	65,625	61,923	58,007	54,663	51,917	49,923	48,989	48,629	48,355	48,201
17	VA Heart of Texas Health Care Network	46,412	46,179	45,983	45,365	44,205	42,907	41,102	39,368	37,923	36,749	35,727	35,172	34,922	34,736	34,638
18	VA Southwest Health Care Network	29,681	30,428	30,843	30,971	30,598	29,588	28,357	27,322	26,480	25,856	25,271	24,896	24,715	24,580	24,513
19	Rocky Mountain Network	27,469	27,913	28,134	28,202	28,003	27,117	25,793	24,474	23,278	22,267	21,408	21,025	20,851	20,721	20,648
20	Northwest Network	38,859	39,610	40,045	40,239	39,884	38,894	37,542	36,386	35,326	34,473	33,668	33,154	32,898	32,699	32,587
21	Sierra Pacific Network	32,581	32,969	33,052	32,872	32,557	31,596	30,344	29,318	28,484	27,855	27,303	26,921	26,732	26,588	26,522
22	Desert Pacific Healthcare Network	52,166	52,908	53,237	53,649	53,564	52,928	52,000	51,225	50,540	49,913	49,101	48,471	48,114	47,831	47,666
23	VA Midwest Health Care Network	34,629	35,224	35,796	36,186	36,260	35,067	32,595	29,912	27,477	25,135	23,474	22,959	22,790	22,666	22,599
30 TO 34 YEARS	**Total**	1,069,813	1,057,946	1,033,276	1,005,899	989,530	988,783	994,130	998,531	992,115	973,527	942,103	900,885	860,732	829,969	807,608
1	VA New England Healthcare System	35,876	35,248	34,559	33,779	33,527	33,720	33,927	34,034	33,493	32,485	31,084	29,362	27,668	26,424	25,549
2	VA Healthcare Network Upstate New York	18,380	17,973	17,407	16,922	16,669	17,037	17,303	17,419	17,178	16,756	16,053	15,181	14,419	13,900	13,523
3	VA NY/NJ Veterans Healthcare Network	31,567	30,700	29,343	27,786	26,500	25,281	24,452	23,754	23,156	22,424	21,658	20,736	19,795	19,100	18,642
4	VA Healthcare - VISN 4	49,142	47,660	45,858	43,986	42,467	42,037	42,293	42,498	42,412	41,772	40,354	38,298	36,216	34,424	33,055
5	VA Capitol Health Care Network	40,997	39,807	38,451	37,003	36,298	36,194	36,516	37,123	37,537	37,483	36,926	36,223	35,413	34,705	34,342
6	VA Mid-Atlantic Health Care Network	76,385	75,898	75,355	74,822	75,131	76,445	78,383	79,317	78,879	77,426	75,333	72,416	70,125	68,571	67,501
7	VA Southeast Network	73,698	72,557	70,879	69,264	69,172	70,508	72,196	73,663	74,071	73,161	70,708	67,047	63,389	60,603	58,582
8	VA Sunshine Healthcare Network	61,148	59,977	57,973	55,829	54,410	54,020	54,037	54,227	53,727	52,456	50,516	48,416	46,411	45,075	44,253
9	VA Mid South Healthcare Network	45,305	45,140	44,578	43,864	43,737	44,309	44,862	45,218	44,658	43,225	41,157	38,423	35,764	33,876	32,462
10	VA Healthcare System of Ohio	33,849	33,226	32,195	31,150	30,601	30,345	30,345	30,346	29,885	28,913	27,730	26,286	24,822	23,808	23,086
11	Veterans In Partnership	45,713	45,540	44,474	43,233	42,400	42,164	42,115	42,179	41,835	40,662	38,832	36,556	34,288	32,458	31,246
12	VA Great Lakes Health Care System	39,695	39,412	38,413	37,189	35,899	35,182	34,687	34,398	33,717	33,025	31,844	30,382	28,893	27,742	26,741
15	VA Heartland Network	40,489	40,272	39,771	39,033	38,684	38,847	39,264	39,284	38,936	38,008	36,433	34,402	32,507	31,016	29,865
16	South Central VA Health Care Network	101,764	100,326	96,683	93,049	89,937	88,787	88,747	89,431	89,151	87,790	84,634	80,507	76,138	72,612	69,968
17	VA Heart of Texas Health Care Network	70,147	70,297	69,225	67,941	67,254	66,375	65,752	65,368	64,291	62,510	60,809	58,591	56,391	54,749	53,602
18	VA Southwest Health Care Network	44,044	43,612	42,646	41,584	40,889	40,984	41,500	41,732	41,556	40,831	39,584	38,155	36,907	35,999	35,428
19	Rocky Mountain Network	39,944	39,876	39,287	38,649	37,964	38,220	38,439	38,544	38,331	37,792	36,660	35,102	33,538	32,217	31,215
20	Northwest Network	55,762	55,811	55,153	54,152	53,864	54,275	54,661	54,879	54,606	53,690	52,258	50,517	48,956	47,769	46,962
21	Sierra Pacific Network	49,439	48,624	47,249	45,740	44,452	44,077	44,083	43,968	43,416	42,673	41,437	39,998	38,768	37,896	37,390
22	Desert Pacific Healthcare Network	71,632	70,566	68,465	66,212	65,289	65,239	65,426	65,533	65,555	64,952	64,034	62,932	61,909	61,154	60,681
23	VA Midwest Health Care Network	44,837	45,425	45,311	44,710	44,385	44,736	45,143	45,616	45,728	45,492	44,060	41,355	38,418	35,873	33,517
35 TO 39 YEARS	**Total**	1,077,475	1,094,850	1,122,265	1,145,089	1,163,499	1,164,358	1,148,884	1,124,177	1,094,889	1,075,326	1,072,087	1,075,573	1,077,805	1,071,697	1,055,180
1	VA New England Healthcare System	38,620	38,243	38,130	38,290	38,283	37,761	37,044	36,376	35,559	35,222	35,346	35,499	35,538	35,015	34,079
2	VA Healthcare Network Upstate New York	19,020	19,176	19,471	19,706	19,769	19,342	18,884	18,317	17,810	17,510	17,831	18,059	18,142	17,902	17,507
3	VA NY/NJ Veterans Healthcare Network	29,293	29,848	30,530	30,679	30,700	30,223	29,368	28,148	26,737	25,548	24,446	23,698	23,062	22,541	21,922
4	VA Healthcare - VISN 4	50,713	51,326	52,256	52,796	53,331	52,766	51,142	49,313	47,392	45,775	45,303	45,532	45,693	45,619	45,046
5	VA Capitol Health Care Network	43,897	45,047	45,928	46,723	46,757	46,128	44,762	43,438	41,889	41,035	40,823	41,044	41,521	41,961	42,051
6	VA Mid-Atlantic Health Care Network	79,256	81,064	82,990	84,511	85,819	86,074	85,110	84,435	83,444	83,184	84,009	85,568	86,120	85,712	84,487
7	VA Southeast Network	79,405	80,243	82,004	83,265	83,600	83,083	81,608	79,868	78,096	77,849	79,148	80,817	82,207	82,673	81,917
8	VA Sunshine Healthcare Network	65,710	65,905	66,915	67,516	67,768	67,316	65,954	63,970	61,696	60,111	59,597	59,521	59,556	59,039	57,860
9	VA Mid South Healthcare Network	47,488	47,892	48,762	49,779	50,859	50,855	50,511	49,897	49,041	48,746	49,201	49,652	49,904	49,358	47,970
10	VA Healthcare System of Ohio	34,845	34,386	34,774	35,169	35,651	35,262	34,569	33,570	32,542	31,969	31,698	31,691	31,683	31,252	30,352
11	Veterans In Partnership	47,222	45,999	46,301	46,678	47,367	47,425	47,168	46,138	44,893	43,970	43,711	43,644	43,674	43,372	42,312
12	VA Great Lakes Health Care System	38,326	38,612	39,423	40,313	41,178	41,585	41,240	40,262	39,002	37,644	36,912	36,404	36,088	35,443	34,817
15	VA Heartland Network	40,624	41,187	42,156	43,143	44,147	44,340	43,951	43,427	42,579	42,089	42,115	42,446	42,360	42,033	41,196
16	South Central VA Health Care Network	99,767	102,392	105,919	108,271	110,724	111,065	109,279	105,619	101,782	98,332	97,013	96,825	97,360	97,112	95,933
17	VA Heart of Texas Health Care Network	69,100	71,496	74,442	77,027	79,237	80,527	80,437	79,301	77,887	77,012	75,873	75,071	74,501	73,359	71,590
18	VA Southwest Health Care Network	42,484	43,796	45,443	46,857	48,262	48,807	48,228	47,252	46,206	45,431	45,418	45,920	46,064	45,828	45,131
19	Rocky Mountain Network	39,894	41,177	42,810	44,028	45,195	45,503	45,268	44,634	43,844	42,917	43,027	43,126	43,094	42,882	42,409
20	Northwest Network	55,532	56,876	58,547	60,361	61,691	62,377	62,196	61,462	60,253	59,722	59,924	60,155	60,223	59,945	59,138
21	Sierra Pacific Network	48,061	49,288	50,684	51,887	52,730	52,676	51,674	50,308	48,685	47,206	46,601	46,427	46,143	45,587	44,959
22	Desert Pacific Healthcare Network	65,886	67,526	69,811	71,286	71,960	71,697	70,477	68,545	66,402	65,413	65,217	65,295	65,315	65,351	64,905
23	VA Midwest Health Care Network	42,332	43,369	44,970	46,804	48,472	49,545	50,014	49,897	49,150	48,642	48,873	49,179	49,557	49,713	49,599

Table 37. Veterans in the Population: Living Veterans, by Veteran Integrated Service Network, by Age Group, 2013–Projected 2043—*Continued*

(Number.)

Age group and VISN	VISN description	2028	2029	2030	2031	2032	2033	2034	2035	2036	2037	2038	2039	2040	2041	2042	2043
25 TO 29 YEARS	**Total**	561,349	559,166	556,905	554,679	552,623	550,913	549,601	548,658	548,093	547,698	547,465	547,398	547,529	547,894	548,521	549,434
1	VA New England Healthcare System	18,006	17,928	17,846	17,767	17,696	17,638	17,594	17,567	17,553	17,546	17,545	17,550	17,559	17,575	17,599	17,631
2	VA Healthcare Network Upstate New York	9,897	9,855	9,814	9,773	9,735	9,706	9,684	9,668	9,659	9,655	9,652	9,652	9,654	9,661	9,674	9,692
3	VA NY/NJ Veterans Healthcare Network	13,812	13,764	13,709	13,656	13,605	13,560	13,524	13,499	13,482	13,469	13,460	13,458	13,461	13,468	13,482	13,501
4	VA Healthcare - VISN 4	23,139	23,048	22,953	22,859	22,771	22,700	22,646	22,606	22,583	22,568	22,560	22,557	22,562	22,577	22,604	22,644
5	VA Capitol Health Care Network	21,753	21,680	21,601	21,521	21,446	21,383	21,334	21,297	21,274	21,255	21,240	21,229	21,227	21,232	21,247	21,273
6	VA Mid-Atlantic Health Care Network	48,730	48,542	48,355	48,173	48,007	47,869	47,764	47,686	47,639	47,605	47,582	47,572	47,583	47,615	47,668	47,746
7	VA Southeast Network	38,972	38,848	38,716	38,578	38,445	38,332	38,244	38,167	38,113	38,070	38,034	38,006	37,998	38,008	38,039	38,092
8	VA Sunshine Healthcare Network	30,369	30,255	30,137	30,019	29,910	29,819	29,749	29,697	29,664	29,642	29,627	29,620	29,625	29,643	29,675	29,724
9	VA Mid South Healthcare Network	21,204	21,118	21,031	20,945	20,866	20,802	20,755	20,720	20,700	20,687	20,679	20,676	20,681	20,695	20,719	20,755
10	VA Healthcare System of Ohio	16,659	16,588	16,512	16,439	16,371	16,313	16,269	16,241	16,226	16,216	16,214	16,219	16,228	16,245	16,267	16,297
11	Veterans In Partnership	22,458	22,355	22,249	22,147	22,057	21,984	21,930	21,897	21,882	21,876	21,878	21,887	21,901	21,924	21,957	22,001
12	VA Great Lakes Health Care System	19,359	19,292	19,218	19,145	19,074	19,012	18,963	18,925	18,898	18,879	18,865	18,858	18,860	18,871	18,891	18,921
15	VA Heartland Network	20,507	20,429	20,348	20,268	20,194	20,132	20,084	20,048	20,025	20,009	19,997	19,992	19,994	20,005	20,027	20,059
16	South Central VA Health Care Network	48,030	47,835	47,630	47,429	47,245	47,091	46,975	46,897	46,854	46,828	46,818	46,824	46,844	46,882	46,941	47,024
17	VA Heart of Texas Health Care Network	34,527	34,398	34,263	34,131	34,008	33,900	33,815	33,755	33,715	33,683	33,663	33,657	33,665	33,686	33,722	33,771
18	VA Southwest Health Care Network	24,436	24,346	24,253	24,159	24,071	24,001	23,947	23,904	23,878	23,861	23,847	23,837	23,837	23,848	23,872	23,910
19	Rocky Mountain Network	20,569	20,480	20,390	20,303	20,224	20,161	20,114	20,083	20,068	20,058	20,055	20,058	20,065	20,080	20,105	20,140
20	Northwest Network	32,463	32,324	32,181	32,043	31,919	31,817	31,740	31,691	31,665	31,649	31,643	31,649	31,663	31,690	31,731	31,788
21	Sierra Pacific Network	26,447	26,359	26,265	26,171	26,080	26,004	25,944	25,895	25,861	25,833	25,811	25,795	25,792	25,800	25,821	25,857
22	Desert Pacific Healthcare Network	47,483	47,278	47,072	46,875	46,700	46,555	46,444	46,376	46,341	46,322	46,320	46,337	46,366	46,414	46,482	46,573
23	VA Midwest Health Care Network	22,528	22,445	22,362	22,278	22,199	22,133	22,082	22,039	22,011	21,990	21,974	21,964	21,964	21,975	21,998	22,035
30 TO 34 YEARS	**Total**	790,033	781,548	778,342	776,002	773,645	771,216	768,627	766,058	763,622	761,288	759,206	757,383	755,770	754,373	753,188	752,204
1	VA New England Healthcare System	24,902	24,612	24,509	24,430	24,348	24,262	24,171	24,080	23,995	23,915	23,844	23,784	23,735	23,694	23,661	23,636
2	VA Healthcare Network Upstate New York	13,186	13,033	12,968	12,920	12,875	12,829	12,780	12,733	12,689	12,647	12,612	12,582	12,555	12,533	12,515	12,500
3	VA NY/NJ Veterans Healthcare Network	18,330	18,115	18,041	17,987	17,934	17,881	17,826	17,768	17,714	17,660	17,609	17,564	17,525	17,491	17,461	17,436
4	VA Healthcare - VISN 4	32,074	31,653	31,513	31,410	31,310	31,208	31,100	30,991	30,888	30,788	30,701	30,627	30,560	30,505	30,460	30,423
5	VA Capitol Health Care Network	33,995	33,725	33,616	33,540	33,457	33,371	33,277	33,181	33,090	33,000	32,919	32,846	32,777	32,715	32,659	32,609
6	VA Mid-Atlantic Health Care Network	66,467	65,871	65,575	65,359	65,152	64,949	64,738	64,537	64,348	64,167	64,006	63,862	63,728	63,609	63,504	63,413
7	VA Southeast Network	57,019	56,361	56,160	56,024	55,886	55,744	55,588	55,430	55,274	55,117	54,975	54,847	54,721	54,607	54,507	54,417
8	VA Sunshine Healthcare Network	43,578	43,164	42,999	42,880	42,758	42,631	42,493	42,357	42,225	42,099	41,986	41,888	41,797	41,719	41,652	41,595
9	VA Mid South Healthcare Network	31,428	31,067	30,951	30,864	30,771	30,672	30,566	30,463	30,365	30,271	30,189	30,118	30,054	29,998	29,952	29,913
10	VA Healthcare System of Ohio	22,561	22,264	22,162	22,086	22,009	21,931	21,847	21,762	21,682	21,606	21,538	21,480	21,435	21,397	21,367	21,346
11	Veterans In Partnership	30,383	30,008	29,869	29,764	29,657	29,545	29,427	29,311	29,202	29,101	29,013	28,940	28,882	28,835	28,799	28,773
12	VA Great Lakes Health Care System	26,015	25,648	25,533	25,452	25,377	25,302	25,223	25,141	25,062	24,983	24,911	24,847	24,789	24,739	24,697	24,661
15	VA Heartland Network	29,093	28,758	28,642	28,559	28,474	28,386	28,292	28,199	28,110	28,025	27,949	27,882	27,820	27,766	27,720	27,681
16	South Central VA Health Care Network	68,081	67,245	66,967	66,760	66,549	66,329	66,096	65,860	65,638	65,427	65,239	65,078	64,945	64,834	64,742	64,672
17	VA Heart of Texas Health Care Network	52,607	52,105	51,910	51,771	51,620	51,464	51,297	51,131	50,976	50,826	50,687	50,562	50,455	50,359	50,273	50,203
18	VA Southwest Health Care Network	34,893	34,564	34,427	34,332	34,239	34,141	34,033	33,925	33,820	33,719	33,631	33,555	33,482	33,419	33,366	33,318
19	Rocky Mountain Network	30,363	30,016	29,878	29,779	29,681	29,579	29,472	29,367	29,269	29,176	29,095	29,026	28,966	28,916	28,874	28,840
20	Northwest Network	46,210	45,762	45,564	45,416	45,265	45,106	44,939	44,774	44,620	44,477	44,349	44,239	44,148	44,071	44,006	43,956
21	Sierra Pacific Network	36,956	36,659	36,532	36,436	36,339	36,241	36,136	36,031	35,930	35,829	35,737	35,654	35,573	35,500	35,435	35,377
22	Desert Pacific Healthcare Network	60,030	59,534	59,277	59,079	58,881	58,674	58,456	58,243	58,046	57,865	57,704	57,565	57,453	57,359	57,282	57,225
23	VA Midwest Health Care Network	31,861	31,384	31,250	31,156	31,063	30,970	30,871	30,775	30,681	30,591	30,510	30,438	30,368	30,307	30,255	30,209
35 TO 39 YEARS	**Total**	1,026,548	988,902	952,284	924,507	902,117	884,542	876,062	872,879	870,604	868,288	865,850	863,190	860,474	857,787	855,215	852,902
1	VA New England Healthcare System	32,783	31,207	29,667	28,551	27,707	27,078	26,798	26,699	26,624	26,547	26,463	26,372	26,278	26,186	26,100	26,023
2	VA Healthcare Network Upstate New York	16,847	16,032	15,324	14,850	14,479	14,147	13,998	13,936	13,891	13,849	13,804	13,755	13,706	13,658	13,613	13,574
3	VA NY/NJ Veterans Healthcare Network	21,282	20,525	19,754	19,191	18,781	18,503	18,309	18,240	18,188	18,138	18,089	18,038	17,985	17,933	17,882	17,833
4	VA Healthcare - VISN 4	43,707	41,767	39,799	38,109	36,734	35,748	35,323	35,181	35,079	34,979	34,875	34,763	34,648	34,533	34,424	34,328
5	VA Capitol Health Care Network	41,667	41,205	40,623	40,111	39,758	39,422	39,145	39,026	38,940	38,849	38,755	38,660	38,563	38,466	38,368	38,279
6	VA Mid-Atlantic Health Care Network	82,674	80,053	78,062	76,754	75,673	74,652	74,073	73,795	73,602	73,412	73,216	72,996	72,775	72,558	72,351	72,166
7	VA Southeast Network	79,649	76,187	72,735	70,121	68,042	66,424	65,735	65,523	65,382	65,238	65,086	64,919	64,745	64,566	64,387	64,222
8	VA Sunshine Healthcare Network	56,045	54,147	52,362	51,209	50,413	49,750	49,334	49,166	49,047	48,925	48,795	48,652	48,507	48,360	48,219	48,092
9	VA Mid South Healthcare Network	45,981	43,339	40,764	38,949	37,490	36,427	36,057	35,943	35,862	35,771	35,671	35,557	35,441	35,325	35,215	35,118
10	VA Healthcare System of Ohio	29,270	27,941	26,582	25,657	24,949	24,432	24,141	24,039	23,964	23,888	23,809	23,725	23,637	23,552	23,473	23,400
11	Veterans In Partnership	40,609	38,502	36,405	34,722	33,548	32,711	32,346	32,212	32,113	32,011	31,903	31,786	31,666	31,551	31,443	31,350
12	VA Great Lakes Health Care System	33,727	32,373	30,994	29,941	28,951	28,232	27,865	27,750	27,669	27,594	27,520	27,441	27,358	27,274	27,191	27,114
15	VA Heartland Network	39,747	37,854	36,095	34,715	33,561	32,786	32,452	32,338	32,259	32,177	32,089	31,990	31,890	31,789	31,693	31,607
16	South Central VA Health Care Network	92,959	89,113	85,030	81,734	79,076	77,189	76,343	76,063	75,858	75,646	75,421	75,176	74,921	74,672	74,436	74,225
17	VA Heart of Texas Health Care Network	70,027	67,973	65,912	64,414	63,204	62,146	61,608	61,393	61,241	61,077	60,906	60,724	60,541	60,363	60,191	60,029
18	VA Southwest Health Care Network	43,959	42,651	41,552	40,785	40,221	39,692	39,357	39,223	39,133	39,044	38,947	38,839	38,727	38,611	38,498	38,401
19	Rocky Mountain Network	41,370	39,919	38,462	37,199	36,155	35,259	34,900	34,761	34,661	34,562	34,457	34,343	34,228	34,116	34,010	33,917
20	Northwest Network	57,830	56,243	54,843	53,810	52,982	52,219	51,771	51,578	51,438	51,291	51,133	50,958	50,780	50,606	50,445	50,301
21	Sierra Pacific Network	43,899	42,711	41,722	41,054	40,584	40,193	39,909	39,785	39,693	39,600	39,504	39,400	39,292	39,183	39,075	38,977
22	Desert Pacific Healthcare Network	64,242	63,485	62,778	62,286	61,876	61,297	60,845	60,611	60,433	60,252	60,061	59,857	59,653	59,458	59,277	59,114
23	VA Midwest Health Care Network	48,274	45,673	42,819	40,345	37,932	36,235	35,751	35,618	35,527	35,436	35,343	35,238	35,134	35,027	34,923	34,831

Table 37. Veterans in the Population: Living Veterans, by Veteran Integrated Service Network, by Age Group, 2013–Projected 2043—*Continued*

(Number.)

Age group and VISN	VISN description	2013	2014	2015	2016	2017	2018	2019	2020	2021	2022	2023	2024	2025	2026	2027
40 TO 44 YEARS	**Total**	1,377,770	1,313,037	1,233,924	1,187,405	1,166,689	1,167,802	1,180,624	1,208,168	1,231,102	1,249,921	1,252,338	1,238,332	1,214,221	1,186,586	1,169,096
1	VA New England Healthcare System	49,362	47,012	44,013	41,694	40,244	39,681	39,188	39,089	39,259	39,262	38,800	38,142	37,503	36,752	36,483
2	VA Healthcare Network Upstate New York	24,233	22,465	20,866	20,022	19,656	19,634	19,737	20,024	20,258	20,324	19,918	19,483	18,927	18,443	18,162
3	VA NY/NJ Veterans Healthcare Network	32,777	30,683	28,705	27,810	27,380	27,639	28,069	28,685	28,822	28,858	28,457	27,722	26,646	25,391	24,352
4	VA Healthcare - VISN 4	65,656	61,583	57,424	54,865	53,664	53,465	53,927	54,852	55,424	56,001	55,501	53,946	52,158	50,286	48,739
5	VA Capitol Health Care Network	53,657	52,280	50,021	48,816	48,600	49,348	50,212	51,097	51,899	51,945	51,422	50,170	48,898	47,481	46,805
6	VA Mid-Atlantic Health Care Network	101,821	99,424	95,109	92,414	91,246	91,403	92,523	94,384	95,699	96,863	97,103	96,095	95,259	94,389	94,277
7	VA Southeast Network	106,177	101,900	95,757	91,810	89,871	89,588	90,045	91,827	93,121	93,481	93,054	91,719	90,069	88,372	88,319
8	VA Sunshine Healthcare Network	84,500	81,076	76,396	73,633	72,348	72,085	72,031	73,035	73,742	74,062	73,724	72,448	70,539	68,345	66,871
9	VA Mid South Healthcare Network	65,295	62,231	58,022	55,077	53,274	52,781	52,952	53,820	54,827	55,914	55,940	55,636	55,010	54,177	53,951
10	VA Healthcare System of Ohio	50,203	46,312	41,860	38,873	36,615	35,823	35,304	35,680	36,084	36,584	36,254	35,626	34,692	33,726	33,215
11	Veterans In Partnership	70,291	64,565	58,001	53,043	49,804	47,891	46,637	46,964	47,353	48,071	48,170	47,967	46,984	45,832	44,981
12	VA Great Lakes Health Care System	52,216	48,019	43,727	41,023	39,753	39,311	39,504	40,311	41,210	42,107	42,519	42,211	41,250	40,047	38,779
15	VA Heartland Network	53,565	51,053	47,969	45,683	44,523	44,584	44,975	45,964	46,896	47,858	48,073	47,682	47,139	46,348	45,937
16	South Central VA Health Care Network	124,738	119,369	112,714	109,561	108,467	109,354	111,613	115,253	117,622	120,147	120,583	118,909	115,243	111,497	108,147
17	VA Heart of Texas Health Care Network	85,164	82,930	79,229	77,677	77,512	78,615	80,788	83,892	86,586	88,895	90,412	90,438	89,325	87,989	87,273
18	VA Southwest Health Care Network	52,298	50,558	48,294	47,248	46,905	47,486	48,628	50,290	51,754	53,270	53,984	53,503	52,614	51,691	51,019
19	Rocky Mountain Network	49,918	48,064	45,541	44,353	44,371	44,814	45,991	47,693	48,944	50,160	50,475	50,231	49,545	48,786	47,890
20	Northwest Network	70,582	67,241	63,481	61,519	61,033	61,367	62,439	64,122	65,948	67,257	68,010	67,880	67,102	65,920	65,450
21	Sierra Pacific Network	56,905	54,071	51,210	50,176	50,060	50,667	51,628	52,978	54,110	54,885	54,875	53,926	52,566	51,034	49,659
22	Desert Pacific Healthcare Network	72,693	69,991	66,839	65,639	65,470	66,157	67,423	69,561	71,055	71,828	71,826	70,875	69,178	67,212	66,357
23	VA Midwest Health Care Network	55,718	52,212	48,744	46,467	45,892	46,111	47,007	48,647	50,487	52,152	53,240	53,724	53,573	52,870	52,429
45 TO 49 YEARS	**Total**	1,625,754	1,587,894	1,580,049	1,555,295	1,511,631	1,451,281	1,384,339	1,307,782	1,262,814	1,242,628	1,244,455	1,257,693	1,284,874	1,308,002	1,327,013
1	VA New England Healthcare System	63,490	58,977	56,371	54,296	51,939	49,519	47,189	44,363	42,172	40,797	40,290	39,836	39,742	39,910	39,910
2	VA Healthcare Network Upstate New York	33,905	31,733	29,986	28,149	26,335	24,453	22,711	21,186	20,385	20,039	20,030	20,142	20,423	20,647	20,708
3	VA NY/NJ Veterans Healthcare Network	42,978	39,614	37,182	34,935	32,887	30,878	28,924	27,152	26,349	25,953	26,190	26,586	27,139	27,256	27,283
4	VA Healthcare - VISN 4	86,283	81,739	78,598	75,040	71,241	67,354	63,261	59,216	56,760	55,613	55,469	55,966	56,907	57,482	58,060
5	VA Capitol Health Care Network	63,492	61,740	61,423	60,758	60,017	58,427	56,858	54,780	53,661	53,475	54,232	55,099	55,951	56,746	56,806
6	VA Mid-Atlantic Health Care Network	114,044	113,228	114,692	115,767	115,488	113,693	110,769	106,472	103,642	102,263	102,267	103,222	104,859	106,146	107,298
7	VA Southeast Network	122,717	121,143	121,967	121,599	119,767	115,950	111,327	105,191	101,232	99,248	98,984	99,459	101,227	102,569	102,946
8	VA Sunshine Healthcare Network	102,608	99,000	97,978	96,241	93,713	90,275	86,678	82,020	79,342	78,104	77,938	77,940	78,983	79,759	80,105
9	VA Mid South Healthcare Network	76,134	74,889	75,433	74,990	73,350	70,607	67,318	63,074	60,046	58,169	57,641	57,782	58,613	59,659	60,778
10	VA Healthcare System of Ohio	63,786	61,382	60,033	57,475	54,354	50,288	46,476	42,206	39,357	37,194	36,457	35,989	36,370	36,769	37,264
11	Veterans In Partnership	87,871	83,875	81,856	78,979	74,609	69,584	64,057	57,832	53,149	50,084	48,303	47,145	47,492	47,885	48,604
12	VA Great Lakes Health Care System	64,539	62,524	61,522	59,328	55,874	51,691	47,620	43,557	41,021	39,837	39,460	39,677	40,478	41,357	42,245
15	VA Heartland Network	62,039	61,086	61,281	60,945	59,560	57,179	54,530	51,507	49,218	48,019	48,063	48,439	49,376	50,310	51,272
16	South Central VA Health Care Network	131,895	134,018	137,982	139,495	137,756	134,017	128,253	121,711	118,574	117,444	118,360	120,658	124,263	126,683	129,274
17	VA Heart of Texas Health Care Network	85,924	88,017	91,615	93,695	94,183	92,994	90,473	86,778	85,226	85,061	86,195	88,452	91,634	94,449	96,833
18	VA Southwest Health Care Network	58,661	58,530	59,546	59,452	58,636	57,068	55,161	52,913	51,954	51,668	52,365	53,587	55,322	56,825	58,406
19	Rocky Mountain Network	55,465	55,298	56,124	55,885	55,101	53,604	51,631	49,175	48,040	48,102	48,603	49,826	51,538	52,830	54,096
20	Northwest Network	84,323	82,797	82,697	80,960	78,401	74,675	71,166	67,518	65,612	65,136	65,498	66,578	68,237	70,060	71,342
21	Sierra Pacific Network	72,472	69,416	67,242	64,435	61,432	58,242	55,404	52,757	51,839	51,752	52,397	53,343	54,628	55,709	56,431
22	Desert Pacific Healthcare Network	82,197	79,794	78,793	77,115	74,796	72,500	69,817	67,027	66,121	66,125	66,941	68,294	70,407	71,811	72,542
23	VA Midwest Health Care Network	70,929	69,095	67,728	65,755	62,191	58,285	54,715	51,346	49,113	48,543	48,773	49,671	51,286	53,138	54,807

Age group and VISN	VISN description	2013	2014	2015	2016	2017	2018	2019	2020	2021	2022	2023	2024	2025	2026	2027
45 TO 49 YEARS	**Total**	1,625,754	1,587,894	1,580,049	1,555,295	1,511,631	1,451,281	1,384,339	1,307,782	1,262,814	1,242,628	1,244,455	1,257,693	1,284,874	1,308,002	1,327,013
1	VA New England Healthcare System	63,490	58,977	56,371	54,296	51,939	49,519	47,189	44,363	42,172	40,797	40,290	39,836	39,742	39,910	39,910
2	VA Healthcare Network Upstate New York	33,905	31,733	29,986	28,149	26,335	24,453	22,711	21,186	20,385	20,039	20,030	20,142	20,423	20,647	20,708
3	VA NY/NJ Veterans Healthcare Network	42,978	39,614	37,182	34,935	32,887	30,878	28,924	27,152	26,349	25,953	26,190	26,586	27,139	27,256	27,283
4	VA Healthcare - VISN 4	86,283	81,739	78,598	75,040	71,241	67,354	63,261	59,216	56,760	55,613	55,469	55,966	56,907	57,482	58,060
5	VA Capitol Health Care Network	63,492	61,740	61,423	60,758	60,017	58,427	56,858	54,780	53,661	53,475	54,232	55,099	55,951	56,746	56,806
6	VA Mid-Atlantic Health Care Network	114,044	113,228	114,692	115,767	115,488	113,693	110,769	106,472	103,642	102,263	102,267	103,222	104,859	106,146	107,298
7	VA Southeast Network	122,717	121,143	121,967	121,599	119,767	115,950	111,327	105,191	101,232	99,248	98,984	99,459	101,227	102,569	102,946
8	VA Sunshine Healthcare Network	102,608	99,000	97,978	96,241	93,713	90,275	86,678	82,020	79,342	78,104	77,938	77,940	78,983	79,759	80,105
9	VA Mid South Healthcare Network	76,134	74,889	75,433	74,990	73,350	70,607	67,318	63,074	60,046	58,169	57,641	57,782	58,613	59,659	60,778
10	VA Healthcare System of Ohio	63,786	61,382	60,033	57,475	54,354	50,288	46,476	42,206	39,357	37,194	36,457	35,989	36,370	36,769	37,264
11	Veterans In Partnership	87,871	83,875	81,856	78,979	74,609	69,584	64,057	57,832	53,149	50,084	48,303	47,145	47,492	47,885	48,604
12	VA Great Lakes Health Care System	64,539	62,524	61,522	59,328	55,874	51,691	47,620	43,557	41,021	39,837	39,460	39,677	40,478	41,357	42,245
15	VA Heartland Network	62,039	61,086	61,281	60,945	59,560	57,179	54,530	51,507	49,218	48,019	48,063	48,439	49,376	50,310	51,272
16	South Central VA Health Care Network	131,895	134,018	137,982	139,495	137,756	134,017	128,253	121,711	118,574	117,444	118,360	120,658	124,263	126,683	129,274
17	VA Heart of Texas Health Care Network	85,924	88,017	91,615	93,695	94,183	92,994	90,473	86,778	85,226	85,061	86,195	88,452	91,634	94,449	96,833
18	VA Southwest Health Care Network	58,661	58,530	59,546	59,452	58,636	57,068	55,161	52,913	51,954	51,668	52,365	53,587	55,322	56,825	58,406
19	Rocky Mountain Network	55,465	55,298	56,124	55,885	55,101	53,604	51,631	49,175	48,040	48,102	48,603	49,826	51,538	52,830	54,096
20	Northwest Network	84,323	82,797	82,697	80,960	78,401	74,675	71,166	67,518	65,612	65,136	65,498	66,578	68,237	70,060	71,342
21	Sierra Pacific Network	72,472	69,416	67,242	64,435	61,432	58,242	55,404	52,757	51,839	51,752	52,397	53,343	54,628	55,709	56,431
22	Desert Pacific Healthcare Network	82,197	79,794	78,793	77,115	74,796	72,500	69,817	67,027	66,121	66,125	66,941	68,294	70,407	71,811	72,542
23	VA Midwest Health Care Network	70,929	69,095	67,728	65,755	62,191	58,285	54,715	51,346	49,113	48,543	48,773	49,671	51,286	53,138	54,807

Table 37. Veterans in the Population: Living Veterans, by Veteran Integrated Service Network, by Age Group, 2013–Projected 2043—*Continued*

(Number.)

Age group and VISN	VISN description	2028	2029	2030	2031	2032	2033	2034	2035	2036	2037	2038	2039	2040	2041	2042	2043
40 TO 44 YEARS	**Total**	1,167,895	1,173,321	1,177,358	1,172,666	1,155,954	1,127,303	1,089,764	1,053,269	1,025,568	1,003,193	985,578	976,959	973,569	971,033	968,476	965,817
1	VA New England Healthcare System	36,663	36,860	36,939	36,463	35,545	34,287	32,767	31,287	30,219	29,409	28,803	28,530	28,429	28,350	28,267	28,180
2	VA Healthcare Network Upstate New York	18,489	18,723	18,820	18,596	18,205	17,562	16,768	16,077	15,617	15,254	14,930	14,785	14,722	14,675	14,631	14,583
3	VA NY/NJ Veterans Healthcare Network	23,403	22,767	22,232	21,802	21,250	20,677	20,001	19,313	18,809	18,446	18,197	18,022	17,957	17,909	17,863	17,818
4	VA Healthcare - VISN 4	48,355	48,651	48,874	48,848	48,267	46,923	44,990	43,030	41,348	39,979	38,995	38,568	38,420	38,309	38,201	38,090
5	VA Capitol Health Care Network	46,766	47,130	47,712	48,235	48,303	47,908	47,462	46,888	46,376	46,030	45,698	45,416	45,296	45,208	45,119	45,025
6	VA Mid-Atlantic Health Care Network	95,243	96,994	97,726	97,451	96,160	94,278	91,589	89,553	88,224	87,118	86,083	85,485	85,176	84,942	84,712	84,478
7	VA Southeast Network	89,863	91,756	93,314	93,915	93,114	90,793	87,254	83,736	81,064	78,931	77,260	76,534	76,297	76,131	75,964	75,791
8	VA Sunshine Healthcare Network	66,481	66,511	66,618	66,161	64,951	63,127	61,254	59,503	58,366	57,594	56,930	56,497	56,309	56,171	56,032	55,888
9	VA Mid South Healthcare Network	54,489	55,013	55,343	54,857	53,432	51,400	48,700	46,061	44,201	42,699	41,606	41,219	41,090	40,990	40,880	40,762
10	VA Healthcare System of Ohio	32,996	33,038	33,085	32,705	31,832	30,791	29,500	28,176	27,275	26,582	26,074	25,788	25,683	25,604	25,525	25,443
11	Veterans In Partnership	44,821	44,837	44,944	44,708	43,689	42,035	39,995	37,964	36,332	35,196	34,385	34,027	33,892	33,788	33,682	33,569
12	VA Great Lakes Health Care System	38,144	37,718	37,471	36,883	36,273	35,210	33,891	32,542	31,513	30,544	29,839	29,476	29,362	29,280	29,205	29,130
15	VA Heartland Network	46,026	46,434	46,418	46,148	45,318	43,878	41,991	40,240	38,864	37,706	36,928	36,589	36,467	36,375	36,281	36,181
16	South Central VA Health Care Network	107,034	107,016	107,728	107,615	106,422	103,398	99,532	95,423	92,097	89,410	87,497	86,622	86,313	86,076	85,835	85,583
17	VA Heart of Texas Health Care Network	86,177	85,452	84,964	83,838	81,940	80,312	78,175	76,025	74,464	73,213	72,105	71,530	71,289	71,113	70,927	70,736
18	VA Southwest Health Care Network	51,049	51,643	51,810	51,557	50,793	49,589	48,270	47,176	46,420	45,857	45,323	44,978	44,839	44,743	44,648	44,545
19	Rocky Mountain Network	48,086	48,256	48,304	48,168	47,695	46,651	45,159	43,660	42,345	41,266	40,336	39,961	39,808	39,695	39,582	39,464
20	Northwest Network	65,726	66,036	66,186	65,956	65,130	63,807	62,209	60,803	59,774	58,936	58,169	57,714	57,505	57,344	57,176	56,999
21	Sierra Pacific Network	49,110	48,992	48,784	48,305	47,690	46,664	45,544	44,616	43,992	43,553	43,187	42,908	42,779	42,679	42,580	42,479
22	Desert Pacific Healthcare Network	66,220	66,347	66,463	66,595	66,163	65,544	64,865	64,227	63,786	63,424	62,894	62,466	62,236	62,056	61,874	61,685
23	VA Midwest Health Care Network	52,754	53,146	53,623	53,860	53,782	52,467	49,847	46,971	44,483	42,046	40,337	39,845	39,701	39,597	39,493	39,387
45 TO 49 YEARS	**Total**	1,329,837	1,316,429	1,293,127	1,266,158	1,248,626	1,247,231	1,252,401	1,256,206	1,251,397	1,234,742	1,206,325	1,169,123	1,132,922	1,105,360	1,083,076	1,065,508
1	VA New England Healthcare System	39,472	38,850	38,241	37,523	37,257	37,421	37,598	37,665	37,204	36,327	35,125	33,677	32,268	31,251	30,479	29,900
2	VA Healthcare Network Upstate New York	20,312	19,889	19,351	18,882	18,603	18,910	19,128	19,219	19,001	18,626	18,008	17,243	16,575	16,129	15,776	15,463
3	VA NY/NJ Veterans Healthcare Network	26,914	26,246	25,268	24,128	23,179	22,320	21,740	21,258	20,875	20,383	19,874	19,276	18,669	18,224	17,906	17,688
4	VA Healthcare - VISN 4	57,573	56,047	54,290	52,453	50,919	50,545	50,832	51,050	51,023	50,451	49,122	47,219	45,285	43,625	42,273	41,301
5	VA Capitol Health Care Network	56,334	55,159	53,962	52,613	51,915	51,866	52,178	52,708	53,190	53,244	52,842	52,426	51,888	51,408	51,088	50,788
6	VA Mid-Atlantic Health Care Network	107,538	106,528	105,710	104,836	104,649	105,529	107,233	107,918	107,600	106,266	104,337	101,582	99,484	98,099	96,950	95,887
7	VA Southeast Network	102,506	101,178	99,550	97,841	97,764	99,343	101,246	102,797	103,397	102,576	100,226	96,635	93,078	90,367	88,197	86,487
8	VA Sunshine Healthcare Network	79,789	78,541	76,692	74,508	73,039	72,646	72,689	72,777	72,305	71,077	69,248	67,401	65,675	64,547	63,786	63,122
9	VA Mid South Healthcare Network	60,812	60,516	59,893	59,034	58,790	59,327	59,848	60,177	59,684	58,226	56,157	53,401	50,696	48,783	47,236	46,110
10	VA Healthcare System of Ohio	36,950	36,343	35,447	34,522	34,022	33,811	33,853	33,903	33,539	32,698	31,699	30,452	29,170	28,296	27,622	27,126
11	Veterans In Partnership	48,712	48,531	47,598	46,497	45,661	45,522	45,547	45,662	45,448	44,477	42,881	40,912	38,950	37,368	36,270	35,486
12	VA Great Lakes Health Care System	42,646	42,367	41,452	40,294	39,069	38,474	38,071	37,842	37,279	36,695	35,673	34,401	33,099	32,109	31,172	30,491
15	VA Heartland Network	51,495	51,106	50,579	49,799	49,379	49,452	49,851	49,825	49,553	48,730	47,302	45,425	43,681	42,306	41,148	40,367
16	South Central VA Health Care Network	129,722	128,070	124,405	120,658	117,242	116,136	116,117	116,847	116,734	115,543	112,485	108,582	104,430	101,056	98,331	96,389
17	VA Heart of Texas Health Care Network	98,479	98,550	97,465	96,158	95,441	94,267	93,482	92,944	91,756	89,775	88,116	85,951	83,763	82,178	80,911	79,775
18	VA Southwest Health Care Network	59,186	58,727	57,878	57,019	56,357	56,333	56,932	57,053	56,728	55,905	54,675	53,339	52,247	51,499	50,938	50,404
19	Rocky Mountain Network	54,422	54,202	53,546	52,817	51,893	52,088	52,243	52,284	52,142	51,666	50,626	49,118	47,602	46,252	45,153	44,196
20	Northwest Network	72,088	71,968	71,185	69,984	69,482	69,703	69,971	70,096	69,860	69,047	67,743	66,160	64,763	63,736	62,892	62,123
21	Sierra Pacific Network	56,426	55,531	54,243	52,777	51,439	50,872	50,725	50,507	50,034	49,447	48,469	47,418	46,546	45,961	45,548	45,209
22	Desert Pacific Healthcare Network	72,562	71,678	70,103	68,246	67,401	67,218	67,284	67,362	67,482	67,070	66,497	65,881	65,292	64,880	64,547	64,056
23	VA Midwest Health Care Network	55,899	56,400	56,268	55,570	55,123	55,448	55,835	56,313	56,564	56,513	55,219	52,623	49,762	47,286	44,851	43,142

Age group and VISN	VISN description	2028	2029	2030	2031	2032	2033	2034	2035	2036	2037	2038	2039	2040	2041	2042	2043
45 TO 49 YEARS	**Total**	1,329,837	1,316,429	1,293,127	1,266,158	1,248,626	1,247,231	1,252,401	1,256,206	1,251,397	1,234,742	1,206,325	1,169,123	1,132,922	1,105,360	1,083,076	1,065,508
1	VA New England Healthcare System	39,472	38,850	38,241	37,523	37,257	37,421	37,598	37,665	37,204	36,327	35,125	33,677	32,268	31,251	30,479	29,900
2	VA Healthcare Network Upstate New York	20,312	19,889	19,351	18,882	18,603	18,910	19,128	19,219	19,001	18,626	18,008	17,243	16,575	16,129	15,776	15,463
3	VA NY/NJ Veterans Healthcare Network	26,914	26,246	25,268	24,128	23,179	22,320	21,740	21,258	20,875	20,383	19,874	19,276	18,669	18,224	17,906	17,688
4	VA Healthcare - VISN 4	57,573	56,047	54,290	52,453	50,919	50,545	50,832	51,050	51,023	50,451	49,122	47,219	45,285	43,625	42,273	41,301
5	VA Capitol Health Care Network	56,334	55,159	53,962	52,613	51,915	51,866	52,178	52,708	53,190	53,244	52,842	52,426	51,888	51,408	51,088	50,788
6	VA Mid-Atlantic Health Care Network	107,538	106,528	105,710	104,836	104,649	105,529	107,233	107,918	107,600	106,266	104,337	101,582	99,484	98,099	96,950	95,887
7	VA Southeast Network	102,506	101,178	99,550	97,841	97,764	99,343	101,246	102,797	103,397	102,576	100,226	96,635	93,078	90,367	88,197	86,487
8	VA Sunshine Healthcare Network	79,789	78,541	76,692	74,508	73,039	72,646	72,689	72,777	72,305	71,077	69,248	67,401	65,675	64,547	63,786	63,122
9	VA Mid South Healthcare Network	60,812	60,516	59,893	59,034	58,790	59,327	59,848	60,177	59,684	58,226	56,157	53,401	50,696	48,783	47,236	46,110
10	VA Healthcare System of Ohio	36,950	36,343	35,447	34,522	34,022	33,811	33,853	33,903	33,539	32,698	31,699	30,452	29,170	28,296	27,622	27,126
11	Veterans In Partnership	48,712	48,531	47,598	46,497	45,661	45,522	45,547	45,662	45,448	44,477	42,881	40,912	38,950	37,368	36,270	35,486
12	VA Great Lakes Health Care System	42,646	42,367	41,452	40,294	39,069	38,474	38,071	37,842	37,279	36,695	35,673	34,401	33,099	32,109	31,172	30,491
15	VA Heartland Network	51,495	51,106	50,579	49,799	49,379	49,452	49,851	49,825	49,553	48,730	47,302	45,425	43,681	42,306	41,148	40,367
16	South Central VA Health Care Network	129,722	128,070	124,405	120,658	117,242	116,136	116,117	116,847	116,734	115,543	112,485	108,582	104,430	101,056	98,331	96,389
17	VA Heart of Texas Health Care Network	98,479	98,550	97,465	96,158	95,441	94,267	93,482	92,944	91,756	89,775	88,116	85,951	83,763	82,178	80,911	79,775
18	VA Southwest Health Care Network	59,186	58,727	57,878	57,019	56,357	56,333	56,932	57,053	56,728	55,905	54,675	53,339	52,247	51,499	50,938	50,404
19	Rocky Mountain Network	54,422	54,202	53,546	52,817	51,893	52,088	52,243	52,284	52,142	51,666	50,626	49,118	47,602	46,252	45,153	44,196
20	Northwest Network	72,088	71,968	71,185	69,984	69,482	69,703	69,971	70,096	69,860	69,047	67,743	66,160	64,763	63,736	62,892	62,123
21	Sierra Pacific Network	56,426	55,531	54,243	52,777	51,439	50,872	50,725	50,507	50,034	49,447	48,469	47,418	46,546	45,961	45,548	45,209
22	Desert Pacific Healthcare Network	72,562	71,678	70,103	68,246	67,401	67,218	67,284	67,362	67,482	67,070	66,497	65,881	65,292	64,880	64,547	64,056
23	VA Midwest Health Care Network	55,899	56,400	56,268	55,570	55,123	55,448	55,835	56,313	56,564	56,513	55,219	52,623	49,762	47,286	44,851	43,142

Table 37. Veterans in the Population: Living Veterans, by Veteran Integrated Service Network, by Age Group, 2013–Projected 2043—*Continued*

(Number.)

Age group and VISN	VISN description	2013	2014	2015	2016	2017	2018	2019	2020	2021	2022	2023	2024	2025	2026	2027
50 TO 54 YEARS																
	Total	1,908,350	1,877,874	1,821,286	1,758,347	1,693,931	1,639,211	1,600,375	1,593,638	1,569,752	1,527,220	1,468,580	1,403,443	1,328,513	1,284,918	1,265,354
1	VA New England Healthcare System	84,258	81,653	77,425	72,324	67,067	61,643	57,304	54,857	52,900	50,674	48,379	46,180	43,505	41,427	40,116
2	VA Healthcare Network Upstate New York	41,296	40,692	39,447	37,759	35,431	33,120	31,011	29,343	27,593	25,865	24,074	22,415	20,960	20,194	19,861
3	VA NY/NJ Veterans Healthcare Network	56,025	53,647	50,664	47,029	43,063	39,449	36,364	34,167	32,132	30,278	28,470	26,703	25,105	24,379	24,006
4	VA Healthcare - VISN 4	100,577	99,994	97,683	94,601	90,313	85,815	81,325	78,294	74,865	71,192	67,452	63,505	59,582	57,201	56,085
5	VA Capitol Health Care Network	77,538	76,286	73,748	70,678	67,522	64,845	62,961	62,693	62,039	61,318	59,806	58,309	56,303	55,232	55,051
6	VA Mid-Atlantic Health Care Network	129,505	129,095	126,844	124,301	121,898	119,383	118,198	119,599	120,390	119,798	117,809	114,689	110,163	107,311	105,876
7	VA Southeast Network	145,066	143,615	139,785	135,339	131,220	128,053	126,210	127,043	126,619	124,727	120,870	116,229	110,020	106,080	104,099
8	VA Sunshine Healthcare Network	134,872	130,267	123,773	116,959	110,387	104,978	101,230	100,223	98,535	96,070	92,712	89,225	84,605	81,963	80,752
9	VA Mid South Healthcare Network	88,563	87,851	85,888	83,746	81,395	79,482	78,096	78,598	78,075	76,343	73,521	70,151	65,833	62,770	60,875
10	VA Healthcare System of Ohio	73,190	72,055	69,665	67,291	64,474	62,188	59,850	58,564	56,141	53,180	49,304	45,682	41,611	38,881	36,800
11	Veterans In Partnership	102,385	101,646	98,548	94,185	89,601	85,055	81,207	79,303	76,581	72,450	67,693	62,471	56,585	52,178	49,292
12	VA Great Lakes Health Care System	71,808	70,860	68,943	66,753	64,424	62,471	60,489	59,519	57,436	54,168	50,211	46,370	42,542	40,156	39,040
15	VA Heartland Network	72,280	71,420	69,472	67,292	65,232	63,478	62,434	62,634	62,240	60,807	58,399	55,733	52,698	50,462	49,279
16	South Central VA Health Care Network	143,173	141,547	138,731	136,532	135,885	136,231	138,070	142,051	143,451	141,602	137,824	132,007	125,437	122,364	121,257
17	VA Heart of Texas Health Care Network	91,957	91,548	90,430	89,838	89,604	90,008	91,975	95,638	97,684	98,143	96,935	94,386	90,626	89,068	88,918
18	VA Southwest Health Care Network	69,417	67,997	65,909	64,022	62,241	61,012	60,804	61,828	61,769	60,982	59,445	57,587	55,371	54,463	54,213
19	Rocky Mountain Network	62,095	61,564	60,475	59,358	57,774	56,945	56,689	57,526	57,283	56,472	54,996	53,055	50,627	49,539	49,653
20	Northwest Network	96,723	95,386	92,934	90,357	87,169	85,148	83,508	83,386	81,671	79,139	75,482	72,041	68,464	66,586	66,111
21	Sierra Pacific Network	90,548	86,979	82,967	78,413	74,112	70,542	67,526	65,471	62,812	59,996	56,979	54,324	51,837	50,995	50,918
22	Desert Pacific Healthcare Network	97,723	94,603	90,082	85,546	81,473	77,853	75,485	74,593	73,196	71,201	69,243	66,918	64,484	63,678	63,700
23	VA Midwest Health Care Network	79,351	79,167	77,873	76,024	73,645	71,512	69,639	68,308	66,340	62,816	58,975	55,465	52,153	49,991	49,453
55 TO 59 YEARS																
	Total	2,007,152	1,989,491	1,954,589	1,915,263	1,882,950	1,861,470	1,831,792	1,777,923	1,717,835	1,656,006	1,603,933	1,566,941	1,560,908	1,538,111	1,497,216
1	VA New England Healthcare System	85,614	86,280	85,665	83,899	81,671	79,725	77,245	73,293	68,513	63,578	58,499	54,440	52,153	50,310	48,218
2	VA Healthcare Network Upstate New York	41,223	41,344	41,070	40,356	39,721	39,441	38,853	37,671	36,088	33,890	31,711	29,724	28,151	26,490	24,848
3	VA NY/NJ Veterans Healthcare Network	57,187	57,192	55,994	54,307	52,355	50,196	48,025	45,374	42,148	38,625	35,399	32,640	30,655	28,826	27,164
4	VA Healthcare - VISN 4	102,063	102,277	101,371	99,679	98,300	97,465	96,905	94,719	91,810	87,726	83,447	79,181	76,314	73,008	69,469
5	VA Capitol Health Care Network	74,686	75,303	75,215	74,907	74,213	73,777	72,527	70,163	67,298	64,325	61,834	60,062	59,772	59,118	58,393
6	VA Mid-Atlantic Health Care Network	130,675	131,604	131,081	130,472	129,793	130,107	129,564	127,255	124,607	122,069	119,427	118,048	119,212	119,879	119,182
7	VA Southeast Network	145,688	147,077	147,334	147,155	146,692	146,523	145,006	141,182	136,678	132,479	129,278	127,363	128,146	127,723	125,853
8	VA Sunshine Healthcare Network	142,255	142,941	141,783	139,432	136,438	133,365	128,861	122,471	115,977	109,687	104,477	100,836	99,905	98,238	95,815
9	VA Mid South Healthcare Network	91,927	91,388	90,482	89,707	89,563	89,683	88,911	86,940	84,759	82,331	80,384	78,954	79,376	78,839	77,096
10	VA Healthcare System of Ohio	75,941	75,236	74,182	72,518	71,106	70,146	69,075	66,838	64,584	61,906	59,764	57,562	56,366	54,059	51,245
11	Veterans In Partnership	103,920	102,882	100,912	99,209	97,823	97,566	96,874	93,978	89,880	85,552	81,278	77,637	75,844	73,283	69,401
12	VA Great Lakes Health Care System	75,455	74,595	72,893	70,879	69,335	68,283	67,428	65,676	63,601	61,370	59,511	57,635	56,724	54,749	51,668
15	VA Heartland Network	75,176	74,447	73,495	72,439	71,573	71,314	70,461	68,575	66,428	64,375	62,644	61,586	61,725	61,334	59,930
16	South Central VA Health Care Network	161,256	157,262	152,256	147,920	144,557	142,833	141,175	138,444	136,201	135,456	135,734	137,473	141,307	142,642	140,784
17	VA Heart of Texas Health Care Network	101,466	99,896	97,643	95,118	93,573	93,218	92,805	91,739	91,064	90,746	91,122	93,071	96,726	98,747	99,203
18	VA Southwest Health Care Network	76,548	75,652	73,835	72,068	70,825	69,748	68,312	66,236	64,425	62,689	61,520	61,378	62,449	62,381	61,594
19	Rocky Mountain Network	66,425	65,361	63,915	62,449	61,743	61,515	60,989	59,959	58,770	57,146	56,306	56,022	56,836	56,599	55,789
20	Northwest Network	107,914	104,641	100,831	97,416	95,650	94,740	93,380	91,012	88,511	85,403	83,446	81,837	81,694	80,005	77,522
21	Sierra Pacific Network	102,713	99,781	95,782	91,752	88,162	84,900	81,546	77,858	73,620	69,606	66,290	63,491	61,562	59,073	56,466
22	Desert Pacific Healthcare Network	108,354	104,696	100,498	96,193	92,576	89,257	86,375	82,290	78,401	74,885	71,760	69,729	69,035	67,754	65,928
23	VA Midwest Health Care Network	80,668	79,634	78,350	77,387	77,282	77,667	77,474	76,251	74,471	72,161	70,102	68,272	66,955	65,055	61,650
60 TO 64 YEARS																
	Total	2,303,000	2,085,187	1,980,933	1,956,181	1,928,430	1,924,252	1,908,006	1,875,856	1,839,386	1,809,686	1,790,128	1,762,667	1,711,669	1,654,712	1,596,067
1	VA New England Healthcare System	92,994	81,622	76,811	77,365	78,455	79,947	80,563	80,030	78,409	76,362	74,564	72,260	68,572	64,107	59,504
2	VA Healthcare Network Upstate New York	46,391	41,191	38,826	38,466	38,133	38,778	38,895	38,653	38,011	37,448	37,213	36,681	35,584	34,092	32,023
3	VA NY/NJ Veterans Healthcare Network	67,258	56,358	51,378	50,131	49,363	50,440	50,424	49,367	47,935	46,234	44,357	42,461	40,143	37,250	34,116
4	VA Healthcare - VISN 4	128,335	111,281	101,686	98,784	96,471	97,174	97,381	96,558	95,043	93,827	93,110	92,656	90,633	87,882	83,998
5	VA Capitol Health Care Network	71,641	67,160	66,000	66,688	67,231	68,232	68,780	68,741	68,454	67,811	67,405	66,270	64,100	61,434	58,672
6	VA Mid-Atlantic Health Care Network	134,462	126,549	124,345	125,902	127,971	129,223	130,116	129,608	128,975	128,256	128,511	127,929	125,569	122,927	120,404
7	VA Southeast Network	152,069	142,375	140,077	142,233	143,348	145,053	146,427	146,723	146,519	146,011	145,806	144,277	140,420	135,956	131,797
8	VA Sunshine Healthcare Network	149,325	136,834	133,493	134,728	136,733	138,263	138,987	137,972	136,018	133,371	130,654	126,540	120,530	114,213	108,107
9	VA Mid South Healthcare Network	107,601	99,613	94,569	92,898	91,507	91,139	90,615	89,746	88,989	88,876	88,989	88,226	86,273	84,118	81,698
10	VA Healthcare System of Ohio	90,545	80,380	75,041	73,420	72,057	72,210	71,568	70,621	69,046	67,716	66,809	65,796	63,665	61,553	59,033
11	Veterans In Partnership	130,582	115,078	105,596	101,660	98,597	98,583	97,626	95,820	94,261	92,991	92,774	92,157	89,423	85,569	81,489
12	VA Great Lakes Health Care System	98,145	84,065	76,525	73,811	70,938	70,928	70,165	68,612	66,733	65,316	64,358	63,583	61,947	60,025	57,926
15	VA Heartland Network	92,046	83,414	78,167	75,774	73,051	72,532	71,853	70,986	69,972	69,148	68,895	68,076	66,242	64,195	62,234
16	South Central VA Health Care Network	187,289	172,527	165,598	163,516	160,119	157,141	153,309	148,541	144,310	141,085	139,397	137,790	135,103	132,953	132,237
17	VA Heart of Texas Health Care Network	106,343	102,023	100,840	102,301	101,528	101,098	99,627	97,484	94,923	93,329	92,907	92,439	91,297	90,679	90,406
18	VA Southwest Health Care Network	91,942	83,177	79,842	78,183	75,886	75,672	74,838	73,080	71,416	70,304	69,315	67,949	65,953	64,168	62,437
19	Rocky Mountain Network	77,651	72,006	68,798	67,614	65,581	64,523	63,532	62,186	60,664	59,881	59,540	58,929	57,819	56,691	55,140
20	Northwest Network	126,581	116,102	111,014	109,336	107,115	104,020	100,919	97,301	94,049	92,385	91,527	90,227	87,951	85,546	82,549
21	Sierra Pacific Network	120,331	108,257	101,616	99,364	96,187	94,297	91,657	88,051	84,374	81,093	78,111	75,030	71,670	67,782	64,105
22	Desert Pacific Healthcare Network	121,051	108,464	102,879	101,554	99,996	97,641	94,325	90,553	86,937	83,943	81,184	78,846	75,386	71,862	68,672
23	VA Midwest Health Care Network	110,418	96,711	87,832	82,453	78,162	77,358	76,398	75,221	74,348	74,299	74,699	74,545	73,391	71,709	69,517

Table 37. Veterans in the Population: Living Veterans, by Veteran Integrated Service Network, by Age Group, 2013–Projected 2043—*Continued*

(Number.)

Age group and VISN	VISN description	2028	2029	2030	2031	2032	2033	2034	2035	2036	2037	2038	2039	2040	2041	2042	2043
50 TO 54 YEARS	**Total**	1,267,477	1,280,732	1,307,642	1,330,540	1,349,154	1,351,893	1,338,763	1,315,985	1,289,672	1,272,645	1,271,450	1,276,673	1,280,501	1,275,829	1,259,577	1,231,809
1	VA New England Healthcare System	39,642	39,210	39,117	39,276	39,261	38,838	38,245	37,660	36,975	36,723	36,879	37,041	37,101	36,664	35,837	34,705
2	VA Healthcare Network Upstate New York	19,852	19,962	20,230	20,442	20,494	20,106	19,695	19,174	18,721	18,449	18,739	18,944	19,030	18,820	18,464	17,878
3	VA NY/NJ Veterans Healthcare Network	24,210	24,559	25,042	25,136	25,144	24,798	24,191	23,308	22,281	21,429	20,666	20,147	19,724	19,392	18,965	18,523
4	VA Healthcare - VISN 4	55,957	56,450	57,381	57,949	58,510	58,024	56,526	54,798	53,003	51,508	51,158	51,444	51,664	51,645	51,094	49,798
5	VA Capitol Health Care Network	55,766	56,584	57,383	58,130	58,138	57,657	56,517	55,367	54,067	53,396	53,366	53,662	54,171	54,647	54,717	54,341
6	VA Mid-Atlantic Health Care Network	105,811	106,690	108,256	109,467	110,550	110,741	109,694	108,841	107,945	107,725	108,558	110,242	110,907	110,569	109,228	107,291
7	VA Southeast Network	103,852	104,338	106,127	107,480	107,826	107,326	105,978	104,343	102,613	102,550	104,187	106,123	107,684	108,304	107,493	105,153
8	VA Sunshine Healthcare Network	80,631	80,642	81,702	82,523	82,857	82,553	81,319	79,544	77,405	76,011	75,652	75,710	75,783	75,309	74,085	72,274
9	VA Mid South Healthcare Network	60,337	60,468	61,306	62,377	63,507	63,533	63,234	62,602	61,718	61,473	62,021	62,544	62,877	62,385	60,911	58,825
10	VA Healthcare System of Ohio	36,097	35,656	36,025	36,411	36,889	36,583	35,994	35,134	34,251	33,777	33,580	33,629	33,689	33,349	32,550	31,605
11	Veterans In Partnership	47,632	46,563	46,927	47,317	48,023	48,129	47,962	47,073	46,026	45,220	45,110	45,150	45,275	45,087	44,173	42,648
12	VA Great Lakes Health Care System	38,701	38,915	39,689	40,537	41,401	41,778	41,520	40,646	39,536	38,368	37,824	37,454	37,252	36,725	36,176	35,206
15	VA Heartland Network	49,335	49,724	50,659	51,577	52,513	52,724	52,324	51,799	51,028	50,618	50,689	51,089	51,065	50,800	49,998	48,600
16	South Central VA Health Care Network	122,210	124,544	128,158	130,586	133,188	133,603	131,948	128,267	124,525	121,096	120,043	120,054	120,821	120,726	119,565	116,511
17	VA Heart of Texas Health Care Network	90,059	92,376	95,642	98,542	100,951	102,681	102,766	101,690	100,404	99,728	98,511	97,702	97,149	95,928	93,901	92,244
18	VA Southwest Health Care Network	54,988	56,242	58,023	59,544	61,169	61,999	61,552	60,735	59,947	59,326	59,261	59,882	59,966	59,573	58,699	57,456
19	Rocky Mountain Network	50,195	51,473	53,227	54,571	55,882	56,196	55,988	55,332	54,621	53,678	53,882	54,032	54,077	53,939	53,474	52,453
20	Northwest Network	66,471	67,529	69,164	70,953	72,178	72,890	72,761	71,955	70,737	70,226	70,411	70,654	70,766	70,534	69,751	68,486
21	Sierra Pacific Network	51,559	52,453	53,662	54,671	55,314	55,288	54,431	53,201	51,798	50,524	49,961	49,804	49,592	49,141	48,599	47,688
22	Desert Pacific Healthcare Network	64,469	65,744	67,696	68,983	69,641	69,653	68,818	67,342	65,587	64,776	64,571	64,596	64,653	64,770	64,392	63,877
23	VA Midwest Health Care Network	49,703	50,609	52,224	54,069	55,719	56,794	57,299	57,174	56,483	56,043	56,381	56,770	57,255	57,524	57,505	56,246
55 TO 59 YEARS	**Total**	1,440,686	1,378,043	1,305,902	1,264,139	1,245,609	1,248,103	1,261,419	1,287,935	1,310,550	1,328,955	1,331,900	1,319,415	1,297,558	1,272,311	1,256,158	1,255,438
1	VA New England Healthcare System	46,044	43,980	41,477	39,528	38,299	37,864	37,460	37,372	37,522	37,500	37,100	36,544	35,989	35,341	35,109	35,262
2	VA Healthcare Network Upstate New York	23,149	21,579	20,203	19,480	19,166	19,159	19,268	19,524	19,722	19,769	19,395	19,002	18,503	18,071	17,810	18,085
3	VA NY/NJ Veterans Healthcare Network	25,545	23,963	22,546	21,899	21,554	21,721	22,023	22,441	22,512	22,509	22,190	21,644	20,856	19,945	19,196	18,528
4	VA Healthcare - VISN 4	65,872	62,088	58,319	56,051	54,991	54,890	55,381	56,294	56,855	57,404	56,931	55,484	53,810	52,078	50,643	50,333
5	VA Capitol Health Care Network	56,948	55,537	53,671	52,669	52,508	53,155	53,909	54,629	55,306	55,279	54,813	53,740	52,659	51,442	50,822	50,835
6	VA Mid-Atlantic Health Care Network	117,176	114,066	109,557	106,721	105,271	105,166	106,000	107,520	108,679	109,736	109,918	108,873	108,025	107,137	106,910	107,721
7	VA Southeast Network	122,032	117,466	111,313	107,426	105,484	105,265	105,776	107,582	108,954	109,300	108,770	107,429	105,821	104,097	104,054	105,754
8	VA Sunshine Healthcare Network	92,516	89,118	84,566	81,984	80,828	80,754	80,788	81,854	82,721	83,058	82,805	81,647	79,985	77,909	76,612	76,275
9	VA Mid South Healthcare Network	74,276	70,916	66,639	63,588	61,710	61,186	61,327	62,174	63,267	64,408	64,438	64,147	63,523	62,631	62,399	62,966
10	VA Healthcare System of Ohio	47,549	44,110	40,240	37,641	35,659	34,993	34,582	34,939	35,313	35,778	35,486	34,922	34,104	33,267	32,822	32,648
11	Veterans In Partnership	64,918	59,996	54,447	50,306	47,597	46,049	45,058	45,427	45,809	46,508	46,622	46,477	45,640	44,651	43,876	43,800
12	VA Great Lakes Health Care System	47,933	44,321	40,733	38,510	37,471	37,171	37,384	38,130	38,951	39,794	40,151	39,919	39,093	38,040	36,935	36,447
15	VA Heartland Network	57,578	54,985	52,045	49,892	48,751	48,825	49,230	50,157	51,055	51,970	52,179	51,784	51,274	50,528	50,138	50,218
16	South Central VA Health Care Network	137,061	131,332	124,934	121,995	120,965	121,963	124,319	127,917	130,347	132,962	133,360	131,728	128,085	124,411	121,036	120,080
17	VA Heart of Texas Health Care Network	97,997	95,470	91,727	90,185	90,074	91,222	93,601	96,946	99,928	102,373	104,199	104,319	103,280	102,052	101,448	100,219
18	VA Southwest Health Care Network	60,054	58,243	56,075	55,237	55,033	55,885	57,171	58,988	60,528	62,206	63,105	62,682	61,920	61,231	60,674	60,585
19	Rocky Mountain Network	54,365	52,504	50,169	49,149	49,323	49,924	51,236	52,999	54,345	55,669	55,963	55,776	55,128	54,449	53,523	53,745
20	Northwest Network	73,946	70,596	67,129	65,301	64,848	65,204	66,243	67,846	69,589	70,761	71,451	71,327	70,519	69,303	68,790	68,955
21	Sierra Pacific Network	53,644	51,193	48,912	48,160	48,109	48,738	49,583	50,715	51,659	52,242	52,217	51,422	50,274	48,963	47,776	47,250
22	Desert Pacific Healthcare Network	64,140	62,021	59,819	59,108	59,150	59,873	61,070	62,871	64,056	64,672	64,698	63,929	62,567	60,931	60,169	59,960
23	VA Midwest Health Care Network	57,944	54,561	51,380	49,309	48,819	49,096	50,010	51,612	53,434	55,058	56,111	56,617	56,504	55,833	55,414	55,771
60 TO 64 YEARS	**Total**	1,546,807	1,512,100	1,507,078	1,485,787	1,446,996	1,393,126	1,333,438	1,264,628	1,225,070	1,207,857	1,210,886	1,224,358	1,250,514	1,272,884	1,291,161	1,294,505
1	VA New England Healthcare System	54,769	50,992	48,862	47,146	45,198	43,162	41,244	38,921	37,111	35,973	35,580	35,210	35,128	35,273	35,247	34,876
2	VA Healthcare Network Upstate New York	29,970	28,103	26,625	25,062	23,517	21,921	20,448	19,159	18,484	18,193	18,190	18,299	18,543	18,730	18,775	18,421
3	VA NY/NJ Veterans Healthcare Network	31,237	28,782	27,001	25,374	23,902	22,473	21,073	19,833	19,263	18,947	19,082	19,343	19,698	19,747	19,733	19,445
4	VA Healthcare - VISN 4	79,929	75,883	73,176	70,027	66,666	63,255	59,677	56,098	53,961	52,974	52,907	53,395	54,291	54,851	55,393	54,945
5	VA Capitol Health Care Network	56,339	54,668	54,341	53,696	52,988	51,649	50,346	48,653	47,734	47,588	48,151	48,823	49,453	50,050	49,997	49,558
6	VA Mid-Atlantic Health Care Network	117,790	116,410	117,543	118,140	117,390	115,405	112,343	107,903	105,145	103,736	103,642	104,472	105,978	107,113	108,165	108,360
7	VA Southeast Network	128,631	126,734	127,533	127,147	125,329	121,583	117,129	111,085	107,290	105,423	105,265	105,826	107,649	109,046	109,410	108,859
8	VA Sunshine Healthcare Network	102,984	99,411	98,525	96,882	94,502	91,276	87,981	83,550	81,054	79,976	79,963	80,022	81,102	82,024	82,361	82,205
9	VA Mid South Healthcare Network	79,783	78,391	78,798	78,274	76,565	73,795	70,487	66,298	63,303	61,475	60,982	61,146	62,006	63,125	64,280	64,324
10	VA Healthcare System of Ohio	57,027	54,951	53,822	51,637	48,970	45,461	42,210	38,549	36,088	34,212	33,591	33,215	33,561	33,925	34,378	34,100
11	Veterans In Partnership	77,466	74,039	72,357	69,941	66,278	62,037	57,386	52,146	48,249	45,700	44,255	43,339	43,719	44,101	44,798	44,918
12	VA Great Lakes Health Care System	56,175	54,414	53,555	51,700	48,817	45,318	41,940	38,601	36,545	35,589	35,335	35,556	36,276	37,069	37,895	38,233
15	VA Heartland Network	60,587	59,589	59,734	59,367	58,021	55,763	53,272	50,457	48,409	47,328	47,424	47,848	48,768	49,646	50,545	50,760
16	South Central VA Health Care Network	132,521	134,246	137,983	139,289	137,490	133,912	128,371	122,225	119,458	118,536	119,585	121,965	125,532	127,954	130,574	130,972
17	VA Heart of Texas Health Care Network	90,831	92,811	96,474	98,487	98,961	97,792	95,322	91,642	90,153	90,108	91,288	93,739	97,158	100,214	102,691	104,620
18	VA Southwest Health Care Network	61,284	61,160	62,232	62,168	61,403	59,886	58,141	56,052	55,295	55,149	56,087	57,413	59,266	60,823	62,553	63,516
19	Rocky Mountain Network	54,362	54,093	54,894	54,687	53,915	52,564	50,804	48,582	47,631	47,846	48,465	49,766	51,512	52,841	54,151	54,439
20	Northwest Network	80,665	79,103	78,952	77,318	74,906	71,444	68,210	64,883	63,132	62,719	63,076	64,098	65,666	67,364	68,494	69,163
21	Sierra Pacific Network	61,059	58,511	56,733	54,464	52,103	49,522	47,297	45,238	44,584	44,569	45,194	46,000	47,069	47,963	48,515	48,510
22	Desert Pacific Healthcare Network	65,829	63,972	63,344	62,190	60,535	58,914	56,995	55,018	54,408	54,481	55,177	56,320	57,995	59,097	59,682	59,725
23	VA Midwest Health Care Network	67,569	65,840	64,596	62,791	59,538	55,993	52,761	49,734	47,773	47,336	47,645	48,563	50,142	51,929	53,525	54,556

Table 37. Veterans in the Population: Living Veterans, by Veteran Integrated Service Network, by Age Group, 2013–Projected 2043—*Continued*

(Number.)

Age group and VISN	VISN description	2013	2014	2015	2016	2017	2018	2019	2020	2021	2022	2023	2024	2025	2026	2027
65 TO 69 YEARS	**Total**	3,151,898	3,195,675	3,120,427	2,767,254	2,441,272	2,157,624	1,957,192	1,862,380	1,841,368	1,817,282	1,814,605	1,800,658	1,771,781	1,738,898	1,712,327
1	VA New England Healthcare System	147,159	146,187	138,966	118,351	98,714	84,630	74,442	70,192	70,809	71,913	73,321	73,912	73,456	71,992	70,138
2	VA Healthcare Network Upstate New York	69,350	69,463	66,509	57,282	49,483	42,584	37,874	35,752	35,492	35,245	35,874	36,021	35,831	35,251	34,752
3	VA NY/NJ Veterans Healthcare Network	117,255	114,451	106,141	87,787	71,603	57,765	48,420	44,178	43,219	42,679	43,683	43,723	42,844	41,589	40,071
4	VA Healthcare - VISN 4	184,213	187,006	183,397	160,923	140,104	119,327	103,626	94,843	92,263	90,256	90,998	91,275	90,592	89,246	88,180
5	VA Capitol Health Care Network	91,077	91,464	88,944	79,790	71,128	63,987	60,021	59,047	59,710	60,256	61,180	61,689	61,669	61,393	60,787
6	VA Mid-Atlantic Health Care Network	177,284	181,966	180,387	161,120	142,315	130,360	122,732	120,646	122,172	124,215	125,431	126,304	125,823	125,247	124,562
7	VA Southeast Network	194,212	199,360	197,623	179,513	162,186	148,144	138,810	136,649	138,782	139,891	141,575	142,925	143,234	143,111	142,654
8	VA Sunshine Healthcare Network	224,720	223,533	213,391	185,648	161,435	142,330	130,460	127,444	128,962	131,188	132,984	134,034	133,434	131,718	129,251
9	VA Mid South Healthcare Network	137,978	142,482	142,257	129,470	115,423	104,133	96,532	91,749	90,230	88,931	88,619	88,153	87,345	86,663	86,617
10	VA Healthcare System of Ohio	124,906	127,560	125,573	111,784	97,371	84,154	74,831	69,953	68,472	67,251	67,393	66,796	65,931	64,515	63,331
11	Veterans In Partnership	182,887	185,142	181,162	161,578	141,492	121,081	106,858	98,217	94,669	91,912	91,950	91,103	89,484	88,112	86,997
12	VA Great Lakes Health Care System	136,798	140,978	138,105	121,540	106,374	90,169	77,387	70,549	68,094	65,496	65,486	64,790	63,352	61,682	60,458
15	VA Heartland Network	123,835	125,640	123,038	110,291	97,754	86,787	78,740	73,874	71,648	69,124	68,657	68,029	67,234	66,328	65,603
16	South Central VA Health Care Network	238,508	244,664	241,619	217,607	196,994	178,454	164,617	158,175	156,227	153,028	150,209	146,589	142,091	138,166	135,244
17	VA Heart of Texas Health Care Network	135,946	138,122	136,826	123,303	112,094	103,624	99,612	98,612	99,999	99,179	98,704	97,223	95,088	92,694	91,231
18	VA Southwest Health Care Network	126,657	129,170	124,677	111,765	100,269	88,968	80,535	77,403	75,946	73,869	73,811	73,140	71,531	69,936	68,908
19	Rocky Mountain Network	103,291	103,508	101,499	90,881	81,316	73,735	68,495	65,541	64,338	62,303	61,192	60,134	58,742	57,358	56,667
20	Northwest Network	163,439	166,614	164,875	148,746	133,136	119,549	109,778	105,087	103,578	101,519	98,621	95,732	92,341	89,320	87,807
21	Sierra Pacific Network	162,743	164,365	159,780	139,996	122,916	108,134	97,388	91,491	89,521	86,723	85,052	82,711	79,481	76,214	73,288
22	Desert Pacific Healthcare Network	168,140	167,666	159,549	137,631	120,519	106,383	95,389	90,525	89,721	88,711	86,968	84,333	81,285	78,125	75,516
23	VA Midwest Health Care Network	141,500	146,332	146,108	132,246	118,646	103,326	90,642	82,453	77,515	73,594	72,897	72,042	70,992	70,238	70,264
70 TO 74 YEARS	**Total**	2,036,905	2,127,179	2,239,849	2,531,807	2,736,936	2,861,351	2,902,386	2,833,712	2,515,481	2,222,901	1,968,036	1,789,068	1,705,792	1,688,947	1,669,107
1	VA New England Healthcare System	98,049	102,043	106,367	118,583	127,221	129,612	128,790	122,369	104,291	87,124	74,848	66,010	62,394	63,045	64,127
2	VA Healthcare Network Upstate New York	43,939	45,931	48,504	55,523	59,713	61,661	61,756	59,089	50,944	44,116	38,043	33,927	32,104	31,925	31,749
3	VA NY/NJ Veterans Healthcare Network	77,120	78,550	81,477	90,896	96,555	97,808	95,431	88,351	73,116	59,693	48,215	40,511	37,066	36,303	35,900
4	VA Healthcare - VISN 4	125,475	129,849	133,400	149,272	159,056	166,077	168,610	165,244	145,161	126,624	108,001	94,003	86,259	84,019	82,331
5	VA Capitol Health Care Network	56,187	58,938	61,694	69,451	75,112	78,653	79,079	76,940	69,176	61,791	55,660	52,250	51,451	52,048	52,547
6	VA Mid-Atlantic Health Care Network	109,479	114,468	121,935	142,329	158,015	166,950	171,299	169,637	151,529	133,955	122,775	115,664	113,792	115,292	117,311
7	VA Southeast Network	125,681	133,333	141,710	159,855	174,496	183,720	188,617	186,843	169,717	153,423	140,163	131,449	129,482	131,603	132,752
8	VA Sunshine Healthcare Network	172,906	175,321	180,842	197,564	204,781	209,083	207,956	198,175	172,530	150,435	132,905	122,107	119,691	121,243	123,489
9	VA Mid South Healthcare Network	84,919	88,992	95,031	109,671	121,708	129,543	133,733	133,446	121,424	108,415	97,902	90,902	86,516	85,213	84,066
10	VA Healthcare System of Ohio	74,748	79,662	84,039	96,124	106,662	112,528	114,960	113,127	100,718	87,798	75,937	67,610	63,260	61,995	60,986
11	Veterans In Partnership	105,751	113,066	122,046	140,119	154,618	164,460	166,565	162,925	145,393	127,490	109,187	96,520	88,880	85,805	83,429
12	VA Great Lakes Health Care System	86,308	88,650	93,361	106,428	115,360	121,861	125,651	123,063	108,299	94,823	80,436	69,140	63,110	61,012	58,793
15	VA Heartland Network	74,918	80,010	85,951	98,289	108,046	113,165	114,846	112,443	100,820	89,449	79,468	72,164	67,775	65,812	63,595
16	South Central VA Health Care Network	151,023	160,243	171,093	194,904	210,599	220,293	226,060	223,234	201,083	182,110	165,100	152,463	146,618	144,997	142,195
17	VA Heart of Texas Health Care Network	85,576	91,557	97,054	111,830	122,358	128,436	130,493	129,222	116,440	105,954	97,934	94,193	93,267	94,675	93,976
18	VA Southwest Health Care Network	83,397	86,491	92,782	104,928	113,769	119,017	121,369	117,129	105,144	94,468	84,024	76,197	73,412	72,141	70,280
19	Rocky Mountain Network	64,501	68,868	73,117	83,061	90,936	95,026	95,293	93,464	83,595	74,772	67,736	62,846	60,060	59,023	57,196
20	Northwest Network	105,830	112,094	117,369	131,429	141,501	150,135	153,051	151,342	136,532	122,246	109,888	101,032	96,835	95,526	93,673
21	Sierra Pacific Network	106,468	108,052	111,918	126,094	136,122	141,909	143,411	139,480	122,156	107,267	94,390	85,076	79,957	78,335	75,982
22	Desert Pacific Healthcare Network	119,461	121,414	125,529	136,819	140,226	143,129	142,652	135,616	117,325	103,103	91,395	82,386	78,582	78,026	77,261
23	VA Midwest Health Care Network	85,171	89,645	94,628	108,638	120,080	128,286	132,764	132,572	120,087	107,843	94,029	82,617	75,282	70,908	67,466
75 TO 79 YEARS	**Total**	1,685,148	1,647,745	1,623,302	1,636,010	1,696,984	1,749,745	1,832,088	1,932,684	2,192,217	2,375,477	2,484,940	2,519,565	2,456,609	2,182,706	1,932,956
1	VA New England Healthcare System	82,137	78,496	76,242	77,245	79,791	81,620	85,098	88,878	99,440	106,945	108,981	108,210	102,622	87,494	73,235
2	VA Healthcare Network Upstate New York	38,538	36,604	35,068	34,334	35,796	36,932	38,697	40,943	47,049	50,731	52,419	52,479	50,147	43,250	37,549
3	VA NY/NJ Veterans Healthcare Network	71,564	67,071	63,191	61,624	61,050	60,705	61,939	64,365	72,095	76,829	77,922	76,023	70,242	58,072	47,411
4	VA Healthcare - VISN 4	103,537	100,471	99,829	100,148	103,781	106,959	110,930	114,148	128,231	136,985	143,252	145,413	142,295	125,065	109,286
5	VA Capitol Health Care Network	43,406	42,556	42,115	42,468	44,412	46,009	48,377	50,691	57,220	62,060	65,034	65,428	63,604	57,251	51,240
6	VA Mid-Atlantic Health Care Network	88,099	89,263	89,386	90,118	94,131	97,384	102,132	109,026	127,731	142,089	150,064	153,784	151,964	135,776	120,213
7	VA Southeast Network	95,423	95,524	96,364	100,493	106,581	112,549	119,655	127,309	143,929	157,420	165,791	170,054	168,124	152,758	138,311
8	VA Sunshine Healthcare Network	151,974	149,274	145,693	145,632	150,723	152,973	155,336	160,406	176,067	183,019	187,281	186,416	177,430	154,437	134,862
9	VA Mid South Healthcare Network	70,327	69,720	69,224	70,202	73,550	75,373	79,188	84,754	98,109	109,068	116,084	119,670	119,229	108,475	97,074
10	VA Healthcare System of Ohio	62,034	59,012	57,960	58,081	60,124	63,675	68,015	71,868	82,450	91,664	96,719	98,695	96,894	86,295	75,348
11	Veterans In Partnership	86,431	83,820	82,387	83,657	86,981	89,918	96,460	104,365	120,123	132,766	141,270	142,953	139,583	124,655	109,510
12	VA Great Lakes Health Care System	72,062	70,460	68,974	68,542	71,015	72,637	74,796	78,906	90,215	98,031	103,593	106,686	104,221	91,759	80,451
15	VA Heartland Network	61,594	59,614	58,361	58,764	61,797	64,810	69,401	74,662	85,583	94,234	98,635	99,978	97,704	87,677	77,964
16	South Central VA Health Care Network	124,597	120,977	118,844	120,067	125,644	132,172	140,545	150,248	171,547	185,583	194,034	198,907	196,087	176,806	160,375
17	VA Heart of Texas Health Care Network	69,953	68,377	68,804	68,759	72,377	76,614	82,167	87,296	100,684	110,222	115,590	117,128	115,611	104,315	95,232
18	VA Southwest Health Care Network	70,138	70,579	70,348	70,051	71,166	74,449	77,388	83,080	94,251	102,475	107,222	109,375	105,522	94,769	85,232
19	Rocky Mountain Network	53,218	52,605	52,245	52,886	54,358	56,272	60,223	64,023	72,814	79,707	83,097	83,110	81,222	72,686	65,173
20	Northwest Network	80,149	79,754	80,713	84,173	89,107	91,998	97,697	102,421	115,109	124,229	131,816	134,252	132,454	119,488	107,086
21	Sierra Pacific Network	85,964	85,655	84,759	85,658	87,228	87,580	89,189	92,650	104,795	113,282	118,068	119,171	115,668	101,330	89,094
22	Desert Pacific Healthcare Network	98,794	95,912	93,093	93,063	95,944	96,061	97,752	101,113	110,867	114,123	116,944	116,878	111,357	96,416	84,849
23	VA Midwest Health Care Network	75,209	72,003	69,702	70,045	71,430	73,056	77,103	81,529	93,908	104,018	111,121	114,957	114,629	103,933	93,462

Table 37. Veterans in the Population: Living Veterans, by Veteran Integrated Service Network, by Age Group, 2013–Projected 2043—*Continued*

(Number.)

Age group and VISN	VISN description	2028	2029	2030	2031	2032	2033	2034	2035	2036	2037	2038	2039	2040	2041	2042	2043
65 TO 69 YEARS	**Total**	1,695,073	1,670,138	1,622,552	1,569,357	1,514,647	1,468,951	1,437,165	1,433,348	1,413,790	1,377,407	1,326,650	1,270,573	1,205,935	1,169,175	1,153,588	1,157,227
1	VA New England Healthcare System	68,502	66,384	62,985	58,876	54,649	50,307	46,856	44,911	43,339	41,551	39,666	37,909	35,788	34,139	33,105	32,761
2	VA Healthcare Network Upstate New York	34,550	34,060	33,039	31,652	29,733	27,830	26,105	24,737	23,288	21,854	20,375	19,014	17,828	17,209	16,946	16,949
3	VA NY/NJ Veterans Healthcare Network	38,416	36,733	34,692	32,144	29,405	26,884	24,742	23,176	21,758	20,477	19,238	18,024	16,962	16,474	16,193	16,302
4	VA Healthcare - VISN 4	87,562	87,183	85,311	82,747	79,106	75,291	71,519	69,008	66,056	62,905	59,710	56,374	53,030	51,056	50,158	50,131
5	VA Capitol Health Care Network	60,397	59,353	57,365	54,925	52,402	50,258	48,722	48,382	47,765	47,088	45,869	44,688	43,177	42,351	42,228	42,716
6	VA Mid-Atlantic Health Care Network	124,823	124,270	121,949	119,361	116,903	114,379	113,049	114,163	114,697	113,909	111,965	108,994	104,690	102,056	100,719	100,643
7	VA Southeast Network	142,510	141,073	137,326	132,979	128,936	125,874	124,057	124,887	124,550	122,804	119,169	114,887	109,041	105,401	103,645	103,557
8	VA Sunshine Healthcare Network	126,740	122,878	117,097	111,014	105,162	100,196	96,735	95,883	94,293	91,991	88,877	85,733	81,476	79,109	78,147	78,199
9	VA Mid South Healthcare Network	86,754	86,038	84,157	82,066	79,705	77,865	76,549	76,953	76,453	74,796	72,103	68,889	64,849	61,957	60,208	59,760
10	VA Healthcare System of Ohio	62,533	61,627	59,660	57,712	55,381	53,537	51,615	50,568	48,525	46,029	42,740	39,712	36,299	34,007	32,261	31,697
11	Veterans In Partnership	86,842	86,311	83,772	80,197	76,409	72,685	69,517	67,968	65,720	62,302	58,336	53,998	49,118	45,509	43,147	41,824
12	VA Great Lakes Health Care System	59,653	59,005	57,536	55,783	53,842	52,224	50,602	49,806	48,084	45,417	42,176	39,062	36,002	34,134	33,271	33,066
15	VA Heartland Network	65,404	64,666	62,944	61,025	59,188	57,655	56,742	56,898	56,561	55,285	53,139	50,778	48,125	46,212	45,206	45,327
16	South Central VA Health Care Network	133,719	132,276	129,756	127,740	127,087	127,405	129,128	132,745	134,004	132,270	128,863	123,572	117,763	115,218	114,420	115,515
17	VA Heart of Texas Health Care Network	90,903	90,537	89,486	88,940	88,727	89,218	91,226	94,872	96,851	97,327	96,199	93,817	90,258	88,850	88,879	90,086
18	VA Southwest Health Care Network	67,967	66,636	64,702	62,971	61,281	60,178	60,090	61,161	61,105	60,369	58,890	57,239	55,265	54,608	54,528	55,546
19	Rocky Mountain Network	56,374	55,835	54,808	53,758	52,307	51,609	51,368	52,154	51,980	51,250	49,986	48,347	46,269	45,407	45,668	46,304
20	Northwest Network	87,029	85,815	83,668	81,393	78,554	76,782	75,305	75,157	73,598	71,280	67,973	64,896	61,757	60,114	59,750	60,110
21	Sierra Pacific Network	70,627	67,842	64,828	61,317	58,004	55,253	52,979	51,368	49,330	47,223	44,896	42,912	41,090	40,542	40,568	41,191
22	Desert Pacific Healthcare Network	73,081	71,037	67,953	64,809	61,962	59,419	57,757	57,204	56,178	54,698	53,244	51,534	49,789	49,282	49,381	50,041
23	VA Midwest Health Care Network	70,689	70,581	69,516	67,949	65,907	64,101	62,501	61,345	59,654	56,583	53,235	50,194	47,360	45,538	45,162	45,503
70 TO 74 YEARS	**Total**	1,667,876	1,656,420	1,631,355	1,602,766	1,579,915	1,565,304	1,543,389	1,500,132	1,451,778	1,402,148	1,361,017	1,332,894	1,330,446	1,313,001	1,279,717	1,233,072
1	VA New England Healthcare System	65,409	65,948	65,562	64,280	62,652	61,207	59,313	56,261	52,580	48,804	44,933	41,871	40,146	38,748	37,154	35,456
2	VA Healthcare Network Upstate New York	32,327	32,477	32,320	31,814	31,390	31,224	30,786	29,861	28,603	26,869	25,154	23,603	22,374	21,065	19,768	18,435
3	VA NY/NJ Veterans Healthcare Network	36,744	36,762	35,998	34,931	33,617	32,200	30,750	29,006	26,827	24,507	22,366	20,557	19,222	18,025	16,948	15,910
4	VA Healthcare - VISN 4	83,056	83,355	82,782	81,634	80,741	80,236	79,940	78,252	75,924	72,600	69,118	65,701	63,439	60,744	57,866	54,950
5	VA Capitol Health Care Network	53,351	53,794	53,778	53,527	52,977	52,618	51,688	49,917	47,746	45,507	43,597	42,230	41,898	41,329	40,704	39,626
6	VA Mid-Atlantic Health Care Network	118,492	119,367	118,972	118,485	117,873	118,151	117,657	115,442	112,981	110,663	108,303	107,076	108,164	108,634	107,834	105,978
7	VA Southeast Network	134,435	135,798	136,190	136,168	135,793	135,721	134,422	130,881	126,770	122,953	120,088	118,417	119,276	119,002	117,368	113,926
8	VA Sunshine Healthcare Network	125,332	126,478	126,084	124,645	122,404	120,129	116,577	111,143	105,414	99,940	95,242	91,972	91,200	89,703	87,526	84,588
9	VA Mid South Healthcare Network	83,837	83,466	82,764	82,184	82,213	82,378	81,734	79,975	78,005	75,770	74,061	72,865	73,267	72,806	71,240	68,687
10	VA Healthcare System of Ohio	61,149	60,647	59,919	58,689	57,677	57,002	56,219	54,454	52,706	50,610	48,967	47,239	46,297	44,436	42,160	39,157
11	Veterans In Partnership	83,516	82,797	81,401	80,244	79,311	79,220	78,784	76,481	73,253	69,830	66,478	63,635	62,250	60,212	57,100	53,482
12	VA Great Lakes Health Care System	58,818	58,237	56,981	55,547	54,536	53,891	53,376	52,092	50,537	48,793	47,342	45,893	45,178	43,619	41,210	38,282
15	VA Heartland Network	63,221	62,693	62,025	61,250	60,642	60,504	59,863	58,291	56,543	54,871	53,491	52,688	52,857	52,558	51,376	49,388
16	South Central VA Health Care Network	139,704	136,474	132,443	128,917	126,366	125,042	123,801	121,505	119,675	119,114	119,476	121,178	124,609	125,793	124,158	120,987
17	VA Heart of Texas Health Care Network	93,622	92,322	90,407	88,241	86,952	86,734	86,484	85,551	85,093	84,949	85,504	87,507	91,060	92,960	93,422	92,357
18	VA Southwest Health Care Network	70,309	69,746	68,263	66,783	65,872	65,010	63,751	61,927	60,298	58,698	57,682	57,644	58,697	58,651	57,960	56,552
19	Rocky Mountain Network	56,211	55,269	54,025	52,808	52,229	51,991	51,534	50,610	49,663	48,344	47,744	47,542	48,299	48,162	47,488	46,340
20	Northwest Network	91,043	88,442	85,370	82,653	81,332	80,657	79,560	77,589	75,498	72,885	71,274	69,924	69,791	68,342	66,170	63,089
21	Sierra Pacific Network	74,567	72,573	69,778	66,964	64,434	62,128	59,683	57,056	53,973	51,070	48,659	46,689	45,273	43,491	41,667	39,636
22	Desert Pacific Healthcare Network	75,841	73,609	71,025	68,349	66,150	64,065	62,333	59,657	56,929	54,459	52,248	50,806	50,334	49,446	48,152	46,879
23	VA Midwest Health Care Network	66,892	66,164	65,267	64,650	64,754	65,196	65,135	64,180	62,760	60,914	59,293	57,857	56,816	55,273	52,446	49,365
75 TO 79 YEARS	**Total**	1,715,259	1,564,201	1,495,700	1,483,898	1,469,264	1,469,433	1,460,839	1,440,510	1,417,379	1,399,270	1,387,941	1,369,870	1,332,241	1,290,250	1,247,379	1,212,359
1	VA New England Healthcare System	63,084	55,846	52,973	53,652	54,688	55,808	56,276	55,968	54,910	53,562	52,356	50,739	48,114	44,956	41,734	38,444
2	VA Healthcare Network Upstate New York	32,443	29,024	27,542	27,454	27,364	27,872	28,020	27,902	27,488	27,157	27,037	26,666	25,862	24,768	23,270	21,794
3	VA NY/NJ Veterans Healthcare Network	38,301	32,248	29,574	29,023	28,766	29,437	29,434	28,798	27,939	26,861	25,710	24,522	23,100	21,323	19,452	17,724
4	VA Healthcare - VISN 4	93,346	81,474	75,008	73,214	71,929	72,614	72,924	72,484	71,581	70,905	70,538	70,342	68,886	66,866	63,962	60,924
5	VA Capitol Health Care Network	46,225	43,452	42,845	43,383	43,838	44,507	44,885	44,882	44,681	44,222	43,917	43,134	41,625	39,780	37,884	36,270
6	VA Mid-Atlantic Health Care Network	110,356	104,163	102,688	104,144	106,090	107,208	108,078	107,819	107,474	106,998	107,318	106,934	104,921	102,691	100,615	98,535
7	VA Southeast Network	126,526	118,941	117,371	119,437	120,631	122,253	123,603	124,096	124,219	123,979	124,003	122,910	119,715	116,009	112,581	110,056
8	VA Sunshine Healthcare Network	119,264	109,788	107,872	109,458	111,663	113,476	114,660	114,485	113,380	111,464	109,515	106,398	101,489	96,307	91,402	87,153
9	VA Mid South Healthcare Network	87,806	81,746	77,993	76,979	76,051	75,914	75,671	75,123	74,690	74,813	75,016	74,485	72,916	71,147	69,139	67,645
10	VA Healthcare System of Ohio	65,285	58,291	54,671	53,677	52,927	53,102	52,708	52,139	51,139	50,342	49,814	49,181	47,665	46,171	44,377	42,993
11	Veterans In Partnership	93,927	83,250	76,896	74,414	72,522	72,644	72,069	70,940	70,049	69,344	69,331	69,003	66,997	64,206	61,252	58,381
12	VA Great Lakes Health Care System	68,364	58,956	53,977	52,309	50,550	50,605	50,147	49,107	47,953	47,187	46,720	46,349	45,275	43,957	42,465	41,233
15	VA Heartland Network	69,380	63,144	59,443	57,827	56,014	55,743	55,338	54,824	54,217	53,758	53,693	53,175	51,802	50,285	48,842	47,673
16	South Central VA Health Care Network	145,707	134,932	130,064	128,843	126,549	124,456	121,731	118,321	115,344	113,271	112,212	111,234	109,248	107,680	107,263	107,693
17	VA Heart of Texas Health Care Network	88,209	85,085	84,463	85,851	85,315	85,089	84,022	82,413	80,574	79,526	79,447	79,336	78,563	78,214	78,159	78,782
18	VA Southwest Health Care Network	75,965	69,026	66,661	65,646	64,097	64,211	63,780	62,490	61,201	60,458	59,725	58,596	56,951	55,492	54,058	53,188
19	Rocky Mountain Network	59,139	54,965	52,625	51,797	50,262	49,434	48,640	47,589	46,592	46,154	45,986	45,630	44,835	44,027	42,891	42,419
20	Northwest Network	96,448	88,889	85,379	84,335	82,760	80,485	78,265	75,626	73,329	72,270	71,733	70,804	69,069	67,239	64,953	63,578
21	Sierra Pacific Network	78,491	70,900	66,747	65,506	63,649	62,510	60,899	58,600	56,307	54,237	52,342	50,300	48,114	45,529	43,107	41,104
22	Desert Pacific Healthcare Network	75,374	68,191	65,223	64,908	64,380	63,287	61,488	59,410	57,269	55,522	53,833	52,443	50,222	47,961	45,917	44,086
23	VA Midwest Health Care Network	81,619	71,889	65,686	62,040	59,217	58,779	58,203	57,495	57,044	57,240	57,695	57,688	56,870	55,640	54,058	52,684

Table 37. Veterans in the Population: Living Veterans, by Veteran Integrated Service Network, by Age Group, 2013–Projected 2043—*Continued*

(Number.)

Age group and VISN	VISN description	2013	2014	2015	2016	2017	2018	2019	2020	2021	2022	2023	2024	2025	2026	2027
80 TO 84 YEARS	**Total**	1,514,202	1,486,228	1,436,873	1,377,425	1,325,702	1,304,387	1,280,590	1,265,936	1,280,379	1,334,880	1,382,247	1,451,209	1,533,421	1,748,019	1,900,351
1	VA New England Healthcare System	78,889	75,733	72,028	66,962	62,828	61,599	59,056	57,558	58,478	60,698	62,345	65,111	68,114	76,591	82,651
2	VA Healthcare Network Upstate New York	33,966	33,253	32,595	31,782	30,532	29,134	27,763	26,703	26,263	27,520	28,521	29,985	31,808	36,734	39,718
3	VA NY/NJ Veterans Healthcare Network	70,174	67,304	63,411	58,269	53,784	50,825	47,707	45,027	44,057	43,877	43,836	44,878	46,781	52,632	56,241
4	VA Healthcare - VISN 4	99,573	95,552	90,269	85,461	81,559	79,579	77,453	77,162	77,708	81,015	83,814	87,146	89,849	101,472	108,756
5	VA Capitol Health Care Network	39,970	38,802	37,098	34,884	32,983	31,967	31,466	31,273	31,641	33,297	34,645	36,524	38,299	43,399	47,242
6	VA Mid-Atlantic Health Care Network	74,321	72,924	71,652	70,559	69,591	70,645	71,817	72,094	72,860	76,472	79,437	83,611	89,466	105,401	117,619
7	VA Southeast Network	79,307	79,882	79,389	77,700	76,663	77,063	77,451	78,343	81,939	87,243	92,406	98,425	104,783	118,965	130,570
8	VA Sunshine Healthcare Network	137,088	135,584	132,389	127,665	123,384	121,424	119,798	117,337	117,899	122,892	125,345	127,683	132,152	145,735	151,878
9	VA Mid South Healthcare Network	61,147	60,931	59,876	57,481	55,322	56,251	55,992	55,761	56,654	59,581	61,329	64,606	69,315	80,634	89,916
10	VA Healthcare System of Ohio	56,498	55,938	53,381	51,243	49,438	47,487	45,346	44,698	44,966	46,787	49,742	53,220	56,280	64,887	72,382
11	Veterans In Partnership	82,081	79,558	75,149	70,915	67,223	66,173	64,452	63,571	64,739	67,618	70,183	75,521	81,861	94,626	104,875
12	VA Great Lakes Health Care System	66,511	64,268	60,631	57,836	55,350	54,709	53,751	52,749	52,554	54,626	56,031	57,796	61,021	70,141	76,549
15	VA Heartland Network	58,115	56,695	54,650	52,131	49,451	47,939	46,531	45,722	46,224	48,839	51,405	55,157	59,377	68,366	75,524
16	South Central VA Health Care Network	105,115	106,575	105,595	102,483	99,727	98,079	95,586	94,211	95,463	100,354	106,072	112,978	120,817	138,523	150,255
17	VA Heart of Texas Health Care Network	60,700	60,786	59,419	58,468	57,180	56,342	55,257	55,811	55,916	59,143	62,812	67,412	71,670	82,958	91,068
18	VA Southwest Health Care Network	60,822	61,186	59,492	58,289	58,005	56,445	57,054	57,022	57,034	58,240	61,211	63,862	68,697	78,231	85,286
19	Rocky Mountain Network	44,848	44,491	43,476	42,641	42,304	41,894	41,540	41,373	41,971	43,284	44,885	48,034	50,983	58,246	63,919
20	Northwest Network	64,490	65,105	65,404	64,220	62,982	63,117	63,024	63,945	66,810	70,962	73,457	78,199	82,029	92,692	100,391
21	Sierra Pacific Network	77,055	74,562	71,380	67,114	64,026	63,880	63,982	63,534	64,265	65,605	66,006	67,314	69,971	79,696	86,453
22	Desert Pacific Healthcare Network	89,716	86,180	81,481	77,328	73,577	71,756	69,753	67,784	68,211	70,830	71,251	72,888	75,703	83,470	86,153
23	VA Midwest Health Care Network	73,816	70,919	68,107	63,993	59,790	58,079	55,812	54,258	54,727	55,996	57,513	60,859	64,446	74,621	82,905
85 YEARS AND OVER	**Total**	1,478,662	1,492,832	1,513,081	1,533,944	1,557,256	1,559,344	1,550,682	1,533,118	1,510,074	1,495,564	1,488,175	1,471,648	1,456,822	1,460,816	1,500,906
1	VA New England Healthcare System	86,295	85,811	85,344	84,788	84,542	82,354	80,263	77,975	74,779	72,546	71,014	68,656	66,935	66,317	67,302
2	VA Healthcare Network Upstate New York	37,262	37,409	37,145	36,589	36,003	35,920	35,594	35,108	34,390	33,410	32,723	31,864	31,121	30,638	31,170
3	VA NY/NJ Veterans Healthcare Network	76,449	74,821	73,294	72,110	71,396	69,673	67,293	64,432	61,099	58,563	56,383	53,626	50,902	49,016	48,204
4	VA Healthcare - VISN 4	102,386	103,394	104,283	104,917	105,466	103,830	101,819	99,062	96,640	94,973	93,197	91,113	89,931	89,634	91,891
5	VA Capitol Health Care Network	40,323	39,987	39,960	40,145	40,429	39,989	39,133	38,174	37,012	36,132	35,414	34,794	34,347	34,184	35,129
6	VA Mid-Atlantic Health Care Network	63,507	66,587	69,518	72,090	74,792	76,062	76,599	77,234	77,803	78,663	80,096	81,104	81,643	82,618	86,010
7	VA Southeast Network	62,503	66,037	69,406	72,875	76,785	79,685	81,875	83,177	83,687	85,085	86,856	88,159	89,287	92,110	96,944
8	VA Sunshine Healthcare Network	139,462	140,354	142,031	144,571	147,011	147,494	147,246	146,500	145,689	145,143	144,819	144,251	142,790	143,279	147,487
9	VA Mid South Healthcare Network	51,892	53,653	55,954	58,318	61,055	62,038	62,750	63,301	62,931	63,081	64,240	64,370	64,500	64,934	67,360
10	VA Healthcare System of Ohio	56,881	56,995	57,911	58,232	58,295	58,291	58,047	57,066	55,968	54,983	53,910	52,540	51,746	51,660	52,781
11	Veterans In Partnership	83,559	84,324	85,554	85,570	86,062	85,090	83,875	81,847	79,207	77,442	76,617	75,183	73,833	73,646	75,317
12	VA Great Lakes Health Care System	69,806	70,008	70,421	70,322	69,975	68,824	67,600	65,730	64,136	62,675	62,017	61,055	59,640	59,119	60,244
15	VA Heartland Network	56,345	57,028	57,952	58,905	59,888	60,034	59,493	58,761	57,713	56,642	55,852	54,680	53,901	53,977	55,603
16	South Central VA Health Care Network	91,942	93,721	96,427	99,943	103,352	106,301	108,237	109,097	108,929	109,020	109,623	108,884	108,325	109,231	113,163
17	VA Heart of Texas Health Care Network	54,643	55,956	57,963	60,016	62,000	63,422	64,175	64,413	64,912	65,074	65,242	64,733	65,184	65,719	68,400
18	VA Southwest Health Care Network	55,543	55,931	57,909	60,128	61,956	63,684	63,998	64,047	64,729	65,818	65,841	66,467	66,453	67,019	68,832
19	Rocky Mountain Network	41,357	42,010	43,193	44,291	45,357	46,163	46,302	46,363	46,404	46,794	46,932	46,647	46,485	47,087	48,480
20	Northwest Network	67,530	67,204	66,435	66,706	68,287	69,378	69,833	69,761	69,376	69,897	70,927	71,214	71,853	73,706	77,182
21	Sierra Pacific Network	80,747	79,752	79,217	79,267	79,476	78,037	76,299	74,476	72,198	70,877	70,368	69,782	68,771	68,384	69,127
22	Desert Pacific Healthcare Network	89,097	88,952	89,208	89,259	88,930	87,434	85,463	83,022	81,026	79,106	77,741	75,957	74,002	73,830	75,205
23	VA Midwest Health Care Network	71,132	72,899	73,957	74,900	76,198	75,641	74,787	73,571	71,446	69,641	68,362	66,569	65,172	64,707	65,077

Note: Numbers from this table should be reported to the nearest 1,000. Numbers and projections are for September 30th of the applicable year.

Table 37. Veterans in the Population: Living Veterans, by Veteran Integrated Service Network, by Age Group, 2013–Projected 2043—*Continued*

(Number.)

Age group and VISN	VISN description	2028	2029	2030	2031	2032	2033	2034	2035	2036	2037	2038	2039	2040	2041	2042	2043
80 TO 84 YEARS	**Total**	1,988,666	2,013,941	1,958,330	1,741,853	1,547,571	1,378,174	1,263,186	1,213,474	1,207,730	1,199,452	1,201,108	1,195,968	1,181,598	1,165,370	1,153,219	1,145,960
1	VA New England Healthcare System	84,190	83,438	78,848	67,242	56,464	48,840	43,506	41,507	42,200	43,152	44,073	44,456	44,246	43,467	42,466	41,563
2	VA Healthcare Network Upstate New York	41,019	40,982	39,024	33,672	29,347	25,432	22,871	21,806	21,818	21,831	22,248	22,391	22,321	22,023	21,809	21,747
3	VA NY/NJ Veterans Healthcare Network	57,003	55,457	50,965	42,083	34,391	27,815	23,524	21,673	21,345	21,238	21,730	21,715	21,231	20,605	19,804	18,954
4	VA Healthcare - VISN 4	113,865	115,417	112,538	98,959	86,695	74,232	65,091	60,248	59,027	58,235	58,858	59,171	58,896	58,297	57,890	57,693
5	VA Capitol Health Care Network	49,513	49,787	48,268	43,511	39,077	35,359	33,349	32,979	33,464	33,878	34,405	34,721	34,746	34,627	34,300	34,081
6	VA Mid-Atlantic Health Care Network	124,115	126,920	124,979	111,741	99,228	91,390	86,617	85,735	87,124	88,929	89,951	90,808	90,747	90,608	90,347	90,735
7	VA Southeast Network	137,593	140,968	138,974	126,330	114,721	105,243	99,374	98,401	100,355	101,588	103,075	104,377	104,989	105,301	105,266	105,415
8	VA Sunshine Healthcare Network	155,578	154,623	146,571	127,553	111,616	98,955	91,443	90,176	91,749	93,841	95,523	96,690	96,756	96,065	94,611	93,109
9	VA Mid South Healthcare Network	95,684	98,419	97,822	89,006	79,927	72,502	67,798	64,964	64,328	63,707	63,679	63,605	63,269	63,037	63,272	63,525
10	VA Healthcare System of Ohio	76,415	77,861	76,177	67,859	59,412	51,629	46,319	43,624	42,967	42,524	42,706	42,442	42,062	41,349	40,815	40,467
11	Veterans In Partnership	111,633	112,802	109,849	98,171	86,484	74,354	66,182	61,437	59,689	58,400	58,550	58,150	57,346	56,778	56,354	56,436
12	VA Great Lakes Health Care System	80,985	83,291	81,091	71,412	62,745	53,451	46,336	42,637	41,483	40,276	40,360	40,041	39,265	38,445	37,959	37,687
15	VA Heartland Network	79,012	79,972	77,956	70,035	62,508	55,769	50,952	48,153	46,989	45,697	45,545	45,294	44,966	44,575	44,300	44,322
16	South Central VA Health Care Network	157,136	160,957	158,357	142,969	130,008	118,511	110,264	106,714	105,991	104,352	102,766	100,701	98,115	95,878	94,410	93,692
17	VA Heart of Texas Health Care Network	95,541	96,609	95,089	85,948	78,859	73,319	71,043	70,815	72,127	71,811	71,729	70,965	69,774	68,385	67,660	67,750
18	VA Southwest Health Care Network	89,163	90,839	87,425	78,585	70,833	63,333	57,778	56,018	55,352	54,237	54,433	54,168	53,163	52,165	51,651	51,111
19	Rocky Mountain Network	66,579	66,503	64,820	58,065	52,274	47,574	44,360	42,607	42,046	40,909	40,283	39,684	38,885	38,169	37,909	37,831
20	Northwest Network	106,529	108,362	106,548	96,131	86,325	78,024	72,226	69,622	68,935	67,737	65,944	64,229	62,174	60,438	59,719	59,366
21	Sierra Pacific Network	90,167	90,905	88,023	77,157	68,000	60,044	54,450	51,432	50,614	49,314	48,486	47,310	45,585	43,897	42,364	40,948
22	Desert Pacific Healthcare Network	88,393	88,278	83,940	72,768	64,174	57,219	52,072	50,028	49,945	49,651	48,901	47,577	46,060	44,515	43,267	42,025
23	VA Midwest Health Care Network	88,555	91,549	91,065	82,657	74,483	65,176	57,631	52,896	50,181	48,144	47,864	47,473	47,000	46,748	47,045	47,504
85 YEARS AND OVER	**Total**	1,539,797	1,585,583	1,639,948	1,802,851	1,940,026	2,022,643	2,059,908	2,041,246	1,983,953	1,923,830	1,845,304	1,780,639	1,730,961	1,693,600	1,661,760	1,628,793
1	VA New England Healthcare System	68,279	69,292	70,802	76,814	81,919	83,493	83,339	80,718	76,346	71,945	67,499	63,795	61,047	59,311	58,077	56,943
2	VA Healthcare Network Upstate New York	31,714	32,444	33,469	36,851	39,398	40,587	40,860	39,905	38,197	36,635	34,472	32,794	31,488	30,595	29,998	29,330
3	VA NY/NJ Veterans Healthcare Network	47,668	47,380	47,636	50,966	53,294	53,670	52,535	49,711	46,000	42,436	38,416	35,136	32,579	30,659	29,197	27,884
4	VA Healthcare - VISN 4	93,547	95,205	96,901	105,553	112,470	117,030	118,715	117,038	112,675	107,974	101,625	96,006	91,562	88,304	85,698	83,227
5	VA Capitol Health Care Network	35,937	37,084	38,175	41,714	45,021	46,957	47,643	46,952	45,744	44,605	43,049	41,960	41,225	40,907	40,760	40,466
6	VA Mid-Atlantic Health Care Network	89,315	93,100	97,669	110,113	121,168	127,376	130,928	131,287	129,018	126,124	123,319	121,304	120,363	119,682	119,536	119,208
7	VA Southeast Network	101,903	107,052	112,172	124,413	135,827	143,400	148,067	148,464	146,195	144,134	140,954	138,833	137,750	137,458	137,462	137,159
8	VA Sunshine Healthcare Network	149,786	151,705	154,493	165,660	173,444	177,498	177,436	172,416	165,527	158,448	151,440	145,763	141,666	139,024	137,338	135,685
9	VA Mid South Healthcare Network	69,652	72,229	75,799	84,516	92,840	98,091	101,061	102,152	100,803	98,915	96,068	93,913	92,158	90,639	89,243	87,916
10	VA Healthcare System of Ohio	54,613	56,522	58,446	64,776	70,904	74,735	76,526	75,926	73,711	71,227	67,667	64,729	62,285	60,509	59,089	57,578
11	Veterans In Partnership	77,325	80,724	84,738	94,007	102,403	108,120	110,483	110,109	107,158	103,556	97,846	93,014	89,233	86,297	83,796	81,159
12	VA Great Lakes Health Care System	61,377	62,433	64,128	70,564	75,986	79,703	81,647	80,697	77,738	74,752	70,210	66,248	63,003	60,530	58,430	56,375
15	VA Heartland Network	57,356	59,606	62,361	69,124	75,391	78,712	80,369	80,066	78,362	76,556	73,264	70,494	68,114	66,279	64,667	63,034
16	South Central VA Health Care Network	118,142	122,846	128,233	141,881	152,847	160,457	165,249	165,528	162,375	158,999	154,531	150,963	148,127	145,480	142,737	139,674
17	VA Heart of Texas Health Care Network	71,429	74,564	78,100	86,830	94,508	99,389	101,469	101,781	100,253	99,519	97,927	97,016	96,720	96,550	96,184	95,561
18	VA Southwest Health Care Network	71,173	73,710	77,271	84,800	91,194	95,234	97,601	96,703	94,682	92,607	89,061	86,085	83,934	82,209	80,532	79,017
19	Rocky Mountain Network	49,846	51,984	53,993	59,702	64,623	67,086	67,992	67,537	66,079	64,770	62,533	60,493	58,821	57,561	56,295	54,885
20	Northwest Network	79,754	83,377	86,437	95,386	103,000	108,467	111,365	110,986	108,656	105,826	102,722	99,903	97,442	95,415	93,148	90,567
21	Sierra Pacific Network	69,678	70,674	72,198	79,039	84,322	87,096	87,949	86,578	83,276	80,042	76,026	72,597	69,731	67,386	65,151	62,913
22	Desert Pacific Healthcare Network	75,290	75,867	77,026	82,775	85,738	87,317	87,488	85,058	81,057	76,928	73,233	70,052	67,480	65,457	63,492	61,647
23	VA Midwest Health Care Network	66,011	67,785	69,900	77,368	83,730	88,225	91,185	91,635	90,102	87,832	83,442	79,540	76,230	73,349	70,930	68,565

Table 38. Summary of Veteran-Related Expenditures, by State, FY2014

(Number; expenditures in thousands of dollars.)

State	Veteran population[1]	Total expenditure	Compensation and pension	Construction	Education and vocational rehabilitation/ employment	Loan guaranty[2]	General operating expenses	Insurance and indemnities	Medical care	Unique patients[3]
Totals	21,894,286	161,228,849	75,265,436	1,535,617	13,680,866	2,046,206	7,601,823	1,674,631	59,424,269	5,829,315
Alabama	413,618	3,191,317	1,875,091	4,992	225,325	0	35,140	29,054	1,021,715	110,616
Alaska	73,397	552,280	244,437	165	74,731	0	6,154	3,855	222,938	18,182
Arizona	532,206	3,607,036	1,666,170	15,452	410,041	0	107,135	33,149	1,375,088	143,785
Arkansas	249,274	2,143,834	1,055,813	7,143	95,186	0	29,631	15,816	940,246	86,718
California	1,851,470	14,318,281	6,376,052	153,525	1,848,364	0	197,940	157,549	5,584,851	460,954
Colorado	413,271	3,073,039	1,447,416	221,644	379,047	0	61,079	32,291	931,562	95,382
Connecticut	213,420	1,171,099	432,271	403	106,709	0	14,238	24,166	593,312	51,073
Delaware	78,099	398,842	199,732	693	38,126	0	3,792	5,711	150,788	15,000
District of Columbia	29,825	2,703,410	90,387	257,897	35,086	0	2,091,541	3,094	225,406	8,598
Florida	1,583,697	11,688,201	5,618,726	80,833	1,043,675	0	149,942	132,732	4,662,293	493,890
Georgia	752,882	5,398,211	3,004,840	1,056	528,777	0	106,881	48,836	1,707,821	189,127
Hawaii	121,007	842,115	388,532	573	167,447	0	16,593	14,822	254,149	25,041
Idaho	132,395	827,990	401,211	995	58,612	0	8,180	7,587	351,404	41,266
Illinois	721,575	4,248,086	1,680,632	17,019	349,069	0	49,986	62,953	2,088,426	182,101
Indiana	476,283	2,667,905	1,239,688	1,549	165,293	0	50,029	24,944	1,186,402	129,308
Iowa	231,655	1,339,350	592,671	379	78,530	0	11,156	18,393	638,221	72,367
Kansas	221,206	1,358,491	632,709	270	113,362	0	25,295	16,883	569,972	58,490
Kentucky	330,599	2,425,358	1,255,748	10,245	155,455	0	40,024	18,858	945,028	101,840
Louisiana	330,145	2,540,466	1,211,754	260,204	146,468	0	26,158	20,187	875,694	88,621
Maine	127,234	959,396	541,754	126	45,924	0	18,616	8,733	344,244	39,859
Maryland	437,762	2,688,111	1,228,854	5,299	364,342	0	23,589	38,630	1,027,397	82,383
Massachusetts	379,772	2,593,152	1,159,009	5,712	209,261	0	29,524	43,491	1,146,155	83,926
Michigan	658,469	3,753,563	1,983,451	17,517	232,514	0	52,983	46,116	1,420,982	150,215
Minnesota	369,149	2,564,646	1,146,384	16,225	151,587	0	83,322	30,815	1,136,313	115,827
Mississippi	220,389	1,657,042	776,679	36,478	100,467	0	30,094	14,544	698,780	69,754
Missouri	494,346	3,440,223	1,651,755	79,828	209,426	0	154,455	32,728	1,312,031	139,929
Montana	99,646	731,755	335,093	250	42,166	0	8,088	7,950	338,208	35,966
Nebraska	143,375	1,136,146	557,741	9,147	70,254	0	36,827	13,012	449,167	47,352
Nevada	228,027	1,780,651	776,443	50,831	108,908	0	12,870	13,406	818,193	69,464
New Hampshire	113,660	674,052	311,022	3,744	58,392	0	6,000	8,979	285,915	28,969
New Jersey	428,396	2,115,578	1,047,058	555	214,108	0	18,716	51,045	784,096	77,128
New Mexico	171,528	1,450,002	794,229	11,767	79,524	0	12,854	11,087	540,540	51,702
New York	892,221	6,123,810	2,396,837	30,504	548,240	0	124,442	92,821	2,930,966	230,159
North Carolina	775,020	5,949,873	3,328,183	8,405	478,939	0	93,726	53,403	1,987,216	214,278
North Dakota	57,395	367,003	171,165	3,970	25,528	0	6,508	4,156	155,677	18,988
Ohio	866,481	7,504,281	2,235,023	21,382	324,969	0	2,549,868	56,928	2,316,111	230,266
Oklahoma	337,571	2,934,748	1,823,983	4,905	155,650	0	121,169	20,467	808,574	92,674
Oregon	331,632	2,542,834	1,282,449	19,124	142,348	0	35,597	23,413	1,039,903	99,502
Pennsylvania	939,069	5,260,391	2,432,807	19,992	376,417	0	158,371	79,167	2,193,637	233,551
Rhode Island	71,966	529,503	232,604	3,355	40,498	0	21,115	6,221	225,710	19,954
South Carolina	417,554	3,289,095	1,868,959	10,942	267,185	0	65,216	31,415	1,045,378	127,365
South Dakota	72,030	619,864	238,175	3,531	31,787	0	11,593	6,103	328,675	29,827
Tennessee	506,340	3,758,888	1,995,305	6,028	269,071	0	63,217	32,085	1,393,181	140,625
Texas	1,680,418	15,394,005	7,282,260	28,798	1,357,830	2,046,206	223,667	110,141	4,345,103	446,303
Utah	151,719	1,029,344	433,073	2,156	120,457	0	56,947	11,521	405,189	35,142
Vermont	48,602	295,362	135,803	1,560	20,321	0	3,796	3,155	130,727	14,919
Virginia	781,388	5,251,707	2,729,280	21,218	931,880	0	63,300	62,360	1,443,669	148,585
Washington	603,623	3,811,479	2,070,141	33,346	392,247	0	71,074	41,739	1,202,932	124,006
West Virginia	167,355	1,826,167	722,958	9,927	49,784	0	318,791	8,505	716,202	59,261
Wisconsin	413,723	2,665,107	1,142,091	11,984	143,544	0	70,816	33,242	1,263,430	120,515
Wyoming	49,708	383,891	152,461	4,144	17,544	0	1,623	2,710	205,410	18,730
Puerto Rico	93,240	1,563,237	816,544	17,830	65,064	0	22,157	2,832	638,810	57,248
Guam	9,453	88,631	51,981	0	15,389	0	0	832	20,430	2,584

[1]Veteran population estimates, as of September 30, 2014, are produced by the VA Office of the Actuary (VetPop 2014).

[2]Prior to FY 08, "Loan Guaranty" expenditures were included in the Education & Vocational Rehabilitation and Employment (E&VRE) programs. Currently, all "Loan Guaranty" expenditures are attributed to Travis County, TX, where all Loan Guaranty payments are processed. VA will continue to improve data collection for future GDX reports to better distribute loan expenditures at the state, county and congressional district levels.

[3]Unique patients are patients who received treatment at a VA health care facility. Data are provided by the Allocation Resource Center (ARC).

Table 39. Summary of Veteran-Related Expenditures, by State, FY2013

(Number; expenditures in thousands of dollars.)

State	Veteran population[1]	Total expenditure	Compensation and pension	Construction	Education and vocational rehabilitation/ employment	Loan guaranty[2]	General operating expenses	Insurance and indemnities	Medical care	Unique patients[3]
Totals	21,882,153	142,822,345	63,574,737	1,330,053	11,949,205	1,385,063	6,889,908	1,699,587	55,993,792	5,690,384
Alabama	414,963	2,824,088	1,580,861	1,922	189,414	0	33,885	29,857	988,150	108,175
Alaska	74,671	501,604	211,260	616	61,850	0	6,686	3,441	217,751	17,304
Arizona	527,400	3,220,905	1,409,346	21,201	343,820	0	108,885	36,145	1,301,507	137,362
Arkansas	250,095	1,946,615	924,671	7,938	79,063	0	31,331	13,484	890,127	86,763
California	1,795,455	12,707,536	5,397,860	145,008	1,599,760	0	192,392	162,956	5,209,559	444,432
Colorado	390,824	2,594,677	1,212,143	112,614	324,347	0	62,854	32,483	850,235	90,822
Connecticut	207,759	1,078,567	365,638	8,332	96,416	0	13,794	24,195	570,192	51,360
Delaware	78,016	362,617	169,963	859	34,331	0	3,895	5,595	147,974	14,676
District of Columbia	31,166	2,295,599	78,699	153,310	31,054	0	1,825,604	2,785	204,146	8,800
Florida	1,520,563	10,430,774	4,728,273	131,870	892,555	0	146,088	139,645	4,392,344	479,193
Georgia	774,464	4,670,709	2,482,164	3,359	453,034	0	109,242	48,822	1,574,087	179,821
Hawaii	116,947	754,680	337,919	1,690	142,729	0	16,013	13,109	243,220	23,825
Idaho	138,108	746,018	334,504	11,690	51,513	0	7,807	8,006	332,499	39,928
Illinois	744,710	3,854,717	1,450,236	18,558	311,330	0	51,835	65,139	1,957,618	180,384
Indiana	490,380	2,477,767	1,092,855	8,783	150,033	0	48,931	27,941	1,149,224	128,499
Iowa	233,815	1,192,889	505,601	79	74,079	0	10,585	18,891	583,653	72,191
Kansas	223,708	1,237,985	529,023	743	103,950	0	27,158	17,340	559,771	58,097
Kentucky	339,334	2,229,580	1,087,772	7,129	139,199	0	37,983	18,871	938,626	101,096
Louisiana	315,342	2,202,388	1,016,206	202,777	120,767	0	26,501	19,941	816,195	86,890
Maine	127,694	873,125	467,398	7	42,577	0	18,277	9,459	335,408	39,358
Maryland	443,076	2,453,557	1,047,226	7,521	333,943	0	24,725	42,512	997,630	82,183
Massachusetts	374,809	2,371,613	985,894	20,552	192,975	0	32,546	41,235	1,098,412	84,345
Michigan	660,773	3,361,961	1,675,388	6,185	208,565	0	51,291	43,961	1,376,571	146,804
Minnesota	360,754	2,336,965	986,609	15,600	133,629	0	82,027	33,370	1,085,731	113,577
Mississippi	225,469	1,470,950	666,715	12,230	88,010	0	29,313	13,394	661,288	69,676
Missouri	497,874	3,025,845	1,386,280	34,423	189,473	0	146,126	32,796	1,236,747	137,008
Montana	101,597	646,509	290,869	8	38,237	0	7,765	7,072	302,558	35,189
Nebraska	138,773	1,023,761	487,975	9,837	63,597	0	36,470	12,589	413,294	47,275
Nevada	225,933	1,573,091	641,969	19,641	95,562	0	13,505	14,516	787,899	65,443
New Hampshire	110,778	613,805	268,735	1,282	50,861	0	6,142	8,473	278,312	28,604
New Jersey	425,094	1,927,021	906,744	6,578	196,113	0	15,868	51,994	749,724	77,179
New Mexico	170,699	1,312,943	686,222	26,571	67,315	0	12,586	12,750	507,499	49,981
New York	885,796	5,621,911	2,063,566	17,521	493,102	0	120,558	94,116	2,833,048	231,161
North Carolina	769,384	5,067,823	2,712,319	21,238	399,186	0	91,538	53,714	1,789,827	205,006
North Dakota	56,213	334,755	149,596	2,623	22,770	0	6,479	3,770	149,518	18,526
Ohio	877,894	6,643,911	1,837,567	34,987	296,446	0	2,202,389	59,096	2,213,426	223,944
Oklahoma	340,395	2,568,390	1,544,376	5,320	131,030	0	121,588	19,958	746,118	90,731
Oregon	322,355	2,283,129	1,100,287	36,702	128,169	0	35,298	23,228	959,445	96,190
Pennsylvania	953,644	4,782,351	2,029,589	49,407	359,065	0	158,258	82,386	2,103,647	232,054
Rhode Island	69,206	474,338	193,988	2,867	35,525	0	19,476	5,928	216,555	20,132
South Carolina	420,968	2,876,324	1,557,784	2,557	223,348	0	63,246	28,310	1,001,079	123,070
South Dakota	75,687	564,489	209,347	1,976	30,364	0	10,392	5,461	306,949	29,744
Tennessee	521,267	3,320,710	1,652,616	6,443	236,754	0	63,014	33,644	1,328,239	135,582
Texas	1,667,740	12,943,393	6,091,910	30,026	1,118,114	1,385,063	220,626	110,750	3,986,903	434,255
Utah	150,771	887,516	350,923	6,163	85,974	0	53,145	10,033	381,279	34,062
Vermont	48,812	273,966	118,286	1,105	20,296	0	3,992	3,340	126,949	14,925
Virginia	840,398	4,653,545	2,291,200	22,761	874,229	0	61,129	60,779	1,343,447	142,605
Washington	602,272	3,384,110	1,788,537	55,674	343,793	0	67,749	41,915	1,086,440	118,461
West Virginia	173,389	1,601,256	625,689	6,525	44,341	0	261,560	9,871	653,270	58,733
Wisconsin	409,419	2,421,849	972,511	12,224	133,679	0	69,991	34,398	1,199,045	118,371
Wyoming	56,518	343,611	127,557	7,264	15,751	0	1,456	3,131	188,453	18,583
Puerto Rico	99,928	1,387,777	697,879	7,756	46,541	0	19,912	2,496	613,193	58,009
Guam	9,055	66,330	46,193	0	10,629	0	0	495	9,012	0

[1]Veteran population estimates, as of September 30, 2013, are produced by the VA Office of the Actuary (VetPop 2011).
[2]Prior to FY 08, "Loan Guaranty" expenditures were included in the Education & Vocational Rehabilitation and Employment (E&VRE) programs. Currently, all "Loan Guaranty" expenditures are attributed to Travis County, TX, where all Loan Guaranty payments are processed. VA will continue to improve data collection for future GDX reports to better distribute loan expenditures at the state, county and congressional district levels.
[3]Unique patients are patients who received treatment at a VA health care facility. Data are provided by the Allocation Resource Center (ARC).

Table 40. Summary of Veteran-Related Expenditures, by State, FY2010

(Number; expenditures in thousands of dollars.)

State	Veteran population[1]	Total expenditure	Compensation and pension	Construction	Education and vocational rehabilitation/ employment	Loan guaranty[2]	General operating expenses	Insurance and indemnities	Medical care	Unique patients[3]
Totals	22,568,578	108,634,691	47,784,622	1,618,367	8,260,115	804,064	6,101,273	1,694,243	42,372,007	5,316,616
Alabama	405,624	2,171,215	1,181,450	15,927	130,271	0	36,119	27,450	779,999	101,842
Alaska	77,025	359,342	167,394	13,678	35,065	0	6,550	3,183	133,472	15,324
Arizona	556,729	2,397,241	1,054,437	7,957	229,540	0	98,142	36,992	970,173	125,972
Arkansas	254,664	1,616,787	761,123	30,269	60,854	0	44,347	14,031	706,162	85,624
California	1,971,959	9,124,852	3,804,601	136,604	991,205	0	190,350	170,694	3,831,398	405,918
Colorado	421,342	1,828,589	904,509	23,454	219,202	0	69,751	30,331	581,342	78,515
Connecticut	229,734	829,125	278,863	2,191	85,897	0	14,254	24,712	423,209	50,193
Delaware	78,247	280,266	128,984	5,650	22,850	0	4,609	4,749	113,424	13,896
District of Columbia	37,268	1,940,241	64,135	133,978	17,653	0	1,538,076	3,200	183,198	9,413
Florida	1,650,876	8,041,289	3,668,460	217,586	600,434	0	150,590	140,465	3,263,755	448,858
Georgia	773,858	3,481,761	1,722,943	15,944	372,060	0	126,946	49,477	1,194,391	158,032
Hawaii	116,166	537,128	243,813	8,467	82,546	0	14,652	13,650	174,000	20,571
Idaho	136,625	576,366	275,862	1,199	37,357	0	9,019	8,709	244,221	35,883
Illinois	782,747	2,985,041	1,039,465	24,889	250,886	0	87,127	65,341	1,517,333	171,289
Indiana	491,605	1,814,121	777,648	10,277	102,092	0	33,056	26,815	864,233	122,335
Iowa	234,552	891,159	378,657	777	48,308	0	11,165	18,573	433,679	69,128
Kansas	225,091	937,195	393,705	7,041	66,962	0	26,950	16,698	425,839	57,075
Kentucky	335,670	1,761,192	886,451	3,220	91,568	0	28,308	21,376	730,268	97,776
Louisiana	304,889	1,585,152	768,087	25,292	86,678	0	28,846	21,346	654,903	83,013
Maine	138,551	743,795	410,056	9,871	39,812	0	18,292	9,282	256,482	38,019
Maryland	471,238	1,784,295	754,755	8,238	205,103	0	35,109	38,788	742,301	76,033
Massachusetts	393,722	1,821,408	775,842	6,970	115,127	0	32,024	42,882	848,563	75,413
Michigan	703,970	2,400,007	1,136,035	25,199	138,822	0	52,016	44,508	1,003,427	133,196
Minnesota	381,309	1,832,705	818,980	7,943	120,999	0	81,536	32,052	771,196	106,039
Mississippi	205,644	1,238,167	502,046	103,067	60,242	0	29,105	15,302	528,405	68,008
Missouri	505,916	2,288,658	1,005,861	23,743	121,905	0	127,581	32,377	977,191	130,997
Montana	102,015	505,710	255,238	5,134	26,064	0	8,196	6,914	204,163	31,832
Nebraska	145,237	861,137	433,235	16,117	47,647	0	28,107	11,218	324,812	44,430
Nevada	243,867	1,264,737	447,347	200,313	62,506	0	14,542	12,763	527,266	57,869
New Hampshire	127,964	492,834	212,753	216	40,149	0	9,161	8,378	222,176	26,569
New Jersey	443,161	1,555,339	733,454	2,262	152,499	0	19,200	49,776	598,149	77,825
New Mexico	174,687	1,057,365	574,985	2,494	55,579	0	12,881	12,511	398,914	46,962
New York	950,417	4,537,260	1,599,625	41,345	370,899	0	138,300	95,470	2,291,622	230,272
North Carolina	765,942	3,769,312	2,000,475	20,887	286,043	0	87,667	49,034	1,325,207	181,529
North Dakota	56,310	251,467	122,247	624	16,561	0	6,770	3,620	101,645	17,990
Ohio	890,340	5,252,743	1,384,310	83,268	211,169	0	1,752,983	62,179	1,758,834	209,055
Oklahoma	324,714	2,073,912	1,230,737	3,125	104,659	0	109,894	20,938	604,559	85,828
Oregon	333,752	1,701,878	844,587	17,621	87,903	0	39,073	23,257	689,436	87,955
Pennsylvania	964,132	3,824,045	1,525,466	100,992	240,643	0	179,177	77,363	1,700,404	237,183
Rhode Island	71,216	361,653	155,147	8,841	19,526	0	12,047	6,427	159,665	19,655
South Carolina	406,729	2,093,514	1,086,181	14,092	160,208	0	51,111	27,575	754,347	110,090
South Dakota	71,762	455,333	179,340	928	18,373	0	10,244	4,994	241,454	29,291
Tennessee	495,766	2,466,606	1,212,897	10,659	143,209	0	64,400	30,682	1,004,758	124,733
Texas	1,693,791	9,402,572	4,460,761	62,975	778,237	804,064	206,882	107,169	2,982,483	396,299
Utah	153,623	675,371	262,497	5,321	54,801	0	48,922	12,931	290,899	31,151
Vermont	52,082	239,217	96,158	6,837	28,810	0	5,155	3,799	98,458	14,312
Virginia	822,312	3,403,757	1,681,764	14,891	559,581	0	112,950	61,590	972,982	126,889
Washington	632,210	2,527,972	1,391,229	33,779	232,021	0	52,932	42,313	775,698	103,232
West Virginia	167,182	1,306,463	506,560	44,885	77,151	0	152,118	9,658	516,090	58,311
Wisconsin	417,654	1,876,977	808,775	30,910	105,741	0	57,209	33,791	840,550	112,788
Wyoming	55,850	262,678	102,431	635	12,106	0	3,144	2,701	141,661	17,855
Puerto Rico	112,699	1,107,564	543,031	19,786	30,360	0	23,685	3,266	487,436	58,349
Guam	8,144	40,177	29,232	0	4,230	0	0	943	5,773	

[1]Veteran population estimates, as of September 30, 2010, are produced by the VA Office of the Actuary (VetPop 2007).
[2]Prior to FY 08, "Loan Guaranty" expenditures were included in the Education & Vocational Rehabilitation and Employment (E&VRE) programs. Currently, all "Loan Guaranty" expenditures are attributed to Travis County, TX, where all Loan Guaranty payments are processed. VA will continue to improve data collection for future GDX reports to better distribute loan expenditures at the state, county and congressional district levels.
[3]Unique patients are patients who received treatment at a VA health care facility. Data are provided by the Allocation Resource Center (ARC).

Table 41. Summary of Veteran-Related Expenditures, by State, FY2005

(Number; expenditures in thousands of dollars.)

State	Veteran population[1]	Total expenditure	Compensation and pension	Education and vocational rehabilitation	Insurance and indemnities	Construction	Medical and general operating expenses
Totals	24,256,800	70,248,954	32,068,270	3,154,748	1,809,417	303,192	32,913,328
Alabama	421,992	1,374,855	781,564	57,566	24,672	2,030	509,023
Alaska	66,537	229,954	112,403	10,577	2,481	1,662	102,831
Arizona	552,963	1,519,913	741,741	85,494	41,157	7,668	643,853
Arkansas	265,532	1,097,049	521,422	30,353	15,499	3,175	526,600
California	2,257,130	5,939,724	2,664,232	304,138	186,061	28,303	2,756,990
Colorado	424,029	1,618,301	557,998	77,084	29,072	7,868	946,279
Connecticut	260,388	601,529	203,599	42,702	28,786	2,400	324,042
Delaware	79,915	196,068	81,726	6,945	5,619	1,997	99,781
District of Columbia	36,056	1,765,921	93,351	15,330	3,302	4,626	1,649,312
Florida	1,768,359	5,156,967	2,547,217	217,636	166,831	19,317	2,205,966
Georgia	758,963	2,049,475	1,080,278	153,708	40,966	14,488	760,034
Hawaii	104,842	324,966	163,804	19,909	15,691	669	124,893
Idaho	132,554	311,236	181,769	16,010	7,999	1,431	104,027
Illinois	874,387	1,892,843	675,043	92,901	74,774	28,889	1,021,236
Indiana	542,505	927,107	464,767	37,635	27,161	735	396,809
Iowa	260,406	636,337	245,947	19,847	22,241	2,565	345,738
Kansas	241,958	658,484	273,066	28,242	17,898	1,930	337,348
Kentucky	355,576	1,008,454	556,571	40,220	17,876	4,350	389,437
Louisiana	361,757	1,258,103	618,578	48,870	23,480	2,288	564,887
Maine	141,416	502,581	294,034	25,408	9,796	2,064	171,278
Maryland	478,543	1,006,511	503,180	60,010	38,276	3,143	401,902
Massachusetts	476,363	1,411,605	606,065	45,021	48,065	4,609	707,845
Michigan	820,485	1,568,758	713,938	60,713	49,199	8,797	736,111
Minnesota	418,386	1,142,723	501,299	38,041	37,363	5,390	560,630
Mississippi	238,279	918,223	392,591	23,899	12,931	2,874	485,929
Missouri	546,416	1,684,861	637,033	55,633	34,509	3,321	954,364
Montana	101,438	285,761	157,711	11,246	7,318	335	109,151
Nebraska	156,667	543,405	260,924	20,985	13,454	2,043	245,998
Nevada	244,205	681,865	299,197	24,943	12,587	7,089	338,050
New Hampshire	129,281	273,725	156,451	15,714	9,549	612	91,399
New Jersey	563,953	1,027,690	525,614	59,300	62,025	2,917	377,834
New Mexico	178,070	709,498	407,879	30,885	13,838	2,073	254,822
New York	1,132,703	3,365,992	1,211,440	151,405	117,364	15,456	1,870,328
North Carolina	761,894	2,251,938	1,264,959	126,828	47,045	3,774	809,331
North Dakota	54,208	195,454	80,266	8,756	4,615	2,422	99,396
Ohio	1,032,095	2,795,896	944,206	86,172	66,439	10,075	1,689,005
Oklahoma	351,072	1,311,128	800,396	64,030	20,572	5,368	420,762
Oregon	362,104	1,143,392	541,793	47,154	23,303	10,515	520,627
Pennsylvania	1,117,004	2,640,348	1,099,113	73,050	93,452	9,491	1,365,242
Rhode Island	88,735	280,626	123,063	6,551	7,530	745	142,737
South Carolina	411,987	1,167,372	636,454	59,358	25,423	3,908	442,228
South Dakota	72,196	365,561	123,022	11,223	5,910	164	225,242
Tennessee	536,574	1,745,736	776,018	58,189	27,342	6,927	877,259
Texas	1,667,370	5,380,225	2,840,910	294,748	104,797	15,795	2,123,974
Utah	148,958	421,822	161,144	20,608	11,306	203	228,561
Vermont	56,743	199,704	69,051	18,430	4,233	85	107,905
Virginia	744,459	1,850,101	1,037,063	136,262	53,033	4,438	619,305
Washington	625,408	1,683,479	958,516	91,717	40,113	15,272	577,861
West Virginia	185,221	893,081	347,552	62,266	10,088	1,239	471,936
Wisconsin	466,054	1,193,763	522,151	36,832	38,839	11,261	584,682
Wyoming	54,341	191,384	64,805	5,515	3,388	1,853	115,823
Puerto Rico	128,322	847,460	445,352	18,689	4,148	2,543	376,727

[1]Veteran population estimated as of September 30, 2005. Data from Office of the Actuary, VA. Data is unrounded.

Table 42. Disability Compensation and Patient Expenditures, FY2000–FY2013

(Dollars; number; percent.)

Fiscal year	Disability compensation					VA healthcare					
	Expenditures	Recipients	Average expenditure per recepient	% Expenditure change from previous year	% Change in recipients from previous year	Patient expenditures	Veteran patients	Nonveteran patients	Average expenditure per patient	% Expenditure change from previous year	% Change in patients from previous year
2000	$14,773,382,340	2,308,186	$6,400	X	X	$16,806,577,327	3,427,925	312,810	$4,493	X	X
2001	$15,806,234,628	2,321,103	$6,810	6.99%	0.56%	$18,632,727,019	3,843,832	305,874	$4,490	10.87%	10.93%
2002	$17,589,232,812	2,398,287	$7,334	11.28%	3.33%	$19,935,388,850	4,246,084	298,269	$4,387	6.99%	9.51%
2003	$19,535,925,552	2,485,229	$7,861	11.07%	3.63%	$21,967,982,313	4,505,433	301,438	$4,570	10.20%	5.78%
2004	$20,591,728,748	2,555,696	$8,057	5.40%	2.84%	$25,198,103,663	4,677,720	301,431	$5,061	14.70%	3.58%
2005	$23,542,487,166	2,636,979	$8,928	14.33%	3.18%	$27,565,765,198	4,806,345	445,322	$5,249	9.40%	5.47%
2006	$25,622,853,876	2,725,824	$9,400	8.84%	3.37%	$28,077,033,706	4,900,800	288,025	$5,411	1.85%	-1.20%
2007	$27,969,259,960	2,844,178	$9,834	9.16%	4.34%	$29,036,286,719	4,950,501	283,225	$5,548	3.42%	0.87%
2008	$30,274,152,913	2,952,285	$10,254	8.24%	3.80%	$33,962,036,284	4,999,106	300,539	$6,408	16.96%	1.26%
2009	$34,102,951,214	3,069,652	$11,110	12.65%	3.98%	$39,348,043,535	5,139,285	308,778	$7,222	15.86%	2.80%
2010	$36,485,965,838	3,210,261	$11,365	6.99%	4.58%	$40,586,657,907	5,351,873	286,731	$7,198	3.15%	3.50%
2011	$39,373,549,773	3,354,741	$11,737	7.91%	4.50%	$42,265,215,266	5,499,498	295,667	$7,293	4.14%	2.78%
2012	$44,358,737,799	3,536,802	$12,542	12.66%	5.43%	$43,028,963,249	5,598,829	297,680	$7,297	1.81%	1.75%
2013	$49,151,877,576	3,743,259	$13,131	10.81%	5.84%	$44,826,036,151	5,720,614	296,487	$7,450	4.18%	2.05%

Note: "Patients" do not include: Veterans who have visits with the Readjustment Counceling Service ONLY; state nursing home patients; and CHAMPVA (nonveteran) patients; nor the associated cost.
X = Not applicable/not available.

Table 43. Number of Veteran Patients, by Healthcare Priority Group, FY2000–FY2014

(Number.)

Fiscal year	1	2	3	4	5	6	7A	7C	8A	8B	8C	8D	8E	8G	Non-enrolled veterans	Nonveterans
2000	441,491	264,535	434,690	145,848	1,397,736	48,440	43,626	530,890	X	X	X	X	X	X	120,669	312,810
2001	482,448	277,036	478,908	162,026	1,512,410	42,791	45,183	782,539	X	X	X	X	X	X	60,491	305,874
2002	539,792	292,323	500,686	156,346	1,542,886	45,304	44,838	1,030,202	X	X	X	X	X	X	93,707	298,269
2003	610,692	306,640	520,264	170,869	1,542,874	53,924	4,324	106,478	43,387	X	1,068,497	X	945	10,063	66,476	301,438
2004	662,952	313,622	527,330	175,953	1,596,958	70,967	4,604	138,563	41,550	X	1,035,910	X	1,617	16,907	90,787	301,431
2005	720,975	326,321	543,246	178,895	1,592,261	99,463	5,641	170,328	40,309	X	1,033,437	X	2,021	14,268	79,180	445,322
2006	768,537	342,023	568,740	177,563	1,575,645	134,425	5,948	162,130	45,519	X	1,104,720	X	2,464	13,086	X	288,025
2007	820,691	358,410	591,165	181,776	1,511,127	156,048	5,966	150,091	47,420	X	1,097,428	X	3,333	27,046	X	283,225
2008	888,470	365,212	585,032	185,997	1,438,971	199,882	5,050	125,902	51,088	X	1,123,232	X	3,355	26,915	X	300,539
2009	981,910	401,033	640,978	187,493	1,410,118	219,796	5,249	117,849	50,536	559	1,085,075	9,223	3,937	25,529	X	308,778
2010	1,071,400	425,937	677,648	189,428	1,447,713	244,504	5,987	135,994	51,609	240	1,073,697	5,889	4,007	17,820	X	286,731
2011	1,179,333	442,665	687,284	191,177	1,440,438	266,374	6,321	146,632	50,799	1,179	1,034,160	27,598	4,363	21,175	X	295,667
2012	1,307,750	456,050	697,548	191,521	1,417,207	272,043	5,574	132,242	50,315	1,487	1,008,326	35,071	4,319	19,376	X	297,680
2013	1,451,707	473,841	721,576	192,241	1,360,567	275,799	6,389	143,898	50,283	1,818	973,357	43,053	4,708	21,377	X	296,487
2014	1,599,196	489,273	741,839	191,385	1,315,571	276,375	7,575	167,290	49,902	2,342	934,860	55,903	4,924	21,255	X	305,411

Note: "Patients" does not include: Veterans who have visits with the Readjustment Counseling Service ONLY; state nursing home patients; and CHAMPVA (nonveteran) patients; nor the associated costs.
X = Not applicable/not available.
See Appendix A for priority group definitions.

Table 44. Average Expenditures[1] Per Patient, by Healthcare Priority Group, FY2000–FY2014

(Dollars.)

Fiscal year	1	2	3	4	5	6	7A	7C	8A	8B	8C	8D	8E	8G	Non-enrolled veterans	Nonveterans
2000	8,441	4,126	3,640	19,448	4,358	2,342	2,108	1,822	X	X	X	X	X	X	1,210	511
2001	8,347	4,146	3,723	18,249	4,471	2,223	2,259	1,870	X	X	X	X	X	X	1,904	587
2002	8,719	3,986	3,608	17,134	4,583	2,163	2,324	1,890	X	X	X	X	X	X	1,929	595
2003	9,058	3,980	3,968	17,083	4,861	2,251	3,793	2,922	2,124	X	1,837	X	1,124	1,074	2,333	674
2004	10,017	4,511	4,130	17,286	5,310	2,313	4,474	3,221	2,468	X	2,143	X	795	1,153	2,538	791
2005	10,228	4,559	4,215	17,400	5,516	2,280	4,702	3,405	2,645	X	2,370	X	870	874	2,710	1,924
2006	10,515	4,678	4,253	17,135	5,669	2,418	4,919	3,644	2,881	X	2,389	X	980	1,266	X	927
2007	10,428	4,671	4,300	17,216	5,921	2,394	4,725	3,855	2,912	X	2,516	X	1,029	1,778	X	896
2008	11,793	5,451	5,046	19,313	6,942	2,725	6,134	4,758	3,320	X	2,887	X	1,205	2,037	X	1,041
2009	12,887	5,853	5,642	21,409	8,057	3,008	6,222	5,224	3,708	3,289	3,261	2,167	1,107	1,967	X	1,165
2010	12,483	5,756	5,418	21,131	8,048	2,909	6,191	5,169	3,528	2,989	3,177	3,187	918	1,286	X	1,202
2011	12,292	5,777	5,457	21,309	8,161	2,961	6,049	5,215	3,555	3,579	3,263	3,046	857	1,313	X	1,234
2012	11,839	5,683	5,409	21,110	8,126	2,960	6,139	5,438	3,658	3,571	3,326	3,024	869	1,307	X	1,295
2013	11,598	5,734	5,546	21,597	8,386	2,983	5,921	5,409	3,786	2,974	3,419	3,159	818	1,324	X	1,276
2014	11,702	5,945	5,773	22,109	8,787	3,104	5,980	5,351	4,032	3,155	3,720	3,521	767	1,111	X	1,068

X = Not applicable/not available.
[1]Average expenditures are calculated as the total expenditures for each Priority Group divided by the number of patients. VHA September 2014 data accessed on 06/18/15.
See Appendix A for priority group definitions.

Table 45. Selected Veterans Health Administration Characteristics, FY2002–FY2013

(Numbers in millions, except where noted.)

Fiscal year	Total enrollees[1]	Outpatient visits[2]	Inpatient admissions (in thousands)
2002	6.8	46.5	564.7
2003	7.1	49.8	567.3
2004	7.3	54.0	589.8
2005	7.7	57.5	585.8
2006	7.9	59.1	568.9
2007	7.8	62.3	589.0
2008	7.8	67.7	641.4
2009	8.1	74.9	662.0
2010	8.3	80.2	682.3
2011	8.6	79.8	692.1
2012	8.8	83.6	703.5
2013	8.9	86.4	694.7

[1]Includes non-enrolled veteran patients.
[2]Includes fee visits.

Table 46. Summary of Veterans Benefits, FY2000–FY2012

(Number; percent.)

Fiscal year	Disability compensation recipients (DCR)	% change in DCR from previous year	Disability pension recipients (DPR)	% change in DPR from previous year	Education beneficiaries (EB)	% change in EB from previous year	Home loans guaranteed (HLG) during fiscal year	% change in HLG from previous year	Life insurance policies[1] (LIP)	% change in LIP from previous year	Vocational rehabilitation and employment (VR&E) participants	% change in VR&E from previous year
2000	2,308,186	X	364,220	X	397,589	X	199,160	X	2,206,834	X	50,281	X
2001	2,321,103	0.56	348,052	-4.44	420,651	5.80	250,009	25.53	2,079,163	-5.79	52,402	4.22
2002	2,398,287	3.33	346,579	-0.42	464,159	10.34	317,251	26.90	1,962,525	-5.61	53,605	2.30
2003	2,485,229	3.63	346,555	-0.01	472,970	1.90	489,418	54.27	1,853,872	-5.54	55,589	3.70
2004	2,555,696	2.84	342,903	-1.05	490,397	3.68	335,788	-31.39	1,750,372	-5.58	55,805	0.39
2005	2,636,979	3.18	335,787	-2.08	498,498	1.65	165,854	-50.61	1,648,195	-5.84	55,228	-1.03
2006	2,725,824	3.37	329,856	-1.77	498,123	-0.08	142,708	-13.96	1,545,436	-6.23	52,982	-4.07
2007	2,844,178	4.34	322,875	-2.12	523,344	5.06	133,313	-6.58	1,446,004	-6.43	98,546	86.00
2008	2,952,282	3.80	315,763	-2.20	541,439	3.46	179,670	34.77	1,347,563	-6.81	103,126	4.65
2009	3,069,652	3.98	314,425	-0.48	564,487	4.26	325,690	81.27	1,254,059	-6.94	110,750	7.39
2010	3,210,261	4.58	313,563	-0.22	800,369	41.79	314,011	-3.59	1,167,081	-6.94	117,130	5.76
2011	3,354,741	4.50	313,665	0.03	923,826	15.43	357,594	13.88	1,085,004	-7.03	116,295	-0.71
2012	3,536,802	5.43	314,790	0.36	945,052	2.30	539,884	50.98	1,006,235	-7.26	121,236	4.25

Note: Totals include the Philippines, Puerto Rico, all other U.S. possessions and foreign countries.
[1]The totals shown here are for the six life insurance programs administered by the Department of Veterans Affairs (USGLI, NSLI, VSLI, VRI, SDVI, and VMLI). Life insurance programs that are administered by Prudential Insurance Company of America and supervised by VA are not included here. For more information on life insurance programs, see the Annual Benefits Reports located at: *http://www.vba.va.gov/REPORTS/abr/index.asp.*

Table 47. Summary of Department of Veterans Affairs Education Program Beneficiaries, FY2000–FY2013

(Number.)

Area and fiscal year	Total beneficiaries	MGIB-AD trainees	MGIB-SR trainees	DEA trainees	VEAP trainees	REAP trainees	Post-9/11 trainees	VRAP trainees
2000	397,589	279,948	70,299	44,820	2,522	X	X	X
2001	420,651	289,771	82,283	46,917	1,680	X	X	X
2002	464,159	323,165	85,766	53,888	1,340	X	X	X
2003	472,970	321,837	88,342	61,874	917	X	X	X
2004	490,397	332,031	88,650	68,920	796	X	X	X
2005	498,498	336,347	87,161	74,267	723	X	X	X
2006	498,123	332,184	66,105	75,460	627	23,747	X	X
2007	523,344	343,751	60,298	77,339	568	41,388	X	X
2008	541,439	354,284	62,390	80,191	560	44,014	X	X
2009	564,487	341,969	63,469	81,327	448	42,881	34,393	X
2010	800,369	247,105	67,373	89,696	286	30,269	365,640	X
2011	923,836	185,220	65,216	90,657	112	27,302	555,329	X
2012	945,052	118,549	60,393	87,707	76	19,774	646,302	12,251
2013	1,091,044	99,755	62,656	89,160	29	17,297	754,229	67,918

Note: State statistics may include individuals who used their education benefits in more than one state. Therefore the national totals in the Annual Benefits Report summary statistics should not be used to reflect the total number of beneficiaries during the fiscal year as these counts are calculated as the sum total of the state statistics.

Table 48. Summary of Department of Veterans Affairs Education Program Beneficiaries, by Geography,[1] FY2000–FY2013

(Number.)

Area and fiscal year	Total beneficiaries	MGIB-AD trainees	MGIB-SR trainees	DEA trainees	VEAP trainees	REAP trainees	Post-9/11 trainees	VRAP trainees
Alabama								
2000	7,889	X	X	X	X	X	X	X
2001	7,645	X	X	X	X	X	X	X
2002	8,064	4,525	2,004	1,512	23	X	X	X
2003	8,284	4,555	1,967	1,746	16	X	X	X
2004	8,671	4,718	1,932	2,008	13	X	X	X
2005	8,980	4,758	2,020	2,192	10	X	X	X
2006	8,623	4,799	1,472	2,342	10	X	X	X
2007	10,489	5,741	1,358	2,419	9	962	X	X
2008	12,006	6,531	1,624	2,606	9	1,236	X	X
2009	12,426	6,718	1,728	2,703	8	1,269	X	X
2010	19,582	5,779	2,075	3,102	5	883	7,738	X
2011	22,551	4,913	2,053	3,332	2	669	11,582	X
2012	24,340	3,679	1,895	3,336	1	521	14,669	239
2013	27,256	2,878	1,848	3,367	1	439	17,409	1,314
Alaska								
2000	1,281	X	X	X	X	X	X	X
2001	1,266	X	X	X	X	X	X	X
2002	1,238	956	161	117	4	X	X	X
2003	1,266	946	169	148	3	X	X	X
2004	1,352	1,001	190	158	3	X	X	X
2005	1,259	922	181	154	2	X	X	X
2006	1,360	1,036	159	163	2	X	X	X
2007	1,386	1,029	147	169	2	39	X	X
2008	1,415	1,024	161	170	2	58	X	X
2009	1,158	776	154	166	2	60	X	X
2010	2,705	561	170	164	1	28	1,781	X
2011	3,312	350	166	192	0	12	2,592	X
2012	3,146	179	143	210	0	6	2,592	16
2013	4,105	124	117	182	0	4	3,585	93
Arizona								
2000	11,238	X	X	X	X	X	X	X
2001	12,129	X	X	X	X	X	X	X
2002	14,404	11,744	1,260	1,370	30	X	X	X
2003	18,361	15,227	1,426	1,687	21	X	X	X
2004	22,230	18,672	1,592	1,949	17	X	X	X
2005	23,856	19,862	1,698	2,283	13	X	X	X
2006	24,532	20,676	1,416	2,426	14	X	X	X
2007	28,606	23,301	1,475	2,625	13	1,192	X	X
2008	32,020	25,782	1,669	2,894	12	1,663	X	X
2009	33,986	26,822	2,005	3,137	11	2,011	X	X
2010	46,743	21,012	2,132	3,571	7	1,433	18,588	X
2011	49,841	15,079	1,965	3,631	3	1,171	27,992	X
2012	44,701	10,031	1,792	3,386	2	975	27,992	523
2013	62,633	6,494	1,661	3,204	1	717	47,824	2,732
Arkansas								
2000	3,886	X	X	X	X	X	X	X
2001	4,155	X	X	X	X	X	X	X
2002	4,630	2,144	1,446	1,032	8		X	X
2003	5,019	2,186	1,626	1,201	6	X	X	X
2004	4,924	2,254	1,351	1,314	5	X	X	X
2005	5,282	2,159	1,664	1,455	4	X	X	X
2006	4,860	2,247	1,070	1,539	4	X	X	X
2007	5,389	2,145	950	1,547	3	744	X	X
2008	5,090	2,060	837	1,568	3	622	X	X
2009	5,513	2,061	988	1,575	3	886	X	X
2010	7,932	1,639	1,219	1,760	2	733	2,579	X
2011	8,357	1,320	1,226	1,781	1	566	3,463	X
2012	7,873	935	1,184	1,770	0	397	3,463	124
2013	9,784	744	1,317	1,787	0	309	5,022	605

Table 48. Summary of Department of Veterans Affairs Education Program Beneficiaries, by Geography,[1] FY2000–FY2013—*Continued*

(Number.)

Area and fiscal year	Total beneficiaries	MGIB-AD trainees	MGIB-SR trainees	DEA trainees	VEAP trainees	REAP trainees	Post-9/11 trainees	VRAP trainees
California								
2000	39,779	X	X	X	X	X	X	X
2001	39,115	X	X	X	X	X	X	X
2002	40,518	31,030	4,652	4,700	136	X	X	X
2003	44,051	33,701	4,771	5,485	94	X	X	X
2004	46,764	35,734	4,768	6,182	80	X	X	X
2005	45,874	34,665	4,484	6,664	61	X	X	X
2006	45,378	35,094	3,568	6,653	63	X	X	X
2007	47,073	35,404	3,131	6,663	57	1,818	X	X
2008	48,756	36,864	3,062	6,883	56	1,891	X	X
2009	46,897	34,942	2,987	7,017	48	1,903	X	X
2010	76,639	20,642	2,977	7,283	31	800	44,906	X
2011	88,420	14,279	3,097	7,119	12	650	63,263	X
2012	83,574	8,781	2,989	6,764	8	617	63,263	1,152
2013	112,838	6,446	3,139	6,667	3	648	88,609	7,326
Colorado								
2000	8,473	X	X	X	X	X	X	X
2001	8,462	X	X	X	X	X	X	X
2002	8,822	7,107	720	966	29	X	X	X
2003	9,401	7,550	726	1,105	20	X	X	X
2004	10,186	8,073	807	1,289	17	X	X	X
2005	11,458	9,090	1,016	1,339	13	X	X	X
2006	11,913	9,645	840	1,415	13	X	X	X
2007	12,894	10,029	782	1,469	12	602	X	X
2008	13,764	10,726	830	1,504	12	692	X	X
2009	13,614	10,389	914	1,569	10	732	X	X
2010	21,485	6,987	905	1,735	7	472	11,379	X
2011	24,794	4,978	861	1,755	3	370	16,827	X
2012	22,749	3,026	792	1,605	2	270	16,827	227
2013	30,323	2,192	799	1,697	1	212	24,414	1,008
Connecticut								
2000	2,796	X	X	X	X	X	X	X
2001	2,802	X	X	X	X	X	X	X
2002	2,757	1,476	1,026	244	11	X	X	X
2003	2,812	1,494	1,030	280	8	X	X	X
2004	2,956	1,560	1,075	314	7	X	X	X
2005	2,977	1,580	1,071	321	5	X	X	X
2006	2,725	1,656	746	318	5	X	X	X
2007	2,968	1,756	536	323	5	348	X	X
2008	3,293	1,905	579	337	5	467	X	X
2009	2,997	1,771	490	357	4	375	X	X
2010	4,350	1,169	507	412	3	51	2,208	X
2011	5,273	915	554	397	130	1	3,276	X
2012	5,105	654	606	408	1	83	3,276	77
2013	6,967	507	569	444	0	67	4,889	491
Delaware								
2000	956	X	X	X	X	X	X	X
2001	1,015	X	X	X	X	X	X	X
2002	1,070	610	321	136	3	X	X	X
2003	1,106	619	326	159	2	X	X	X
2004	1,143	619	346	176	2	X	X	X
2005	1,196	647	340	208	1	X	X	X
2006	1,099	624	261	212	2	X	X	X
2007	1,183	660	223	193	1	106	X	X
2008	1,170	626	207	210	1	126	X	X
2009	1,145	599	169	244	1	132	X	X
2010	1,904	374	176	238	1	54	1,061	X
2011	2,194	249	164	247	0	35	1,499	X
2012	2,115	151	150	258	0	25	1,499	32
2013	2,797	102	163	240	0	20	2,098	174

Table 48. Summary of Department of Veterans Affairs Education Program Beneficiaries, by Geography,[1] FY2000–FY2013—*Continued*

(Number.)

Area and fiscal year	Total beneficiaries	MGIB-AD trainees	MGIB-SR trainees	DEA trainees	VEAP trainees	REAP trainees	Post-9/11 trainees	VRAP trainees
District of Columbia								
2000	985	X	X	X	X	X	X	X
2001	957	X	X	X	X	X	X	X
2002	974	716	115	136	7	X	X	X
2003	1,002	723	120	154	5	X	X	X
2004	1,075	802	109	160	4	X	X	X
2005	1,019	735	110	171	3	X	X	X
2006	1,031	776	76	176	3	X	X	X
2007	1,050	753	62	180	3	52	X	X
2008	1,126	813	54	185	3	71	X	X
2009	1,084	791	48	173	3	69	X	X
2010	2,185	434	50	191	2	23	1,485	X
2011	2,740	267	35	198	1	12	2,227	X
2012	2,712	214	37	197	0	9	2,227	28
2013	4,868	154	53	216	0	8	4,001	436
Florida								
2000	25,556	X	X	X	X	X	X	X
2001	26,598	X	X	X	X	X	X	X
2002	28,394	21,390	3,358	3,568	78	X	X	X
2003	29,551	22,224	3,287	3,986	54	X	X	X
2004	31,815	23,971	3,453	4,346	45	X	X	X
2005	31,791	23,658	3,501	4,597	35	X	X	X
2006	32,193	24,731	2,671	4,755	36	X	X	X
2007	33,963	24,990	2,417	5,096	32	1,428	X	X
2008	36,088	26,343	2,408	5,589	32	1,716	X	X
2009	36,394	26,167	2,678	5,788	28	1,733	X	X
2010	59,519	20,414	2,986	6,582	18	1,227	28,292	X
2011	68,133	14,608	3,020	6,810	7	1,081	42,607	X
2012	62,911	9,454	2,613	6,513	5	818	42,607	901
2013	87,140	6,530	2,575	6,770	2	615	63,947	6,701
Georgia								
2000	13,257	X	X	X	X	X	X	X
2001	14,701	X	X	X	X	X	X	X
2002	15,925	11,987	1,996	1,906	36	X	X	X
2003	17,393	13,152	2,075	2,141	25	X	X	X
2004	16,957	14,367	175	2,394	21	X	X	X
2005	17,697	12,892	2,193	2,596	16	X	X	X
2006	17,812	13,374	1,704	2,717	17	X	X	X
2007	18,978	13,394	1,640	2,889	15	1,040	X	X
2008	18,898	12,753	1,882	3,111	15	1,137	X	X
2009	18,236	11,909	2,128	3,192	13	994	X	X
2010	28,631	9,303	2,473	3,765	8	618	12,464	X
2011	34,815	7,836	2,655	4,015	3	571	19,735	X
2012	32,067	4,568	2,603	3,842	2	420	19,735	897
2013	41,522	3,309	2,626	3,808	1	339	26,763	4,676
Hawaii								
2000	2,946	X	X	X	X	X	X	X
2001	2,976	X	X	X	X	X	X	X
2002	2,957	1,788	869	290	10	X	X	X
2003	3,235	2,044	874	310	7	X	X	X
2004	3,311	2,155	770	380	6	X	X	X
2005	3,016	2,066	559	387	4	X	X	X
2006	2,988	2,084	497	403	4	X	X	X
2007	3,144	1,977	419	400	4	344	X	X
2008	3,055	1,941	416	379	4	315	X	X
2009	2,521	1,591	377	374	3	176	X	X
2010	5,699	802	352	444	2	87	4,012	X
2011	7,166	496	343	387	1	29	5,910	X
2012	6,961	300	330	357	1	22	5,910	41
2013	8,642	253	316	378	0	17	7,549	129

Table 48. Summary of Department of Veterans Affairs Education Program Beneficiaries, by Geography,[1] FY2000–FY2013—*Continued*

(Number.)

Area and fiscal year	Total beneficiaries	MGIB-AD trainees	MGIB-SR trainees	DEA trainees	VEAP trainees	REAP trainees	Post-9/11 trainees	VRAP trainees
Idaho								
2000	2,384	X	X	X	X	X	X	X
2001	2,390	X	X	X	X	X	X	X
2002	2,367	1,453	618	290	6	X	X	X
2003	2,507	1,488	693	322	4	X	X	X
2004	2,708	1,652	695	357	4	X	X	X
2005	2,320	1,453	497	367	3	X	X	X
2006	2,408	1,584	415	406	3	X	X	X
2007	2,744	1,585	391	391	3	374	X	X
2008	2,828	1,598	492	356	3	379	X	X
2009	2,751	1,491	545	376	2	337	X	X
2010	3,945	1,134	618	423	1	193	1,576	X
2011	4,097	904	428	458	1	106	2,200	X
2012	4,045	620	481	420	0	272	2,200	52
2013	5,023	472	460	413	0	244	3,256	178
Illinois								
2000	14,752	X	X	X	X	X	X	X
2001	15,105	X	X	X	X	X	X	X
2002	15,754	10,718	3,944	1,040	52	X	X	X
2003	17,242	11,742	4,185	1,279	36	X	X	X
2004	19,935	14,269	4,080	1,556	30	X	X	X
2005	21,608	15,860	4,013	1,712	23	X	X	X
2006	20,179	15,365	3,055	1,735	24	X	X	X
2007	21,841	15,499	2,596	1,781	22	1,943	X	X
2008	22,159	15,729	2,677	1,886	21	1,846	X	X
2009	21,964	15,659	2,491	2,025	19	1,770	X	X
2010	32,007	12,000	2,653	2,218	12	1,602	13,522	X
2011	32,949	8,859	2,522	2,162	5	1,312	18,089	X
2012	29,990	6,169	2,278	1,974	3	1,025	18,089	452
2013	35,096	4,937	2,535	1,981	1	801	22,520	2,321
Indiana								
2000	5,848	X	X	X	X	X	X	X
2001	6,405	X	X	X	X	X	X	X
2002	6,910	4,102	1,959	826	23	X	X	X
2003	7,086	3,967	2,223	880	16	X	X	X
2004	7,379	4,127	2,292	947	13	X	X	X
2005	6,927	3,747	2,210	960	10	X	X	X
2006	6,578	3,845	1,776	947	10	X	X	X
2007	7,507	3,880	1,614	1,003	9	1,001	X	X
2008	7,451	3,994	1,611	1,018	9	819	X	X
2009	7,809	4,001	1,757	1,085	8	958	X	X
2010	11,972	2,925	1,892	1,249	5	840	5,061	X
2011	13,406	2,238	1,956	1,240	2	658	7,312	X
2012	12,549	1,394	1,872	1,157	1	467	7,312	346
2013	16,075	1,109	1,922	1,173	1	359	10,137	1,374
Iowa								
2000	3,717	X	X	X	X	X	X	X
2001	3,945	X	X	X	X	X	X	X
2002	4,168	2,112	1,682	362	12	X	X	X
2003	4,500	2,295	1,760	436	9	X	X	X
2004	4,962	2,754	1,707	494	7	X	X	X
2005	5,513	3,132	1,849	526	6	X	X	X
2006	3,955	2,292	1,188	469	6	X	X	X
2007	5,166	2,580	1,139	538	5	904	X	X
2008	6,405	3,626	1,313	598	5	863	X	X
2009	9,013	5,694	1,568	719	4	1,028	X	X
2010	14,490	6,237	1,834	889	3	887	4,640	X
2011	17,721	6,045	1,631	980	1	888	8,176	X
2012	16,530	4,648	1,563	1,011	1	1,043	8,176	88
2013	20,809	3,394	1,540	934	0	819	13,729	393

Table 48. Summary of Department of Veterans Affairs Education Program Beneficiaries, by Geography,[1] FY2000–FY2013—*Continued*

(Number.)

Area and fiscal year	Total beneficiaries	MGIB-AD trainees	MGIB-SR trainees	DEA trainees	VEAP trainees	REAP trainees	Post-9/11 trainees	VRAP trainees
Kansas								
2000	4,324	X	X	X	X	X	X	X
2001	4,312	X	X	X	X	X	X	X
2002	4,551	2,927	1,075	537	12	X	X	X
2003	4,856	3,086	1,127	635	8	X	X	X
2004	5,003	3,098	1,180	718	7	X	X	X
2005	4,784	2,901	1,154	724	5	X	X	X
2006	4,544	3,005	867	667	5	X	X	X
2007	4,999	2,995	840	663	5	496	X	X
2008	5,019	3,002	830	653	5	529	X	X
2009	4,947	2,953	771	654	4	565	X	X
2010	7,744	2,354	797	680	3	415	3,495	X
2011	8,722	1,809	697	642	1	336	5,237	X
2012	8,259	1,253	721	623	1	331	5,237	93
2013	10,606	1,076	792	655	0	301	7,393	389
Kentucky								
2000	5,131	X	X	X	X	X	X	X
2001	5,303	X	X	X	X	X	X	X
2002	5,736	3,377	1,391	952	16	X	X	X
2003	5,930	3,448	1,392	1,079	11	X	X	X
2004	6,391	3,726	1,465	1,191	9	X	X	X
2005	5,786	3,239	1,264	1,276	7	X	X	X
2006	5,548	3,244	1,000	1,297	7	X	X	X
2007	6,174	3,280	826	1,431	7	630	X	X
2008	6,454	3,244	1,006	1,549	6	649	X	X
2009	6,388	3,075	1,050	1,588	6	669	X	X
2010	9,589	2,282	1,130	1,819	4	502	3,852	X
2011	10,861	1,802	1,024	1,849	1	380	5,805	X
2012	10,355	1,197	943	1,777	1	348	5,805	284
2013	13,611	1,013	955	1,801	0	319	8,427	1,096
Louisiana								
2000	7,737	X	X	X	X	X	X	X
2001	7,818	X	X	X	X	X	X	X
2002	8,164	4,055	3,043	1,054	12	X	X	X
2003	8,839	4,348	3,196	1,286	9	X	X	X
2004	9,181	4,693	3,052	1,429	7	X	X	X
2005	8,899	4,739	2,514	1,640	6	X	X	X
2006	7,301	4,164	1,647	1,484	6	X	X	X
2007	7,384	3,485	1,395	1,448	5	1,051	X	X
2008	6,066	2,397	1,352	1,449	5	863	X	X
2009	6,651	3,101	1,360	1,470	4	716	X	X
2010	9,528	2,357	1,222	1,564	3	390	3,992	X
2011	10,625	1,788	1,215	1,618	1	322	5,681	X
2012	10,022	1,110	1,157	1,630	1	262	5,681	181
2013	12,513	793	1,119	1,636	0	213	7,940	812
Maine								
2000	1,713	X	X	X	X	X	X	X
2001	1,739	X	X	X	X	X	X	X
2002	1,847	933	329	579	6	X	X	X
2003	1,996	994	356	642	4	X	X	X
2004	2,106	1,055	357	690	4	X	X	X
2005	2,139	1,003	393	740	3	X	X	X
2006	2,051	1,048	288	712	3	X	X	X
2007	2,123	975	231	736	3	178	X	X
2008	2,104	938	261	706	3	196	X	X
2009	1,920	811	274	679	2	154	X	X
2010	2,733	535	286	699	1	68	1,144	X
2011	2,985	407	283	646	1	67	1,581	X
2012	2,896	243	315	651	0	55	1,581	51
2013	3,696	168	323	665	0	47	2,302	191

Table 48. Summary of Department of Veterans Affairs Education Program Beneficiaries, by Geography,[1] FY2000–FY2013—*Continued*

(Number.)

Area and fiscal year	Total beneficiaries	MGIB-AD trainees	MGIB-SR trainees	DEA trainees	VEAP trainees	REAP trainees	Post-9/11 trainees	VRAP trainees
Maryland								
2000	8,229	X	X	X	X	X	X	X
2001	8,929	X	X	X	X	X	X	X
2002	9,445	7,365	1,279	766	35	X	X	X
2003	10,171	8,039	1,260	847	25	X	X	X
2004	10,727	8,553	1,247	906	21	X	X	X
2005	10,762	8,596	1,213	937	16	X	X	X
2006	10,271	8,352	980	923	16	X	X	X
2007	10,874	8,740	778	928	15	413	X	X
2008	11,053	8,836	707	953	15	542	X	X
2009	10,085	7,854	649	979	13	590	X	X
2010	18,078	5,022	683	1,115	8	244	11,006	X
2011	22,402	3,512	629	1,057	3	151	17,050	X
2012	21,613	2,445	689	1,074	136	2	17,050	217
2013	29,047	1,839	716	1,088	1	119	24,111	1,173
Massachusetts								
2000	5,283	X	X	X	X	X	X	X
2001	5,221	X	X	X	X	X	X	X
2002	5,202	2,738	1,550	885	29	X	X	X
2003	5,172	2,739	1,460	953	20	X	X	X
2004	5,475	2,973	1,485	1,000	17	X	X	X
2005	5,181	2,631	1,452	1,085	13	X	X	X
2006	4,948	2,876	1,023	1,035	14	X	X	X
2007	5,707	3,143	883	1,035	12	634	X	X
2008	6,039	3,324	878	1,078	12	747	X	X
2009	6,009	3,331	872	1,046	10	750	X	X
2010	8,792	1,947	854	1,047	7	293	4,644	X
2011	10,468	1,379	759	1,036	3	213	7,078	X
2012	10,108	771	843	1,085	2	199	7,078	130
2013	14,771	470	923	1,072	1	153	11,546	606
Michigan								
2000	9,280	X	X	X	X	X	X	X
2001	9,315	X	X	X	X	X	X	X
2002	9,720	6,949	1,631	1,094	46	X	X	X
2003	9,941	6,930	1,753	1,226	32	X	X	X
2004	10,169	6,903	1,908	1,331	27	X	X	X
2005	9,821	6,534	1,897	1,369	21	X	X	X
2006	9,320	6,328	1,539	1,432	21	X	X	X
2007	9,782	6,083	1,412	1,502	19	766	X	X
2008	9,775	5,760	1,489	1,576	19	931	X	X
2009	9,344	5,254	1,461	1,715	16	898	X	X
2010	13,759	3,426	1,439	1,805	11	444	6,634	X
2011	14,468	2,337	1,260	1,696	4	275	8,896	X
2012	13,889	1,468	1,192	1,682	3	210	8,896	438
2013	19,012	1,097	1,322	1,848	1	198	12,503	2,043
Minnesota								
2000	5,741	X	X	X	X	X	X	X
2001	6,173	X	X	X	X	X	X	X
2002	6,325	3,111	2,321	864	29	X	X	X
2003	6,793	3,278	2,450	1,045	20	X	X	X
2004	7,137	3,579	2,371	1,170	17	X	X	X
2005	7,793	3,886	2,663	1,231	13	X	X	X
2006	7,381	4,243	1,854	1,271	13	X	X	X
2007	8,870	4,499	1,802	1,371	12	1,186	X	X
2008	10,097	5,290	1,993	1,440	12	1,362	X	X
2009	9,791	5,185	1,895	1,442	10	1,259	X	X
2010	15,174	3,698	1,957	1,625	7	762	7,125	X
2011	16,574	2,725	1,858	1,613	3	576	9,799	X
2012	15,297	1,788	1,535	1,486	2	567	9,799	120
2013	18,914	1,336	1,774	1,528	1	669	13,087	519

Table 48. Summary of Department of Veterans Affairs Education Program Beneficiaries, by Geography,[1] FY2000–FY2013—*Continued*

(Number.)

Area and fiscal year	Total beneficiaries	MGIB-AD trainees	MGIB-SR trainees	DEA trainees	VEAP trainees	REAP trainees	Post-9/11 trainees	VRAP trainees
Mississippi								
2000	4,183	X	X	X	X	X	X	X
2001	4,317	X	X	X	X	X	X	X
2002	4,613	2,088	1,864	653	8	X	X	X
2003	4,663	2,099	1,865	694	5	X	X	X
2004	4,764	2,158	1,856	746	4	X	X	X
2005	4,359	2,018	1,528	810	3	X	X	X
2006	3,815	1,812	1,184	816	3	X	X	X
2007	4,541	1,735	1,154	805	3	844	X	X
2008	4,559	1,699	1,306	815	3	736	X	X
2009	4,299	1,605	1,247	787	3	657	X	X
2010	7,152	1,307	1,428	916	2	571	2,928	X
2011	8,297	1,052	1,412	995	1	592	4,245	X
2012	7,802	731	1,305	984	0	410	4,245	127
2013	9,585	539	1,395	1,027	0	387	5,738	499
Missouri								
2000	7,409	X	X	X	X	X	X	X
2001	7,808	X	X	X	X	X	X	X
2002	8,394	5,327	2,030	1,002	35	X	X	X
2003	8,715	5,371	2,192	1,128	24	X	X	X
2004	9,240	5,992	1,971	1,257	20	X	X	X
2005	8,737	5,295	2,100	1,326	16	X	X	X
2006	9,307	6,285	1,635	1,371	16	X	X	X
2007	11,655	7,422	1,489	1,440	14	1,290	X	X
2008	12,865	8,212	1,698	1,471	14	1,470	X	X
2009	13,962	8,909	1,797	1,460	12	1,784	X	X
2010	20,821	7,831	2,154	1,673	8	1,643	7,512	X
2011	23,867	6,700	2,129	1,701	3	1,742	11,592	X
2012	22,020	4,913	1,991	1,619	2	1,624	11,592	279
2013	29,313	3,809	1,927	1,728	1	1,316	17,434	3,098
Montana								
2000	1,591	X	X	X	X	X	X	X
2001	1,609	X	X	X	X	X	X	X
2002	1,586	946	418	217	5	X	X	X
2003	1,717	1,013	477	223	4	X	X	X
2004	1,751	1,038	443	267	3	X	X	X
2005	1,554	922	351	279	2	X	X	X
2006	1,559	1,003	294	260	2	X	X	X
2007	1,873	1,050	264	294	2	263	X	X
2008	1,956	1,075	328	322	2	229	X	X
2009	1,795	979	338	312	2	164	X	X
2010	2,712	651	372	359	1	78	1,251	X
2011	2,859	465	315	372	0	37	1,670	X
2012	2,697	294	304	344	0	61	1,670	24
2013	3,362	213	309	346	0	70	2,311	113
Nebraska								
2000	3,630	X	X	X	X	X	X	X
2001	3,703	X	X	X	X	X	X	X
2002	3,809	2,277	985	537	10	X	X	X
2003	3,954	2,252	1,073	622	7	X	X	X
2004	4,287	2,435	1,136	710	6	X	X	X
2005	4,219	2,394	1,078	742	5	X	X	X
2006	3,983	2,534	710	734	5	X	X	X
2007	5,099	3,046	644	772	4	633	X	X
2008	5,456	3,129	775	812	4	736	X	X
2009	5,416	3,145	799	806	4	662	X	X
2010	6,892	2,295	854	854	2	404	2,483	X
2011	7,395	1,792	752	821	1	316	3,713	X
2012	6,729	1,176	730	734	1	320	3,713	55
2013	8,344	977	784	754	0	259	5,229	341

Table 48. Summary of Department of Veterans Affairs Education Program Beneficiaries, by Geography,[1] FY2000–FY2013—*Continued*

(Number.)

Area and fiscal year	Total beneficiaries	MGIB-AD trainees	MGIB-SR trainees	DEA trainees	VEAP trainees	REAP trainees	Post-9/11 trainees	VRAP trainees
Nevada								
2000	2,803	X	X	X	X	X	X	X
2001	2,895	X	X	X	X	X	X	X
2002	3,088	2,441	314	327	6	X	X	X
2003	3,442	2,640	385	413	4	X	X	X
2004	3,792	2,851	442	496	3	X	X	X
2005	3,743	2,785	415	540	3	X	X	X
2006	3,836	2,909	378	546	3	X	X	X
2007	3,859	2,856	313	523	2	165	X	X
2008	3,885	2,850	326	518	2	189	X	X
2009	3,728	2,647	353	550	2	176	X	X
2010	5,728	1,711	411	589	1	97	2,919	X
2011	6,430	1,175	410	585	1	79	4,180	X
2012	6,094	751	386	558	0	100	4,180	119
2013	7,861	552	412	579	0	142	5,495	681
New Hampshire								
2000	1,256	X	X	X	X	X	X	X
2001	1,227	X	X	X	X	X	X	X
2002	1,284	792	219	267	6	X	X	X
2003	1,279	786	198	291	4	X	X	X
2004	1,369	853	216	297	3	X	X	X
2005	1,286	760	234	289	3	X	X	X
2006	1,251	752	214	282	3	X	X	X
2007	1,303	750	172	258	2	121	X	X
2008	1,357	776	181	273	2	125	X	X
2009	1,326	706	231	263	2	124	X	X
2010	2,090	425	245	264	1	54	1,101	X
2011	2,496	301	184	240	1	34	1,736	X
2012	2,497	242	207	257	0	38	1,736	17
2013	4,694	255	244	297	0	34	3,793	71
New Jersey								
2000	4,487	X	X	X	X	X	X	X
2001	4,618	X	X	X	X	X	X	X
2002	4,777	2,786	1,342	628	21	X	X	X
2003	5,120	2,905	1,480	720	15	X	X	X
2004	5,547	3,270	1,501	763	13	X	X	X
2005	5,263	3,074	1,341	838	10	X	X	X
2006	5,346	3,432	1,103	801	10	X	X	X
2007	5,904	3,566	923	791	9	615	X	X
2008	6,187	3,748	920	834	9	676	X	X
2009	5,511	3,473	754	833	8	443	X	X
2010	9,058	2,274	947	901	5	312	4,619	X
2011	9,939	1,446	987	821	2	179	6,504	X
2012	9,527	793	1,042	838	1	145	6,504	204
2013	12,853	549	1,185	849	0	96	9,168	1,006
New Mexico								
2000	4,043	X	X	X	X	X	X	X
2001	3,969	X	X	X	X	X	X	X
2002	4,142	2,761	518	851	12	X	X	X
2003	4,481	2,830	555	1,088	8	X	X	X
2004	4,871	2,959	591	1,314	7	X	X	X
2005	4,897	2,812	612	1,468	5	X	X	X
2006	4,842	2,896	470	1,471	5	X	X	X
2007	4,765	2,782	398	1,372	5	208	X	X
2008	4,723	2,730	382	1,381	5	225	X	X
2009	4,551	2,623	415	1,304	4	205	X	X
2010	6,401	2,116	462	1,322	3	126	2,372	X
2011	6,657	1,619	441	1,232	1	108	3,256	X
2012	6,123	1,129	410	1,174	1	85	3,256	68
2013	7,539	903	409	1,201	0	108	4,423	495

Table 48. Summary of Department of Veterans Affairs Education Program Beneficiaries, by Geography,[1] FY2000–FY2013—*Continued*

(Number.)

Area and fiscal year	Total beneficiaries	MGIB-AD trainees	MGIB-SR trainees	DEA trainees	VEAP trainees	REAP trainees	Post-9/11 trainees	VRAP trainees
New York								
2000	11,529	X	X	X	X	X	X	X
2001	12,191	X	X	X	X	X	X	X
2002	12,792	7,474	3,385	1,872	61	X	X	X
2003	13,333	7,681	3,414	2,196	42	X	X	X
2004	14,255	8,501	3,328	2,390	36	X	X	X
2005	13,620	8,059	2,996	2,538	27	X	X	X
2006	13,894	8,974	2,448	2,444	28	X	X	X
2007	15,201	9,446	2,024	2,430	25	1,276	X	X
2008	15,223	9,679	1,823	2,474	25	1,222	X	X
2009	13,967	8,795	1,695	2,319	22	1,136	X	X
2010	22,678	5,420	1,937	2,517	14	591	12,199	X
2011	25,768	3,765	1,785	2,513	5	408	17,292	X
2012	24,961	2,507	1,738	2,604	4	330	17,292	486
2013	35,202	1,837	1,834	2,636	1	296	26,244	2,354
North Carolina								
2000	12,682	X	X	X	X	X	X	X
2001	12,883	X	X	X	X	X	X	X
2002	13,960	9,960	1,807	2,161	32	X	X	X
2003	14,912	10,399	1,820	2,670	23	X	X	X
2004	15,172	10,515	1,523	3,115	19	X	X	X
2005	15,794	10,462	1,812	3,505	15	X	X	X
2006	15,179	10,242	1,280	3,642	15	X	X	X
2007	16,552	10,447	1,222	3,865	14	1,004	X	X
2008	16,148	10,423	1,376	3,938	13	398	X	X
2009	15,730	9,785	1,327	3,861	12	745	X	X
2010	24,508	7,973	1,598	4,267	7	595	10,068	X
2011	28,642	6,567	1,651	4,303	3	579	15,539	X
2012	26,946	4,729	1,514	4,136	2	421	15,539	605
2013	36,177	3,894	1,511	4,163	1	411	22,841	3,356
North Dakota								
2000	1,783	X	X	X	X	X	X	X
2001	1,847	X	X	X	X	X	X	X
2002	1,825	722	915	183	5	X	X	X
2003	1,898	744	949	202	3	X	X	X
2004	1,917	742	939	233	3	X	X	X
2005	1,882	729	897	254	2	X	X	X
2006	1,489	721	528	238	2	X	X	X
2007	1,919	721	564	262	2	370	X	X
2008	1,913	752	578	252	2	329	X	X
2009	1,778	679	526	250	2	321	X	X
2010	2,420	519	529	259	1	255	857	X
2011	2,740	399	573	227	0	247	1,294	X
2012	2,458	266	493	203	0	189	1,294	13
2013	2,814	194	537	212	0	148	1,705	18
Ohio								
2000	12,466	X	X	X	X	X	X	X
2001	13,176	X	X	X	X	X	X	X
2002	14,064	8,910	3,787	1,317	50	X	X	X
2003	14,468	8,588	4,378	1,467	35	X	X	X
2004	14,794	8,801	4,355	1,609	29	X	X	X
2005	13,993	8,048	4,189	1,733	23	X	X	X
2006	12,808	7,981	3,119	1,685	23	X	X	X
2007	14,149	7,906	2,779	1,746	21	1,697	X	X
2008	13,836	7,717	2,693	1,800	21	1,605	X	X
2009	13,314	7,250	2,673	1,781	18	1,592	X	X
2010	20,625	5,295	3,160	1,991	11	1,174	8,994	X
2011	22,279	3,803	2,802	1,989	4	981	12,700	X
2012	20,605	2,524	2,325	1,955	3	751	12,700	347
2013	26,959	1,733	2,520	1,910	1	858	17,420	2,517

Table 48. Summary of Department of Veterans Affairs Education Program Beneficiaries, by Geography,[1] FY2000–FY2013—*Continued*

(Number.)

Area and fiscal year	Total beneficiaries	MGIB-AD trainees	MGIB-SR trainees	DEA trainees	VEAP trainees	REAP trainees	Post-9/11 trainees	VRAP trainees
Oklahoma								
2000	8,387	X	X	X	X	X	X	X
2001	8,492	X	X	X	X	X	X	X
2002	8,708	4,898	2,153	1,641	16	X	X	X
2003	9,367	5,102	2,350	1,904	11	X	X	X
2004	9,999	5,445	2,422	2,123	9	X	X	X
2005	9,844	5,160	2,506	2,171	7	X	X	X
2006	9,247	5,198	1,764	2,278	7	X	X	X
2007	9,616	4,995	1,528	2,285	7	801	X	X
2008	8,905	4,768	1,265	2,197	6	669	X	X
2009	9,206	4,765	1,251	2,160	6	1,024	X	X
2010	12,708	3,943	1,418	2,314	4	900	4,129	X
2011	13,246	3,142	1,241	2,357	1	606	5,899	X
2012	12,015	2,135	1,074	2,242	1	560	5,899	104
2013	15,127	1,765	1,076	2,218	0	587	8,883	598
Oregon								
2000	4,932	X	X	X	X	X	X	X
2001	5,432	X	X	X	X	X	X	X
2002	5,113	3,349	964	781	19	X	X	X
2003	5,921	3,868	1,079	961	13	X	X	X
2004	6,067	3,988	978	1,090	11	X	X	X
2005	5,757	3,551	1,033	1,164	9	X	X	X
2006	5,647	3,683	784	1,171	9	X	X	X
2007	5,813	3,558	711	1,131	8	405	X	X
2008	5,972	3,656	760	1,138	8	410	X	X
2009	5,870	3,623	664	1,241	7	335	X	X
2010	8,616	2,437	638	1,382	4	218	3,937	X
2011	10,400	1,848	621	1,414	2	269	6,246	X
2012	9,816	1,180	599	1,434	1	206	6,246	150
2013	12,154	673	562	1,349	0	135	8,491	944
Pennsylvania								
2000	11,440	X	X	X	X	X	X	X
2001	11,724	X	X	X	X	X	X	X
2002	11,984	6,738	3,652	1,544	50	X	X	X
2003	12,308	6,645	3,935	1,693	35	X	X	X
2004	13,943	7,787	4,302	1,825	29	X	X	X
2005	12,998	6,788	4,088	2,099	23	X	X	X
2006	12,565	7,469	3,011	2,062	23	X	X	X
2007	14,478	7,895	2,628	2,068	21	1,866	X	X
2008	14,484	8,182	2,499	2,096	21	1,686	X	X
2009	13,011	7,660	2,009	2,025	18	1,299	X	X
2010	21,998	4,904	2,353	2,225	11	690	11,815	X
2011	24,888	3,395	2,325	2,274	4	429	16,461	X
2012	23,561	1,839	2,404	2,252	3	288	16,461	314
2013	30,183	1,314	2,511	2,323	1	186	22,432	1,416
Rhode Island								
2000	1,138	X	X	X	X	X	X	X
2001	1,136	X	X	X	X	X	X	X
2002	1,155	596	319	234	6	X	X	X
2003	1,173	636	284	249	4	X	X	X
2004	1,195	654	299	238	4	X	X	X
2005	1,181	611	318	249	3	X	X	X
2006	1,092	591	238	260	3	X	X	X
2007	1,220	648	197	252	3	120	X	X
2008	1,205	605	199	258	3	140	X	X
2009	1,175	555	203	226	2	189	X	X
2010	1,848	333	238	243	1	80	953	X
2011	2,132	211	224	210	1	62	1,424	X
2012	2,043	136	211	211	0	48	1,424	13
2013	2,680	83	217	213	0	43	2,016	108

Table 48. Summary of Department of Veterans Affairs Education Program Beneficiaries, by Geography,[1] FY2000–FY2013—*Continued*

(Number.)

Area and fiscal year	Total beneficiaries	MGIB-AD trainees	MGIB-SR trainees	DEA trainees	VEAP trainees	REAP trainees	Post-9/11 trainees	VRAP trainees
South Carolina								
2000	6,826	X	X	X	X	X	X	X
2001	7,029	X	X	X	X	X	X	X
2002	7,249	4,508	1,530	1,193	18	X	X	X
2003	7,450	4,570	1,564	1,303	13	X	X	X
2004	7,592	4,708	1,480	1,393	11	X	X	X
2005	7,314	4,251	1,547	1,508	8	X	X	X
2006	7,028	4,353	1,104	1,563	8	X	X	X
2007	7,840	4,330	1,144	1,703	8	655	X	X
2008	7,997	4,250	1,222	1,804	8	713	X	X
2009	7,872	3,966	1,343	1,867	7	689	X	X
2010	13,056	2,852	1,597	2,195	4	341	6,067	X
2011	15,341	1,950	1,575	2,395	2	248	9,171	X
2012	14,847	1,237	1,505	2,343	1	233	9,171	357
2013	19,801	909	1,519	2,593	0	252	12,725	1,803
South Dakota								
2000	1,699	X	X	X	X	X	X	X
2001	1,802	X	X	X	X	X	X	X
2002	1,804	720	882	198	4	X	X	X
2003	1,851	750	906	192	3	X	X	X
2004	1,893	821	834	235	3	X	X	X
2005	1,890	708	927	253	2	X	X	X
2006	1,721	809	631	279	2	X	X	X
2007	2,110	796	605	296	2	411	X	X
2008	2,092	789	673	290	2	338	X	X
2009	1,992	783	634	266	2	307	X	X
2010	2,585	564	684	284	1	226	826	X
2011	2,866	442	674	284	0	192	1,274	X
2012	2,605	287	589	261	0	180	1,274	14
2013	3,225	229	576	262	0	185	1,912	61
Tennessee								
2000	7,137	X	X	X	X	X	X	X
2001	7,243	X	X	X	X	X	X	X
2002	7,770	5,248	1,363	1,138	21	X	X	X
2003	8,100	5,330	1,475	1,280	15	X	X	X
2004	8,348	5,542	1,434	1,360	12	X	X	X
2005	8,142	5,358	1,299	1,475	10	X	X	X
2006	7,865	5,184	1,152	1,519	10	X	X	X
2007	8,441	4,830	1,158	1,634	9	810	X	X
2008	8,969	5,174	1,391	1,636	9	759	X	X
2009	8,757	4,987	1,368	1,680	8	714	X	X
2010	13,740	3,430	1,382	1,829	5	481	6,613	X
2011	16,404	2,591	1,360	1,808	2	538	10,105	X
2012	15,403	1,599	1,264	1,759	1	408	10,105	267
2013	20,369	1,333	1,315	1,894	0	305	13,895	1,627
Texas								
2000	32,568	X	X	X	X	X	X	X
2001	32,583	X	X	X	X	X	X	X
2002	34,710	26,121	4,122	4,389	78	X	X	X
2003	38,392	28,500	4,373	5,465	54	X	X	X
2004	41,765	30,624	4,661	6,434	46	X	X	X
2005	41,628	30,141	4,361	7,091	35	X	X	X
2006	41,290	30,395	3,371	7,488	36	X	X	X
2007	42,173	29,504	3,038	7,365	33	2,233	X	X
2008	42,562	29,686	3,112	7,423	32	2,309	X	X
2009	40,402	27,894	3,101	7,392	28	1,987	X	X
2010	67,015	19,027	3,244	8,041	18	1,089	35,596	X
2011	76,878	14,575	3,255	8,204	7	899	49,938	X
2012	71,331	9,809	2,875	7,737	5	700	49,938	267
2013	94,506	7,988	2,939	7,913	2	569	69,957	5,138

Table 48. Summary of Department of Veterans Affairs Education Program Beneficiaries, by Geography,[1] FY2000–FY2013—*Continued*

(Number.)

Area and fiscal year	Total beneficiaries	MGIB-AD trainees	MGIB-SR trainees	DEA trainees	VEAP trainees	REAP trainees	Post-9/11 trainees	VRAP trainees
Utah								
2000	3,451	X	X	X	X	X	X	X
2001	3,610	X	X	X	X	X	X	X
2002	3,720	1,814	1,411	487	8	X	X	X
2003	3,998	1,896	1,556	541	5	X	X	X
2004	4,241	2,015	1,651	571	4	X	X	X
2005	4,493	2,152	1,703	635	3	X	X	X
2006	4,266	2,427	1,176	659	4	X	X	X
2007	5,107	2,670	1,092	632	3	710	X	X
2008	5,168	2,729	1,064	631	3	741	X	X
2009	5,345	2,811	1,106	668	3	757	X	X
2010	7,832	2,250	1,170	744	2	533	3,133	X
2011	8,346	1,819	1,063	714	1	385	4,364	X
2012	7,965	1,483	1,000	696	0	397	4,364	25
2013	10,609	1,286	1,005	697	0	361	7,050	210
Vermont								
2000	556	X	X	X	X	X	X	X
2001	555	X	X	X	X	X	X	X
2002	509	253	156	98	2	X	X	X
2003	547	262	168	116	1	X	X	X
2004	610	320	174	115	1	X	X	X
2005	618	339	161	117	1	X	X	X
2006	664	414	144	105	1	X	X	X
2007	850	492	137	120	1	100	X	X
2008	887	508	138	133	1	107	X	X
2009	768	435	120	121	1	91	X	X
2010	1,272	316	104	125	0	37	690	X
2011	1,625	241	120	116	0	29	1,119	X
2012	1,562	149	153	112	0	22	1,119	7
2013	2,077	105	201	117	0	15	1,609	30
Virginia								
2000	15,792	X	X	X	X	X	X	X
2001	16,111	X	X	X	X	X	X	X
2002	17,429	13,540	2,096	1,748	45	X	X	X
2003	18,470	14,406	2,122	1,911	31	X	X	X
2004	19,758	15,410	2,214	2,108	26	X	X	X
2005	19,682	15,371	2,049	2,242	20	X	X	X
2006	19,246	15,288	1,621	2,317	20	X	X	X
2007	20,676	15,825	1,350	2,461	19	1,021	X	X
2008	21,493	16,158	1,343	2,744	18	1,230	X	X
2009	20,541	15,030	1,358	2,880	16	1,257	X	X
2010	42,092	10,092	1,549	3,322	10	693	26,426	X
2011	51,474	7,160	1,489	3,420	4	518	38,883	X
2012	50,024	5,071	1,588	3,617	3	452	38,883	410
2013	63,665	3,824	1,652	3,768	1	383	52,002	2,035
Washington								
2000	11,069	X	X	X	X	X	X	X
2001	11,097	X	X	X	X	X	X	X
2002	11,302	8,192	1,393	1,682	35	X	X	X
2003	12,391	8,871	1,596	1,899	25	X	X	X
2004	12,810	9,188	1,530	2,071	21	X	X	X
2005	12,336	8,457	1,678	2,185	16	X	X	X
2006	12,056	8,727	1,182	2,131	16	X	X	X
2007	12,208	8,433	1,006	2,001	15	753	X	X
2008	12,410	8,712	934	2,064	15	685	X	X
2009	11,492	7,969	769	2,192	13	549	X	X
2010	18,729	5,059	743	2,381	8	307	10,231	X
2011	21,854	3,487	719	2,408	3	186	15,051	X
2012	20,287	1,865	710	2,201	2	151	15,051	307
2013	25,972	1,248	721	2,238	1	98	19,966	1,700

Table 48. Summary of Department of Veterans Affairs Education Program Beneficiaries, by Geography,[1] FY2000–FY2013—*Continued*

(Number.)

Area and fiscal year	Total beneficiaries	MGIB-AD trainees	MGIB-SR trainees	DEA trainees	VEAP trainees	REAP trainees	Post-9/11 trainees	VRAP trainees
West Virginia								
2000	2,487	X	X	X	X	X	X	X
2001	2,665	X	X	X	X	X	X	X
2002	2,839	1,238	1,067	529	5	X	X	X
2003	3,421	1,663	1,168	586	4	X	X	X
2004	4,037	2,310	1,057	667	3	X	X	X
2005	4,340	2,513	1,096	729	2	X	X	X
2006	4,440	2,865	835	737	3	X	X	X
2007	6,365	3,988	834	739	2	802	X	X
2008	8,103	5,373	946	742	2	1,040	X	X
2009	8,840	6,040	896	724	2	1,178	X	X
2010	12,917	5,834	1,075	840	1	1,022	4,145	X
2011	14,941	5,278	980	899	1	976	6,807	X
2012	13,965	4,322	1,023	899	0	848	6,807	66
2013	22,130	3,690	1,036	895	0	716	15,521	272
Wisconsin								
2000	6,075	X	X	X	X	X	X	X
2001	6,273	X	X	X	X	X	X	X
2002	6,488	3,217	2,456	792	23	X	X	X
2003	6,599	3,210	2,550	823	16	X	X	X
2004	6,982	3,450	2,604	914	14	X	X	X
2005	6,653	3,159	2,506	978	10	X	X	X
2006	6,046	3,302	1,670	1,063	11	X	X	X
2007	7,833	3,782	1,426	1,223	10	1,392	X	X
2008	8,427	4,173	1,606	1,242	10	1,396	X	X
2009	8,081	4,156	1,547	1,281	8	1,089	X	X
2010	12,308	3,131	1,509	1,402	5	825	5,436	X
2011	12,315	1,517	1,456	1,381	2	604	7,355	X
2012	11,412	813	1,385	1,281	1	428	7,355	149
2013	13,125	652	1,520	1,305	1	354	8,565	728
Wyoming								
2000	909	X	X	X	X	X	X	X
2001	940	X	X	X	X	X	X	X
2002	978	627	243	105	3	X	X	X
2003	1,122	695	289	136	2	X	X	X
2004	1,103	688	277	136	2	X	X	X
2005	1,067	674	249	143	1	X	X	X
2006	1,002	653	199	149	1	X	X	X
2007	1,064	625	195	139	1	104	X	X
2008	1,140	679	207	126	1	127	X	X
2009	1,117	686	212	118	1	100	X	X
2010	1,487	561	227	150	1	84	464	X
2011	1,590	456	191	145	0	109	689	X
2012	1,430	337	188	115	0	84	689	17
2013	2,009	312	208	141	0	68	1,218	62
Puerto Rico								
2000	3,910	X	X	X	X	X	X	X
2001	4,051	X	X	X	X	X	X	X
2002	4,078	702	1,608	1,758	10	X	X	X
2003	4,008	745	1,507	1,749	7	X	X	X
2004	3,991	763	1,505	1,717	6	X	X	X
2005	4,049	806	1,569	1,670	4	X	X	X
2006	3,750	878	1,270	1,598	4	X	X	X
2007	4,292	920	1,000	1,646	4	722	X	X
2008	4,542	929	1,063	1,645	4	901	X	X
2009	4,424	822	1,107	1,565	3	927	X	X
2010	5,129	635	1,285	1,580	2	670	957	X
2011	5,707	487	1,413	1,574	1	667	1,565	X
2012	5,753	364	1,604	1,544	1	671	1,565	4
2013	6,880	242	1,717	1,572	0	630	2,586	133

Table 48. Summary of Department of Veterans Affairs Education Program Beneficiaries, by Geography,[1] FY2000–FY2013—*Continued*

(Number.)

Area and fiscal year	Total beneficiaries	MGIB-AD trainees	MGIB-SR trainees	DEA trainees	VEAP trainees	REAP trainees	Post-9/11 trainees	VRAP trainees
Philippines								
2000	X	X	X	X	X	X	X	X
2001	X	X	X	X	X	X	X	X
2002	545	381	1	163	0	X	X	X
2003	446	318	0	128	0	X	X	X
2004	373	293	0	80	0	X	X	X
2005	332	288	0	44	0	X	X	X
2006	338	311	1	26	0	X	X	X
2007	328	319	1	8	0	0	X	X
2008	325	317	0	8	0	0	X	X
2009	318	311	0	6	0	1	X	X
2010	472	291	0	10	0	0	171	X
2011	630	243	2	14	0	1	370	X
2012	575	194	2	8	0	1	370	0
2013	775	147	1	13	0	0	605	9

Note: State statistics may include individuals who used their education benefit in more than one state therefore the totals may differ from the national fiscal year totals.
X = Not applicable/not available.
[1]Details of educational program type were not available by geographies prior to 2003.

Table 49. Service-Connected Disabled Veterans, by Disability Rating Group, FY1986–FY2013

(Number.)

Fiscal year	Total veterans with a service-connected disability	0 to 20 percent	30 to 40 percent	50 to 60 percent	70 to 100 percent
1986	2,225,289	1,255,399	495,655	224,588	249,647
1987	2,212,303	1,251,733	491,932	221,480	247,158
1988	2,198,857	1,246,938	488,117	218,394	245,407
1989	2,191,549	1,245,045	485,456	215,972	245,076
1990	2,184,262	1,242,103	483,479	214,399	244,281
1991	2,179,122	1,242,386	480,368	213,029	243,339
1992	2,180,936	1,245,352	479,501	212,178	243,905
1993	2,197,635	1,254,732	483,034	212,802	247,067
1994	2,217,908	1,266,403	487,251	213,807	250,447
1995	2,235,675	1,271,698	490,581	215,381	258,015
1996	2,252,980	1,272,924	494,802	217,648	267,606
1997	2,262,771	1,266,042	496,067	221,015	279,647
1998	2,277,049	1,255,055	499,907	226,586	295,501
1999	2,294,453	1,242,621	503,341	233,897	314,594
2000	2,308,186	1,227,207	506,019	241,260	333,700
2001	2,321,103	1,211,807	509,110	248,104	352,082
2002	2,398,287	1,209,274	527,820	266,886	394,307
2003	2,485,229	1,204,038	546,157	287,978	447,056
2004	2,555,696	1,200,715	558,306	304,341	492,334
2005	2,636,979	1,199,271	573,994	324,637	539,077
2006	2,725,824	1,207,358	594,765	345,832	577,869
2007	2,844,178	1,229,001	621,440	371,622	622,115
2008	2,952,285	1,237,868	643,882	398,679	671,856
2009	3,069,652	1,244,230	665,211	427,902	732,309
2010	3,210,261	1,258,882	689,599	459,657	802,123
2011	3,354,741	1,258,987	711,305	492,692	891,757
2012	3,536,802	1,266,501	729,813	532,192	1,008,296
2013	3,743,259	1,281,492	749,531	572,421	1,139,815

Table 50. National Cemetery Administration Summary of Veteran Interments, FY2000–FY2013

(Number.)

Fiscal year	Total veteran interments at national cemeteries	Interment type		Percent change, year to year, total interments
		Casket	Cremain[1]	
2000	57,202	36,398	20,674	X
2001	58,027	37,467	20,560	1.4
2002	61,093	37,814	23,279	5.3
2003	61,137	37,765	23,372	0.1
2004	62,854	38,149	24,705	2.8
2005	62,330	37,520	24,810	-0.8
2006	64,765	37,869	26,896	3.9
2007	67,126	37,951	29,175	3.6
2008	68,684	38,275	30,409	2.3
2009	70,784	37,384	33,400	3.1
2010	74,292	38,442	35,850	5.0
2011	77,478	38,880	38,598	4.3
2012	77,833	38,315	39,518	0.5
2013	81,530	39,011	42,519	4.7

X = Not applicable/not available.
[1]Cremains are cremated remains. Cremains include in-ground cremains, columbaria, and scatter cremains.

Table 51. National Cemetery Administration Summary of Veteran and Nonveteran[1] Interments, FY2000–FY2013

(Number.)

Fiscal year	Total interments at national cemeteries	Interment type	
		Casket	Cremain[2]
2000	82,717	53,898	28,819
2001	84,822	55,601	29,221
2002	89,329	56,422	32,907
2003	89,755	56,495	33,260
2004	93,033	57,480	35,553
2005	93,245	57,201	36,044
2006	96,797	57,620	39,177
2007	100,185	57,845	42,340
2008	103,275	58,725	44,550
2009	106,361	57,634	48,727
2010	111,807	59,503	52,304
2011	117,412	61,036	56,376
2012	118,158	59,710	58,448
2013	124,787	61,656	63,131

[1]Nonveteran includes dependents, active duty servicemembers, and reservists.
[2]Cremains are cremated remains. Cremains include in-ground cremains, columbaria, and scatter cremains.

Table 52. National Cemetery Administration Summary of Veteran, Nonveteran, and Dependent Interments, by Cemetery Type, FY2000–FY2013

(Number.)

Fiscal year	Total veteran, nonveteran, and dependent interments at national and state cemeteries	Veterans and Nonveterans[1]		Interment type		Percent change, year to year, total interments
		National	State grant	National	State grant	
2000	97,071	57,249	10,941	25,468	3,413	X
2001	100,231	58,183	11,690	26,639	3,719	3.3
2002	106,506	61,296	13,024	28,033	4,153	6.3
2003	107,947	61,382	13,614	28,374	4,578	1.4
2004	112,279	63,165	14,345	29,868	4,901	4.0
2005	114,127	62,650	15,658	30,595	5,224	1.6
2006	119,231	65,128	16,738	31,669	5,696	4.5
2007	123,443	67,555	17,139	32,630	6,119	3.5
2008	128,101	68,977	18,149	34,298	6,677	3.8
2009	133,161	71,051	19,353	35,310	7,447	4.0
2010	139,652	74,564	20,238	37,243	7,607	4.9
2011	146,903	77,814	21,296	39,598	8,195	5.2
2012	149,321	77,833	22,430	40,326	8,732	1.6
2013	156,792	81,530	22,865	43,257	9,140	5.0

X = Not applicable/not available.
[1]Nonveteran includes active duty servicemembers and reservists.

Table 53. Veteran Employees in Federal Agencies, FY2012

(Number; Percent.)

Executive agency	On-board veterans					Veteran new hires				
	Overall rank	Employees who are veterans	Employees who are veterans with preference	Employees who are disabled veterans[1]	Employees who are 30% or more disabled veterans	Overall rank	New hires who are veterans	New hires who are veterans with preference	New hires who are disabled veterans	New hires who are 30% or more disabled veterans
Total	X	29.7	24.9	9.8	5.4	X	28.9	25.7	11.1	6.6
Agriculture	13	11.2	10.3	3.4	1.6	14	8.0	7.3	2.6	1.3
Commerce	11	11.6	9.9	2.9	1.1	12	11.0	10.2	3.7	1.4
Defense	1	46.8	39.9	15.5	9.4	1	45.9	40.6	14.9	10.3
Education	14	9.7	8.0	2.0	1.3	13	10.5	9.2	4.4	3.7
Energy	6	21.3	17.6	5.9	2.7	7	18.7	14.9	5.9	2.7
HHS	15	6.6	6.3	2.3	1.1	15	7.3	6.9	2.7	1.4
Homeland Security	4	27.4	22.4	6.4	3.1	6	24.9	22.4	8.0	4.7
HUD	10	14.3	13.2	5.0	3.0	11	12.9	11.5	7.1	3.8
Interior	9	15.9	14.0	5.8	2.1	9	14.7	13.4	5.2	2.4
Justice	5	23.8	17.2	4.3	2.0	5	27.4	25.5	7.9	4.4
Labor	7	19.8	18.3	8.7	4.7	4	30.4	28.6	15.5	9.7
State	8	18.8	16.2	6.0	3.1	8	16.6	12.7	5.1	2.6
Transportation	2	35.9	26.5	8.0	3.2	3	33.8	30.6	12.2	6.8
Treasury	12	11.3	9.3	3.6	1.7	10	13.6	12.8	6.7	3.6
Veterans Affairs	3	32.2	25.8	13.1	6.7	2	34.0	29.7	18.0	9.5

X = Not applicable/not available.
[1]The disabled veteran classification includes those with a compensable service-connected disability of 30% or more.

Table 54. Compensation and Pension Recipients, by County, FY2014

(Number of recipients.)

State and county	Compensation					Total, pension	Compensation or pension								
	Total	0 to 20 percent	30 to 40 percent	50 to 60 percent	70 to 100 percent		Total	Male	Female	Less than 35 years	35 to 44 years	45 to 54 years	55 to 64 years	65 to 74 years	75 years and over
Total	2,225,289	1,255,399	495,655	224,588	249,647										
Alabama															
Autauga	1,756	499	362	292	603	56	1,812	1,579	232	126	230	478	412	360	205
Baldwin	3,471	1,276	727	529	939	246	3,717	3,481	236	260	283	554	652	1,201	766
Barbour	502	133	95	77	197	47	549	500	49	33	55	96	129	148	88
Bibb	249	69	51	31	98	53	302	281	21	22	34	41	56	105	44
Blount	626	194	128	109	195	84	710	688	22	44	69	99	134	239	124
Bullock	143	44	23	22	54	20	164	144	20	13	13	23	48	38	29
Butler	312	73	46	55	138	47	359	329	30	30	49	49	81	97	53
Calhoun	2,992	969	598	484	941	187	3,178	2,856	323	203	258	490	895	926	404
Chambers	568	135	87	85	262	72	640	594	46	47	61	76	156	201	99
Cherokee	294	91	55	34	114	48	342	324	18	26	22	26	66	131	71
Chilton	563	139	101	95	228	173	736	702	34	70	67	71	146	215	167
Choctaw	210	54	37	29	90	58	268	241	27	20	25	39	49	81	54
Clarke	348	100	61	74	113	46	394	362	32	39	52	63	83	99	58
Clay	216	60	51	35	71	28	245	235	10	20	17	34	49	78	47
Cleburne	188	56	35	20	77	25	213	205	*	12	15	25	36	91	34
Coffee	2,470	667	497	421	885	66	2,536	2,260	277	198	357	608	601	508	265
Colbert	889	270	178	116	325	148	1,037	996	41	71	79	109	214	332	231
Conecuh	252	55	53	42	102	27	279	261	18	16	29	46	61	89	38
Coosa	180	44	34	25	76	30	210	185	24	19	12	35	60	55	29
Covington	701	204	133	119	245	91	792	758	34	56	54	106	174	238	164
Crenshaw	225	55	47	36	87	26	251	233	18	21	22	33	52	73	49
Cullman	1,172	391	272	183	325	170	1,342	1,266	76	114	118	152	261	425	272
Dale	2,317	620	460	386	851	78	2,395	2,130	265	228	309	428	607	534	288
Dallas	626	164	106	97	259	77	703	612	91	61	60	144	152	172	114
De Kalb	705	211	152	118	225	132	837	796	41	74	69	69	161	302	163
Elmore	2,562	745	507	435	875	95	2,657	2,314	343	209	316	630	626	576	299
Escambia	571	163	114	100	194	83	654	618	36	37	57	95	141	216	108
Etowah	1,501	432	267	209	593	255	1,756	1,663	93	104	133	215	385	582	337
Fayette	298	73	58	45	122	53	350	332	19	33	34	53	69	96	66
Franklin	265	60	59	50	96	67	332	317	15	32	26	30	70	103	71
Geneva	688	176	141	114	257	72	759	720	39	44	65	122	153	247	129
Greene	120	29	21	18	52	40	160	148	12	*	11	30	40	40	32
Hale	227	55	47	38	87	41	268	249	19	22	32	38	64	80	32
Henry	349	76	77	65	131	53	401	374	27	23	49	71	74	104	81
Houston	2,236	630	473	334	799	185	2,421	2,222	199	218	297	424	532	597	353
Jackson	526	166	100	90	170	81	607	581	26	43	34	64	111	239	116
Jefferson	8,232	2,528	1,727	1,349	2,629	1,362	9,594	8,703	891	750	888	1,524	2,342	2,745	1,343
Lamar	216	59	41	43	73	36	252	238	14	17	15	43	62	64	51
Lauderdale	1,187	416	234	180	357	192	1,379	1,301	78	123	103	149	253	466	283
Lawrence	356	112	69	59	117	43	399	378	21	33	33	43	73	142	76
Lee	3,013	713	518	469	1,312	145	3,157	2,842	315	405	462	657	695	621	316
Limestone	1,641	557	361	294	430	77	1,718	1,580	138	126	215	429	385	401	161
Lowndes	190	47	44	28	72	20	210	186	25	20	35	35	66	32	23
Macon	513	119	98	72	224	60	573	521	52	36	48	89	175	145	80
Madison	9,364	3,041	2,203	1,582	2,537	301	9,665	8,619	1,046	708	1,057	2,596	2,537	1,923	844
Marengo	326	81	56	63	126	75	401	365	36	32	54	50	91	111	63
Marion	318	79	82	59	98	69	387	376	11	22	38	51	86	108	82
Marshall	1,231	380	265	205	380	172	1,403	1,341	62	97	91	173	341	460	241
Mobile	6,617	2,347	1,405	995	1,870	716	7,333	6,737	596	565	733	1,263	1,612	2,063	1,095
Monroe	268	62	46	57	103	44	312	289	23	30	28	44	68	83	59
Montgomery	6,276	1,696	1,192	1,050	2,337	305	6,581	5,515	1,066	534	799	1,403	1,695	1,352	796
Morgan	1,669	578	365	261	464	234	1,903	1,785	118	159	186	273	375	572	336
Perry	123	27	29	21	46	33	156	144	12	10	16	22	33	36	39
Pickens	329	50	64	49	166	34	363	327	36	24	43	69	80	99	48
Pike	493	131	97	82	183	45	538	497	41	42	53	93	131	152	67
Randolph	319	107	64	41	107	42	361	340	21	29	15	36	70	135	76
Russell	2,433	506	396	385	1,146	110	2,543	2,169	373	388	428	633	488	389	217
Saint Clair	1,106	365	230	187	323	102	1,207	1,137	70	119	131	189	237	371	159
Shelby	2,304	841	486	367	610	233	2,537	2,314	223	230	296	418	446	699	447
Sumter	154	40	26	31	57	26	180	160	20	14	12	29	63	40	22
Talladega	1,177	380	237	200	360	144	1,321	1,219	102	97	135	189	327	392	182
Tallapoosa	773	220	124	98	330	105	878	824	54	63	69	96	197	265	188
Tuscaloosa	2,592	670	504	430	988	281	2,873	2,585	288	284	313	464	675	766	372
Walker	1,037	292	197	169	379	165	1,202	1,163	39	65	87	137	219	454	239
Washington	221	63	41	37	80	30	251	239	12	20	15	33	36	102	45
Wilcox	120	22	21	22	55	28	149	141	*	14	13	22	33	40	26
Winston	301	99	57	55	89	56	356	338	18	35	35	32	71	113	70

Table 54. Compensation and Pension Recipients, by County, FY2014—*Continued*

(Number of recipients.)

State and county	Compensation					Total, pension	Compensation or pension								
	Total	0 to 20 percent	30 to 40 percent	50 to 60 percent	70 to 100 percent		Total	Male	Female	Less than 35 years	35 to 44 years	45 to 54 years	55 to 64 years	65 to 74 years	75 years and over
Alabama cnt'd															
Unknown	*	*	*	*	*	*	*	*	*	*	*	*	*	*	*
Alaska															
Aleutians East	*	*	*	*	*	*	*	*	*	*	*	*	*	*	*
Aleutians West	19	11	*	*	*	*	19	18	*	*	*	*	*	*	*
Anchorage	8,250	2,365	1,780	1,622	2,483	123	8,373	7,218	1,155	1,396	1,172	2,103	1,900	1,396	406
Bethel	64	29	17	*	10	*	72	63	*	*	*	19	13	20	*
Bristol Bay	23	*	*	*	*	*	23	23	*	*	*	*	*	*	*
Denali	32	10	*	*	*	*	33	30	*	*	*	12	*	*	*
Dillingham	30	14	*	*	*	*	32	30	*	*	*	*	*	11	*
Fairbanks North Star	3,219	897	707	652	963	30	3,249	2,778	471	861	558	780	612	372	65
Haines	31	*	*	*	*	*	34	33	*	*	*	*	*	14	*
Hoonah Angoon	32	12	*	*	10	*	32	30	*	*	*	*	*	18	*
Juneau	380	135	89	59	97	16	396	366	30	49	47	83	101	98	18
Kenai Peninsula	1,184	381	238	192	373	47	1,231	1,149	82	95	98	175	316	409	138
Ketchikan Gateway	187	64	30	30	63	13	200	184	16	13	14	54	59	46	14
Kodiak Island	217	70	48	39	60	*	220	203	17	19	28	70	54	39	10
Lake And Peninsula	14	*	*	*	*	*	14	13	*	*	*	*	*	*	*
Matanuska Susitna	2,787	804	572	553	858	49	2,836	2,572	264	360	430	759	598	533	155
Nome	38	18	14	*	*	*	45	43	*	*	*	*	10	22	*
North Slope	27	10	10	*	*	*	28	26	*	*	*	*	*	*	*
Northwest Arctic	13	*	*	*	*	*	16	15	*	*	*	*	*	*	*
Petersburg	43	19	13	*	*	*	45	43	*	*	*	*	10	19	*
Prince Of Wales Hyder	57	24	15	*	10	10	67	63	*	*	*	*	*	28	15
Sitka	104	34	25	14	31	*	104	96	*	*	17	17	26	28	*
Skagway	*	*	*	*	*	*	*	*	*	*	*	*	*	*	*
Southeast Fairbanks	199	58	39	41	61	*	205	185	20	25	28	41	45	46	20
Valdez Cordova	150	67	23	23	37	*	153	146	*	16	19	29	32	40	17
Wade Hampton	23	11	*	*	*	*	29	28	*	*	*	*	*	11	*
Wrangell	24	*	*	*	*	*	29	26	*	*	*	*	*	13	*
Yakutat	*	*	*	*	*	*	*	*	*	*	*	*	*	*	*
Yukon Koyukuk	41	15	*	*	10	*	43	40	*	*	*	*	*	17	*
Unknown	*	*	*	*	*	*	*	*	*	*	*	*	*	*	*
Arizona															
Apache	576	146	91	78	261	93	669	628	41	80	45	54	109	288	92
Cochise	6,626	2,020	1,536	1,168	1,902	163	6,789	5,865	924	724	873	1,380	1,512	1,456	843
Coconino	1,177	425	222	181	349	110	1,287	1,172	115	202	132	141	235	423	152
Gila	818	245	142	129	302	79	897	839	58	44	34	66	173	404	175
Graham	422	133	97	70	122	24	446	422	24	43	46	55	81	142	79
Greenlee	112	37	22	21	32	*	120	116	*	10	14	17	18	46	15
La Paz	302	96	47	54	105	71	373	357	16	13	*	13	75	163	100
Maricopa	45,214	15,830	8,936	6,948	13,500	2,764	47,978	43,843	4,135	6,541	5,872	7,119	8,521	12,688	7,219
Mohave	3,573	1,143	605	504	1,321	386	3,959	3,769	190	237	237	338	817	1,633	695
Navajo	1,158	365	202	146	445	117	1,275	1,193	82	102	104	115	275	465	212
Pima	17,640	6,094	3,769	2,840	4,937	1,083	18,723	16,867	1,856	1,787	1,929	3,116	3,738	4,838	3,302
Pinal	5,326	1,779	1,026	772	1,749	277	5,603	5,193	410	619	648	683	964	1,828	859
Santa Cruz	346	122	69	55	100	24	370	354	16	34	35	45	54	128	74
Yavapai	4,352	1,399	711	621	1,621	471	4,823	4,514	309	357	263	416	970	1,851	965
Yuma	3,552	1,150	835	601	966	148	3,700	3,417	283	626	530	592	585	775	592
Unknown	30	*	*	*	14	*	32	30	*	*	*	*	*	*	*
Arkansas															
Arkansas	216	49	41	47	79	32	248	243	*	17	30	35	57	73	35
Ashley	272	62	67	38	105	32	304	278	26	34	37	46	64	94	29
Baxter	789	214	137	125	313	73	862	815	47	69	62	110	147	301	172
Benton	2,648	773	494	417	963	176	2,824	2,629	195	341	341	418	459	810	453
Boone	577	161	96	92	228	50	627	590	37	71	53	82	117	191	113
Bradley	132	28	20	19	65	15	147	135	12	12	18	18	32	47	20
Calhoun	53	11	11	*	23	*	61	57	*	*	10	11	*	15	*
Carroll	353	99	46	59	149	38	391	369	22	23	28	36	86	155	63
Chicot	156	31	26	39	60	33	189	173	16	*	19	28	61	52	21
Clark	245	77	37	33	98	32	277	263	14	30	25	32	51	89	50
Clay	286	67	46	45	128	38	324	313	11	28	22	47	67	101	59
Cleburne	484	120	98	80	186	54	538	506	32	39	29	51	112	178	129
Cleveland	140	37	14	26	63	*	149	141	*	10	11	28	31	48	21
Columbia	261	63	37	42	119	33	294	269	25	34	31	30	68	92	39
Conway	328	77	52	53	146	39	367	345	22	32	27	46	79	126	57
Craighead	1,046	285	181	164	416	88	1,134	1,086	48	141	144	145	204	351	149
Crawford	1,072	257	175	171	469	80	1,152	1,073	79	124	120	182	234	329	163

Table 54. Compensation and Pension Recipients, by County, FY2014—*Continued*

(Number of recipients.)

State and county	Compensation: Total	Compensation: 0 to 20 percent	Compensation: 30 to 40 percent	Compensation: 50 to 60 percent	Compensation: 70 to 100 percent	Total, pension	Compensation or pension: Total	Male	Female	Less than 35 years	35 to 44 years	45 to 54 years	55 to 64 years	65 to 74 years	75 years and over
Arkansas cnt'd															
Crittenden	599	152	130	88	229	60	659	602	57	66	77	141	143	173	59
Cross	232	57	38	39	98	23	255	241	14	28	34	49	51	68	25
Dallas	91	18	20	17	36	11	102	96	*	*	10	19	20	31	15
Desha	181	38	30	40	73	13	194	173	21	17	25	28	55	46	23
Drew	255	55	44	48	108	25	280	257	23	32	32	40	62	74	40
Faulkner	1,698	431	338	276	652	90	1,788	1,638	150	213	246	336	343	433	216
Franklin	296	72	42	36	146	27	323	310	13	23	29	50	57	104	60
Fulton	233	54	45	43	91	22	255	248	*	25	15	27	46	95	47
Garland	1,646	497	299	241	610	202	1,848	1,731	117	142	161	226	391	588	341
Grant	286	65	49	58	114	33	319	295	24	41	34	53	57	81	53
Greene	691	144	118	128	301	44	735	710	25	93	77	86	147	236	95
Hempstead	235	56	40	42	97	29	264	247	17	14	20	35	66	82	47
Hot Spring	458	111	93	82	172	69	527	508	19	47	44	74	102	188	72
Howard	149	38	33	29	49	11	160	151	*	*	20	27	31	49	24
Independence	473	96	94	83	200	62	535	513	22	56	61	57	110	149	102
Izard	216	60	37	33	86	24	240	235	*	20	11	26	57	87	39
Jackson	196	53	18	30	95	30	226	216	10	23	21	23	39	70	50
Jefferson	1,389	339	227	219	604	112	1,501	1,355	146	121	174	289	373	408	135
Johnson	367	100	59	57	151	32	399	380	19	43	32	61	85	119	59
Lafayette	84	21	16	17	30	10	94	89	*	*	*	*	30	34	10
Lawrence	245	50	54	46	95	38	283	270	13	27	31	34	50	87	54
Lee	85	21	17	18	29	*	94	87	*	*	*	13	27	33	12
Lincoln	136	39	33	20	44	20	156	147	*	10	20	15	28	60	23
Little River	181	47	34	26	74	15	196	182	14	19	15	26	31	82	23
Logan	356	89	67	51	149	44	400	384	16	30	41	49	94	121	65
Lonoke	2,381	537	481	426	936	59	2,440	2,179	261	253	396	695	474	442	180
Madison	189	47	35	29	78	27	216	209	*	15	13	25	50	79	34
Marion	372	92	64	52	164	39	411	394	17	26	23	43	109	147	63
Miller	563	165	111	81	206	80	643	598	45	69	70	93	147	182	82
Mississippi	584	136	102	108	238	76	660	621	39	47	55	95	170	198	95
Monroe	110	34	15	15	46	20	130	120	10	10	*	21	32	39	19
Montgomery	178	34	35	27	82	23	201	191	10	16	*	16	43	69	47
Nevada	129	33	23	16	57	16	145	134	11	12	16	24	25	43	25
Newton	117	34	20	14	49	22	139	130	*	*	*	18	33	45	29
Ouachita	365	89	74	59	143	52	417	388	29	44	33	62	114	110	54
Perry	183	43	32	29	79	24	207	194	13	17	22	24	47	68	29
Phillips	230	56	41	37	96	35	265	238	27	31	24	52	61	78	19
Pike	129	29	26	16	58	23	152	141	11	*	16	22	23	55	27
Poinsett	253	62	45	37	109	44	297	287	10	23	26	36	77	96	39
Polk	412	102	68	63	179	58	470	452	18	40	40	43	108	139	100
Pope	800	231	167	137	265	58	858	799	59	114	99	122	164	244	115
Prairie	110	27	12	15	56	10	120	111	*	*	12	12	30	38	20
Pulaski	8,478	2,148	1,567	1,368	3,395	665	9,143	7,998	1,145	894	1,150	1,733	2,348	1,992	1,026
Randolph	341	78	63	63	137	52	393	373	20	36	33	46	74	125	79
Saint Francis	305	88	39	40	138	41	346	327	19	20	26	72	80	110	38
Saline	1,775	518	317	292	647	103	1,878	1,720	158	217	246	297	337	539	242
Scott	162	32	37	26	67	17	179	174	*	18	19	17	46	55	24
Searcy	154	38	20	32	64	29	183	176	*	*	*	28	30	63	46
Sebastian	1,818	497	330	275	716	180	1,998	1,864	134	189	245	315	407	546	296
Sevier	160	34	28	31	67	19	179	172	*	13	21	23	34	58	30
Sharp	399	99	55	56	189	54	452	429	23	29	23	45	98	168	90
Stone	268	61	44	40	123	39	307	290	17	14	18	33	64	117	61
Union	460	126	85	84	165	59	519	483	36	44	47	82	123	161	62
Van Buren	338	91	64	54	129	58	396	374	22	23	22	37	91	147	76
Washington	2,192	659	394	345	795	228	2,420	2,223	197	315	271	354	526	603	351
White	1,290	310	243	207	530	115	1,405	1,307	98	150	159	224	311	381	180
Woodruff	91	21	11	17	42	22	113	108	*	*	*	15	25	41	17
Yell	270	73	46	45	106	23	293	275	18	34	28	36	54	97	44
California															
Alameda	8,378	2,915	1,518	1,205	2,740	975	9,353	8,614	739	1,086	849	1,129	1,928	2,708	1,652
Alpine	*	*	*	*	*	*	*	*	*	*	*	*	*	*	*
Amador	526	169	117	76	164	37	563	542	21	30	37	46	108	233	109
Butte	2,767	883	462	381	1,041	382	3,149	2,955	194	336	239	257	606	1,051	660
Calaveras	733	222	112	120	279	60	793	754	39	58	50	72	138	337	137
Colusa	153	46	28	22	57	*	161	150	11	23	19	18	22	54	25
Contra Costa	8,384	3,320	1,553	1,173	2,338	630	9,014	8,413	601	922	762	1,176	1,612	2,651	1,887
Del Norte	575	203	86	67	219	48	623	592	31	50	31	60	131	227	124
El Dorado	2,345	902	412	346	685	168	2,513	2,373	140	211	181	228	439	918	534
Fresno	8,122	3,043	1,395	1,257	2,427	782	8,904	8,422	482	1,108	800	918	1,751	2,734	1,593

Table 54. Compensation and Pension Recipients, by County, FY2014—*Continued*

(Number of recipients.)

State and county	Compensation					Total, pension	Compensation or pension								
	Total	0 to 20 percent	30 to 40 percent	50 to 60 percent	70 to 100 percent		Total	Male	Female	Less than 35 years	35 to 44 years	45 to 54 years	55 to 64 years	65 to 74 years	75 years and over
California cnt'd															
Glenn	268	93	43	33	99	23	291	273	18	36	26	17	62	80	70
Humboldt	1,859	566	283	242	768	308	2,167	2,021	146	206	160	191	507	784	318
Imperial	1,630	556	349	283	441	89	1,719	1,606	113	433	315	226	266	327	152
Inyo	210	63	40	25	82	33	243	228	15	24	21	15	47	85	51
Kern	8,447	2,854	1,604	1,256	2,734	781	9,228	8,602	627	1,413	1,103	1,286	1,860	2,458	1,105
Kings	3,073	1,231	666	471	705	97	3,170	2,827	343	504	455	751	644	543	272
Lake	1,156	385	149	158	464	203	1,359	1,296	63	84	80	105	282	534	273
Lassen	456	160	81	68	147	42	498	473	25	62	59	58	94	152	73
Los Angeles	44,940	15,372	8,243	6,318	15,006	6,538	51,478	47,935	3,543	8,072	5,893	5,807	9,264	13,679	8,755
Madera	1,644	595	290	262	497	90	1,734	1,649	85	184	122	124	329	666	309
Marin	1,350	568	235	168	379	202	1,552	1,453	99	99	89	128	217	553	466
Mariposa	352	134	57	36	125	29	381	358	23	23	22	26	73	151	86
Mendocino	1,133	332	164	140	497	169	1,302	1,244	58	69	73	83	258	540	279
Merced	2,226	836	409	358	623	148	2,374	2,236	138	254	183	238	476	715	508
Modoc	155	47	33	20	55	15	170	163	*	*	15	14	31	71	32
Mono	113	38	20	22	33	*	121	115	*	17	14	17	17	41	15
Monterey	4,425	1,311	724	656	1,733	194	4,619	4,207	412	476	345	596	959	1,267	973
Napa	1,309	516	223	204	366	218	1,527	1,442	85	126	107	141	260	497	396
Nevada	1,618	641	253	227	497	112	1,730	1,631	99	133	111	137	264	688	397
Orange	18,230	6,726	3,528	2,544	5,433	1,446	19,676	18,531	1,145	3,403	2,167	2,011	2,707	5,558	3,830
Placer	4,282	1,618	891	603	1,170	324	4,606	4,254	353	513	440	605	741	1,317	989
Plumas	326	124	53	45	104	45	371	357	14	15	*	25	82	168	72
Riverside	29,847	9,439	5,567	4,733	10,108	1,980	31,827	29,410	2,417	4,421	4,427	5,387	5,315	7,250	5,022
Sacramento	16,106	5,661	3,168	2,302	4,975	1,469	17,575	16,056	1,519	2,052	1,763	2,323	3,662	4,656	3,117
San Benito	517	143	62	72	240	19	536	503	33	67	52	54	91	197	75
San Bernardino	20,722	6,357	4,055	3,163	7,147	1,812	22,534	20,803	1,731	3,937	2,834	2,843	4,265	5,847	2,805
San Diego	67,147	21,589	14,387	11,373	19,798	2,788	69,935	62,159	7,776	14,281	10,367	13,237	13,729	11,394	6,925
San Francisco	3,046	1,094	539	419	994	831	3,877	3,627	250	387	321	363	832	1,143	831
San Joaquin	5,528	1,674	956	869	2,029	590	6,118	5,708	410	794	640	771	1,292	1,791	830
San Luis Obispo	3,109	1,163	561	414	971	273	3,382	3,211	171	338	263	360	583	1,154	684
San Mateo	3,293	1,204	585	423	1,080	361	3,654	3,441	213	406	323	386	634	1,083	822
Santa Barbara	4,149	1,505	808	615	1,221	304	4,453	4,108	345	538	455	634	792	1,119	914
Santa Clara	7,763	2,543	1,289	1,079	2,853	679	8,442	7,926	516	1,062	762	936	1,572	2,544	1,564
Santa Cruz	1,758	533	213	254	759	196	1,954	1,835	119	184	156	154	331	748	381
Shasta	3,465	1,059	542	454	1,410	300	3,766	3,537	229	371	331	345	709	1,301	708
Sierra	41	15	*	*	13	*	46	43	*	*	*	*	*	24	*
Siskiyou	758	247	149	96	266	113	872	823	49	62	62	68	156	350	173
Solano	10,525	3,399	2,040	1,737	3,349	373	10,898	9,757	1,141	1,088	1,037	1,884	2,581	2,558	1,748
Sonoma	4,025	1,458	640	502	1,425	515	4,540	4,272	268	442	292	435	829	1,615	925
Stanislaus	4,180	1,278	623	607	1,672	414	4,594	4,312	282	734	457	448	871	1,410	673
Sutter	1,615	529	299	261	526	86	1,701	1,542	159	209	183	269	354	419	267
Tehama	959	308	163	131	357	96	1,054	996	58	107	91	93	194	358	211
Trinity	231	67	39	36	89	40	271	262	*	15	12	16	66	125	37
Tulare	4,459	1,875	809	614	1,160	303	4,762	4,542	220	571	480	430	875	1,529	875
Tuolumne	931	269	127	116	419	90	1,021	976	45	91	56	78	173	420	203
Ventura	7,217	2,384	1,426	1,070	2,337	508	7,724	7,189	536	1,007	885	1,120	1,292	2,115	1,305
Yolo	1,712	654	340	246	472	172	1,883	1,732	151	216	187	258	349	502	372
Yuba	1,702	474	350	288	590	104	1,806	1,568	239	289	222	355	341	387	211
Unknown	*	*	*	*	*	*	*	*	*	*	*	*	*	*	*
Colorado															
Adams	5,241	1,787	1,070	816	1,568	301	5,542	5,026	516	811	784	832	1,056	1,433	623
Alamosa	189	41	38	27	83	24	213	202	11	22	16	24	46	60	45
Arapahoe	8,176	2,812	1,680	1,287	2,397	334	8,511	7,421	1,090	1,150	1,174	1,619	1,716	1,879	970
Archuleta	208	72	28	28	80	13	221	206	15	11	16	11	50	92	41
Baca	31	*	*	*	16	*	32	30	*	*	*	*	*	*	11
Bent	141	27	22	15	77	12	153	146	*	*	11	13	44	55	22
Boulder	2,046	786	419	293	549	165	2,211	2,012	199	306	213	271	367	633	419
Broomfield	551	201	105	97	148	31	582	535	47	98	72	80	92	146	94
Chaffee	277	107	63	37	70	14	291	277	14	19	17	30	42	111	71
Cheyenne	14	*	*	*	*	*	14	13	*	*	*	*	*	*	*
Clear Creek	129	48	24	20	37	*	132	121	11	20	10	22	30	39	11
Conejos	105	25	16	14	50	23	128	121	*	*	14	12	25	39	30
Costilla	76	16	10	*	42	15	91	84	*	*	*	*	24	39	14
Crowley	73	23	*	11	35	11	84	76	*	*	10	10	22	29	10
Custer	108	43	14	13	38	*	114	106	*	*	*	13	24	53	13
Delta	608	245	129	68	166	49	657	630	27	39	33	53	116	239	176
Denver	5,854	1,944	1,154	851	1,905	794	6,648	5,999	649	803	749	851	1,394	1,728	1,123
Dolores	32	12	*	*	10	*	40	39	*	*	*	*	*	15	*
Douglas	3,736	1,425	820	551	941	66	3,802	3,449	353	477	647	852	638	821	368

Table 54. Compensation and Pension Recipients, by County, FY2014—*Continued*

(Number of recipients.)

State and county	Compensation					Total, pension	Compensation or pension								
	Total	0 to 20 percent	30 to 40 percent	50 to 60 percent	70 to 100 percent		Total	Male	Female	Less than 35 years	35 to 44 years	45 to 54 years	55 to 64 years	65 to 74 years	75 years and over
Colorado cnt'd															
Eagle	165	71	32	22	40	*	172	156	16	14	20	28	25	66	19
El Paso	35,268	9,212	7,495	6,609	11,952	540	35,808	30,875	4,933	6,221	5,780	9,505	7,021	4,589	2,690
Elbert	389	125	72	64	128	*	398	347	51	48	45	78	79	124	23
Fremont	1,076	320	195	158	403	51	1,127	1,053	74	85	105	175	208	354	200
Garfield	523	264	104	55	101	25	548	514	34	65	62	55	80	200	87
Gilpin	66	15	15	11	25	*	70	60	10	*	11	17	10	19	*
Grand	120	46	25	18	31	*	129	115	14	10	11	10	36	44	18
Gunnison	144	61	26	21	36	*	153	143	10	28	*	14	26	54	22
Hinsdale	*	*	*	*	*	*	*	*	*	*	*	*	*	*	*
Huerfano	135	33	29	17	56	31	166	157	*	*	*	13	36	73	37
Jackson	15	*	*	*	*	*	15	15	*	*	*	*	*	*	*
Jefferson	5,749	2,102	1,171	813	1,663	330	6,079	5,568	512	861	634	759	1,093	1,742	988
Kiowa	11	*	*	*	*	*	11	10	*	*	*	*	*	*	*
Kit Carson	52	17	14	*	13	*	56	52	*	*	*	*	11	19	11
La Plata	569	181	106	74	208	48	617	571	46	68	46	71	116	225	90
Lake	75	25	19	*	22	*	78	69	*	10	*	*	17	26	10
Larimer	4,444	1,831	841	622	1,150	227	4,671	4,303	368	656	448	558	804	1,321	879
Las Animas	245	50	37	22	136	30	275	265	10	14	19	27	54	115	46
Lincoln	52	20	*	*	17	*	59	53	*	*	*	11	10	19	14
Logan	218	89	51	26	52	11	229	215	14	26	18	27	45	67	45
Mesa	3,017	1,359	583	390	685	146	3,163	2,951	212	340	294	379	546	940	663
Mineral	13	*	*	*	*	*	13	13	*	*	*	*	*	*	*
Moffat	166	72	42	17	35	12	178	170	*	20	18	14	35	67	22
Montezuma	306	104	54	35	113	39	345	322	23	31	29	43	60	121	61
Montrose	759	322	150	105	182	26	785	736	49	62	59	72	131	295	166
Morgan	246	98	47	38	63	13	259	251	*	25	21	33	42	83	55
Otero	326	66	56	43	161	33	359	339	20	23	23	43	81	126	63
Ouray	62	37	11	*	*	*	68	67	*	*	*	*	15	27	14
Park	432	140	63	56	172	13	445	405	40	37	24	57	129	153	44
Phillips	29	14	*	*	*	*	30	30	*	*	*	*	*	*	11
Pitkin	71	36	12	*	20	*	77	74	*	*	*	*	12	33	20
Prowers	115	19	24	20	52	13	128	120	*	13	10	13	24	46	22
Pueblo	3,359	841	534	488	1,496	299	3,658	3,395	263	341	420	513	786	1,053	545
Rio Blanco	101	49	17	13	22	*	105	98	*	10	10	11	18	35	21
Rio Grande	183	54	30	21	78	37	220	209	11	15	10	34	39	82	40
Routt	166	79	33	28	26	*	170	160	10	14	15	17	26	72	25
Saguache	60	17	12	*	23	*	69	63	*	*	*	*	16	28	15
San Juan	*	*	*	*	*	*	*	*	*	*	*	*	*	*	*
San Miguel	34	19	*	*	*	*	39	35	*	*	*	*	*	15	*
Sedgwick	42	25	*	*	*	*	45	43	*	*	*	*	*	17	10
Summit	117	59	22	19	17	*	124	112	12	12	13	18	22	33	26
Teller	973	292	186	173	323	18	991	890	101	62	92	212	295	240	91
Washington	38	11	10	*	10	*	42	41	*	*	*	*	*	14	10
Weld	2,756	1,093	517	390	756	160	2,916	2,679	236	435	370	406	512	774	416
Yuma	79	19	22	15	23	*	86	84	*	10	*	*	18	24	25
Unknown	*	*	*	*	*	*	*	*	*	*	*	*	*	*	*
Connecticut															
Fairfield	3,803	1,568	714	535	986	344	4,147	3,919	228	515	382	386	524	1,272	1,068
Hartford	6,325	2,538	1,186	823	1,778	592	6,917	6,448	469	876	722	806	1,200	1,961	1,351
Litchfield	1,534	625	279	194	436	107	1,641	1,544	97	219	150	142	263	575	289
Middlesex	1,336	508	264	188	376	94	1,431	1,342	88	187	152	179	229	447	236
New Haven	6,080	2,301	1,099	868	1,812	640	6,720	6,277	443	856	634	763	1,181	1,954	1,328
New London	3,912	1,271	832	667	1,142	158	4,069	3,743	327	538	594	836	754	875	473
Tolland	1,165	472	233	164	296	50	1,215	1,120	95	186	151	170	194	370	144
Windham	1,223	431	208	199	385	89	1,312	1,233	79	170	155	206	231	390	160
Unknown	*	*	*	*	*	*	*	*	*	*	*	*	*	*	*
Delaware															
Kent	4,331	1,415	962	756	1,198	105	4,435	3,886	549	378	524	1,141	973	914	505
New Castle	4,753	1,621	965	696	1,471	280	5,034	4,567	467	472	538	880	1,091	1,418	634
Sussex	2,552	895	512	344	801	122	2,674	2,470	204	162	186	338	540	981	464
District of Columbia															
District of Columbia	4,450	1,464	888	642	1,456	699	5,149	4,496	653	478	629	769	1,196	1,243	832
Florida															
Alachua	3,249	1,197	642	508	902	426	3,675	3,313	362	387	379	536	869	990	514
Baker	371	153	73	56	89	27	398	368	30	27	42	71	101	114	42
Bay	7,412	2,580	1,645	1,187	2,000	273	7,685	6,892	793	494	746	1,870	1,825	1,738	1,012

Table 54. Compensation and Pension Recipients, by County, FY2014—*Continued*

(Number of recipients.)

State and county	Compensation					Total, pension	Compensation or pension								
	Total	0 to 20 percent	30 to 40 percent	50 to 60 percent	70 to 100 percent		Total	Male	Female	Less than 35 years	35 to 44 years	45 to 54 years	55 to 64 years	65 to 74 years	75 years and over
Florida cnt'd															
Bradford	432	143	98	75	115	47	478	443	35	25	55	81	104	152	61
Brevard	16,402	5,586	3,118	2,355	5,343	920	17,322	15,803	1,519	1,029	1,531	3,001	3,875	4,600	3,284
Broward	13,359	4,624	2,485	1,957	4,293	1,957	15,316	13,982	1,334	1,780	1,636	2,065	2,817	3,784	3,231
Calhoun	189	62	38	31	58	22	211	196	15	15	15	29	35	78	39
Charlotte	3,678	1,228	663	523	1,263	311	3,989	3,791	198	171	193	362	637	1,597	1,027
Citrus	3,230	1,119	669	466	976	354	3,584	3,393	191	179	206	321	641	1,276	961
Clay	8,315	2,979	1,875	1,416	2,045	154	8,469	7,408	1,061	613	1,138	2,543	1,956	1,515	704
Collier	3,369	1,328	601	473	967	250	3,619	3,456	163	222	210	277	515	1,273	1,122
Columbia	1,536	522	310	237	467	174	1,710	1,569	141	124	148	224	432	510	272
Desoto	346	104	66	53	123	66	412	398	14	12	18	33	80	162	107
Dixie	288	82	56	50	100	61	348	335	13	22	11	22	69	150	74
Duval	21,280	7,859	4,768	3,472	5,181	1,039	22,319	19,480	2,839	2,399	3,295	5,934	4,935	3,921	1,834
Escambia	11,704	4,107	2,523	1,857	3,216	532	12,236	10,812	1,424	928	1,234	2,654	2,952	2,872	1,595
Flagler	1,971	640	391	296	644	128	2,099	1,952	147	161	188	246	361	756	387
Franklin	185	56	42	34	53	35	220	211	*	*	17	10	54	88	43
Gadsden	691	257	144	101	189	102	793	737	56	38	71	131	228	241	84
Gilchrist	299	106	53	41	100	33	332	305	27	38	20	43	71	111	49
Glades	153	47	25	18	63	22	175	172	*	*	*	*	35	78	42
Gulf	392	142	78	63	109	19	411	384	27	10	31	66	98	148	58
Hamilton	226	93	37	32	64	36	262	247	15	14	20	30	67	96	35
Hardee	202	69	33	29	71	32	234	222	12	19	21	17	27	95	55
Hendry	318	139	49	34	96	35	353	332	21	24	26	23	77	148	55
Hernando	4,386	1,586	755	589	1,455	351	4,737	4,454	283	285	322	502	779	1,603	1,243
Highlands	2,018	683	394	273	668	261	2,279	2,160	119	107	103	193	414	770	691
Hillsborough	21,771	7,331	4,519	3,478	6,443	1,726	23,497	20,647	2,851	2,359	2,885	5,124	5,175	5,139	2,811
Holmes	508	170	96	72	170	69	577	559	18	22	37	56	118	208	136
Indian River	2,591	918	487	367	819	235	2,826	2,664	162	160	143	248	483	996	795
Jackson	922	277	223	140	282	87	1,009	930	79	69	86	126	275	290	163
Jefferson	256	96	59	29	72	31	287	261	26	27	18	37	72	89	44
Lafayette	59	18	12	12	17	12	71	67	*	*	*	*	16	27	*
Lake	5,679	2,039	1,098	831	1,711	502	6,181	5,810	371	402	472	710	1,077	2,035	1,482
Lee	9,279	3,448	1,686	1,327	2,818	872	10,151	9,554	597	700	747	989	1,801	3,715	2,199
Leon	3,111	1,243	685	466	717	266	3,377	3,036	341	300	379	577	811	907	403
Levy	916	316	167	149	283	127	1,043	978	65	68	73	94	238	386	183
Liberty	95	38	19	14	24	10	105	104	*	*	10	*	27	34	21
Madison	284	92	57	48	87	43	327	308	19	19	27	44	82	115	40
Manatee	5,262	1,955	971	753	1,583	522	5,784	5,433	351	370	429	601	999	1,940	1,444
Marion	6,462	2,308	1,288	917	1,949	666	7,128	6,643	485	401	476	739	1,336	2,462	1,714
Martin	1,873	706	326	242	599	221	2,094	1,984	110	119	113	154	296	720	692
Miami-Dade	11,560	3,822	2,074	1,689	3,975	1,438	12,998	11,836	1,162	2,110	1,650	1,961	2,780	2,847	1,650
Monroe	1,408	484	249	242	433	156	1,564	1,434	130	139	135	254	344	488	204
Nassau	1,500	546	357	235	362	68	1,568	1,454	114	121	157	348	314	449	178
Okaloosa	14,191	5,043	3,290	2,395	3,463	205	14,396	12,531	1,865	1,260	1,668	4,058	3,295	2,352	1,762
Okeechobee	555	179	105	79	192	93	648	615	33	39	34	63	123	238	151
Orange	15,237	5,169	3,030	2,362	4,676	1,061	16,298	14,695	1,604	1,960	1,884	2,657	3,628	3,840	2,329
Osceola	4,626	1,376	851	681	1,718	290	4,916	4,521	395	473	617	822	1,129	1,275	599
Palm Beach	12,872	4,964	2,328	1,722	3,858	1,803	14,675	13,778	898	1,200	1,061	1,385	2,127	3,894	5,003
Pasco	9,542	3,299	1,796	1,430	3,017	863	10,405	9,644	761	739	904	1,432	1,988	3,234	2,108
Pinellas	17,514	6,185	3,156	2,413	5,760	2,161	19,675	17,976	1,699	1,310	1,480	2,545	4,189	5,898	4,249
Polk	8,979	3,270	1,721	1,294	2,695	807	9,786	9,162	625	673	833	1,308	1,942	3,186	1,845
Putnam	1,479	502	308	226	444	169	1,648	1,537	111	85	110	196	392	588	277
Saint Johns	3,372	1,305	680	512	875	183	3,555	3,246	309	231	390	714	677	987	555
Saint Lucie	4,934	1,664	859	689	1,722	444	5,378	4,998	380	416	426	661	979	1,653	1,242
Santa Rosa	8,090	2,713	1,788	1,371	2,219	178	8,269	7,304	964	620	1,066	2,597	1,735	1,436	812
Sarasota	6,081	2,444	1,053	779	1,805	635	6,717	6,365	352	331	370	551	979	2,363	2,118
Seminole	5,839	2,132	1,190	869	1,648	402	6,241	5,656	585	687	685	945	1,298	1,570	1,055
Sumter	2,850	1,085	585	392	788	164	3,014	2,881	133	52	81	170	401	1,525	785
Suwannee	790	267	163	127	232	92	882	819	63	51	48	111	209	293	169
Taylor	375	125	68	64	118	50	426	407	19	18	39	53	92	147	77
Union	210	78	38	38	56	11	221	206	15	21	11	29	61	69	30
Volusia	9,563	3,195	1,769	1,396	3,204	1,103	10,666	9,944	722	876	834	1,242	2,280	3,428	2,006
Wakulla	501	179	115	76	131	56	557	514	43	45	59	78	123	180	72
Walton	1,538	558	328	220	433	67	1,605	1,444	161	90	140	288	350	475	261
Washington	640	179	137	105	219	40	680	638	42	24	51	108	176	205	116
Unknown	*	*	*	*	*	*	*	*	*	*	*	*	*	*	*
Georgia															
Appling	187	56	42	31	58	36	223	210	13	16	25	28	40	79	35
Atkinson	79	27	11	12	29	21	100	92	*	*	*	*	31	39	*
Bacon	128	37	24	28	39	16	144	138	*	13	18	16	24	55	18

Table 54. Compensation and Pension Recipients, by County, FY2014—*Continued*

(Number of recipients.)

State and county	Compensation					Total, pension	Compensation or pension								
	Total	0 to 20 percent	30 to 40 percent	50 to 60 percent	70 to 100 percent		Total	Male	Female	Less than 35 years	35 to 44 years	45 to 54 years	55 to 64 years	65 to 74 years	75 years and over
Georgia cnt'd															
Baker	51	19	*	*	21	*	53	47	*	*	*	*	14	19	*
Baldwin	539	157	117	76	189	78	616	556	60	53	49	102	159	183	71
Banks	180	65	19	26	69	18	198	193	*	13	12	19	42	82	30
Barrow	744	265	152	109	218	59	803	737	66	100	121	139	154	209	80
Bartow	1,238	416	235	188	399	125	1,363	1,271	92	133	136	213	279	446	155
Ben Hill	252	73	49	32	98	32	284	269	15	21	28	37	71	81	46
Berrien	379	117	88	66	108	37	416	383	33	43	46	81	71	122	53
Bibb	2,298	726	476	361	735	337	2,635	2,381	254	179	247	511	737	664	297
Bleckley	178	50	33	26	69	14	192	180	12	12	14	45	38	58	24
Brantley	261	75	56	54	76	31	292	279	13	31	24	29	80	89	38
Brooks	255	76	54	40	85	33	288	268	20	14	24	49	74	81	46
Bryan	1,270	336	257	233	444	18	1,288	1,073	215	160	308	395	241	147	38
Bulloch	845	254	179	147	265	61	906	819	87	126	110	155	213	212	89
Burke	412	97	75	61	179	32	444	403	41	36	41	78	114	126	49
Butts	331	109	55	46	121	37	368	346	22	27	31	50	76	141	44
Calhoun	73	16	17	16	24	12	85	83	*	*	*	15	26	28	*
Camden	2,298	717	567	456	558	55	2,353	2,110	243	311	441	803	415	286	97
Candler	121	38	28	15	40	19	141	126	15	14	13	24	27	35	27
Carroll	1,236	416	201	184	436	109	1,345	1,237	108	122	161	219	267	410	165
Catoosa	785	260	131	94	300	75	860	805	55	52	86	124	160	300	138
Charlton	183	79	32	33	39	18	201	188	13	20	13	32	45	66	25
Chatham	6,413	1,812	1,292	1,030	2,280	288	6,701	5,655	1,046	1,358	1,045	1,311	1,254	1,238	495
Chattahoochee	535	89	77	98	272	*	544	461	83	225	122	90	58	32	18
Chattooga	322	103	63	42	114	42	364	354	10	21	17	27	89	126	84
Cherokee	2,536	944	517	379	696	143	2,679	2,510	169	261	387	410	468	825	326
Clarke	905	306	172	117	309	127	1,031	933	99	122	111	129	247	285	137
Clay	47	16	11	*	14	*	51	44	*	*	*	*	15	18	*
Clayton	5,231	1,560	1,007	852	1,812	282	5,513	4,408	1,105	473	734	1,471	1,565	1,004	264
Clinch	75	28	17	*	24	*	82	76	*	*	11	*	20	24	12
Cobb	7,596	2,765	1,525	1,176	2,129	474	8,070	7,004	1,066	960	1,168	1,682	1,572	1,842	845
Coffee	430	132	76	64	158	61	491	465	26	40	40	76	120	154	61
Colquitt	508	173	96	80	159	72	580	543	37	36	56	77	133	195	83
Columbia	5,735	1,424	1,167	1,001	2,143	72	5,807	4,691	1,116	722	1,062	1,589	1,106	918	409
Cook	297	91	67	51	87	30	327	296	31	27	44	59	68	83	46
Coweta	1,956	646	416	285	609	96	2,052	1,864	188	191	238	425	439	574	186
Crawford	179	63	34	33	49	19	198	187	11	16	23	34	45	65	15
Crisp	224	66	54	26	78	51	275	257	18	15	21	41	62	90	46
Dade	184	60	31	28	65	18	201	192	*	20	15	26	36	68	37
Dawson	288	102	40	46	100	24	312	299	13	25	33	39	59	120	36
Decatur	308	114	72	51	71	29	337	305	32	43	40	46	72	99	37
Dekalb	8,175	2,595	1,584	1,258	2,737	831	9,005	7,640	1,366	801	1,077	1,939	2,359	2,108	720
Dodge	236	74	47	37	78	33	269	247	22	19	32	52	58	78	30
Dooly	117	26	23	20	48	15	132	117	15	12	11	25	29	37	18
Dougherty	1,844	479	412	313	640	132	1,976	1,771	205	204	240	401	484	449	199
Douglas	2,429	724	491	361	853	99	2,528	2,116	412	219	390	688	526	539	166
Early	148	41	26	16	65	13	161	147	14	15	15	30	34	47	20
Echols	35	12	*	*	10	*	38	36	*	*	*	*	*	11	*
Effingham	1,057	343	199	158	356	23	1,080	978	102	149	197	244	219	224	47
Elbert	253	69	49	35	100	37	290	272	18	13	28	31	67	101	50
Emanuel	267	74	55	46	92	42	309	281	28	27	31	54	71	89	37
Evans	129	34	24	27	44	13	142	136	*	14	*	22	42	38	17
Fannin	419	147	57	61	154	47	466	448	18	23	21	34	87	211	90
Fayette	2,231	769	472	322	667	56	2,287	2,031	256	135	198	494	627	603	229
Floyd	1,021	325	207	143	346	151	1,172	1,099	73	91	75	128	247	417	214
Forsyth	1,181	491	236	161	293	81	1,262	1,174	87	108	152	235	212	364	189
Franklin	237	72	52	28	86	42	279	269	10	21	17	19	55	108	60
Fulton	8,414	2,691	1,655	1,246	2,823	1,203	9,617	8,338	1,280	920	1,288	1,822	2,183	2,411	990
Gilmer	449	134	67	76	172	64	513	497	16	24	24	42	98	218	106
Glascock	27	*	*	*	*	*	30	29	*	*	*	*	*	*	*
Glynn	1,402	487	291	213	411	102	1,504	1,367	137	111	165	263	333	435	197
Gordon	531	173	93	91	173	54	585	568	17	49	41	59	108	232	96
Grady	264	85	59	32	88	39	304	285	19	33	26	36	62	99	47
Greene	215	76	31	27	81	24	240	224	16	*	15	15	57	107	38
Gwinnett	7,324	2,595	1,452	1,116	2,160	340	7,664	6,575	1,089	977	1,300	1,722	1,507	1,565	591
Habersham	519	169	82	87	182	49	568	548	20	46	40	56	96	198	132
Hall	1,732	624	317	224	568	155	1,886	1,761	126	162	180	255	338	669	282
Hancock	117	36	17	15	49	17	134	128	*	*	*	20	31	54	17
Haralson	321	108	62	40	111	32	353	330	23	28	30	52	86	119	37
Harris	1,174	277	235	182	480	28	1,202	1,084	118	61	141	343	285	259	114
Hart	278	90	39	38	111	32	310	296	14	16	30	19	70	120	54

Table 54. Compensation and Pension Recipients, by County, FY2014—*Continued*

(Number of recipients.)

State and county	Compensation					Total, pension	Compensation or pension								
	Total	0 to 20 percent	30 to 40 percent	50 to 60 percent	70 to 100 percent		Total	Male	Female	Less than 35 years	35 to 44 years	45 to 54 years	55 to 64 years	65 to 74 years	75 years and over
Georgia cnt'd															
Heard	144	52	25	16	51	11	155	150	*	*	13	24	35	53	21
Henry	4,553	1,282	853	733	1,685	114	4,667	3,841	826	379	723	1,414	1,030	852	267
Houston	7,425	2,160	1,667	1,333	2,264	144	7,569	6,437	1,132	615	1,007	2,476	1,816	1,081	572
Irwin	112	33	23	18	37	12	124	118	*	*	16	18	20	41	20
Jackson	804	284	143	126	251	62	866	802	64	93	82	134	149	299	109
Jasper	175	49	30	33	63	18	193	180	13	13	19	35	41	63	22
Jeff Davis	140	37	26	26	51	34	174	164	10	13	10	15	40	70	26
Jefferson	230	58	42	28	102	26	256	236	20	17	21	40	65	81	32
Jenkins	97	30	13	12	42	14	111	105	*	12	*	19	20	35	17
Johnson	92	27	25	12	28	12	104	102	*	*	14	17	17	28	20
Jones	377	126	68	75	108	40	416	380	36	40	44	79	100	115	38
Lamar	275	82	40	47	106	26	301	281	20	28	34	41	57	103	38
Lanier	243	70	53	43	77	19	261	226	35	30	43	55	58	49	27
Laurens	868	217	178	146	327	118	986	900	86	76	110	158	273	251	117
Lee	689	180	165	115	228	18	707	636	70	74	123	216	126	133	34
Liberty	5,164	1,087	1,030	965	2,080	41	5,205	4,187	1,018	1,408	998	1,301	962	426	109
Lincoln	169	46	34	32	57	10	179	164	15	12	13	22	51	54	27
Long	803	171	124	166	342	14	817	680	137	192	197	212	135	65	16
Lowndes	2,650	811	566	521	753	173	2,823	2,443	381	363	398	643	625	488	306
Lumpkin	424	117	85	76	147	30	454	441	14	59	32	69	94	132	68
Macon	139	50	30	23	36	19	158	140	18	10	12	37	42	41	16
Madison	383	125	55	65	137	47	430	408	22	33	37	63	83	147	65
Marion	196	36	35	35	89	*	205	188	17	17	19	48	51	54	15
Mcduffie	378	104	72	49	153	18	396	358	38	24	41	74	93	118	46
Mcintosh	197	58	40	28	71	28	225	209	16	13	22	27	45	96	22
Meriwether	312	94	65	46	107	31	343	326	17	28	26	51	93	103	41
Miller	50	17	*	12	15	12	62	57	*	*	*	*	12	19	12
Mitchell	210	65	52	36	57	33	243	224	19	17	24	44	49	77	32
Monroe	350	110	64	62	113	34	383	364	20	26	39	52	94	131	42
Montgomery	90	18	18	16	38	18	108	102	*	*	10	24	27	29	11
Morgan	226	68	50	33	75	24	250	240	10	13	21	28	55	100	33
Murray	418	127	59	78	154	47	465	440	25	39	29	52	93	189	63
Muscogee	9,249	2,010	1,642	1,456	4,141	350	9,599	8,266	1,333	1,179	1,299	2,199	2,433	1,515	973
Newton	1,701	496	300	286	619	113	1,814	1,601	213	141	256	429	369	478	141
Oconee	330	107	69	61	93	28	358	343	15	29	32	52	81	108	55
Oglethorpe	206	52	49	34	71	20	226	211	15	17	11	25	48	85	40
Paulding	2,160	707	415	339	699	102	2,262	2,028	234	268	375	551	426	484	158
Peach	583	148	133	105	198	41	624	553	71	46	59	152	173	141	54
Pickens	379	133	58	65	123	42	421	407	14	34	26	36	81	173	71
Pierce	280	74	57	42	107	37	317	300	17	25	26	38	73	106	49
Pike	242	94	52	29	67	18	260	244	16	24	18	37	48	92	41
Polk	443	141	86	54	161	55	497	467	30	35	40	63	101	174	84
Pulaski	144	38	27	24	55	17	161	146	15	11	*	31	39	54	22
Putnam	350	124	51	70	105	36	386	372	14	13	24	43	85	159	61
Quitman	45	11	*	10	17	*	52	51	*	*	*	*	14	16	14
Rabun	276	90	58	41	87	28	305	297	*	10	14	24	39	140	75
Randolph	97	34	13	13	37	13	110	106	*	*	10	19	26	29	19
Richmond	8,031	1,945	1,477	1,229	3,380	344	8,375	6,802	1,572	970	996	1,752	2,369	1,516	769
Rockdale	1,588	507	262	252	566	85	1,673	1,443	230	124	192	444	367	392	153
Schley	40	16	*	*	12	*	46	42	*	*	*	*	12	*	*
Screven	161	49	33	23	56	23	184	167	17	13	20	25	46	56	24
Seminole	123	36	23	14	50	19	142	131	11	*	*	22	34	48	23
Spalding	888	281	177	132	297	110	998	922	75	87	96	123	219	346	126
Stephens	301	101	60	40	100	55	357	339	18	25	15	37	74	139	65
Stewart	77	21	11	13	32	*	81	74	*	*	*	15	27	17	*
Sumter	372	108	71	62	131	57	429	398	31	29	48	79	117	106	50
Talbot	145	30	30	19	67	10	155	145	10	11	*	24	56	37	22
Taliaferro	20	*	*	*	*	*	23	21	*	*	*	*	*	*	*
Tattnall	428	117	82	54	175	30	458	407	51	53	54	99	102	121	29
Taylor	102	27	21	16	38	17	119	114	*	*	*	11	22	49	22
Telfair	149	34	28	21	66	36	185	180	*	*	*	28	55	57	29
Terrell	138	41	32	19	46	*	144	133	11	*	22	41	27	35	12
Thomas	627	233	119	94	181	110	737	674	63	52	76	122	180	215	92
Tift	511	157	106	71	177	70	581	531	50	53	61	105	124	169	69
Toombs	332	109	56	59	108	45	376	355	21	36	44	75	89	80	53
Towns	194	64	35	12	83	25	219	214	*	*	*	*	38	98	63
Treutlen	60	19	12	10	19	10	70	68	*	*	*	11	18	16	10
Troup	1,034	327	196	164	347	97	1,131	1,041	90	78	124	182	228	351	168
Turner	114	29	24	25	36	19	133	120	13	16	12	20	41	32	11
Twiggs	120	35	25	22	38	*	127	115	13	10	*	25	36	38	10

Table 54. Compensation and Pension Recipients, by County, FY2014—*Continued*

(Number of recipients.)

State and county	Compensation					Total, pension	Compensation or pension								
	Total	0 to 20 percent	30 to 40 percent	50 to 60 percent	70 to 100 percent		Total	Male	Female	Less than 35 years	35 to 44 years	45 to 54 years	55 to 64 years	65 to 74 years	75 years and over
Georgia cnt'd															
Union	494	173	78	65	178	51	544	518	26	17	24	42	91	224	146
Upson	363	95	55	61	152	60	423	401	22	30	38	51	81	152	71
Walker	811	269	136	108	299	99	910	874	36	58	72	101	196	344	139
Walton	995	339	186	149	321	82	1,077	1,015	62	103	113	179	208	327	147
Ware	543	172	98	97	176	98	641	584	57	46	59	90	154	205	88
Warren	76	27	15	*	25	10	86	80	*	*	*	13	25	26	11
Washington	257	72	43	41	101	36	293	257	36	36	22	35	61	112	27
Wayne	488	126	106	87	169	30	518	487	31	53	63	86	113	146	57
Webster	32	*	*	*	14	*	34	32	*	*	*	*	13	12	*
Wheeler	79	18	16	10	35	12	91	84	*	*	*	10	26	31	10
White	385	130	81	51	123	44	429	411	18	28	29	49	73	162	88
Whitfield	824	323	157	106	238	110	935	902	33	99	60	81	179	345	170
Wilcox	88	25	13	21	29	15	103	98	*	10	*	12	25	28	21
Wilkes	151	45	26	20	60	23	174	154	20	20	*	21	37	60	27
Wilkinson	139	34	24	19	62	*	148	137	11	17	16	21	27	50	17
Worth	300	96	55	61	87	28	328	308	20	25	22	72	71	96	41
Unknown	*	*	*	*	*	*	*	*	*	*	*	*	*	*	*
Hawaii															
Hawaii	2,437	736	387	306	1,008	156	2,593	2,464	129	148	154	279	531	1,079	400
Honolulu	19,381	6,182	4,000	3,228	5,971	386	19,767	17,533	2,234	2,909	2,551	3,978	3,850	3,803	2,667
Kauai	854	318	157	108	271	45	899	859	40	36	47	102	182	365	166
Maui	1,674	502	255	198	719	70	1,744	1,674	70	91	89	171	367	709	317
Idaho															
Ada	6,308	2,328	1,386	956	1,638	351	6,658	6,024	634	797	944	1,169	1,291	1,607	849
Adams	73	30	12	10	21	*	77	72	*	*	*	10	14	31	12
Bannock	1,080	424	217	160	279	73	1,153	1,090	63	136	135	137	235	329	181
Bear Lake	57	25	*	10	14	*	62	60	*	*	*	*	*	22	11
Benewah	179	65	33	31	50	13	192	181	11	19	*	18	27	88	30
Bingham	451	178	78	73	122	28	479	452	27	50	49	63	92	152	73
Blaine	98	39	26	13	20	14	112	108	*	13	*	14	17	38	23
Boise	201	66	36	27	71	11	212	195	17	13	14	35	50	85	15
Bonner	672	254	118	88	212	68	740	713	27	38	43	77	156	296	129
Bonneville	1,117	438	247	166	266	56	1,173	1,111	62	159	176	159	213	289	177
Boundary	197	68	44	25	60	25	222	211	11	14	17	21	56	85	29
Butte	31	17	*	*	*	*	33	32	*	*	*	*	*	17	*
Camas	*	*	*	*	*	*	*	*	*	*	*	*	*	*	*
Canyon	2,637	930	596	404	707	149	2,786	2,569	217	332	362	506	531	721	334
Caribou	61	26	12	*	15	*	63	61	*	*	*	*	14	26	11
Cassia	165	50	32	30	53	10	175	164	11	20	18	23	16	62	36
Clark	*	*	*	*	*	*	*	*	*	*	*	*	*	*	*
Clearwater	212	71	51	35	55	14	226	221	*	15	*	23	42	100	37
Custer	64	17	19	*	19	10	74	69	*	*	*	*	20	25	13
Elmore	1,429	411	322	290	406	26	1,455	1,243	212	164	167	477	329	208	110
Franklin	94	30	23	18	23	*	99	96	*	*	*	12	18	38	13
Fremont	137	42	23	34	38	13	150	145	*	17	*	24	19	54	27
Gem	336	115	59	54	108	25	361	335	26	28	41	53	64	110	65
Gooding	141	51	32	20	38	14	155	147	*	16	11	17	26	44	41
Idaho	273	97	61	45	70	22	295	288	*	14	13	29	57	127	54
Jefferson	242	86	52	44	60	15	257	245	12	37	31	37	36	71	44
Jerome	188	75	45	24	44	16	204	189	15	25	16	22	42	65	34
Kootenai	2,610	923	517	449	721	159	2,769	2,579	190	288	288	361	525	861	446
Latah	366	150	77	61	78	19	385	357	28	59	51	50	74	98	53
Lemhi	171	46	40	24	61	18	189	180	*	*	*	20	37	83	38
Lewis	136	44	21	24	47	10	146	141	*	*	*	15	32	57	30
Lincoln	49	12	16	*	12	11	60	55	*	*	*	*	12	20	10
Madison	141	50	27	27	37	*	147	141	*	25	11	16	24	47	24
Minidoka	132	49	33	19	31	13	145	142	*	14	12	18	26	46	29
Nez Perce	681	248	145	116	172	63	744	706	38	65	78	88	118	224	171
Oneida	50	18	*	11	15	*	53	51	*	*	*	*	10	14	15
Owyhee	114	41	28	19	26	15	129	122	*	10	*	22	29	45	20
Payette	329	118	86	47	78	40	369	343	26	38	33	54	58	110	76
Power	77	27	15	17	18	10	87	81	*	*	10	*	20	23	17
Shoshone	248	78	54	37	79	27	275	267	*	17	21	33	49	107	48
Teton	51	23	11	*	12	*	53	52	*	*	*	*	*	19	*
Twin Falls	780	283	178	115	204	63	843	778	65	129	89	94	144	219	168
Valley	126	51	31	16	28	*	132	124	*	10	12	15	19	57	19
Washington	161	56	36	26	43	16	177	170	*	17	13	23	26	62	36

Table 54. Compensation and Pension Recipients, by County, FY2014—*Continued*

(Number of recipients.)

State and county	Compensation					Total, pension	Compensation or pension								
	Total	0 to 20 percent	30 to 40 percent	50 to 60 percent	70 to 100 percent		Total	Male	Female	Less than 35 years	35 to 44 years	45 to 54 years	55 to 64 years	65 to 74 years	75 years and over
Illinois															
Adams	777	295	152	111	219	102	879	825	54	120	91	84	144	299	141
Alexander	113	38	16	16	43	15	128	124	*	*	*	18	34	47	17
Bond	190	73	30	27	60	20	210	202	*	19	15	27	50	71	27
Boone	355	133	83	53	86	19	374	348	26	46	40	44	61	122	61
Brown	50	18	*	*	14	*	55	55	*	*	*	*	14	17	*
Bureau	271	106	55	43	67	39	310	290	20	29	31	43	44	102	60
Calhoun	55	17	12	10	16	10	65	62	*	*	*	*	12	25	16
Carroll	167	57	38	25	47	*	176	162	14	24	21	21	28	58	24
Cass	131	29	22	28	52	*	140	133	*	11	12	*	33	62	15
Champaign	1,388	485	282	228	393	99	1,487	1,350	137	228	183	216	262	363	235
Christian	353	111	80	59	103	34	387	366	21	57	37	43	65	127	58
Clark	182	53	33	34	62	22	204	194	10	23	15	28	41	67	30
Clay	150	49	34	22	45	18	168	163	*	13	24	16	29	59	27
Clinton	652	228	143	105	175	33	685	610	75	48	71	175	141	165	85
Coles	477	151	93	71	162	37	514	484	30	71	60	56	94	164	69
Cook	24,185	8,290	4,570	3,351	7,974	4,031	28,216	26,072	2,144	3,468	2,833	3,344	5,490	9,034	4,042
Crawford	200	69	38	26	67	19	219	206	13	26	15	23	33	86	36
Cumberland	113	42	24	12	35	12	125	119	*	16	12	10	24	44	19
Dekalb	635	227	118	84	206	30	665	602	63	160	90	69	89	192	65
Dewitt	166	60	28	30	48	14	180	159	21	23	20	16	32	64	25
Douglas	128	42	19	19	48	12	140	133	*	23	12	17	18	49	20
Dupage	3,692	1,341	709	486	1,157	251	3,943	3,685	258	677	445	382	524	1,295	617
Edgar	202	56	44	31	71	18	220	212	*	22	14	27	40	81	36
Edwards	77	28	12	12	25	*	86	84	*	*	*	*	20	36	15
Effingham	278	82	71	37	88	24	302	286	16	61	16	31	49	100	45
Fayette	185	55	41	33	56	16	201	193	*	25	19	30	36	70	21
Ford	133	40	29	21	43	*	138	130	*	22	12	*	32	42	22
Franklin	673	197	114	107	255	84	756	726	31	84	54	66	141	288	124
Fulton	344	126	68	45	105	40	384	356	28	54	43	44	58	126	59
Gallatin	88	25	20	11	32	*	94	93	*	*	*	*	15	40	19
Greene	127	37	22	17	51	*	134	125	*	13	*	17	31	51	18
Grundy	339	116	57	47	120	10	349	327	22	81	46	29	50	110	32
Hamilton	111	28	17	23	43	17	128	124	*	*	*	11	23	54	26
Hancock	211	64	43	38	66	22	233	220	13	31	20	24	42	93	24
Hardin	59	17	12	*	21	*	67	65	*	*	*	*	10	34	*
Henderson	78	28	13	15	22	11	89	86	*	*	*	18	10	40	13
Henry	515	184	92	82	156	40	555	522	33	53	69	82	104	182	64
Iroquois	241	77	52	38	74	13	254	236	18	32	17	28	42	99	36
Jackson	698	230	132	113	223	68	766	691	75	142	104	94	123	220	82
Jasper	83	22	23	14	24	*	88	84	*	12	*	*	17	29	15
Jefferson	534	188	91	92	163	49	583	553	30	59	63	65	87	221	88
Jersey	227	72	43	31	81	31	259	245	14	21	18	29	47	106	37
Jo Daviess	202	81	40	36	45	17	219	210	*	18	17	23	36	85	40
Johnson	228	77	39	37	75	14	242	230	12	23	22	27	49	91	30
Kane	2,126	769	391	290	677	148	2,274	2,114	160	428	267	266	298	742	273
Kankakee	839	260	156	115	308	97	936	877	59	114	95	122	178	319	108
Kendall	708	252	138	105	212	32	740	672	68	149	146	107	84	192	62
Knox	530	158	126	83	163	58	588	562	26	61	49	79	102	213	84
La Salle	968	311	156	138	363	96	1,064	1,016	48	133	104	130	182	371	144
Lake	5,357	1,758	1,152	845	1,603	297	5,654	4,944	710	783	760	1,164	1,081	1,302	562
Lawrence	155	55	40	20	40	16	171	160	11	13	16	21	30	60	31
Lee	293	124	59	34	76	30	323	298	25	47	47	32	61	93	43
Livingston	293	101	56	40	96	25	318	304	14	34	36	30	65	117	36
Logan	215	71	44	31	69	17	232	216	16	30	19	34	41	76	32
Macon	1,095	328	221	180	366	129	1,224	1,151	73	142	107	134	236	464	141
Macoupin	587	192	104	100	191	37	625	597	28	80	58	60	111	244	70
Madison	3,366	1,199	743	511	914	261	3,628	3,299	329	382	398	696	717	1,045	390
Marion	507	154	94	88	171	60	567	542	25	59	51	58	106	206	86
Marshall	103	30	18	16	39	*	108	102	*	13	12	19	17	34	13
Mason	161	40	36	19	66	11	172	163	*	17	11	29	33	65	17
Massac	190	50	37	26	77	16	206	190	16	27	20	17	30	82	30
Mcdonough	396	141	80	62	113	34	430	409	21	86	43	46	72	135	48
Mchenry	1,856	656	394	273	532	113	1,969	1,838	131	322	238	260	265	665	218
Mclean	1,164	392	244	191	337	75	1,239	1,145	94	232	160	140	196	376	134
Menard	125	40	25	27	33	*	129	123	*	14	19	21	12	43	20
Mercer	195	70	37	27	61	10	205	196	*	25	21	24	30	83	22
Monroe	348	114	73	57	104	14	362	336	26	27	44	69	66	110	46
Montgomery	304	109	55	58	82	25	329	309	20	39	34	22	59	122	53
Morgan	375	94	74	66	141	35	410	391	19	43	30	45	63	180	49
Moultrie	123	30	19	14	60	*	131	123	*	19	15	17	25	33	22

Table 54. Compensation and Pension Recipients, by County, FY2014—*Continued*

(Number of recipients.)

State and county	Compensation: Total	Compensation: 0 to 20 percent	Compensation: 30 to 40 percent	Compensation: 50 to 60 percent	Compensation: 70 to 100 percent	Total, pension	Compensation or pension: Total	Male	Female	Less than 35 years	35 to 44 years	45 to 54 years	55 to 64 years	65 to 74 years	75 years and over
Illinois cnt'd															
Ogle	475	175	114	74	112	43	518	485	33	78	53	65	80	171	71
Peoria	1,494	557	281	226	430	153	1,647	1,508	139	228	225	264	278	455	197
Perry	274	86	46	48	94	21	295	279	16	37	26	31	47	100	54
Piatt	143	55	30	21	37	*	150	136	14	16	16	17	27	50	24
Pike	169	48	35	26	60	23	192	185	*	15	13	18	30	81	35
Pope	55	22	*	12	14	*	62	58	*	*	*	10	10	25	*
Pulaski	106	31	18	14	43	10	116	111	*	*	*	17	22	42	23
Putnam	58	24	*	11	18	*	60	57	*	12	*	*	*	20	*
Randolph	369	128	56	75	110	33	402	387	15	47	34	48	65	161	47
Richland	178	69	33	32	44	19	197	189	*	28	17	15	32	75	30
Rock Island	1,586	553	321	247	465	127	1,713	1,580	133	238	194	284	344	481	170
Saint Clair	7,406	2,418	1,637	1,268	2,082	308	7,713	6,511	1,202	619	990	2,330	1,844	1,370	559
Saline	363	116	68	54	125	62	425	409	16	35	36	45	72	152	85
Sangamon	1,845	634	389	290	532	151	1,996	1,837	159	288	245	267	385	581	230
Schuyler	90	25	15	19	31	*	98	92	*	*	11	11	11	47	10
Scott	43	18	*	*	13	11	54	53	*	*	*	*	*	18	14
Shelby	229	82	43	36	68	23	252	236	16	27	21	26	47	95	36
Stark	54	28	*	10	*	*	58	55	*	*	11	*	*	19	*
Stephenson	474	202	98	59	115	48	522	498	24	59	37	62	95	169	99
Tazewell	1,212	406	254	189	363	75	1,287	1,207	80	219	164	175	194	406	129
Union	255	84	60	27	84	21	276	260	16	20	27	32	57	103	37
Vermilion	1,012	281	201	152	378	138	1,150	1,073	77	107	112	139	271	345	176
Wabash	120	37	32	19	32	17	137	129	*	18	10	16	20	47	26
Warren	147	51	26	23	47	15	162	156	*	19	14	17	42	53	17
Washington	201	66	40	47	48	12	213	201	12	19	22	26	44	71	31
Wayne	175	73	27	25	50	17	192	188	*	11	16	14	30	86	35
White	199	64	37	31	67	21	220	212	*	23	14	*	37	99	38
Whiteside	583	219	118	80	166	51	634	590	44	76	68	95	110	196	89
Will	3,830	1,356	664	501	1,308	265	4,095	3,783	312	559	568	584	637	1,291	453
Williamson	1,123	360	215	186	362	94	1,218	1,145	73	132	125	174	215	393	178
Winnebago	2,517	987	513	362	655	219	2,736	2,529	207	298	264	350	497	923	404
Woodford	307	115	54	48	90	*	316	293	23	49	41	38	40	107	41
Unknown	*	*	*	*	*	*	*	*	*	*	*	*	*	*	*
Indiana															
Adams	220	107	41	25	47	16	236	225	11	28	18	18	42	90	40
Allen	4,046	1,889	774	547	836	334	4,380	4,110	270	495	468	617	846	1,332	621
Bartholomew	867	368	193	115	191	50	917	866	51	74	99	139	177	284	143
Benton	68	24	11	11	22	*	73	69	*	12	11	*	18	16	*
Blackford	251	107	57	36	51	14	265	255	10	26	19	37	42	90	51
Boone	472	191	102	65	114	36	508	483	25	74	65	90	71	121	87
Brown	329	133	52	54	90	15	344	332	12	18	27	48	83	117	51
Carroll	242	89	53	33	66	13	255	249	*	26	22	30	60	85	31
Cass	666	316	136	93	121	30	696	665	31	64	49	85	146	220	132
Clark	1,647	703	328	235	381	114	1,761	1,635	126	161	202	306	382	507	203
Clay	381	156	76	48	101	18	399	383	16	35	42	53	72	134	63
Clinton	310	128	66	33	83	19	329	316	13	32	25	50	62	118	42
Crawford	160	82	18	26	34	11	171	164	*	14	*	21	50	49	30
Daviess	350	142	76	48	84	26	376	356	20	46	32	60	69	103	66
De Kalb	726	354	139	96	137	31	758	729	29	51	55	90	123	302	136
Dearborn	635	265	156	86	128	30	665	639	26	70	71	76	121	227	100
Decatur	234	88	55	40	51	10	244	228	16	26	25	37	45	77	34
Delaware	1,513	636	306	207	364	94	1,607	1,531	76	139	144	209	323	519	272
Dubois	374	165	76	50	83	23	397	373	24	67	41	53	76	101	59
Elkhart	1,832	815	386	234	397	119	1,951	1,877	74	199	156	243	386	660	307
Fayette	269	106	42	31	90	21	290	278	12	29	31	35	47	105	43
Floyd	1,186	586	223	152	226	47	1,233	1,169	64	102	146	195	253	382	156
Fountain	154	53	28	25	48	14	168	163	*	18	20	23	22	58	27
Franklin	258	100	67	32	59	10	268	260	*	23	21	31	52	90	51
Fulton	300	139	65	32	64	25	325	310	15	31	19	28	64	117	66
Gibson	359	132	75	53	99	30	389	371	18	49	54	40	66	125	55
Grant	1,973	936	338	252	447	118	2,091	2,008	83	90	131	247	446	713	464
Greene	615	255	126	86	148	31	646	614	32	66	69	109	123	206	73
Hamilton	2,623	1,099	550	361	613	113	2,736	2,496	240	310	407	580	468	652	318
Hancock	1,108	423	240	157	287	35	1,143	1,054	89	146	131	224	203	334	104
Harrison	709	313	146	85	164	15	724	687	37	74	71	109	140	231	98
Hendricks	2,046	889	429	284	445	103	2,149	2,001	148	232	307	423	370	555	262
Henry	632	253	129	91	159	48	680	653	27	51	60	106	107	236	120
Howard	2,003	1,122	339	230	312	96	2,099	1,992	107	138	168	314	433	663	382
Huntington	630	299	133	90	108	36	666	641	24	54	46	88	112	225	139

Table 54. Compensation and Pension Recipients, by County, FY2014—*Continued*

(Number of recipients.)

State and county	Compensation					Total, pension	Compensation or pension								
	Total	0 to 20 percent	30 to 40 percent	50 to 60 percent	70 to 100 percent		Total	Male	Female	Less than 35 years	35 to 44 years	45 to 54 years	55 to 64 years	65 to 74 years	75 years and over
Indiana cnt'd															
Jackson	417	174	96	57	90	38	455	436	19	49	33	82	76	147	68
Jasper	265	104	52	35	74	12	277	262	15	36	38	43	46	93	21
Jay	202	85	37	30	50	17	219	210	*	24	12	31	35	76	41
Jefferson	546	272	101	60	113	26	572	552	20	34	48	71	97	224	98
Jennings	360	124	82	48	106	31	391	379	12	28	37	63	73	138	52
Johnson	1,940	792	409	266	473	99	2,039	1,890	149	266	276	349	352	552	243
Knox	559	231	107	88	133	48	607	584	23	42	51	82	121	186	125
Kosciusko	727	314	148	114	151	50	777	740	37	72	70	83	139	279	134
La Porte	993	391	225	116	261	83	1,076	1,026	50	119	96	159	199	371	132
Lagrange	277	113	53	44	67	18	295	279	16	27	13	22	66	119	48
Lake	4,039	1,388	809	639	1,203	369	4,408	4,110	298	475	472	664	847	1,409	541
Lawrence	713	256	158	100	199	30	743	706	37	83	90	142	134	207	86
Madison	2,086	892	405	293	497	124	2,210	2,106	104	174	185	340	426	748	338
Marion	10,826	4,046	2,313	1,671	2,796	1,077	11,903	10,740	1,163	1,166	1,226	2,208	2,959	2,964	1,380
Marshall	462	194	91	66	111	18	480	459	21	46	36	53	82	189	74
Martin	190	71	45	25	49	14	204	196	*	19	15	46	50	57	17
Miami	1,435	849	242	156	189	29	1,464	1,394	70	85	102	263	290	462	262
Monroe	1,234	518	248	190	278	80	1,314	1,214	100	159	168	208	261	318	200
Montgomery	340	143	74	53	70	32	372	352	20	39	31	54	81	107	60
Morgan	1,055	452	213	154	236	41	1,096	1,038	58	124	127	186	229	317	113
Newton	117	46	19	16	36	*	126	120	*	12	13	18	23	42	18
Noble	584	272	114	86	112	26	610	584	26	57	54	57	115	231	96
Ohio	73	25	20	12	16	*	79	74	*	*	*	15	14	25	14
Orange	252	122	45	30	55	15	267	261	*	18	27	32	60	89	42
Owen	338	130	66	41	101	29	367	351	16	34	22	47	93	126	45
Parke	240	108	40	35	56	15	255	246	*	22	12	35	59	90	36
Perry	255	114	47	39	55	15	270	252	18	19	27	33	58	90	43
Pike	140	58	27	15	40	12	152	150	*	16	17	17	28	53	21
Porter	1,402	505	292	220	385	75	1,477	1,394	83	214	183	228	236	480	136
Posey	277	91	68	34	84	14	291	277	14	36	27	42	47	98	41
Pulaski	146	54	37	15	40	10	156	146	10	11	18	15	25	64	23
Putnam	559	236	120	76	127	22	582	553	29	47	50	100	132	172	80
Randolph	282	107	61	37	77	29	311	301	10	21	20	46	53	110	61
Ripley	298	124	58	48	68	20	318	299	19	25	24	39	63	111	56
Rush	172	72	36	27	37	12	184	176	*	18	18	39	33	56	20
Scott	313	118	64	50	81	24	337	321	16	36	36	44	82	107	31
Shelby	516	185	122	78	131	31	547	513	34	58	62	89	108	157	72
Spencer	264	86	42	51	85	14	277	267	11	32	25	32	55	110	23
St Joseph	3,040	1,497	584	362	597	173	3,213	3,056	157	290	249	392	616	1,136	530
Starke	241	90	45	40	66	20	261	249	12	29	21	28	52	102	29
Steuben	503	220	99	66	118	21	524	509	15	37	38	54	94	221	80
Sullivan	284	108	55	53	68	19	303	293	10	27	28	50	61	97	40
Switzerland	106	40	18	15	33	*	115	111	*	12	10	12	21	45	15
Tippecanoe	1,252	479	257	190	326	124	1,376	1,267	109	221	193	220	229	354	159
Tipton	263	132	53	29	49	*	270	260	10	18	16	39	41	107	49
Union	89	39	14	12	24	*	96	93	*	*	*	18	25	24	17
Vanderburgh	2,021	711	460	322	528	227	2,248	2,111	137	273	245	277	400	653	400
Vermillion	220	71	45	33	71	12	232	221	11	25	23	39	48	78	19
Vigo	1,244	504	231	166	344	112	1,356	1,283	73	141	129	219	306	386	175
Wabash	571	270	107	76	118	36	607	594	13	32	45	54	83	243	150
Warren	89	32	17	14	26	*	94	90	*	*	*	20	15	30	12
Warrick	724	239	156	110	219	34	758	718	40	85	96	113	118	251	95
Washington	372	158	71	51	92	19	391	370	21	39	32	64	86	116	54
Wayne	802	262	179	126	235	73	875	835	40	71	86	131	186	302	99
Wells	386	171	81	61	73	*	395	382	13	34	31	45	65	157	63
White	311	127	62	42	80	17	328	308	20	28	34	31	51	118	66
Whitley	462	219	93	51	99	16	478	459	19	39	49	51	72	187	80
Iowa															
Adair	80	27	15	15	22	11	91	87	*	*	*	*	*	37	22
Adams	49	21	*	12	11	*	54	54	*	*	*	*	10	15	11
Allamakee	174	61	39	20	54	21	195	182	13	22	10	16	33	77	37
Appanoose	214	91	55	24	44	35	249	245	*	17	16	22	30	77	87
Audubon	92	26	27	15	24	*	97	91	*	10	*	16	13	34	20
Benton	257	98	52	34	73	13	270	255	15	34	37	36	47	74	42
Black Hawk	1,149	423	229	155	342	144	1,293	1,210	83	154	126	199	246	370	198
Boone	388	181	78	55	74	18	406	390	16	49	32	65	81	101	78
Bremer	199	66	36	38	59	10	209	201	*	26	22	35	23	67	35
Buchanan	183	83	32	23	45	14	197	192	*	30	23	28	22	68	26
Buena Vista	254	98	64	47	45	17	271	263	*	20	15	17	37	96	86

Table 54. Compensation and Pension Recipients, by County, FY2014—*Continued*

(Number of recipients.)

State and county	Compensation					Total, pension	Compensation or pension								
	Total	0 to 20 percent	30 to 40 percent	50 to 60 percent	70 to 100 percent		Total	Male	Female	Less than 35 years	35 to 44 years	45 to 54 years	55 to 64 years	65 to 74 years	75 years and over
Iowa cnt'd															
Butler	183	62	51	33	37	13	196	191	*	21	17	17	30	77	34
Calhoun	135	76	23	*	29	15	150	146	*	*	*	16	28	50	40
Carroll	229	102	66	24	37	21	250	241	*	28	21	24	40	81	56
Cass	212	89	46	30	47	18	230	221	*	22	14	25	36	77	56
Cedar	213	92	44	27	50	15	228	209	19	32	33	31	38	64	30
Cerro Gordo	808	340	152	129	187	111	919	882	37	62	63	85	149	263	297
Cherokee	208	97	33	28	50	*	212	205	*	14	14	22	43	71	48
Chickasaw	135	43	37	14	41	*	143	137	*	*	11	19	34	50	20
Clarke	180	80	36	30	34	20	200	187	13	14	12	20	26	70	58
Clay	192	83	41	36	32	32	224	214	10	27	18	20	27	73	59
Clayton	215	76	38	43	58	20	235	221	14	32	24	26	41	83	29
Clinton	524	172	115	81	156	50	574	540	34	67	69	72	120	180	66
Crawford	243	116	50	38	39	16	259	250	*	20	11	26	39	92	71
Dallas	677	284	158	105	131	30	707	663	44	104	87	99	113	191	113
Davis	98	37	20	14	27	13	111	102	*	12	*	*	12	37	38
Decatur	118	53	18	18	29	10	128	118	10	*	*	11	21	41	38
Delaware	158	53	36	26	43	17	175	165	10	22	*	28	27	60	29
Des Moines	430	142	93	69	126	49	479	448	31	65	42	72	85	150	65
Dickinson	205	92	35	22	56	34	239	232	*	15	13	19	38	94	59
Dubuque	1,037	330	212	172	323	71	1,108	1,037	71	141	104	170	196	341	154
Emmet	130	56	30	17	27	11	141	134	*	22	14	10	21	47	27
Fayette	207	77	45	30	55	27	234	221	13	23	26	29	37	74	45
Floyd	261	93	55	42	71	26	287	274	13	24	19	33	45	100	66
Franklin	141	53	23	25	40	11	152	147	*	11	*	12	22	56	42
Fremont	121	38	27	17	39	14	135	129	*	*	17	16	21	46	26
Greene	118	47	22	18	31	10	128	119	*	14	*	23	23	34	30
Grundy	122	51	31	13	27	12	134	126	*	12	17	18	18	39	30
Guthrie	167	61	34	28	44	19	186	180	*	10	13	29	29	51	54
Hamilton	240	95	58	37	50	15	255	247	*	28	12	19	41	85	69
Hancock	170	73	47	14	36	*	179	170	*	11	15	10	22	62	59
Hardin	220	103	55	30	32	12	232	227	*	21	19	22	39	76	54
Harrison	273	114	52	40	67	20	292	278	14	26	19	34	57	94	63
Henry	246	69	62	49	66	15	261	249	12	34	32	45	43	76	31
Howard	102	35	19	15	33	12	114	105	*	11	*	15	22	32	26
Humboldt	119	49	22	19	29	*	128	123	*	13	10	14	27	34	30
Ida	88	28	19	14	27	*	96	90	*	11	*	10	20	33	14
Iowa	148	54	34	24	36	21	169	159	10	29	15	20	30	51	24
Jackson	230	75	50	31	74	15	245	232	13	19	24	37	49	87	29
Jasper	445	184	116	61	84	29	474	452	22	40	34	58	83	166	93
Jefferson	136	41	29	21	45	32	168	154	14	25	17	20	15	66	25
Johnson	826	302	199	140	185	78	904	840	64	191	106	136	154	213	103
Jones	247	88	41	45	73	18	265	252	13	36	24	34	42	93	35
Keokuk	101	40	24	12	25	19	120	117	*	15	*	13	24	34	27
Kossuth	230	102	41	32	55	22	252	244	*	22	15	26	21	81	87
Lee	403	121	81	77	124	48	451	420	31	72	51	63	69	143	53
Linn	2,053	745	435	321	552	181	2,234	2,055	179	341	227	366	382	617	300
Louisa	119	44	30	19	26	*	128	121	*	*	14	20	24	49	12
Lucas	109	49	19	15	26	10	119	114	*	13	*	19	32	24	22
Lyon	110	44	16	21	29	*	115	107	*	12	10	13	17	43	20
Madison	210	92	50	22	47	12	222	214	*	25	17	31	34	83	31
Mahaska	251	115	41	31	64	28	279	273	*	13	17	37	57	84	70
Marion	617	292	88	85	152	53	670	639	31	28	45	64	139	228	166
Marshall	491	218	102	60	111	101	592	562	30	52	29	59	108	195	149
Mills	346	121	75	55	95	*	354	327	27	40	31	62	80	89	52
Mitchell	139	57	26	25	31	26	165	156	*	17	*	21	27	43	50
Monona	130	42	35	21	32	13	143	135	*	15	*	13	32	45	29
Monroe	138	48	33	16	41	*	146	143	*	11	*	15	23	58	32
Montgomery	179	65	46	22	46	14	193	184	*	21	13	26	34	54	44
Muscatine	358	133	75	50	100	29	387	362	25	43	47	57	73	124	42
Obrien	171	76	34	23	38	14	185	180	*	15	11	16	28	77	38
Osceola	65	28	14	10	13	11	76	74	*	*	*	*	11	24	22
Page	170	61	34	30	45	19	189	180	*	17	*	23	27	60	53
Palo Alto	155	59	36	23	37	18	173	167	*	11	*	12	23	71	49
Plymouth	214	87	49	29	49	22	236	221	15	19	*	36	48	73	52
Pocahontas	86	31	22	*	24	16	102	98	*	*	*	14	12	35	26
Polk	4,832	1,972	1,038	780	1,041	472	5,303	4,944	360	643	541	703	1,055	1,522	838
Pottawattamie	1,766	717	354	284	411	121	1,887	1,764	123	169	170	258	362	567	359
Poweshiek	142	52	35	15	40	16	158	150	*	17	17	14	31	58	21
Ringgold	65	22	16	11	16	*	72	72	*	*	*	*	14	28	18
Sac	189	86	44	23	36	20	209	201	*	*	*	13	30	68	83

Table 54. Compensation and Pension Recipients, by County, FY2014—*Continued*

(Number of recipients.)

State and county	Compensation					Total, pension	Compensation or pension								
	Total	0 to 20 percent	30 to 40 percent	50 to 60 percent	70 to 100 percent		Total	Male	Female	Less than 35 years	35 to 44 years	45 to 54 years	55 to 64 years	65 to 74 years	75 years and over
Iowa cnt'd															
Scott	1,858	625	404	336	493	141	1,999	1,811	188	306	284	332	346	537	193
Shelby	214	106	37	29	42	10	224	214	10	14	*	16	37	67	80
Sioux	231	104	48	33	46	20	251	242	*	22	16	19	26	92	76
Story	734	319	166	125	124	47	781	732	49	123	88	67	124	227	152
Tama	181	64	31	28	58	21	202	189	13	21	17	25	27	75	37
Taylor	85	33	17	15	20	*	91	84	*	*	*	10	20	30	17
Union	189	83	35	27	44	17	206	198	*	23	15	19	37	70	42
Van Buren	95	32	24	16	23	*	104	97	*	*	12	*	25	33	21
Wapello	400	143	79	79	99	58	458	445	13	38	25	56	89	136	114
Warren	734	338	146	106	143	31	765	721	44	65	87	107	137	232	136
Washington	233	73	45	54	61	27	260	236	24	38	30	30	41	81	40
Wayne	76	33	13	*	22	18	94	92	*	*	*	*	18	23	34
Webster	556	247	113	70	126	32	588	565	23	56	47	64	116	195	110
Winnebago	179	68	41	25	45	16	195	189	*	19	12	23	25	54	62
Winneshiek	161	46	38	32	45	11	172	166	*	23	10	14	22	56	47
Woodbury	993	422	222	144	205	134	1,127	1,061	66	119	99	144	211	372	181
Worth	137	70	24	13	30	*	144	141	*	*	13	10	27	56	32
Wright	168	65	34	27	42	18	186	177	*	22	*	16	32	52	59
Unknown	*	*	*	*	*	*	*	*	*	*	*	*	*	*	*
Kansas															
Allen	141	49	27	17	48	22	163	155	*	10	19	16	36	50	32
Anderson	71	31	*	12	20	*	74	73	*	*	*	11	13	26	15
Atchison	191	78	33	24	56	17	208	198	10	17	12	38	43	57	41
Barber	53	17	15	*	14	*	57	55	*	10	*	*	*	15	17
Barton	240	89	53	35	63	29	269	257	12	22	21	16	52	111	47
Bourbon	156	61	32	19	44	18	174	163	11	17	21	16	25	59	36
Brown	127	42	28	13	44	*	136	131	*	11	13	21	25	45	21
Butler	841	332	173	139	197	45	886	803	83	107	119	176	180	203	101
Chase	26	*	*	*	10	*	30	29	*	*	*	*	*	10	*
Chautauqua	38	15	*	*	11	*	47	46	*	*	*	*	13	10	14
Cherokee	237	82	39	45	71	23	260	248	12	24	16	29	59	85	47
Cheyenne	32	19	*	*	*	*	38	36	*	*	*	*	*	16	13
Clark	20	*	*	*	*	*	23	22	*	*	*	*	*	11	*
Clay	293	70	52	53	118	*	300	274	26	49	48	79	52	45	27
Cloud	99	29	17	21	32	10	109	106	*	*	12	14	15	35	25
Coffey	105	38	18	11	38	13	118	109	*	13	15	17	16	44	13
Comanche	16	*	*	*	*	*	18	18	*	*	*	*	*	10	*
Cowley	385	147	82	59	97	49	434	412	22	59	45	52	78	122	78
Crawford	359	137	65	54	103	44	403	376	27	39	33	44	77	137	73
Decatur	26	*	*	*	*	*	29	28	*	*	*	*	*	*	10
Dickinson	595	155	116	92	232	36	631	571	60	88	117	145	120	109	52
Doniphan	85	33	18	14	20	*	88	86	*	10	*	*	15	30	15
Douglas	804	255	172	121	256	61	865	801	64	140	94	127	146	239	119
Edwards	23	*	*	*	*	*	25	23	*	*	*	*	*	*	*
Elk	47	13	*	*	22	*	49	45	*	*	*	*	12	14	*
Ellis	203	93	45	25	40	27	230	213	17	38	21	18	33	71	49
Ellsworth	73	27	15	10	21	*	79	77	*	*	*	*	13	31	13
Finney	177	78	40	22	37	16	193	186	*	24	14	24	38	63	30
Ford	187	71	44	25	47	21	208	198	10	32	23	20	38	61	34
Franklin	273	98	43	39	93	20	293	282	11	34	25	44	51	88	51
Geary	3,160	694	641	583	1,242	39	3,199	2,677	522	1,081	609	676	431	269	133
Gove	18	*	*	*	*	*	21	19	*	*	*	*	*	*	10
Graham	14	*	*	*	*	*	19	18	*	*	*	*	*	*	*
Grant	27	*	*	*	*	*	30	30	*	*	*	*	*	*	*
Gray	17	*	*	*	*	*	19	18	*	*	*	*	*	11	*
Greeley	*	*	*	*	*	*	10	*	*	*	*	*	*	*	*
Greenwood	88	40	23	*	18	11	99	90	*	*	12	*	26	31	20
Hamilton	15	*	*	*	*	*	17	17	*	*	*	*	*	*	*
Harper	45	19	*	*	13	10	55	53	*	*	*	*	21	13	*
Harvey	290	85	69	59	77	32	322	295	27	50	36	40	65	79	52
Haskell	19	10	*	*	*	*	20	20	*	*	*	*	*	*	*
Hodgeman	18	*	*	*	*	*	18	17	*	*	*	*	*	*	10
Jackson	234	75	51	28	80	10	244	227	17	21	25	35	60	68	35
Jefferson	307	91	61	42	113	20	327	301	26	26	31	49	84	104	33
Jewell	45	22	*	*	13	*	49	47	*	*	*	*	*	18	15
Johnson	4,306	1,579	901	642	1,184	244	4,550	4,218	332	578	596	631	738	1,259	746
Kearny	25	*	*	*	10	*	26	24	*	*	*	*	*	*	*
Kingman	88	39	17	11	21	*	94	88	*	15	*	13	16	33	11
Kiowa	13	*	*	*	*	*	15	15	*	*	*	*	*	*	*

Table 54. Compensation and Pension Recipients, by County, FY2014—*Continued*

(Number of recipients.)

State and county	Compensation					Total, pension	Compensation or pension								
	Total	0 to 20 percent	30 to 40 percent	50 to 60 percent	70 to 100 percent		Total	Male	Female	Less than 35 years	35 to 44 years	45 to 54 years	55 to 64 years	65 to 74 years	75 years and over
Kansas cnt'd															
Labette	177	72	31	20	54	31	208	196	12	14	13	28	31	87	35
Lane	13	*	*	*	*	*	13	13	*	*	*	*	*	*	*
Leavenworth	3,159	994	639	517	1,009	104	3,263	2,899	364	282	337	780	915	686	263
Lincoln	36	12	11	*	*	*	39	38	*	*	*	*	10	11	*
Linn	170	58	24	27	61	16	186	177	*	22	11	20	36	64	33
Logan	12	*	*	*	*	*	17	16	*	*	*	*	*	*	*
Lyon	294	96	60	44	94	32	326	308	18	42	36	27	42	119	60
Marion	110	46	19	17	28	20	130	121	*	17	12	14	18	45	24
Marshall	130	49	19	18	44	10	140	134	*	13	*	15	21	45	37
Mcpherson	217	94	46	24	53	22	239	224	15	35	21	32	50	64	37
Meade	22	*	*	*	*	*	24	21	*	*	*	*	*	*	*
Miami	334	118	55	57	104	19	353	332	21	48	30	49	61	100	65
Mitchell	56	20	13	11	12	*	61	58	*	11	*	*	*	25	12
Montgomery	418	168	85	59	106	56	474	457	17	39	44	62	93	159	77
Morris	149	31	29	23	66	10	159	144	15	24	18	23	41	27	26
Morton	14	*	*	*	*	*	14	13	*	*	*	*	*	*	*
Nemaha	89	30	19	*	32	*	95	91	*	*	*	*	15	32	26
Neosho	150	49	37	21	43	18	168	160	*	14	13	17	38	52	34
Ness	25	10	*	*	*	*	28	26	*	*	*	*	*	*	*
Norton	54	21	13	*	16	*	63	60	*	*	*	*	*	18	21
Osage	244	86	50	36	72	23	267	249	18	19	27	37	53	84	47
Osborne	34	14	*	*	12	*	43	42	*	*	*	*	*	17	12
Ottawa	73	24	11	16	22	*	78	75	*	*	*	12	16	19	16
Pawnee	72	29	13	*	23	*	78	77	*	*	*	*	13	27	12
Phillips	74	28	15	11	20	10	84	82	*	*	*	*	*	33	23
Pottawatomie	422	138	91	68	124	*	431	393	38	46	72	96	70	109	38
Pratt	68	23	20	*	19	*	76	71	*	14	10	*	16	17	15
Rawlins	21	11	*	*	*	*	22	21	*	*	*	*	*	10	*
Reno	619	223	122	78	196	68	687	648	39	77	60	75	119	226	129
Republic	64	21	22	*	14	*	70	66	*	*	*	*	12	24	18
Rice	104	38	19	14	33	*	113	107	*	13	11	*	30	31	19
Riley	1,490	432	284	284	491	16	1,506	1,295	211	411	259	279	273	189	95
Rooks	61	21	15	*	22	*	70	68	*	*	*	*	10	33	11
Rush	32	13	*	*	10	*	38	36	*	*	*	*	13	12	*
Russell	73	19	19	*	26	13	86	84	*	*	*	*	14	30	22
Saline	620	245	125	88	162	66	686	650	36	60	77	103	116	213	117
Scott	28	11	*	*	*	*	29	29	*	*	*	*	*	14	*
Sedgwick	5,857	2,241	1,208	887	1,521	497	6,354	5,772	582	794	774	1,118	1,312	1,514	840
Seward	78	23	16	19	20	15	93	91	*	19	*	10	15	30	12
Shawnee	2,708	750	442	388	1,128	235	2,943	2,691	252	274	289	452	633	863	432
Sheridan	16	*	*	*	*	*	20	19	*	*	*	*	*	*	*
Sherman	57	23	13	*	14	*	62	58	*	*	*	13	10	23	*
Smith	44	15	11	*	15	10	54	53	*	*	*	*	10	14	19
Stafford	46	14	*	*	19	*	54	53	*	*	*	*	*	24	*
Stanton	*	*	*	*	*	*	*	*	*	*	*	*	*	*	*
Stevens	29	10	10	*	*	*	29	29	*	*	*	*	*	*	*
Sumner	268	107	57	29	75	25	293	273	20	26	28	30	68	91	49
Thomas	61	29	12	*	11	*	68	65	*	*	*	*	10	19	14
Trego	26	*	*	*	*	*	30	30	*	*	*	*	*	12	10
Wabaunsee	138	39	25	20	54	*	142	132	10	12	14	31	38	40	*
Wallace	13	*	*	*	*	*	17	16	*	*	*	*	*	*	*
Washington	71	31	*	14	20	*	78	75	*	*	*	*	10	26	24
Wichita	11	*	*	*	*	*	12	12	*	*	*	*	*	*	*
Wilson	96	35	19	10	32	14	110	104	*	11	*	11	19	41	22
Woodson	44	15	*	10	13	*	52	48	*	*	*	*	*	15	13
Wyandotte	1,449	461	255	212	521	196	1,645	1,557	88	139	119	234	420	506	227
Kentucky															
Adair	202	58	32	36	76	31	233	224	*	16	20	23	43	87	44
Allen	271	88	40	40	103	15	286	269	17	26	30	36	58	100	36
Anderson	288	93	42	50	103	13	301	286	15	28	37	53	44	105	34
Ballard	116	37	20	18	41	11	127	124	*	17	12	14	18	44	22
Barren	458	99	96	67	196	50	508	489	19	41	50	61	89	165	102
Bath	132	39	19	20	54	20	152	147	*	11	17	17	16	62	29
Bell	332	76	51	56	149	55	387	372	15	29	30	40	73	159	56
Boone	1,380	515	332	209	323	71	1,451	1,364	87	195	191	235	267	422	140
Bourbon	216	70	39	31	76	24	240	227	13	23	21	35	37	86	38
Boyd	859	296	151	123	290	70	929	885	44	72	97	105	186	321	147
Boyle	339	98	68	61	112	24	363	345	18	22	43	62	64	113	59
Bracken	94	32	24	15	23	*	99	95	*	*	10	20	22	32	*

Table 54. Compensation and Pension Recipients, by County, FY2014—*Continued*

(Number of recipients.)

State and county	Compensation					Total, pension	Compensation or pension								
	Total	0 to 20 percent	30 to 40 percent	50 to 60 percent	70 to 100 percent		Total	Male	Female	Less than 35 years	35 to 44 years	45 to 54 years	55 to 64 years	65 to 74 years	75 years and over
Kentucky cnt'd															
Breathitt	155	38	13	15	89	18	173	170	*	14	12	21	32	65	29
Breckinridge	363	101	62	60	140	33	396	375	21	26	29	62	96	133	50
Bullitt	1,105	422	207	188	288	50	1,155	1,085	70	117	153	238	208	353	85
Butler	192	61	21	36	74	19	211	203	*	14	19	22	38	89	29
Caldwell	170	55	29	24	62	11	181	176	*	14	21	27	28	55	36
Calloway	449	125	87	80	157	36	485	457	28	47	34	55	91	162	96
Campbell	863	339	210	133	181	98	961	917	44	100	70	129	218	304	140
Carlisle	70	24	11	15	20	*	76	75	*	*	*	*	12	29	20
Carroll	117	54	21	15	27	11	128	124	*	*	*	17	28	51	18
Carter	342	98	55	42	147	33	375	369	*	24	26	48	68	146	63
Casey	190	56	30	25	79	30	220	213	*	15	25	17	42	78	43
Christian	3,152	676	595	602	1,279	76	3,228	2,780	448	1,169	641	487	424	339	168
Clark	517	161	100	88	168	35	552	510	42	61	59	96	97	153	86
Clay	195	38	34	38	85	39	234	226	*	14	24	26	46	87	37
Clinton	127	33	31	21	42	22	149	148	*	*	10	13	28	57	33
Crittenden	127	27	12	22	66	*	132	127	*	*	*	13	23	62	18
Cumberland	96	29	18	*	40	13	109	108	*	*	*	13	20	43	28
Daviess	1,131	337	209	202	383	139	1,270	1,209	61	169	135	167	220	362	218
Edmonson	168	52	22	21	73	22	190	186	*	12	18	30	37	66	26
Elliott	62	24	*	10	19	*	66	64	*	*	*	*	15	21	16
Estill	184	41	26	24	93	22	206	193	13	27	23	19	45	70	22
Fayette	2,866	937	588	434	907	270	3,136	2,847	289	411	399	455	648	803	420
Fleming	157	38	26	31	62	29	186	174	12	15	14	17	37	70	33
Floyd	459	102	67	64	226	42	501	492	*	33	40	43	94	219	72
Franklin	558	165	110	84	199	41	599	549	50	51	48	103	127	170	100
Fulton	101	26	19	16	40	12	113	111	*	*	*	13	30	43	15
Gallatin	54	23	*	*	15	*	57	56	*	*	*	*	11	23	*
Garrard	240	82	43	32	83	19	259	247	12	28	28	31	52	81	39
Grant	287	88	71	41	87	28	315	301	14	39	24	45	67	108	32
Graves	464	134	101	72	157	56	520	492	28	39	39	71	97	172	102
Grayson	345	106	66	51	122	29	374	354	20	27	31	63	82	128	43
Green	140	51	26	18	45	26	166	160	*	*	10	21	33	56	36
Greenup	613	196	113	100	203	59	671	643	28	42	57	94	132	231	115
Hancock	103	42	22	11	28	10	113	107	*	*	16	19	21	36	14
Hardin	6,304	1,430	1,241	1,153	2,479	103	6,407	5,611	795	652	883	1,803	1,526	1,016	525
Harlan	472	95	45	70	262	57	529	520	*	44	39	51	100	224	71
Harrison	237	77	46	28	86	18	255	242	13	18	28	36	51	97	25
Hart	251	75	46	45	85	40	291	274	17	22	27	42	77	87	36
Henderson	453	148	103	66	136	57	510	485	25	50	40	74	92	159	95
Henry	179	64	44	30	41	18	197	182	15	19	*	34	40	75	21
Hickman	60	12	15	*	27	12	72	69	*	*	*	11	14	28	*
Hopkins	645	196	111	99	239	49	694	670	24	42	69	104	126	234	119
Jackson	134	29	22	22	61	21	155	148	*	10	12	14	28	54	37
Jefferson	8,733	3,263	1,780	1,295	2,396	950	9,684	8,851	833	771	1,095	1,703	2,213	2,576	1,325
Jessamine	567	166	110	86	205	58	625	590	35	61	82	102	114	183	83
Johnson	387	99	53	37	198	26	413	401	12	34	30	41	59	185	64
Kenton	1,515	592	311	241	371	178	1,693	1,584	109	206	189	247	341	516	194
Knott	188	42	29	19	98	18	206	201	*	10	13	16	30	94	43
Knox	353	90	46	57	160	45	399	385	14	29	34	44	79	154	58
Larue	224	76	51	23	74	*	233	215	18	16	29	37	49	79	23
Laurel	885	224	157	130	374	89	974	943	31	90	116	111	193	317	146
Lawrence	233	54	30	39	110	17	250	241	*	19	17	18	61	100	34
Lee	91	23	*	14	47	23	114	111	*	*	*	*	28	47	19
Leslie	109	28	17	21	43	18	127	124	*	*	11	15	24	46	23
Letcher	291	75	39	38	139	42	333	329	*	12	26	14	64	158	59
Lewis	166	55	31	17	63	29	194	186	*	*	20	19	44	67	37
Lincoln	318	82	63	57	116	51	369	354	15	28	41	56	63	122	59
Livingston	129	33	24	22	50	15	144	138	*	*	14	22	30	52	17
Logan	311	92	52	55	112	25	336	318	18	36	27	37	58	126	52
Lyon	139	45	23	19	52	*	147	141	*	*	12	19	28	50	30
Madison	1,262	345	247	194	476	68	1,330	1,239	91	198	185	231	266	318	132
Magoffin	95	27	18	*	42	21	116	113	*	14	*	*	21	50	19
Marion	188	57	35	36	60	23	211	200	11	19	21	39	41	64	27
Marshall	449	143	86	71	149	29	478	455	23	39	39	57	94	174	75
Martin	104	19	16	13	56	10	114	114	*	*	13	*	22	52	15
Mason	149	47	25	13	64	33	182	171	11	11	20	25	40	59	27
Mccracken	846	265	156	130	295	92	938	892	46	94	95	108	184	300	157
Mccreary	293	68	44	40	141	43	336	333	*	34	20	52	77	107	46
Mclean	85	25	17	17	26	18	103	97	*	*	10	10	20	34	22
Meade	1,317	334	229	246	509	22	1,339	1,205	135	177	204	360	307	212	78

Table 54. Compensation and Pension Recipients, by County, FY2014—*Continued*

(Number of recipients.)

State and county	Compensation: Total	Compensation: 0 to 20 percent	Compensation: 30 to 40 percent	Compensation: 50 to 60 percent	Compensation: 70 to 100 percent	Total, pension	Compensation or pension: Total	Male	Female	Less than 35 years	35 to 44 years	45 to 54 years	55 to 64 years	65 to 74 years	75 years and over
Kentucky cnt'd															
Menifee	94	24	13	16	41	11	105	102	*	*	*	18	16	42	14
Mercer	256	74	54	37	91	23	279	265	14	26	27	48	54	83	41
Metcalfe	110	37	18	15	40	28	138	129	*	*	*	*	30	47	35
Monroe	98	32	16	12	38	11	109	108	*	*	*	10	35	36	14
Montgomery	342	109	64	49	120	31	373	359	14	41	49	48	63	113	59
Morgan	127	29	24	22	52	17	144	140	*	*	*	17	14	67	28
Muhlenberg	368	110	62	60	136	26	394	376	18	24	33	56	74	143	64
Nelson	512	188	92	79	153	47	559	523	36	47	58	83	126	177	68
Nicholas	100	31	28	10	31	10	110	106	*	*	11	15	19	30	27
Ohio	300	81	55	43	121	49	349	339	10	22	26	34	57	151	58
Oldham	603	249	121	75	158	27	630	582	48	51	72	142	114	186	65
Owen	116	43	26	18	29	14	130	126	*	10	10	17	27	39	27
Owsley	61	10	*	13	32	10	71	69	*	*	*	*	14	22	17
Pendleton	167	59	37	25	46	17	184	175	*	16	17	21	41	66	23
Perry	424	96	49	64	215	50	474	461	13	25	30	49	83	200	87
Pike	791	188	103	106	394	81	872	858	14	71	60	68	124	403	146
Powell	192	37	26	25	104	10	202	195	*	29	21	22	28	75	27
Pulaski	982	264	160	158	400	100	1,082	1,025	57	91	98	160	220	338	175
Robertson	29	11	*	*	*	*	34	33	*	*	*	*	*	15	*
Rockcastle	203	60	31	33	79	28	231	226	*	14	20	26	52	76	43
Rowan	259	71	53	37	98	25	284	271	13	29	25	29	67	90	44
Russell	231	69	32	35	95	34	265	259	*	19	22	21	49	98	56
Scott	492	169	99	63	161	28	520	489	31	48	72	90	107	149	54
Shelby	421	144	95	61	121	17	439	413	25	37	52	69	81	146	53
Simpson	241	82	32	31	96	23	264	253	11	28	22	27	55	94	38
Spencer	224	91	43	32	58	14	238	222	16	29	27	39	55	66	22
Taylor	290	78	47	53	112	32	322	304	18	33	23	44	68	102	52
Todd	208	57	36	34	81	11	219	206	13	20	30	45	50	59	15
Trigg	384	93	77	67	147	14	398	363	35	33	55	78	65	120	46
Trimble	119	45	18	19	37	*	128	123	*	*	14	*	16	59	23
Union	182	56	34	39	53	10	192	185	*	22	12	17	31	81	29
Warren	1,271	411	237	142	481	73	1,344	1,269	75	132	146	189	246	447	184
Washington	121	28	26	23	44	*	127	120	*	*	19	17	25	51	10
Wayne	280	74	38	45	123	33	313	306	*	27	21	42	73	103	47
Webster	149	49	28	27	45	10	159	154	*	*	13	16	37	57	27
Whitley	527	105	91	71	260	60	587	561	26	51	50	66	108	215	96
Wolfe	82	13	12	13	44	*	91	90	*	13	*	11	14	30	16
Woodford	273	95	47	42	89	28	301	283	18	21	35	45	60	97	43
Unknown	*	*	*	*	*	*	*	*	*	*	*	*	*	*	*
Louisiana															
Acadia	520	164	92	81	183	119	638	595	44	82	74	69	126	168	120
Allen	271	71	45	50	105	44	315	298	17	35	30	31	66	89	63
Ascension	1,001	294	179	182	346	80	1,081	995	86	137	181	187	167	288	121
Assumption	158	45	28	17	68	30	188	176	12	14	21	18	32	69	34
Avoyelles	552	129	101	99	223	105	657	624	33	50	66	95	124	192	130
Beauregard	1,079	233	187	187	473	42	1,121	1,001	120	139	194	220	214	242	113
Bienville	207	56	33	41	77	22	229	202	27	23	18	33	43	58	54
Bossier	3,853	1,152	803	672	1,226	138	3,991	3,476	515	438	564	966	737	712	573
Caddo	3,970	1,134	791	653	1,392	528	4,498	4,055	443	472	545	715	981	1,154	631
Calcasieu	2,270	750	410	349	762	250	2,520	2,343	178	336	282	353	495	731	323
Caldwell	120	34	21	16	49	22	142	136	*	10	15	18	21	54	24
Cameron	52	16	11	*	17	*	59	57	*	10	*	*	*	28	*
Catahoula	112	22	21	16	53	29	141	133	*	11	11	16	28	52	23
Claiborne	185	48	25	35	77	24	209	194	15	13	23	21	50	80	22
Concordia	210	52	34	34	90	51	261	245	16	13	28	26	48	93	53
De Soto	355	111	66	49	129	50	405	377	28	36	46	56	73	143	51
East Baton Rouge	4,175	1,255	686	644	1,590	506	4,681	4,256	425	570	517	626	1,025	1,328	613
East Carroll	62	14	12	15	21	12	74	65	*	*	11	*	18	29	*
East Feliciana	198	59	24	18	97	55	253	239	14	21	22	30	51	88	41
Evangeline	315	87	50	42	136	50	365	337	28	41	33	38	65	114	74
Franklin	216	54	35	40	87	64	280	270	10	13	17	28	50	111	61
Grant	382	97	69	74	142	39	421	387	34	51	34	50	91	141	54
Iberia	612	175	99	99	239	128	740	682	58	70	99	83	144	220	124
Iberville	317	99	50	50	118	48	365	352	13	27	31	40	69	152	46
Jackson	217	52	41	35	89	26	243	228	15	28	19	25	36	76	59
Jefferson	4,045	1,238	764	605	1,438	424	4,469	4,009	460	438	557	671	927	1,279	597
Jefferson Davis	315	92	52	53	118	77	392	373	19	32	42	45	66	118	89
La Salle	162	40	20	22	80	37	199	192	*	16	11	21	33	76	42
Lafayette	2,185	673	413	351	748	284	2,469	2,227	242	405	390	328	413	592	341

Table 54. Compensation and Pension Recipients, by County, FY2014—*Continued*

(Number of recipients.)

State and county	Compensation					Total, pension	Compensation or pension								
	Total	0 to 20 percent	30 to 40 percent	50 to 60 percent	70 to 100 percent		Total	Male	Female	Less than 35 years	35 to 44 years	45 to 54 years	55 to 64 years	65 to 74 years	75 years and over
Louisiana cnt'd															
Lafourche	654	168	103	92	291	61	715	673	42	81	66	61	98	289	120
Lincoln	363	97	93	51	122	61	424	391	33	48	49	59	88	112	68
Livingston	1,098	349	190	168	391	94	1,192	1,128	64	174	162	152	183	363	158
Madison	117	36	26	20	35	33	150	142	*	15	*	17	34	61	16
Morehouse	303	99	54	43	107	75	378	353	25	33	34	51	61	136	63
Natchitoches	517	129	93	89	206	99	616	575	41	53	49	70	112	225	107
Orleans	3,854	1,060	697	604	1,493	668	4,522	4,115	407	346	472	740	1,099	1,337	527
Ouachita	1,821	474	328	301	718	323	2,144	1,997	147	220	230	277	459	618	340
Plaquemines	270	83	47	49	91	16	286	247	39	43	63	71	39	44	26
Pointe Coupee	202	68	31	29	74	31	233	220	13	20	10	17	38	103	45
Rapides	2,870	737	480	450	1,203	239	3,109	2,819	290	309	319	490	750	795	446
Red River	77	19	13	13	32	13	90	85	*	12	*	17	13	22	19
Richland	183	50	39	26	69	51	234	218	16	22	16	28	49	77	42
Sabine	395	104	67	71	153	48	443	416	27	35	32	42	79	168	87
Saint Bernard	277	78	57	45	97	32	309	280	29	49	37	37	51	96	39
Saint Charles	464	160	87	81	136	48	512	475	37	47	65	84	91	147	78
Saint Helena	116	31	20	10	55	25	141	130	11	*	19	16	37	47	13
Saint James	169	47	26	21	75	20	189	174	15	10	23	22	35	83	16
Saint Landry	1,013	268	189	170	386	235	1,248	1,162	86	120	146	164	256	347	215
Saint Martin	508	141	94	76	197	82	590	555	35	70	74	71	115	175	85
Saint Mary	398	136	55	71	136	68	466	427	39	57	62	56	78	147	66
Saint Tammany	3,414	1,045	584	537	1,248	222	3,636	3,316	320	335	452	671	718	995	465
St John The Baptist	461	119	77	72	193	53	514	466	48	50	55	86	107	146	70
Tangipahoa	1,215	357	205	184	469	153	1,368	1,238	130	154	164	170	261	431	188
Tensas	42	12	11	*	13	12	54	52	*	*	*	*	12	17	12
Terrebonne	878	266	164	129	319	99	977	893	84	159	130	118	145	301	124
Union	267	73	47	35	112	57	324	313	11	18	22	31	64	118	71
Vermilion	499	162	88	77	172	124	623	588	35	90	62	88	91	165	127
Vernon	3,307	618	530	548	1,611	44	3,352	2,822	530	1,010	583	613	492	450	203
Washington	630	142	107	119	262	96	726	674	52	61	72	80	154	261	98
Webster	606	157	133	101	215	83	689	631	58	49	46	103	142	240	109
West Baton Rouge	224	62	39	31	92	30	254	240	14	32	19	36	50	97	20
West Carroll	104	35	17	22	30	45	149	146	*	15	*	12	23	52	42
West Feliciana	74	26	15	11	22	10	84	81	*	11	*	14	18	26	10
Winn	194	57	34	28	75	32	226	219	*	18	19	35	30	81	43
Unknown	*	*	*	*	*	*	*	*	*	*	*	*	*	*	*
Maine															
Androscoggin	2,210	699	420	299	792	122	2,332	2,181	151	228	270	354	481	627	371
Aroostook	1,725	468	300	230	727	144	1,869	1,784	85	113	154	265	433	641	263
Cumberland	3,885	1,204	732	549	1,400	294	4,179	3,876	303	371	418	637	793	1,217	743
Franklin	539	167	88	86	198	53	592	543	49	55	58	65	123	184	107
Hancock	895	284	149	125	337	69	964	895	69	49	84	142	184	335	170
Kennebec	3,135	897	515	453	1,270	188	3,323	3,045	278	293	387	518	713	922	490
Knox	714	248	123	107	236	41	755	710	45	30	62	101	132	245	185
Lincoln	734	211	126	112	285	43	777	727	50	48	56	99	167	264	143
Oxford	941	276	147	146	372	99	1,040	978	62	89	86	130	253	333	149
Penobscot	2,992	836	516	428	1,212	244	3,236	3,006	230	292	291	479	677	983	514
Piscataquis	433	120	71	49	193	46	479	447	32	22	27	42	107	199	82
Sagadahoc	1,054	295	216	168	375	30	1,084	989	95	81	115	263	243	257	125
Somerset	1,033	323	139	142	429	89	1,122	1,053	69	80	103	138	228	384	189
Waldo	755	239	121	104	291	67	822	771	51	75	56	96	180	276	139
Washington	835	208	123	116	388	91	926	876	50	55	70	121	204	317	158
York	3,289	1,009	650	447	1,183	177	3,466	3,238	228	320	372	497	667	1,047	563
Maryland															
Allegany	952	282	194	140	337	87	1,039	992	47	95	98	130	207	347	163
Anne Arundel	10,868	3,418	2,373	1,929	3,148	220	11,088	8,961	2,127	1,367	1,960	2,835	2,220	1,840	861
Baltimore	7,349	2,499	1,552	1,130	2,169	467	7,816	6,917	899	803	1,035	1,335	1,540	2,040	1,060
Baltimore City	4,665	1,456	1,000	666	1,542	1,019	5,684	5,085	599	408	496	891	1,617	1,584	686
Calvert	1,707	573	401	314	419	25	1,732	1,526	206	180	259	546	352	275	120
Caroline	353	139	62	54	98	23	376	348	28	39	31	49	99	109	48
Carroll	1,560	557	362	227	414	39	1,599	1,436	163	190	230	317	262	416	183
Cecil	1,471	449	308	206	508	104	1,575	1,436	139	132	178	344	371	404	146
Charles	5,025	1,346	1,146	957	1,576	56	5,081	3,920	1,162	425	950	1,928	1,027	542	209
Dorchester	377	120	78	59	120	43	420	385	35	31	35	53	100	133	68
Frederick	3,189	1,009	682	563	933	90	3,279	2,815	464	439	470	701	634	725	309
Garrett	403	116	74	70	142	32	435	411	24	24	35	58	96	173	48
Harford	4,288	1,232	974	715	1,366	132	4,420	3,847	573	390	617	1,091	1,036	918	365
Howard	3,291	1,112	720	564	895	81	3,373	2,766	607	460	619	833	577	597	285

Table 54. Compensation and Pension Recipients, by County, FY2014—*Continued*

(Number of recipients.)

State and county	Compensation					Total, pension	Compensation or pension								
	Total	0 to 20 percent	30 to 40 percent	50 to 60 percent	70 to 100 percent		Total	Male	Female	Less than 35 years	35 to 44 years	45 to 54 years	55 to 64 years	65 to 74 years	75 years and over
Maryland cnt'd															
Kent	183	61	41	23	58	14	197	185	12	10	10	27	43	72	35
Montgomery	7,156	2,473	1,517	1,061	2,106	197	7,353	6,071	1,283	1,030	1,074	1,314	1,397	1,524	1,015
Prince George's	14,993	4,360	3,116	2,451	5,065	429	15,422	12,542	2,880	1,326	1,993	3,882	3,519	3,370	1,330
Queen Anne's	496	161	108	81	146	32	528	473	55	42	65	104	106	135	76
Saint Mary's	3,159	1,038	779	557	785	52	3,211	2,818	393	384	614	1,069	662	340	142
Somerset	283	85	50	45	103	34	317	296	21	25	26	45	66	105	50
Talbot	407	155	76	63	113	33	440	408	32	31	33	61	77	140	98
Washington	1,821	651	408	259	504	110	1,931	1,760	171	214	263	331	407	472	244
Wicomico	1,005	332	208	142	323	95	1,100	1,009	91	118	110	180	233	312	147
Worcester	743	282	155	94	212	44	787	736	51	40	52	100	151	290	154
Massachusetts															
Barnstable	3,657	1,501	603	495	1,058	184	3,841	3,649	192	205	192	307	562	1,276	1,297
Berkshire	1,307	513	225	160	409	133	1,440	1,370	70	106	94	152	246	469	373
Bristol	5,493	1,933	1,014	766	1,780	416	5,909	5,609	300	610	499	688	1,022	1,805	1,284
Dukes	116	48	19	19	30	*	125	121	*	*	10	10	15	55	27
Essex	5,907	2,233	1,082	790	1,802	350	6,257	5,961	296	689	476	615	992	1,858	1,626
Franklin	850	285	121	135	309	56	906	855	51	73	69	99	189	340	136
Hampden	5,159	1,848	870	677	1,764	450	5,609	5,292	317	523	490	729	1,108	1,633	1,125
Hampshire	1,593	558	300	197	538	133	1,726	1,607	119	152	139	216	346	528	344
Middlesex	10,978	4,239	2,021	1,394	3,324	631	11,609	10,953	656	1,273	916	1,189	1,860	3,235	3,132
Nantucket	44	19	*	*	10	*	47	45	*	*	*	*	*	20	11
Norfolk	5,790	2,125	1,022	778	1,865	276	6,066	5,790	276	717	471	592	922	1,686	1,677
Plymouth	6,181	2,171	1,042	826	2,142	326	6,507	6,198	309	669	543	674	1,165	2,116	1,337
Suffolk	4,292	1,498	735	577	1,482	496	4,788	4,511	277	784	470	463	837	1,180	1,054
Worcester	7,904	2,755	1,481	1,071	2,597	472	8,376	7,920	456	940	801	1,020	1,371	2,430	1,809
Unknown	*	*	*	*	*	*	*	*	*	*	*	*	*	*	*
Michigan															
Alcona	275	91	55	38	91	30	305	295	10	22	11	38	58	122	54
Alger	185	64	32	26	63	13	199	190	*	*	15	19	47	68	40
Allegan	832	252	133	148	299	67	898	849	49	132	89	88	152	328	109
Alpena	427	147	88	73	118	27	454	428	26	31	30	65	94	166	68
Antrim	315	114	58	37	106	31	346	336	10	36	23	34	65	126	60
Arenac	248	84	53	29	82	23	271	265	*	17	14	27	65	99	49
Baraga	174	52	32	34	56	16	190	181	*	22	11	24	41	62	30
Barry	606	187	107	98	213	54	660	631	29	81	59	78	122	243	76
Bay	1,506	551	267	192	496	139	1,645	1,549	96	122	151	204	308	608	252
Benzie	274	87	62	41	84	23	297	280	17	21	21	37	50	114	54
Berrien	1,408	412	266	206	524	136	1,544	1,452	92	175	143	193	291	544	197
Branch	466	121	83	78	184	57	523	496	27	55	41	59	113	191	64
Calhoun	1,761	434	314	244	769	216	1,977	1,823	154	172	158	305	471	655	216
Cass	519	170	106	87	156	39	558	529	29	58	38	73	118	213	57
Charlevoix	321	116	60	51	94	*	327	314	13	24	25	36	43	137	62
Cheboygan	501	137	83	86	195	43	545	528	17	27	29	48	91	234	115
Chippewa	654	215	143	120	176	51	705	658	47	62	58	89	164	210	121
Clare	546	183	84	90	190	59	605	582	23	55	23	65	117	243	102
Clinton	537	179	101	82	176	32	570	533	37	79	60	75	106	181	66
Crawford	264	78	48	48	90	20	285	270	15	24	20	45	60	91	44
Delta	825	235	155	126	309	52	877	831	46	75	75	102	157	317	151
Dickinson	552	174	93	96	189	57	609	568	41	61	59	90	123	170	106
Eaton	1,032	295	192	164	382	73	1,105	1,026	79	155	123	149	203	356	119
Emmet	393	152	73	39	130	33	426	410	16	33	28	47	71	165	81
Genesee	4,020	1,349	735	599	1,337	483	4,503	4,240	263	439	456	606	879	1,495	626
Gladwin	493	154	108	56	175	41	534	515	19	38	36	54	104	201	101
Gogebic	255	81	49	46	79	33	288	269	19	25	20	32	53	98	60
Grand Traverse	1,069	383	217	142	327	107	1,176	1,122	54	123	109	145	191	379	228
Gratiot	507	180	102	63	162	37	544	531	13	40	35	59	89	212	108
Hillsdale	461	138	91	80	152	43	504	480	24	45	48	54	111	168	77
Houghton	478	133	100	71	174	56	534	503	31	63	43	62	97	200	69
Huron	417	151	74	58	134	36	453	442	11	29	35	38	80	168	103
Ingham	2,112	639	408	319	746	282	2,394	2,214	180	303	229	327	473	750	309
Ionia	522	149	102	74	197	45	567	529	38	80	51	67	115	205	49
Iosco	558	212	87	74	185	43	601	563	38	40	39	58	133	215	116
Iron	266	86	41	38	101	22	288	277	11	12	18	33	57	119	49
Isabella	554	185	100	74	196	42	596	566	30	77	56	65	114	199	85
Jackson	1,824	607	348	291	578	182	2,006	1,876	130	192	191	252	387	663	319
Kalamazoo	1,873	571	358	293	651	160	2,033	1,880	153	303	216	295	363	617	238
Kalkaska	258	78	33	45	102	22	279	269	10	21	14	31	82	85	47
Kent	4,110	1,333	718	635	1,424	633	4,742	4,401	341	658	416	551	918	1,494	704

Table 54. Compensation and Pension Recipients, by County, FY2014—*Continued*

(Number of recipients.)

State and county	Compensation					Total, pension	Compensation or pension								
	Total	0 to 20 percent	30 to 40 percent	50 to 60 percent	70 to 100 percent		Total	Male	Female	Less than 35 years	35 to 44 years	45 to 54 years	55 to 64 years	65 to 74 years	75 years and over
Michigan cnt'd															
Keweenaw	36	14	*	*	*	*	42	41	*	*	*	*	*	18	10
Lake	180	52	31	29	68	20	200	194	*	*	14	20	35	92	31
Lapeer	1,119	473	193	154	299	77	1,196	1,147	49	96	107	136	215	461	181
Leelanau	254	91	57	43	63	26	280	269	11	21	17	18	40	102	81
Lenawee	1,161	395	246	174	346	75	1,235	1,176	59	134	129	154	199	405	215
Livingston	1,787	654	377	270	486	115	1,902	1,794	109	220	166	240	323	684	268
Luce	83	21	13	14	35	13	96	90	*	11	*	10	11	39	20
Mackinac	167	43	30	26	68	14	181	178	*	*	10	29	38	61	37
Macomb	7,817	2,778	1,590	1,241	2,208	798	8,615	8,086	529	762	805	1,096	1,465	2,971	1,514
Manistee	364	121	51	50	142	31	395	372	23	28	31	53	68	156	59
Marquette	1,372	395	284	210	483	140	1,512	1,420	92	165	147	166	297	475	260
Mason	338	88	58	60	132	35	373	351	22	28	29	49	64	154	49
Mecosta	403	117	71	63	152	31	434	416	18	42	24	54	88	178	48
Menominee	416	117	78	73	148	42	458	442	16	36	28	58	105	149	82
Midland	1,038	376	214	142	307	53	1,091	1,040	51	120	112	116	194	341	207
Missaukee	181	54	32	32	63	18	199	190	*	20	11	20	43	71	34
Monroe	1,529	552	319	240	417	99	1,628	1,549	78	167	155	218	293	576	218
Montcalm	619	168	114	95	243	55	674	626	49	80	74	81	128	242	70
Montmorency	185	64	23	32	66	21	206	203	*	*	13	12	45	90	38
Muskegon	1,870	509	363	296	702	187	2,057	1,920	137	229	162	298	458	672	238
Newaygo	627	156	117	98	256	59	686	648	38	82	35	73	155	257	84
Oakland	8,177	3,090	1,653	1,146	2,288	902	9,080	8,513	567	832	767	1,091	1,480	3,223	1,680
Oceana	295	87	53	49	106	34	329	313	17	33	20	41	67	116	53
Ogemaw	361	111	69	55	126	51	412	397	15	24	36	38	81	176	57
Ontonagon	182	48	38	26	70	15	197	187	10	14	14	26	40	69	34
Osceola	267	85	47	38	97	22	289	277	12	27	19	22	60	126	35
Oscoda	163	47	35	20	61	16	179	172	*	14	*	12	40	76	29
Otsego	304	107	58	40	99	34	338	310	28	21	36	48	68	113	52
Ottawa	1,643	530	308	265	539	149	1,792	1,674	118	299	183	203	286	541	279
Presque Isle	265	97	54	40	75	15	280	268	12	19	15	18	54	120	54
Roscommon	433	134	87	58	154	50	482	471	11	31	29	38	90	199	96
Saginaw	2,319	800	400	323	795	219	2,539	2,371	167	207	255	373	459	843	399
Saint Clair	2,332	991	458	331	552	196	2,528	2,416	112	211	168	296	499	930	424
Saint Joseph	549	160	115	78	196	57	606	570	36	56	46	65	109	243	87
Sanilac	506	191	93	74	148	43	549	525	24	37	34	59	96	212	111
Schoolcraft	143	40	28	24	51	13	156	144	12	*	15	23	30	56	24
Shiawassee	809	302	157	106	244	55	864	823	41	102	78	121	140	297	126
Tuscola	698	256	108	101	234	68	766	735	31	72	60	113	163	264	95
Van Buren	750	215	135	122	278	71	821	772	49	97	71	125	146	288	94
Washtenaw	1,991	728	377	307	579	188	2,179	1,981	198	283	238	303	352	692	309
Wayne	13,984	4,892	2,853	2,000	4,239	2,582	16,566	15,481	1,085	1,248	1,408	2,179	3,662	5,657	2,407
Wexford	409	119	78	66	146	48	457	428	29	51	36	68	85	147	70
Unknown	*	*	*	*	*	*	*	*	*	*	*	*	*	*	*
Minnesota															
Aitkin	436	203	72	41	121	28	464	449	15	12	19	31	75	170	157
Anoka	6,015	3,334	987	582	1,112	135	6,150	5,887	263	584	422	657	1,150	2,232	1,102
Becker	743	326	135	99	183	63	806	777	29	55	57	74	161	288	169
Beltrami	778	281	142	99	256	48	826	789	37	83	67	67	155	295	159
Benton	1,020	509	139	110	262	31	1,051	999	52	122	75	137	221	324	172
Big Stone	210	135	24	22	30	*	215	211	*	15	*	18	34	79	61
Blue Earth	1,005	528	161	118	198	27	1,032	992	40	141	79	106	172	311	223
Brown	658	372	114	59	114	33	691	665	26	67	30	47	111	218	218
Carlton	928	439	148	105	236	27	955	916	39	68	81	124	184	294	204
Carver	965	553	175	87	150	14	980	946	34	103	63	96	185	342	191
Cass	1,075	484	153	136	302	74	1,149	1,109	40	45	48	82	212	436	326
Chippewa	202	96	35	28	43	*	210	202	*	17	12	19	29	56	77
Chisago	908	455	149	108	196	33	941	905	36	89	91	99	175	314	172
Clay	921	421	151	128	221	51	972	901	71	111	98	129	171	286	176
Clearwater	197	82	35	29	51	29	225	216	10	12	11	15	45	89	54
Cook	117	54	19	11	33	*	121	118	*	*	*	*	12	66	32
Cottonwood	261	132	52	37	40	*	267	263	*	15	11	19	27	103	91
Crow Wing	1,843	849	298	209	486	76	1,919	1,855	64	139	102	174	357	613	534
Dakota	6,204	3,100	1,121	720	1,264	160	6,364	5,958	406	608	613	849	1,180	1,981	1,130
Dodge	313	160	57	47	49	*	322	309	13	31	22	38	69	83	79
Douglas	779	392	137	90	160	45	824	797	27	71	40	66	135	302	210
Faribault	272	133	51	31	57	17	289	270	19	32	17	27	41	90	82
Fillmore	396	198	86	42	71	10	406	392	14	35	20	30	55	152	114
Freeborn	763	442	143	70	108	26	790	770	20	42	24	67	114	283	258
Goodhue	872	476	165	92	139	24	896	861	35	84	53	97	154	282	225

Table 54. Compensation and Pension Recipients, by County, FY2014—*Continued*

(Number of recipients.)

State and county	Compensation					Total, pension	Compensation or pension								
	Total	0 to 20 percent	30 to 40 percent	50 to 60 percent	70 to 100 percent		Total	Male	Female	Less than 35 years	35 to 44 years	45 to 54 years	55 to 64 years	65 to 74 years	75 years and over
Minnesota cnt'd															
Grant	147	72	27	21	27	12	159	155	*	*	10	*	25	61	48
Hennepin	11,183	5,747	1,973	1,184	2,279	719	11,902	11,230	672	1,154	829	1,181	2,087	3,820	2,827
Houston	414	229	62	39	84	13	427	409	18	16	29	38	74	147	123
Hubbard	602	286	72	76	168	33	635	606	29	35	20	48	122	252	158
Isanti	958	544	137	97	180	25	983	946	37	78	61	95	200	357	191
Itasca	1,302	623	218	158	302	70	1,372	1,329	43	76	69	111	262	487	364
Jackson	158	71	28	30	29	*	167	155	12	15	16	17	23	60	36
Kanabec	475	220	71	53	131	25	500	485	15	24	27	39	103	181	125
Kandiyohi	905	476	148	88	194	38	943	916	27	65	37	57	166	323	294
Kittson	51	17	*	*	16	*	53	53	*	*	*	*	*	23	*
Koochiching	264	128	38	32	66	12	276	265	11	19	14	29	48	104	62
Lac Qui Parle	206	108	34	25	39	*	212	207	*	23	*	10	31	76	63
Lake	277	128	54	30	65	15	292	281	11	13	14	18	47	98	102
Lake Of The Woods	85	29	16	16	24	*	89	87	*	*	*	*	21	41	12
Le Sueur	514	286	81	54	93	16	530	509	21	44	31	47	106	183	118
Lincoln	75	30	12	11	22	11	86	85	*	*	*	*	15	29	26
Lyon	363	168	68	39	88	22	385	366	19	53	27	27	62	131	85
Mahnomen	69	20	17	13	19	15	84	78	*	*	*	*	18	35	21
Marshall	150	55	28	25	42	*	157	153	*	14	*	16	29	62	28
Martin	508	275	79	45	109	18	526	514	12	40	28	47	80	177	153
Mcleod	625	319	127	63	116	*	632	609	23	59	40	69	91	223	150
Meeker	495	249	83	58	105	21	516	490	26	39	26	49	93	181	128
Mille Lacs	898	503	124	98	174	27	925	888	37	78	48	91	194	285	228
Morrison	1,307	681	191	149	286	38	1,345	1,274	71	117	90	155	297	399	287
Mower	795	409	150	86	150	20	815	784	31	52	43	64	130	263	263
Murray	157	81	34	19	23	16	173	163	10	18	*	17	23	55	51
Nicollet	683	410	102	58	112	10	693	673	20	61	45	56	102	277	151
Nobles	232	104	49	33	46	22	254	247	*	19	15	21	52	91	56
Norman	130	54	22	15	39	10	140	134	*	*	*	25	21	45	34
Olmsted	1,779	956	334	194	295	57	1,836	1,725	111	217	172	191	276	562	418
Otter Tail	1,201	511	192	155	343	78	1,279	1,212	67	83	59	126	232	459	316
Pennington	231	97	43	35	56	*	240	230	10	40	14	23	46	72	45
Pine	732	361	123	83	165	23	756	724	32	53	31	75	156	266	174
Pipestone	95	46	21	10	18	*	102	96	*	*	*	*	14	31	31
Polk	456	194	95	66	101	36	492	469	23	39	34	67	88	168	96
Pope	237	120	39	26	53	*	246	234	12	21	15	19	34	82	76
Ramsey	5,023	2,489	873	602	1,059	389	5,412	5,107	304	561	390	536	993	1,672	1,258
Red Lake	58	22	*	*	21	*	62	58	*	*	*	*	*	27	13
Redwood	353	171	52	48	82	*	361	353	*	30	17	24	68	112	109
Renville	320	138	51	43	88	20	340	329	11	32	15	21	57	119	96
Rice	934	517	162	88	167	27	961	910	51	59	70	105	163	335	228
Rock	113	54	23	13	23	11	124	120	*	17	10	14	14	44	25
Roseau	210	87	33	36	54	*	219	207	12	18	20	25	47	76	33
Saint Louis	4,365	2,155	755	476	979	239	4,603	4,403	200	364	336	499	851	1,565	989
Scott	2,023	1,131	324	221	347	38	2,061	1,959	102	232	188	237	333	668	401
Sherburne	1,924	1,024	303	192	406	50	1,974	1,880	94	199	178	251	392	600	353
Sibley	318	200	42	29	46	*	324	311	13	25	13	32	48	109	95
Stearns	3,967	2,074	518	425	951	101	4,068	3,873	195	379	235	393	824	1,301	934
Steele	584	296	112	82	94	25	609	583	26	60	47	75	106	179	142
Stevens	122	67	16	19	20	*	128	123	*	15	*	10	22	38	36
Swift	218	104	37	19	58	12	230	222	*	23	17	19	39	71	61
Todd	753	357	125	76	194	39	792	762	30	45	37	56	155	261	237
Traverse	81	31	19	*	23	*	90	88	*	11	*	*	17	26	28
Wabasha	568	313	75	62	118	*	577	547	30	45	17	60	96	206	154
Wadena	465	225	66	63	111	33	498	481	17	27	26	51	83	181	130
Waseca	478	300	76	42	60	*	487	471	16	28	34	48	96	174	107
Washington	3,232	1,653	580	382	617	69	3,301	3,111	190	332	275	424	594	1,055	618
Watonwan	304	185	54	20	45	*	311	300	11	27	14	20	51	100	99
Wilkin	103	51	23	11	18	*	106	103	*	12	*	10	17	44	19
Winona	521	222	102	62	136	38	559	528	31	69	40	51	83	200	116
Wright	1,860	935	304	219	401	44	1,904	1,825	79	189	169	214	333	663	335
Yellow Medicine	192	86	26	30	50	*	199	196	*	13	*	14	32	60	72
Mississippi															
Adams	393	106	81	60	146	72	465	430	35	25	32	61	134	157	56
Alcorn	375	99	72	52	152	48	423	408	15	39	27	44	64	163	86
Amite	162	47	24	25	66	23	185	175	10	14	23	27	38	53	30
Attala	218	57	39	40	82	41	259	242	17	14	18	27	40	90	70
Benton	45	10	10	*	22	*	51	51	*	*	*	*	13	18	10
Bolivar	247	70	44	32	101	44	291	274	17	24	25	45	73	81	43

Table 54. Compensation and Pension Recipients, by County, FY2014—*Continued*

(Number of recipients.)

State and county	Compensation					Total, pension	Compensation or pension								
	Total	0 to 20 percent	30 to 40 percent	50 to 60 percent	70 to 100 percent		Total	Male	Female	Less than 35 years	35 to 44 years	45 to 54 years	55 to 64 years	65 to 74 years	75 years and over
Mississippi cnt'd															
Calhoun	166	31	30	31	74	15	181	171	10	17	18	12	38	47	49
Carroll	98	22	28	13	34	11	109	105	*	*	10	20	16	44	10
Chickasaw	152	52	26	22	52	20	171	162	10	18	21	19	32	53	29
Choctaw	75	27	12	14	22	14	89	86	*	*	13	*	21	24	18
Claiborne	83	25	17	13	28	19	102	93	*	*	*	15	26	28	18
Clarke	191	51	34	31	75	35	226	216	10	15	19	38	35	74	45
Clay	194	51	43	28	72	13	207	192	15	11	27	31	48	64	25
Coahoma	217	62	25	32	98	36	253	230	23	12	29	48	67	66	31
Copiah	389	120	74	71	124	58	447	418	29	33	30	56	114	143	71
Covington	226	62	36	38	90	39	265	239	26	20	33	21	59	73	59
Desoto	1,757	552	378	278	549	111	1,868	1,712	156	209	253	366	327	512	201
Forrest	1,054	298	192	186	378	152	1,206	1,083	123	134	137	232	259	284	157
Franklin	73	29	12	*	23	10	83	74	*	*	11	10	*	33	13
George	232	85	44	37	66	24	256	246	10	15	20	41	40	98	41
Greene	145	47	24	26	48	19	164	159	*	*	14	22	42	58	19
Grenada	253	95	41	33	84	32	285	261	24	23	30	61	56	75	40
Hancock	631	218	134	88	191	75	706	663	43	54	69	102	151	197	133
Harrison	5,624	1,801	1,172	979	1,673	301	5,925	5,114	812	616	723	1,269	1,253	1,241	819
Hinds	2,787	832	540	426	989	392	3,179	2,835	344	230	339	586	808	812	403
Holmes	120	31	19	21	49	29	149	137	12	10	11	22	34	45	27
Humphreys	76	18	15	*	35	17	93	85	*	15	*	15	17	26	13
Issaquena	*	*	*	*	*	*	*	*	*	*	*	*	*	*	*
Itawamba	178	48	41	27	61	22	200	192	*	24	17	15	44	64	35
Jackson	3,213	1,148	705	527	832	165	3,378	2,996	382	218	386	830	701	817	425
Jasper	191	48	42	41	60	28	219	207	12	19	15	33	40	79	33
Jefferson	51	13	11	11	16	*	60	56	*	*	*	*	13	17	12
Jefferson Davis	121	39	28	18	36	22	143	128	15	10	17	30	31	36	19
Jones	725	232	140	102	251	120	845	802	43	49	59	111	189	263	173
Kemper	106	38	22	19	27	18	124	114	10	*	13	19	27	37	23
Lafayette	312	95	66	66	85	38	350	321	29	32	29	54	83	82	70
Lamar	794	221	147	149	277	42	836	753	83	73	138	197	156	175	96
Lauderdale	1,103	330	246	174	353	93	1,196	1,077	119	83	158	192	289	278	196
Lawrence	180	57	27	28	68	32	212	206	*	20	20	30	45	60	37
Leake	226	57	40	36	93	32	258	241	17	18	31	30	51	78	50
Lee	755	233	136	110	276	87	843	796	47	76	93	122	176	246	129
Leflore	244	72	55	39	78	42	286	267	19	22	29	59	71	78	27
Lincoln	331	95	67	54	114	52	382	359	23	37	43	48	83	107	62
Lowndes	1,277	423	263	204	387	65	1,342	1,215	127	142	139	264	299	322	176
Madison	1,010	339	200	173	298	94	1,104	1,004	100	83	140	214	237	264	165
Marion	267	74	52	42	99	42	309	281	28	24	27	39	64	101	53
Marshall	320	90	56	44	130	50	370	343	27	13	21	64	88	126	57
Monroe	425	116	78	74	156	40	465	439	26	42	41	70	96	142	72
Montgomery	159	46	30	23	60	20	179	172	*	19	27	17	43	50	23
Neshoba	279	79	41	52	107	51	330	309	21	20	33	41	63	104	69
Newton	297	86	49	52	110	24	321	305	16	26	33	56	71	83	52
Noxubee	74	17	16	12	29	*	82	76	*	*	*	15	20	24	13
Oktibbeha	365	131	65	50	119	28	393	365	28	66	43	63	82	91	48
Panola	284	82	53	40	109	40	324	306	18	34	20	49	72	101	48
Pearl River	951	315	211	158	267	99	1,050	967	83	71	85	144	218	335	195
Perry	174	48	32	31	63	15	189	174	15	12	17	28	42	51	39
Pike	431	125	72	79	155	61	492	446	46	49	43	76	114	138	72
Pontotoc	257	78	43	37	99	26	283	274	*	23	29	29	47	103	51
Prentiss	215	58	47	33	77	28	243	232	12	27	22	22	45	77	50
Quitman	76	14	11	10	41	15	91	84	*	*	*	14	26	28	13
Rankin	1,755	630	320	261	544	114	1,869	1,705	164	173	258	304	419	472	243
Scott	244	82	38	44	80	39	283	274	*	19	23	37	57	86	60
Sharkey	40	15	*	*	13	10	50	48	*	*	*	*	13	14	10
Simpson	318	92	59	43	124	40	358	337	21	36	35	44	82	112	48
Smith	168	49	34	25	60	28	196	186	10	17	14	28	37	50	50
Stone	290	90	75	49	76	29	319	298	21	26	28	57	74	90	44
Sunflower	190	61	34	20	75	31	221	206	15	24	24	42	55	57	19
Tallahatchie	102	19	21	14	48	14	116	109	*	14	13	18	26	27	18
Tate	273	80	64	42	87	29	302	286	16	31	30	46	59	93	43
Tippah	191	62	30	24	75	19	210	204	*	17	14	26	43	77	33
Tishomingo	190	55	40	24	71	24	214	210	*	19	15	25	45	73	37
Tunica	113	25	17	20	51	21	134	124	10	*	10	27	38	39	14
Union	239	80	45	44	70	28	267	258	*	19	11	30	57	93	57
Walthall	145	47	27	18	53	20	165	156	*	16	14	23	33	47	32
Warren	503	176	91	75	161	59	562	504	58	48	82	90	134	154	53
Washington	479	151	93	74	161	121	600	552	48	49	56	102	164	148	81

Table 54. Compensation and Pension Recipients, by County, FY2014—*Continued*

(Number of recipients.)

State and county	Compensation					Total, pension	Compensation or pension								
	Total	0 to 20 percent	30 to 40 percent	50 to 60 percent	70 to 100 percent		Total	Male	Female	Less than 35 years	35 to 44 years	45 to 54 years	55 to 64 years	65 to 74 years	75 years and over
Mississippi cnt'd															
Wayne	201	64	37	37	63	46	247	237	10	10	21	36	46	83	51
Webster	136	49	24	20	42	15	151	149	*	*	*	32	26	49	31
Wilkinson	61	16	*	*	28	13	74	72	*	10	*	*	15	24	16
Winston	190	67	32	29	62	42	232	216	16	15	20	45	46	53	53
Yalobusha	171	43	36	20	72	30	201	192	*	*	17	28	45	62	41
Yazoo	273	85	45	45	98	43	316	294	22	28	32	63	83	55	55
Missouri															
Adair	255	108	48	39	60	40	295	285	10	29	20	27	46	97	76
Andrew	198	86	32	30	50	16	214	205	*	20	20	30	41	63	39
Atchison	67	26	11	*	26	12	79	77	*	*	*	*	12	28	23
Audrain	406	185	79	61	81	45	451	437	14	23	28	35	84	168	113
Barry	476	159	95	78	145	47	523	500	23	37	22	53	123	190	99
Barton	143	38	34	20	51	14	157	149	*	11	14	11	33	62	26
Bates	206	73	39	30	64	29	235	227	*	20	16	21	43	81	54
Benton	572	201	86	88	197	30	602	576	27	21	27	54	112	257	131
Bollinger	186	69	35	38	44	28	214	209	*	12	13	21	50	69	49
Boone	2,120	792	423	318	587	146	2,266	2,076	190	282	235	305	449	615	380
Buchanan	1,035	395	189	167	284	139	1,174	1,113	61	99	82	130	254	363	246
Butler	912	282	166	130	335	151	1,063	1,001	62	68	69	134	261	348	183
Caldwell	146	60	27	21	38	18	164	158	*	11	*	14	31	64	36
Callaway	899	371	178	119	231	41	940	904	36	73	67	131	194	322	150
Camden	858	334	136	115	272	38	896	852	44	36	64	78	156	388	174
Cape Girardeau	1,021	378	214	162	267	109	1,130	1,066	64	126	100	133	212	347	212
Carroll	151	54	24	21	52	14	165	163	*	*	*	15	28	57	48
Carter	139	51	28	29	31	13	152	142	10	*	*	16	40	48	33
Cass	1,589	548	315	246	480	65	1,654	1,550	104	190	190	276	278	453	266
Cedar	285	87	57	43	98	30	315	302	13	13	20	28	72	123	59
Chariton	141	63	30	15	33	10	151	146	*	*	*	13	23	53	52
Christian	1,188	396	232	194	365	59	1,247	1,160	86	122	179	196	240	352	157
Clark	84	25	15	13	31	*	89	86	*	11	*	10	12	35	14
Clay	3,001	1,043	589	464	905	147	3,148	2,930	218	394	390	452	532	946	434
Clinton	287	106	50	46	85	25	312	299	13	35	30	31	48	97	71
Cole	1,288	562	260	171	295	48	1,336	1,237	99	125	105	196	286	404	219
Cooper	330	136	65	55	74	27	357	333	24	26	30	31	71	119	79
Crawford	443	161	91	60	131	43	487	470	17	25	29	50	104	162	117
Dade	127	47	16	22	42	*	135	128	*	*	10	*	31	54	24
Dallas	338	101	64	55	118	37	374	348	26	20	26	38	94	135	62
Daviess	147	62	32	12	41	*	154	149	*	10	*	14	24	52	48
Dekalb	143	51	33	19	40	20	163	156	*	12	11	22	31	45	42
Dent	312	102	57	47	106	20	332	313	19	16	27	47	67	116	59
Douglas	198	72	34	33	59	26	224	211	13	14	15	28	48	86	33
Dunklin	433	128	80	78	147	83	516	501	15	34	33	57	109	185	98
Franklin	1,144	416	233	162	333	107	1,251	1,173	78	146	98	158	210	416	224
Gasconade	255	117	43	40	55	26	281	274	*	18	16	26	51	84	86
Gentry	86	36	13	11	26	15	101	96	*	*	*	12	27	26	22
Greene	3,466	1,185	690	577	1,014	355	3,821	3,556	265	486	393	526	736	1,027	651
Grundy	188	93	40	20	35	17	205	201	*	10	*	21	31	68	66
Harrison	134	58	25	19	32	19	153	146	*	10	*	16	22	52	43
Henry	483	132	101	87	163	41	524	498	26	42	41	64	87	185	105
Hickory	170	60	25	24	61	24	194	187	*	*	*	15	34	81	57
Holt	66	24	10	13	19	*	74	72	*	*	*	*	15	27	15
Howard	169	59	29	20	61	14	183	178	*	*	13	19	30	72	42
Howell	761	244	145	125	247	83	843	799	45	59	85	84	165	291	160
Iron	178	55	35	28	60	24	202	191	11	16	15	14	46	71	40
Jackson	8,112	2,739	1,544	1,176	2,653	778	8,890	8,222	668	827	859	1,199	1,997	2,615	1,388
Jasper	1,359	473	269	209	409	193	1,552	1,462	90	142	167	194	329	452	268
Jefferson	2,806	1,005	593	427	779	173	2,979	2,807	171	335	332	390	579	1,046	294
Johnson	1,546	468	368	284	426	45	1,591	1,388	203	238	221	451	294	254	133
Knox	100	41	21	18	20	12	112	112	*	*	*	*	18	48	28
Laclede	923	262	174	184	302	40	963	912	51	97	92	163	173	286	151
Lafayette	492	180	83	96	133	30	522	496	26	52	40	62	108	172	88
Lawrence	556	167	110	85	193	71	627	585	42	53	63	72	115	203	120
Lewis	135	40	29	22	44	10	145	137	*	17	*	13	28	53	27
Lincoln	624	239	131	87	167	60	684	659	25	79	71	94	124	226	90
Linn	246	116	40	39	51	18	264	252	12	12	17	21	42	93	79
Livingston	225	92	37	42	54	22	247	239	*	23	17	21	37	69	79
Macon	305	108	62	47	88	21	326	315	11	24	24	36	47	119	76
Madison	246	84	55	38	69	24	270	254	16	11	18	41	51	107	42
Maries	263	84	53	53	72	15	278	262	16	29	18	46	55	76	54

Table 54. Compensation and Pension Recipients, by County, FY2014—*Continued*

(Number of recipients.)

State and county	Compensation					Total, pension	Compensation or pension								
	Total	0 to 20 percent	30 to 40 percent	50 to 60 percent	70 to 100 percent		Total	Male	Female	Less than 35 years	35 to 44 years	45 to 54 years	55 to 64 years	65 to 74 years	75 years and over
Missouri cnt'd															
Marion	413	159	71	55	128	49	462	450	12	54	27	35	84	179	83
Mcdonald	234	69	48	32	85	29	263	255	*	24	23	34	51	89	42
Mercer	81	35	12	15	19	13	94	88	*	*	*	*	20	27	31
Miller	545	205	95	89	156	27	572	557	15	46	33	75	117	182	117
Mississippi	141	37	35	30	39	27	168	162	*	14	*	15	36	64	32
Moniteau	230	95	48	34	53	10	240	230	10	19	17	22	41	85	56
Monroe	153	60	29	27	37	17	170	163	*	14	*	20	29	68	34
Montgomery	192	72	32	32	56	15	207	200	*	13	14	19	51	55	53
Morgan	525	184	94	78	169	55	581	559	22	24	17	48	134	223	134
New Madrid	245	84	46	39	76	28	273	260	13	18	26	30	57	98	44
Newton	719	256	144	111	208	91	811	773	38	74	79	98	137	270	152
Nodaway	192	69	40	31	52	18	210	198	12	24	14	26	24	75	47
Oregon	195	57	32	38	68	23	218	213	*	14	*	16	43	81	55
Osage	201	78	45	29	48	11	212	191	21	15	15	28	30	83	41
Ozark	192	67	28	35	62	36	229	214	15	15	10	19	58	79	47
Pemiscot	220	55	55	31	79	40	260	247	13	16	13	34	61	91	45
Perry	234	70	60	35	69	18	252	245	*	33	14	20	41	84	60
Pettis	891	349	144	135	262	49	939	881	58	84	72	145	163	274	201
Phelps	1,217	377	230	183	427	74	1,290	1,215	75	109	111	239	259	354	218
Pike	247	105	45	29	68	18	265	260	*	12	21	22	44	103	62
Platte	1,497	523	297	220	457	69	1,566	1,437	129	176	185	304	300	424	176
Polk	419	129	87	80	123	34	453	426	27	40	41	55	89	156	72
Pulaski	3,976	785	717	659	1,815	33	4,009	3,402	607	749	713	1,101	762	483	201
Putnam	76	25	19	*	24	*	85	81	*	*	*	*	13	31	24
Ralls	194	79	38	17	59	*	202	196	*	12	19	18	32	93	28
Randolph	446	166	81	60	138	50	496	481	15	46	38	54	89	170	98
Ray	362	142	59	57	104	12	374	365	*	26	34	48	57	137	72
Reynolds	153	43	26	26	58	15	168	162	*	*	*	20	38	64	32
Ripley	257	67	53	48	89	38	295	281	14	18	*	38	75	96	59
Saint Charles	3,912	1,541	791	601	979	203	4,115	3,825	290	499	448	548	727	1,302	589
Saint Clair	190	55	37	24	74	23	213	204	*	16	10	17	39	81	50
Saint Francois	977	318	191	146	322	115	1,092	1,044	48	115	119	143	242	324	148
Saint Louis	9,112	3,360	1,856	1,370	2,525	996	10,108	9,217	891	882	900	1,346	1,956	3,194	1,829
Saint Louis City	2,748	940	551	414	842	845	3,593	3,264	329	286	301	494	1,077	973	461
Sainte Genevieve	220	83	49	30	58	33	253	240	13	23	15	26	47	102	40
Saline	345	124	80	55	86	21	366	355	11	33	23	39	67	126	78
Schuyler	60	23	*	12	18	*	63	59	*	*	*	10	15	20	10
Scotland	62	23	*	*	21	*	65	63	*	*	*	*	12	16	18
Scott	652	199	137	109	207	69	720	689	31	65	54	86	153	246	116
Shannon	145	45	29	31	40	27	172	168	*	*	*	18	30	79	34
Shelby	104	48	18	11	27	*	110	109	*	*	*	*	19	44	25
Stoddard	611	197	124	113	177	54	665	634	31	49	54	71	116	239	136
Stone	499	181	96	63	158	42	541	507	34	27	25	45	101	236	106
Sullivan	91	37	19	13	22	11	102	101	*	*	*	10	18	36	28
Taney	771	260	133	114	264	89	860	819	41	60	63	102	177	305	153
Texas	863	253	170	139	301	53	916	854	62	77	65	172	207	265	130
Vernon	256	104	41	38	73	37	293	277	16	27	16	34	62	93	61
Warren	385	141	79	72	93	26	411	387	24	46	32	25	79	157	72
Washington	319	102	78	47	91	38	357	343	14	31	23	53	79	127	43
Wayne	290	78	50	58	103	46	336	326	10	21	10	32	79	128	66
Webster	533	178	96	96	163	42	575	535	40	59	49	91	133	165	78
Worth	31	14	*	*	*	*	35	33	*	*	*	*	*	14	13
Wright	358	108	57	51	142	46	404	390	14	27	16	38	92	148	83
Unknown	*	*	*	*	*	*	*	*	*	*	*	*	*	*	*
Montana															
Beaverhead	169	75	32	20	42	18	187	177	10	15	24	11	30	68	39
Big Horn	101	30	18	20	33	14	115	105	10	*	*	18	26	50	*
Blaine	120	36	26	11	47	*	129	126	*	10	*	16	26	42	27
Broadwater	142	52	27	21	42	10	152	145	*	12	19	22	32	48	19
Carbon	161	54	46	25	36	16	177	167	10	10	10	25	35	58	39
Carter	*	*	*	*	*	*	*	*	*	*	*	*	*	*	*
Cascade	3,697	1,269	866	639	923	122	3,819	3,405	414	479	486	858	757	756	483
Chouteau	89	37	16	12	24	*	92	81	11	*	11	11	23	23	15
Custer	213	65	56	32	60	22	235	223	12	20	20	33	42	80	40
Daniels	25	*	*	*	*	*	26	25	*	*	*	*	*	*	10
Dawson	117	42	29	18	28	15	132	123	*	13	10	14	26	46	23
Deer Lodge	202	76	47	35	44	16	218	204	14	11	23	29	43	71	41
Fallon	29	14	*	*	*	*	33	33	*	*	*	*	*	*	*
Fergus	247	88	65	38	56	16	263	246	17	13	21	19	43	98	69

Table 54. Compensation and Pension Recipients, by County, FY2014—*Continued*

(Number of recipients.)

State and county	Compensation					Total, pension	Compensation or pension								
	Total	0 to 20 percent	30 to 40 percent	50 to 60 percent	70 to 100 percent		Total	Male	Female	Less than 35 years	35 to 44 years	45 to 54 years	55 to 64 years	65 to 74 years	75 years and over
Montana cnt'd															
Flathead	1,570	572	342	249	408	141	1,711	1,597	114	178	205	225	357	506	241
Gallatin	1,239	540	277	178	244	54	1,293	1,205	88	227	152	153	192	330	239
Garfield	11	*	*	*	*	*	13	13	*	*	*	*	*	*	*
Glacier	181	69	34	33	45	17	198	189	*	21	19	26	30	62	40
Golden Valley	23	*	*	*	*	*	26	23	*	*	*	*	*	*	*
Granite	73	28	17	16	12	*	79	77	*	*	*	*	12	30	17
Hill	325	148	64	44	69	16	341	316	25	28	34	42	77	105	55
Jefferson	290	106	68	37	79	17	307	277	30	19	35	38	99	83	32
Judith Basin	52	16	14	10	12	*	55	53	*	*	*	*	*	25	13
Lake	440	146	83	76	134	50	490	458	32	43	28	56	88	183	91
Lewis And Clark	1,732	604	354	282	492	104	1,836	1,661	175	189	216	335	414	475	207
Liberty	15	*	*	*	*	*	16	16	*	*	*	*	*	*	*
Lincoln	460	137	92	73	158	40	500	479	21	41	32	49	116	202	60
Madison	120	45	18	15	42	15	135	131	*	*	*	*	27	54	30
Mccone	*	*	*	*	*	*	11	10	*	*	*	*	*	*	*
Meagher	39	14	*	*	12	*	47	46	*	*	*	*	*	23	10
Mineral	80	26	14	*	33	11	91	86	*	*	*	*	22	36	18
Missoula	1,818	675	395	262	486	131	1,949	1,775	174	326	223	248	343	574	235
Musselshell	108	32	23	18	35	11	119	110	*	*	*	17	35	42	10
Park	261	102	61	38	60	14	275	261	14	24	26	33	50	89	52
Petroleum	10	*	*	*	*	*	11	11	*	*	*	*	*	*	*
Phillips	56	23	18	*	*	10	66	62	*	*	10	*	15	18	14
Pondera	102	37	20	17	28	10	112	108	*	*	*	10	18	46	23
Powder River	18	*	*	*	*	*	21	20	*	*	*	*	*	*	*
Powell	168	61	36	31	40	10	178	170	*	15	16	22	39	57	29
Prairie	30	13	*	*	*	*	35	32	*	*	*	*	*	10	*
Ravalli	1,028	354	195	149	330	51	1,079	1,017	62	84	83	136	198	397	181
Richland	115	46	26	18	25	11	126	122	*	23	20	13	16	40	14
Roosevelt	118	51	32	16	19	13	131	119	12	17	16	11	29	42	16
Rosebud	108	41	29	*	32	12	120	110	10	18	*	18	16	48	14
Sanders	268	87	50	35	96	30	298	284	14	13	13	28	60	132	52
Sheridan	35	16	*	*	*	*	38	32	*	*	*	*	10	11	*
Silver Bow	614	217	154	89	154	69	683	630	53	62	68	113	133	193	113
Stillwater	153	57	37	21	38	*	159	151	*	17	11	16	34	60	21
Sweet Grass	69	20	21	12	16	*	74	68	*	*	*	*	*	30	15
Teton	108	46	21	14	27	*	114	108	*	*	*	12	24	40	21
Toole	91	35	18	21	17	*	96	92	*	13	10	*	16	36	12
Treasure	*	*	*	*	*	*	*	*	*	*	*	*	*	*	*
Valley	119	42	26	14	37	*	128	117	11	*	*	13	25	47	25
Wheatland	46	16	12	*	14	*	54	52	*	*	*	*	16	19	10
Wibaux	*	*	*	*	*	*	12	12	*	*	*	*	*	*	*
Yellowstone	2,539	933	565	394	647	193	2,732	2,523	209	398	359	384	500	729	361
Nebraska															
Adams	739	360	118	109	152	22	761	728	33	75	37	62	122	243	220
Antelope	186	84	30	25	47	*	192	189	*	*	*	19	26	59	70
Arthur	*	*	*	*	*	*	*	*	*	*	*	*	*	*	*
Banner	26	13	*	*	*	*	28	28	*	*	*	*	*	10	*
Blaine	*	*	*	*	*	*	*	*	*	*	*	*	*	*	*
Boone	188	109	24	15	40	*	190	185	*	10	*	12	12	79	75
Box Butte	187	75	36	34	42	*	194	184	10	28	23	26	28	57	32
Boyd	56	27	*	10	10	*	62	60	*	*	*	*	*	23	23
Brown	92	37	18	13	24	*	96	95	*	*	*	*	*	33	47
Buffalo	852	397	156	94	205	16	868	829	39	108	66	76	116	285	213
Burt	114	46	17	21	30	*	122	117	*	12	*	13	23	32	34
Butler	200	110	20	27	43	*	206	200	*	12	*	21	31	59	75
Cass	989	371	215	174	229	*	997	919	78	68	105	208	205	280	130
Cedar	151	71	25	15	40	12	163	160	*	15	*	18	23	52	52
Chase	53	17	14	*	18	*	58	53	*	10	*	*	*	19	16
Cherry	86	34	18	*	25	*	91	86	*	*	11	10	14	33	20
Cheyenne	258	164	38	18	38	*	262	253	*	23	14	20	41	90	74
Clay	140	63	21	26	30	*	147	146	*	*	*	10	25	45	50
Colfax	94	49	22	10	12	*	98	98	*	*	*	*	10	38	36
Cuming	157	63	31	23	39	12	169	161	*	14	10	14	17	51	62
Custer	312	138	51	45	78	13	325	319	*	11	15	13	54	119	111
Dakota	286	144	48	32	62	14	300	285	15	27	20	28	46	108	71
Dawes	162	54	36	28	44	14	176	167	*	19	12	23	30	46	46
Dawson	320	153	57	40	70	12	332	322	10	32	17	25	41	123	93
Deuel	55	31	11	*	10	*	56	53	*	*	*	*	*	22	18
Dixon	82	39	20	12	11	*	90	83	*	*	*	*	10	33	28

Table 54. Compensation and Pension Recipients, by County, FY2014—*Continued*

(Number of recipients.)

State and county	Compensation					Total, pension	Compensation or pension								
	Total	0 to 20 percent	30 to 40 percent	50 to 60 percent	70 to 100 percent		Total	Male	Female	Less than 35 years	35 to 44 years	45 to 54 years	55 to 64 years	65 to 74 years	75 years and over
Nebraska cnt'd															
Dodge	772	365	154	99	154	37	809	788	21	68	62	77	120	246	234
Douglas	6,834	2,668	1,390	995	1,781	467	7,301	6,760	541	809	834	1,177	1,320	1,859	1,290
Dundy	32	10	*	*	11	*	33	32	*	*	*	*	*	*	10
Fillmore	217	108	34	26	49	*	223	219	*	11	10	15	23	73	90
Franklin	139	68	26	18	27	*	140	135	*	*	*	*	15	58	49
Frontier	54	21	*	*	17	*	54	52	*	*	*	*	*	17	16
Furnas	168	93	21	19	35	*	170	161	*	*	*	13	19	67	59
Gage	733	370	138	75	150	20	753	724	29	40	52	62	107	223	267
Garden	42	13	11	10	*	*	44	39	*	*	*	*	*	15	15
Garfield	60	32	*	10	*	*	65	62	*	*	*	*	11	26	20
Gosper	64	30	*	*	17	*	65	64	*	*	*	*	*	27	25
Grant	13	*	*	*	*	*	14	14	*	*	*	*	*	*	*
Greeley	83	42	*	17	18	*	84	82	*	*	*	*	10	30	35
Hall	1,913	1,051	296	208	358	84	1,997	1,912	85	149	119	194	295	691	547
Hamilton	308	164	35	50	59	*	315	305	10	23	15	33	49	94	101
Harlan	136	76	21	13	26	*	138	136	*	*	*	*	18	54	50
Hayes	18	12	*	*	*	*	19	19	*	*	*	*	*	*	*
Hitchcock	82	41	*	10	22	*	83	81	*	*	*	*	*	32	30
Holt	242	109	47	30	56	*	249	241	*	19	*	*	35	86	93
Hooker	15	*	*	*	*	*	15	15	*	*	*	*	*	*	*
Howard	278	145	40	33	60	*	283	276	*	10	12	15	39	110	97
Jefferson	180	79	31	27	43	*	187	181	*	*	*	11	29	68	61
Johnson	61	25	10	11	15	*	69	66	*	12	*	*	10	12	24
Kearney	108	51	15	16	26	*	110	106	*	*	*	13	17	30	36
Keith	149	69	20	24	36	*	153	147	*	14	12	*	30	50	37
Keya Paha	25	11	*	*	*	*	28	27	*	*	*	*	*	13	12
Kimball	75	34	13	13	15	*	80	78	*	*	*	*	14	21	28
Knox	248	112	44	45	47	10	258	249	*	15	13	18	32	95	85
Lancaster	5,260	2,423	988	692	1,157	193	5,453	5,101	352	673	453	621	929	1,514	1,256
Lincoln	721	314	137	91	179	26	747	718	29	73	63	78	133	227	169
Logan	13	*	*	*	*	*	14	14	*	*	*	*	*	*	*
Loup	30	19	*	*	*	*	30	29	*	*	*	*	*	17	*
Madison	447	205	90	67	85	33	480	455	25	57	31	32	74	159	127
Mcpherson	*	*	*	*	*	*	*	*	*	*	*	*	*	*	*
Merrick	342	183	58	45	56	*	344	333	11	14	15	22	48	123	122
Morrill	114	54	24	19	17	*	118	116	*	10	10	11	18	33	36
Nance	99	59	12	*	19	*	101	96	*	*	*	*	18	32	41
Nemaha	91	35	24	16	16	*	94	88	*	*	*	13	20	25	20
Nuckolls	126	63	24	13	26	*	129	124	*	*	*	*	10	45	58
Otoe	364	165	65	52	82	*	373	357	16	45	20	45	55	109	99
Pawnee	59	30	14	*	*	*	61	56	*	*	*	*	*	16	20
Perkins	47	22	12	*	*	*	48	45	*	*	*	*	*	17	11
Phelps	331	188	61	40	42	*	337	328	*	25	17	14	38	126	117
Pierce	104	55	17	12	20	*	112	107	*	*	*	11	13	29	46
Platte	575	318	104	79	74	10	585	570	15	40	41	38	76	215	175
Polk	180	103	25	24	28	*	184	180	*	10	*	*	29	59	70
Red Willow	331	150	49	47	85	*	334	325	*	15	13	29	43	112	122
Richardson	195	67	42	35	51	16	211	203	*	11	10	11	44	76	59
Rock	14	*	*	*	*	*	15	15	*	*	*	*	*	*	10
Saline	260	109	55	38	58	*	268	256	12	16	14	23	56	84	75
Sarpy	7,280	2,393	1,626	1,318	1,943	56	7,336	6,300	1,036	778	1,048	2,122	1,581	1,161	646
Saunders	632	325	123	71	113	14	646	622	24	49	40	76	101	196	184
Scotts Bluff	943	465	178	122	178	27	970	931	39	88	63	89	149	303	278
Seward	467	275	71	45	76	*	474	461	13	37	32	54	70	163	116
Sheridan	102	28	22	14	38	*	109	104	*	13	*	*	16	40	25
Sherman	142	82	14	18	28	*	144	143	*	10	*	*	17	46	56
Sioux	23	13	*	*	*	*	24	22	*	*	*	*	*	11	*
Stanton	97	46	18	13	19	*	102	97	*	*	*	*	21	31	30
Thayer	136	71	24	19	22	*	139	134	*	*	*	13	20	46	49
Thomas	12	*	*	*	*	*	13	12	*	*	*	*	*	*	*
Thurston	50	25	*	*	11	*	58	57	*	*	*	*	10	24	13
Valley	110	54	12	15	29	*	118	115	*	*	*	10	19	38	44
Washington	323	133	70	50	70	10	333	319	14	30	37	43	57	97	68
Wayne	130	68	22	18	22	*	134	129	*	12	*	*	16	48	43
Webster	124	54	21	21	28	*	127	122	*	11	*	15	20	35	40
Wheeler	21	13	*	*	*	*	21	21	*	*	*	*	*	*	*
York	643	419	97	55	72	*	651	641	10	33	23	50	101	220	224
Nevada															
Carson City	776	261	154	94	267	73	849	795	54	78	64	92	171	294	150

Table 54. Compensation and Pension Recipients, by County, FY2014—*Continued*

(Number of recipients.)

State and county	Compensation					Total, pension	Compensation or pension								
	Total	0 to 20 percent	30 to 40 percent	50 to 60 percent	70 to 100 percent		Total	Male	Female	Less than 35 years	35 to 44 years	45 to 54 years	55 to 64 years	65 to 74 years	75 years and over
Nevada cnt'd															
Churchill	1,027	318	230	158	321	44	1,071	962	109	118	135	228	232	246	112
Clark	28,534	9,051	5,427	4,293	9,763	1,984	30,518	27,511	3,007	3,088	3,645	5,320	6,402	8,112	3,946
Douglas	767	261	161	102	243	52	818	760	58	88	77	85	131	287	151
Elko	575	255	115	71	134	35	610	567	43	98	61	70	130	183	66
Esmeralda	*	*	*	*	*	*	13	12	*	*	*	*	*	*	*
Eureka	19	12	*	*	*	*	20	20	*	*	*	*	*	11	*
Humboldt	167	63	33	24	47	12	179	170	*	20	18	16	44	71	10
Lander	51	18	11	*	13	*	56	53	*	*	*	*	12	24	*
Lincoln	47	21	*	*	12	*	51	47	*	*	*	*	*	27	*
Lyon	1,259	385	242	186	446	69	1,328	1,202	126	140	133	191	266	424	175
Mineral	107	36	18	15	38	12	119	112	*	14	*	10	23	53	16
Nye	1,241	363	208	169	501	90	1,331	1,241	90	55	72	129	276	532	267
Pershing	78	24	15	*	32	*	86	85	*	*	*	10	16	36	11
Storey	92	28	14	17	32	*	96	87	*	10	*	13	19	36	12
Washoe	5,988	2,115	1,088	872	1,914	664	6,652	6,148	504	725	589	777	1,414	2,227	920
White Pine	122	43	33	13	33	16	138	135	*	14	10	17	30	39	28
New Hampshire															
Belknap	971	375	198	131	268	83	1,054	993	61	89	84	118	219	357	187
Carroll	772	269	144	122	237	33	805	768	37	46	73	100	133	297	155
Cheshire	930	305	178	158	289	42	972	901	71	92	97	140	196	298	149
Coos	619	194	120	92	213	42	661	624	37	57	70	79	144	201	110
Grafton	1,217	425	230	167	395	70	1,287	1,208	79	89	130	187	278	364	239
Hillsborough	5,089	1,931	1,020	749	1,389	245	5,334	4,940	394	649	571	761	1,083	1,410	858
Merrimack	1,936	720	402	275	538	107	2,043	1,888	155	237	220	288	421	541	335
Rockingham	3,742	1,442	772	569	959	155	3,897	3,670	227	378	390	494	730	1,156	749
Strafford	1,818	619	402	273	524	116	1,934	1,798	136	195	173	293	420	535	318
Sullivan	680	234	122	106	218	36	716	655	61	55	71	109	172	193	116
New Jersey															
Atlantic	2,054	664	384	301	705	183	2,237	2,105	132	192	167	264	415	779	419
Bergen	3,763	1,493	648	504	1,118	277	4,040	3,888	152	476	319	307	480	1,226	1,229
Burlington	6,314	1,778	1,216	972	2,347	222	6,536	5,848	688	638	673	1,221	1,293	1,625	1,084
Camden	3,984	1,222	678	572	1,513	353	4,337	4,007	330	414	418	603	871	1,343	687
Cape May	1,317	454	256	152	455	73	1,390	1,336	54	77	80	122	220	615	276
Cumberland	1,049	355	204	166	324	92	1,141	1,074	67	95	103	136	201	422	184
Essex	3,734	1,343	638	523	1,230	444	4,178	3,833	345	443	389	526	815	1,195	806
Gloucester	2,564	771	467	366	960	159	2,723	2,550	173	273	262	332	509	926	421
Hudson	2,011	676	376	314	645	188	2,199	2,029	170	397	292	226	369	544	370
Hunterdon	669	270	105	82	212	33	702	669	33	55	44	61	95	281	166
Mercer	1,938	690	325	267	656	136	2,073	1,950	123	175	191	230	370	731	376
Middlesex	3,797	1,474	705	488	1,130	210	4,008	3,802	205	484	343	369	589	1,290	929
Monmouth	4,140	1,553	773	554	1,260	231	4,371	4,165	206	417	300	447	695	1,531	976
Morris	2,101	866	378	282	575	101	2,202	2,103	99	242	187	181	253	732	605
Ocean	6,265	2,220	1,035	887	2,123	269	6,534	6,270	264	490	424	589	885	2,368	1,771
Passaic	1,928	708	338	272	610	145	2,073	1,956	117	308	194	187	274	630	476
Salem	627	203	111	101	211	37	664	617	47	59	76	82	103	255	87
Somerset	1,459	595	242	172	449	106	1,565	1,480	85	150	132	164	237	504	376
Sussex	1,061	372	178	149	362	37	1,098	1,042	56	129	104	118	144	467	135
Union	2,550	1,004	473	311	762	184	2,734	2,556	178	325	246	326	481	782	572
Warren	807	301	127	103	276	39	846	805	41	92	60	89	132	305	168
Unknown	*	*	*	*	*	*	*	*	*	*	*	*	*	*	*
New Mexico															
Bernalillo	12,023	3,163	1,901	1,728	5,231	773	12,796	11,656	1,140	1,137	1,289	2,053	2,809	3,462	2,041
Catron	57	*	*	10	34	*	59	56	*	*	*	*	14	30	*
Chaves	757	212	129	119	297	75	832	794	38	63	61	100	190	261	157
Cibola	388	88	46	55	199	49	437	415	22	22	37	42	100	153	83
Colfax	230	47	26	24	133	36	266	257	*	12	19	25	54	105	51
Curry	1,341	347	261	250	483	39	1,380	1,187	193	213	179	287	300	256	145
De Baca	35	*	*	*	15	*	39	38	*	*	*	*	*	11	10
Dona Ana	3,337	956	668	585	1,129	188	3,525	3,255	270	440	393	495	741	954	500
Eddy	573	177	113	74	209	52	625	576	49	65	58	82	143	202	75
Grant	517	128	59	88	242	60	577	546	31	37	41	46	116	246	91
Guadalupe	73	14	*	*	45	12	85	83	*	*	*	12	19	20	22
Harding	15	*	*	*	*	*	19	19	*	*	*	*	*	*	*
Hidalgo	62	20	11	11	20	*	69	63	*	*	*	*	20	15	14
Lea	497	155	94	88	160	56	553	519	34	74	60	66	93	159	101
Lincoln	342	105	46	42	149	34	376	346	30	17	30	39	67	154	69
Los Alamos	173	78	35	22	38	*	176	166	10	17	21	28	48	38	24

Table 54. Compensation and Pension Recipients, by County, FY2014—*Continued*

(Number of recipients.)

State and county	Compensation					Total, pension	Compensation or pension								
	Total	0 to 20 percent	30 to 40 percent	50 to 60 percent	70 to 100 percent		Total	Male	Female	Less than 35 years	35 to 44 years	45 to 54 years	55 to 64 years	65 to 74 years	75 years and over
New Mexico cnt'd															
Luna	290	84	47	44	115	43	333	323	10	10	22	19	72	125	85
Mckinley	675	136	109	103	327	107	782	722	60	93	88	68	129	269	135
Mora	110	16	11	14	69	12	122	111	11	*	*	21	28	36	28
Otero	2,407	673	500	420	813	82	2,489	2,180	309	311	263	506	545	545	318
Quay	176	45	15	22	94	26	202	196	*	11	14	20	40	78	39
Rio Arriba	442	86	55	58	243	53	495	473	22	27	29	55	102	189	93
Roosevelt	245	62	45	47	91	14	259	231	28	43	28	44	58	45	41
San Juan	1,227	329	181	191	526	113	1,340	1,246	94	167	173	160	230	432	178
San Miguel	485	71	49	67	298	64	549	520	29	29	48	93	118	178	83
Sandoval	3,109	846	484	399	1,379	113	3,222	2,937	284	269	378	604	727	868	376
Santa Fe	1,895	450	280	204	961	141	2,036	1,884	152	130	130	257	425	728	364
Sierra	268	72	36	34	126	51	319	301	18	10	11	24	71	126	77
Socorro	280	59	30	44	147	25	305	287	18	23	11	33	82	113	43
Taos	515	82	54	70	309	47	562	528	34	25	34	61	98	237	107
Torrance	245	46	28	33	137	19	264	244	20	12	14	48	71	82	36
Union	52	14	*	*	26	11	63	60	*	*	*	*	11	27	10
Valencia	1,664	426	250	233	755	80	1,744	1,622	122	114	177	262	406	545	240
New York															
Albany	2,496	942	486	338	730	289	2,785	2,562	223	296	261	335	567	828	495
Allegany	647	175	125	78	269	69	716	670	46	75	87	83	138	234	99
Bronx	4,515	1,415	748	659	1,693	985	5,500	4,999	501	682	556	695	1,290	1,472	804
Broome	1,790	605	352	275	558	171	1,961	1,846	115	239	221	196	349	597	359
Cattaraugus	1,129	284	182	188	475	120	1,249	1,177	72	167	113	139	237	439	154
Cayuga	854	302	186	111	255	76	930	856	74	113	107	109	167	277	157
Chautauqua	1,714	430	290	276	718	251	1,965	1,838	127	241	179	195	365	648	337
Chemung	1,268	367	218	191	492	107	1,375	1,285	90	164	135	167	257	455	196
Chenango	529	192	91	83	163	58	587	548	39	62	46	79	121	199	80
Clinton	1,451	539	333	186	393	91	1,542	1,453	89	125	143	198	389	441	245
Columbia	559	230	110	72	147	63	622	587	35	47	37	56	119	233	130
Cortland	505	175	101	67	162	50	555	524	31	79	51	66	107	190	61
Delaware	489	196	84	75	135	63	552	522	30	49	37	46	108	206	105
Dutchess	2,187	834	349	284	720	152	2,339	2,214	125	247	169	243	416	828	434
Erie	9,623	2,753	1,617	1,356	3,897	1,029	10,652	9,933	719	1,172	1,008	1,279	1,956	3,456	1,777
Essex	524	197	106	89	131	63	587	561	26	36	43	73	134	179	121
Franklin	666	224	124	80	238	84	750	707	43	69	61	102	166	241	111
Fulton	574	205	111	86	172	61	635	594	41	64	68	75	136	180	111
Genesee	720	244	128	106	242	64	784	732	52	103	72	81	123	279	125
Greene	496	190	91	58	157	52	548	526	22	41	37	55	102	203	110
Hamilton	49	22	10	*	11	*	54	50	*	*	*	*	13	19	12
Herkimer	786	257	148	149	232	72	859	815	44	79	78	103	159	284	155
Jefferson	4,382	965	898	794	1,725	111	4,493	3,887	606	1,393	919	932	544	499	206
Kings	6,915	2,193	1,207	969	2,546	1,244	8,159	7,408	751	1,132	908	939	1,637	2,284	1,257
Lewis	406	97	93	70	146	27	433	392	41	67	72	74	79	96	45
Livingston	552	192	121	73	166	43	595	557	38	77	53	57	99	226	83
Madison	746	272	147	119	209	54	800	747	53	84	77	114	143	257	125
Monroe	5,283	2,033	1,065	746	1,439	636	5,919	5,528	391	748	523	689	955	1,829	1,174
Montgomery	574	200	108	100	166	55	628	580	48	78	48	81	119	189	114
Nassau	5,969	2,543	1,218	780	1,429	565	6,534	6,260	274	574	442	456	797	2,286	1,977
New York	4,273	1,557	799	589	1,328	1,115	5,388	5,021	367	611	456	522	944	1,475	1,378
Niagara	2,511	729	402	393	987	198	2,709	2,509	200	333	270	358	484	884	379
Oneida	3,058	1,058	613	479	908	216	3,274	3,063	211	302	258	480	702	1,002	530
Onondaga	4,149	1,437	850	591	1,271	525	4,674	4,314	360	572	490	634	859	1,255	860
Ontario	1,170	428	236	141	365	127	1,297	1,209	88	128	109	170	233	430	228
Orange	3,263	1,074	598	472	1,119	199	3,462	3,202	260	391	357	496	585	1,043	589
Orleans	502	148	78	75	201	26	528	493	35	56	41	77	95	186	73
Oswego	1,493	524	315	209	445	136	1,628	1,529	99	209	194	246	305	447	227
Otsego	696	242	141	104	209	73	769	736	33	77	61	77	141	287	125
Putnam	633	229	127	88	189	20	653	628	25	65	47	50	92	273	125
Queens	6,756	2,342	1,276	936	2,202	852	7,608	7,008	600	1,108	841	791	1,200	2,093	1,571
Rensselaer	1,575	592	307	242	434	108	1,683	1,579	104	177	157	214	321	558	256
Richmond	2,537	791	396	347	1,003	167	2,704	2,598	106	286	213	209	449	1,030	517
Rockland	1,519	573	286	203	457	78	1,597	1,537	60	150	131	144	165	582	423
Saint Lawrence	1,735	465	335	260	675	125	1,860	1,743	117	217	263	306	338	530	206
Saratoga	2,225	861	461	312	591	139	2,364	2,180	184	268	243	375	415	709	353
Schenectady	1,272	518	239	163	353	135	1,408	1,305	103	146	133	206	299	376	247
Schoharie	350	118	82	47	102	28	378	362	16	38	30	38	74	131	67
Schuyler	240	71	53	37	79	17	257	240	17	27	26	35	49	82	38
Seneca	424	149	84	63	128	38	462	432	30	51	36	62	116	133	64
Steuben	1,575	461	281	244	589	159	1,734	1,624	110	202	161	233	410	516	212

Table 54. Compensation and Pension Recipients, by County, FY2014—*Continued*

(Number of recipients.)

State and county	Compensation					Total, pension	Compensation or pension								
	Total	0 to 20 percent	30 to 40 percent	50 to 60 percent	70 to 100 percent		Total	Male	Female	Less than 35 years	35 to 44 years	45 to 54 years	55 to 64 years	65 to 74 years	75 years and over
New York cnt'd															
Suffolk	9,618	3,847	1,935	1,302	2,533	795	10,412	9,972	440	888	746	919	1,500	4,053	2,303
Sullivan	754	301	132	94	227	75	829	790	39	64	61	91	155	307	151
Tioga	535	190	106	85	153	27	562	518	44	70	65	89	105	169	64
Tompkins	520	191	93	82	154	38	558	521	37	73	52	71	90	202	70
Ulster	1,371	517	263	181	410	136	1,507	1,422	85	100	137	155	297	533	285
Warren	763	256	164	122	221	69	832	783	49	102	72	104	161	238	155
Washington	696	269	135	105	187	52	748	702	46	83	75	103	131	237	119
Wayne	1,008	377	185	142	304	68	1,076	1,016	60	147	104	118	201	355	151
Westchester	3,840	1,458	622	511	1,249	409	4,249	4,039	210	357	291	353	619	1,381	1,244
Wyoming	467	150	70	67	180	32	499	476	23	63	38	60	88	200	50
Yates	311	98	50	51	112	28	339	318	21	35	24	32	65	121	62
Unknown	*	*	*	*	*	*	*	*	*	*	*	*	*	*	*
North Carolina															
Alamance	1,569	523	325	202	519	127	1,696	1,560	136	145	186	253	319	550	243
Alexander	480	149	93	76	162	46	526	504	22	43	33	56	105	203	86
Alleghany	167	72	25	27	43	13	180	177	*	*	*	*	38	80	41
Anson	291	80	46	40	125	35	326	318	*	17	20	41	72	133	43
Ashe	382	132	68	56	126	57	439	420	19	15	23	38	84	183	96
Avery	197	63	31	27	76	22	219	212	*	11	12	17	25	96	58
Beaufort	796	233	141	109	313	87	883	825	58	58	61	108	189	319	148
Bertie	195	48	33	32	82	27	222	201	21	14	21	33	61	67	26
Bladen	532	138	96	74	223	55	586	543	43	38	56	96	152	181	64
Brunswick	2,456	705	455	363	933	122	2,578	2,450	128	146	218	304	453	1,034	423
Buncombe	3,243	1,029	606	474	1,133	319	3,561	3,264	297	275	277	441	824	1,128	616
Burke	1,214	395	211	178	430	114	1,328	1,260	68	95	106	146	268	515	198
Cabarrus	2,391	848	480	364	699	147	2,538	2,339	199	257	315	453	441	727	344
Caldwell	1,096	360	193	176	367	130	1,226	1,164	62	102	107	154	238	423	202
Camden	351	85	66	74	126	*	356	313	43	18	44	138	74	56	26
Carteret	2,880	842	567	467	1,005	80	2,960	2,760	200	271	286	515	579	861	447
Caswell	304	79	62	53	109	32	335	314	21	24	36	35	77	116	47
Catawba	2,017	692	395	320	610	196	2,213	2,087	126	212	196	267	373	805	360
Chatham	646	249	117	83	197	33	679	622	57	65	76	87	118	228	103
Cherokee	557	178	88	84	207	46	603	578	25	30	19	49	111	262	132
Chowan	231	72	43	34	82	20	251	237	14	22	20	31	64	74	40
Clay	198	58	39	24	77	15	213	207	*	*	13	15	37	88	52
Cleveland	1,318	380	247	220	471	150	1,468	1,392	76	117	126	165	326	531	201
Columbus	872	210	161	137	364	100	972	904	68	73	75	153	232	301	138
Craven	4,693	1,122	982	862	1,727	81	4,773	4,213	561	1,171	641	912	871	751	427
Cumberland	23,800	5,060	4,713	4,211	9,816	341	24,141	19,843	4,297	3,927	3,526	6,365	5,381	3,162	1,779
Currituck	802	220	165	148	269	14	816	736	80	49	81	256	186	182	62
Dare	417	154	83	68	112	18	435	404	31	22	30	50	82	157	94
Davidson	1,714	563	371	251	528	156	1,870	1,761	109	213	198	230	362	632	234
Davie	514	186	107	70	151	36	550	517	33	33	46	59	107	192	113
Duplin	932	237	174	145	376	64	996	922	73	124	85	143	214	294	136
Durham	2,864	837	532	404	1,091	218	3,082	2,710	371	296	358	529	761	816	322
Edgecombe	715	170	111	119	315	76	791	723	68	55	71	105	203	268	89
Forsyth	4,155	1,365	810	642	1,337	341	4,496	4,092	404	449	479	702	969	1,273	624
Franklin	721	229	118	98	276	34	755	700	55	63	104	138	153	232	65
Gaston	2,670	886	498	417	869	215	2,885	2,693	192	271	267	348	609	995	395
Gates	254	77	45	54	78	16	270	241	29	23	39	59	63	58	28
Graham	109	27	20	15	47	12	121	119	*	*	*	*	20	59	29
Granville	686	202	134	96	254	50	736	678	58	65	69	154	154	218	76
Greene	255	56	36	41	122	16	271	247	24	15	31	54	60	87	23
Guilford	5,040	1,601	991	735	1,712	477	5,517	4,967	550	521	621	919	1,197	1,584	676
Halifax	788	197	134	118	339	81	869	801	68	52	70	110	262	258	117
Harnett	4,323	937	877	770	1,740	87	4,410	3,724	686	668	865	1,213	792	603	268
Haywood	1,238	387	221	198	432	66	1,304	1,250	54	82	81	168	240	500	232
Henderson	1,472	506	282	212	473	112	1,585	1,478	107	107	118	169	288	524	379
Hertford	316	65	60	59	132	29	345	326	19	20	26	60	105	94	40
Hoke	2,766	549	562	490	1,164	22	2,788	2,239	549	539	598	783	511	259	97
Hyde	68	16	12	*	32	11	79	74	*	*	*	*	22	26	17
Iredell	1,860	630	370	268	593	119	1,979	1,850	129	220	202	284	340	660	273
Jackson	499	137	80	82	200	53	552	526	26	46	36	55	83	220	112
Johnston	2,788	844	543	427	974	113	2,901	2,631	270	295	414	583	650	708	252
Jones	312	67	42	59	143	15	327	297	30	47	36	52	84	76	31
Lee	1,125	295	223	190	417	45	1,170	1,030	140	127	163	251	238	277	114
Lenoir	1,186	280	179	183	545	83	1,269	1,167	102	112	110	213	303	370	161
Lincoln	917	341	187	139	250	55	971	918	53	94	78	130	172	353	144
Macon	660	205	133	89	233	59	719	678	41	37	46	67	124	248	197

Table 54. Compensation and Pension Recipients, by County, FY2014—*Continued*

(Number of recipients.)

State and county	Compensation					Total, pension	Compensation or pension								
	Total	0 to 20 percent	30 to 40 percent	50 to 60 percent	70 to 100 percent		Total	Male	Female	Less than 35 years	35 to 44 years	45 to 54 years	55 to 64 years	65 to 74 years	75 years and over
North Carolina cnt'd															
Madison	252	70	39	40	103	24	276	263	13	17	25	29	52	112	41
Martin	325	63	49	38	175	28	353	331	22	23	24	49	78	134	45
Mcdowell	730	197	132	102	299	91	821	785	36	49	63	85	174	317	133
Mecklenburg	8,661	2,799	1,652	1,348	2,863	596	9,257	8,097	1,160	1,130	1,292	1,714	1,921	2,273	927
Mitchell	185	47	35	29	74	23	208	201	*	12	10	19	33	76	58
Montgomery	317	80	54	49	134	28	345	326	19	25	34	32	80	124	51
Moore	2,361	660	468	396	836	95	2,456	2,195	260	189	306	591	476	547	347
Nash	1,306	330	212	184	580	83	1,389	1,269	120	121	156	211	300	425	176
New Hanover	3,278	938	660	481	1,200	226	3,504	3,217	287	525	395	509	624	931	521
Northampton	260	73	52	45	90	31	291	269	22	13	20	39	81	94	44
Onslow	15,385	2,648	2,852	2,983	6,902	114	15,499	13,457	2,042	5,740	2,492	2,969	2,280	1,296	722
Orange	870	309	169	123	269	67	937	840	97	94	101	119	196	297	131
Pamlico	373	116	69	46	141	28	401	388	13	21	19	44	85	148	83
Pasquotank	1,181	364	252	220	345	35	1,216	1,075	141	107	170	331	293	222	93
Pender	1,248	320	242	181	505	59	1,307	1,197	110	185	188	220	239	332	143
Perquimans	318	96	54	62	106	21	339	311	28	29	27	56	87	101	39
Person	472	122	84	67	199	30	502	473	29	35	44	58	103	191	71
Pitt	2,427	625	441	388	973	161	2,588	2,341	247	306	306	445	606	660	265
Polk	276	80	50	37	109	19	295	283	12	13	15	29	50	125	62
Randolph	1,516	459	294	224	539	102	1,617	1,542	75	140	141	203	311	616	207
Richmond	916	206	166	115	430	99	1,015	963	52	65	76	136	278	326	134
Robeson	1,930	476	346	330	778	151	2,081	1,898	184	199	237	333	526	566	222
Rockingham	1,090	313	209	163	405	99	1,189	1,113	76	106	95	151	249	419	169
Rowan	2,325	730	431	353	810	216	2,541	2,327	214	171	232	308	601	864	364
Rutherford	1,012	282	158	123	449	75	1,087	1,028	59	87	60	96	214	448	183
Sampson	1,046	242	170	159	475	102	1,149	1,059	90	62	96	185	296	346	162
Scotland	637	156	136	88	257	49	686	634	52	48	60	113	190	202	73
Stanly	683	225	142	99	216	43	726	685	41	61	60	83	150	263	109
Stokes	489	153	84	87	165	38	527	503	24	46	40	62	92	207	81
Surry	846	234	160	141	311	94	940	905	35	83	60	84	164	347	201
Swain	215	71	45	32	67	22	237	216	21	15	18	28	43	88	45
Transylvania	414	119	75	74	146	19	433	408	25	24	27	22	89	189	82
Tyrrell	33	*	14	*	*	*	36	31	*	*	*	*	*	12	*
Union	1,917	669	370	296	582	106	2,023	1,867	156	176	276	340	380	643	208
Vance	571	151	100	91	229	41	612	562	50	43	53	80	165	209	62
Wake	9,019	2,986	1,880	1,382	2,772	466	9,485	8,320	1,165	1,110	1,552	1,973	1,901	2,034	916
Warren	303	71	37	58	137	34	337	311	26	19	19	40	96	119	43
Washington	198	53	30	35	80	10	208	200	*	10	13	32	36	82	35
Watauga	579	182	114	105	178	68	647	616	31	47	32	53	93	259	163
Wayne	3,861	1,111	741	665	1,345	109	3,971	3,447	524	394	469	938	961	784	424
Wilkes	844	257	166	128	293	122	966	918	48	71	53	81	182	397	182
Wilson	1,154	283	195	168	508	96	1,250	1,143	107	103	118	179	327	386	137
Yadkin	449	164	91	64	130	48	496	478	18	43	49	63	87	173	82
Yancey	339	104	47	47	141	26	365	352	13	16	15	30	60	149	95
North Dakota															
Adams	30	10	*	*	*	*	32	28	*	*	*	*	*	10	*
Barnes	198	94	35	30	39	11	209	197	12	20	*	23	45	67	47
Benson	70	23	14	11	22	13	83	80	*	*	*	*	12	34	18
Billings	12	*	*	*	*	*	12	11	*	*	*	*	*	*	*
Bottineau	124	41	29	19	35	*	130	124	*	10	13	29	20	40	18
Bowman	31	14	*	*	*	*	31	30	*	*	*	*	*	11	*
Burke	28	*	*	*	*	*	30	28	*	*	*	*	*	13	*
Burleigh	1,267	531	254	201	281	58	1,325	1,220	105	172	146	218	231	352	206
Cass	2,764	1,331	503	342	588	111	2,875	2,676	199	380	318	362	504	773	537
Cavalier	35	12	11	*	*	*	36	36	*	*	*	*	*	16	*
Dickey	60	33	*	*	11	*	62	58	*	*	*	*	12	23	10
Divide	36	13	12	*	*	*	39	39	*	*	*	*	*	10	*
Dunn	53	15	*	12	18	*	56	53	*	*	*	*	*	21	*
Eddy	34	14	*	*	*	*	38	37	*	*	*	*	*	21	*
Emmons	46	15	10	*	16	11	57	54	*	*	*	*	10	24	14
Foster	34	19	*	*	*	*	37	35	*	*	*	*	*	*	*
Golden Valley	22	*	*	*	*	*	23	22	*	*	*	*	*	*	*
Grand Forks	1,353	462	315	243	333	39	1,392	1,249	143	180	188	293	287	289	155
Grant	31	*	*	*	10	*	38	38	*	*	*	*	*	13	13
Griggs	70	33	12	12	13	*	75	73	*	*	*	*	12	26	28
Hettinger	37	17	*	*	13	*	39	37	*	11	*	*	*	*	*
Kidder	26	*	*	*	11	*	27	26	*	*	*	*	*	10	*
Lamoure	48	21	16	*	10	*	51	49	*	*	*	10	*	12	16
Logan	29	*	*	*	*	*	33	32	*	*	*	*	*	*	*

Table 54. Compensation and Pension Recipients, by County, FY2014—*Continued*

(Number of recipients.)

State and county	Compensation					Total, pension	Compensation or pension								
	Total	0 to 20 percent	30 to 40 percent	50 to 60 percent	70 to 100 percent		Total	Male	Female	Less than 35 years	35 to 44 years	45 to 54 years	55 to 64 years	65 to 74 years	75 years and over
North Dakota cnt'd															
Mchenry	106	30	27	20	29	*	114	101	13	13	15	18	20	31	17
Mcintosh	41	16	*	*	14	*	50	48	*	*	*	*	*	13	16
Mckenzie	71	28	12	10	21	*	77	74	*	10	*	*	20	30	*
Mclean	174	81	32	17	44	*	180	163	17	18	17	16	39	66	24
Mercer	121	53	22	18	28	*	125	120	*	25	*	*	37	40	11
Morton	492	197	100	77	118	28	520	489	31	62	61	58	100	159	80
Mountrail	133	51	35	21	26	*	139	129	10	19	22	17	21	45	15
Nelson	71	25	12	13	21	*	73	67	*	*	*	*	19	23	15
Oliver	23	*	*	*	*	*	23	21	*	*	*	*	*	10	*
Pembina	101	37	24	12	28	11	112	104	*	*	*	12	22	39	24
Pierce	64	22	15	10	17	*	69	64	*	10	*	10	14	23	10
Ramsey	173	63	31	21	58	*	182	170	12	12	13	21	39	58	39
Ransom	97	34	17	22	24	19	116	115	*	*	*	11	22	39	30
Renville	62	24	12	14	12	*	65	60	*	*	*	22	14	16	*
Richland	218	102	40	26	50	13	231	223	*	24	13	22	55	79	38
Rolette	119	32	21	19	47	*	126	120	*	14	13	15	33	37	14
Sargent	59	24	13	*	14	*	60	57	*	*	*	*	*	22	*
Sheridan	17	*	*	*	*	*	18	17	*	*	*	*	*	*	*
Sioux	39	14	*	*	13	*	45	40	*	*	*	*	*	15	*
Slope	*	*	*	*	*	*	10	10	*	*	*	*	*	*	*
Stark	304	111	65	43	85	21	325	304	21	58	34	40	53	83	57
Steele	54	26	*	*	13	*	57	55	*	*	*	*	20	19	*
Stutsman	333	149	73	41	70	31	364	348	16	44	28	35	65	108	83
Towner	44	16	12	*	*	*	46	43	*	*	*	*	*	14	11
Traill	148	62	26	19	42	14	162	152	11	11	24	28	26	39	35
Walsh	144	55	27	23	39	15	159	151	*	12	*	19	26	54	44
Ward	1,660	544	400	320	396	52	1,712	1,492	220	328	252	422	301	256	153
Wells	57	18	16	*	16	*	60	58	*	*	*	*	11	20	15
Williams	305	119	69	47	70	13	318	308	10	56	52	41	59	73	37
Ohio															
Adams	372	138	69	59	107	68	440	429	11	22	28	51	79	179	81
Allen	1,057	357	241	150	310	180	1,237	1,160	77	152	132	161	245	368	180
Ashland	590	229	110	83	168	62	652	620	32	64	49	81	117	243	98
Ashtabula	1,254	439	231	183	401	196	1,450	1,360	90	186	124	188	309	467	175
Athens	598	175	131	78	214	128	726	690	36	69	83	75	178	234	86
Auglaize	467	155	109	76	127	46	514	495	19	83	70	57	77	157	69
Belmont	772	269	149	116	238	123	895	853	42	56	77	104	158	343	157
Brown	544	204	134	76	130	70	614	582	32	68	46	88	114	212	86
Butler	4,040	1,562	931	595	952	307	4,347	4,095	252	546	474	588	807	1,379	552
Carroll	350	134	62	49	105	31	381	364	17	41	27	53	64	147	49
Champaign	403	158	72	74	99	49	452	419	33	43	47	71	98	140	53
Clark	2,283	830	482	336	635	204	2,487	2,273	214	164	234	383	593	736	374
Clermont	2,460	949	580	350	581	146	2,605	2,461	144	332	275	317	469	884	327
Clinton	574	184	121	99	169	43	617	590	27	73	58	97	130	178	81
Columbiana	1,296	457	266	181	392	180	1,476	1,397	79	143	123	195	303	520	193
Coshocton	460	161	119	51	129	52	512	487	25	54	35	44	100	199	80
Crawford	438	158	85	58	138	76	514	493	21	46	39	56	94	191	88
Cuyahoga	10,943	4,041	2,240	1,548	3,114	2,540	13,483	12,476	1,007	1,191	1,150	1,716	3,278	3,970	2,173
Darke	499	168	117	76	138	51	550	527	23	63	52	87	76	186	86
Defiance	580	274	127	62	117	41	621	599	22	59	64	54	99	245	99
Delaware	1,139	465	238	178	259	69	1,208	1,138	70	129	147	206	221	366	139
Erie	758	249	167	115	226	191	949	885	64	87	93	105	193	308	162
Fairfield	1,676	602	349	269	456	144	1,821	1,689	132	220	249	295	303	560	193
Fayette	305	87	61	60	97	36	342	328	14	47	36	29	72	119	38
Franklin	10,525	3,884	2,277	1,538	2,827	1,384	11,910	10,836	1,074	1,408	1,317	1,755	2,589	3,342	1,497
Fulton	397	150	79	70	98	31	428	400	28	54	42	56	87	141	47
Gallia	407	119	84	59	145	54	461	439	22	37	43	53	90	168	70
Geauga	724	296	157	86	185	70	793	753	40	85	59	86	137	305	122
Greene	4,630	1,665	1,018	784	1,163	121	4,751	4,130	621	335	496	1,280	1,159	998	481
Guernsey	547	169	107	78	193	81	628	597	31	58	49	74	110	242	95
Hamilton	6,272	2,456	1,445	918	1,454	1,123	7,395	6,897	498	813	589	877	1,675	2,251	1,186
Hancock	579	217	133	78	150	67	645	606	39	82	62	75	103	209	114
Hardin	283	103	47	39	94	28	310	299	11	33	35	37	55	116	34
Harrison	180	69	31	26	54	24	204	194	10	21	15	18	43	80	27
Henry	218	78	43	47	50	17	235	221	14	30	30	23	46	73	33
Highland	525	159	108	74	184	81	605	578	27	47	54	86	128	196	95
Hocking	370	127	76	48	119	32	402	383	19	36	32	54	94	145	41
Holmes	184	48	40	30	65	20	204	198	*	24	15	24	34	84	23
Huron	589	213	130	72	173	63	652	609	43	84	59	80	130	228	71

Table 54. Compensation and Pension Recipients, by County, FY2014—*Continued*

(Number of recipients.)

State and county	Compensation					Total, pension	Compensation or pension								
	Total	0 to 20 percent	30 to 40 percent	50 to 60 percent	70 to 100 percent		Total	Male	Female	Less than 35 years	35 to 44 years	45 to 54 years	55 to 64 years	65 to 74 years	75 years and over
Ohio cnt'd															
Jackson	476	129	90	64	193	85	561	549	12	40	36	75	126	216	68
Jefferson	802	293	161	119	229	124	926	882	44	65	77	113	180	356	135
Knox	598	234	137	89	137	57	654	618	36	67	63	89	131	208	97
Lake	2,317	905	470	306	636	249	2,566	2,427	139	319	263	263	428	900	393
Lawrence	1,040	288	203	149	400	127	1,167	1,118	49	94	133	165	242	393	139
Licking	2,354	1,018	480	313	543	176	2,530	2,387	143	251	248	380	524	798	328
Logan	443	158	105	57	123	45	488	462	26	54	47	51	91	176	69
Lorain	3,014	1,132	570	450	862	281	3,295	3,059	236	344	397	467	596	1,066	425
Lucas	3,187	1,157	654	460	916	529	3,716	3,454	262	368	363	494	771	1,158	561
Madison	380	142	76	60	102	34	413	393	20	48	37	58	60	147	63
Mahoning	2,343	857	509	309	668	524	2,868	2,707	160	206	236	376	569	929	552
Marion	598	210	128	76	184	90	688	651	37	66	53	94	140	241	94
Medina	1,513	591	289	216	417	116	1,629	1,541	88	203	189	195	256	582	204
Meigs	276	68	63	43	102	41	317	302	15	25	29	40	73	110	40
Mercer	370	130	76	61	103	38	408	395	13	53	37	42	67	146	63
Miami	1,127	400	241	173	313	84	1,211	1,124	87	147	133	195	210	365	161
Monroe	185	63	28	30	64	29	214	206	*	10	14	19	45	90	36
Montgomery	7,932	2,719	1,729	1,248	2,235	866	8,797	7,808	989	753	955	1,762	2,102	2,105	1,119
Morgan	220	68	43	44	65	37	257	244	13	30	18	24	44	97	44
Morrow	396	137	100	64	94	43	439	416	23	45	37	63	87	151	56
Muskingum	941	327	198	150	266	137	1,078	1,019	59	129	95	125	236	355	138
Noble	150	41	38	27	44	15	165	158	*	22	18	22	22	51	29
Ottawa	521	197	115	78	131	32	553	533	20	60	52	63	88	214	76
Paulding	197	74	35	27	61	12	209	200	*	16	15	27	34	94	23
Perry	380	141	76	65	97	51	431	408	23	57	44	51	75	158	46
Pickaway	684	223	146	106	209	74	758	716	42	86	68	86	161	258	99
Pike	496	186	84	75	150	69	565	543	21	43	52	73	122	188	86
Portage	1,584	596	327	222	439	144	1,727	1,639	88	214	151	213	331	610	209
Preble	489	172	84	77	156	26	515	480	35	70	55	58	105	164	63
Putnam	210	77	54	34	45	15	225	218	*	32	28	24	30	78	33
Richland	1,390	529	296	185	380	203	1,593	1,505	88	157	142	183	335	529	247
Ross	1,200	367	259	162	412	183	1,383	1,295	88	138	137	199	357	419	133
Sandusky	646	258	140	100	148	57	703	660	43	84	67	88	118	258	88
Scioto	1,117	345	210	179	383	160	1,277	1,220	57	123	123	168	244	439	180
Seneca	539	228	118	61	133	51	591	565	26	71	54	68	114	202	81
Shelby	437	174	86	66	111	33	470	448	22	70	38	53	86	169	54
Stark	3,449	1,334	679	501	934	552	4,001	3,751	250	401	417	502	756	1,289	635
Summit	4,616	1,713	931	641	1,330	720	5,336	4,965	371	637	489	630	1,118	1,699	763
Trumbull	2,394	850	447	376	721	305	2,699	2,557	142	243	254	305	528	993	375
Tuscarawas	1,081	384	218	176	303	116	1,197	1,149	48	133	103	132	215	439	174
Union	508	214	107	72	115	21	529	500	29	67	46	89	106	171	51
Van Wert	295	114	65	40	76	25	320	304	16	32	35	36	56	108	53
Vinton	175	34	37	32	72	26	201	195	*	17	14	23	44	80	23
Warren	1,925	755	428	313	430	110	2,036	1,888	148	230	254	361	371	596	223
Washington	724	199	144	128	253	69	793	759	34	96	73	118	144	261	101
Wayne	969	371	201	142	255	121	1,090	1,037	53	136	99	126	219	386	124
Williams	464	199	100	56	109	29	493	469	24	53	46	64	82	170	79
Wood	899	363	195	128	213	74	973	921	52	131	103	126	164	305	144
Wyandot	195	69	45	31	50	28	224	216	*	32	15	24	51	78	23
Oklahoma															
Adair	349	77	42	48	182	34	383	368	15	27	27	39	77	149	64
Alfalfa	65	28	13	*	20	*	73	69	*	*	*	*	14	21	16
Atoka	235	48	37	48	102	19	254	242	12	14	22	29	50	89	50
Beaver	41	14	*	*	14	*	44	38	*	*	*	*	*	16	*
Beckham	226	75	42	25	84	31	257	247	10	29	21	25	54	71	57
Blaine	142	46	23	23	50	15	157	149	*	12	*	18	35	59	24
Bryan	682	155	115	109	303	66	748	717	31	62	55	71	141	264	155
Caddo	543	162	79	78	224	49	592	568	24	55	59	59	106	208	105
Canadian	2,648	800	440	412	996	77	2,726	2,518	208	364	422	464	461	741	272
Carter	790	235	116	134	305	88	878	843	35	63	88	88	159	313	167
Cherokee	1,064	250	156	169	488	71	1,135	1,082	52	107	90	106	235	408	188
Choctaw	273	60	44	47	122	41	314	307	*	23	18	29	43	129	72
Cimarron	15	*	*	*	*	*	17	17	*	*	*	*	*	*	*
Cleveland	6,978	2,123	1,253	1,107	2,495	225	7,203	6,587	616	947	966	1,313	1,284	1,763	930
Coal	102	25	17	19	41	*	110	106	*	*	11	12	17	36	32
Comanche	9,271	1,531	1,496	1,571	4,673	162	9,433	8,275	1,158	1,478	1,508	2,219	2,013	1,323	891
Cotton	195	51	27	30	87	12	207	195	12	16	25	31	37	60	38
Craig	278	93	29	37	119	28	306	296	10	16	17	31	70	121	51
Creek	1,358	407	212	212	527	76	1,434	1,377	57	112	139	152	272	554	204

Table 54. Compensation and Pension Recipients, by County, FY2014—*Continued*

(Number of recipients.)

State and county	Compensation					Total, pension	Compensation or pension								
	Total	0 to 20 percent	30 to 40 percent	50 to 60 percent	70 to 100 percent		Total	Male	Female	Less than 35 years	35 to 44 years	45 to 54 years	55 to 64 years	65 to 74 years	75 years and over
Oklahoma cnt'd															
Custer	351	102	62	56	131	44	395	381	14	54	38	27	72	122	82
Delaware	797	171	127	120	379	81	878	843	35	37	58	84	133	397	169
Dewey	59	10	17	*	28	*	63	58	*	*	*	*	*	29	11
Ellis	42	12	*	*	20	*	45	42	*	*	*	*	*	22	*
Garfield	1,156	372	208	200	376	61	1,217	1,112	105	149	132	179	263	297	196
Garvin	724	216	100	102	306	30	754	730	24	35	48	50	130	292	199
Grady	1,201	394	177	199	432	56	1,257	1,189	69	104	123	164	232	434	200
Grant	57	21	*	*	19	*	59	58	*	*	*	*	10	18	14
Greer	138	42	22	19	55	19	157	146	11	*	16	18	23	55	36
Harmon	52	19	10	*	15	*	55	53	*	*	*	*	14	17	*
Harper	36	*	*	*	12	*	40	40	*	*	*	*	*	16	11
Haskell	315	66	55	46	148	27	342	334	*	17	18	18	67	149	73
Hughes	342	79	41	61	161	31	373	354	19	12	30	35	78	123	95
Jackson	1,299	360	297	239	403	46	1,345	1,187	158	154	153	264	357	261	156
Jefferson	109	32	10	14	53	11	120	120	*	*	*	*	23	51	29
Johnston	231	48	34	36	113	27	258	250	*	19	15	23	56	98	47
Kay	767	255	146	96	270	66	833	798	35	83	77	71	161	284	157
Kingfisher	155	56	20	24	55	11	166	155	11	24	23	20	23	52	24
Kiowa	221	58	39	35	89	17	238	228	10	20	13	26	55	72	52
Latimer	307	68	36	45	158	32	339	331	*	16	19	28	87	124	65
Leflore	998	237	140	169	452	103	1,101	1,057	44	71	86	94	211	424	215
Lincoln	782	226	124	126	306	48	830	782	49	72	64	113	174	284	122
Logan	846	246	140	138	322	39	885	831	54	92	96	126	171	292	106
Love	143	39	10	26	68	13	156	149	*	12	13	16	27	68	20
Major	83	28	14	*	32	*	91	86	*	17	*	10	11	33	11
Marshall	297	66	36	59	136	25	322	309	13	21	18	26	65	127	65
Mayes	841	238	130	113	360	69	910	877	33	77	73	77	186	336	161
Mcclain	1,103	328	169	159	447	24	1,126	1,083	43	85	97	151	187	402	204
Mccurtain	461	93	67	84	217	67	528	511	17	27	28	49	98	226	100
Mcintosh	746	174	101	99	372	50	796	770	26	31	46	66	170	288	195
Murray	339	94	57	52	136	41	380	367	13	20	23	33	77	129	98
Muskogee	2,209	578	324	377	930	161	2,370	2,218	152	202	208	290	526	736	408
Noble	155	47	28	20	60	10	165	162	*	19	13	18	25	62	28
Nowata	179	48	25	31	75	15	194	188	*	23	*	13	36	68	46
Okfuskee	223	57	42	44	80	29	252	240	12	13	12	22	53	102	50
Oklahoma	15,521	4,610	2,812	2,496	5,604	1,026	16,547	14,944	1,603	1,897	1,977	2,737	3,701	4,099	2,135
Okmulgee	985	247	164	164	410	98	1,083	1,030	53	85	67	109	239	374	209
Osage	902	274	139	141	348	40	943	904	39	63	65	90	169	384	171
Ottawa	686	227	104	84	271	52	738	710	28	48	61	72	143	292	122
Pawnee	341	111	47	61	122	15	356	337	19	25	25	21	78	140	67
Payne	924	297	172	158	297	45	969	908	61	145	101	98	167	283	175
Pittsburg	1,214	335	203	181	495	81	1,295	1,240	55	97	111	158	263	403	263
Pontotoc	786	193	136	113	344	49	835	792	43	80	65	71	136	297	186
Pottawatomie	1,830	514	273	283	760	91	1,921	1,805	116	180	189	268	403	621	260
Pushmataha	303	73	47	47	136	27	330	322	*	16	18	24	67	137	68
Roger Mills	38	13	*	*	15	*	40	40	*	*	*	*	*	19	10
Rogers	1,922	625	300	287	711	88	2,010	1,891	119	194	195	262	407	668	284
Seminole	518	151	67	74	226	56	574	551	23	34	31	67	110	218	114
Sequoyah	1,016	246	120	146	504	74	1,090	1,036	54	69	82	122	225	390	202
Stephens	1,219	315	188	218	498	52	1,271	1,220	51	107	97	130	242	401	293
Texas	138	58	27	17	36	*	141	129	12	15	22	11	16	51	26
Tillman	185	50	38	27	70	19	204	191	13	19	32	29	28	57	39
Tulsa	8,769	2,972	1,456	1,327	3,014	739	9,507	8,883	625	1,053	1,067	1,211	1,861	2,848	1,468
Wagoner	1,651	483	244	266	658	71	1,722	1,631	91	170	195	227	306	586	238
Washington	1,024	318	154	163	389	63	1,087	1,049	38	85	100	96	172	374	260
Washita	148	38	31	24	55	23	171	166	*	13	13	14	23	57	51
Woods	89	35	17	12	25	*	98	95	*	13	10	*	15	31	20
Woodward	281	98	64	52	67	13	294	279	15	39	35	25	46	81	68
Oregon															
Baker	457	161	90	76	130	42	499	467	32	37	41	52	95	162	111
Benton	944	338	186	134	286	98	1,042	963	79	139	124	122	198	301	158
Clackamas	4,944	1,625	1,013	750	1,556	326	5,270	4,902	367	678	584	675	1,025	1,598	706
Clatsop	696	206	125	115	249	78	774	722	52	68	83	99	166	249	109
Columbia	1,093	337	222	188	346	67	1,160	1,086	74	110	138	138	243	404	125
Coos	1,686	388	226	200	872	152	1,838	1,733	105	149	131	186	418	651	303
Crook	492	147	116	82	147	32	524	500	24	40	39	50	117	199	79
Curry	594	169	90	59	276	56	650	621	29	40	25	55	126	275	128
Deschutes	2,790	869	537	472	912	161	2,951	2,751	200	370	285	340	541	969	446

Table 54. Compensation and Pension Recipients, by County, FY2014—*Continued*

(Number of recipients.)

State and county	Compensation					Total, pension	Compensation or pension								
	Total	0 to 20 percent	30 to 40 percent	50 to 60 percent	70 to 100 percent		Total	Male	Female	Less than 35 years	35 to 44 years	45 to 54 years	55 to 64 years	65 to 74 years	75 years and over
Oregon cnt'd															
Douglas	3,667	733	471	432	2,031	280	3,947	3,660	287	300	327	388	850	1,373	708
Gilliam	54	19	*	*	22	*	58	55	*	*	*	*	*	21	13
Grant	157	46	38	24	49	*	164	159	*	*	11	17	29	75	23
Harney	150	56	19	14	61	20	170	161	*	10	12	20	32	66	30
Hood River	256	77	60	40	79	13	269	261	*	20	25	22	49	94	59
Jackson	4,589	1,445	765	682	1,697	541	5,130	4,790	340	440	461	611	1,177	1,628	810
Jefferson	426	130	76	73	148	18	444	420	25	31	28	33	103	188	62
Josephine	2,207	589	364	369	885	264	2,471	2,323	148	220	178	224	492	871	484
Klamath	2,121	648	345	298	831	166	2,287	2,149	138	193	155	290	490	792	366
Lake	216	58	31	25	102	25	241	232	*	16	14	16	45	112	38
Lane	6,335	1,778	942	841	2,774	578	6,913	6,353	560	755	691	822	1,487	2,142	1,015
Lincoln	1,131	365	214	165	387	119	1,250	1,185	65	63	77	109	276	505	220
Linn	2,534	823	499	401	811	191	2,725	2,536	189	297	319	336	587	824	360
Malheur	323	110	65	46	102	45	368	351	17	37	27	38	76	119	71
Marion	4,540	1,378	901	778	1,483	317	4,857	4,470	387	559	548	678	1,020	1,351	700
Morrow	189	65	32	28	64	*	198	188	10	11	15	23	45	62	42
Multnomah	7,258	2,440	1,379	1,112	2,327	986	8,244	7,559	685	972	958	1,002	1,801	2,484	1,026
Polk	1,202	376	246	185	395	79	1,281	1,180	101	170	145	169	226	395	175
Sherman	39	18	*	*	11	*	46	44	*	*	*	*	10	16	12
Tillamook	601	176	114	90	221	66	667	634	33	31	37	52	167	259	120
Umatilla	1,316	425	268	228	395	106	1,422	1,351	71	156	138	177	265	433	251
Union	507	158	86	83	180	38	545	524	21	49	63	55	107	181	89
Wallowa	202	74	32	25	71	23	225	212	13	*	13	20	34	91	57
Wasco	424	143	79	66	136	51	475	444	31	47	38	50	84	172	84
Washington	6,113	2,107	1,314	935	1,756	335	6,448	5,947	501	987	915	950	1,163	1,599	832
Wheeler	35	18	*	*	*	*	38	34	*	*	*	*	14	12	10
Yamhill	1,354	441	266	229	417	82	1,436	1,332	104	203	183	185	268	399	198
Unknown	19	*	*	*	*	*	19	17	*	*	*	*	*	*	*
Other Foreign Countries	7,929	2,341	1,878	1,418	2,292	418	8,347	7,794	553	487	821	1,923	1,405	1,320	2,386
Other U.S. Territories	2,492	658	435	355	1,044	96	2,588	2,368	220	221	240	497	728	670	232
Pennsylvania															
Adams	972	353	218	145	255	44	1,016	929	87	113	73	169	200	292	166
Allegheny	9,520	4,051	2,008	1,244	2,216	1,928	11,448	10,710	738	1,117	937	1,306	2,232	3,385	2,464
Armstrong	673	266	124	95	188	118	791	742	49	56	55	93	172	281	134
Beaver	1,793	722	388	251	432	239	2,032	1,915	117	165	189	256	343	716	360
Bedford	601	193	124	98	187	60	662	631	31	66	50	79	125	240	102
Berks	2,860	1,013	582	397	868	323	3,184	2,976	208	342	320	358	577	956	628
Blair	1,795	573	318	285	619	289	2,084	1,953	131	199	206	247	381	682	366
Bradford	735	226	141	109	259	54	789	729	60	104	85	102	133	253	111
Bucks	4,800	1,646	923	673	1,558	263	5,063	4,792	271	490	436	578	884	1,833	838
Butler	1,784	721	389	244	430	249	2,034	1,907	126	194	164	295	418	635	325
Cambria	1,726	556	363	275	532	271	1,997	1,895	102	187	213	200	360	650	387
Cameron	71	23	15	10	23	*	80	74	*	12	*	*	11	25	19
Carbon	753	255	121	104	273	54	807	765	42	70	74	82	140	292	149
Centre	1,090	375	241	162	313	65	1,155	1,065	90	207	102	169	188	311	178
Chester	3,575	1,231	634	497	1,213	340	3,915	3,653	262	364	354	527	740	1,267	659
Clarion	366	143	76	56	90	54	419	395	24	42	41	58	69	163	46
Clearfield	920	285	202	134	298	103	1,023	969	54	119	111	119	157	342	174
Clinton	616	208	122	109	176	54	670	638	32	63	68	82	102	197	157
Columbia	692	249	151	94	199	70	763	718	45	79	86	91	116	246	144
Crawford	1,045	352	215	160	318	133	1,178	1,115	63	123	124	142	184	426	179
Cumberland	3,177	1,100	690	542	846	170	3,348	3,044	304	297	338	669	730	787	527
Dauphin	2,889	984	615	441	849	273	3,162	2,863	299	298	321	547	673	870	451
Delaware	3,711	1,149	654	557	1,351	414	4,124	3,831	293	398	357	516	837	1,338	676
Elk	343	108	83	44	108	41	384	360	24	48	33	38	52	125	88
Erie	3,131	1,084	597	513	937	383	3,514	3,276	238	468	347	456	610	1,074	559
Fayette	1,589	533	310	230	517	330	1,919	1,845	74	132	151	211	360	670	394
Forest	79	20	16	13	29	14	93	88	*	*	*	12	12	36	18
Franklin	2,082	746	451	340	544	90	2,172	2,006	166	202	241	419	406	562	340
Fulton	128	47	20	22	39	15	143	132	11	16	12	15	30	49	21
Greene	412	126	77	57	152	58	470	441	29	35	55	41	65	185	89
Huntingdon	525	177	110	80	157	46	571	541	29	58	53	60	94	216	89
Indiana	866	288	186	136	256	115	982	922	60	135	97	94	143	339	174
Jefferson	465	164	103	73	125	79	543	510	33	71	48	56	90	166	112
Juniata	139	47	17	27	48	22	161	146	15	21	15	*	21	65	30
Lackawanna	2,364	787	437	342	799	258	2,622	2,508	114	266	228	227	425	804	670

Table 54. Compensation and Pension Recipients, by County, FY2014—*Continued*

(Number of recipients.)

State and county	Compensation					Total, pension	Compensation or pension								
	Total	0 to 20 percent	30 to 40 percent	50 to 60 percent	70 to 100 percent		Total	Male	Female	Less than 35 years	35 to 44 years	45 to 54 years	55 to 64 years	65 to 74 years	75 years and over
Pennsylvania cnt'd															
Lancaster	3,393	1,235	676	448	1,034	353	3,746	3,468	278	518	398	424	669	1,070	667
Lawrence	863	343	165	123	232	152	1,016	959	57	90	107	141	169	312	197
Lebanon	1,752	560	323	245	624	168	1,920	1,755	165	156	197	324	436	545	262
Lehigh	2,359	833	428	324	774	262	2,621	2,467	154	285	268	307	458	796	505
Luzerne	3,984	1,308	725	618	1,332	436	4,420	4,194	226	375	351	480	716	1,377	1,117
Lycoming	1,241	424	251	203	364	137	1,378	1,277	101	191	151	184	231	373	248
Mckean	554	173	99	82	200	84	638	603	35	51	50	78	122	220	117
Mercer	1,138	445	241	156	296	186	1,324	1,231	93	144	102	166	248	409	255
Mifflin	405	130	65	56	154	47	452	431	21	28	39	67	94	157	65
Monroe	1,537	466	268	206	597	101	1,638	1,536	102	175	156	206	313	587	199
Montgomery	5,317	1,880	996	740	1,700	405	5,722	5,315	407	578	545	699	904	1,913	1,082
Montour	199	69	30	29	71	25	225	208	17	39	23	30	36	62	35
Northampton	2,068	747	366	256	698	193	2,261	2,125	135	234	211	252	363	794	405
Northumberland	919	342	165	130	282	112	1,031	968	63	98	101	130	176	313	212
Perry	520	185	99	69	167	36	556	518	38	56	56	97	113	167	67
Philadelphia	10,844	2,878	1,750	1,476	4,740	2,303	13,147	12,116	1,031	1,058	1,015	1,814	3,480	3,983	1,794
Pike	763	241	132	103	287	44	807	770	37	70	68	98	143	300	127
Potter	246	62	47	36	101	25	271	257	14	29	22	30	65	92	34
Schuylkill	1,680	519	341	228	592	175	1,855	1,753	102	125	156	204	299	668	402
Snyder	269	99	40	48	82	17	286	274	12	26	26	37	49	96	52
Somerset	828	285	164	131	248	113	941	895	46	86	90	117	152	333	162
Sullivan	53	21	10	*	17	10	63	60	*	*	*	*	*	24	14
Susquehanna	479	153	80	84	162	34	513	490	23	50	36	43	90	201	92
Tioga	513	135	99	92	187	49	562	536	26	64	65	76	92	184	81
Union	283	116	59	44	64	31	314	290	24	37	28	54	45	84	66
Venango	715	260	142	104	209	56	771	730	41	72	70	108	163	263	95
Warren	596	194	118	97	187	73	669	639	30	91	56	79	99	250	94
Washington	1,810	713	405	250	442	289	2,099	1,995	104	197	189	221	323	746	422
Wayne	650	214	109	104	223	41	692	654	38	60	50	64	126	274	116
Westmoreland	3,386	1,336	731	475	844	418	3,804	3,595	209	311	327	477	645	1,291	751
Wyoming	299	98	51	41	109	21	320	302	18	35	28	32	56	125	44
York	3,923	1,416	801	629	1,077	294	4,217	3,851	366	495	544	737	745	1,151	543
Unknown	*	*	*	*	*	*	*	*	*	*	*	*	*	*	*
Rhode Island															
Bristol	491	182	89	67	153	61	552	516	36	50	46	69	100	155	132
Kent	2,298	818	407	314	759	164	2,462	2,323	139	242	234	280	463	732	510
Newport	1,467	471	310	242	444	68	1,535	1,394	141	123	133	253	336	440	250
Providence	5,835	2,030	1,096	853	1,856	605	6,440	6,099	341	677	540	747	1,129	1,863	1,481
Washington	1,582	555	285	232	510	70	1,652	1,560	92	147	121	241	292	535	315
South Carolina															
Abbeville	425	85	67	73	200	35	460	437	23	32	33	54	101	156	84
Aiken	2,672	802	486	405	978	135	2,807	2,571	237	300	329	390	547	893	348
Allendale	112	31	26	21	34	17	129	118	11	*	14	23	34	37	15
Anderson	2,453	672	460	401	920	235	2,688	2,541	147	195	234	357	484	939	478
Bamberg	219	48	40	34	97	25	244	235	*	14	20	30	52	96	32
Barnwell	265	55	46	48	116	11	276	256	20	26	30	50	46	100	24
Beaufort	4,680	1,383	993	758	1,546	160	4,840	4,241	599	811	666	767	813	1,147	634
Berkeley	5,636	1,675	1,137	979	1,845	187	5,823	5,135	688	752	875	1,260	1,263	1,173	497
Calhoun	246	68	40	35	103	27	273	256	17	17	19	45	68	95	29
Charleston	6,259	1,911	1,262	991	2,095	494	6,754	6,019	735	699	713	1,159	1,601	1,750	829
Cherokee	727	182	138	115	291	122	849	807	42	50	61	101	198	296	143
Chester	478	115	81	67	215	60	538	513	25	31	40	60	113	205	89
Chesterfield	563	146	102	97	218	60	623	575	48	50	64	79	153	209	68
Clarendon	804	212	136	141	315	73	877	832	45	52	74	108	192	288	163
Colleton	722	166	149	111	296	67	789	724	65	70	73	137	164	218	126
Darlington	935	227	146	166	396	89	1,024	965	59	73	94	140	243	353	121
Dillon	376	88	56	63	169	54	430	397	33	38	52	68	105	115	51
Dorchester	5,232	1,551	1,079	909	1,693	102	5,335	4,681	653	568	822	1,437	1,124	997	386
Edgefield	404	104	51	79	171	24	429	405	24	49	44	86	76	134	41
Fairfield	394	91	69	65	169	36	430	407	23	20	31	72	102	139	66
Florence	2,215	566	369	373	907	207	2,421	2,232	189	200	256	420	579	694	273
Georgetown	986	317	159	154	356	106	1,093	1,017	76	88	71	143	211	401	178
Greenville	5,372	1,718	1,037	873	1,744	545	5,917	5,449	468	549	662	938	1,072	1,752	945
Greenwood	897	230	138	115	414	85	982	925	57	76	72	116	187	361	169
Hampton	266	71	43	41	110	20	286	258	28	26	35	46	55	87	37
Horry	5,312	1,599	899	755	2,060	328	5,640	5,317	323	412	444	659	1,089	2,121	915
Jasper	363	101	61	59	142	32	395	352	43	37	40	69	85	107	57
Kershaw	1,905	436	338	324	806	78	1,984	1,787	197	130	240	418	445	530	220

Table 54. Compensation and Pension Recipients, by County, FY2014—*Continued*

(Number of recipients.)

State and county	Compensation					Total, pension	Compensation or pension								
	Total	0 to 20 percent	30 to 40 percent	50 to 60 percent	70 to 100 percent		Total	Male	Female	Less than 35 years	35 to 44 years	45 to 54 years	55 to 64 years	65 to 74 years	75 years and over
South Carolina cnt'd															
Lancaster	1,026	302	171	164	390	89	1,115	1,064	52	67	104	137	216	402	188
Laurens	1,034	243	163	166	463	102	1,136	1,069	67	77	96	159	239	374	191
Lee	307	71	46	48	142	20	327	304	23	25	32	53	79	117	21
Lexington	4,615	1,271	825	789	1,730	273	4,888	4,437	451	541	626	873	982	1,290	574
Marion	548	113	97	110	228	68	616	573	43	52	59	109	162	171	63
Marlboro	375	90	59	61	165	43	418	383	35	37	44	59	107	126	45
Mccormick	222	59	40	39	84	17	239	218	21	*	16	37	52	84	41
Newberry	509	115	102	89	203	44	553	521	32	45	45	72	88	220	83
Oconee	967	299	148	134	386	132	1,099	1,049	50	68	70	127	174	420	240
Orangeburg	1,603	390	276	271	666	186	1,788	1,621	168	125	174	259	406	589	236
Pickens	1,414	452	256	221	485	146	1,560	1,498	62	138	133	170	304	519	296
Richland	12,097	2,573	2,012	1,974	5,538	544	12,641	10,503	2,139	1,204	1,637	3,056	3,079	2,478	1,185
Saluda	276	63	46	47	119	25	301	286	14	11	17	47	59	113	54
Spartanburg	3,402	985	603	542	1,272	369	3,771	3,534	237	370	341	535	751	1,235	539
Sumter	4,648	1,173	893	892	1,690	174	4,822	4,085	736	552	615	1,247	1,108	839	461
Union	361	93	59	66	143	44	405	386	19	30	38	60	95	116	65
Williamsburg	609	131	107	107	264	55	664	612	52	63	75	104	154	202	66
York	2,814	898	537	423	956	186	3,000	2,774	226	306	365	485	576	924	344
South Dakota															
Aurora	50	16	*	10	15	*	57	55	*	*	*	*	*	13	17
Beadle	217	100	34	37	46	29	246	230	16	25	24	21	61	72	43
Bennett	32	12	*	*	11	*	39	36	*	*	*	*	*	13	11
Bon Homme	90	34	28	16	12	12	102	99	*	14	*	15	16	26	24
Brookings	313	153	58	38	64	23	336	313	23	68	39	36	56	93	44
Brown	467	181	102	69	115	35	502	470	32	70	62	67	89	139	75
Brule	58	27	10	*	12	*	60	56	*	*	*	*	12	12	14
Buffalo	16	*	*	*	*	*	22	22	*	*	*	*	*	*	*
Butte	190	62	29	25	74	19	209	192	17	19	14	27	52	69	28
Campbell	21	*	*	*	*	*	24	22	*	*	*	*	*	11	*
Charles Mix	96	37	19	18	22	15	111	109	*	*	10	10	16	36	30
Clark	47	12	14	*	14	*	54	52	*	*	*	*	10	23	14
Clay	132	43	34	16	39	15	147	137	10	30	19	16	26	39	17
Codington	350	150	68	62	70	32	382	353	29	42	50	48	76	111	55
Corson	40	11	10	*	14	*	48	48	*	*	*	*	*	16	*
Custer	221	80	43	32	66	11	232	216	16	20	19	24	53	86	30
Davison	246	105	50	40	51	19	265	250	15	35	26	33	51	75	45
Day	102	31	20	11	40	11	113	110	*	10	*	12	20	42	22
Deuel	72	37	11	*	17	10	82	76	*	*	14	12	15	19	16
Dewey	49	12	*	10	19	20	69	66	*	*	*	*	13	23	13
Douglas	33	13	*	*	10	*	36	36	*	*	*	*	*	10	11
Edmunds	43	19	12	*	10	*	48	48	*	*	*	*	11	11	*
Fall River	300	90	49	50	111	68	368	336	32	11	29	45	96	117	70
Faulk	28	15	*	*	*	*	30	28	*	*	*	*	*	*	*
Grant	126	60	17	22	27	10	136	130	*	13	10	16	19	50	28
Gregory	70	33	10	*	20	*	78	75	*	*	*	10	10	25	20
Haakon	19	*	*	*	*	*	20	19	*	*	*	*	*	*	*
Hamlin	68	25	16	*	19	10	78	70	*	*	*	10	12	26	15
Hand	62	32	13	*	*	*	68	63	*	*	*	*	*	23	23
Hanson	71	30	16	13	12	*	75	71	*	*	*	*	14	36	11
Harding	*	*	*	*	*	*	10	10	*	*	*	*	*	*	*
Hughes	230	98	50	40	42	18	248	232	16	30	27	31	55	62	43
Hutchinson	83	27	22	14	20	12	95	90	*	10	13	10	15	23	24
Hyde	23	11	*	*	*	*	25	23	*	*	*	*	*	11	*
Jackson	21	*	*	*	*	*	28	24	*	*	*	*	*	*	*
Jerauld	25	12	*	*	*	*	29	29	*	*	*	*	*	12	*
Jones	*	*	*	*	*	*	*	*	*	*	*	*	*	*	*
Kingsbury	75	24	13	21	17	*	82	81	*	12	*	12	13	24	16
Lake	198	79	43	27	49	*	204	191	13	26	20	29	33	66	30
Lawrence	456	157	94	77	128	39	495	458	37	45	55	61	117	139	78
Lincoln	559	217	116	86	140	26	585	525	60	107	84	104	97	120	73
Lyman	45	19	10	*	*	*	49	47	*	*	*	*	*	18	*
Marshall	39	16	*	*	10	12	51	50	*	*	*	*	*	12	21
Mccook	84	37	13	16	18	10	94	90	*	14	*	14	20	21	20
Mcpherson	39	13	*	*	11	*	43	41	*	*	*	*	11	*	13
Meade	942	286	190	153	312	41	983	860	124	128	123	204	218	225	84
Mellette	12	*	*	*	*	*	18	18	*	*	*	*	*	*	*
Miner	34	*	*	*	10	*	36	35	*	*	*	*	*	16	*
Minnehaha	2,769	1,086	594	405	684	173	2,942	2,703	239	405	357	432	585	768	394
Moody	93	33	21	13	26	*	100	93	*	13	*	12	20	32	14

Table 54. Compensation and Pension Recipients, by County, FY2014—*Continued*

(Number of recipients.)

State and county	Compensation: Total	0 to 20 percent	30 to 40 percent	50 to 60 percent	70 to 100 percent	Total, pension	Compensation or pension: Total	Male	Female	Less than 35 years	35 to 44 years	45 to 54 years	55 to 64 years	65 to 74 years	75 years and over
South Dakota cnt'd															
Pennington	3,270	1,120	768	566	817	142	3,412	3,025	387	481	430	697	737	699	368
Perkins	52	19	15	*	*	*	56	50	*	*	*	*	*	17	11
Potter	34	11	*	10	*	*	35	33	*	*	*	*	*	12	*
Roberts	154	56	20	29	49	33	187	181	*	13	17	19	26	61	51
Sanborn	29	12	10	*	*	*	35	35	*	*	*	*	*	11	10
Shannon	137	26	28	25	58	37	174	159	15	14	15	24	30	55	36
Spink	73	25	18	13	17	13	86	81	*	*	*	13	18	28	13
Stanley	43	17	*	*	*	*	45	43	*	*	*	*	*	16	*
Sully	26	*	*	*	*	*	27	25	*	*	*	*	*	*	*
Todd	85	27	18	11	29	26	111	102	*	*	10	11	27	39	18
Tripp	73	25	20	12	16	10	83	80	*	*	*	*	16	22	23
Turner	125	45	29	17	34	14	139	133	*	16	*	19	22	41	36
Union	172	69	40	21	42	13	185	172	13	26	20	29	32	50	28
Walworth	81	29	14	12	26	11	92	84	*	*	*	11	15	31	20
Yankton	266	103	42	48	73	27	293	269	24	27	22	47	58	83	55
Ziebach	*	*	*	*	*	*	11	10	*	*	*	*	*	*	*
Tennessee															
Anderson	1,291	435	258	194	404	106	1,397	1,302	95	132	154	220	275	441	175
Bedford	493	153	100	72	168	34	527	484	43	33	56	80	114	179	65
Benton	291	74	42	57	118	41	332	319	13	21	30	39	69	128	45
Bledsoe	153	48	18	20	67	16	169	164	*	*	*	22	38	79	18
Blount	2,122	746	386	292	697	139	2,261	2,140	121	164	193	312	458	739	395
Bradley	1,138	380	183	161	414	108	1,246	1,174	72	98	142	175	240	413	178
Campbell	852	229	115	111	396	72	924	901	23	48	59	86	184	363	183
Cannon	184	56	29	27	72	17	202	186	15	15	16	26	44	70	30
Carroll	427	110	88	71	158	41	468	445	23	43	44	70	100	146	65
Carter	1,320	334	225	222	539	111	1,431	1,365	66	85	104	157	282	544	258
Cheatham	700	210	151	104	236	40	739	688	51	69	105	139	139	218	70
Chester	214	77	37	29	70	26	239	224	15	21	17	36	53	75	38
Claiborne	550	140	78	75	257	51	601	570	31	43	42	85	100	248	82
Clay	101	28	11	17	45	16	117	114	*	*	11	13	25	41	18
Cocke	682	173	110	112	287	80	762	720	42	46	49	95	165	302	105
Coffee	914	325	152	135	302	59	973	905	68	69	75	174	212	306	137
Crockett	153	37	33	21	61	12	165	155	10	10	12	27	36	55	24
Cumberland	1,216	444	206	160	405	105	1,321	1,260	61	50	61	116	241	551	302
Davidson	6,010	1,996	1,090	874	2,050	739	6,749	6,079	670	734	784	1,073	1,630	1,732	794
Decatur	203	63	47	32	61	30	233	225	*	14	11	19	40	101	48
Dekalb	177	59	32	20	66	16	193	183	10	29	12	23	31	68	30
Dickson	752	250	124	119	259	47	799	753	46	71	76	119	176	250	106
Dyer	550	194	104	62	190	75	625	601	24	49	40	70	144	220	102
Fayette	475	153	88	77	157	48	523	495	28	44	41	82	113	175	68
Fentress	293	70	55	44	124	56	349	334	15	16	19	43	83	133	55
Franklin	726	240	109	111	266	58	784	732	52	52	52	125	175	246	134
Gibson	589	191	103	93	203	79	668	633	35	42	46	100	147	227	107
Giles	461	141	82	68	170	35	496	465	31	36	48	55	102	168	87
Grainger	343	102	61	49	131	25	368	356	12	23	21	45	83	147	49
Greene	1,186	372	216	191	407	103	1,289	1,237	52	88	80	141	268	498	214
Grundy	155	36	19	20	80	19	174	167	*	16	11	21	27	68	31
Hamblen	993	344	184	125	341	95	1,088	1,038	50	64	93	124	187	439	182
Hamilton	3,786	1,224	627	572	1,363	423	4,208	3,923	286	323	430	646	899	1,356	553
Hancock	79	21	19	*	33	12	91	85	*	*	*	10	16	43	*
Hardeman	314	82	69	47	116	33	347	320	27	12	26	45	91	121	52
Hardin	431	125	90	69	146	53	484	464	20	32	29	52	89	191	90
Hawkins	1,157	341	200	198	418	70	1,228	1,190	38	58	86	151	241	498	193
Haywood	225	69	36	56	64	28	253	233	20	12	25	44	69	72	31
Henderson	305	101	45	46	113	31	336	317	19	29	20	43	66	122	56
Henry	655	175	120	106	254	51	706	673	33	52	58	82	152	250	112
Hickman	301	105	49	44	103	37	338	317	21	16	19	53	92	120	38
Houston	164	45	21	26	72	*	173	166	*	10	20	17	42	66	18
Humphreys	340	107	51	52	130	22	362	342	20	28	23	52	84	123	52
Jackson	182	63	26	27	66	32	214	202	12	11	16	20	50	80	37
Jefferson	911	285	155	126	344	71	982	935	47	73	59	123	195	382	149
Johnson	413	121	73	72	147	31	444	426	18	20	31	49	82	167	95
Knox	5,442	1,858	1,066	847	1,671	504	5,945	5,554	391	573	647	866	1,162	1,817	880
Lake	59	17	10	10	22	12	71	71	*	*	*	10	18	18	14
Lauderdale	301	98	51	37	115	39	340	325	15	22	18	47	70	135	48
Lawrence	538	153	96	67	222	76	613	576	37	59	45	62	133	215	100
Lewis	200	71	20	28	81	14	214	202	12	16	22	20	46	86	24
Lincoln	471	166	93	67	145	38	509	472	37	37	33	77	131	158	73

Table 54. Compensation and Pension Recipients, by County, FY2014—*Continued*

(Number of recipients.)

State and county	Compensation					Total, pension	Compensation or pension								
	Total	0 to 20 percent	30 to 40 percent	50 to 60 percent	70 to 100 percent		Total	Male	Female	Less than 35 years	35 to 44 years	45 to 54 years	55 to 64 years	65 to 74 years	75 years and over
Tennessee cnt'd															
Loudon	741	263	147	102	229	52	792	740	52	54	67	92	144	301	134
Macon	237	66	40	34	96	37	274	262	12	20	25	28	51	99	49
Madison	1,146	373	224	177	372	164	1,310	1,201	109	91	126	200	285	402	205
Marion	384	110	56	59	159	36	420	396	24	27	32	64	80	164	53
Marshall	371	117	64	57	133	47	418	400	18	37	38	53	99	132	59
Maury	926	311	182	115	319	73	999	939	60	101	90	113	220	334	141
Mcminn	794	227	131	123	313	85	879	819	60	68	92	124	162	315	118
Mcnairy	397	115	71	72	140	62	459	432	27	20	30	52	87	174	97
Meigs	177	48	34	20	75	19	196	191	*	18	14	21	42	76	25
Monroe	713	186	133	115	279	70	783	747	36	54	47	89	159	336	97
Montgomery	14,516	3,194	2,847	2,624	5,851	124	14,640	12,262	2,378	3,458	2,907	3,710	2,491	1,396	677
Moore	90	24	21	*	37	*	91	85	*	11	*	11	12	34	16
Morgan	379	113	72	56	138	26	406	382	23	39	30	51	90	150	46
Obion	454	160	87	69	138	46	500	472	28	36	57	75	93	166	73
Overton	268	68	52	41	106	40	308	296	12	22	14	35	78	103	56
Perry	163	39	28	21	75	*	172	168	*	*	16	16	47	68	19
Pickett	117	31	16	21	49	*	123	119	*	12	*	16	25	43	23
Polk	238	80	38	30	90	24	262	254	*	10	18	22	56	114	41
Putnam	905	317	157	97	334	106	1,011	954	58	94	91	125	206	319	176
Rhea	419	131	81	54	153	54	473	446	27	35	43	72	87	156	80
Roane	880	304	156	106	314	91	970	922	48	65	69	131	226	339	141
Robertson	962	294	190	139	339	61	1,023	952	71	118	138	166	190	299	111
Rutherford	3,660	1,225	682	539	1,213	202	3,862	3,474	388	513	541	778	779	855	395
Scott	306	77	51	40	138	34	340	335	*	16	19	42	78	132	53
Sequatchie	243	56	32	45	110	20	263	250	13	15	18	33	54	118	25
Sevier	1,568	534	262	229	544	138	1,706	1,627	79	116	125	208	329	669	259
Shelby	10,245	3,345	2,052	1,433	3,415	1,352	11,596	10,331	1,265	871	1,168	2,344	3,052	2,968	1,193
Smith	207	49	41	47	70	17	224	204	20	31	28	36	43	61	25
Stewart	700	172	146	135	248	16	716	658	58	53	87	190	174	155	57
Sullivan	2,927	926	535	450	1,016	237	3,164	3,035	129	209	275	409	586	1,125	559
Sumner	2,084	700	385	309	690	125	2,209	2,054	155	248	253	346	427	668	267
Tipton	1,525	436	315	280	494	51	1,576	1,394	182	77	148	497	401	327	126
Trousdale	107	32	21	18	36	13	120	113	*	*	13	17	21	38	22
Unicoi	390	109	66	56	159	45	435	420	15	31	32	42	83	161	86
Union	268	91	40	44	92	30	299	283	15	20	17	34	68	128	31
Van Buren	102	20	26	12	44	10	112	106	*	*	*	12	25	48	17
Warren	474	130	90	74	180	57	531	509	22	39	36	81	105	188	82
Washington	2,574	771	470	412	921	250	2,824	2,644	180	226	235	401	641	915	406
Wayne	209	63	29	31	86	27	236	231	*	20	20	31	45	74	46
Weakley	415	131	80	78	126	41	456	427	29	39	43	80	96	136	62
White	364	117	63	52	131	56	419	392	27	53	32	40	80	134	81
Williamson	1,473	568	291	210	404	82	1,556	1,464	92	160	227	249	258	449	211
Wilson	1,812	624	363	221	604	91	1,903	1,775	128	193	206	307	381	627	189
Unknown	*	*	*	*	*	*	*	*	*	*	*	*	*	*	*
Texas															
Anderson	690	179	113	112	286	85	775	731	44	60	43	78	141	296	157
Andrews	124	45	32	22	25	*	128	126	*	28	12	14	21	23	30
Angelina	1,233	332	207	171	523	90	1,323	1,236	87	151	141	134	230	439	227
Aransas	556	162	96	91	207	39	595	556	39	43	34	51	110	236	121
Archer	162	45	29	30	58	*	169	155	14	15	18	26	27	50	32
Armstrong	24	*	*	*	*	*	24	22	*	*	*	*	*	*	*
Atascosa	954	248	179	134	393	38	992	912	80	80	113	137	193	316	153
Austin	260	74	48	41	97	31	291	267	24	27	29	26	65	93	51
Bailey	46	16	10	*	16	*	51	49	*	*	*	*	*	11	20
Bandera	634	163	119	97	255	27	661	614	47	36	42	93	125	238	126
Bastrop	1,240	406	257	193	384	93	1,333	1,213	120	116	121	202	314	401	178
Baylor	67	26	*	*	24	11	78	75	*	10	*	*	12	29	19
Bee	404	115	68	81	140	31	435	413	22	44	51	55	84	155	46
Bell	26,477	5,268	4,713	4,844	11,652	521	26,998	21,867	5,132	5,747	5,298	6,700	4,853	2,941	1,459
Bexar	55,572	14,003	10,109	9,589	21,872	1,522	57,094	48,609	8,485	6,325	7,929	12,395	12,671	11,306	6,463
Blanco	171	58	30	27	56	*	175	160	15	*	16	18	33	64	38
Borden	*	*	*	*	*	*	*	*	*	*	*	*	*	*	*
Bosque	315	106	52	35	122	30	345	323	22	28	22	22	70	151	51
Bowie	1,774	450	335	293	696	154	1,928	1,787	141	156	232	304	411	564	260
Brazoria	3,704	1,128	689	604	1,283	187	3,891	3,518	373	600	546	544	629	1,131	440
Brazos	1,695	555	352	282	506	108	1,803	1,639	163	337	214	228	321	448	255
Brewster	115	37	24	14	40	12	127	117	10	16	*	12	32	41	18
Briscoe	18	*	*	*	*	*	21	21	*	*	*	*	*	*	*
Brooks	86	27	*	14	36	*	95	91	*	*	*	*	16	38	19

Table 54. Compensation and Pension Recipients, by County, FY2014—*Continued*

(Number of recipients.)

State and county	Compensation					Total, pension	Compensation or pension								
	Total	0 to 20 percent	30 to 40 percent	50 to 60 percent	70 to 100 percent		Total	Male	Female	Less than 35 years	35 to 44 years	45 to 54 years	55 to 64 years	65 to 74 years	75 years and over
Texas cnt'd															
Brown	640	190	130	105	215	78	718	682	36	70	70	71	119	257	131
Burleson	246	69	51	45	81	38	284	266	18	23	15	34	54	96	62
Burnet	786	268	156	112	250	59	845	796	50	77	65	76	152	269	205
Caldwell	582	169	107	103	203	43	625	584	41	56	53	72	127	196	121
Calhoun	295	77	43	38	137	26	321	307	14	23	21	22	54	148	53
Callahan	293	91	58	36	107	23	316	298	17	15	25	43	61	93	78
Cameron	4,569	1,396	666	662	1,845	244	4,813	4,590	223	685	615	515	842	1,380	773
Camp	139	38	22	18	61	30	169	155	14	14	12	16	25	66	36
Carson	81	25	13	15	28	*	83	79	*	13	*	*	11	25	19
Cass	532	137	93	91	211	60	592	563	29	46	60	63	117	218	87
Castro	39	*	*	*	15	*	40	37	*	*	*	*	*	15	*
Chambers	382	124	75	67	115	36	418	390	27	53	64	56	78	118	47
Cherokee	520	149	95	81	194	75	594	563	31	48	51	54	116	207	118
Childress	80	29	13	13	25	10	90	82	*	11	*	13	16	27	14
Clay	256	74	42	47	92	11	267	253	14	22	30	39	48	83	45
Cochran	32	*	*	*	14	*	33	30	*	*	*	*	*	14	*
Coke	50	18	11	*	12	*	55	51	*	*	*	*	*	22	13
Coleman	144	48	27	23	46	18	162	156	*	*	*	16	41	52	38
Collin	6,608	2,418	1,417	1,025	1,749	297	6,905	6,227	679	949	1,200	1,245	1,124	1,628	759
Collingsworth	30	13	*	*	*	*	32	32	*	*	*	*	*	*	*
Colorado	204	63	39	33	69	25	229	215	14	12	16	18	49	83	51
Comal	4,032	1,110	729	690	1,504	95	4,127	3,621	506	276	425	878	917	1,098	533
Comanche	225	64	39	27	95	25	250	235	15	21	17	19	43	85	65
Concho	42	*	11	*	18	*	43	40	*	*	*	*	*	23	*
Cooke	373	111	76	64	121	40	413	396	16	36	35	26	86	162	66
Coryell	5,788	1,169	1,068	1,056	2,495	62	5,850	4,919	931	1,208	1,153	1,322	1,087	713	367
Cottle	18	*	*	*	*	*	24	23	*	*	*	*	*	*	*
Crane	33	*	*	*	13	*	39	34	*	*	*	*	*	18	*
Crockett	29	*	*	*	11	*	31	30	*	*	*	*	*	*	*
Crosby	51	15	*	13	14	*	56	54	*	*	*	*	*	20	*
Culberson	25	*	*	*	10	*	30	29	*	*	*	*	*	13	*
Dallam	61	19	14	*	22	*	69	64	*	12	10	*	16	14	12
Dallas	17,906	5,733	3,530	2,780	5,863	2,322	20,228	18,115	2,114	2,481	2,603	3,029	4,520	5,211	2,381
Dawson	99	33	18	11	37	10	109	105	*	*	13	17	18	25	27
De Witt	278	88	44	44	102	31	309	295	14	22	26	30	61	100	70
Deaf Smith	95	36	19	12	28	17	112	107	*	11	11	11	22	20	37
Delta	67	22	13	*	23	10	77	76	*	*	*	*	18	32	15
Denton	6,534	2,357	1,381	989	1,808	302	6,836	6,207	629	1,135	1,139	1,201	1,117	1,594	648
Dickens	33	*	*	*	13	*	37	34	*	*	*	*	11	*	10
Dimmit	103	28	22	15	38	14	117	113	*	12	10	14	12	50	19
Donley	45	10	*	*	23	*	49	45	*	*	*	*	*	20	11
Duval	120	37	17	14	52	*	129	126	*	*	13	*	16	64	24
Eastland	295	86	47	48	114	38	333	320	13	35	20	28	59	123	68
Ector	1,090	363	224	161	341	112	1,202	1,124	77	220	164	111	197	330	179
Edwards	22	*	*	*	*	*	24	24	*	*	*	*	*	12	*
El Paso	19,552	4,586	3,673	3,388	7,906	628	20,180	17,806	2,374	3,992	3,220	3,598	3,772	3,536	2,061
Ellis	1,847	559	370	302	616	126	1,973	1,809	164	234	287	295	409	543	206
Erath	346	90	68	45	143	36	382	355	27	60	33	37	63	121	68
Falls	329	89	62	45	133	40	369	341	28	14	27	59	97	112	60
Fannin	608	164	122	99	223	101	709	664	45	63	58	78	174	229	107
Fayette	301	88	52	43	118	34	335	323	12	31	19	25	42	132	86
Fisher	66	23	13	*	25	10	76	75	*	*	*	*	11	27	24
Floyd	45	14	*	*	16	*	53	50	*	*	*	*	13	14	13
Foard	16	*	*	*	*	*	16	16	*	*	*	*	*	*	*
Fort Bend	5,077	1,548	976	846	1,707	241	5,318	4,784	535	777	915	978	881	1,313	456
Franklin	130	37	25	18	50	12	142	137	*	14	11	13	36	50	18
Freestone	254	74	43	38	99	26	280	267	13	24	17	26	59	110	44
Frio	129	40	16	21	52	*	135	128	*	16	11	21	26	47	14
Gaines	80	31	17	11	21	*	85	82	*	*	*	11	18	26	16
Galveston	3,784	1,256	689	592	1,247	278	4,062	3,712	350	527	510	554	808	1,196	465
Garza	34	10	*	10	*	*	36	34	*	*	*	*	*	13	*
Gillespie	442	150	75	67	150	38	480	448	32	24	32	25	69	179	151
Glasscock	*	*	*	*	*	*	*	*	*	*	*	*	*	*	*
Goliad	102	30	13	15	44	*	110	106	*	12	*	*	19	43	24
Gonzales	191	58	32	34	67	20	211	195	16	21	18	12	45	87	28
Gray	217	60	44	45	68	23	240	229	11	31	24	21	46	74	44
Grayson	1,750	507	314	274	656	221	1,971	1,849	122	172	178	184	383	680	375
Gregg	1,223	381	248	169	426	144	1,367	1,258	109	166	143	151	264	403	240
Grimes	306	98	43	58	107	25	331	311	20	35	20	35	73	120	48
Guadalupe	6,925	1,488	1,247	1,297	2,893	68	6,993	5,894	1,099	464	968	2,318	1,508	1,144	590

Table 54. Compensation and Pension Recipients, by County, FY2014—*Continued*

(Number of recipients.)

State and county	Compensation					Total, pension	Compensation or pension								
	Total	0 to 20 percent	30 to 40 percent	50 to 60 percent	70 to 100 percent		Total	Male	Female	Less than 35 years	35 to 44 years	45 to 54 years	55 to 64 years	65 to 74 years	75 years and over
Texas cnt'd															
Hale	250	73	41	34	102	28	278	266	12	35	24	24	60	83	52
Hall	30	*	*	*	10	*	34	34	*	*	*	*	*	12	*
Hamilton	116	32	24	16	44	15	131	119	12	10	11	16	28	41	25
Hansford	21	*	*	*	*	*	23	20	*	*	*	*	*	*	*
Hardeman	48	11	13	*	18	*	50	44	*	11	*	*	*	17	*
Hardin	720	209	150	117	244	66	786	738	48	120	89	92	118	275	92
Harris	31,523	10,177	5,961	4,989	10,396	3,094	34,617	31,097	3,520	5,755	5,182	4,769	6,315	9,070	3,516
Harrison	920	267	173	147	332	96	1,016	934	82	84	107	133	218	324	149
Hartley	32	10	*	*	13	*	34	31	*	*	*	*	*	11	*
Haskell	68	21	14	10	23	*	76	73	*	*	*	*	*	28	20
Hays	2,638	846	562	400	829	109	2,747	2,471	276	417	375	440	529	682	303
Hemphill	20	13	*	*	*	*	22	20	*	*	*	*	*	*	*
Henderson	1,066	312	210	147	397	159	1,225	1,158	67	119	80	99	265	437	223
Hidalgo	6,303	1,977	991	882	2,453	356	6,659	6,390	269	878	808	739	1,069	1,919	1,243
Hill	617	174	115	92	236	61	678	654	24	55	36	65	131	251	140
Hockley	214	66	41	32	75	25	239	229	10	23	19	28	50	80	39
Hood	900	285	198	144	273	84	984	925	59	93	71	99	188	318	215
Hopkins	373	107	71	69	126	63	436	408	28	49	28	47	76	141	95
Houston	324	63	56	59	146	39	363	346	17	33	25	38	59	134	74
Howard	636	200	128	90	218	54	690	643	47	56	68	74	140	181	171
Hudspeth	38	*	*	*	14	*	41	38	*	*	*	*	10	10	*
Hunt	1,195	371	235	196	393	123	1,318	1,228	90	140	155	184	260	397	181
Hutchinson	259	77	54	41	87	30	289	275	14	43	27	28	47	98	46
Irion	28	*	*	*	14	*	28	26	*	*	*	*	*	*	*
Jack	79	32	18	10	19	*	88	83	*	*	*	14	14	31	15
Jackson	145	36	29	29	51	13	158	151	*	29	16	19	13	48	33
Jasper	451	140	65	79	167	48	499	470	29	52	43	46	74	203	81
Jeff Davis	31	*	*	*	11	*	35	33	*	*	*	*	*	15	*
Jefferson	2,870	867	568	472	963	405	3,275	2,993	282	343	373	483	692	946	438
Jim Hogg	54	12	*	*	30	*	62	60	*	*	*	*	11	23	14
Jim Wells	539	145	100	85	209	51	590	569	21	53	55	61	94	231	96
Johnson	1,870	640	363	260	607	132	2,002	1,840	162	270	240	258	390	587	257
Jones	282	78	45	54	105	32	314	287	27	29	34	47	46	95	63
Karnes	142	37	27	20	58	16	158	152	*	16	*	18	32	53	31
Kaufman	1,253	373	230	217	433	131	1,384	1,286	98	195	205	168	263	427	126
Kendall	829	265	152	143	269	21	851	767	83	51	84	173	179	231	133
Kenedy	*	*	*	*	*	*	*	*	*	*	*	*	*	*	*
Kent	*	*	*	*	*	*	13	13	*	*	*	*	*	*	*
Kerr	1,249	360	199	185	505	89	1,338	1,249	89	87	79	113	238	440	381
Kimble	54	17	*	12	19	*	62	59	*	*	*	*	*	28	15
King	*	*	*	*	*	*	*	*	*	*	*	*	*	*	*
Kinney	106	35	17	17	37	*	111	108	*	*	*	*	21	31	40
Kleberg	562	181	120	82	179	25	587	552	35	80	70	67	112	176	82
Knox	36	13	*	*	13	*	42	40	*	*	*	*	*	16	11
La Salle	36	15	*	*	13	*	42	41	*	*	*	*	13	16	*
Lamar	669	183	137	112	237	107	776	730	46	82	67	85	131	264	147
Lamb	116	41	21	21	33	14	130	122	*	*	16	17	24	28	36
Lampasas	1,481	353	290	243	594	30	1,511	1,311	200	107	211	380	362	299	151
Lavaca	216	54	32	43	87	29	244	230	14	16	11	20	41	85	72
Lee	192	54	40	24	74	16	208	200	*	12	15	22	45	66	48
Leon	276	89	43	49	95	25	301	294	*	15	17	29	56	124	60
Liberty	901	281	167	127	326	107	1,008	946	62	111	92	112	193	377	123
Limestone	319	95	66	55	103	47	366	348	18	24	28	37	85	127	65
Lipscomb	20	11	*	*	*	*	23	22	*	*	*	*	*	*	*
Live Oak	133	36	21	22	54	*	138	132	*	12	15	16	20	50	25
Llano	393	130	70	56	137	36	429	398	31	22	33	32	84	144	114
Lubbock	3,248	1,034	545	503	1,166	286	3,534	3,267	267	513	409	409	694	932	577
Lynn	32	*	*	10	10	*	35	34	*	*	*	*	*	15	*
Madison	115	39	20	18	38	20	135	127	*	*	16	12	24	48	26
Marion	190	41	32	31	86	33	223	203	20	*	17	26	39	81	53
Martin	37	11	*	*	13	*	42	41	*	10	*	*	*	13	*
Mason	39	10	*	*	18	*	45	45	*	*	*	*	*	21	13
Matagorda	433	150	76	53	154	53	486	465	21	52	32	25	111	197	69
Maverick	318	101	63	49	105	29	347	335	12	57	57	28	56	96	53
Mcculloch	102	25	19	23	35	10	111	105	*	15	*	*	18	47	19
Mclennan	4,600	1,219	775	714	1,893	383	4,983	4,645	339	475	486	700	1,205	1,367	750
Mcmullen	*	*	*	*	*	*	*	*	*	*	*	*	*	*	*
Medina	1,293	360	214	214	504	37	1,330	1,199	131	89	121	248	339	368	164
Menard	27	*	*	*	11	*	31	31	*	*	*	*	*	15	11
Midland	1,297	470	257	187	384	121	1,418	1,332	87	265	180	161	259	310	244

Table 54. Compensation and Pension Recipients, by County, FY2014—*Continued*

(Number of recipients.)

State and county	Compensation					Total, pension	Compensation or pension								
	Total	0 to 20 percent	30 to 40 percent	50 to 60 percent	70 to 100 percent		Total	Male	Female	Less than 35 years	35 to 44 years	45 to 54 years	55 to 64 years	65 to 74 years	75 years and over
Texas cnt'd															
Milam	364	114	57	69	124	51	415	401	14	23	20	56	79	146	91
Mills	68	24	*	12	23	11	79	74	*	*	*	*	18	26	20
Mitchell	81	29	*	17	27	18	99	96	*	10	*	12	15	27	29
Montague	295	88	47	56	105	33	328	320	*	22	29	32	51	126	69
Montgomery	5,321	1,710	1,013	904	1,695	363	5,684	5,229	455	861	766	792	943	1,654	663
Moore	139	47	36	19	37	16	155	149	*	31	13	13	27	37	34
Morris	195	47	35	30	83	31	226	215	11	19	20	23	55	75	34
Motley	18	*	*	*	*	*	20	19	*	*	*	*	*	*	*
Nacogdoches	676	212	126	96	242	85	760	717	43	90	73	64	155	259	120
Navarro	612	167	117	96	232	90	702	665	37	67	60	69	165	238	103
Newton	165	50	18	31	66	21	186	182	*	13	13	23	48	69	20
Nolan	209	60	45	37	68	21	230	217	13	21	24	23	47	74	42
Nueces	7,373	2,185	1,452	1,257	2,479	371	7,744	7,169	575	865	1,044	1,248	1,599	2,114	871
Ochiltree	57	19	14	14	10	*	61	59	*	10	*	*	*	24	*
Oldham	20	*	*	*	*	*	20	20	*	*	*	*	*	*	*
Orange	1,527	472	272	222	561	97	1,624	1,548	76	162	150	180	297	536	298
Palo Pinto	373	104	64	63	142	35	408	384	24	29	36	33	101	146	63
Panola	244	81	42	35	86	37	281	269	12	26	29	33	57	78	58
Parker	1,916	604	370	314	629	118	2,034	1,888	146	194	228	331	418	595	268
Parmer	43	*	*	11	14	*	47	45	*	*	*	*	*	11	*
Pecos	106	35	24	18	29	*	114	106	*	22	13	15	19	31	14
Polk	860	270	139	126	325	73	933	876	57	61	54	66	141	399	212
Potter	1,332	419	239	237	436	194	1,526	1,420	106	181	149	183	329	431	252
Presidio	54	11	11	13	19	*	54	52	*	*	*	*	*	22	*
Rains	218	62	32	43	80	20	238	223	15	14	23	23	57	87	33
Randall	1,921	626	410	321	565	96	2,017	1,882	135	337	276	285	344	494	281
Reagan	26	10	*	*	*	*	26	24	*	*	*	*	*	*	*
Real	53	17	10	*	24	*	58	56	*	*	*	*	14	19	*
Red River	173	46	33	23	71	37	210	198	12	15	16	21	46	62	50
Reeves	79	21	15	15	28	15	94	93	*	10	*	*	26	32	12
Refugio	128	37	18	16	57	*	136	128	*	*	10	12	21	58	27
Roberts	*	*	*	*	*	*	*	*	*	*	*	*	*	*	*
Robertson	210	64	30	35	80	38	248	231	17	16	15	22	54	97	43
Rockwall	1,082	378	229	150	325	44	1,126	1,035	91	155	205	218	186	257	104
Runnels	135	37	23	24	51	11	146	137	*	14	*	16	27	48	33
Rusk	536	155	96	87	197	50	586	556	30	58	58	65	95	199	110
Sabine	252	80	42	42	88	18	270	263	*	13	13	11	48	114	71
San Augustine	135	37	18	20	60	14	149	141	*	13	13	11	29	55	28
San Jacinto	396	111	57	54	174	39	436	417	19	37	38	40	95	168	57
San Patricio	1,483	394	310	264	515	73	1,556	1,445	111	146	238	367	253	384	168
San Saba	59	26	*	*	17	*	63	61	*	*	*	*	10	21	13
Schleicher	24	*	*	*	*	*	26	24	*	*	*	*	*	10	*
Scurry	140	56	26	24	34	*	147	138	*	27	18	18	16	43	25
Shackelford	40	12	*	13	*	*	44	40	*	*	*	*	*	12	*
Shelby	204	65	34	42	63	34	238	223	15	25	19	26	47	74	47
Sherman	10	*	*	*	*	*	10	10	*	*	*	*	*	*	*
Smith	2,456	773	472	407	804	301	2,757	2,559	199	246	310	331	584	779	508
Somervell	86	33	18	11	24	11	97	95	*	13	11	10	14	31	18
Starr	230	61	36	26	107	51	281	275	*	34	29	24	45	79	70
Stephens	92	30	17	11	34	12	104	100	*	*	*	*	20	46	16
Sterling	*	*	*	*	*	*	*	*	*	*	*	*	*	*	*
Stonewall	*	*	*	*	*	*	13	13	*	*	*	*	*	*	*
Sutton	32	10	*	*	13	*	34	32	*	*	*	*	*	13	*
Swisher	68	23	12	10	23	14	82	77	*	*	*	11	12	28	18
Tarrant	22,378	7,478	4,577	3,586	6,737	1,736	24,114	21,533	2,581	3,211	3,545	4,328	4,844	5,382	2,802
Taylor	3,789	1,093	682	678	1,337	147	3,936	3,538	399	515	491	780	744	791	615
Terrell	21	*	*	*	*	*	23	23	*	*	*	*	*	*	*
Terry	86	26	10	16	34	14	100	97	*	*	10	*	23	32	22
Throckmorton	19	*	*	*	*	*	21	21	*	*	*	*	*	12	*
Titus	275	73	51	37	114	26	301	288	13	38	29	36	50	102	46
Tom Green	2,681	869	545	445	822	124	2,805	2,493	313	403	338	482	500	626	456
Travis	10,845	3,681	2,189	1,613	3,362	769	11,613	10,410	1,203	1,800	1,573	1,649	2,233	2,682	1,674
Trinity	266	67	36	46	117	40	306	295	11	18	19	21	62	118	68
Tyler	268	86	45	41	96	29	297	279	18	23	21	30	64	113	46
Upshur	476	131	82	76	187	61	537	505	32	55	50	62	120	158	92
Upton	34	*	*	*	13	*	36	33	*	*	*	*	*	18	*
Uvalde	307	91	58	52	106	28	335	318	17	33	35	33	58	124	52
Val Verde	967	278	191	182	316	33	1,000	926	74	144	145	154	175	245	137
Van Zandt	668	191	131	122	224	76	744	709	35	69	52	77	148	279	119
Victoria	1,201	344	216	186	455	86	1,287	1,200	87	170	143	109	212	428	224

Table 54. Compensation and Pension Recipients, by County, FY2014—*Continued*

(Number of recipients.)

State and county	Compensation					Total, pension	Compensation or pension								
	Total	0 to 20 percent	30 to 40 percent	50 to 60 percent	70 to 100 percent		Total	Male	Female	Less than 35 years	35 to 44 years	45 to 54 years	55 to 64 years	65 to 74 years	75 years and over
Texas cnt'd															
Walker	638	209	133	103	193	50	688	642	46	92	79	75	127	218	96
Waller	319	106	52	52	109	25	344	318	26	39	41	43	71	106	45
Ward	115	43	20	15	37	*	122	116	*	*	13	16	13	52	23
Washington	385	120	73	65	127	39	424	401	23	38	36	30	80	153	87
Webb	1,929	596	303	321	709	104	2,033	1,964	69	339	243	195	343	588	325
Wharton	318	105	61	43	109	35	353	338	15	31	24	43	60	141	54
Wheeler	54	20	11	*	17	*	58	53	*	*	*	*	*	25	12
Wichita	3,972	1,050	828	723	1,371	147	4,119	3,607	512	438	499	887	866	830	599
Wilbarger	177	44	28	35	70	23	200	188	12	14	15	24	38	70	39
Willacy	218	68	33	38	79	24	242	236	*	21	25	14	53	82	47
Williamson	7,421	2,450	1,544	1,223	2,205	238	7,659	6,809	850	1,119	1,330	1,406	1,249	1,670	885
Wilson	1,506	397	268	240	601	38	1,544	1,353	191	109	173	348	384	372	157
Winkler	53	15	14	*	17	*	54	49	*	*	*	*	11	15	*
Wise	770	262	139	112	256	48	818	770	47	77	87	97	168	285	104
Wood	680	193	119	122	246	71	751	716	35	69	46	68	131	295	142
Yoakum	37	10	*	*	16	*	43	42	*	*	*	*	*	15	*
Young	188	63	37	28	60	31	219	209	10	25	12	20	36	67	59
Zapata	98	27	16	16	39	15	113	110	*	*	*	*	21	49	31
Zavala	65	18	15	13	19	15	80	77	*	*	*	*	10	33	20
Unknown	*	*	*	*	*	*	*	*	*	*	*	*	*	*	*
Utah															
Beaver	43	12	10	*	13	*	50	49	*	*	*	*	12	13	10
Box Elder	401	158	75	65	103	21	422	399	23	58	40	52	82	112	78
Cache	528	170	113	91	154	43	571	540	31	110	63	62	78	154	104
Carbon	268	83	47	46	92	23	291	278	13	23	22	30	52	117	47
Daggett	*	*	*	*	*	*	*	*	*	*	*	*	*	*	*
Davis	4,915	1,617	1,035	915	1,347	120	5,035	4,537	498	626	732	1,337	982	869	489
Duchesne	142	41	31	26	44	20	162	155	*	26	13	14	36	52	21
Emery	59	17	15	11	16	*	64	62	*	*	*	*	18	21	*
Garfield	41	13	11	*	13	*	46	46	*	*	*	*	11	16	14
Grand	96	32	21	17	26	14	110	104	*	*	*	*	22	47	17
Iron	369	122	65	60	122	20	389	369	20	37	38	42	82	137	52
Juab	74	18	16	13	27	*	80	76	*	12	*	*	15	32	*
Kane	100	29	19	15	37	*	105	101	*	*	*	*	24	46	19
Millard	83	26	20	16	21	12	95	92	*	12	*	*	17	28	20
Morgan	109	38	23	21	27	*	110	99	11	*	*	21	24	32	17
Piute	10	*	*	*	*	*	11	11	*	*	*	*	*	*	*
Rich	11	*	*	*	*	*	11	11	*	*	*	*	*	*	*
Salt Lake	7,260	2,477	1,446	1,147	2,190	739	7,999	7,412	587	1,191	1,047	1,025	1,558	2,056	1,116
San Juan	72	30	17	*	17	*	81	77	*	*	*	11	12	25	19
Sanpete	178	61	33	24	60	24	202	198	*	27	17	13	36	71	38
Sevier	187	71	27	28	61	20	207	203	*	22	22	18	41	69	35
Summit	216	80	49	35	52	11	227	211	16	17	21	37	42	75	35
Tooele	796	278	156	119	243	32	828	768	60	96	133	156	189	196	58
Uintah	197	75	44	35	43	14	211	201	10	27	20	30	33	72	29
Utah	2,517	847	495	421	754	157	2,674	2,523	151	441	377	339	446	656	415
Wasatch	119	31	29	29	30	*	125	121	*	10	18	15	26	43	13
Washington	1,517	507	253	226	531	156	1,673	1,582	91	136	136	124	240	587	449
Wayne	*	*	*	*	*	*	12	12	*	*	*	*	*	*	*
Weber	3,493	1,104	724	623	1,043	173	3,666	3,295	371	453	506	792	763	759	392
Unknown	*	*	*	*	*	*	*	*	*	*	*	*	*	*	*
Vermont															
Addison	291	100	49	40	102	11	302	284	18	22	31	44	52	102	51
Bennington	392	137	54	54	147	32	424	401	23	27	32	47	79	157	81
Caledonia	402	132	70	78	122	23	425	390	35	37	44	46	97	139	62
Chittenden	1,397	481	263	219	434	58	1,455	1,341	114	163	150	262	271	373	234
Essex	130	39	16	20	55	10	140	134	*	*	*	21	30	58	18
Franklin	519	149	94	88	188	26	545	510	35	53	59	117	112	126	77
Grand Isle	84	25	19	13	27	*	89	86	*	13	10	14	16	29	*
Lamoille	246	77	44	47	78	21	267	253	14	24	33	37	51	85	37
Orange	405	143	57	54	151	15	420	383	37	32	34	73	93	129	58
Orleans	404	120	70	71	143	27	431	409	22	38	27	63	94	150	59
Rutland	789	254	133	138	264	44	833	785	48	76	60	136	158	294	109
Washington	700	235	141	107	217	35	735	689	46	72	80	110	153	195	124
Windham	397	119	62	63	153	32	429	409	20	33	25	60	74	159	78
Windsor	809	265	153	106	285	39	848	793	55	51	80	106	214	263	132

Table 54. Compensation and Pension Recipients, by County, FY2014—*Continued*

(Number of recipients.)

State and county	Compensation: Total	Compensation: 0 to 20 percent	Compensation: 30 to 40 percent	Compensation: 50 to 60 percent	Compensation: 70 to 100 percent	Total, pension	Compensation or pension: Total	Male	Female	Less than 35 years	35 to 44 years	45 to 54 years	55 to 64 years	65 to 74 years	75 years and over
Virginia															
Accomack	458	141	85	79	153	57	515	470	45	34	56	96	131	134	64
Albemarle	901	319	189	151	243	54	955	834	121	140	136	163	141	232	142
Alexandria City	2,276	717	538	418	602	43	2,319	1,805	514	361	397	525	508	332	193
Alleghany	267	83	54	43	87	21	288	276	12	13	25	32	67	104	46
Amelia	200	53	33	35	79	14	214	194	20	21	13	33	49	68	30
Amherst	382	119	73	63	127	40	422	394	28	41	33	51	88	144	65
Appomattox	149	55	32	14	48	12	161	153	*	18	13	20	28	56	26
Arlington	2,359	796	548	388	627	47	2,406	1,988	418	368	409	514	503	363	248
Augusta	845	290	185	121	249	73	918	871	47	87	66	105	182	341	136
Bath	59	22	13	*	15	10	69	65	*	*	*	*	*	27	20
Bedford	973	357	193	154	269	59	1,032	970	62	88	90	142	201	355	156
Bedford City	78	21	19	15	23	11	90	79	11	*	16	10	20	16	18
Bland	115	30	26	15	44	*	122	120	*	*	*	18	19	60	14
Botetourt	484	153	87	82	161	13	497	469	28	29	55	75	98	157	83
Bristol	263	84	45	46	88	42	305	297	*	20	22	40	45	109	69
Brunswick	214	56	47	35	76	26	240	219	21	20	17	23	54	83	43
Buchanan	281	48	41	47	145	29	310	303	*	28	30	27	36	136	53
Buckingham	170	48	31	29	61	17	187	178	*	16	14	23	34	62	37
Buena Vista City	61	17	21	10	13	*	65	62	*	*	*	*	*	28	19
Campbell	635	218	140	83	194	60	695	662	34	65	66	85	138	228	113
Caroline	583	160	114	100	209	23	606	539	67	73	87	141	133	131	41
Carroll	352	103	67	43	139	29	382	365	17	42	29	37	67	145	61
Charles City	121	36	20	17	48	*	128	116	11	11	*	17	28	51	11
Charlotte	179	61	31	24	63	18	197	186	11	16	16	28	40	63	34
Charlottesville City	200	71	52	27	50	24	224	199	25	29	31	30	45	50	40
Chesapeake City	8,627	2,165	1,931	1,755	2,776	167	8,794	7,352	1,442	924	1,444	2,984	1,914	1,103	425
Chesterfield	5,552	1,572	1,143	921	1,915	161	5,713	4,868	845	522	806	1,402	1,245	1,285	451
Clarke	171	58	36	32	45	*	177	163	14	20	14	29	35	50	29
Colonial Heights City	487	141	101	97	149	14	501	440	61	51	62	96	103	106	84
Covington City	95	25	16	17	37	14	109	102	*	*	*	12	18	48	17
Craig	82	21	11	12	38	*	91	83	*	*	*	12	13	36	15
Culpeper	622	223	149	80	170	26	648	584	64	66	101	127	115	166	73
Cumberland	113	32	21	17	43	10	123	107	16	14	10	23	22	37	17
Danville City	559	180	105	84	190	99	657	608	49	52	47	87	143	221	106
Dickenson	255	65	36	44	110	20	275	264	11	21	33	21	47	106	47
Dinwiddie	625	142	127	99	258	25	651	560	91	47	88	169	137	165	44
Emporia City	54	18	13	*	19	*	61	55	*	*	*	*	20	17	*
Essex	132	45	22	23	42	*	140	133	*	*	15	27	23	44	22
Fairfax	17,939	6,058	4,209	3,027	4,645	186	18,125	15,265	2,860	1,754	2,342	4,400	4,399	3,246	1,983
Fairfax City	305	127	67	44	68	*	314	280	34	22	30	53	82	66	62
Falls Church City	149	49	37	26	37	*	155	137	18	16	18	30	32	35	24
Fauquier	911	344	222	126	218	22	933	843	90	99	115	214	182	216	106
Floyd	194	72	35	24	63	24	218	205	13	12	19	27	46	79	35
Fluvanna	331	126	66	52	87	16	347	315	32	36	33	55	61	96	66
Franklin	771	238	133	109	291	56	827	781	46	60	58	110	161	308	129
Franklin City	147	46	28	28	45	12	159	140	19	27	21	36	36	29	10
Frederick	1,038	352	240	174	272	33	1,071	983	88	120	135	188	173	319	136
Fredericksburg City	461	151	93	69	148	18	479	408	71	75	90	124	89	66	35
Galax City	79	25	18	14	22	*	88	86	*	*	*	*	19	28	17
Giles	238	68	40	38	92	24	262	248	14	21	26	24	40	102	49
Gloucester	1,146	355	213	203	374	22	1,168	1,048	120	84	115	311	305	253	100
Goochland	191	65	33	27	66	14	205	193	12	12	21	29	37	82	23
Grayson	220	60	43	37	80	26	247	238	*	18	12	23	55	82	56
Greene	258	83	70	35	70	*	262	236	26	32	47	65	44	49	25
Greensville	147	41	22	20	64	13	160	146	14	11	13	16	50	58	12
Halifax	526	126	96	89	215	43	569	533	36	47	40	72	111	228	70
Hampton City	6,722	1,798	1,423	1,190	2,311	242	6,964	5,597	1,367	825	997	1,757	1,706	1,067	610
Hanover	895	314	176	154	252	31	926	856	70	98	89	174	159	290	116
Harrisonburg City	192	80	34	27	51	28	220	199	21	39	17	29	40	61	35
Henrico	3,142	1,008	663	498	972	171	3,313	2,936	376	359	404	595	691	841	421
Henry	640	200	140	99	201	79	719	684	35	63	54	61	154	266	121
Highland	23	*	*	*	*	*	28	27	*	*	*	*	*	12	*
Hopewell City	644	168	135	111	231	26	670	558	112	73	97	148	144	135	73
Isle Of Wight	1,092	320	246	219	307	26	1,118	950	168	84	143	343	288	191	69
James City	1,927	607	436	327	557	21	1,948	1,746	201	93	199	441	425	460	329
King And Queen	83	23	11	17	32	*	86	79	*	*	*	11	27	28	*
King George	735	217	179	152	187	16	751	663	88	71	156	244	152	102	26
King William	177	50	42	20	65	*	186	176	10	23	26	29	34	59	15
Lancaster	175	60	31	31	53	18	193	186	*	11	11	18	30	72	51

Table 54. Compensation and Pension Recipients, by County, FY2014—*Continued*

(Number of recipients.)

State and county	Compensation					Total, pension	Compensation or pension								
	Total	0 to 20 percent	30 to 40 percent	50 to 60 percent	70 to 100 percent		Total	Male	Female	Less than 35 years	35 to 44 years	45 to 54 years	55 to 64 years	65 to 74 years	75 years and over
Virginia cnt'd															
Lee	377	101	69	61	146	45	422	410	12	27	45	45	82	175	48
Lexington City	61	23	17	*	13	*	67	60	*	*	*	*	*	25	16
Loudoun	3,709	1,467	899	539	804	46	3,755	3,257	498	443	698	1,038	730	549	297
Louisa	450	145	77	74	154	29	480	439	40	36	39	68	103	174	59
Lunenburg	204	62	41	27	74	17	221	207	14	18	16	40	56	61	30
Lynchburg City	699	228	146	118	208	102	801	732	69	86	63	120	185	209	138
Madison	126	45	22	20	39	*	134	130	*	*	12	15	33	41	26
Manassas City	441	145	102	70	125	12	453	388	65	78	68	100	107	66	35
Manassas Park City	178	63	41	28	46	*	183	150	33	31	35	53	32	25	*
Martinsville City	147	58	25	17	47	30	177	165	12	11	*	25	47	61	22
Mathews	148	57	19	21	51	*	155	143	12	*	*	23	25	55	35
Mecklenburg	515	155	94	77	189	38	553	517	36	44	46	64	115	220	64
Middlesex	165	51	36	24	53	10	175	168	*	10	*	21	35	68	32
Montgomery	705	239	156	120	190	41	746	685	61	79	103	104	156	204	98
Nelson	182	72	34	24	52	23	205	200	*	10	11	14	34	94	42
New Kent	366	104	81	59	122	*	372	333	40	29	47	68	96	103	30
Newport News City	7,654	1,993	1,656	1,474	2,532	236	7,890	6,391	1,500	1,139	1,352	2,077	1,751	1,050	521
Norfolk City	7,124	1,906	1,606	1,347	2,264	355	7,479	5,937	1,542	1,458	1,406	1,748	1,574	903	388
Northampton	129	54	24	18	33	17	146	132	14	*	*	18	46	41	31
Northumberland	175	65	35	20	55	*	183	177	*	*	*	17	26	72	54
Norton City	41	17	*	*	16	*	43	41	*	*	*	*	*	18	*
Nottoway	231	58	46	38	89	21	252	234	18	19	23	48	50	79	33
Orange	616	204	118	102	192	28	643	571	73	70	101	111	116	153	93
Page	240	79	43	32	86	25	265	250	15	22	19	32	32	106	54
Patrick	219	61	43	37	78	29	248	237	11	21	21	18	41	104	43
Petersburg City	1,009	254	191	146	418	54	1,063	882	181	104	105	195	297	247	115
Pittsylvania	848	262	156	128	302	79	927	872	55	90	75	112	180	346	124
Poquoson City	438	154	107	66	111	*	443	393	50	17	42	105	116	98	65
Portsmouth City	2,919	772	615	586	946	172	3,091	2,546	545	481	540	736	660	451	222
Powhatan	309	106	57	52	94	11	320	297	23	32	26	56	57	110	39
Prince Edward	227	59	43	36	90	31	259	240	19	19	16	35	61	80	47
Prince George	1,648	375	317	300	656	14	1,662	1,332	330	227	253	400	365	310	106
Prince William	11,998	3,604	2,780	2,105	3,509	119	12,117	9,861	2,256	1,382	2,031	3,819	2,791	1,532	560
Pulaski	447	137	95	60	155	35	482	461	21	36	40	62	72	180	92
Radford City	97	29	31	12	26	11	108	99	*	21	14	13	16	29	16
Rappahannock	77	31	13	10	23	*	82	76	*	*	*	*	14	34	16
Richmond	95	25	14	18	38	17	112	105	*	11	*	13	24	31	25
Richmond City	1,970	611	434	292	633	323	2,293	2,016	277	223	205	285	668	621	292
Roanoke	1,352	442	264	206	440	67	1,419	1,320	99	109	152	214	249	414	281
Roanoke City	1,361	399	284	217	461	219	1,580	1,426	154	135	160	214	441	413	217
Rockbridge	308	106	53	48	102	33	341	328	13	13	24	44	65	126	70
Rockingham	630	228	147	86	169	56	685	641	45	78	53	91	118	213	132
Russell	293	86	56	52	99	29	322	308	14	24	27	43	50	118	60
Salem	343	119	53	50	122	21	364	337	27	32	38	53	88	94	60
Scott	286	78	51	39	118	34	320	310	10	17	25	26	57	124	71
Shenandoah	551	181	119	77	174	39	590	559	31	59	61	73	102	200	95
Smyth	439	110	86	83	160	41	480	467	13	33	34	54	73	193	93
Southampton	298	80	72	52	94	16	314	281	33	26	51	65	69	76	26
Spotsylvania	3,785	1,096	868	671	1,150	59	3,844	3,359	485	422	671	1,252	788	519	192
Stafford	6,283	1,600	1,466	1,232	1,985	37	6,320	5,301	1,019	726	1,038	2,473	1,330	587	166
Staunton City	287	93	63	47	84	37	324	298	26	34	23	46	71	100	51
Suffolk City	3,517	895	715	705	1,202	78	3,595	2,938	657	346	654	1,271	757	425	142
Surry	119	35	22	12	50	*	126	117	*	*	14	25	26	41	12
Sussex	178	50	49	20	59	11	189	167	22	12	17	51	49	40	19
Tazewell	787	187	126	110	364	68	855	824	31	49	80	86	161	349	130
Virginia Beach City	22,300	5,935	5,048	4,553	6,765	270	22,570	18,946	3,624	2,744	3,952	7,233	4,792	2,665	1,184
Warren	530	217	110	75	128	22	552	507	45	55	71	103	107	151	64
Washington	805	231	156	129	289	78	883	844	39	51	87	90	139	354	162
Waynesboro City	241	90	49	26	76	20	261	246	15	16	24	41	46	82	52
Westmoreland	283	97	62	35	89	12	295	276	19	24	32	44	70	80	45
Williamsburg City	181	63	38	30	50	12	193	172	21	15	22	28	44	52	32
Winchester City	225	98	48	25	54	23	248	225	23	30	23	41	50	58	46
Wise	635	143	106	107	279	54	689	670	19	67	71	87	97	260	105
Wythe	372	98	83	49	142	27	399	378	21	26	32	42	74	156	69
York	3,147	982	703	619	843	14	3,162	2,732	429	204	372	997	888	486	214
Washington															
Adams	102	30	19	16	37	*	110	105	*	11	*	11	29	33	20
Asotin	433	167	100	48	118	23	456	430	26	46	43	55	72	144	96
Benton	2,577	1,055	504	365	653	95	2,672	2,506	166	332	304	347	476	830	381

Table 54. Compensation and Pension Recipients, by County, FY2014—*Continued*

(Number of recipients.)

State and county	Compensation					Total, pension	Compensation or pension								
	Total	0 to 20 percent	30 to 40 percent	50 to 60 percent	70 to 100 percent		Total	Male	Female	Less than 35 years	35 to 44 years	45 to 54 years	55 to 64 years	65 to 74 years	75 years and over
Washington cnt'd															
Chelan	793	284	145	104	260	58	851	798	53	86	72	71	145	323	153
Clallam	1,462	479	263	206	514	106	1,568	1,460	108	104	111	149	307	565	331
Clark	6,791	2,411	1,399	1,096	1,885	401	7,192	6,566	626	896	928	1,142	1,380	2,024	820
Columbia	81	27	21	*	27	*	86	78	*	*	*	11	17	36	10
Cowlitz	1,597	475	329	265	529	148	1,745	1,631	114	186	160	221	352	575	251
Douglas	411	140	75	72	124	12	423	400	23	58	40	40	65	149	71
Ferry	169	38	29	27	75	23	192	179	13	*	11	17	48	85	25
Franklin	726	310	121	104	191	20	746	702	44	125	101	83	110	218	109
Garfield	42	16	*	*	13	*	45	44	*	*	*	*	*	17	*
Grant	839	299	153	127	260	68	907	866	41	84	86	117	172	289	159
Grays Harbor	1,392	459	234	213	487	104	1,496	1,400	96	99	115	172	332	548	231
Island	4,039	1,025	810	822	1,382	51	4,090	3,561	529	602	600	1,050	818	643	377
Jefferson	589	180	105	93	211	40	629	588	41	26	36	59	137	263	108
King	15,664	5,768	3,183	2,210	4,503	1,461	17,124	15,577	1,547	2,184	2,178	2,511	3,419	4,561	2,271
Kitsap	11,484	3,571	2,687	2,138	3,088	256	11,740	10,641	1,099	1,290	1,587	3,254	2,742	2,079	788
Kittitas	412	132	81	61	138	32	444	411	33	54	46	59	72	157	56
Klickitat	328	100	65	51	112	22	350	329	21	29	34	40	62	143	42
Lewis	1,400	438	256	215	491	88	1,488	1,401	87	119	143	180	314	477	255
Lincoln	213	60	36	41	76	*	221	212	*	15	18	32	54	75	27
Mason	1,605	493	328	261	522	65	1,670	1,522	148	125	173	334	380	477	180
Okanogan	689	190	106	97	296	48	737	697	40	45	48	84	166	296	98
Pacific	387	111	68	58	150	34	421	393	28	25	19	43	70	178	86
Pend Oreille	296	92	45	56	102	30	326	304	22	14	16	42	56	147	50
Pierce	29,225	8,437	5,899	4,787	10,102	833	30,059	26,399	3,660	4,793	4,259	5,961	6,336	5,751	2,956
San Juan	155	55	35	18	47	*	163	151	12	*	*	17	25	74	35
Skagit	2,122	627	439	319	737	77	2,199	2,006	193	218	269	432	449	582	249
Skamania	172	63	41	24	44	18	190	180	10	20	16	26	37	63	28
Snohomish	10,279	3,569	2,051	1,642	3,017	492	10,771	9,777	994	1,494	1,613	2,041	2,096	2,531	993
Spokane	9,797	3,351	1,982	1,589	2,876	619	10,416	9,431	985	1,091	1,174	2,025	2,280	2,507	1,337
Stevens	997	300	173	177	346	55	1,052	971	81	52	83	161	253	356	147
Thurston	10,323	2,790	2,162	1,824	3,547	207	10,530	9,189	1,341	1,421	1,589	2,413	2,338	1,902	867
Wahkiakum	76	22	13	18	23	*	81	78	*	*	*	*	14	33	18
Walla Walla	817	251	159	121	286	86	903	835	68	80	98	123	163	280	159
Whatcom	2,617	902	461	380	874	164	2,781	2,579	202	296	305	398	529	875	377
Whitman	313	135	51	48	79	16	329	292	37	59	37	48	54	81	50
Yakima	2,383	761	469	402	751	159	2,542	2,388	154	285	251	279	488	844	395
West Virginia															
Barbour	228	56	45	37	90	28	256	244	12	20	21	25	46	102	42
Berkeley	2,208	617	407	356	829	158	2,366	2,162	204	231	283	448	599	599	206
Boone	347	92	46	55	154	31	378	372	*	23	38	31	79	163	44
Braxton	275	77	43	40	115	33	309	295	14	15	23	42	68	108	53
Brooke	247	95	51	29	72	27	275	262	13	14	30	36	41	102	51
Cabell	1,485	442	250	230	563	202	1,688	1,598	90	160	187	212	369	505	255
Calhoun	108	22	17	14	55	26	134	125	*	*	*	12	28	54	21
Clay	181	50	33	29	69	17	198	195	*	16	16	17	31	85	33
Doddridge	150	38	17	31	64	14	164	153	11	13	13	23	30	61	24
Fayette	1,094	303	173	172	446	76	1,170	1,123	47	74	107	137	223	454	175
Gilmer	102	29	21	18	34	*	111	108	*	*	14	23	22	36	*
Grant	157	32	34	33	58	19	176	169	*	13	22	19	34	54	34
Greenbrier	819	253	168	132	266	67	886	841	45	66	75	85	176	308	176
Hampshire	349	99	66	60	124	42	391	372	19	28	28	40	93	144	57
Hancock	343	130	66	53	94	35	377	354	23	32	41	56	57	129	62
Hardy	207	52	38	30	87	25	232	219	13	15	13	24	43	89	48
Harrison	1,231	336	206	220	469	122	1,353	1,276	77	106	143	197	267	434	206
Jackson	392	101	71	61	159	33	425	406	19	40	45	60	87	124	69
Jefferson	893	263	214	136	280	44	937	846	91	102	139	190	203	224	79
Kanawha	2,685	841	482	405	957	266	2,951	2,795	156	200	326	349	600	1,039	434
Lewis	333	90	66	36	141	40	373	354	20	33	30	47	75	131	57
Lincoln	298	69	43	40	146	43	341	331	10	22	29	48	76	131	35
Logan	605	120	91	85	309	36	641	632	*	42	50	41	144	299	65
Marion	938	231	169	141	397	75	1,013	962	51	93	117	142	179	339	142
Marshall	319	110	63	54	92	38	357	344	13	32	26	49	66	125	59
Mason	402	127	77	48	150	23	425	413	12	35	36	52	85	172	45
Mcdowell	344	72	49	46	177	24	368	357	11	14	22	41	88	154	49
Mercer	1,373	342	215	188	628	110	1,483	1,439	44	120	127	149	303	505	279
Mineral	439	115	81	60	183	37	476	461	15	31	39	64	105	175	61
Mingo	346	68	47	50	181	40	386	378	*	17	35	21	89	178	46
Monongalia	937	241	176	138	382	64	1,001	939	62	186	127	131	136	317	104
Monroe	282	78	48	41	115	20	302	291	11	19	22	37	50	110	64

Table 54. Compensation and Pension Recipients, by County, FY2014—*Continued*

(Number of recipients.)

State and county	Compensation					Total, pension	Compensation or pension								
	Total	0 to 20 percent	30 to 40 percent	50 to 60 percent	70 to 100 percent		Total	Male	Female	Less than 35 years	35 to 44 years	45 to 54 years	55 to 64 years	65 to 74 years	75 years and over
West Virginia cnt'd															
Morgan	290	83	47	48	112	12	302	281	21	22	27	53	55	105	40
Nicholas	646	167	118	102	259	36	682	665	17	51	70	79	120	255	106
Ohio	460	174	87	78	121	75	535	507	28	42	47	52	105	195	94
Pendleton	113	34	14	24	41	17	130	118	12	*	15	23	22	43	19
Pleasants	111	25	21	19	46	*	120	116	*	*	14	14	14	49	20
Pocahontas	188	63	36	26	63	16	204	197	*	*	17	16	48	78	36
Preston	583	129	103	93	258	56	639	601	38	54	78	84	105	232	86
Putnam	778	241	167	109	261	31	809	763	46	82	118	118	136	260	95
Raleigh	1,913	484	300	270	859	126	2,039	1,943	96	130	242	248	425	701	292
Randolph	471	114	77	67	213	52	523	496	27	39	57	67	89	210	61
Ritchie	184	46	35	21	82	23	207	196	11	*	22	30	45	81	20
Roane	232	50	42	41	99	34	266	250	16	14	29	30	59	92	42
Summers	340	87	76	39	138	30	370	354	16	26	36	34	80	120	74
Taylor	276	62	41	53	120	28	304	285	19	31	40	42	52	106	33
Tucker	97	32	15	11	39	11	108	103	*	*	14	11	16	45	18
Tyler	138	41	29	20	48	16	154	145	*	10	16	15	33	67	13
Upshur	467	137	72	72	186	40	507	475	32	31	51	66	100	201	58
Wayne	743	208	125	100	310	88	830	803	27	57	75	112	166	270	150
Webster	189	46	30	22	91	33	222	217	*	17	12	13	46	91	43
Wetzel	200	54	29	37	80	22	222	212	10	20	27	29	45	79	21
Wirt	98	29	20	14	35	*	106	100	*	10	13	16	15	41	10
Wood	1,251	333	213	174	531	83	1,334	1,268	66	137	153	207	277	410	149
Wyoming	366	99	47	59	161	21	387	374	13	15	37	36	86	170	41
Wisconsin															
Adams	476	177	85	92	122	42	518	492	26	40	34	45	91	196	112
Ashland	236	96	43	30	67	27	263	253	10	13	22	38	68	73	49
Barron	701	262	142	103	194	65	766	726	40	82	52	82	142	264	144
Bayfield	340	155	71	36	78	17	357	341	16	18	13	30	78	138	80
Brown	2,595	863	616	403	714	175	2,770	2,556	215	447	358	426	473	744	323
Buffalo	253	111	51	32	59	14	268	258	10	30	13	28	52	92	52
Burnett	434	188	82	64	100	37	471	459	12	22	23	35	83	191	117
Calumet	443	149	102	83	109	17	461	422	38	64	52	80	78	134	52
Chippewa	864	385	177	102	200	96	960	905	55	110	78	147	150	300	174
Clark	499	191	98	77	133	31	530	498	32	39	37	53	82	173	146
Columbia	731	303	183	86	159	49	781	715	65	105	78	115	136	228	118
Crawford	224	78	51	23	72	21	245	233	12	19	16	26	55	89	40
Dane	3,906	1,540	852	600	914	332	4,238	3,839	399	665	464	590	816	1,079	624
Dodge	857	356	180	130	191	67	924	872	52	142	99	134	167	244	138
Door	322	131	48	47	96	21	343	324	19	23	25	21	58	153	63
Douglas	903	354	171	107	271	50	953	908	45	93	77	101	216	299	166
Dunn	530	216	99	77	138	23	553	524	29	84	46	82	91	171	79
Eau Claire	1,106	437	233	168	268	76	1,182	1,096	86	184	128	158	209	338	164
Florence	117	27	24	21	45	14	131	124	*	*	*	16	29	44	27
Fond Du Lac	1,005	385	241	138	241	74	1,079	997	82	171	100	151	204	335	118
Forest	265	70	51	38	106	21	286	273	13	17	10	34	60	99	66
Grant	447	177	108	61	101	42	489	463	26	74	37	65	73	163	77
Green	421	171	90	61	99	23	444	425	19	51	34	50	76	154	78
Green Lake	195	69	42	33	51	13	208	196	12	19	14	19	33	80	43
Iowa	234	86	54	28	66	14	248	232	16	24	22	24	43	96	39
Iron	112	30	22	24	36	14	126	121	*	*	*	13	27	41	28
Jackson	436	164	84	62	126	30	466	443	23	37	43	62	106	135	83
Jefferson	893	380	180	120	213	53	946	880	66	133	106	140	176	270	121
Juneau	489	199	84	79	127	41	530	499	31	49	35	64	117	169	96
Kenosha	2,025	623	442	338	622	134	2,160	1,933	227	267	308	467	417	495	205
Kewaunee	295	119	54	41	81	31	326	315	11	31	28	34	60	112	61
La Crosse	1,802	680	389	268	465	93	1,895	1,759	136	259	160	242	363	502	369
Lafayette	140	50	33	20	37	13	153	143	10	24	14	13	21	47	34
Langlade	380	137	73	59	111	42	422	405	17	21	32	42	80	148	99
Lincoln	485	141	94	87	163	38	523	494	29	58	46	65	92	156	106
Manitowoc	963	341	212	143	267	61	1,024	936	88	143	99	153	166	308	155
Marathon	1,630	656	328	248	397	87	1,716	1,601	115	233	171	240	283	476	313
Marinette	824	262	157	142	263	74	898	842	56	95	79	100	184	280	160
Marquette	270	89	59	37	85	20	290	270	20	22	23	32	71	96	46
Menominee	47	*	11	*	19	15	62	58	*	*	*	*	15	20	*
Milwaukee	8,496	2,813	1,622	1,285	2,776	1,219	9,715	8,824	891	1,209	1,061	1,394	2,345	2,524	1,181
Monroe	1,536	469	316	265	486	117	1,653	1,496	157	152	198	371	395	385	152
Oconto	622	205	118	95	204	47	669	625	44	77	52	72	124	250	94
Oneida	666	230	137	99	200	61	727	683	44	66	60	87	137	234	143
Outagamie	1,833	669	415	255	494	117	1,951	1,785	165	362	250	276	325	519	218

Table 54. Compensation and Pension Recipients, by County, FY2014—*Continued*

(Number of recipients.)

State and county	Compensation					Total, pension	Compensation or pension								
	Total	0 to 20 percent	30 to 40 percent	50 to 60 percent	70 to 100 percent		Total	Male	Female	Less than 35 years	35 to 44 years	45 to 54 years	55 to 64 years	65 to 74 years	75 years and over
Wisconsin cnt'd															
Ozaukee	686	291	136	92	167	34	720	667	53	103	66	107	106	229	109
Pepin	132	64	25	14	29	12	144	133	11	11	*	17	26	52	33
Pierce	555	254	117	62	123	14	569	534	36	60	63	75	116	188	68
Polk	809	370	169	90	180	50	859	820	39	72	52	100	171	290	174
Portage	1,041	464	212	146	219	42	1,083	1,020	63	138	106	122	185	345	186
Price	263	113	52	36	62	23	286	268	18	16	18	37	59	104	52
Racine	1,943	694	421	294	535	212	2,156	2,005	151	276	256	329	431	555	308
Richland	210	85	36	25	64	18	228	214	14	19	12	27	47	72	51
Rock	1,727	661	389	252	424	109	1,836	1,714	122	251	194	278	368	541	204
Rusk	276	111	57	34	74	38	314	300	14	16	20	33	57	113	74
Saint Croix	1,221	544	258	155	264	34	1,255	1,164	91	161	144	189	233	383	144
Sauk	714	279	154	95	186	43	757	700	57	91	67	101	128	245	125
Sawyer	349	153	62	36	98	28	377	368	*	22	*	38	65	152	91
Shawano	533	183	98	74	178	57	590	542	48	59	51	70	97	209	104
Sheboygan	903	350	177	143	233	50	953	879	74	136	92	143	173	280	128
Taylor	275	107	60	40	68	23	298	279	19	30	19	31	63	90	65
Trempealeau	436	184	86	70	96	43	479	460	19	41	23	41	90	178	106
Vernon	396	163	72	64	97	30	426	399	27	30	32	43	95	150	76
Vilas	477	176	94	73	134	38	515	491	24	32	26	40	74	219	124
Walworth	955	348	193	157	257	115	1,071	989	81	146	97	138	179	321	189
Washburn	362	151	61	44	105	43	404	385	19	26	24	41	76	142	95
Washington	1,117	441	265	174	237	50	1,167	1,086	81	194	117	165	187	346	158
Waukesha	2,928	1,105	663	406	755	189	3,117	2,916	201	443	292	386	503	983	509
Waupaca	715	243	118	102	252	178	892	837	55	78	57	106	171	282	199
Waushara	451	177	98	63	113	37	488	467	21	27	24	54	98	165	120
Winnebago	1,842	708	397	287	450	166	2,007	1,854	153	342	199	297	358	548	264
Wood	1,175	493	237	178	267	71	1,246	1,176	71	172	94	143	191	384	263
Unknown	*	*	*	*	*	*	*	*	*	*	*	*	*	*	*
Wyoming															
Albany	440	163	109	50	118	20	460	426	34	119	44	64	74	112	46
Big Horn	124	46	27	19	32	10	134	128	*	13	19	18	27	40	17
Campbell	459	185	112	57	105	11	470	435	35	93	74	86	75	115	26
Carbon	209	84	35	38	52	18	227	215	12	31	15	28	50	76	27
Converse	158	74	32	22	30	*	167	158	*	17	17	20	35	52	26
Crook	84	33	18	16	17	*	86	74	12	*	10	12	14	24	17
Fremont	503	189	93	61	160	21	524	492	32	79	50	55	97	183	60
Goshen	273	119	48	41	65	*	282	267	15	20	29	30	49	100	51
Hot Springs	75	28	12	13	22	*	83	79	*	*	*	10	19	26	16
Johnson	133	46	26	16	45	25	158	146	12	*	15	19	38	54	23
Laramie	3,514	1,290	744	611	869	109	3,623	3,217	406	447	403	844	784	735	409
Lincoln	140	60	28	20	32	*	145	133	12	16	17	12	33	44	22
Natrona	1,008	398	234	165	211	70	1,078	1,002	76	149	169	140	204	264	150
Niobrara	31	*	*	*	*	*	35	32	*	*	*	*	11	13	*
Park	407	149	79	60	119	15	422	393	29	47	39	57	72	154	53
Platte	182	73	40	29	40	10	192	183	*	17	17	22	28	67	40
Sheridan	612	209	116	88	199	42	654	597	57	71	63	91	128	224	77
Sublette	82	31	24	10	17	*	84	79	*	*	14	12	10	31	*
Sweetwater	515	219	105	77	114	15	530	500	30	94	88	57	75	175	41
Teton	98	45	18	18	17	*	99	94	*	14	*	13	16	31	16
Uinta	235	99	46	35	55	14	249	230	19	27	30	27	53	93	18
Washakie	86	45	12	*	21	*	93	84	*	18	*	13	12	33	12
Weston	106	32	37	15	22	*	112	102	10	15	23	10	17	36	11
Puerto Rico															
All counties	17,254	4,285	2,676	2,458	7,835	7,737	24,991	24,242	749	917	1,424	2,429	4,624	6,888	8,707
Unknown	99	55	22	*	13	*	99	92	*	*	*	26	30	22	10

* = Fewer than 10 recipients.

APPENDIX A. TABLE NOTES AND METHODOLOGY

Tables 1–25.

***Sources*: 5-Year American Community Surveys, 2009–2013, 2008–2012, 2007–2011, 2006–2010, 2005–2009; 3-Year American Community Surveys, 2011–2013; 2010–2012; 2009–2011; 2008–2010; 2007–2009; 1-Year American Community Surveys, 2013, 2012, 2011, 2010, 2009.**

Data are based on a sample and are subject to sampling variability. The degree of uncertainty for an estimate arising from sampling variability is represented through the use of a margin of error. The value shown here is the 90 percent margin of error. The margin of error can be interpreted roughly as providing a 90 percent probability that the interval defined by the estimate minus the margin of error and the estimate plus the margin of error (the lower and upper confidence bounds) contains the true value. In addition to sampling variability, the ACS estimates are subject to nonsampling error. The effect of nonsampling error is not represented in these tables. For more information about sample size and data quality, please see: http://www.census.gov/acs/www/methodology/sample-size-and-data-quality/.

Estimates of urban and rural population, housing units, and characteristics reflect boundaries of urban areas defined based on Census 2010 data. As a result, data for urban and rural areas from the ACS do not necessarily reflect the results of ongoing urbanization. For more information about geographical changes, please see: http://www.census.gov/programs-surveys/acs/technical-documentation/table-and-geography-changes.html.

Although the American Community Survey (ACS) produces population, demographic, and housing unit estimates, it is the Census Bureau's Population Estimates Program that produces and disseminates the official estimates of the population for the nation, states, counties, cities, and towns and estimates of housing units for states and counties.

While American Community Survey (ACS) data (including 1-, 3-, and 5-year estimates) ending between 2010 and 2012 generally reflect the December 2009 Office of Management and Budget (OMB) definitions of metropolitan and micropolitan statistical areas, in certain instances the names, codes, and boundaries of the principal cities shown in ACS tables may differ from the OMB definitions due to differences in the effective dates of the geographic entities. Data for surveys ending in 2013 generally reflect the February 2013 Office of Management and Budget (OMB) definitions of metropolitan and micropolitan statistical areas, and data ending in 2009 generally reflect the same from November 2008.

For more information about the ACS's technical documentation procedures, please see: http://www.census.gov/programs-surveys/acs/technical-documentation.html/.

Special Note on Table 8

***Source*: See General Notes for American Community Survey tables.**

The Census Bureau introduced a new set of disability questions in the 2008 ACS questionnaire. Accordingly, comparisons of disability data from 2008 or later with data from prior years are not recommended. For more information on these questions and their evaluation in the 2006 ACS Content Test, please see the Evaluation Report Covering Disability at https://www.census.gov/people/disability/files/2008ACS_disability.pdf.

Table 26.

***Source*: Current Population Survey (CPS) via Bureau of Labor Statistics (BLS)**

The household survey provides information on the labor force, employment, and unemployment that appears in the "A" tables, marked HOUSEHOLD DATA. It is a sample survey of about 60,000 eligible households conducted by the U.S. Census Bureau for the U.S. Bureau of Labor Statistics (BLS).

Household survey

The sample is selected to reflect the entire civilian noninstitutional population. Based on responses to a series of questions on work and job search activities, each person 16 years and over in a sample household is classified as employed, unemployed, or not in the labor force. People are classified as employed if they did any work at all as paid employees during the reference week; worked in their own business, profession, or on their own farm; or worked without pay at least 15 hours in a family business or farm. People are also counted as employed if they were temporarily absent from their jobs because of illness, bad weather, vacation, labor-management disputes, or personal reasons. People are classified as unemployed if they meet all of the following criteria: they had no employment during the reference week; they were available for work at that time; and they made specific efforts to find employment sometime during the 4-week period ending with the reference week. Persons laid off from a job and expecting recall need not be looking for work to be counted as unemployed. The unemployment data derived from the household survey in no way depend upon the eligibility for or receipt of unemployment insurance benefits.

The civilian labor force is the sum of employed and unemployed persons. Those persons not classified as employed or unemployed are not in the labor force. The unemployment rate is the number unemployed as a percent of the labor force. The labor force participation rate is the labor force as a percent of the population, and the employment-population ratio is the employed as a percent of the population. Additional information about the household survey can be found at www.bls.gov/cps/documentation.htm.

Employment estimates

The numerous conceptual and methodological differences between the household and establishment surveys (used in other BLS products) result in important distinctions in the employment estimates derived from the surveys. Among these are:

- The household survey includes agricultural workers, self-employed workers whose businesses are unincorporated, unpaid family workers, and private household workers among the employed. These groups are excluded from the establishment survey.
- The household survey includes people on unpaid leave among the employed. The establishment survey does not.
- The household survey is limited to workers 16 years of age and older. The establishment survey is not limited by age.
- The household survey has no duplication of individuals, because individuals are counted only once, even if they hold more than one job. In the establishment survey, employees working at more than one job and thus appearing on more than one payroll are counted separately for each appearance.

Seasonal adjustment

Over the course of a year, the size of the nation's labor force and the levels of employment and unemployment undergo regularly occurring fluctuations. These events may result from seasonal changes in weather, major holidays, and the opening and closing of schools. The effect of such seasonal variation can be very large. Because these seasonal events follow a more or less regular pattern each year, their influence on the level of a series can be tempered by adjusting for regular seasonal variation. These adjustments make nonseasonal developments, such as declines in employment or increases in the participation of women in the labor force, easier to spot. For example, in the household survey, the large number of youth entering the labor force each June is likely to obscure any other changes that have taken place relative to May, making it difficult to determine if the level of economic activity has risen or declined. Similarly, in the establishment survey, payroll employment in education declines by about 20 percent at the end of the spring term and later rises with the start of the fall term, obscuring the underlying employment trends in the industry. Because seasonal employment changes at the end and beginning of the school year can be estimated, the statistics can be adjusted to make underlying employment patterns more discernable. The seasonally adjusted figures provide a more useful tool with which to analyze changes in month-to-month economic activity.

Many seasonally adjusted series are independently adjusted in both the household and establishment surveys. However, the adjusted series for many major estimates, such as total payroll employment, employment in most major sectors, total employment, and unemployment are computed by aggregating independently adjusted component series. For example, total unemployment is derived by summing the adjusted series for four major age-sex components; this differs from the unemployment estimate that would be obtained by directly adjusting the total or by combining the duration, reasons, or more detailed age categories.

For both the household and establishment surveys, a concurrent seasonal adjustment methodology is used in which new seasonal factors are calculated each month using all relevant data, up to and including the data for the current month. In the household survey, new seasonal factors are used to adjust only the current month's data. In the establishment survey, however, new seasonal factors are used each month to adjust the three most recent monthly estimates. The prior two months are routinely revised to incorporate additional sample reports and recalculated seasonal adjustment factors. In both surveys, 5-year revisions to historical data are made once a year.

Reliability of the estimates

Statistics based on the household and establishment surveys are subject to both sampling and nonsampling error. When a sample, rather than the entire population, is surveyed, there is a chance that the sample estimates may differ from the true population values they represent. The component of this difference that occurs because samples differ by chance is known as sampling error, and its variability is measured by the standard error of the estimate. There is about a 90-percent chance, or level of confidence, that an estimate based on a sample will differ by no more than 1.6 standard errors from the true population value because of sampling error. BLS analyses are generally conducted at the 90-percent level of confidence.

For example, the confidence interval for the monthly change in total nonfarm employment from the establishment survey is on the order of plus or minus 105,000. Suppose the estimate of nonfarm employment increases by 50,000 from one month to the next. The 90-percent confidence interval on the monthly change would range from -55,000 to +155,000 (50,000 +/- 105,000). These figures do not mean that the sample results are off by these magnitudes, but rather that there is about a 90-percent chance that the true over-the-month change lies within this interval. Since this range includes values of less than zero, we could not say with confidence that nonfarm employment had, in fact, increased that month. If, however, the reported nonfarm employment rise was 250,000, then all of the values within the 90- percent confidence interval would be greater than zero. In this case, it is likely (at least a 90-percent chance) that nonfarm employment had, in fact, risen that month. At an unemployment rate of around 6.0 percent, the 90-percent confidence interval for the monthly change in unemployment as measured by the household survey is about +/- 300,000, and for the monthly change in the unemployment rate it is about +/- 0.2 percentage point.

In general, estimates involving many individuals or establishments have lower standard errors (relative to the size of the estimate) than estimates, that are based on a small number of observations. The precision of estimates also is improved when the data are cumulated over time, such as for quarterly and annual averages.

The household and establishment surveys are also affected by nonsampling error, which can occur for many reasons, including the failure to sample a segment of the population, inability to obtain information for all respondents in the sample, inability or unwillingness of respondents to provide correct information on a timely basis, mistakes made by respondents, and errors made in the collection or processing of the data.

For example, in the establishment survey, estimates for the most recent two months are based on incomplete returns; for this reason, these estimates are labeled preliminary in the tables. It is only after two successive revisions to a monthly estimate, when nearly all sample reports have been received, that the estimate is considered final. Another major source of nonsampling error in the establishment survey is the inability to capture, on a timely basis, employment generated by new firms. To correct for this systematic underestimation of employment growth, an estimation procedure with two components is used to account for business births. The first component excludes employment losses from business deaths from sample-based estimation in order to offset the missing employment gains from business births. This is incorporated into the sample-based estimation procedure by simply not reflecting sample units going out of business, but imputing to them the same employment trend as the other firms in the sample. This procedure accounts for most of the net birth/death employment.

The second component is an ARIMA time series model designed to estimate the residual net birth/death employment not accounted for by the imputation. The historical time series used to create and test the ARIMA model was derived from the unemployment insurance universe micro-level database, and reflects the actual residual net of births and deaths over the past five years.

The sample-based estimates from the establishment survey are adjusted once a year (on a lagged basis) to universe counts of payroll employment obtained from administrative records of the unemployment insurance program. The difference between the March sample-based employment estimates and the March universe counts is known as a benchmark revision and serves as a rough proxy for total survey error. The new benchmarks also incorporate changes in the classification of industries. Over the past decade, absolute benchmark revisions for total nonfarm employment have averaged 0.3 percent, with a range from -0.7 percent to 0.6 percent.

Tables 27 and 28.

***Source*: Current Population Survey (CPS) via Bureau of Labor Statistics (BLS)**

The data in this release were collected through the Current Population Survey (CPS). The CPS—a monthly survey of about 60,000 eligible households conducted by the U.S. Census Bureau for the Bureau of Labor Statistics—obtains information on employment and unemployment among the nation's civilian noninstitutional population age 16 and over. Most of the data in this release are annual averages for 2014, compiled from the results of the monthly survey. In August 2014, a supplement to the CPS collected additional information about veterans on topics such as service-connected disability, veterans' Reserve or National Guard status, and veterans who served in Iraq and/or Afghanistan. The supplement was co-sponsored by the U.S. Department of Veterans Affairs and by the U.S. Department of Labor's Veterans' Employment and Training Service. Questions were asked of persons 17 years of age and older regarding their prior service in the U.S. Armed Forces. Data are tabulated for persons 18 years of age and older.

The definitions underlying the data in this release are as follows:

Veterans are men and women who previously served on active duty in the U.S. Armed Forces and who were civilians at the time they were surveyed. Members of the Reserve and National Guard are counted as veterans if they had ever been called to active duty. Persons who are on active duty at the time of the survey are outside the scope of the survey and thus not in the estimates shown here, as are persons who reside in institutions, such as nursing homes and prisons. Nonveterans are men and women who never served on active duty in the U.S. Armed Forces.

World War II, Korean War, Vietnam-era, and Gulf War-era veterans are men and women who served in the U.S. Armed

Forces during these periods of service, regardless of where in the world they served. Veterans who served in more than one wartime period are classified in the most recent one.

Veterans of other service periods are men and women who served in the U.S. Armed Forces at any time other than World War II, the Korean War, the Vietnam era, or the Gulf War era. Although U.S. Armed Forces were engaged in several armed conflicts during other service periods, these conflicts were more limited in scope and included a smaller proportion of the Armed Forces than the selected wartime periods. Veterans who served during one of the selected wartime periods and during another period are classified in the wartime period.

Veteran status is obtained from responses to the question, "Did you ever serve on active duty in the U.S. Armed Forces?"

Period of service identifies when a veteran served in the Armed Forces, but not the location of their service. It is obtained from answers to the question asked of veterans, "When did you serve on active duty in the U.S. Armed Forces?"

The following service periods are identified:

Gulf War era II—September 2001–present
Gulf War era I—August 1990–August 2001
Vietnam era—August 1964–April 1975
Korean War—July 1950–January 1955
World War II—December 1941–December 1946
Other service periods—All other time periods

Veterans could have served anywhere in the world during these periods of service. Veterans are counted only in one period of service, their most recent wartime period. Veterans who served in more than one wartime period are classified in the most recent one. Veterans who served in both a wartime period and any other service period are classified in the wartime period. The period-of-service definitions are modified occasionally to reflect changes in law, regulations, and program needs of the survey sponsors. Veterans who served in Iraq, Afghanistan, or both are individuals who served in Iraq at any time since March 2003, in Afghanistan at any time since October 2001, or in both locations. Service in Iraq or Afghanistan is determined by answers to two questions: "Did you serve in Iraq, off the coast of Iraq, or did you fly missions over Iraq at any time since March 2003?" and "Did you serve in Afghanistan, or did you fly missions over Afghanistan, at any time since October 2001?"

Presence of service-connected disability is determined by answers to the question, "Has the Department of Veterans Affairs (VA) or Department of Defense (DoD) determined that you have a service-connected disability, that is, a health condition or impairment caused or made worse by any of your military service?" Service-connected disability rating is based on answers to the question, "What is your current service-connected disability rating?" Answers can range from 0 to 100 percent, in increments of 10 percentage points. Ratings are determined by the VA or DoD from a rating schedule published in the Code of Federal Regulations, Title 38, "Pensions, Bonuses, and Veterans' Relief," Part 4—"Schedule for Rating Disabilities." The rating schedule is "primarily a guide in the evaluation of disability resulting from all types of diseases and injuries encountered as a result of or incident to military service. The percentage ratings represent as far as can practicably be determined the average impairment in earning capacity resulting from such diseases and injuries and their residual conditions in civil occupations." Part 4 contains a listing of hundreds of possible disorders and assigns ratings of 0 through 100 percent, with instructions for rating multiple disorders.

Reserve and National Guard membership refers only to Gulf War-era veterans who are current or past members of the Reserve or National Guard. Members of the Reserve and National Guard are counted as veterans if they had ever been called to active duty. These data do not refer to all persons who may have ever served in the Reserve or National Guard. Reserve or National Guard status is obtained from answers to two questions. Gulf War-era veterans were asked: "Was any of your active service the result of a call-up from the Reserve or National Guard?" If the answer was no, they were asked, "Have you ever been a member of the Reserve or National Guard?" A 'yes' response to either question classified persons as "Current or past member of the Reserve or National Guard." A 'no' response to the latter question classified persons as "Never a member of the Reserve or National Guard."

Reliability of the estimates statistics based on the CPS are subject to both sampling and nonsampling error. When a sample, rather than the entire population, is surveyed, there is a chance that the sample estimates will differ from the true population values they represent. The component of this difference that occurs because samples differ by chance is known as sampling error, and its variability is measured by the standard error of the estimate. There is about a 90-percent chance, or level of confidence, that an estimate based on a sample will differ by no more than 1.6 standard errors from the true population value because of sampling error. BLS analyses are generally conducted at the 90-percent level of confidence.

The CPS data also are affected by nonsampling error. Nonsampling error can occur for many reasons, including the failure to sample a segment of the population, the inability to obtain information for all respondents in the sample, the inability or unwillingness of respondents to provide correct information, and errors made in the collection or processing of the data.

Information about the reliability of national data from the CPS and estimating standard errors is available at www.bls.gov/cps/

documentation.htm#reliability. For a discussion of the reliability of state estimates from the CPS, such as those in table 6 of this release, see www.bls.gov/opub/gp/gpapndb.htm.

Tables 29, 30, 31, 32, 33, 34, 35, 36, 37.

***Source*: National Center for Veterans Analysis and Statistics, Department of Veterans Affairs**

The Veteran Population Projection Model 2014 (VetPop2014) provides the latest official Veteran population projection from the Department of Veterans Affairs (VA). VetPop2014 is an actuarial projection model developed by the Office of the Actuary (OACT) for Veteran population projection from Fiscal Year FY2014 to FY2043. Using the best available Veteran data by the end of FY2013, VetPop2014 provides living Veteran counts by key demographic characteristics such as age, gender, period of service, and race/ethnicity at various geographic levels. VetPop2014 is the 7th generation of the OACT Veteran Population Projection Model with significant improvements in data, methodology, and modeling processes.

The VetPop2014 actuarial model uses both Veteran record-level data and survey data from a wide variety of sources including VA, Department of Defense (DoD), U.S. Census Bureau, Department of Treasury's Internal Revenue Service (IRS), and the Social Security Administration (SSA).

These data sources enabled OACT to develop the VetPop2014 Model using advanced actuarial and predictive modeling methods for three critical modules—the Separation Module, the Mortality Module, and the Migration Module.

Military separations from the Armed Forces provide new entrants to the Veteran population. Thus, the Separation Module is an essential component of the Veteran Population Projection Model. Based on DoD's annual military separation data from FY1980 to FY2013, VetPop2014 Separation Module first developed a set of Time Series Models to project annual separations for various age and gender groups. Additionally, due to distinct differences in the characteristics of Active and Reserve Components, Time Series Models were developed for these two components' separations. The projected separations from Active and Reserve Components by gender and age groups were then aggregated to the national level. VetPop2014 Model then used historical county separation data based on VA administrative records along with migration information from the IRS to project the county level separation from FY2014 to FY2044 using predictive modeling techniques.

The VetPop2011 Mortality Module is based on mortality experience data such as Veteran specific experience from VA administrative data and U.S. population experience data from SSA. Mortality projections are developed for each single year of age and gender using the Lee-Carter Model combined with credibility weighting and smoothing techniques. VetPop2014 projected lower mortality rates than previous projections for older Veterans due to longevity improvement. As a result of the longevity improvement, VetPop2014 projected a relatively larger Veteran population in the future.

The Migration Module at the county level is a critical component to the bottom-up VetPop2014 model. Like the VetPop2011 Migration Module, VetPop2014 Migration Module developed the county Veteran migration models for various age and gender cohorts using historical longitudinal data from VA, IRS, and ACS. The VetPop2014 Migration Module made adjustment in the migration rates for older veterans in counties due to the availability of more creditable data. Overall, the migration rate changes were minimal.

The 2014 Veteran Population Projection includes not only the living civilian Veterans but also Veterans who are currently serving in the military. Due to the latest data enhancements, the VetPop2014 projected more living Veterans in the future compared to VetPop2011. Overall, while the male Veteran population steadily decreases, woman and minority Veteran population are projected to increase over the next 30 years. Another noticeable trend for the Veteran population is the projected higher growths in the Southern and Western regions.

Tables 38, 39, 40, 41.

***Source*: National Center for Veterans Analysis and Statistics, Department of Veterans Affairs**

Each fiscal year the Department of Veterans Affairs' Office of Policy and Planning publishes the annual Geographic Distribution of VA Expenditures (GDX) Report for the public and all stakeholders. The GDX report provides the estimated dollar expenditures for major VA programs at the state, county, and Congressional District levels. Expenditure data are grouped by the following categories: Compensation and Pension; Education and Vocational Rehabilitation and Employment; Insurance and Indemnities; Construction and Related Costs; General Operating Expenses and Related Costs; Loan Guaranty; and Medical Expenditures. The GDX Report also includes Veteran population estimates at the state, county and Congressional District level and the number of unique patients who used VA health care services.

Expenditure data sources include: USASpending.gov for Compensation & Pension (C&P) and Education and Vocational Rehabilitation and Employment (EVRE) Benefits; Veterans Benefits Administration Insurance Center for the Insurance costs; the VA Financial Management System (FMS) for Construction, Medical Research, General Operating Expenses, and certain C&P and Readjustment data; and the Allocation Resource Center (ARC) for Medical Care costs.

Definitions

Compensation and Pension: For the purposes of the GDX Report, Compensation and Pension (C&P) applies to benefits expenditures for the following categories: compensation payments, pension payments, Dependency and Indemnity Compensation, and burial allowances.

Construction: For the purposes of the GDX Report, Construction applies to construction expenditures, which include funding for Major Projects, Minor Projects, Grants for Construction of State Extended Care Facilities, and Grants for Construction of State Veterans Cemeteries.

Education & Vocational Rehabilitation & Employment: Though Education and Vocational Rehabilitation and Employment (E&VRE) are separate programs, they are combined into one category for display purposes in the Geographic Distribution of VA Expenditures (GDX) Report. Expenditures in this category include: automobile and adaptive equipment, specially adapted housing, Survivors' and Dependents' Educational Assistance (Chapter 35), Vocational Rehabilitation for Disabled Veterans (Chapter 31), Post-Vietnam Era Veterans' Educational Assistance (Chapter 32), Montgomery G.I. Bill for Selected Reserves (Chapter 1606), Reserve Educational Assistance Program (Chapter 1607), Montgomery G.I. Bill (Chapter 30), and Post-9/11 Veterans Educational Assistance (Chapter 33).

General Operating Expense: General Operating Expenses represent the costs necessary to provide administration and oversight for the benefits provided by VA. This includes costs for overhead and human resources. This category does not include payments made directly to beneficiaries.

Insurance and Indemnity (I&I): For the purposes of the GDX Report, Insurance and Indemnity (I&I) consists of VA expenditures for death claims, matured endowments, dividends, cash surrender payments, total disability income provision payments, and total and permanent disability benefits payments.

Loan Guaranty Program: This VA benefits program provides assistance to Veterans, certain spouses, and servicemembers to enable them to buy and retain homes. Assistance is provided through VA's partial guaranty of loans made by private lenders in lieu of the substantial down payment and private mortgage insurance required in conventional mortgage transactions. This protection means that in most cases qualified Veterans can obtain a loan without making a down payment.

Medical Care: With respect to the GDX Report, medical care consists of operating expenses incurred through the provision of healthcare services to Veterans. The specific programs reported for this category are: medical care, General Post Fund, medical and prosthetic research, and miscellaneous accounts.

Unique Patients: A Veteran patient is counted as a unique in each division from which they receive care. For example, if a patient receives Primary Care at one VA facility and specialty care from another VA facility, he/she will be counted as a unique patient in each division.

Table 42.

***Source*: Department of Veterans Affairs, Veterans Benefits Administration, Annual Benefits Reports, 2000 to 2013; Veterans Health Administration, Office of Policy and Planning, Table A: VHA Enrollment, Expenditures, and Patients National Vital Signs, September Reporting 2000 to 2013. Prepared by the National Center for Veterans Analysis and Statistics.**

Tables 43, 44, 45.

***Source*: Department of Veterans Affairs, Veterans Health Administration, Office of Policy and Planning. Prepared by the National Center for Veterans Analysis and Statistics.**

Definition of Healthcare Priority Groups

The number of veterans who can be enrolled in the health care program is determined by the amount of money Congress gives VA each year. Since funds are limited, VA sets up Priority Groups to make sure that certain groups of veterans are able to be enrolled before others.

Once enrollment is sought, eligibility is verified. Based on specific eligibility status, each veteran is assigned a Priority Group. The Priority Groups range from 1–8 with 1 being the highest priority for enrollment. Based on eligibility and income, some veterans may have to agree to pay copay to be placed in certain Priority Groups and some veterans may not be eligible for enrollment.

Veterans are sometimes eligible for more than one Enrollment Priority Group. In that case, VA will always place them in the highest applicable Priority Group.

Priority Group 1

- Veterans with VA-rated service-connected disabilities 50% or more disabling
- Veterans determined by VA to be unemployable due to service-connected conditions

Priority Group 2

- Veterans with VA-rated service-connected disabilities 30% or 40% disabling

Priority Group 3

- Veterans who are Former Prisoners of War (POWs)
- Veterans awarded a Purple Heart medal
- Veterans whose discharge was for a disability that was incurred or aggravated in the line of duty
- Veterans with VA-rated service-connected disabilities 10% or 20% disabling
- Veterans awarded special eligibility classification under Title 38, U.S.C., § 1151, "benefits for individuals disabled by treatment or vocational rehabilitation"
- Veterans awarded the Medal Of Honor (MOH)

Priority Group 4

- Veterans who are receiving aid and attendance or housebound benefits from VA
- Veterans who have been determined by VA to be catastrophically disabled

Priority Group 5

- Nonservice-connected veterans and noncompensable service-connected veterans rated 0% disabled by VA with annual income below the VA's and geographically (based resident ZIP code) adjusted income limits.
- Veterans receiving VA pension benefits
- Veterans eligible for Medicaid programs

Priority Group 6

- Compensable 0% service-connected veterans
- Veterans exposed to Ionizing Radiation during atmospheric testing or during the occupation of Hiroshima and Nagasaki
- Project 112/SHAD participants
- Veterans who served in the Republic of Vietnam between January 9, 1962, and May 7, 1975
- Veterans of the Persian Gulf War who served between August 2, 1990 and November 11, 1998
- *Veterans who served on active duty at Camp Lejeune for not fewer than 30 days beginning August 1, 1953 and ending December 31, 1987
- Veterans who served in a theater of combat operations after November 11, 1998 as follows:
  - Currently enrolled veterans and new enrollees who were discharged from active duty on or after January 28, 2003, are eligible for the enhanced benefits for 5 years post discharge.
  - Combat Veterans who were discharged between January 2009 and January 2011 and did not enroll in the VA health care during their 5-year period of eligibility have an additional one year to enroll and receive care. The additional one-year eligibility period began February 12, 2015 with the signing of the Clay Hunt Suicide Prevention for America Veterans Act.

Note: At the end of this enhanced enrollment priority group placement time period Veterans will be assigned to the highest Priority Group their unique eligibility status at that time qualifies for.

**Note:* While eligible for Priority Group (PG) 6; until system changes are implemented veterans will be assigned to PG 7 or 8 depending on your income.

Priority Group 7

- Veterans with gross household income below the geographically adjusted income limits (GMT) for their resident location and who agree to pay copays

Priority Group 8

- Veterans with gross household income above the VA and the geographically-adjusted income limits for their resident location and who agree to pay copays

Veterans eligible for enrollment:

Noncompensable 0% service-connected:

- *Subpriority a*: Enrolled as of January 16, 2003, and who have remained enrolled since that date and/or placed in this sub priority due to changed eligibility status
- *Subpriority b*: Enrolled on or after June 15, 2009, whose income exceeds the current VA or geographic income limits by 10% or less

Nonservice-connected and:

- *Subpriority c*: Enrolled as of January 16, 2003, and who have remained enrolled since that date and/or placed in this sub priority due to changed eligibility status
- *Subpriority d*: Enrolled on or after June 15, 2009 whose income exceeds the current VA or geographic income limits by 10% or less

Veterans not eligible for enrollment:

Veterans not meeting the criteria above:

- *Subpriority e*: Noncompensable 0% service-connected (eligible for care of their SC condition only)
- *Subpriority g*: Nonservice-connected

Table 46.

***Source*: Department of Veterans Affairs, Veterans Benefits Administration, Annual Benefits Reports, 2000 to 2012. Prepared by the National Center for Veterans Analysis and Statistics.**

Definitions:

Disability Compensation: The compensation program provides monthly benefits to veterans in recognition of the effects of disabilities, diseases, or injuries incurred or aggravated during active military service.

Disability Pension: Disability pension is payable to certain wartime veterans who are permanently and totally disabled, or age 65 and older.

Education Programs: Education programs provide Veterans, servicemembers, reservists, and certain family members of veterans with educational resources to supplement opportunities missed because of military service. There are seven active education programs.

Home Loan Guaranty: The objective of the VA Home Loan Guaranty program is to help eligible veterans, active duty personnel, surviving spouses, and members of the Reserves and National Guard purchase, retain, and adapt homes in recognition of their service to the nation.

Life Insurance Policies: The life insurance programs provide servicemembers and their families with universally available life insurance (available to all servicemembers and their families without underwriting), as well as traumatic injury protection insurance for servicemember.

Vocational Rehabilitation and Employment: The VR&E Program provides a wide range of vocational and employment services to Veterans, active-duty servicemembers and eligible dependents. These services are designed to help servicemembers and Veterans choose a career path and assist them in achieving their employment goals.

Tables 47 and 48.

***Sources*: Department of Veterans Affairs, Veterans Benefits Administration, Annual Benefits Reports, 2000 to 2013; Prepared by the National Center for Veterans Analysis and Statistics.**

Definitions:

MGIB-AD: The Montgomery GI Bill-Active Duty Educational Assistance Program (Chapter 30 of Title 38, U.S. Code), which provides educational assistance to persons who served on active duty in the Armed Forces.

MGIB-SR: The Montgomery GI Bill-Selected Reserve Educational Assistance Program (Chapter 1606 of Title 10, U.S. Code) which provides educational assistance to members of the Selected Reserve or the Ready Reserve of any of the reserve components of the Armed Forces.

DEA: Survivors' and Dependents' Educational Assistance (DEA)—Under Chapter 35 of Title 38, U.S. Code, a monetary educational benefit payable to eligible dependents and survivors of veterans.

VEAP: The Veterans Educational Assistance Program (Chapter 32 of Title 38, U.S. Code) is a contributory educational assistance program for post-Vietnam Era veterans.

REAP: The Reserve Educational Assistance Program (Chapter 1607 of Title 10, U.S. Code) which provides educational assistance to members of the Guard and Reserves who serve on active duty in support of a contingency operation under federal authority on or after September 11, 2001.

Post-9/11: The Post-9/11 GI Bill (Chapter 33, sections 3301 - 3324, of Title 38, U.S. Code) is a new educational assistance program, effective August 1, 2009, which provides financial support for education and housing to individuals with at least 90 days of aggregate service on or after September 11, 2001, or individuals discharged with a service-connected disability after 30 days.

VRAP: Veterans Retraining Assistance Program (VRAP) offers 12 months of training assistance for veterans who: (1) are at least 35 but not more than 60 years old; (2) are unemployed on the date of application; (3) received an other than dishonorable discharge; (4) are not eligible for any other VA education benefit program; (5) are not in receipt of VA compensation due to unemployability; (6) are not enrolled in a federal or state job training program.

Table 49.

***Source*: Department of Veterans Affairs, Veterans Benefits Administration; 1985–1998: COIN CP-127 Reports; 1999–2013: Annual Benefits Reports.**

Definitions:

Disability Compensation: A monetary benefit paid to Veterans who are disabled by an injury or illness that was incurred or aggravated during active military service. These disabilities are considered to be service-connected. Disability compensation varies with the degree of disability and the number of a Veteran's dependents, and is paid monthly. Veterans with certain severe disabilities may be eligible for additional special monthly compensation. The benefits are not subject to federal or state income tax. The payment of military retirement pay, disability severance pay and separation incentive payments known as SSB (Special Separation Benefits) and VSI (Voluntary Separation Incentives), and Combat-Related Special Compensation affect the amount of VA compensation paid to disabled Veterans. To be eligible, the service of the Veteran must have been terminated through separation or discharge under conditions other than dishonorable.

Service Connected Disability: Veterans who are disabled by an injury or illness that was incurred or aggravated during active military service. These disabilities are considered to be service-connected.

For more information on how the Department of Veterans Affairs determines disability ratings, please see: http://www.benefits.va.gov/warms/bookc.asp.

Tables 50, 51, 52.

***Source*: Department of Veterans Affairs, National Cemetery Administration, Policy and Planning Service. Data are compiled from NCA's Burial Operations Support System (BOSS) and Management and Decision Support System (MADSS)**

Definitions:

National Cemetery Administration (NCA): A VA organizational component that honor our Nation's Veterans with final resting places in national shrines and with lasting tributes that commemorate their service to our Nation. NCA provides interment of eligible Service members, Veterans, Reservists, National Guard members, and eligible family members in national cemeteries, and furnishes headstones and markers for the graves of Veterans throughout the United States and the world. Additionally, NCA administers the State Cemetery Grants Program, which provides grants to states and tribal governments for establishing, expanding, and improving state Veterans' cemeteries. Finally, NCA provides Presidential Memorial Certificates to Veterans' loved ones to honor the service of honorably discharged deceased service members or Veterans.

Table 53.

***Source*: Veterans Employed in the Federal Executive Branch: Fiscal Year 2012; prepared by the National Center for Veterans Analysis and Statistics, January 2015**

Table 54.

***Source*: National Center for Veterans Analysis and Statistics.**

APPENDIX B. IMPORTANT WEB SITES FOR VETERANS AND ASSISTANCE PROVIDERS

Cultural, Data-Related, and Archival Resources

eVetRecs

http://vetrecs.archives.gov

http://www.archives.gov/veterans/military-service-records/

This site provides instructions on requesting information from a military record and is intended for veterans or the next of kin of a deceased former member of the military. The site also links to guidance on requests from the general public, which requires a different procedure. The eVetRecs site includes information on how the National Archives protects the privacy and security of veterans' and military personnel records.

Nationwide Gravesite Locator

http://gravelocator.cem.va.gov/

The Nationwide Gravesite Locator has burial records from many sources. It includes burial locations of veterans and their family members in VA National Cemeteries, state veterans cemeteries, other military and Department of Interior cemeteries, and for veterans buried in private cemeteries (1997 to present) when the grave is marked with a government grave marker. Researchers can search the database by name, birth or death date, and cemetery name.

Veterans History Project

http://www.loc.gov/vets/

The Veterans History Project collects, presents, and preserves firsthand accounts from veterans of World War I, World War II, the Korean War, the Vietnam War, the Persian Gulf War, and the current conflicts in Afghanistan and Iraq. The accounts include letters, photographs, and oral histories in audio and video formats. Records describing the collections can be searched in a database, and digitized collections can be viewed or listened to online. The site also includes information on how to submit veterans' stories to the collection.

National Center for Veterans Analysis and Statistics

http://www.va.gov/vetdata/

This site provides current and projected veterans demographics at the national, state, county, and congressional district level. It also provides data on Veterans Administration expenditures by geographic area and links to other surveys and statistics on the veteran population.

National Personnel Records Center (NPRC)

http://www.archives.gov/st-louis/

http://www.archives.gov/veterans/military-service-records/

NPRC in St. Louis is a central repository for federal civil service and military personnel records. Its Web site describes the collections and how to request information. The records themselves are not available online. A special site, eVetRecs, allows veterans and the next of kin of deceased veterans to request records online. The eVetRecs site is available at the second URL listed above.

Employment and Business

America's Heroes at Work

http://www.americasheroesatwork.gov/

The America's Heroes at Work project is designed to provide support for employers of returning service members living with traumatic brain injury (TBI) or post-traumatic stress disorder (PTSD). The site includes answers to frequently asked questions, fact sheets, and training presentations to inform audiences about TBI and PTSD. The site also includes success stories for veterans and employers.

Center for Veterans Enterprise

http://www.vetbiz.gov/

The Center for Veterans Enterprise works to promote veteran-owned businesses. Its Web site includes the VA VOSB Verification Program Document Submission Web Portal and the Vendor Information Pages (VIP).

Elaws—Employment Laws Assistance for Workers and Small Businesses

http://www.dol.gov/elaws/

The Elaws Advisors are interactive tools designed to help employees and employers understand their respective rights and responsibilities under the laws and regulations administered by the Department of Labor. Each Elaws Advisor provides information about a specific law or regulation. The Advisor imitates the interaction that an individual might have with an employment law expert. It asks questions, provides information, and directs the user to the appropriate resolutions based on the user's responses. Featured expertise includes the Fair Labor Standards Act, Family and Medical Leave Act, Veterans' Preference, and Worker Adjustment and Retraining Notification (WARN) Act.

FedsHireVets.gov

http://fedshirevets.gov/

FedsHireVets.gov is part of the Veterans Employment Initiative, established by executive order in 2009. The Web site is intended to be a central source for federal employment information for veterans, transitioning service members and their families, and federal hiring managers. The site has a section for individuals looking for a job and for agency human resources personnel looking to hire. It also has a directory of Veteran Employment Program Offices.

GovLoans.gov

http://govloans.gov/

GovLoans.gov is a central location for information about federal loan programs. Major sections cover topics such as agriculture, business, disaster relief, education, housing, and veterans' loans. The site is a cooperative effort between the Departments of Agriculture, Commerce, Education, Housing and Urban Development, and Veterans Affairs, as well as the Small Business Administration. It is hosted by the Department of Labor's GovBenefits.gov Web site. GovLoans.gov is also available in Spanish.

USAJOBS

http://www.usajobs.gov/

The core of the USAJOBS Web site is a database of current federal government employment opportunities. These openings can be searched by keyword or by other criteria, including by agency, occupational grouping, salary, or state. Users can create and store a resume online for applying for federal jobs and set up a profile to receive automated job alerts. The site has special sections for veterans, students, senior executives, and individuals with disabilities.

Veterans' Employment and Training Service (VETS)

http://www.dol.gov/vets/welcome.html

VETS advocates for veterans in the employment marketplace. Materials on the VETS Web site include the text of laws and regulations concerning veterans' employment, information about the Veterans Preference for federal jobs, grants announcements, and information about the Uniformed Services Employment and Reemployment Rights Act (USERRA).

Federal Agencies and Military Branches and Programs

Defense Threat Reduction Agency (DTRA)

http://www.dtra.mil/

The full name of this Web site is Defense Threat Reduction Agency & USSTRATCOM Center for Combating WMD. These entities' names are abbreviated DTRA and SSC-WMD, respectively, and they work closely together. DTRA addresses the threat of weapons of mass destruction (chemical, biological, radiological, nuclear, and high explosives) with combat support, technology development, threat control, and threat reduction. SSC-WMD coordinates counter-WMD activities at U.S. military locations around the world. Each mission link on the home page provides further information on DTRA's work. The Web site includes current information on DTRA research grants and business opportunities. The site also has information on the Nuclear Test Personnel Review to assist veterans who received doses of radiation while participating in U.S. atmospheric nuclear tests during the Cold War era.

Department of Housing and Urban Development (HUD)

http://www.hud.gov/

HUD's Web site describes the agency's programs in housing and community development. Under the heading State Info, the site has information for residents of each of the 50 states, the District of Columbia, Puerto Rico, and the Virgin Islands. Another main section of the site, Topic Areas, provides information on numerous topics, including avoiding foreclosure, buying a home, fair lending practices, homes for sale, housing discrimination, housing research and data sets, rental assistance, and veterans information. Under Resources, the site has an extensive online library of information and tools including a Loan Estimator Calculator, a Lender Locator, and a database of HUD-approved appraisers. The site also has an A to Z index and is available in Spanish.

Department of Homeland Security (DHS)

http://www.dhs.gov/

DHS was formed in January 2003 by consolidating many existing agencies and agency divisions whose missions relate to domestic defense. The DHS Web site organizes information into major sections under the Topics link, including Preventing Terrorism, Border Security, Cybersecurity, Civil Rights and Civil Liberties, and Immigration Enforcement. Each of these sections has publications, grants, laws, program links, and background information as appropriate. A complete list of links to component agencies and offices is provided in the About DHS section along with budget information, an organization chart, and guidance on major laws and regulations.

Information is also organized on the home page (under "How Do I?"), with links to frequently asked questions, including "Find Overseas Travel Alerts" and "Report Cyber Incidents". As Cabinet departments are required to do, DHS maintains an Open Government page.

Department of Veterans Affairs (VA)

http://www.va.gov/

Major sections of the VA Web site in the Veterans Services section include Health, Benefits, and Burials & Memorials. The site has direct links to topics in demand, such as prescriptions, VA forms, and federal jobs for veterans. The site also has a directory of VA locations and a link to online services. The About VA section has organization information, congressional testimony, and budget information.

More institutional information is provided in the News Room sections. Because it is Cabinet-level department, the VA also has an Open Government section on its Web site.

This site should prove useful to veterans and people involved in assisting them. Using the site map will help to uncover all of the available information.

United States Air Force

http://www.af.mil/

This Web site is the central point for information about the United States Air Force. The home pages includes links to featured news stories, topics of interest, and information about its senior leadership. The News section links to commentaries, photos, art, and Air Force TV. The About Us section includes a CSAF Reading List, biographies, and an events schedule.

United States Army

http://www.army.mil/

This is the central Web site for the Army. The site links to Army news services, video and images, publications, and the Army Live blog. Under the Info heading, the Organization section connects users to major commands and units; it also links to installations and facilities, including airfields, barracks, camps, libraries, medical centers, institutes, museums, and more. Also listed under Info, the References section links to official Army strategic documents, other Army publications, and libraries. Other sections cover Army history and heritage, career management, veterans' service organizations, and community outreach. The A-Z section provides a helpful alphabetical listing of Army Web sites.

This well-designed and well-organized site should be one of the first stopping points for anyone seeking information about the Army, its bases, or related news. It is also a good resource for active servicemembers, reservists, and those who have retired from the Army.

United States Marine Corps (USMC)

http://www.marines.mil/

The official USMC Web site focuses on current news, featuring articles written by Marines. Major sections provide information about the USMC Headquarters and links to individual units' Web pages. The site connects to other USMC sites of interest on recruiting, careers, community relations, and quality of life issues.

United States Navy

http://www.navy.mil/

The official Web site of the Navy features Navy news, leadership biographies, photos, videos, and policy documents such as the Secretary of the Navy's Posture Statement. Under the About heading, the site provides Status of the Navy statistics and links to fun facts and a command directory. This section also has organizational information, profiles of current and past Navy ships, and fact sheets on Navy aircraft, weapons systems, submarines, missiles, ships, and other topics. Under Media, the site has archived, digitized copies of all issues of the Navy magazine *All Hands* going back to its start in 1922.

Health and Support Resources

Armed Forces Retirement Home

http://www.afrh.gov/

The Armed Forces Retirement Home consists of two campuses, one in Washington, D.C., and one in Gulfport, Miss. The Gulfport campus was damaged by Hurricane Katrina; it was renovated and has reopened. The site has information about both facilities.

GulfLINK

http://www.gulflink.osd.mil/

GulfLINK has news and information on illnesses reported by veterans of the Persian Gulf War of 1991. The Library section of the site includes case narratives, *Environmental Exposure Reports*, and RAND research reports. The site also has information on services for veterans, medical evaluation programs, and a summary of medical issues relating to symptoms among Gulf War veterans.

Health Care—Veterans Health Administration

http://www1.va.gov/health/

The VHA Web site is part of the larger Veterans Administration site. It provides consumer-oriented information and services, with sections on applying for care, refilling a prescription, finding a VA health facility, a crisis prevention hotline for veterans, and more. In the A-Z index, the site links to VHA information on specific topics, such as dental care, prescriptions, prosthetics and sensory aids, health promotion, and VA medical research.

Hospital and Medical Facility Finder, Department of Veterans Affairs

http://www.va.gov/directory/guide/home.asp?isflash=1

This Web site provides a field that enables users to search by state/territory, address, facility, and range of distance for VA health facilities. The site also features a clickable map as an alternative search feature.

National Center for PTSD

http://www.ptsd.va.gov/

The VA's National Center for Post-Traumatic Stress Disorder (PTSD) provides this Web site as an educational resource concerning PTSD and other consequences of traumatic stress. The primary audiences are veterans and their families, researchers, and mental health care providers. The Web site offers information on assessment, treatment, and VA services. In addition to combat stress, reactions to trauma caused by natural disasters, abuse, and other factors are discussed. The site offers free online access to PILOTS, a database indexing the literature on PTSD and other mental health consequences of exposure to traumatic events.

National Resource Directory

https://www.nrd.gov/

The subtitle of the National Resource Directory Web site is "Connecting Wounded Warriors, Service Members, Veterans, Their Families and Caregivers with Those Who Support Them." The Departments of Defense, Labor, and Veterans Affairs maintain the site. It links to information on benefits and compensation, education and training, employment, health care, family and caregiver support, and other topics. The linked information is from federal, state and local government agencies, veterans' service and benefit organizations, non-profit community-based and faith-based organizations, academic institutions, professional associations, and philanthropic organizations.

Returning Service Members (OEF/OIF)

http://www.oefoif.va.gov/

This VA Web site provides information on benefits and transition assistance available for service members returning from Operation Iraqi Freedom and Operation Enduring Freedom. The site has special sections for returning members of the Guard and Reserve and for families of returning service members.

Servicemembers.gov

http://www.justice.gov/crt/spec_topics/military/

This Web site explains the major laws that support the rights of veterans and military service members: the Uniformed Services Employment and Reemployment Rights Act (USERRA), the Uniformed and Overseas Citizen Absentee Voting Act (UOCAVA), and the Servicemembers Civil Relief Act (SCRA). The site has brochures about protecting servicemember rights and returning servicemembers with disabilities.

TRICARE, Military Health System

http://www.tricare.mil

TRICARE is the health care benefit for the military. This Web site provides information and documents for TRICARE beneficiaries and providers, including a directory of providers. TRICARE beneficiaries can also log into the TRICARE Online service to conduct transactions such as scheduling appointments.

Veterans Benefits Administration (VBA)

http://www.vba.va.gov/

The VBA Web site is part of the larger Department of Veterans Affairs (VA) Web site. Major sections of the site cover education benefits, home loans, compensation and pensions, survivors' benefits, vocational rehabilitation, employment, and life insurance. The site links to forms, manuals, publications, and benefits fact sheets.

Wounded Warrior Regiment

http://www.woundedwarriorregiment.org/

Established in 2006, the Wounded Warrior Regiment "serves Marines who are wounded in combat, fall ill, or are injured in the line of duty. This includes active duty, reserve, and veteran Marines." (From the Web site) The site has information for both Marines and their families.

Housing

VA Loan Guaranty Home Loan Program

http://www.benefits.va.gov/homeloans/

http://www.homeloans.va.gov/

The VA Loan Guaranty Service is the organization within the Veterans Benefits Administration charged with the responsibility of administering the home loan program. The VA home loan program helps veterans finance the purchase of homes through favorable loan terms and competitive interest rates. The Web site provides information for home buyers, lenders, loan servicers, and real estate professionals. It has online videos, pamphlets, and disaster advice for VA borrowers. The site also has information on grants for specially adapted housing.

Legislative and Judicial Resources

GI Bill Web site

http://www.gibill.va.gov/

The GI Bill Web site provides information on the range of education benefits for active duty and reserve servicemembers, veterans, survivors, and dependents. The site outlines the steps for applying and provides tools, such as benefits comparison tools, to encourage informed planning. The site has a history of the original GI Bill, the Servicemembers' Readjustment Act of 1944, which preceded the current program.

House Committee on Veterans' Affairs

http://veterans.house.gov/

Visitors to this Web site can learn more about the goals and policy forwarded by the Committee on Veterans' Affairs in the House of Representatives. The Web site also features a hearings schedule, a media center, and a section for veterans.

Senate Committee on Veterans' Affairs

http://www.veterans.senate.gov/

This Web site provides information about the Senate Committee on Veterans' Affairs's policy, legislation, and members. A featured items section provides links to news topics of interest on the subject of veterans' affairs.

U.S. Court of Appeals for Veterans Claims

http://www.uscourts.cavc.gov/

The court reviews final decisions of the Board of Veterans' Appeals, which largely consist of cases concerning entitlement to benefits. The court's Web site has information on how to appeal, court rules, forms, and fees. Orders and opinions are online from 2000 to present, with archives for previous years. Audio files for oral arguments are online beginning with 2005.

Veterans Jobs Caucus

http://denham.house.gov/HireAVet

This Web site links to the bicameral, bipartisan Veterans Jobs Caucus. According to the Web site, its primary initiative is the "I Hire Veterans" program. Visitors to the site can learn more about its mission, its members, and related veterans organizations.

INDEX